Cover to Cover
CHALLENGE

Jason L. Bell

Cover to Cover Challenge – Jason L. Bell
Copyright © 2018
First edition published 2018
All rights reserved. No part of this book may be reproduced, stored in a retrieval system, or transmitted in any form or by any means – electronic, mechanical, photocopying, recording, or otherwise, without written permission from the publisher.
Scripture taken from the New King James Version®. Copyright © 1982 by Thomas Nelson. Used by permission. All rights reserved.
Cover Design: Robert Reed (nVIUS Graphics, Inc.)

Printed in the United States of America
Jason Bell
547 Scott Avenue South
Rainsville, Alabama 35986

RELIGION / Biblical Studies / Bible Study Guides
ISBN: 978-1-72108-839-3 & 978-1-62245-586-7
10   9   8   7   6   5   4   3   2   1
Available where books are sold

Table of Contents

Foreword vii
Preface ix
Before You Get Started… xi
Week 1 1
Week 2 9
Week 3 17
Week 4 25
Week 5 32
Week 6 38
Week 7 44
Week 8 50
Week 9 57
Week 10 65
Week 11 72
Week 12 78
Week 13 84
Week 14 91
Week 15 98
Week 16 104
Week 17 111
Week 18 117
Week 19 125
Week 20 131
Week 21 137
Week 22 142
Week 23 147
Week 24 153
Week 25 159
Week 26 165
Week 27 170
Week 28 176
Week 29 180
Week 30 186
Week 31 193
Week 32 199
Week 33 205
Week 34 210
Week 35 216
Week 36 221
Week 37 228
Week 38 234
Week 39 240
Week 40 247
Week 41 253
Week 42 259
Week 43 265
Week 44 272
Week 45 280
Week 46 288
Week 47 295
Week 48 301
Week 49 306
Week 50 313
Week 51 319
Week 52 324
Bibliography 329
Meet the Author 331

*For the loves of my life
my wife Amber
my daughter Jacey
my son Noah.*

Foreword

As the secretary at Nazareth Baptist Church, I have been afforded a behind the scenes look at the commitment, time, and effort that went into *Cover to Cover Challenge* and *Cover to Cover Challenge NT*. In observing, I have been greatly blessed by Bro. Jason's commitment to preparation of this project and by witnessing his desire to lead others to study God's Word. His interpretive guidance and daily narratives are easily understood by new Bible readers, and they promise to shed new light on scriptures others may have read many times.

God used His Word and Bro. Jason's commentary to minister to me personally during some especially challenging times over the past two years. Many weeks while I was unable to be at home and at my home church, God spoke comfort to me through this study. His Word is filled with promises to provide and to deliver. It is the definitive source of truth for our lives. As you read these Bible verses and Bro. Jason's commentary, I pray that you and your church family are blessed by them as I and mine have been.

Kathy Higdon

* * * *

As we study Scripture, we learn that there are boundless benefits for believers within the pages of the Bible. While not an exhaustive list, consider a few prominent advantages that the study of God's Word provides to us. First, Psalm 119:11 tells us that the Psalmist studied Scripture so that he might not sin against the Lord. In Ephesians, Paul goes a step further and identifies the Word as the "sword of the Spirit" and depicts it as a critical offensive weapon in an ongoing spiritual battle.

However, it is even more than a weapon; it is also a tool that can give us greater insight into God's will, as Samuel experienced in 1 Samuel 3:21. It was through the Word that the Lord revealed Himself, and it is through the same Word that the Lord continues to speak to us today. The Psalmist echoes this truth in 119:105, calling it a "lamp unto my feet and a light unto my path."

In addition to serving as a weapon and a tool, Scripture is also a platform for believers. Peter charges us in 1 Peter 3:15, to study the Word and "always be ready to give a defense to everyone who asks you a reason for the hope that is in you." When we wear and represent the name of Christ, we have a responsibility to know what it is that we believe. Paul affirms that thought in 1 Timothy 2:15 as he reminds us that we have a responsibility to study in order to show ourselves approved unto God. You can't truly believe what you don't know or haven't studied.

Finally, Scripture is a blueprint. Jesus tells us in John 15:7 that the study of His Word will lead to a more effective and successful prayer life. However, this is a deeper truth than what it may appear on the surface. Studying the Scriptures is a process. And that process has a changing effect upon the heart, mind, and soul of the one who spends time in the pages of the Living Word. The evidence of the change is in the different prayers that we will pray after we have spent time in the Word. As we align our thoughts with His thoughts, our desires change. And as we calibrate to His guidance, we see more clearly what we need to pray for. That clarity is essential to a successful Christian life, and it is only possible through the study of Scripture.

May God give you a renewed desire for His Word as you study from Cover to Cover.

Kevin Willoughby

Preface

Thank you for participating in the *Cover to Cover Challenge*! Our prayer, first and foremost, is that the Lord will use this challenge to bring glory to His name. He alone is worthy of our praise! I am convinced there is nothing greater you and I can do together than to read and study the Word of God. Before we get into the benefits of reading the Word, let me introduce you to the *Cover to Cover Challenge*.

The *Cover to Cover Challenge* is designed to take you through the Bible in 52 weeks. Each day you will read from a different grouping that will span the entire Bible. On Sundays, for example, you will be reading from the Psalms to help you prepare for worship that day. Monday's reading will be from the Torah (Law), Tuesday- Old Testament History, Wednesday-Gospels/History, Thursday- Wisdom, Friday- Prophecy, and Saturday's reading will be from the New Testament letters. In addition to the daily Bible reading plan, this book contains commentary to help you put what you are reading in context. This will be especially helpful when you begin to read the History and Prophetic books, so you can see where they fit into the overall scheme of the Old Testament. If you are a pastor and your church is going through this together, you can preach from it every week. If you are a Sunday School teacher or small group leader, you can take your group through the Bible and teach a lesson from the readings for the week. You may be thinking "What is the benefit of doing this?" There are many, but I would like to share a few with you as I bring this introduction to a close. First, you will be blessed. Psalm 119:2 says "Blessed are those who keep His testimonies, who seek Him with their whole heart!" Second, you will grow closer to the Lord because all Scripture points to Him (Luke 24:27). Third, reading through the Word allows the Holy Spirit to teach us. Jesus promised this to the disciples in John 14:26. Fourth, the reading of Scripture prompts prayer. As the psalmist in Psalm 119:125 cried out, "I am your servant; give me understanding, that I may know your testimonies." In addition to praying for understanding, each believer in Jesus should pray for one another. In the trying times we live in, there is nothing more comforting than knowing God's Word and knowing people are praying for you. Finally, the reading of God's Word gives us life. Again the psalmist declares, "I will never forget Your precepts, for by them You have given me life" (Psalm 119:93). Isn't it great to know you have been given life by the Savior? John 1:4 reminds us that "In Him (Jesus) was life, and the life was the light of men." Real, true, and eternal life is found in knowing Jesus, and there is no greater way to know Him than through His Word.

Reading the Bible from cover to cover in a year can be a challenging endeavor, but together we can do it. Feel free to share what God is doing in your life through this challenge on the Nazareth Baptist Church Facebook page, or send us an email at c2c@nazarethbaptistchurch.com. God Bless each of you, and I pray the Lord is glorified and works in your life through His Word!

Before You Get Started...

The *Cover to Cover Challenge* was not my idea. God gave it to me as I was praying for a vision for our church in May 2016. Over the course of these past couple of years God's Word has impacted us as individuals, our families, and our church. I pray that it does the same for you. This endeavor could not have been done without the following people who have sacrificed their time to make this challenge possible. I thank and love each one of you.

First and most important I would like to thank my Lord and Savior Jesus Christ for saving me and calling me into the ministry. All the honor and glory belongs to Him. I would like to thank my family for their prayers, encouragement and love they have shown me. William and Roxie Bell (parents), Jeff and Jennifer Bell (brother), Justin and Jill Shifflett (sister), Bobby and Elaine Chester (in-laws), Randy and Lisa Chester (brother-in-law) and Rodney and Michelle Chester (brother-in-law). The Lord has been good to our whole family. To Teresa Presley and Mary Etta Bailey for spending long hours organizing 7,000 pages of commentary for me to read and for helping me finalize and compile the Bible reading plans. To Leanne Timmons for editing and proofreading each week of the *Cover to Cover Challenge*. To our youth/worship pastor Robert Reed who designed the graphics and made sure the week's commentary was posted online and emailed out. If you ever need a graphics designer Robert is your man (reed@nviusgraphics.com). To Kathy Higdon our church secretary who stayed late and worked over to proofread, print, fold, and insert the *Cover to Cover Challenge* newsletters each week. To Kevin Willoughby for his friendship, teaching, and ideas through the years. To each member of Nazareth Baptist Church for their prayers, encouragement, and for participating in the *Cover to Cover Challenge*. Special thanks to our deacons: Danny (Ann) Ashley, Michael (Teresa) Brooks, Ralph (Linda) Hall, Dennis (Sandra) Hicks, Jayson (Emily) Higdon, Paul (Kristi) Higdon, Darrell (Darlene) Johnson, Josh (Lindsay) Little, Chris (Karin) Millican, Gerald (Margie) Owens, Bob (Katy) Powers, Mike (Carrel) Reed, Robert (Regina) Sims, and Jim Tumlin. It is my honor to serve and lead alongside each of you. Finally, to Bro. Charles Jones for inspiring a young preacher to be a student of God's Word and a servant to the Savior.

Cover to Cover Challenge

Week 1

Sunday • Psalms 1-5

Welcome to the *Cover to Cover Challenge*! Once again, thank you for your commitment to read the entire Bible in one year. It will be challenging, but rewarding. You will see your relationship with the Lord grow. Pray that the Lord will be honored and glorified through this, and pray that the Holy Spirit will speak in the hearts of all who are participating.

We will begin each week on Sunday reading from the book of Psalms. The main focus of this book is to lead us to worship our Lord and Savior. In the Hebrew Bible, the literal title is simply Praises. God's "book of hymns" spans from the time of Moses (Ps. 90) to the period after the exile (Ps. 126). It is also composed by many authors ranging from David, who wrote half of them, to Solomon, and Moses and others. In this book we find the authors of the Psalms in many different situations but it is God who is still in control. The Psalms should inspire us all to worship the Lord because no matter what situation we find ourselves in, He is still sovereign over it all!

Psalm 1 is the perfect introduction to the book of Psalms and to the *Cover to Cover Challenge*. Verses 1-3 introduce us to the life of the godly man who avoids the well-worn path of sinners, stays in the Word of God, and experiences a life blessing from the Lord. In contrast, verse 4 describes the life of the ungodly and verse 5 describes the fate of the ungodly. In conclusion, verse 6 reminds us of Matthew 7:13-14. There are two ways, only one leads to life- and that is with Jesus.

Psalm 2 will probably remind you of the time we live in. Verses 1-3 display the rebellion of man against God and how they want nothing to do with God or His people. God's reaction to the plans of the wicked are recorded in verses 4-6. God will laugh at their plans, but notice in verse 6 He is going to send His King (Jesus) to deal with the problem in verses 7-9. It is Jesus who will deal with the sin problem as He rules the nations with a rod of iron. Verses 10-12 are addressed to those who are leaders and urge them to serve the Lord.

Psalm 3 is our first Psalm with a superscription of the context of when it was written. Pay close attention to this, because it will help you understand this passage of Scripture. Verses 1-2 describe the plight the psalmist finds himself in. Verses 3-6 show the psalmist praising God for who He is, and show what great faith he has in God. Verses 7-8 record the desperate prayer of David for God to save him from his troubles.

Psalm 4 begins with a call for God to hear the prayer that is about to be spoken in the middle of a stressful situation. Notice the advice given verses 2-5 regarding finding yourself in a stressful situation. The Lord will hear you when you call (v3), do not sin (v4), think about the situation and wait (v4), and trust in the Lord (v5). Verses 6-8 describe the results of trusting in God during these times. It is God who gives gladness (v7) during these times in our life, peace (v8), and safety (v8).

Psalm 5, just like Psalm 4, begins with a call for God to hear the prayer of the psalmist. In verses 1-3, David pours his heart out for God to hear his prayer that he will offer every morning. In verses 4-6, David praises God for His holiness, and in verse 7 David worships God based upon His covenant love (mercy). In verses 8-12 David asks for God to make a path for him with no obstacles (v8), describes the characteristics of the wicked (v9), asks God to judge the wicked (v10), and petitions God to protect and give to joy to those who love Him (v11,12).

Monday • Genesis 1-4

Genesis is also known as the book of origins or the book of beginnings. It introduces us to the revelation of God. Genesis details for us the beginnings of the universe, life, blessing, sin, covenants, marriage, government, and most importantly salvation. Most people believe Genesis was written by Moses sometime after the exodus from Egypt. This would allow the children of Israel to see that the God who delivered them from the hands of the Egyptians is the same God who created the heavens and the earth. If there is a book in the Bible that lays the foundation for what is to come it is the book of Genesis. Everything begins here.

Genesis 1 records the creation of the universe, which I am sure you are all familiar with. The creation story actually goes from 1:1-2:3. The height of His creation is recorded in verse 27 as God creates man in His image. Verse 28 is the beginning of the marriage covenant that is between one man and one woman which will be highlighted more in chapter 2.

Chapter 2 takes us a little deeper into the story of creation as Genesis begins to highlight the sixth day when God made man and woman. We get glimpses of the beauty of Eden, the trees, the rivers, and all that comprised the paradise that God had prepared for man. Chapter 2 sets the stage for chapter 3 as God provides a warning not to eat of the tree of the knowledge of good and evil and the consequences of doing so. Chapter 2 ends with the creation of woman for the man. It is a breathtaking portrait of the marriage covenant God has given us to celebrate with our spouses.

Genesis 3 is important to the whole of Scripture. The fall of man is one of the most heartbreaking, yet glorious stories in the Bible. We read of the serpent (Satan) doubting (v1), denying (v3), and distorting (v5) God's Word- all things he continues to do today. Adam and Eve quench their desire (v6) to have the fruit, and we see sin enter into the hearts of man. In the midst of sorrow there is hope. God will send a Savior, a Redeemer if you will, to pay the price for sin (v15). God's mercy is seen for the first time in providing clothing for Adam and Eve before they are banished from the garden forever.

Genesis 4 introduces us to the first family as they begin to have children. In the story of Cain and Abel you will see the effects of sin and judgment of sin. The greatest thing about chapter 4 happens in verses 25 and 26 as Eve gives birth Seth and men begin to call upon the name of the Lord. It is through the line of Seth that the Redeemer will be born.

Tuesday • Joshua 1-6

Joshua, whose name means "Jehovah saves", is set aside as the leader of the Israelites after the death of Moses (Deut. 34; Num. 27:12-23). He was born under slavery in Egypt and will be a key figure in leading the Israelites into Canaan, defeating those who oppose God and separating the land among the 12 tribes. This is done for two primary reasons. First, it shows God to be truthful to His Word in fulfilling the covenant He made with Abraham

(Gen. 12:7, 15:18-21, 17:8). Second, it will be a judgment on those who oppose God which serve as a testimony to the Israelites that they are followers of the one true God. Joshua is the first of the historical books in the Old Testament. Paul instructs us in 1 Corinthians 10:1-13 to learn from the examples set by them.

Joshua 1:1-9 records God's encouragement to Joshua as he begins leading the children of Israel. These promises are for all of us who belong to the Lord. But, notice the central part is in verses 7 and 8-it is the Word of God. The rest of the chapter (v10-18) shows Joshua preparing the Israelites to leave and enter the Promised Land.

At the beginning of chapter 2 Joshua sends two spies to Jericho. Rahab agrees to help the spies hide from the king's men in exchange for them sparing her and her family when they come to conquer Jericho.

Led by the Ark of the Covenant (which symbolized the presence of God) and the Levites the Israelites will cross over the Jordan River in chapter 3. The exodus began with the parting of the Red Sea and concludes with the parting of the Jordan River as the people of Israel to enter the Promised Land. God is once again making His presence known among those He calls His own.

Two memorials for what God has done for the children of Israel are built in chapter 4. One man from each tribe will be chosen to take a stone from the river and build a memorial on the bank of the Jordan River. This will allow future generations to know what God had done for the people of Israel. The second is built by Joshua in the middle of the river where the priests stood. As God promised in 3:7, Joshua is now great in the eyes of the people of Israel.

Joshua 5 begins with the Israelites entering the land of Canaan, the Amorites and Canaanites are petrified. God purifies the male population in verses 2-9, and they celebrate the Passover for the first time in Canaan in verse 10. The provision of manna stops as the people eat from the land God is giving them. As chapter 5 closes, Joshua stands in the presence of the commander of the Lord's army which many believe is the Lord Jesus Christ.

In Joshua 6 we will read the story of the fall of Jericho. Jericho was built on a hill and normally would have taken many months to conquer for even the best army. This battle taught the Israelites that obedience to the Lord brings true victory. Just as promised in chapter 2, Rahab the harlot is spared along with her family. Joshua pronounces a curse on anyone who tries to rebuild Jericho. Read 1 Kings 16:34 and you will see someone who tried.

Wednesday • Matthew 1-4

The Gospel of Matthew was written between AD 63 and AD 70 from Antioch of Syria. Antioch of Syria would become the center of the Gentile missionary effort, and send out the first missionaries (Acts 13). Matthew, formerly known as Levi the tax collector, left everything to follow Jesus. In the gospel that bears his name, Matthew offers firsthand testimony to demonstrate that Jesus fulfills the prophecies regarding the Messiah. It is the most Jewish of all the Gospels, but also shows a need for the gospel to go to the nations. Matthew quotes or alludes to the Old Testament over 60 times to connect his claim of Jesus' messiahship. There are other substantial clues that point to a Jewish audience. Matthew is the only gospel writer to repeatedly refer to "the kingdom of heaven", whereas the others use "the kingdom of God". Jesus is called "the Son of David" in Matthew's gospel. Matthew is separated into five major discourses which each end with "when Jesus had ended these sayings". The five discourses include: the Sermon on the Mount (ch. 5-7), the sending out of the twelve (ch. 10), the parables of the kingdom (ch. 13), the child-like faith of a believer (ch. 18), and the Olivet Discourse (ch. 24,25).

Matthew and Luke are the only Gospels to record a genealogy and a birth narrative. This genealogy shows that Jesus is the Messiah by linking Jesus with David. While most are not interested in reading the genealogy, to a Jew it was important to know where and who your descendants were. Notice the names in the list and the remarkable stories that are recorded of them in Scripture. Abraham, Isaac, and Jacob are familiar stories to us-but look at some of the other names. Tamar (Gen. 38), Rahab (Josh. 2), Ruth, and Bathsheba (2 Sam. 11) are surprising names found in the genealogy of Jesus. Matthew's birth narrative focuses on Joseph and his many dreams (v18-25). Betrothal was treated the same as marriage even though the couple lived apart. Joseph is described as a just man (law abiding) who did not want to shame Mary (v19). The birth narrative concentrates on Joseph, the angels, and dreams (20). The mission of Jesus is to save His people from their sins (v21). What was prophesied in the OT is now going to become a reality-people are going to be saved from their sin (Isa. 53; Jer. 31:31-34; Ez. 36:24-31). While Isaiah 7:14 was fulfilled in Isaiah's day, Matthew sees the ultimate fulfillment of this prophecy in Jesus. The name Immanuel shows that Jesus is God, and His presence will be with His people.

Matthew 2 continues the birth narrative from chapter 1. In this section of the text we meet the wise men. These men are following a star in the east in order to encounter the King of the Jews (v1-6). These verses and the fact that Herod died in 4 B.C. help us to date the timing of Jesus' birth. Most people believe that the star mentioned in verse 2 is a reference to Numbers 24:17, concerning the prophecy of a rising star out of Jacob. Scripture and history show Herod to be a violent, ruthless, and suspicious man. Being an Idumean, Herod would have naturally feared a king who was rising up from the Jews. Micah 5:2 is quoted to show the origin of Jesus' birth and also to directly link Him as the Son of David. There are also allusions to 2 Samuel 5:2 that describe David's role as the shepherd of Israel. In verses 7-12 Herod asks about the king, pretending to want to worship Him. Verses 9-10 show that the star moved to guide the wise men. The gifts that they brought to the Child were fit for a king (Ps. 45:8, 72:15, Isa. 60:6). Joseph is also warned about Herod in a dream, and flees to Egypt in response to that dream (v13-15). Verse 15 is a quotation from Hosea 11:1. In Hosea we see God deliver His people from bondage to Egypt. In the same manner, God would call His Son from Egypt to deliver His people from their sin. When Herod realizes he has been deceived, he orders all male children under the age of two to be killed (v16-18). Jeremiah 31:15 is quoted here, originally referencing those who were going into exile. The passage goes on to explain that there would be hope for their future despite their current circumstances. Matthew may be showing that God is using the disaster with Herod to bring forth the One who would provide ultimate deliverance and joy to them. After the death of Herod, Joseph once again receives a warning in a dream. In response to the dream Joseph and his family go to Galilee and reside in the city of Nazareth (v. 19-23).

John the Baptist becomes the focal point in chapter 3. His primary task was to prepare the way for Jesus. He was also to preach to the people about repentance and judgment (v1-2). The word repent means "to change the mind" and it was meant to be done immediately (at hand). Verse 3 was originally directed at those coming out of exile (Isa. 40:3). Here it refers to the coming of Jesus, who would bring forgiveness of sins. Verse 4 shows that John was dressed similar to the OT prophets (2 Kings 1:8). Many people were coming to John to be baptized in order to show that they had repented of their sins (v5-6). Because of this, the Pharisees and Sadducees investigated John and his message (v7-8). John shows them that they depended only on being Abraham's descendants for their salvation (v9). Verses 10-11 show that only those who place faith in Christ will bear fruit as proof that they have repented of their sins and be baptized by the Holy Spirit (Gal. 3:6-7). Those who do not repent and bear fruit will experience the judgment of God (v12). In verses 13-17 Jesus comes to John for baptism, and we read that all three members of the Trinity are present. By coming forth for baptism Jesus is identifying with His people and with the message that John is preaching. John's message and Jesus' message are both a call to repent (4:17). Jesus begins His public ministry when the Holy Spirit descends on Him. In the first three chapters Matthew has shown us that Jesus is the Davidic Messiah, the Son of God, and a Servant who has begun his mission to die for the sins of the world.

Chapter 4 contains the temptation (testing) of Jesus, the beginning of His ministry, and the calling of the first four disciples. Jesus is led by the Spirit into the wilderness, where He is tempted by Satan (v1-2). The 40 days and nights of fasting should bring to mind Moses (Ex. 34:28) and Elijah (1 Kgs 19:8). Verses 3-4 show that Jesus was obedient to the Father and to His plan. Verses 5-7 show that Jesus trusted in the Father's plan, and verses 8-10 show that Jesus was loyal to the Father's plan. With each of the temptations, Satan is tempting Jesus (as he does us) to act independently of God. Satan even twists Scripture (v6) to try and get Jesus to succumb to the temptation. Notice how Jesus responds…"It is written". When temptations come our way there is nothing greater that we can do than to quote Scripture. Jesus went through this testing so that you and I would know how to defeat temptation from Satan when it comes (Heb. 4:15).

Verses 12-17 record the beginning of Jesus' ministry and His message, "Repent for the kingdom of heaven is at hand!" Capernaum would become the "home base" of Jesus' ministry, which may be due to His rejection in Nazareth (Luke 4:16-30). The quotation of Isaiah 9:1-2 is also significant because the rest of the passage in Isaiah shows the birth of the Messiah. Jesus calls Peter, Andrew, James, and John to become fishers of men in verses 18-22. Jesus was not only calling them to listen and learn from Him, but to become active in the ministry. Chapter 4 ends with a description of His ministry. Notice in verse 23 that Jesus taught, preached, healed, and that He was followed by a great multitude (v25).

Thursday • Job 1-2

It is not known when Job was written, but we are given clues to the time period Job lived in. The book of Job never mentions Abraham or the covenant God made with him. Job's wealth is in accordance with his livestock, he acts as a priest for his family, and his age at the end all point toward Job living during the patriarchal period, possibly before Abraham. The story of Job is an enduring lesson for all believers who are suffering. We all have talked about the suffering of Job. Maybe even entertained the idea we have suffered worse. Even in the New Testament we read that suffering is a reality in a believer's life. Job invites us to see "that the sufferings of this present time are not worthy to be compared with the glory which shall be revealed in us" (Rom. 8:18) and that we should "count it all joy when you fall into various trials, knowing that the testing of your faith produces patience… but let patience have its perfect work, that you may be perfect and complete, lacking nothing" (James 1:2-4).

In the first chapter we meet Job and learn about his faith and his family (v1-5). Beginning in verse 6 we leave earth for the heavens and witness a conversation between God and Satan concerning Job (Zech. 3 records another heavenly confrontation). During this conversation (v8-12) you should notice it is God who initiates the dialogue. Satan believes Job only serves God because God has blessed him tremendously. God then gives Satan permission to touch all of Job's possessions. Notice Satan cannot touch anything unless he is given permission by God. Verses 13-19 record four catastrophes where Job loses his animals, servants, and his children. Job's reaction to the dreadful news is recorded in verses 20-22. Tearing the robe and shaving of the head are symbols of extreme grief. All Job has left is his wife and his health but even this is about to change.

Job 2 records another conversation between God and Satan concerning Job (v1-10). Satan asks for permission to touch Job's body and God agrees, but Satan is not given permission to take his life. He goes to the ash heap and takes broken pottery to scrape the boils off to release the infection and relieve his pain. His own wife tells him to curse (blaspheme) God and die but Job does not. Eliphaz, Bildad, Zophar come to mourn alongside Job during his time of great grief (v11-13). Verse 13 says that they sat silent by him for seven days as his pain was still increasing. In times of great sadness we want to say something to help with the pain, but oftentimes it is the power of our presence and silence that speaks the loudest.

Friday • Obadiah

Obadiah is the shortest book in the Old Testament. Obadiah means "servant of the Lord" or "worshiper of the Lord". Obadiah, like Nahum and Jonah pronounces judgment on a hostile nation instead of Israel. Edom is also a representative term of all the nations that oppose God and His people (Ps. 83:5-18, 137:7; Jer. 49:7-22; Lam. 4:21,22; Joel 3:19; Mal. 1:2-5). Edom is guilty according to Obadiah of not helping Judah during a time of invasion. Obadiah is one of the hardest books to place an exact date on, but there are two time periods associated with it. First, many believe Obadiah and Joel prophesied during the times of Elijah and Elisha in the ninth century. In 2 Kings 8:20-22 and 2 Chronicles 21:16-17, Jerusalem is attacked by the Philistines and the Arabs while Edom sits idly by doing nothing to help. Second, Obadiah could have been written during the fall of Jerusalem in 586 BC when the Babylonians, led by Nebuchadnezzar invaded taking them into captivity (2 Chronicles 36:20; Ez. 25:13-14). There is much evidence to support both but Obadiah never mentions the Babylonians by name (as other prophets do), the destruction of the Temple, or the taking of the people into captivity so the first option is preferred here. Either context brings out the message of Obadiah.

The Israel/Edom conflict actually began in Genesis 25 in the womb of Rebekah. The Edomites are descendants of Esau who is remembered for selling his birthright (Gen. 25:30) and marrying women outside the covenant (Gen. 26:34; 28:9). The Edomites always opposed Israel and were a continual thorn in their side. They participated in the destruction of Jerusalem in 586 BC and were driven out of the area later by the Babylonians where they became known as the Idumeans. What is significant about this? Herod the Great, king of Judea, whom you read about at the birth of Christ was an Idumean. Esau/Edom was still standing in the way of God's plan for His people! Obadiah predicts that Edom will one day no longer exist (v10, 18). This came to fulfillment in 70 AD as Rome, led by Titus, destroyed Jerusalem and the Idumeans were erased from history.

Verses 1-9 cover the punishment of Edom. Verse 1 confirms that the message is from the Lord, not Obadiah. Verses 3-4 give one reason for God's judgment-is their pride (James 4:6). The capital of Edom was Petra. The capital's location-hidden in the mountains and the fortresses of rocks protecting it caused the Edomites to gloat over their security. Verse 5-6 detail when their enemy comes there will be nothing left of their city. Verse 7 relates that those who were their friends and benefited from alliances with Edom will be the ones to come against them. Edom was known for its men of wisdom (Eliphaz, Job's friend was from there), and in verses 8-9 we are told that God will eliminate the wise men and the warriors.

Verses 10-14 describe the sins of Edom. Verse 10 gives an overall scope of their sins in that they committed "violence against your brother Jacob (Israel)". What were the sins? They offered no help (v11), were happy over it (v12), would help those attacking Jacob (v13), and they prevented any from escaping Judah (v14).

Day of the Lord prophecies have a near and far fulfillment. Here in verse 15, Edom will get paid back for their sins against Jacob which is the near fulfillment. Edom, serves as an example of nations who oppose God. In verse 16 we are told that these nations will "drink continually". This is a reference to the judgment of God on those who oppose Him.

Verses 17-21 detail the future plight of Jacob and Edom. Edom will be "consumed" by Jacob as the Lord's people repossess the land. Many believe this will be fulfilled in the future kingdom when the Lord Jesus will rule with a rod of iron.

Saturday • James 1-2

The letter of James was written around AD 44-50 and is the earliest of the New Testament books. James is the half-brother of Jesus. He had formerly rejected Jesus (John 7:5), but would come to believe later in life (1 Cor. 15:7). Paul, in Galatians 2:9, calls James one of the pillars of the church. This letter is written to the "twelve tribes" (Jews outside of Jerusalem) which have been scattered, perhaps due to persecution following the martyrdom of Stephen and the sudden advancement of the church (v1). He writes to encourage them in the midst of this situation. James' letter is practical, simple, and straightforward. He touches on the ethical teachings of the Sermon on the Mount throughout the letter.

James 1:2-8 opens with the discussion of the purpose of trials in a believer's life. James says that trials produce patience or endurance in our lives. In fact, he said trials complete who we are. Trials become the way that believers are developed into maturity. Next, he discusses asking for wisdom and provides instruction on how to ask (Prov. 2:6; Matt. 7:7). All prayers should be asked in faith (Matt. 21:21-22). A person who asks without faith (doubting) is like a person being tossed back and forth by the waves, unstable in all his ways.

James 1:9-11 discusses trials of the rich and poor. Both will suffer trials of different kinds, both are equal in God's eyes, and both must live their lives with a heavenly perspective as opposed to an earthly one. The blessing of enduring temptation and a description of temptation is found in verses 12-16. All people are tempted, but the one who endures is blessed (v12). Those who endure are given a crown of life (eternal life) which shows victory over suffering and temptations (Rev. 2:10). God does not tempt us, nor is He tempted by evil (v13). Each of us is tempted when we are drawn away (draw out from hiding place) by our own desires (fleshly, selfish) and enticed (bait the hook). It is the desires of our flesh that draw us out and make us vulnerable, while Satan baits the hook (v14). Verse 15 describes the rest of the process. When desire is fully grown we sin, and when sin is brought to completion it brings forth death (Rom. 6:23). Verse 16 is a warning not to wander or go astray. Verses 17-18 are reminders that every blessing we receive is from God- who never changes. Verse 19 serves as a warning to watch our speech, and verse 20 is a warning against anger. By putting these two together, James is showing that it is often uncontrolled anger that leads to us saying harmful words (Prov. 10:19, 15:1, 17:27).

James 1:21-27 begins another passage about the effects of God's Word. Verses 21-22 say that we are to receive it, or let it take up residence in our lives. The word "filthiness" in verse 21 describes clothes that need to be removed (Zech. 3:3-4). James does this to show that after one has believed the word they are to remain in it. The word is not only to be heard, but obeyed (v22, Luke 11:28, Rom. 2:13). Verses 23-24 instruct us to assess our lives in the mirror of God's Word, while verse 25 encourages us to apply what we have learned to our lives. Verses 26-27 instruct us to live out what we have learned by having self-control (v26), love for others (v27), and by living a clean life (v27).

James 2:1-13 refers to showing favoritism toward anyone based upon financial status. It would also include race, how they dress, or social status. James contends that God does not even show partiality (favoritism), so the Christian must also not (v1, Deut. 10:17-18; Rom. 2:11; Eph. 6:9). The situation is described in verses 2-3. James says that the basis for this attitude is evil thoughts (v4). In fact, God has chosen the poor and they are rich (those that know Him) in His sight (Matt. 5:3). James also points out to them that the people they are showing partiality to are the same ones who are oppressing them. He also points out that they are blaspheming the name of Christ (v6-7). James announces in verses 8-9 that if you want to fulfill the law you will love your neighbor as yourself, but once you hold one person higher than another based upon these things you have sinned. Some believe it is called the "royal law" because the law of love comes from the King of heaven. Jesus extended the law of love to include all people (Luke 10:25-27), even our enemies (Matt. 5:44). Failure to love results in failing to keep the whole law and renders the person guilty before God (v10-11). In verse 12 James calls to mind that a Christian will be judged based upon the word of God. This section concludes with an appeal to show mercy on all people, which alludes back to Matthew 5:7. Those who have shown no mercy should expect no mercy in the judgment, but those who show mercy display evidence of Christ in their life.

James 2:14-26 is about faith that produces works. The issue that James discusses here is the difference between real faith and a dead faith. His argument here proves that real faith in Christ will produce works. It is also important to point out that James is not saying faith does not save. What he is pointing out is that if someone claims to have faith, but has no works, then that type of faith (dead) cannot save them. He gives an example in verses 15-16. A need is brought to the person, but they refuse to meet the need and literally tell the person "good luck" and send them away. James says that kind of faith is dead because there are no works to show for it (v17). In verse 18 James contends that he can show how real and genuine someone's faith is by his or her works. James is not saying that works saved him, but that works prove the genuineness of his faith. He also shows that any person (even a demon) can claim belief in God and it not be genuine (v19-20). James offers the example of Abraham, who was willing to offer Isaac upon the altar as a sacrifice after placing his faith in God (v21-23). Rahab from the book of Joshua is also used as an example of someone whose works display their faith (v25). Both the examples of Abraham and Rahab show that their faith produced works. In verse 26 James once again reiterates his point- faith without works is dead, showing what type of faith the person has.

Cover to Cover CHALLENGE

Week 2

Sunday • Psalms 6-8

I pray you have enjoyed reading and studying God's Word this week with the *Cover to Cover Challenge*. Our prayer is that while you read that God will speak to you thru the Scriptures and that His name is honored and glorified. As always we will begin each week with the Psalms.

When you read Psalm 6 it is apparent David is suffering from persecution (v10) from his enemies. It is possible he is suffering over something he may have done (v1). Whichever is the case David sees no end in sight (v3). In verses 1-3 he cries out to God to restore him though the trouble he is experiencing has shaken him to his core (v2). Verses 4-5 record David crying out to God based upon His mercy (unfailing love, covenant love). David feels as if he is going to die, and reminds God that if he does die he cannot recall all the great deeds God has done for him (5). In verses 6-7, David cries "all night" and his grief is beginning to overtake him. David is assured God has heard his prayer and will deal with his enemies in verses 8-10.

In Psalm 7 David prays for deliverance from his enemies. Verses 1-2 describe David placing his trust in the Lord to deliver him from his enemies. David believes he has not caused this to come upon himself, but if he has done wrong he will willingly suffer the consequences (3-5). In verses 6-13 David asks God to judge his enemies. Verses 6-8 show him asking the Lord four times to "Arise", "Lift Yourself up", "Rise up", and "return on high" to do justice to those who persecute him. David prays for God, in His righteousness, to defend him in verses 9-10. Verse 11-13 points toward the wrath of God which will be poured out upon the wicked (John 3:36; Rom. 1:18, 2:5; Eph. 5:6). Also, in verses 12-13, God is pictured as a righteous warrior ready to avenge. God will pay the wicked back for their evil deeds in verses 14-16. This is called God's retribution (Proverbs 26:27). Finally in verse 17, David praises God for His righteousness. It is God who will deliver the upright and cause the wicked to fall.

Psalm 8 praises God for His role in creation. Verses 1-2 praise God because He is the Redeemer and also that He is Lord over all the earth. Verse 2 highlights the fact that no enemy can overcome His rule. In verses 3-4 David is essentially saying, "Lord when I look at Your creation-the sun, moon, and stars-why do You care for me and give me good things?" Verse 5 is a reminder of our status as children of God because we have been made in the image of God (Gen. 1:26-27). Verses 6-8 speak of man's dominion over the earth to rule and to care for it (Gen. 1:28) and the psalm closes in verse 9 with praise to God. This is also a Messianic psalm pointing toward the first coming of Christ.

Monday • Genesis 5-9

The story of Lamech from Genesis 4 ties in with Genesis 5. Cain's genealogy is recorded in 4:16-24 of Genesis. Lamech is the seventh in Cain's line which makes him a representative of Cain's family tree. Lamech had these traits: he acted independently of God, was a polygamist, was prideful, and a murderer. The genealogy in chapter five follows Seth who is born to Adam and Eve at the closing of chapter four. The seventh from Adam in this line is Enoch who represents his line. If you will notice in verse 22, he "walked with God". Enoch was dependent on God and is remembered by you and me for being taken to heaven without dying (Heb. 11:5). This is the testimony of two family trees. One lived as if God didn't exist, while the other was living for God. Genesis 5:29-32 introduce us to Noah whom the next three chapters will be about.

Genesis 6:1-8 tell of the extreme wickedness of Noah's day. Jesus said in Matthew 24:37-39 that this will characterize the time of His coming as well. Noah ("Rest") is described for us in verses 8-10. He "found grace in the eyes of the Lord", he was just, blameless, and he walked (dependent on) with God. God instructs Noah to build the ark (450x75x45) to prepare for the coming of the flood (v17). God established a covenant with Noah and his family in verse 18. God alone is responsible to uphold the covenant.

Chapter 6 ends with the obedience of Noah to God's plan. Verses 5, 9, and 17 of chapter 7 also speak of Noah's obedience. 2 Peter 2:5 tells us that Noah was a preacher of righteousness. If it took Noah 120 years to build the ark, and during that time he was warning people of the coming destruction-what would it have been like once God shut the door of the ark and the rain began to fall?

In chapter 8 the flood waters begin to recede and God "remembered Noah". Not that God had forgotten Noah, but the word "remembered" means God was acting on Noah's behalf to deliver him. In verses 20-22 Noah builds an altar and sacrifices to the Lord. God promises never to destroy every living thing again.

At the beginning of chapter 9 God reiterates the command to "be fruitful and multiply" to Noah and his family. Animal life becomes a part of man's diet and God speaks of "life that is in the blood". The sanctity of human life is discussed in verses 5-6. Also in verse 6 most see the institution of human government. In verses 8-17, God details the covenant (mentioned 7x) he is making with Noah. God places the rainbow in the cloud to remind Himself and man that He will never destroy every living creature again in verse 13. The rainbow is a sign of God's grace, His promise, and His presence. Noah after the incident with Ham pronounces a curse upon him and his descendants and blesses Shem and Japheth (20-29).

Tuesday • Joshua 7-10

As Joshua 7 begins, the children of Israel (still under the leadership of Joshua) are defeated at Ai ("Ruins"). Ai was a much smaller foe than Jericho, and the Israelites should have had no problem defeating them. Joshua goes to the Lord in verses 7-9. Notice he has an attitude of defeat, and recommends they should have never crossed the Jordan. He asks God if He wants them to be destroyed and have His name diminished among the nations. In verse 10-15 God speaks to Joshua and tells him that someone has sinned and broken the covenant and God prescribes the death penalty for the one who committed the crime. Verses 16-26 describe how the people come by families before the Lord, and it is revealed that it is Achan who has sinned. Achan admits he was the one who broke covenant with God, and the evidence is presented (20-23). All of his family and possessions are brought to the Valley of Achor ("Disaster") where they were stoned, burned with fire, and buried under stones. God takes sin seriously, and wants His people to guard themselves from it.

Chapter 8 begins with God telling Joshua "not to be afraid or dismayed" and how the defeat of Ai will be accomplished. In verses 3-8, Joshua gives the orders on how the battle will be fought while verses 9-29 relay the details of the battle. Joshua builds an altar (to bless God for victory and the land) to the Lord and reads from the Book of the Law reminding the people of the blessings and curses. They copied the Law on stones in verse 32 in obedience to what Moses had earlier commanded them to do (Deut. 27:4).

Joshua 9:1-15 records the peace agreement with the Gibeonites. God had instructed them not to make a treaty with anyone in the land (Deut. 7:1-3, 20:16-18). The Gibeonites tricked them into believing they had come from a faraway land. Verse 14 records the fact that the men of Israel did not seek God in this matter. In verses 16-27 the trickery is discovered. Because of the treaty made with them, Joshua cannot destroy them. Instead he makes the Gibeonites woodcutters and water carriers (they were known for their wells) for the children of Israel. King Saul violates this treaty in 2 Samuel 21:1-9 and suffers the wrath of God. Also some Gibeonites helped Nehemiah rebuild the wall (Neh. 3:7).

In Joshua 10:1-15 five kings come together to punish the Gibeonites for making a treaty with Israel which causes them to lose one of their allies. God intercedes in the battle as verse 11 says "large hailstones from heaven" fell, killing more people than Joshua and the army did. Verses 12-15 record the miracle of the sun standing still. This reminded the Israelites that it was the Lord who fought for them and who was winning the battle for them. All the kings of the nations who came against the Gibeonites are executed in verses16-27. Verse 25 is a reminder to the children of Israel that if they continued to follow God He would give them victory. Verses 29-43 record victories in battle and names the lands conquered by the Israelites.

Wednesday • Matthew 5-7

The book of Matthew contains the greatest sermon in scripture, which is preached by the greatest preacher to ever live. The Sermon on the Mount records ethical teachings of Jesus, which He used to counter the teachings of the Pharisees. This sermon contains qualities of living a Spirit-filled and Spirit-led life, the way to truly have joy, and it also shows the need to be born again. After calling the disciples it was important that Jesus lay the foundation of what a true disciple was.

Matthew 5:1-12 records nine "blessed" statements made by Jesus. The term "blessed" refers to inward happiness despite outward circumstances. I will give some examples of how to read these in the hope of shedding more light on them: "Blessed (inward happiness) are the poor (dependent on someone else for well-being), for theirs (alone) is the kingdom of heaven". Only those who realize they are poor in spirit will receive the kingdom of heaven (Isa. 66:2). Verse 4 tells us those who mourn are those who experience grief and sorrow in their lives for any number of reasons. We read that they will be comforted. This verse may also refer to Isaiah 61:2. Verse 6 would say "Blessed (inward happiness) are those who hunger and thirst (for the whole thing) for righteousness, for they (alone) shall be filled (satisfied, complete)". If you live out verses 1-9 you can expect 10-12 to happen. Persecution would be experienced by Jesus, by the early church, and even by us in the world we live in today. Jesus warned His disciples (and us) that true disciples would be persecuted (John 15:18-21). There is reason to rejoice, even in the midst of persecution. The word "glad" means "to run and jump with joy". Verses 13-16 explain that if we have the characteristics found in verses 1-12 we will become the salt and light of the earth and we will be lights in a world filled with darkness. These verses show that the disciples are effective at influencing those around them, they are preserving those around them, and they are revealing the gospel to the world. Christ fulfilling the law is the subject of verses 17-20. Verse 18 shows the importance of God's Word in our lives and its eternal value. As the psalmist says "Forever O Lord Your word is settled in heaven" (Ps. 119:89).Verse 20 is important because it explains that the only way to have your righteousness exceed that of the Pharisees is to believe in Jesus.

In verses 21-26 we are warned about anger and reconciling with those that we have a disagreement with. A person living this kind of life cannot worship (v23-24) God, nor can they have their prayers answered (Mark 11:20-26). An attitude of forgiveness and reconciliation should be found in the lives of believers. Adultery and marriage are the subjects of verses 27-32. Jesus equates looking at a woman to lust after her to adultery. Verses 31-32 can be better explained by referring to Matthew 19. In both passages Jesus refers to Deuteronomy 24:1-4 and the writing of divorcement given by Moses, which was misinterpreted by the Jews. Many Jewish men believed that they could divorce for any reason. Jesus corrects their flawed view of marriage and divorce by citing Genesis 1:27 and Genesis 2:24. He also alludes to Malachi 2:16 in verses 4-6. Jesus, within this context, teaches that the only reason for divorce is adultery. Verses 33-37 discuss being a person of your word (truthfulness). If a person is true to their word, there is no reason for an oath. Verses 38-42 warn against seeking revenge and retaliating against those who may have wronged you. Chapter 5 closes with an admonishment to love all people, including your enemies (43-48). This type of love will show the world that a person is a disciple of Jesus.

In 6:1-18, Jesus begins speaking about our motives behind our deeds. The three greatest things a Jew in Jesus' day could do were: good deeds (1-4), pray (8-14), and fast (16-18). In verses 1-4 Jesus gives a warning to not to do acts of mercy to be seen by others, because this is the wrong motive. He ascribes the same warning to prayer (v5-9) and fasting (v16-18). Verses 9-13 refer to the Lord's Prayer. This is an example of how a disciple of Jesus should pray. It covers praising God (v9), having concern for His kingdom (v10), God's will (v10), the disciples' needs (v11), forgiveness (v12), guidance (v13), and deliverance from evil (v13). Verses 19-21 warn of where your true treasure lies. Verses 22-24 continue the same theme of eyeing earthly treasures and letting them become your master. A divided loyalty is no loyalty at all. The key to the Sermon on the Mount is found in verses 25-34. While the main subject of these verses is worry, verse 33 contains the antidote to keep us from worrying (easier said than done I know). We are to "seek first the kingdom of God and His righteousness". Doing this makes our worrying come into perspective. Verse 27 shows that worrying will not add any time to your life. In fact, worrying and stress will take years off of your life.

Matthew 7:1-6 warns about being critical of others when we ourselves have sin, and may be doing the same thing we condemn others for. Many people will partially quote this and say "we shouldn't judge others". This saying is only partially true. We should not judge others in the sense that we are continually finding faults in others or have condemning attitudes toward them. The parable in 18:23-35 demonstrates this perfectly. On the other hand we are to use righteous judgment (John 7:24). An illustration of this is in verses 15-20. The way we can tell if someone is a false teacher is by making a judgment based upon their fruit. Judgment is also needed in verse 6. One must know what is holy/pearl in order not to cast it before dogs/swine. Verses 7-12 are about being persistent in your prayer life (Luke 18:1-8), the goodness of God, and what we call the Golden Rule. Verses 7-8 the words ask, seek, and knock are in the present tense which shows that prayer is to be continual. In verses 9-11 the goodness of God is compared to the goodness of man. While man is evil and gives good gifts God is not evil and most certainly will answer the prayers of those who belong to Him. Verse 12 summarizes all of the teachings of Jesus up to this point. If you want people to treat you well you treat them well. In conclusion the Sermon on the Mount ends with four sections. By these a genuine disciple can be known. In the first Jesus warns of two gates (v13-14). These verses warn not to enter the wide gate which leads to destruction but to go by the narrow gate which is difficult. The word "difficult" means "restricted". Today many believe there are many ways to heaven (broad way). There is only one way to heaven and that is through Jesus Christ (restricted, John 14:6). Next are two types of fruit (v15-21). The false prophets mentioned look like sheep, sound like sheep, and may even seem to walk like sheep but are not. How can believers tell between a false shepherd and a true shepherd? It is by looking at their fruit. Verses 21-23 seem to shock people and proceed from verse 19 concerning judgment. Verse 21 shows that not everyone who calls Jesus Lord is a child of God. Verse 22 takes it a step further and shows that not everyone who has preached/taught or performed miracles is a child of God. Even Satan can masquerade as an angel of light and perform miracles (2 Cor. 11:14). Verse 23 is the key because Jesus says they "practice lawlessness". You cannot habitually practice sin and be a child of God. Will we sin? Yes. But will you stay in it? Absolutely not. These people have deceived themselves and that is a great travesty (James 1:16, 22). The final section in verses 24-27 reflects obedience to Jesus' words. Both hear His words but only one does them. Verses 28-29 show that Jesus taught with authority and in the coming chapters His works will demonstrate that authority.

Thursday • Job 3-4

When we last saw Job he was in the ash heap at the edge of town (where the lepers and beggars stayed) broken, distraught, and depressed over the great losses he had suffered. Whether in sickness or the loss of a loved one, we all have felt as if we were Job at one point or another. In Job chapter 3 we will see Job speak from the depth of his heart and receive a glimpse of the pain he must be suffering. In chapter 4 Eliphaz will be the first of Job's friends to speak.

Job wishes the day he was born never happened and describes the day of his birth as a day of darkness (v3-4). He goes back even farther wishing that he would have never been conceived (v10). In verse 11 Job wishes that he had died at birth. Verses 14-19 make it seem as if Job would welcome death at this point, if God so chose to allow him to die. Throughout chapter 3 Job laments over his situation, and in verses 20-23 he wonders why God even lets him live. He describes his feelings in verses 24-26 and you get a picture of the physical and mental pain he is suffering.

Job chapter 4 opens with Eliphaz the Temanite speaking. He speaks of the type of man Job is (v3-4, 6,) but in verses 7-9 Eliphaz seems to indicate that Job wouldn't be going through this if he hadn't sinned. Eliphaz believes Job must have done something very bad to be experiencing this much pain. Just because we suffer does not mean we have sinned (John 9:1-3). Verse 17 adds to this accusation. Of course no man can be more righteous than God, and no one can be more pure than Him. The point that Eliphaz is making to Job is that you have sinned, you are not righteous enough, you need to repent, and get your life straightened out.

Friday • Joel

Like Obadiah, the book of Joel ("the Lord is God") can refer to two time periods. Some date it during the time of Uzziah (792-740 BC), while others place it during the reign of Joash (835-796 BC). The time period during the reign of Joash may be preferred based upon writing style and the lack of naming any world powers. The setting for Joel includes the recent plague of locust and drought. It ravished all areas of society and Joel took it as a warning of things to come if the people did not repent. It is against this backdrop Joel warns of the coming Day of the Lord. When the Day of the Lord is mentioned it will normally have a historic near event it is referring to (locust plague) and a fulfillment in the future. Often it is characterized by clouds and darkness, signs in the skies, and described as "terrible" or "dreadful". The Day of the Lord is mentioned nineteen times in the OT, with Joel giving the most extensive description, and four times in the New Testament (Acts 2:20; 1 Thess. 5:2; 2 Thess. 2:2; 2 Pet. 3:10). One of the main themes in Joel is that when sin becomes great among His people God will judge it. This judgment will be through natural disasters and political means.

Joel chapter 1 opens with a description of the locust plague (1-4). Joel will warn the general population (v5), farmers (v11), and priests (v13) that it is their spiritual condition that has brought all this upon them. It had even come to the point that there wasn't enough crop production to perform the grain and drink offering (v8-10). Joel instructs the priests to call a fast and cry out in repentance over their current spiritual state because the Day of the Lord is at hand (v14-15). Verses 16-18 tell that even the animals groan, which further describes the plight of the people as a result of the locust plague. Joel cries out to God for deliverance as the dry and decaying fields reflect the people's hearts.

In Joel 2:1-11, Joel pictures an invading army overcoming and devouring everything in their path, claiming that "nothing will escape them". In verses 7-11 he describes the near invincibility of the incoming army and the destruction they will cause in the land. God, through Joel, calls upon the people to repent in verses 12-17 so they can be spared this judgment. Joel will again ask that the people be called together to repent with the priests who are leading the way (v15-17). Verses 18-27 confirm what will happen when the people repent. God will restore all that has been lost through the plague of locust (v18-19), the invading army will not come (v20), and all the people will rejoice in the Lord (v23) as He blesses them abundantly again. In verses 28-30 we see the outpouring of the Spirit which shows the people have been spiritually renewed (Acts 2:16). Earthly and heavenly signs will show the presence of God (v30-31) and people will call upon the name of the Lord to be saved (v32, Rom. 10:13).

Joel 3:1-8 is a reference to the coming judgment of the nations when the Lord will gather all of them together and judge them in the Valley of Jehoshaphat (Valley of Judgment). The sins of the nations are: scattering God's people (v2), dividing the land (v2), and treating His people unkindly (v3). Verses 4-8 record that God will repay them for how they have treated His people. What they have done will be turned back to them. The message of verses 1-8 is to be told to all the nations (9-12) as their wickedness has become great (v13). It is in the valley of decision (v14) the nations will know that the Lord is great. During this time those who belong to the Lord will experience His blessings, while those who do not will experience His retribution. Joel closes verses 18-21 with the blessings of God's people as God will "dwell" (tabernacle, *shekinah*) with His people forever.

Saturday • James 3-5

James 3 opens with a warning for those who want to be teachers. The role of teacher is prominent in the New Testament and in the early church (1 Cor. 12:28; Acts 13:1; Rom. 12:7; Eph. 4:11). Teachers in the early church taught doctrine (2 Tim. 2:2). Some would seek to be teachers for the wrong reasons, so James is offering a strict warning that this office is not for everyone but for those who have been gifted to teach.

Verses 2-12 concern the use of our tongue. James admits that all people misuse the tongue (v2). Proverbs has much to say in respect of the power of our words (10:8, 11; 16:27-28; 18:7-8). The tongue is small, like a bridle or rudder (v3-4), but it can do great things (v5). The issue here is control. Our tongue is also like a fire- it can destroy with its influence, corrupt the whole body, and corrupt the lives of those around us (v6; Matt. 15:11, 18-19). James uses the word *gehenna* for hell here, which refers to the final destination of the wicked for punishment. Lies, rumors, and gossip have harmed many Christians and churches. We can tame animals, but no man can tame his own tongue (v7-8). Like a venomous snake, the tongue is full of poison (Ps. 140:3). Verses 9-11 urge us to use our tongue to praise God, bless others, and not to harm others with cursing because they are made in the image of God. The word for "curse" actually expresses a desire for someone to be cut off from God and suffer eternal punishment.

Verses 13-18 cover two types of wisdom. James has already spoken in 1:5 that wisdom is available to all and comes from God (Prov. 2:6). In verses 14-16, earthly wisdom is characterized as extremely jealous (criticize and harm others) and self-seeking (v14). Its origin is earthly not heavenly, unspiritual rather than spiritual, and of the devil instead of coming from God (v15). Verse 16 tells us that where envy and self-seeking are found there will be disorder and evil. Verses 17-18 give us the characteristics of heavenly wisdom: it is pure (morally and spiritually), peaceable (between man and God), gentle (opposite of self), willing to yield (listen and heed others), full of mercy and good deeds (performs good deeds), without prejudice (no favoritism), and without hypocrisy (genuine).

James 4:1-10 discusses those who have adopted a worldly attitude. It is primarily speaking to those who seek pleasure in their life and have no concern for God. The word for "pleasure" in verse 1 means someone who has "evil tendencies". These people lust for things and do not get them, even to the point of murdering (v2). Some never ask, while others ask and do not receive because they ask with wrong motives wanting only their pleasures fulfilled (v3). Verse 4 begins a call to repentance. By calling them adulterers and adulteresses, James is calling out those who have placed their own desires ahead of God's purpose for their life (v4). In Jeremiah, and especially Hosea, God repeatedly calls His people out for their spiritual adultery with the world. Verse 4 also shows that God will judge those who take this path. Verse 5 may make more sense if we read it as "God jealously longs for the Spirit that He made to live in us". God has a strong desire for the lives of His people to follow Him. The answer to their worldly, self-righteous attitudes is found in verse 6- humility. Verses 7-10 contain 10 commands to cure the ailments of verses 1-6. These are (1) submit to God, (2) resist the devil, (3) draw near to God, (4) cleanse your hands, (5) purify your hearts, (6) lament, (7) mourn, (8) weep, (9) joy to gloom, and (10) humble yourselves. These terms are also used in Joel 2:12 and 2 Corinthians 7:10 to describe real repentance. Verses 11-12 warn against continual fault finding in others. James also says that the person who speaks against his brother denies the authority of God's word. When this is done, the person is saying that they are a better judge than God.

Verses 13-17 warn against leaving God out of your plans and believing you can live without God. James is not condemning them for being wealthy, but for their arrogant attitude. Proverbs 27:1 warns against this type of attitude and Jesus also spoke about it in a parable (Luke 12:16-20). Verse 15 encourages this person to place themselves and their plans under the will of God. The word "boast" in verse 16 refers to confidence in your own knowledge. These people are claiming to know better than God for what is best for their life. Verse 17 warns that they have been told what is right, and if they fail to do it they will be sinning. It also shows that the sins we commit are serious, but there will be condemnation for sins of omission as well (Matt. 25:31-46).

James 5:1-6 is a warning to the rich of the miseries that are about to come upon them. The book of Amos in the Old Testament and Luke's gospel in the New Testament address the dangers of wealth more than any other books. Again, wealth does not bring judgment, but the misuse of their wealth does. Jesus even warns in Matthew 19:16-24 of the misuse of riches. Verse 1 shows that the misery that is coming on them is not an earthly suffering, but is condemnation that will come at the final judgment. The crimes they are guilty of are: accumulating wealth (v2-3), not paying wages (v4), living in luxury and caring only for self (v5), and the murder of innocent people (v6). Verse 5 also shows that they have "fattened" themselves for their own coming judgment with their luxurious living.

Verses 7-11 deal with the subject of patience and give examples of the farmer (v7), the prophets (v10), and Job (v11). All believers must wait patiently on the Lord during any circumstance (v8). Still under the theme of the coming of the Lord, James warns Christians not to speak against a fellow believer because the return of Christ is imminent (v9). The warning of oath-keeping coincides with Matthew 5:34-37, which addresses being a person of your word.

Verses 13-16 detail the importance of prayer no matter what point of life you are in. Suffering, cheerfulness, and sickness are all occasions for prayer; which can result in healing, confessing sin, and forgiveness. The anointing with oil may also symbolize the setting aside of the person for God to hear the prayer made on their behalf. These types of prayers according to James are "powerful and effective". Verses 17-18 are a fitting example of prayer. Elijah was human just like we are. Look at the prayer he had answered-not once, but twice. It is a great example of placing your faith and trust in God, even if it sounds impossible to others. In verses 19-20, James urges the reader to help those who have wandered away from the truth. It will save them from death (possibly physical, but probably spiritual) and cover a multitude of sin (forgiveness).

Cover to Cover Challenge

Week 3

Sunday • Psalms 9-11

This begins week 3 of the *Cover to Cover Challenge*! I pray the Lord is using it for His honor and glory in your life and that the Holy Spirit is speaking to you through His Word. The Jewish people after the time of Nehemiah/Ezra were known as "people of the book". May the same thing be said about you and me!

Psalm 9 is a psalm of praise for God's righteous rule and judgments. In verses 1-2 David praises God, tells of His works, is glad and rejoices, and sings praises to His name. God as the "Most High" speaks of God being all-powerful and ruling from the heavens. Some translate it "God who does wonders". David asks for God to show Himself to his enemies so they will turn back (v3). In verses 4-6 David acknowledges that it is God who fights for him. A theme in many Psalms and other OT books is found in verses 7-10. Against the backdrop of God's eternal reign, we read that His judgment will be just against the wicked and that the upright can run to Him for safety because God will <u>never</u> forsake His own. In verses 11-14, David calls on all people to join him in praising God (v11). God will always hear the cry of His people (v12). This is followed by a plea for God's help so that David can tell others what God has done for him (v13-14). The retribution of God against the wicked is the theme of verses 15-18. In closing, David calls out to God. He ask God to not allow the wicked to prevail, but that they be judged so they too may realize they are men and not "gods".

Psalm 10 continues the theme of God's justice upon the wicked. David opens up the psalm in verse 1 by asking God (my translation) "Where are You when the wicked do such terrible things?" In verses 2-11 David describes the acts and characteristics that define the wicked. They are: pridefulness (v2), renouncing the Lord (3), not seeking God nor thinking about Him (v4), not caring for the Word (v5), never seeing hard times (v6), having a perverse mouth (v7), hiding to prey on the innocent (v 8-10), and believing they have no accountability (v11,13). David affirms to himself that God does see the deeds of the wicked, and he cries out for God's justice (v12-15). In verses 16-18 David praises God for His kingship, for hearing the cries of the oppressed, and for His justice.

Psalm 11 paints a familiar portrait that applies to our day. In verses 1-3 David places his trust in God, but questions why the wicked (those who do not know God) persecute the upright (those who know God). Verse 3 is saying "If the foundations (society) are (is) destroyed what are the righteous (God's people) to do?" David reminds the people that God is still on the throne (v4), that He hates the deeds of the wicked (v5), and that judgment is coming for those who oppose Him (v6). David knows that the Lord is righteous, that He loves righteousness, and that it is the righteous whom He enjoys intimate fellowship with (v7).

Monday • Genesis 10-14

The curse of Canaan and blessings of Shem and Ham found at the end of chapter 9 are the focus of chapters 10-11. Genealogies of Noah's three sons are recorded in chapter 10 and chapter 11:10-26. Chapter 10 is referred to as the "Table of Nations" as 70 nations will descend from Noah's three sons. At the close of Genesis (46:27), Abraham's list will also include 70 descendants. This shows that Abraham's "seed" reached the number of nations. In chapter 10, beginning with verse 6, you will notice that the descendants of Ham become a perpetual thorn in the side of the Israelites for years to come (9:25). Most of the people you have read about Joshua conquering would fit this description. Nimrod ("Rebel") is highlighted and there are familiar names that follow. The "land of Shinar" would become known as Babel and Babylon, both of which are enemies of God throughout Scripture. Babylon is the center of false religion. The people of Babylon are rooted in idolatry and magic. They were known for their extreme cruelty, arrogance, and self-confidence.

Chapter 11:1-9 contains the famous story of Babel ("confusion"). The people refused to scatter over the face of the earth and gathered in the land of Shinar to build a city and a place of worship for themselves (ziggurat). God confuses their language and they are forced to scatter over the face of the earth. In verses 10-26 the line of Shem is traced ending with Abram and his family. Genesis 11:27-32 introduces us to the main characters of the coming chapters. Verse 30 is a key element to the story of Abram and his descendants to come (Isaac/Rebekah, Jacob/Rachel).

The story of Abram begins in chapter 12. The Abrahamic Covenant is recorded in verses 1-3. Seven promises are highlighted in this covenant. Each time, it is reaffirmed that it will always contain the promise of a seed, land, a nation, and blessings. God will remain faithful to His promises. Abram builds the first altar in the Promised Land to worship the Lord at Bethel ("House of God") in verse 8. Genesis 12:10-20 records Abram and Sarai traveling to Egypt because of a famine in the land. Abram's deceitfulness results in Pharaoh experiencing plagues because God's desire is to protect Sarai and His promise (v17).

Chapter 13 prepares us for some of the following chapters. It is here that Abram and his nephew Lot separate because both of their possessions have grown so large (v6-7). Verses 10-12 are important because they explain the background for Sodom and Gomorrah which we will read in chapters 18-19. In verses 14-18, God reaffirms the promises of land and descendants and Abram again builds an altar to the Lord in Hebron and worships Him there.

In chapter 14 Lot is captured (v12) as a result of the wars in the region between many of the kings in the area (v1-11). Abraham is told of Lot's capture and proceeds to rescue him from the hands of the armies (v14-17). Melchizedek ("Righteous King") is introduced in verses 18-20. Melchizedek and Abraham both worship "God the Most High" and both acknowledge that it is He who has delivered the enemy into Abram's hand. In verses 21-24 Abram denies the king's offer for the spoils acknowledging that he is dependent upon God.

Tuesday • Joshua 11-15

After conquering the Southern regions Joshua will begin his conquest of the Northern land in chapter 11. Hazor is believed to be the largest and most formidable city of the area. In verses 1-5 they are leading the charge against the Israelites. The Lord speaks to Joshua once again to reaffirm His promise to him (v6). The battle is fought and quickly decided (v7-9). In verses 10-15 the land was conquered and Joshua's obedience is highlighted (v14-15). Some of the cities were not destroyed, and were immediately ready for the Israelites to live in fulfilling Deuteronomy 6:10-11. In verses 16-23 it is recorded again that Joshua had control of the whole region. God hardened the hearts of the enemies of Israel so that they would wage war against Israel. This shows the judgment of God on a people who had already rejected Him and exploited extreme wickedness. The chapter closes with the declaration that "the land was at rest from war", noting a time of peace.

Chapter 12:1-6 recalls the victories of Moses before the crossing of the Jordan River. Sihon and Og were both kings of the Amorites (Num. 21:21-35). It is from this land that Moses viewed the Promised Land. Verses 7-24 record the kings killed by Joshua. God is fulfilling His promise of land from Genesis 12 which you read earlier this week.

Joshua 13 describes the land that has yet to be conquered by Joshua (v1-5). Much of this area will be won by David. God once again promises to drive out those who currently possess the land, and gives an order to divide the land (v6-7). The word "divide" in verse 6 refers to casting lots and places the decision for the land solely in the hands of God. In verses 9-14 Reuben, Gad, and the half tribe of Manasseh receive the land of Sihon and Og which is east of the Jordan. Verses 15-21 concern the land given to Reuben. Beth Peor (v20) is remembered as being one of the places Balaam attempted to curse the Israelites (Num.23). It is also the place Moses had delivered his farewell speech (Deut. 3:29). In taking over the land it is noted Balaam is killed by the children of Israel (Num. 22-24). Gad's inheritance is recorded in verses 24-28 and the inheritance of the half tribe of Manasseh is recorded in verses 29-33.

The land west of the Jordan is divided in Joshua 14. According to verse 1, Eleazar the priest aids Joshua in dividing the land. Caleb's inheritance is covered verses 6-15. According to the age of Caleb the conquest by Joshua and the children of Israel spanned seven years. Three times in this passage it is noted that Caleb "followed the Lord my God". Joshua and Caleb were living examples of faithfulness and obedience.

Joshua 15 begins the division of the land among the remaining tribes west of the Jordan. In verses 13-19 an additional story about Caleb is introduced. This story concerns God's promise to Caleb (Numbers 14:24) that he would inherit the land he explored. Othniel is mentioned in verse 17 and would later become one of the judges of Israel (Judges 3:7-11).

Wednesday • Matthew 8-10

Matthew 8 turns us toward the miracles of Jesus. Jesus heals a leper in verses 1-4. Because of their disease lepers were forbidden to be around people (Lev. 13-14). This kept it from spreading and also made them ceremonially unclean. Verse 4 show that Jesus did not want anyone to misunderstand what His true mission was. Although Jesus healed many people of physical ailments His main mission was to die for sinful man. Next Jesus meets the centurion who has a servant who is sick (v5-13). This Gentile (who is also ceremonially unclean being a Gentile) is praised for his great faith (v10) which was demonstrated by his belief that Jesus could just speak the word and his servant be healed. Verse 10 also contains one of only two times in scripture Jesus is said to have "marveled" at someone's faith. Here He praises the Gentiles faith while in Mark 6:6 He "marvels" over the people of Israel and their lack of faith. Verses 11-12 challenge the Jews dangerous belief that they are already assured of participating in the messianic banquet (Isa. 25:6-9). Jesus says the banquet will be for all who believe in Him including Gentiles. Jesus heals Peter's mother-in-law in verses 14-15. She most likely represents a third group that was marginalized in society-women. This is followed by a summary of Jesus' ministry up until that point (v16-17) in which he quotes the Suffering Servant passage of Isaiah 53. Matthew does this to show Jesus' power to heal physically but also to show that the main mission of the Suffering Servant is to heal people of their sin. Jesus lays out the cost of discipleship in verses 18-22, emphasizing counting the cost of following Him.

Verses 19-20 show that the life of the disciple is to share in the life of Jesus. Verses 21-22 show that the loyalty of the disciple is to Jesus and takes precedence over family. Jesus' demand may sound harsh but even in the OT neither the Nazarite or High Priest could attend their fathers funeral (Num. 6:6-7, Lev. 20:11). The "dead burying their own dead" are those who are spiritually dead and have no relationship to with Jesus. This also shows the urgency of becoming a disciple. Jesus shows His authority over nature as He calms the sea in verses 23-27. The "great tempest" is not the typical word for storm. The word here refers to a violent shaking and demonstrates the seriousness of what was taking place. The OT makes it clear that it is God who controls the sea (Job 38:8-11; Ps. 29:3-4) and God who answers the disciples question in verse 27. The phrase "O you of little faith" is always used (Matt. 6:30, 14:31, 16:8) in the context of worrying disciples. Chapter 8 closes with the healing of two demon possessed men, which displays Jesus' power over demonic forces (v28-34). Jesus commanding them to go into the swine offered visible proof to what had taken place.

One of the greatest miracles Jesus ever performed begins chapter 9. It is very significant because it proves that Jesus has the power to forgive sin (v1-8). Jesus forgives the man's sin which cannot be seen with the human eye. The scribes accuse Him of blasphemy because this was something only God could do (Isa. 43:25, 44:22). Knowing their thoughts, Jesus heals the man proving that He had the power to forgive sin. In verses 9-13 Jesus calls Matthew (Levi, Mark 2:14). Tax collectors were hated because they were known for extorting people and taking advantage of any situation for gain. Tax collectors were also ceremonially unclean and deemed outcasts by the Jews. It is here Jesus is charged with eating with sinners (v11). The quoting of Hosea 6:6 shows that Jesus is warning them that performing supposed religious duties do not exceed the call of God to love. God has always desired mercy (love) and not sacrifice. References to the Messianic banquet are used again in verses 14-17. God has always been the bridegroom, even in the OT (Isa. 54:5-6; Hosea 2:16-20) and Jesus is announcing that the time of the Messiah has come. Verses 16-17 are a reference to the new and living way introduced by Jesus, which could not be placed into the old wineskins of Judaism. Matthew 9:18-26 tell the story of the woman who was healed from her hemorrhaging (which made her ceremonially unclean) and of Jesus raising a little girl back to life. Raising the girl back to life proved that Jesus even has the power to raise the dead. As Jesus heals the two blind men in verses 27-31 He is called the "Son of David" (Messiah) for the first time. What is interesting about this is two blind men could "see" better than many others of their day. After Jesus heals the man who was mute (v32-34) He is accused of healing with the power of Satan. What is also notable in verse 33 is the contrast between the present leadership (Pharisees) and the authority Jesus had in healing power. They were basically saying when our leaders speak nothing happens but when Jesus speaks people are healed. Verses 35-36 show Jesus' compassion for the people. The people were "weary and scattered" which means harassed and helpless or torn and thrown down. They were unprotected from the false shepherds of Israel who lacked leadership abilities (Num. 27:17; 1 Kgs 22:17; Ez. 34:5). Verses 37-38 and the prayer for laborers to work in the harvest prepares the way for chapter 10 which focuses on the disciples and their mission.

Chapter 10 opens with the calling and commissioning of the disciples (v1-4). In verses 5-15 they are sent out to the house of Israel only (v6). The message they preached (v7) was the same message of Jesus and John the Baptist. Verse 8 covers their ministry and verses 9-10 show the provision of God. God's judgment is based upon the people's acceptance or refusal of the message (v11-15). In verses 16-26, Jesus speaks of the coming persecution, confrontation with enemies, and the help of the Holy Spirit during these times. Jesus teaches the disciples about the type of character they should have. They are to preach all He has told them (v27), not to fear persecution but to fear God (v28), and the care of God for them in verses 29-31. In verses 32-33, Jesus teaches the importance of confessing Him and not disowning Him before men. Jesus teaches more important truths of following Him in verses 34-39 which will involve conflict. These truths include loving Him over all others which is the choice true disciples must make. This choice also has consequences. Chapter 10 closes with a reward for those who receive the prophet and his message.

Thursday • Job 5-6

Eliphaz is still speaking to Job here in chapter 5. Eliphaz will continue with his point that Job is suffering because he is a sinner. In verses 1-7 Eliphaz tells Job not even one of God's angels would answer him because he is acting foolishly (v1-2). He is convinced that Job is reaping a harvest he has sown (v3-5) because trouble doesn't just come out of the blue (v6-7). In verses 8-16 Eliphaz tells Job to speak to God, because God will do what is right if Job will repent (v8-9). We read that God does many wonderful things (v9) and that He is just (v10-16). What is implied by this is that Job is getting what he deserves. Eliphaz's train of thought in verses 17-27 continues along the same path. He assures Job that God is trying to correct him (v17). In the rest of the chapter, Eliphaz explains to Job that God chastises His people, but that He is always there for them.

It is Job's turn to speak again in chapter 6. In verses 1-4 he has a complaint against God and in verses 5-7 he has a complaint against his friends because he wants to hear the right words from them. Job once again asks God to end his life in verses 8-10, and in verses 11-13 Job is becoming impatient in the trial he is suffering. In verses 14-21, Job continues complaining again about the counsel of his friends and pleads for kindness from them. He complains in verses 24-27 about his friends and wants them to tell him exactly what sin he has committed. Chapter 6 closes with verses 28-30. In these verses, Job appeals to his friends and ask them to show him compassion.

Friday • Jonah

The book of Jonah ("Dove") takes place during the reign of Jeroboam II (793- 758 BC). This makes him either a contemporary of Amos, or from a time prior to him. During this time the Northern Kingdom was enjoying a prosperous time of peace, but was in severe decline spiritually. Their religion had become a mere ritual and was filled with idolatry. Jonah is the only prophet sent to a foreign nation to deliver a message of repentance. Nineveh, the recipient of Jonah's message, was founded by Nimrod (Gen. 10:6-12) and was the capital of Assyria. Nineveh was famous for being the enemy of both the northern and southern kingdoms of Israel. The prophet Nahum would also prophesy against Nineveh, but to no avail. Nineveh would later be destroyed by Nebuchadnezzar for its unwillingness to repent at the message of Nahum. One theme reoccurring throughout Jonah is the sovereignty of God.

Jonah 1 opens with God's call to Jonah, who immediately flees in the opposite direction (v1-4). Jonah is also credited with being the only prophet to reject the call of God. A great storm arises on the sea (prepared just for Jonah) while Jonah is traveling to Tarshish (v4). The mariners cast lots to see who the cause of the storm is, and it falls upon Jonah (v7). In verses 10-15 Jonah is thrown into the sea at his own request (v12) and the storm stops. After being tossed from the boat Jonah is swallowed by a great fish (prepared just for Jonah). Jesus uses Jonah's time in the belly of the fish to compare to the three days and nights He was in the heart of the earth (Matt. 12:40).

Jonah 2 records the prayer of Jonah from inside the fish. It is a prayer concerning the dire situation he is in. What Jonah feels inside the belly of the fish is the same feeling the Ninevites will have when they hear the message Jonah will bring them. They too are in a dire situation but do not realize it yet. Those who do not know Christ are in the same situation, but like the Ninevites, they may not know it yet.

At the beginning of chapter 3, Jonah is again commissioned to go to Nineveh to preach a message of repentance (v1-4). In verses 5-10 all the people repent, starting with the king and continuing down to all the people of the land. With Jonah's obedience and the repentance of the Ninevites, the disaster that was to come upon the Nineveh was averted.

Jonah's reaction to the repentance of the Ninevites begins chapter 4. Jonah is angry and confesses that he knew God would be merciful on the people if they would repent (v2). Jonah goes even further expressing even a desire to die because of what has happened (v3). It would seem from his reaction Jonah, being an Israelite, did not want the Ninevites to repent over their previous treatment of them. God causes a plant (prepared just for Jonah) to rise up protecting Jonah from the heat (v6), which Jonah is thankful for. The next day God prepares a worm (prepared just for Jonah) to destroy the plant in verse 7. In verse 8 a hot scorching wind (prepared just for Jonah) begins to blow and again Jonah claims to want to die. Jonah had pity for the plant which he had no part in making, but none for the Ninevites. 2 Peter 3:9 reads "The Lord is not slack concerning His promise, as some count slackness, but is longsuffering toward us, not willing that any should perish but that all should come to repentance."

Saturday • Galatians 1-3

The book of Galatians is the first letter written by Paul. Most date the book between 47-52 AD. A group of people called the Judaizers had crept in and taught false doctrine concerning salvation. They taught that in addition to faith in Christ a person must obey the Mosaic Law, be circumcised, and follow other Jewish regulations. This would turn Christianity into a works based system. Some of the themes in Galatians are: justification by faith alone, religious liberty, walking in the Spirit, true versus false gospel, law versus grace, and Paul defending his apostleship.

From the opening of Galatians 1, Paul begins to defend his apostleship (v1-2). For the false gospel of the Judaizers to be more effective they would challenge the authority of Paul and his apostleship. Verses 3-5 form a doxology that shows Jesus as the Savior of all men according to God's plan. In verses 6-10 Paul is astonished (shocked) that the Galatians would turn away from the true gospel so quickly (v6). The word "turn away" means "move to another place" and was used in Paul's day to describe a traitor. Notice also that they are not turning away from Paul, but God Himself by adding to the gospel of grace. In verse 7 "not another" means another of the same kind. Paul is clarifying that there is only one gospel and it was the gospel he preached to them. They were taking the gospel of grace and turning it into a works based system. He warns them by pronouncing a curse in verses 8-9 not to believe anyone, including himself or an angel, who preaches a different gospel than the one he has already given them. The term *anathema esto* carries the meaning of being delivered over to God's wrath. Heretics in the early church were labeled this. Verse 10 hints that the Judaizers who opposed Paul were accusing him of preaching only to profit himself.

Closing out the chapter in verses 11-24, Paul gives information about where he received the gospel he preaches (v11-12). Paul's message came straight from Jesus Christ, not from being taught by the apostles. He tells of his former life spent persecuting the church (v13-14) and how God called him from his mother's womb (v15; Jer. 1:5; Isa. 49:1). The term "destroy" literally means "to make havoc of or to extinguish". Paul is speaking of his pre-converted life because it is another example that the gospel he preached did not originate with him. The reason for this calling is so he would be used to "reveal" Christ among the Gentiles (v16; Acts 9:15). In verse 17 Paul also shows that the apostles did not teach him the gospel because it was three years before he had any personal contact with them. In verses 18-24, Paul recounts meeting with Peter and James and how his conversion glorified God.

In Galatians 2:1-10 Paul continues his defense of the gospel and his apostleship. After fourteen years, Paul goes to Jerusalem and preaches the gospel there (v1). The word "communicated" in verse 2 means "to lay before someone to consider". Paul may have brought Titus along to show that the Gentiles were being converted through his ministry and to demonstrate that law keeping and circumcision did not have a roll in salvation (v3). Paul wanted them to hear the gospel he preached, and from there he and Barnabas are sent out (v7-9). The false brethren of verses 4-5 who are gradually sneaking (secretly) in are the Judaizers. The word "spy" means "to discover a weak point and expose it". They were watching the Christians just so they could expose them later, especially in the case of Titus whom they proclaimed needed to be circumcised. What is more than likely the case was that the Judaizers were infiltrating ("secretly") the church to cause confusion over the matters of salvation. Also the "liberty" Paul speaks of is not license to do as one pleases. This liberty is grounded in the truth of the gospel. In verses 6-10 Paul recounts his meeting with the leaders of the church made up of Peter, James, and John. In verse 6 Paul is saying that they were not any different from him because they were all apostles who preached the same message. In verse 7 Paul makes a distinction between him and Peter and their ministries, and in verse 8 Paul shows that it is God who gave them not only their ministry but their message. Peter, James, and John also approved of Paul's ministry to the Gentiles (v9).

Paul's confrontation with Peter is covered in verses 11-21. What was at stake here was the truth of the gospel and the unity of the church. Peter was eating with Gentiles until the Jews came in, and then he would remove himself from them (v11-12). Peter's actions implied that the Gentiles must live like the Jews, which led other Jews to do the same thing (v13). Peter's actions would have also caused quite a controversy because he was a leader in the church. Paul refutes Peter's actions because they betray the truth of the gospel (v14-15). For Peter and the others to continue their actions would imply a different gospel because Gentiles would have to become Jews in order to be saved. Paul introduces us to justification by faith in verse 16. Justification is a gracious act of God, where man is declared justified based upon the finished work of Christ not law keeping (Rom. 3:24; Eph. 2:8-10). Paul makes his point clear in verses 17-21- we are saved by grace through faith not the law. Verses 17-18 also refute Peter's actions of refusing to have fellowship with Gentiles. In verse 19 Paul is not saying that God's law has no meaning, rather Paul is saying that obedience to the law no longer defines him but his obedience to Christ does. He belongs to Christ and that relationship defines who he is now. This can be seen in verse 20. In verse 21 Paul is in effect saying "if the law saves then Christ death means nothing". People are not saved by the law but by grace.

Galatians 3:1-9 further explains justification by faith. The word "bewitched" in verse 1 means "to hold someone spellbound". Even the Galatians' own testimonies should be a witness to them of the truth (v2-5). In these verses Paul also appeals to the work of the Holy Spirit in their lives. Verse 2 concerns how they received the Spirit, verse 3 their sanctification, and verses 4-5 testify of the miracles they had experienced. Paul argues with them from this standpoint because none of those things can be experienced by keeping the law. In the argument of these first few verses Paul is trying to get them to see how they came to Christ in the first place-by grace through faith. No one can be made righteous according to the law and this is where Paul now turns with the example of Abraham. It could be that the Judaizers were telling people that in order to be a true son of Abraham circumcision would be needed. In verse 6, Paul is saying "You believed just like Abraham believed and it was accounted to him for righteousness". The Galatians were only made right with God because of their faith in Jesus Christ. In verses 7-9 Paul takes us back to Genesis 12:1-3. All those who believe (whether Jew or Gentile) are the spiritual children of Abraham because they have exercised faith.

In verses 10-14 Paul argues against the law making anyone righteous. In verse 10 those who live by the law are cursed because it is impossible to obey the law (Deut. 27:26). Verse 11 shows that only those who live by faith will be declared righteous (Hab. 2:4).The law and faith are not two ways to God because those who live by the law must keep it which is again impossible (v12; Lev. 18:5). Verse 13 shows that Jesus redeemed (bought back, paid the price) us from the curse of the law (Deut. 21:23). Verse 14 shows that all the nations are blessed through Abraham just as God promised in Genesis 12:1-3 which includes salvation through Christ and the promise of the Holy Spirit. In summary Paul explains in these verses that Jesus is the end of the law because He brought completion to the law in that what the law could not do (declare righteous) Jesus did by bearing the curse of the law that would fall on everyone. The promise was given to Abraham and he believed even before there was a law (v15-18). What is the purpose of the law? Paul explains it in verses 19-25. Verse 19 shows that the law was given because of transgressions. This could mean that the law functioned to keep sin "in check" before the coming of Christ. Another meaning is that it showed that sin was bad and the law showed how bad sin truly is (Rom. 5:20). The angels role in giving the law is not entirely clear but it is scriptural (Acts 7:38; Heb. 1, 2:2). Even in the book of Revelation an angel received the words from Christ who in turn gave them to John (Rev. 1:1-2). The law also functions as our schoolmaster pointing out our sinfulness and guiding us to Christ (v24). In verses 26-29 Paul discusses sonship and being an heir whether they are Jews or Gentiles. All are sons through faith in Jesus Christ.

Cover to Cover CHALLENGE

Week 4

Sunday • Psalm 12-17

Welcome to week four of the *Cover to Cover Challenge*! At the completion of this week you will have finished 5 books of the Bible. We hope you have been blessed by reading and studying God's Word. As always, our prayer is that the Lord is glorified through this. We also pray that the Holy Spirit is moving in your life, in your family, and in your church.

Psalm 12 is a prayer of deliverance from the ungodly. David cries out to God in verse 1 "Where have all the godly people gone?" In verses 2-4 David describes the speech of the ungodly. They disobey, use flattery, and are double-hearted (deceiving). Verse 5 is a call for the Lord to help those who are oppressed by the ungodly. David recalls the words of the Lord in verse 6, calling them "pure words" (flawless). In verses 7-8, David is assured that the Lord will protect His children even if wickedness reigns.

Psalm 13 is about how we experience the faithfulness of God during times of suffering. The term "how long" is used four times, emphasizing David's plea for God to move on his behalf. In verses 3-4, David asks God to answer (consider) his plea. David does not want to die or have his enemies say they have won. In verses 5-6 states that he will trust, rejoice, and sing to the Lord because He has cared for him.

Psalm 14 concerns God's triumph over the wicked. The "fool" is someone who acts independently of God. Here, David describes the fool as being corrupt, performing detestable acts in defiance of God, and as being incapable of doing good. In verses 2-3, David describes God looking down to earth to see if anyone is seeking Him. God sees that all have turned away (Rom. 3:10-12). The foolish of the world devour (eat up) God's people in verse 4. God is pictured looking down in judgment in verses 5-6. God sees the foolish, who will fear God, while the righteous are in the presence of God and run to Him as their refuge.

In Psalm 15 David details the characteristics of those who enjoy fellowship with God (v1). Verse 2 covers positive characteristics such as walking uprightly (faithful lifestyle), working righteousness (do what is right), and speaking the truth from their heart (integrity). Verse 3 covers what they do not do: backbite (slander), purposely hurt their neighbor, and lay traps for them. The godly man is able to discern between those who are reprobates (vile) and those who honor the Lord. Those who honor the Lord are characterized by staying true to their word (v4). The godly also do not charge extraordinary interest rates (usury) or take bribes (v5). The psalm closes with a promise that whoever lives this way "will not be moved" (shaken).

Psalm 16 concentrates on trusting the Lord. This trust is described in verses 1-4. David asks the Lord to preserve him (v1, watch over), states that he is nothing apart from God (v2), rejoices in community with other believers (v3), and does not speak of the acts of the wicked (v4). In verses 5-6, David praises God for upholding him and for His many blessings. David again expresses praise to God in verses 7-8 because of His counsel and the fact He will not allow David to be moved (shaken). David continues to rejoice in verses 9-11 because he dwells securely in hope (v9), God still preserves him even in death (v10), and because God shows him the way of life by His presence (v11). These verses are quoted in Acts 2:27, 31 and Acts 13:35 in reference to Jesus' resurrection.

Psalm 17 is a prayer about the righteousness of God. In verses 1-5 David cries out for God to hear, attend (listen), and give ear to his words. He asks God to vindicate him (v2), examine his heart (v3), and because he has stayed away from the violent man (v4). In verses 6-9 David prays for God to protect him, knowing that God will answer the prayer. David describes the wicked as having a hard heart, being arrogant in speech (v10), pursuing the righteous (v11), and being violent (v12). Verses 15 is about being in the presence of the Lord.

Monday • Genesis 15-19

In Genesis 15 God affirms His covenant with Abram. In verses 1-4 Abram may be afraid that God is not going to fulfill the covenant He has made, but God promises him that it will be one from his own body that will fulfill the covenant. Abram had placed his faith in God (v6). In verses 7-16, the details of the covenant are once again shared. In verses 18-21 God gives the dimensions for the land to be inherited (what you have read in Joshua).

Genesis 16 contains the story of Hagar. Sarai, believing she would have no children, convinces Abram to lie with her servant Hagar (v1-3). Hagar conceives a child which makes her despised in Sarai's eyes so she sends her away (v4-6). Hagar is greeted by the Angel of the Lord (pre-incarnate appearance of Christ), and is told to return to Sarai (v7-9). The Angel of the Lord promises her that she will have many descendants, she will name her son Ishmael, and that he will fight with every man (v10-12). Ishmael means "He has heard" and Hagar calls God "El Roi" because He saw her in her affliction (v13-15). The chapter closes with a reference Abram's age. The journey began when he was 75, and he is now 86.

Abram is 99 years old at the beginning of chapter 17. This chapter is the "name" chapter, and discusses the name changes that are related to the covenant God made with Abram. In verses 1-8, God reiterates the covenant and changes Abram's name to Abraham ("father of many nations"). In verses 9-14, God gives Abraham the sign of the covenant and commands Abraham to circumcise every male. Abraham fulfills this in verses 22-27. In verses 15-19 and verse 21, Sarai's name is changed to Sarah ("Princess"). God also promises to fulfill the covenant by giving them a son who will be born a year later. Abraham and Sarah are to name their son Isaac ("Laughter").

Two angels who are accompanied by the Lord visit Abraham in Genesis 18:1-8. Sarah overhears a conversation between the Lord and Abraham of her coming pregnancy (v9-10). Sarah laughs at the notion she can have any children (v11-15). Her laughter implies the impossibility of pregnancy due to her age. While the two angels move toward Sodom, Abraham is left to have a time of intercession for the righteous in Sodom before the Lord (v16-33). Notice his humble attitude in verse 27 as he intercedes. This paves the way for the events in chapter 19.

Genesis 19 opens with the angels coming to Sodom to judge it, and to rescue Lot because of Abraham's intercessory prayer (v1-11). The wickedness of Sodom, and its influence on Lot are also recorded in these verses-Lev. 18:22, 29, 20:13, Rom. 1:26; 1 Cor. 6:9; 2 Pet. 2:6-7. In verses 12-28, Sodom and Gomorrah are destroyed for their wickedness as Lot and his wife and daughters escape. They were warned by the angels to not look back. Lot's wife is turned into a pillar of salt for her disobedience (Luke 9:62, 17:28-32). Just as God "remembered" (deliver, act on behalf of) Noah, He remembers Abraham in verse 29. From the sin committed in verses 30-38 come two of Israel's future enemies, the Moabites and the Ammonites.

Tuesday • Joshua 16-20

Joshua 16 contains the inheritance of Ephraim and West Manasseh. One thing to consider here is verse 10. According to God's command in Deuteronomy 20:16, they were to drive out the inhabitants of the land. This would also be the case in chapter 17:1-13 for the other half tribe of Manasseh. While the Canaanites were forced laborers to the children of Israel the command of God was being violated. The tribes of Ephraim and Manasseh complain in Joshua 17:14-18 about the land allotted to them because of foreigners in the area. Joshua reminds them in verse 17 that they can drive the foreigners out of the land.

In chapter 18 three representatives are sent from the 7 remaining tribes to survey the land. This land is given out in 18:11-28 and chapters 19-20. Joshua receives his inheritance in 19:49-51. Joshua 20 concerns the cities of refuge. These cities were for those who had accidently killed someone. They provided refuge for them so that the killing would not be avenged, and they would receive a fair trial (Num. 35:25). If the person was found guilty then they would receive the just punishment. If they were found guilty of manslaughter (accident) then they were to stay in the city of refuge until the death of the high priest (v6). There were 3 cities of refuge on each side of the Jordan River.

Wednesday • Matthew 11-13

In Matthew 11:1-6, we see John the Baptist sending two of his disciples to question Jesus concerning Him being the Messiah, and we see Jesus' response. Jesus assures them that He is the fulfilling the mission God had sent for Him to do (Isa. 61:1-2). Jesus affirms that He is the Coming One through His miracles you read about last week (ch.8-9), His teachings (ch.5-7), and His mission (ch.10). In verses 7-15 Jesus speaks of the greatness of John the Baptist. John the Baptist was not unstable (v7) or weak (v8) but walked in the ways of an OT prophet who called people to repentance and prepared the way for Jesus (v9-10, 15; Mal. 4:5-6). Verses 16-19 characterize the generation that rejects Jesus and John the Baptist. In verses 20-24 Jesus rebukes (denounces-very strong word) those cities where most of His miracles took place. Tyre and Sidon were known for Baal worship (Isa. 23; Ez. 26-28) and you are familiar with the story of Sodom (Gen. 19). Jesus is essentially saying that if they had seen the miracles those cities had seen, they would have repented. Those who experienced Jesus ministry would be under greater judgment (Luke 12:35-48). Matthew 10:25-30 contains one of the most known passages in all of Scripture. After Jesus thanks God for the people whom God revealed His will to, He speaks about those who have labored hard and carry heavy burdens. This invitation is for all to have rest. This passage can be an invitation to those who are not saved to come to Jesus and lay the burden of sin down. It can also refer to those who already know Jesus, inviting them to come to Him and have the rest (refresh, revived) that only He can give.

Matthew 12 begins with two confrontations over the Sabbath (v1-8, 9-14). The Pharisees had their own traditions about Sabbath-keeping and work. He uses the example of David from 1 Samuel 21:1-6 and Numbers 28:9-10. Verse 6 is the key verse: the One who is greater than the temple was here, Jesus is the Lord of the Sabbath. The healing of the withered hand on the Sabbath in verses 9-14 showed the Pharisees own inconsistency. They would rescue their own animal on the Sabbath but not allow a man to be healed on it. From this point forward, the Pharisees will even be more opposed to Jesus (v14). In verses 15-21, Jesus is the prophesied Servant from Isaiah 42:1-4. This presents Jesus as gentle (v19) and just (v20). Jesus heals a demon possessed man in verses 22-24, and it gives an opportunity for the Pharisees to accuse Jesus of healing with Satan's power. In verses 25-30, Jesus explains that His power comes from God (v28), and that He is the one who has come to bind the strong man (v29, Isa.

49:24-26). Verse 30 is proof that a person cannot remain neutral. Either Jesus or Satan must be chosen because there is no middle ground.

In verses 33-37, we are taken back to Matthew 7:15-20 which focused on works and here focuses on words. The "brood of vipers" may be translated "offspring of Satan". Jesus concludes that evil (works and words) comes from a man's heart, and that man will give an account for every word spoken. Jesus speaks again to this generation concerning signs in verses 38-42. They are asking Him to perform a sign immediately to prove who He is and prove His authority. Jesus points forward to His death, burial, and resurrection with the sign of Jonah. The sign of Jonah and of Jesus will show that they were commissioned by God for a divine purpose. He condemns this generation because of their lack of repentance by comparing them with Nineveh and the Queen of Sheba (1 Kgs. 10:1-13) who was wise enough to listen to Jonah's message and Solomon's wisdom. Verses 43-45 coincide with verses 29-30. Both give a warning of remaining neutral when hearing about Jesus. Chapter 12 closes with an appeal to do the will of the Father so that you can be a part of the family of God (v 46-50; 2 Pet. 3:9).

Chapter 13 covers the parables of the kingdom. Verses 1-9 cover the parable of the sower and verses 18-23 explain it. In one soil the seed never penetrates but is snatched away by Satan (v19), in another the seed doesn't take root because of trials (v20-21), and in a third the seed is choked out by caring for the world (v22). Only one is received in good ground and produces fruit (v23). This parable shows that there is nothing wrong with the message it is the one who receives it with the issue. Many things in life can obscure the message of the gospel. But it is encouraging to know that some will receive it. Going back to verses 10-17 Jesus explains the reason He speaks in parables the mysteries of the kingdom. Jesus speaks in parables to conceal the truth by quoting Isaiah 6:9-10 which covers the Israelites failure to respond to the prophet. The parable of the wheat and tares in verses 24-30 is explained in verses 36-43. On an interesting note the tare was probably called a darnel. Wheat and a darnel looked the same until the head appeared. If anyone planted darnel in a wheat field and was caught they would be put to death under Roman law. The parable of the mustard seed (v31-32) is concerned with the growth of the kingdom and explains that it will start off small but grow very large. The parable of the leaven (v33) is about the permeating effects of the kingdom on the world. Matthew inserts that Jesus' speaking in parables is fulfillment of prophecy in verses 34-35 (Ps. 78:2). The parables of the hidden treasure and pearl of great price are similar in that both deal with the worth of the kingdom and the lengths one would go to get it. The parable of the dragnet (v47-52) is similar to the good/bad fruit and wheat/tares explaining again the judgment of both groups. The dragnet was large which was placed between two boats and dragged to shore. Verses 51-52 instruct the disciples to teach others the truths they are learning to others. Chapter 13 ends with Jesus being rejected at Nazareth because of their unbelief (v53-58).

Thursday • Job 7-8

In chapter 6 Job was complaining about the insensitive words that Eliphaz spoke in chapter 5. Here in chapter 7, Job continues his complaint about life and directs it toward God. Job describes his life of suffering in verses 1-2, comparing it to hard work but with no benefit. In verses 3-4 Job sees his life as useless and full of misery (v3-4). He describes the problems that arise from having boils (v5), and in verses 6-10 Job speaks of how his life is passing by in the midst of his suffering. Job even complains that when he does sleep he has nightmares (v14) and he still longs for the death that will end his suffering (v15-16). In verses 17-21, Job believes that the only reason he exists is for God to cause him great suffering.

With much harsher words than Eliphaz, Bildad speaks in chapter 8. Bildad will speak bluntly to Job throughout the chapter, agreeing with Eliphaz that not only has Job sinned but his family has as well. In verse 2 Bildad basically tells Job he is full of hot air. In verses 3-7 Bildad begins to build his case that God is just (He is), but gives the wrong application. He says "Job you and your kids got what you deserved, but if you repent God will prosper you again". Bildad appeals to tradition handed down from the past that his conclusion is right (v8-10). In verses 11-19, Bildad describes those who do not know God with scenes from nature. The hypocrites (godless) have no nourishment (v11-12), have no support (v14-15), and will be uprooted or wither away (v16-18). Bildad closes out his speech in verses 20-22 the same way he began: "Job you must have sinned, repent and turn back to God".

Friday • Amos 1-5

Amos ("Burden") was from Judah (Southern Kingdom) and was called to deliver a message to the Northern Kingdom. Through the information Amos gives in verse 1, which includes the kings of each kingdom and mentioning the earthquake (760 BC), a more precise time period can be associated with the book. Amos is more than likely a contemporary of Isaiah, Jonah, Hosea, and possibly Joel. The Northern Kingdom is enjoying a time of economic prosperity, peace with its neighbors, and is expanding its borders. At the same time, it also was decaying spiritually and ethically. Their worship had become corrupt, which led to their treatment of others being corrupt as well (Deut. 6:5; Lev. 19:18). Amos' message of repentance will deal with these issues.

Amos chapters 1-2 deal with the judgment of the nations. Amos begins with the farthest from the Northern Kingdom, Damascus (Syria, v3-5), and works his way toward Judah and Israel. Those hearing his message were delighted God was going to judge those nations (v 1:3-2:3) until they heard their own names called out for judgment (v2:4-2:16). At the beginning of each judgment oracle you will read "For three transgressions of (blank), and for four, I will not turn away its punishment". Some believe this is symbolic of an infinite number of sins, signifying that God has had enough and will judge. Others view it as three sins fill the cup while the fourth overflows it, so God is pouring out His judgment. Either way, judgment is coming unless they repent. In Amos 2:6-16 God, through Amos, speaks to Israel. They are guilty of exploiting the poor (v6), greed and sexual sin (v7), and disregarding God's law (v8). They committed these sins despite God pouring His grace out upon them in the past (v9-12). In verses 13-16, God pronounces judgment upon them because of their many sins (v13) and says that none will be able to escape (v14-16).

In Amos 3:1-2, God calls out the "whole family" referring possibly to both Israel and Judah, although the message is aimed at Israel. The word "known" in verse 2 means "chosen" or "to have an intimate relationship with." God had chosen them to be His people and because they had repeatedly sinned they will experience God's punishment (Deut. 28-29 Bless/Curse). In verses 3-8 we see cause and effect statements referring to Israel's sin (cause) and God's judgment against them (effect). In verses 9-10 God calls the Philistines and Egyptians to witness what He is about to do to Israel. Verse 11 is a prophecy which was fulfilled by the Assyrians in 722 BC when they took Israel (Northern Kingdom) captive. In verses 13-15, God will dismantle their altars (meaningless worship) and tear down their expensive homes (exploiting poor).

Amos 4:1-3 is a judgment on the rich oppressing the poor while verses 4-5 deal with corrupt worship. In verses 6-13 Amos again refers to Israel's past sufferings which God was using to warn them that judgment was coming. God allowed these things to happen so they would see their sin and repent.

Amos 5:1-3 is what we would call a eulogy for fallen Israel foretelling its tragic fall. In verses 4-17, God urges Israel to "Seek Me and live". The word "seek" refers to turning to God in trust. He warns them not to return to their corrupt worship (v5) and their injustice (v7, 10-11). In the midst of these rebukes, Amos praises God for His creative power in verses 8-9. Amos encourages them to not only seek good but to do good in verses 14-15. Verses 16-17 are a picture of the people weeping because God has judged them. The Day of the Lord is mentioned in verses 18-20 (Joel). Amos condemns them of their worthless worship in verses 21-27 because they have turned from worshipping God to idolatry.

Saturday • Galatians 4-6

Galatians 4 continues the theme found at the end of chapter 3:26-29. This theme concerns being a son and an heir according to the promise. Paul explains the concept from the vantage point of being an underage heir (son) who is placed under guardians and stewards until they are at a mature age to inherit what rightfully is theirs (v1-2). Before they are mature they have no more rights than that of a slave. In verses 3-5, Paul is saying that "we were all under bondage at one time to tradition (or Judaism), but at the right time (fullness of time) God sent Jesus to purchase (redeem) us from being slaves to those systems so that He could adopt us as sons". We are assured of this because God has given us His Holy Spirit (v6; Rom. 8:15-16). It is because of Jesus' death that we are no longer slaves, but sons (v7). He continues his argument in verses 8-11 by asking "why are you turning back to the things that cannot save (Law, circumcision)?" In doing this they are putting themselves back into bondage (becoming a slave) to the law which is something Christ has set them free from (to be a son). In verses 12-20, Paul expresses his concern for their spiritual welfare because they have listened to false teachings. Paul urges them to become like him –to be free from the law and live in the liberty provided by Christ. Verses 13-16 show the care and affection the people in Galatia had for Paul at the beginning. They now perceived him as an enemy. Most believe from these verses that Paul may have had a debilitating eye disease such as ophthalmia which not only causes eye problems but disfigures the face. He warns the Galatians in verse 17 that the false teachers are only wanting to use them for their benefit, while at the same time separating them from the truth that Paul preached. He really wants them to correct their behavior because he is deeply concerned about where they are headed if they continue to believe a false gospel.

In verses 22-31 Paul gives examples, through the analogy of Hagar and Sarah, to describe those who live according to the law, and those who live according to the promise. These five sets of twos represent those who follow the law (Hagar, Ishmael, law, Mt. Sinai, earthly Jerusalem) and those of the promise (Sarah, Isaac, promise, Mt. Zion, heavenly Jerusalem). The children of Hagar are destined to be slaves, while those who have believed in Christ are children of the promise. Paul's point is "Why do you want to live under bondage when you have received grace?" Paul's advice for them is to abandon the false gospel they are believing and be children of the promise who are free (v30-31). This will take us into his discussion about liberty in chapter 5.

In Galatians 5:1-2 Paul proclaims that Jesus has set us free from living in bondage to the law (2 Cor. 3:17). In verses 2-6 Paul discusses the subject of circumcision. He writes that circumcision does not aid their salvation (v2). As a matter of fact, it brings with it the burden of keeping the law perfectly (v3). Verse 4 is not speaking of justification, but sanctification. He is telling the Galatians that they are rejecting grace and living under the law, and that they are depending on their own works for salvation. Verses 5-6 show that their identity is not found in obedience to the law or circumcision, but in Christ. In verses 7-9 Paul is telling them that this teaching (Judaizers) does not come from God and that a little bit of false teaching will spread and influence all. The Judaizers had even accused Paul of preaching in favor of circumcision, but if that is the case Paul asked why he was still being persecuted (v11). Paul speaks of walking in liberty in verse 13, but tells them to be careful and not use it as a license to sin (v14-15).

In verses 16-26 Paul explains to them how to cure their problems with legalism and license among the church- walk in the Spirit. Walking in the Spirit means to listen, obey, and follow the Holy Spirit. Paul shows the spiritual battle that takes place between the flesh and the Spirit in verse 17. He also adds that those who follow the leadership of the Spirit are not under the law (v18; Rom. 8:3-4). The works of those who live according to the flesh are listed in verses 19-21. Notice also in verse 21 that those who practice such things will not inherit the kingdom of God (1 Cor. 6:9-10; Rev. 22:15). In contrast to the works of the flesh the fruit of the Spirit is listed in verses 22-23: love (willful, sacrificial), joy (based upon promises of God), peace (with God/man), longsuffering (endurance), kindness (generous), goodness (benefit others), faithfulness (in word and deed), gentleness (encourage others), and self-control (resist fleshly desires). The believer in Jesus Christ is to crucify his flesh (v24), consistently walk in the Spirit (v25), and challenge himself to live a godly life (v26).

Galatians 6:1-10 concerns living out the Spirit-filled life and displaying the fruit of the Spirit to others. Paul instructs them to help those who are overtaken by sin (v1). The word "restore" means to "put in order, to restore to former condition". Instead of bashing people for their sin Paul says to help them get their life back on track. Paul also instructs them to help others carry their burdens (heavy) which all people have (v2). They are also to keep from deceiving themselves by being conceited (v3). Verse 4 is about examining one's own life. Verse 5 does not contradict verse 2. Verse 2 is referring to heavy loads that all believers need help carrying and the word for "load" in verse 5 is referring to something the size of a backpack that each individual must carry on their own. Today verse 6 could apply to attending worship and Sunday School, participating in the class, and passing on what is being taught. In verses 7-8 Paul warns them not to deceive themselves into thinking that they will get away with mocking ("turn nose up") at God. If a person sows in the flesh he will reap corruption but those who sow to the Spirit will have everlasting life. The word "corruption" actually means "rotting flesh". Also standing behind verses 7-8 is the thought of judgment which all people unbeliever and believer alike will have (Heb. 9:27;1 Cor. 3:10-15; Rev. 20:10-15). Verse 9 is an encouragement to those who are sowing to the Spirit. Paul urges them not to give up because at the right time God will give them a harvest.

In verses 11-13, Paul addresses those whom are under the influence of the Judaizers. Some want to be circumcised so they will not suffer persecution (v12), but Paul warns them that even they do not keep the law (v13). The only reason the Judaizers wanted them to be circumcised was so they could brag about those who have defected to their side. In verse 14, Paul claims that because of Christ this world has nothing to offer him, and this world has no power over him. If Paul was going to "brag" on anything it would be Jesus and the cross. One final time Paul addresses the issue of circumcision in verse 15. Paul says neither group gains anything by circumcision or uncircumcision. Only by being born-again (new creation) can one live the Christian life (2 Cor. 5:17). Paul closes the letter to Galatians by addressing his readers one final time. He tells them to walk (live) according to this rule (Gospel), and he prays for peace and mercy to be upon them (v16-18).

Cover to Cover Challenge

Week 5

Sunday • Psalm 18-20

Congratulations! You have successfully completed the readings for the first month. As always pray the Lord will be honored and glorified through this. While we are reading through the different genres of the Bible each week, I pray you notice how it all overlaps and how certain themes are repeated. Continue to pray that the Lord speaks to each of us as we study God's Word from cover to cover!

Psalm 18 concerns David and his deliverance from his enemies. In verses 1-3, David declares his love (used for a mother's love) for God and tells the reader who God is to him. Because of who God is David trusts (v3) and calls upon Him (v3) to deliver him from his enemies. In verses 4-6, David describes the situation he is in with strong language that refers to his death. David declares how God is going to help him in verses 7-15. God will move heaven and earth to help David, and no one can oppose Him. In verses 16-19, God delivers David from his enemies. In verses 20-24 David declares his faithfulness to God, and in verses 25-29 David speaks of God's faithfulness to him. David discusses the Lord's goodness to those who belong to Him in verses 30-36, and tells how He helps them. In verses 37-42 David claims victory over his enemies because of the strength God had given him, and in verses 43-45 David declares the results of the victory God had given him. In verses 46-50, David reflects on what God has done for him and the deliverance he has experienced by the Lord's hand.

Psalm 19 is about God revealing Himself through creation (v1-6) and through His word (v7-11). These verses also tell where David stands in light of both of these truths (v12-14). David speaks of God's glory being shown in the heavens (v1) and tells how it continually calls out to the whole world to speak of His glory (v2-6). This aspect of God's revelation is called God's general revelation. This is because all people can know there is a God by the evidence of creation and their own conscious (Rom. 1-2). David moves on to the Word of God which is also called His special revelation. The only way for anyone to be saved is to hear God's Word and it be revealed to them through the Holy Spirit. David lists four benefits of knowing God's Word. The benefits are converting the soul (v7 revive, restore), gaining wisdom (v7), rejoicing of the heart (v8), and enlightening the eyes (guidance). When David reflects upon these truths in verses 12-14, he asks God to cleanse him of sin (v12), keep him away from sin (v13), and not let sin dominate him (v13-14).

Psalm 20 is a prayer for victory in the face of a stressful situation. In verses 1-4 David cries out for God's help. Some believe that this may be a prayer of the people on behalf of David for God to help him in his kingly duties. This prayer is for God to answer, defend, help, and strengthen him (v1-2). Setting up "banners" signifies God's victory over his enemies because David knows who fights for him. In verses 6-8, David's trust in God is not just because He answers prayers, but because of who God is. The psalm closes with an appeal for God to save them from their situation.

Monday • Genesis 20-23

In Genesis 20, Abraham journeys to the land of Gerar (Philistines) where Sarah is taken by Abimelech. Abraham and Sarah lie (Gen. 12) about their relationship with one another. God warns Abimelech through a dream that he should return Sarah to Abraham. In verse 6, God actually protects Abimelech from sinning against Him because of the promise He has made to Abraham and Sarah concerning their future son. Another lesson is learned when we see a pagan king rebuke Abraham for his deceitfulness (v9-11). Abimelech heeds the warning from God and judgment is averted.

In Genesis 21:1-7, the birth of Isaac is recorded just as God had said (repeated 3x in first two verses), showing that God fulfilled His promise. In verses 8-13, at the feast celebrating Isaac's weaning, God reminds Abraham that the promise will go through Isaac. He then reminds Abraham that He will also bless Ismael. Hagar and Ishmael are sent away and the Angel of the Lord appears to her once more (Gen. 16, "The God who sees"). The Angel of the Lord comes with a promise to make him a great nation. Abraham is still living among the Philistines as chapter 21 closes.

In Genesis 22:1-14, we see God testing Abraham's faith by asking him to offer Isaac, his only son, to him as a sacrifice. Abraham's obedience and faith can be seen in verse 8 as he answers Isaac's question concerning the sacrifice they will be making. Hebrews 11:17-19 goes into greater detail about Abraham's faith. It states that Abraham believed that if Isaac were killed, God would raise him from the dead. This foreshadows the sacrifice that God would make by giving His one and only Son as a substitute for you and me. In verses 15-19, God renews the promises He has made with Abraham that he will receive a blessing, descendants, and land. The genealogy of Nahor is mentioned at the end of the chapter to introduce us to Rebekah who would become Isaac's bride.

Genesis 23 records the death of Sarah but also shows how Abraham came into possession of land in Canaan. The cave of Machpelah would be an important burial place for many of the patriarchs and their wives (Gen. 49:30-32, 50:13).

Tuesday • Joshua 21-24

In Joshua 21:1-8, cities were given to the Levites from every tribe as the Lord had promised in Numbers 35:1-8. Aaron (v9-19), the Kohathites (20-26), the Gershonites (v27-33) and the Merarites (v34-40) all received their allotment of cities from each tribe on both sides of the Jordan. The fulfillment of the promises given by God is recorded in verses 43-45. The land was theirs (v43), and they were at peace with their enemies (v44) just as God had promised them in Deuteronomy 12:9-10.

The eastern tribes of Reuben, Gad, and half-tribe of Manasseh return to the land allotted them in 22:1-9. In verse 5, Joshua reminds them to obey God's Word given through His prophet Moses by recalling Deuteronomy 6:1-5. These tribes build an altar by the Jordan River which was interpreted by the other tribes as being an act of apostasy (v10-14). One representative from each of the other ten tribes goes to speak with them about the altar they built (v15-20). The "sin of Peor" mentioned in verse 17 is recorded in Numbers 25, as the Israelites were drawn in to worshipping pagan deities and committing immorality. In verses 21-29, the eastern tribes give an explanation for building the altar. It was built as a witness (testimony) that they worshipped God and were a part of the children of Israel. The chapter closes with further explanation that the children of Israel on both sides of the Jordan River worshiped the same God and shared a common place of worship.

Joshua's farewell address is recorded in chapter 23. In verses 1-11, Joshua recalls that they were able to witness to God working on their behalf as they possessed the land and that they should remain loyal to God. The word "holdfast" describes an intimate binding relationship that Israel should have with God. The consequences of being unfaithful to God are reiterated in verses 12-16.

In Joshua 24, the covenant is renewed at Shechem. Joshua recites the history of Israel beginning with Abraham and continuing to the present day in verses 1-13. The "hornet" in verse 12 is believed to be the fear of the Lord which was sent out to bring great fear upon Israel's enemies (Ex. 23:28). In verses 14-24, Joshua once again calls the people to be loyal to the Lord because this will be the only way they will continue to experience His presence and blessing. Joshua sets up a stone in verses 25-28 as a reminder of the promises of God and the people's declaration to obey them. The book of Joshua closes with the burial of Joshua (v29-30), a report of the faithfulness of the Israelites (v31), reburial of Joseph's bones (v32; Gen. 50:24-25), and the death of Eleazar the high priest.

Wednesday • Matthew 14-16

In Matthew 14:1-12 we read the backstory of why John the Baptist is in prison (Mark 6:14-29). John the Baptist is the last of the OT prophets, and is a model for all disciples of Christ. John the Baptist death was against Jewish law because he had no trial and that he was also beheaded. The feeding of the 5,000 is covered in verses 13-21 (found in all 4 Gospels) and reveals God's compassion and power. During the exodus God provided food for the people (Ex. 16) and Elisha fed 100 men with only 20 loaves (2 Kgs. 4:42-44). Many Jews also believed that manna would return when the Messiah appeared. Jesus reveals His power over nature in verses 22-33, as He walks on water to the disciples during a raging storm in the early hours of the morning (3-6 AM). Notice also during this busy and hectic day that Jesus took time to go off alone and pray (v23). In verse 27, "It is I" is better translated "I AM" (Ex. 3:14; Isa. 51:12). Peter briefly walks on water (v29), but sinks once he takes his eyes off Jesus (v30). The main point of this story occurs in verse 33 as the disciples proclaim "Truly You are the Son of God". In verses 34-36 a summary of Jesus' ministry is once again given, showing us that He reaches out to all people.

Confrontation with the Pharisees regarding teaching is found at the beginning of chapter 15. The Pharisees believed that their tradition was on par with Scripture. In verses 3-6, Jesus clarifies the distinctions between their tradition and the actual words of God. The issue here is over ceremonial washing of the hands before a meal which was their tradition as opposed to what God's word says about treatment of parents (Matt. 23:16-17). The Pharisees were more concerned with their outward appearance than the inward condition of their hearts (7-9; Isa. 29:13). Jesus goes on to explain that it is what comes from the heart that causes defilement (v10-20). This also shows the Pharisees failure to see Jesus as the Messiah and their failure to lead people to the true word of God. The teachings of the Pharisees will only lead others to be like them and both will be led to destruction (v14). Jesus heals a Gentile woman's daughter in verses 21-28. The point of the story is Jesus initially came to Israel, so the Israelites get fed first. The woman understands, claiming that all she wants is the crumbs that fall from the master's table which demonstrates her faith. The healings in verses 29-31and the feeding of the 4,000 (v32-39) take place in Gentile territory. Mark 7:31 and the wording of verse 31 in Matthew ("and they glorified the God of Israel") both seem to confirm this.

The religious leaders of the day once again ask for Jesus to perform a sign in chapter 16:1-4. The signs He has been performing testify to who He is and demonstrate that the Messiah and His kingdom are here. The religious leaders of the day only wanted Him to perform signs in hopes they could trap or accuse Him of doing wrong. Jesus warns the disciples of the doctrine and teachings (leaven) of the Pharisees and Sadducees in verses 5-12, showing the side effects of false doctrine. Here the leaven represents the false teaching of the religious leaders (1 Cor. 5:6-8, Gal 5:9). In the Gentile region of Caesarea Philippi it is revealed to Peter, not by signs or wonders, but from the Father Himself who Jesus is (v13-20). Even Herod thought He was John the Baptist risen from the dead, while others thought He was just a forerunner of the Messiah (Elijah). Jesus is the rock on which the church is built, not Peter. The "binding" and "loosing" is based upon God's authority from the principles found in God's Word. Those who fail to repent are still "bound" to their sin while those who repent are "loosed" from their sin. Jesus begins to discuss His coming death openly with the disciples in verses 21-23. Peter is rebuked for his statement because it was against the will of God. Jesus must die and be raised to complete the mission the Father sent Him on. In verses 24-27 we see the characteristics of being one of His disciples. To "deny himself" literally means "to renounce his right to life". A true disciple of Christ will give up his own desires to follow God's will for their life.

Thursday • Job 9-10

Bildad spoke some very harsh words to Job in chapter 8. He told him that he was full of hot air (v2) and that he, along with his children, was getting what he deserved (v3-7). Job doesn't really respond to Bildad's accusations in these chapters, although he does agree that some of what Bildad said is true (v1). Job opens up chapter 9 by speaking about God's power in verses 1-13. In these verses Job says that God shakes the earth (v6), He makes the pillars tremble (v6), He speaks to the sun and it does not shine (v7), and He stretches out the heavens. All of these examples show His complete control of creation. Job laments in verses 14-20 that if he only understood what God was doing, he may be able to bear his suffering. In verses 21-24, Job wonders if God even cares. To Job, God treats the blameless and wicked the same as he is being treated. Job's suffering is to the point where he cannot even wear a smile (v27). Job claims that even if he could cleanse himself, all God will do is put him back into the pit (v31). In verses 32-35, Job again wishes he understood what God was doing. Here, Job speaks for the first time of a mediator. Job wanted someone to plead his case of innocence.

In chapter 10, Job continues to lament over his condition and the burden it has become. Once again he wants to know why he is suffering such horrible things (v1-3). Job even wonders if God is just a mortal man like him (v3-5), and if God is being just toward him (v6-7). Job just simply cannot understand why the One who made him is allowing such horrible things to happen to him (v8-17). Job reverts back to wishing he had never been born, and wishes God would just leave him alone (v18-22).

Friday • Amos 6-9

In Amos 6:1-7, Amos condemns Israel and Judah for believing that there is no nation better than them (v1-2). Because they are unwilling to hear the message (v3), Amos condemns them for their luxurious living and announces that they will soon be exiled (v4-7). This captivity is further described in verses 8-11. Because of their pride (v8), none will be left as God promises to break them in pieces (v11). The people of Israel have turned justice into poison and righteousness into bitterness (v12). They believe they have accumulated their wealth on their own (v13). Assyria will be the nation that God raises up against them (v14).

Chapter 7 opens up with a series of visions given to Amos. The first two, locusts (v1-3) and fire (v4-6), are averted due to Amos' intercessory prayer. In verses 7-9, a plumb line is mentioned. The purpose of a plumb line was to measure a vertical wall. God is using a plumb line here to measure the faithfulness of His people, and they have failed the test. One reason they failed the test is they are not willing to hear the words of Amos who was a sent to them to speak the words of God (v10-17).

Chapter 8 also opens up with a vision but this time it is a basket of fruit symbolizing the people of Israel are ripe for judgment (v1-14). Their crimes are recounted in verses 4-6. In verses 10-14 Amos describes their destruction as a funeral for an only son and predicts a famine of hearing the words of the Lord.

Judgment comes in chapter 9:1-6 as God begins with the false religion they had allowed among them. We read that none of them will escape His hand. Israel, although blessed by God, would learn that they were no better than other nations who deserved judgment for forsaking God (v7). In verses 8-12, God will restore Israel and a remnant of Israel will return to the land. Notice that the Gentiles will be included in what God is doing (v12). The kingdom will be restored and God will bless them abundantly (v13-15). God will bless His people through the promises given to Abraham (Gen. 12:1-3), David (2 Sam. 7), and through the coming of the Messiah.

Saturday • 1 Thessalonians 1-3

Paul wrote this letter around 50-52 AD to the church at Thessalonica. He visited Thessalonica on his second missionary journey with Silas and Timothy and preached there for three Sabbaths (Acts 17:2). It was a thriving city on the main highway of Rome, had a population of over 250,000 people, and also contained a large seaport. Murder, immorality, and many crimes in general were so common that people built houses with only one door. Christianity coming to this city would have provided many evangelistic opportunities for the gospel to be carried to other places. It is a letter written to provide hope and encouragement to a persecuted people, made up largely of Gentiles. It is worth noting that each chapter ends with a reference to the coming of the Lord Jesus Christ.

In chapter 1, Paul commends the church in verses 3-4 for their work of faith (deeds done after salvation), labor of love (motivated by love for God and others), and patience of hope (hope in Christ to endure persecution). The people witnessed the working of the Holy Spirit (v5). They had also become examples to the whole region of enduring persecution and being witnesses of the Lord (v6-7). The word "example" also carries the meaning of being a" model or a pattern" to follow. Their witness had "sounded forth" which means it "spread further out and was spreading wider" (v8). The whole region was a witness to what the Lord was doing among the people of Thessalonica (v9). Paul praises them for turning to God from their false religions (v9). Chapter 1 ends with a reference to the return of Christ. The word "wait" means to "wait expectantly or to look forward to with confidence". Paul also wants them to know that they will be rescued from the wrath to come in the future.

In chapter 2:1-12, Paul describes his affection for the people of Thessalonica and tells how they in turn treated them. When Paul had visited them (Acts 17) he was forced to leave them as well as other cities because of opposition to the gospel. But he wanted them to know that his preaching of the gospel was not in vain (a failure) because they were still able to preach the gospel boldly (v1-2). He also wanted them to know the preaching they heard was not wrong, was not with an impure motive, and they were not trying to trick people (v3). The word for "deceit" means to "catch with bait". The message they preached came from and was approved by God and his aim was to preach the gospel to them while being pleasing to God (v4). They also did not try to flatter people, come with greedy motives ("cloak of covetousness"), or seek only man's approval (v5-6). Paul's only mission was to preach the gospel and not be a burden on the people of Thessalonica (v7-9). Verses 10-12 describe their ministry in Thessalonica. They had behaved devoutly (set apart for God), justly (conform to God's word), and blamelessly (without cause for reproach). Through their preaching they also exhorted (encouraged), comforted, and charged them to live lives worthy of God (v11-12).

In verses 13-16, Paul praises them for how they received the message of the gospel. It was not Paul's word but God's word that worked in them. They had become "imitators" of fellow Christians despite the constant persecution they were under. In verses 17-20 Paul expresses his desire to see them again, but he knows that Satan has hindered his effort. Paul took great pride and joy in the people of Thessalonica because despite their constant persecution they were still standing for Christ.

Paul expresses concern for the people of Thessalonica in chapter 3. In verses 1-5 Paul has sent Timothy to bring encouragement and comfort to them, and to see how they were doing. Timothy's main mission was to strengthen and encourage the believers in Thessalonica. Timothy's report of their well-being in verses 6-10 shows that despite the persecution they are under, they are still thriving in faith and love toward all. Paul expresses a deep desire to see them again and build up what they may lack in their faith (v10). Paul closes out chapter 3 in verses 11-13 with a prayer. In verse 11 he repeats his prayer to see them again. The word "direct" means "to clear the obstacles." He prays for their love to not only grow, but overflow (abound) for one another (v12) so they may stand blameless before the Lord at His coming (v13).

Cover to Cover Challenge

Week 6

Sunday • Psalm 21-23

Welcome to week 6 of the *Cover to Cover Challenge*! Psalm 119:2 says "Blessed are those who keep His testimonies, who seek Him with the whole heart!" Keep seeking God! What an encouragement to each of us as we continue to study the Word of God together. Let us keep praying for the Lord to be glorified, and for the Lord to speak to each of us as we seek His face.

Psalm 21 may have been written to celebrate the victory won in Psalm 20. This psalm concentrates on God giving victory to the king. In verses 1-2, David leads the people to praise God for the strength He has provided them in defeating their enemies. God gives the king many gifts in verses 3-6, because the king trusts in Him (v7). The king knows it is because of God's unfailing love (mercy) that he cannot be shaken (moved). It is through the king and his people that God rules and establishes His kingdom on earth (v8-12). God will destroy all those who oppose Him (v10). In verse 13, all the people praise God for His strength and the blessings He has given them.

Psalm 22 is probably well-known to each of us, as a messianic psalm, foretelling the events of the cross. While it does foreshadow the sufferings of Christ, David is writing about himself and a trial he is suffering through. The first 21 verses of this psalm are a lament, while the final 10 focus on praising God. In verses 1-2 David wonders why God is allowing these things to happen to him, essentially asking "Where are You?" In verses 3-5, David exclaims that God has helped His people in the past and that is why he can trust in God. David speaks about how his enemies look at him in verses 6-8, as he becomes the object of ridicule. In verses 9-11, David knows he owes his very existence to God he also knows that it is God who has been faithful to him even from his mother's womb. In verses 12-21, David describes the strength of his enemies and their hostile intent. David is presenting himself as being a broken man on the edge of death surrounded by his enemies. In verses 19-21, David begins to shift his focus from his enemies to his Lord because only the Lord can deliver him. In verses 22-31, David praises God and calls on all people to worship Him (v27).

Psalm 23 is also a well-known psalm to each of us. Some believe David wrote this psalm after he had grown old was and looking back over the times the Lord had delivered him. David opens up the psalm by declaring that the Lord was his Shepherd and that he will not lack any good thing. Lying down in green pastures represents a place of rest. Sheep will not lay down unless they are: free from fear, hunger, and pests. Jesus promises this same rest in Matthew 11. David also claims that God "restores his soul" or revive his spirit. His Shepherd will lead him down paths (well-worn path) of righteousness because sheep are prone to wander. David knows that even when trouble comes, he does not have to fear because his shepherd is with him everywhere he goes. The rod and staff are symbols of the Shepherd's presence. His Shepherd also prepares a table for him (sign of being in covenant) and anoints his head with oil (divine favor). David knows he has been blessed in abundance (cup runs over) by his Shepherd. Because of this David that knows goodness and mercy will pursue him (follow) during his life, and that as long as he lives he will dwell in the Lord's presence forever (Ps. 27:4).

Monday • Genesis 24-26

After the death of Sarah in Genesis 23, the story now turns to finding a bride for Isaac. Isaac is the one whom the promises will continue through. Abraham explains the plan to find a wife for Isaac to his oldest servant in Genesis 24:1-9. There are two conditions that must be met. First, Isaac was not to marry a Canaanite. The second was that he was not to return to the land of his ancestors, because Canaan would be their home. The servant travels to the city of Nahor and prays very specifically for God to show him a bride for Isaac (v10-27). God answers the servant's prayer even before he is finished praying. In Genesis 22:20-24 the writer of Genesis had already introduced us to Rebekah, who would be Isaac's wife. Abraham's servant recalls the story to Rebekah's household, and how God had answered his prayer (v28-49). In verses 50-61, Rebekah's family affirms that it was the provision of the Lord that had brought them together. Isaac takes Rebekah to be his wife in verses 62-67.

In Genesis 25 we are told about other children Abraham had with his wife Keturah (v1-6). Abraham's death is recorded in verses 7-11, but we are told that the blessing will continue through Isaac. In verses 12-18 we are told about Ishmael and his descendants. This shows that God fulfilled His promise to Abraham and Hagar (Gen. 17:20, 21:18). The next passage details the barrenness of Rebekah, Isaac's prayer, and the birth of twin sons (v19-28). The barrenness of Sarah, Rebekah, Rachel, and Leah show that the promise of blessing is not achieved by human effort, but is based upon the promises and provision of God. Descendants of Jacob and Esau will make up two nations who despise one another. Esau rejects his birthright in verses 29-34 with the aid of some deceiving measures by Jacob. God's choice of Jacob turned out to be the wishes of both.

Isaac's life begins to show similarities with his father Abraham in chapter 26. The story of Isaac and Abimelech mirrors that of Abraham (12:10-20, 20:1-10). It is doubtful that the Abimelech's in each story are the same, considering close to 90 years have passed. Abimelech may be a title, like a king or a prince rather than a proper name. A famine has driven Isaac from the land and he ends up in Gerar a Philistine city. God reaffirms the covenant He made with Abraham to Isaac in verses 1-5. Both Abraham and Isaac stay in Gerar, both call their wife their sister, and both are rebuked by a pagan king (v6-11). In verses 13-22, God blesses Isaac with great wealth which angers the Philistines as they begin to stop up the wells that Abraham had dug. God renews His promises to Isaac again in verses 23-25, and Isaac builds an altar to the Lord and worships Him. In verses 26-31, Abimelech acknowledges the Lord is with Isaac and signs a treaty with him. Both Abimelech's prosper because they have dwelt with Abraham and Isaac, and because God promised they would be a blessing to others. Chapter 26 ends with a reference to Esau and his marriage to foreign women which sets up the stories to come in chapter 27 (v32-35).

Tuesday • Judges 1-5

The book of Judges ("deliverer" or "savior") continues the story of the children of Israel as they possess the Promised Land. It will recount some of the deeds from the book of Joshua through Samuel. If one could call the book of Joshua the "book of obedience" then surely Judges could be called the" book of disobedience".

Prominent in the book of Judges, is the "sin cycle". The children of Israel will sin, be slaves to foreign invaders because of their sin, cry out to God, God will send a deliverer, and they will have peace for a specified number of years. There will be 7 of these cycles throughout the book of Judges. It is believed that the book of Judges covers around 400 years, and will lead up to the dawn of the monarchy.

Judges 1 opens up with the tribe of Judah continuing to conquer the inhabitants of the Promised Land (v1-7). If you are wondering about verses 6-7 the cutting off of thumbs and the big toes would have made him incapable of fighting. It is listed as payback for what he had done to others. In verses 8-15 they continue to take cities away from their enemies, and we are reminded again of Othniel which is a repeated story from Joshua 15:15-19. Judah and Simeon join forces in verses 16-18. Verses 19-21 recount the failure of some tribes to inhabit some of the land. Ephraim captures the city of Bethel in verses 22-26. The rest of the chapter records the failure of the other tribes to drive out the Canaanites and Amorites.

Judges 2 begins with an appearance of the Angel of the Lord (pre-incarnate Christ) in verses 1-5. The Angel of the Lord tells them that the reason they are not successful is because they have broken their covenant with God. Notice in verse 6 that this happened while Joshua was still alive. Things will get much worse after the death of Joshua and those who were leaders alongside him (v7-9). In verses 10-23 the "sin cycle" mentioned in the opening is described.

A description of the remaining people of the land is given in verses 1-6 of chapter 3. They are left to test Israel and to train Israel for later battles. Marrying foreign people was forbidden because it would lead to worshipping their gods. Othniel was the first judge to deliver Israel from foreign invaders (v7-11). Cush is the father of Nimrod (Gen.10) and founder of Babylon. Rishathaim means "double evil". Eglon and the Moabites are the next foreigners to oppress Israel (Gen. 19:37). The 80 years of peace after Ehud and his armies defeat Eglon is the longest period of peace listed in Judges (v12-30). An oxgoad is a stick tipped with bronze used for prodding animals (v31), and is used by Shamgar to defeat the Philistines.

Judges 4-5 covers the story of Deborah and Barak. They would lead the children of Israel to defeat the Canaanites who were led by Jabin and Sisera (v1-5). Deborah is told by God to call on Barak to lead the army but he refuses to go unless Deborah goes with him (v6-8). Because of his lack of faith, Deborah tells him the honor of killing Sisera would go to a woman whose name is Jael (v18). After Barak and his army defeat the Canaanites, Sisera is greeted by Jael and she hides him in her tent (v14-20). This is where she drives a tent peg through his temple (v21). This battle is retold in poetic form in chapter 5. It is a song of praise to God for delivering their enemies into their hands (v1-5).

Wednesday • Matthew 17-19

The opposition of the Pharisees increases in Matthew 14-16 as Jesus continues doing miracles and teaching His doctrine. After the prediction of His death, Jesus is transfigured before Peter, James, and John on the mountain in chapter 17:1-8. The word "transfigured" means that something on the inside becomes visible from the outside. Clouds in Scripture point to the presence of God (Ex. 13:21-22, 40:34-38). Moses and Elijah also appear, representing the law and the prophets which foretold the coming of the Messiah. Luke tells us that they were discussing Jesus' death (Luke 9:31). Jesus once more relates the ministry of John the Baptist to Elijah's ministry (v9-13; Mal. 4:6).

Jesus rebukes His disciples for their lack of faith in verses 14-21. In this passage, the unbelief of the disciples and the type of power that is available to those who have faith comes into focus. This passage also shows that the disciples had divine authority to cast the demon out, but they lacked the faith required to exercise that authority. Jesus predicts His death for the second time in verses 22-23. The temple tax mentioned in verses 24-27 is for the upkeep of the temple and is paid by every male between the ages of 20-50 (Ex. 30:11-16). Sons of royalty, rabbis, and priests were exempt from the tax. This is why Jesus asks Peter the question found in verse 25. Jesus' point is that because He is the Son of God He should not have to pay the tax. However, Jesus pays the tax to avoid offending anyone (1 Cor. 9:12, 20).

In Matthew 18:1-5, Jesus uses a little child to teach about how one must come to Him. In verses 6-9, Jesus warns about causing the "little ones" (disciples) to sin, saying that it would be better for that person to die first. The world entices His disciples to sin (v7), and even a disciple can fall into sin (v8-9, 5:29-30). We should take care to not cause other believers to stumble in their walk with the Lord. Jesus cares for all of His sheep, especially the one who may go astray (v10-14). Jesus teaches the path of restoring a broken relationship in verses 15-20, which is based on OT principles (Lev 19:17; Deut. 19:15). This three step process is not to render someone guilty in order to excommunicate them, but to persuade them to repent. If the person fails to listen, fellowship with that person is to be avoided. Jewish rabbis taught that a person can forgive a repeated sin three times, but on the fourth there was no forgiveness given. Peter thought he was being generous with his seven times (v21-22). This teaching leads to the parable of the unforgiving servant in verses 23-35. This parable teaches mercy and forgiveness, and also reminds the reader that we have been forgiven for much more than we deserve. From God's perspective forgiveness is unlimited, and so we must be willing to forgive others as God has forgiven us. Unforgiveness is one of the greatest hindrances of prayer (Mark 11:25-26).

Matthew notes at the beginning of chapter 19 that Jesus is moving closer to Jerusalem and that He still has many followers (v1-2). The Pharisees once again ask Jesus a question about divorce. This question is designed to trap Him. The Pharisees refer to Deuteronomy 24:1-4 and the writing of divorcement given by Moses, but they misinterpret it as a command. Many Jewish men believed they could divorce for any reason. Divorce was never commanded, only allowed because of the hardness of their hearts. Jesus corrects their flawed view of marriage and divorce by citing Genesis 1:27, Genesis 2:24, and by alluding to Malachi 2:16 in verses 4-6. Jesus, within this context, teaches that the only reason for divorce is adultery. Verses 11-12 are not teaching that all people have to be celibate, but that celibacy is a special calling for some so they can concentrate on kingdom work. In verses 13-15 Jesus again reminds the disciples of the object lesson He taught them earlier about little children.

The tragic story of the rich young ruler who was unwilling to separate himself from his riches to follow Christ is found in verses 16-22 (Matt. 6:24). No one can "work" their way to heaven. Jewish leaders believed if a man was rich he was blessed by God and was surely going to heaven. Jesus teaches the opposite (v23-26). No amount of riches will get someone into heaven but it can keep them out. The simple truth here is that salvation is impossible without Jesus. Chapter 19 closes with Jesus teaching His disciples about their place in the kingdom and the reward they will receive (v27-30).

Thursday • Job 11-13

Zophar will speak for the first time in Job 11. He continues the same argument presented by Eliphaz and Bildad that Job was a sinner and needed to repent. In verses 1-12, Zophar believes that Job is claiming he is flawless. He believed that Job needed to be in the position he was in because apparently, Job must have forgotten his sin. Zophar believes that there is a much better chance of a wild donkey being born tame than Job gaining wisdom (v11-12). In verses 13-20 Zophar tells Job that his only hope is to repent and his suffering would cease. Suffering is not necessarily a sign of sin in a person's life. This is the mistake the three friends keep making when addressing Job.

Job speaks to all of his friends in 12:1-13:19, and speaks to God in 13:20-14:22. Job rebukes his friends and their so-called wisdom by stating that he knows as much as they do (v1-3). In verses 4-6 Job wants to know why all of this is happening to him, and not to those who deserve such pain. Job believes the whole world suffers from injustice (v7-12). In verses 13-25 Job speaks about God's sovereignty and the fact that God can do whatever He wants. That is all true, but Job still wants to know why he suffers so much pain.

In Job 13:1-6 he again claims to know exactly what his friends know (v1-2), but accuses them of lying. He claims that the best way they could show wisdom is to keep quiet (v3-5). In verses 6-12 Job accuses his friends of being deceitful in pleading their case to him before God, because what they believe about Job is wrong. Job again asks for an opportunity to have his case heard before God (v13-19). Job begins his plea to God in verses 20-28. Job asks God to respond to his pleas and to show him his sin (v20-23). He claims that God is hiding from him and treating him like he is an enemy (v24) and that God is holding sins from his youth against him (v26). Job wants to understand why all of this is going on in his life.

Friday • Hosea 1-7

Hosea ("Salvation") was a prophet to the northern kingdom of Israel during the reigns of the kings listed in verse 1. During the reigns of these kings there was great financial prosperity, and many people were becoming wealthy. This led to a religious decline that brought with it social injustice. Amos preached against the same things, but the people were unwilling to listen to his message. Hosea will also address the southern kingdom (Judah), but the message is primarily aimed at Israel. Hosea's marriage to Gomer illustrates God's faithful relationship to Israel even though they have turned away from Him.

In Hosea 1:1-9 God instructs Hosea to marry a woman of harlotry to illustrate His relationship with Israel. Three children are born to them and each name is symbolic. Jezreel is where Jehu slaughtered the house of Ahab in 2 Kings 9-10. The punishment of his sin was that one day Israel would cease to be a nation. Lo-Ruhamah means "not loved", signifying that God would no longer show love to them, but judge them. Lo-Ammi means "not my people", and it is symbolic of the people going after other gods and God disowning them. After this, in 1:10-2:1, God will fulfill His promises given to Abraham. All of Israel will once again be one and they will once again be "My people" and "My loved ones".

In Hosea 2:2-13 God addresses the people of Israel to bring charges against their mother (Israel as a nation). This is also a picture of Hosea and Gomer. Gomer going after other lovers was exactly what Israel was doing by going after other gods. The people received blessings from God, but they only turned and gave them to a false god (v8). Because of her sins, God promises to bring shame (lewdness) upon Israel (v10), destroy their empty religion (v11), destroy their way of life (v12), and punish them for forgetting God (v13). God predicts a day of blessing upon Israel after her captivity (v14-23), and promises a better relationship with Him built upon righteousness, justice, love, compassion, and faithfulness (v19-20).

Hosea is pictured as buying back his wife in Hosea 3, and at the same time this shows God's unfailing love for Israel. In verses 4-5 we read that Israel will one day turn to God, but this is still a future event-even from our own day. Hosea 4:1-4 shows God charging Israel as being untrustworthy, lacking of compassion, and not knowing God. God addresses the sins of the priests and prophets in verses 5-11, and of the people in verses 12-19. Both groups have an appetite for evil that cannot be filled (v11).

In Hosea 5:1-7 God warns the priests, the people, and the king of the coming judgment because of their spiritual and physical harlotry. In verses 8-15, God warns both Ephraim (Israel, north) and Judah (south) of the consequences of their sin. Verses 12-13 show that the judgment had already begun because the northern kingdom had already sought to build an alliance with Assyria (2 Kings 15) instead of asking God for help.

Hosea 6:1-3 is a future prayer of repentance, in which the people of Israel urge each other to go to God and have their wounds healed. Hosea lists many sins of the people in verses 4-11 such as covenant breaking, robbery, murder, and prostitution.

When God shows the people their sin, they still choose to remain in it according to Hosea 7:1-7. God compares their lust to a heated oven that stays hot until morning. All of this resulted in society committing sins against one another. In verses 8-16 outsiders have come in by marriage and led them to worship false gods. The people give no thought of returning to God (v10), and when they do turn it is to other gods (v16).

Saturday • 1 Thessalonians 4-5

Paul encourages the people to keep excelling in being pleasing to God in verses 4:1-8. Verse 1 is written as a command. Walking in a way that is pleasing to God is not optional for a Christian. Coming from a pagan background, many people may have been involved in ritual prostitution (v3). Fornication and adultery would have been viewed in their culture as a normal way of life. What was at stake is their sanctification-their continued maturity toward being like Christ. Paul speaks to them about having self-control over their passion (desires) and lust (out of control craving). The word "defraud" means to take pleasure at someone else's expense (v6). Paul reminds them to be led of the Holy Spirit which lives in them (v8). In verses 9-12 Paul teaches them to love one another, and prays for their love to grow more and more (stretch out to the limit, love as much as you can). Christians from the early church were known for living pure lives and for loving one another.

In verses 13-18, it appears that Paul is answering a question the Thessalonians had about loved ones who had already passed away when Christ returns. Paul deals with the reality of the situation in verse 13 which is his not wanting them to be uninformed (ignorant). Those who have no hope are those who do not believe in Jesus. In verses 14-15, Paul deals with the resurrection and their belief in it (2 Cor. 5:8). Without the resurrection there would be no salvation available and we would all be hopeless. In verse 16 there is a revealing as Christ returns to take all of those who belong to Him to glory. In verse 17 we are told about a reunion of all those who believe in Christ. The word "caught up" means to claim for one's self, move to a new place, and to rescue from danger. Verse 18 shows that there is relationship. We are to comfort one another with these promises from Christ Himself.

The first few verses in 1 Thessalonians 5:1-11 deal with a subject known as the Day of the Lord. No one knows when this Day (time period) will come, but it will be sudden. His coming will be unexpected and unpredictable even for believers (v2). Even Jesus said that no one knows the hour or day of His coming. When the Day does arrive it will not overtake them because they are not of the darkness, but are sons of the light and day (v4-5). In verses 6-8 Paul instructs believers to watch (be alert) and be sober (self-control) while waiting for the Lord's return. The people of God are not appointed (destined) for wrath, but obtain (gain) salvation through Jesus (v9). Paul's aim with these words is for believers to comfort (encourage) and edify (build up) one another (v11).

Verses 12-22 contain exhortations that cover a variety of subjects. In verses 12-13, Paul encourages believers to respect and value those who are leaders because of what they do. The word "esteem" means "to hold them in love exceedingly". Believers are also to warn those who are out of line (unruly), comfort those who are discouraged (fainthearted), cling to those who are burdened (uphold the weak), and not to be short tempered (v14). No one is to pay back evil with evil (v15), they are to rejoice in every situation (v16), have a prayerful attitude (v17), be thankful (v18), not neglect or ignore the Spirit (v19), listen to proclamations of the Word (v20), measure everything by what Scripture says (v21), cling to what is good (v21), and stay away from anything that appears to be evil (v22). Paul closes the letter with a prayer for God to keep using the Thessalonians. He also asks for prayer for himself, and encourages the reading of his letter in all of the churches in Thessalonica (v23-28).

Cover to Cover Challenge

Week 7

Sunday • Psalm 24-26

Welcome to week 7 of the *Cover to Cover Challenge*! I pray that the Holy Spirit is teaching you great and mighty things from the Word of God. There is nothing greater that any of us can do than to be in the Word of God, and allow the Lord to speak to us through it. Continue to pray for the Lord to use this for His glory, and to work in the lives of all those participating. God Bless!

Psalm 24 is known as the "King of Glory" psalm and can be divided into three parts. In verses 1-2, God is the Creator who rules over the earth. In the next set of verses (v3-6), God is described as being holy. The terms "clean hands" and "pure hearts" describe those who live according to God's Word (v3-4). In verses 5-6 we see that those who live according to God's Word enjoy the promises of the covenant, which drives them to continually seek God's face. The last part (v7-10), describes God as the King of glory and the divine warrior who fights for His people.

Psalm 25 is a prayer for deliverance, guidance, and forgiveness. In verses 1-3, David submits himself to the Lord and prays for the wicked to not be able to overpower him. David knows that anyone who has ever placed trust in the Lord has never been disappointed. David prays for God's guidance and forgiveness in verses 4-7. Notice three things he asks God to do-"show me Your ways", "teach me your paths", and "lead me in Your truth" (v4-5). David asks God to remember His past dealings with His people (v6), and to forget the sins of his youth (v7). In verses 8-11, the theme of guidance and forgiveness is repeated. Those who follow God's guidance will enjoy the benefits of being taught by God (v12), and enjoy the blessings of the covenant (v13-14). In verses 15-22 we return to the theme of deliverance and forgiveness as David prays to be delivered from his enemies (v15), and to be forgiven of his sins (v18).

Psalm 26 is a prayer for vindication. David is asking God to declare him to be innocent and avenge the wicked (v1-3). He asks God to examine his heart and mind, because he knows he is walking according to what the Lord desires. David says that he does not even associate with the wicked in any way (v4-5). In verses 6-8, David declares his innocence and praises the Lord for all He has done for him. David declares he does not want to be judged with the wicked (v9-10) but desires to walk with the Lord (v11-12).

WEEK 7

Monday • Genesis 27-30

Genesis 27 continues the story of Jacob ("Deceitful") and Esau. Jacob has already received Esau's birthright, and in this chapter we will see how he deceives Isaac into giving him the blessing of the firstborn. The story unfolds in verses 1-26 as Rebekah overhears a conversation between Isaac and Esau. Isaac's inability to see clearly is a crucial part of the story. Rebekah comes up with a plan for Jacob to deceive Isaac by dressing him like Esau. The plan goes as intended, and Jacob receives the blessing in verses 27-29. The blessing echoes the covenant that God has made with Abraham and Isaac. In verses 30-40, Esau discovers that Jacob has stolen his blessing. Esau makes plans to kill Jacob and Rebekah sends Jacob to find a wife from her brother's family (v41-46).

Genesis 28 begins with Isaac blessing Jacob, which again echoes the covenant made by God with Abraham and Isaac (v1-5). Esau marries one of Ishmael's daughters for spite (v8), which will set up the story coming in chapters 32-33. The older sons (Ishmael and Esau) intermarry, while the younger sons (Isaac and Jacob) inherit the blessing. This shows that God, not man, is in control of the circumstances. The vision of Jacob's ladder affirms that the covenant that God made with Abraham and Isaac is now extended to Jacob. Jacob calls the place Bethel ("House of God"), and will return there in chapter 35 where God will reafirm the covenant with him.

Jacob begins his journey to Padan Aram in Genesis 29. In verses 1-14 he meets Rachel at the well. The story is similar to Abraham's servant finding a bride for Isaac (ch. 24). Jacob, the deceiver, is now deceived by Laban in verses 15-30. After working for Laban for seven years in order to marry Rachel, Laban deceives Jacob into marrying his oldest daughter Leah first. Jacob agrees to work seven more years in order to marry Rachel. The end of the chapter sets up the next chapter by stating that Jacob loved Rachel more than Leah. The Lord is in control, and we are reminded of that in verse 31 as God opens Leah's womb to bear children, but Rachel is barren. From 29:31-30:24, Jacob has children by each of his wives and their maids. The Lord opens up Rachel's womb and she gives birth to Joseph. He will become the focal point of Genesis in chapter 37. In Genesis 30:25-43 Jacob and Laban reach an agreement for him to leave with his family. The story of the sheep is summed up in verse 43. It is God who blessed Jacob (by increasing his wealth through livestock) just as He had blessed Abraham (12:16) and Isaac (26:14). God's promise of blessings has now been proven true through Abraham, Isaac, and Jacob.

Tuesday • Judges 6-10

Deborah and Barak defeated the Canaanites in chapters 4-5, and the land had rest for 40 years. For the fourth time, the children of Israel have entered the "sin cycle" at the beginning of chapter 6. The Midianites and Amalekites are both oppressing Israel at harvest time by stealing all of their crops and livestock (v1-7). After they cry out to the Lord for deliverance, He sends a prophet to tell them why they are oppressed (v8-10). The story of Gideon dominates the next 4 chapters. In verses 11-24, the Angel of the Lord (pre-incarnate Christ) appears to Gideon while he is threshing grain in a winepress. The Angel of the Lord calls Gideon a "mighty man of valor", but to the reader Gideon is far from it. In verse 15 we learn that Gideon is from the smallest tribe, his family is the weakest in that tribe, and he is the weakest in his family. Gideon asks for a sign (which he will do often) that it truly is the Lord who is speaking with him. After confirming that He is the Lord, Gideon builds an altar and names it Jehovah Shalom ("The Lord is Peace"). In verses 25-32 the Lord asks Gideon to destroy the altar for Baal worship, and he does. In verses 33-35, Gideon is filled with the Holy Spirit and gathers an army together from other tribes. Once again, Gideon asks the Lord for a sign to confirm that he is going to defeat the Midianites (v36-40).

Judges 7 begins with God reducing Gideon's army down to 300 (v1-8). God does not want Israel to think they defeated them without His help (v2). In verses 8-14, God gives Gideon a sign to strengthen him before battle by allowing him to overhear a dream and its interpretation. Gideon and his army prepare for battle (v15-18), and begin to defeat the Midianites (v19-25).

In Judges 8 Gideon and his army continue to pursue the Midianites. The people of Succoth and Penuel refuse to help them. Gideon promises to return and punish them after he defeats the Midianites (v1-9), which he does in verses 13-17. After capturing the Midianite kings in verses 10-12, Gideon executes them in verses 18-21. In verses 22-28 Gideon refuses to be their king, but reminds the people that God is to be their king (Ps. 24). Gideon's tragic mistake is making a golden ephod (apron garment used in priestly duties), which led the people to commit idolatry. The closing of chapter 8 prepares us for chapter 9 by introducing Abimelech, who is a son of Gideon, and also shows the children of Israel returning to worship Baal-Berith ('Baal of the covenant").

Abimelech becomes ruler over Shechem and proceeds to kill Gideon's other sons, except for Jotham who managed to hide himself in 9:1-6. The parable of the trees, spoken by Jotham in verses 7-15, is a curse upon Abimelech. The trees probably represent Gideon and others from his family who declined to be king over them. The bramble in verse 15 is Abimelech, and verse 20 is a prophecy of what would happen to Abimelech. In verses 22-29, the Lord sent a spirit of ill will to break the covenant between the people of Shechem and Abimelech. Gaal comes to defeat Abimelech outside of Shechem, but fails in verses 30-41. In verses 42-49, Abimelech attacks the people of Shechem as they go out to gather crops and defeats them. The sowing of salt symbolizes the destruction of the city, and it was not rebuilt until 200 years later under Jeroboam I. Abimelech destroys the rest of Shechem by fire. Moving on to Thebez, Abimelech is killed by a woman who throws a stone down from the tower (v50-57), fulfilling the curse of Jotham.

Judges 10 opens up with the reigns of Tola (v1-2) and Jair (v3-5). Chapter 10 sets up the events of chapters 11-12 and the story of Jephthah. In verses 6-16, God recounts the long list of Israel's sins (v6-7). The "sin cycle" is different here. In verse 13-14 God says that He will deliver them no more, and instructs them to cry out to the gods they are serving. The people demonstrate their repentance by throwing out their idols and by being willing to come to God on His terms (v15-16).

Wednesday • Matthew 20-22

Jesus is still on the journey toward Jerusalem after telling His disciples twice of His impending death. Matthew 20:1-16 is a parable that concerns the sovereignty and grace of God. People were hired to work throughout the day. They were all were paid what was agreed, no matter the time they were hired. For the third time Jesus mentions His death (v17-19), but there is one added statement-how He would die. After being confronted by James and John's mother about giving her sons a place of authority in His kingdom, Jesus takes the opportunity to teach them about serving (v20-28). In verse 28, Jesus states that the purpose for His coming was to give His life as a ransom for many. The word "ransom" means purchasing a slave from the slave market. This means Jesus' death was substitutionary, paying the price for our sin (Isaiah 53). Jesus heals two blind men as He was leaving Jericho in verses 29-34. Even they know that He is the Messiah ("Son of David").

In Matthew 21:1-11 Jesus enters Jerusalem, fulfilling Zechariah 9:9 which refers to the Messiah. In verse 9 the shouts of Hosanna (save, deliver), and Son of David (Messiah) are shouts of praise and adoration for Jesus. Other portions come from Psalm 118:25-26. Jesus cleanses the temple in verses 12-17. Jesus uses Isaiah 56:7 and Jeremiah 7:11 to condemn the practices that were taking place at the temple. They were not using the temple to be a witness to the nations, but to take advantage of the people just as the ancient Israelites had done.

The cursing of the fig tree is an acted parable related to cleansing the temple, which shows His disgust with them (v18-19). A fig tree bears fruit first, then leaves. Jesus went to the fig tree expecting fruit but found none. Likewise, Jesus went to the temple hoping to find prayer and worship of God but He found none. Micah 7:1 also shows a fruitless fig tree that stood for Israel's moral and religious failures. It also teaches the importance of having faith when you pray and not doubting (v20-22). The question of Jesus' authority was designed to trap Him (v23-27). Jesus turns the table by asking them a question concerning John the Baptist. If they answered "from heaven" they had to believe John and his claims about Jesus. The parable of the two sons in verses 28-32 is about the Jewish leadership's (second son) response to John's message compared to the response of the tax collectors and harlots (first son). In the parable of the wicked vinedressers (v33-46) the landowner is God, the vineyard is Israel, the servants are the prophets, and the son is Jesus.

In Matthew 22:1-14 Jesus tells the parable of the wedding banquet. Many are invited, but most refuse to come. It is a parable that speaks not just to Israel and its leaders, but applies even today. There is a high price to pay for refusing the invitation. In verses 15-22, Jesus discusses the proper attitude toward government and God. Again, it was designed to trap ("clever trap") Him with His words. Proper submission should be made to both, but when Caesar desires what belongs to God, God's people must obey God (Acts 5:29; Rom. 13:1-7; 1 Pet. 2:13-17). What is significant about this confrontation was the Herodians and Pharisees were present. Both of these groups represented each side of the question being posed to Jesus. In their thinking Jesus would either oppose taxation or support it. If He opposed it He would be labeled a zealot and be committing treason. If He supported the tax He would be taking side with Rome against His own people.

The Sadducees try once again to trap Jesus with His own words in verses 23-33, concerning a woman who had no children and who married seven brothers. Jesus corrects their beliefs by explaining that they do not understand God's power or His Word. Also it should be noted that the Sadducees believed that the soul perished with the body, so they did not believe in a resurrection. In verses 34-40 it would be the Pharisees turn to try and trap Him. The Pharisees were known for their strict legalism. They made distinctions between "hard" and "easy" commandments, but believed they were all equally binding. In response to their question, Jesus quotes Deut. 6:5 and Lev. 19:18, and giving the highest praise for loving God and loving one another.

In verses 41-46, Jesus turns the tables and asks the Pharisees a question. Jesus explains that He is the Son of David and the Son of God by quoting Psalm 110:1. The Pharisees and others expected more of a political/militant messiah who would come and sit on the throne in Jerusalem. Jesus showed here that He was not only a descendent of David, but that He was David's Lord. This implied a greater authority and a greater throne. From this point forward they would not question Him anymore.

Thursday • Job 13-14

Just to recap from last week, Job speaks to all of his friends in 12:1-13:19, and to God in 13:20-14:22. Job begins his plea to God in verses 20-28. Job asks God to respond to his pleas and to show him his sin (v20-23). He claims that God is hiding from him, treating him like he is an enemy (v24) and holding sins from his youth against him (v26). Job wants to understand why all of this is going on in his life. In chapter 14:1-12, Job pleads for God to show him mercy. Job acknowledges that he has little rest from his pain (v6), and in previous verses admits the frailty of human life (v1-5). In verses 13-17 Job once again asks God to let him die, but this time he wants God to revive him after God's anger has ceased. Job speaks of his hopelessness in verses 18-22.

Friday • Hosea 8-14

Hosea has spent much of the last 3 chapters addressing Israel's sin. Here, in chapter 8, Hosea warns of their coming judgment. Once the invasion would begin, Israel would cry out that they know God out of desperation (v1-3). God judges them because they no longer seek Him for anything, but look to their idols for help (v4-7). The idols mentioned are probably the golden calves at Bethel and Dan, which were set up by Jeroboam. Judgment was already on them because their crops were failing (v7-8). The people were stubborn (v9), and turned to other nations for help (v10). In verses 11-14, God condemns them for offering sacrifices that belonged to Him to their idols, and accuses them of even forgetting who He was.

God continues to warn them of their coming judgment in chapter 9, and of their coming captivity. In verses 1-2, the people of Israel were thanking other gods for their many blessings. For all of their sin, God was sending them back to Egypt (symbolic for Assyria) where they can sacrifice no more (v3-5). In verses 6-9, God promises again that they will be carried captive to Assyria (Egypt, Memphis) because they did not consider the warnings of the prophets God had sent them. In verses 10-17, God recounts punishments that will be brought upon Israel before they go into captivity. Israel's population will decrease (v11-12), they will be murdered, and miscarry children (v13-14). God will no longer love them and will send them away from His house (v15) and they will become like dried up roots (v16) all because of their disobedience (v17).

The theme of captivity continues in chapter 10. As Israel prospered by God's hand they continually turned away from Him, so He will destroy them (v1-2). The northern kingdom of Israel never had a godly king because they never consulted God (v3). They are a deceitful people (v4), who are more concerned over losing their idol than over their sin (v5). Israel would be disgraced and humiliated (v6-7) as the Assyrians will leave nothing standing (v8). In verses 9-15 Hosea addresses Israel's sin and punishment, with the exception of verse 12. Hosea is telling the people to sow righteousness and they would reap mercy, implying it would be hard but they must do it.

Hosea 11:1-7 speaks about Israel's restoration based upon God's love for them. They were called by God (v1) to be His own special people, but they had turned against Him (v2). God raised Israel with compassion and love, and showered them with His grace (v3-4) despite their continued disobedience (v5-7). In verses 8-11 God speaks of His love for Israel, promising that He will never let them go and they will once again turn to Him.

Hosea 12 returns to the subject of Israel's unfaithfulness to God. Much of this is directed at both Israel and Judah. God tells both nations that they should have pursued His blessing as Jacob did, instead of chasing after the wind (v1-6). Instead they were unjust in their dealings with one another (v7-8). The entire land will go into captivity for refusing to hear the prophets (v9-11) but their past history should have led them to be submissive before God despite many hardships (v12-14).

Hosea 13:1-3 discusses the consequences of Baal worship, which is death. In verses 4-6, Hosea reminds Israel of how God helped them during their wilderness journey. In verses 7-8 God will punish Israel for their disobedience, but God still promises to be their king (v9-11). God will redeem His people (v14), but they must be punished and go into captivity (v15-16).

Hosea 14 is a promise of Israel's final restoration. They must acknowledge their sin and trust in the Lord (v1-2,8), because no one else can save them (v3). In response to their repentance, God will bless them and love them unconditionally (v4-7).

Saturday • 2 Thessalonians

Paul's second letter to the Thessalonians was probably written a few weeks/months after the first. It was written in response to the continual persecution and to correct false teaching about the Day of the Lord.

In 2 Thessalonians 1:1-5, Paul prays for the Thessalonians to grow in faith and love in the midst of the persecutions they suffer. Paul had also prayed for this to happen in the previous letter he had sent to them (3:10, 12). He praises them for continuing to endure the persecutions they are experiencing (v4-5). These persecutions are the result of living in a manner worthy of the kingdom of God. In verses 6-12 Paul promises retribution by the Lord against those who are persecuting them. The idea is that God is going to repay those who are persecuting the Thessalonians (v6). The word "repay" carries the meaning of "righting all wrongs" and to "give what is due". The people that God will seek vengeance on are those who do not know God and who have not believed the gospel (v7-8). These people will suffer by never being in the presence of God (hell), while the Thessalonians will glorify the Lord (v9-10). In verse 9 the word "destruction" does not mean annihilation, but to "bring something to complete ruin". They will lose everything that makes life worth living. In verses 11-12 Paul prays that they will continue to live lives worthy of their calling and fulfill God's will for their lives.

2 Thessalonians 2:1-12 discusses the Thessalonians' fear that they are living during the Day of the Lord. It is believed that they may have received word, possibly from false teachers, that the Day of the Lord had begun (v1-2). Paul reminds them that two things must happen before the Day of the Lord begins. First, a great apostasy will take place (v3). Apostasy is simply leaving a known truth (gospel) and embracing error. Second, the man of lawlessness will be revealed (v3, son of perdition, Antichrist). It literally stands for someone who is doomed to be destroyed. Verse 4 may be referring to the "abomination of desolation" spoken of by Daniel (11:31, 12:11) and Jesus (Matt. 24:15). Satan is the one who is behind the "man of lawlessness", and his desire has always been to be worshiped (Isa. 14:12-21). Paul tells them that because these two things haven't happened, they cannot be living during the Day of the Lord (v5). Most believe that the restrainer is the presence and power of the Holy Spirit, which indwells each believer in the body of Christ (v6-7). John's "spirit of antichrist" (1 John 4:3) and the "mystery of lawlessness" of Paul is probably referring to the presence and permeating influence of evil in the world (v8-9). When the "man of lawlessness" does appear, it is the Lord who will "destroy" (make completely powerless) him. Unbelievers will fall prey to the deceptions of the man of lawlessness because they do not believe the truth and they practice unrighteousness (v10-12). In verses 13-17, Paul reminds them of where they stand in their relationship with the Lord. They have been chosen by God, they are being sanctified by the Spirit, they believe the truth, and they have been called by God (v13-14). Paul tells them to stand firm and cling to what he has taught them (v15). Paul encourages the Thessalonians by telling them that the Lord will comfort their hearts and give them strength to do His will (v16-17).

In 2 Thessalonians 3:1-5, Paul asks the Thessalonians to keep praying so they can continue to preach the gospel. He also prays for the Lord to be glorified, and for them to be delivered from the schemes of wicked men (v1-2). It is believed that Paul is in Corinth when he writes, so you know he is in desperate need of prayer. It is because of God's faithfulness they can endure hardships, and Paul prays that the Lord will protect them (v3-5). Paul warns them to stay away from anyone in the church who is not walking according to the gospel (v6). The word "disorderly" refers to a soldier who has fallen out of rank. Paul tells them to mimic (follow us) him (v7-9) in their behavior. In verses 10-12 Paul warns those who are not working. It may be that they believed that the Lord was coming soon so they had quit their jobs to prepare for His return. Paul is encouraging them to work and to make their own living. Paul encourages them to not get discouraged doing things the right way (v13), and to note (mark, do not get mixed up with) anyone not living according to what he has spoken to them (v14-15). Paul prays that the Lord will give them peace both inwardly and outwardly (v16-18).

Cover to Cover Challenge

Week 8

Sunday • Psalm 27-29

Welcome to week 8 of the *Cover to Cover Challenge*! Psalm 119:18 says "Open my eyes, that I may see wondrous things from your law". Each of us should pray this for one another as we study God's Word together. Continue to pray that the Lord will be glorified through the *Cover to Cover Challenge*, and that the Holy Spirit will work mightily in us.

Psalm 27 is a psalm of David's faith in the Lord In verse 1-3, David has complete faith and trust in the Lord. This faith allows him not to be fearful in the face of his enemies. David wants to remain in the presence of the Lord (v4) because he knows that when times of trouble come, God will protect him (v5). In verses 7-12 David cries out for God to be merciful, and that he will be delivered from his enemies. In verses 11-12 David asks the Lord to teach, lead, and deliver him in spite of those who have risen up against him. David knows that the Lord will deliver him from his enemies as he waits (has faith in) the Lord in verses 13-14.

Psalm 28 is a prayer of lament (v1-5) and faith in the Lord (v6-9). David is dependent upon the Lord for help and is asking for the Lord to act now (v1-2). In verses 3-5, David asks the Lord to not judge him with the wicked who have more faith in their works than Lord's. David praises and sings to the Lord for hearing his prayer (v6), for being his strength and shield (v7), and for being his refuge (v8). David closes the psalm with a prayer for the Lord to shepherd His people (v9).

Psalm 29 is a psalm of praise of God's power. In verses 1-2, David is encouraging the praise and worship of God for His glory, strength, and majesty (beauty of holiness). The words in these opening verses form the foundation of praising God for His creation and redemption. It is through "the voice of the Lord" we see His glory, rule, and sovereignty over all (v3-9). God's glory is even on display in judgment, because He is the King of all the earth (v10). We see in these verses that it is God Who protects His people (v11).

Monday • Genesis 31-34

In Genesis 31:1-21 Jacob is instructed by the Lord to return to the land of his fathers (v1-3). We learn in verses 4-13 that God was blessing Jacob for how Laban had been treating him, especially concerning the flocks. Upon hearing Jacob recount the story to them, Rachel and Leah agree that Jacob needs to be obedient to God (v14-21).

We also learn in this passage that Rachel had taken her father's household gods, matching the past deceptive actions of her husband Jacob. In verses 22-42, we learn that God is in control of the whole situation. Jacob and his family leave, only to be pursued by Laban. The story grows suspenseful in verse 32 with Jacob's words to Laban concerning who stole the household gods. The main point of the story is in verse 42. Jacob's wealth did not come from working with Laban, but from God. In verses 43-55, Jacob and Laban make a covenant with one another not to harm each other again and then part ways.

Esau reenters the story in Genesis 32:1-21. The last time we saw Esau, he was wanting to kill Jacob for stealing his birthright and the blessing. Jacob now fears that is what Esau has come to do (v7), and he prays for the Lord to protect them and appeals to the covenant God has made with him (v10-12). Jacob begins to make preparations for the meeting with Esau, but Jacob will be reminded again that God is in control of the situation. In verses 13-22, Jacob sends some of his servants with an elaborate gift for Esau. Jacob's life had been filled with struggles with his brother (ch. 25, 27), his father (ch.27), and Laban (ch. 29-31). In verses 22-32 he will wrestle (struggle) with God for the blessing. The name that Jacob gives to the place (Peniel), and Hosea 12:4 both affirm that Jacob wrestled with God (Angel of the Lord). Jacob's ("Deceiver") name is changes to Israel ("Struggles with God").

In Genesis 33:1-17 Jacob and Esau will meet for the first time in 21 years. Jacob again takes precaution for the meeting, but it is God who has prepared the way. It is not Jacob's preparation, but his earlier prayer that has changed Esau's heart. In verses 18-20, Jacob arrives safely back into the Promised Land and buys land in Shechem. This sets up the story of chapter 34 concerning Dinah.

In chapter 34, Dinah is raped by Shechem the Hivite who also wants to marry her (v1-24). The Hivites wanted to become one with the family of Jacob which was the fear of Abraham (24:3), Rebekah (27:46), and Isaac (28:1). After learning of the rape of their sister, Simeon and Levi carry out a deceptive plan of their own against the men of Shechem (v25-31). It would seem the deception of Jacob had been passed along to his sons. The sign of circumcision was given to be a sign of the unity of the covenant people to remain separate from other nations, but Simeon and Levi use it to kill all the men of Shechem.

Tuesday • Judges 11-16

Judges 10 set the stage for the chapters you are reading this week. In Judges 11:1-11 we meet Jephthah, who is from Gilead. Because he is the illegitimate son of a harlot, he was considered to be the lowest of his family. Jephthah was a skilled fighter (v4-6), but had been banished because of his lineage. The elders of Gilead make him their commander of the army in order to defeat the Ammonites. Jephthah reaches out to the Ammonites in order to negotiate peace over the land Israel currently occupies but the king of the Ammonites refuses (v12-28). Jephthah explains how the Israelites came into occupation of the land in verses 14-26. Jephthah appeals to the Lord as "the Judge" in verse 27, and it will be Him who will decide whose land it truly is. In verses 29-33, the Spirit of the Lord empowers Jephthah for battle just as He did Gideon in chapter 6. Jephthah makes a vow to sacrifice the first thing that comes out of his home after their victory over the Ammonites. Some believe this showed his lack of faith in God's power to enable him to win the battle. After defeating the Ammonites Jephthah returns home, and his daughter (only child) is the first to come from his house. While human sacrifice is forbidden by the Law (Lev. 18:21; Deut. 12:31), it is also a sin to break a vow (Num. 30:2). Some commentators do believe Jepthtah's vow was fulfilled by his daughter taking a vow to remain unmarried.

Judges 12:1-7 begins with Jephthah defeating the Ephraimites after they complain about not being asked to help the Gileadites in battle against Ammonites. Jephthah dies after reigning for 6 years and his reign is followed by Ibzan, Elon, and Abdon (v8-15)

Judges 13:1-14 begins the story of Samson as the Angel of the Lord appears to Manoah's barren wife. Her son Samson was to be a Nazarite ("dedicated") and she was to keep the vows while she was pregnant with him. Numbers 6:1-12 covers the details of the Nazarite vows which Samson would repeatedly break. The Angel of the Lord appears to Manoah and his wife again in verses 15-23, giving them proof of the special circumstances of their son's birth. Samson's birth was predicted by the Lord, he had godly parents, he was dedicated to the Lord as a Nazarite, and he experienced the power of the Lord through His Spirit.

Judges 14:1-9 reveals one of Samson's fatal weaknesses-Philistine women. The Israelites had already been warned not to intermarry with foreigners (Deut. 7:1-3; Judges 3:6) because they would lead the Israelites into adultery (spiritual, physical). We see Samson perform great feats of strength (v5-6) and also violate the Nazarite vow (v7-9). In verses 10-20, Samson poses a riddle to the Philistines at his marriage feast. After threatening his wife, the Philistines receive the answer to the riddle. Empowered by the Spirit of the Lord, Samson kills 30 men and steals their clothes to pay off his debt and loses his wife to his best man.

In Judges 15:1-8, Samson goes to reclaim his wife only to find out she has been given to another man. Samson sets fire to their crops, ruining their harvest. In verses 9-20, the men of Judah bind Samson and bring him to the Philistines, Again, filled with the Spirit of the Lord, Samson kills one thousand Philistines with the jawbone of a donkey (Shamgar, Judges 3:31), but he does acknowledge the victory was because of the Lord.

The story of Samson comes to an end in chapter 16. After he avoids being captured by the Gazites in verses 1-3, we are introduced to Delilah. The leaders of the Philistines offer her a large sum of money to find out what is the source of Samson's strength. In verses 6-20, she tries desperately to find out the source of his great strength before he tells her the truth. The saddest part is that Samson never realized that the Spirit of the Lord had departed from him (v20). In verses 21-31 Samson is captured, has his eyes bored out, and he is forced to work for the Philistines. Samson prays for the Lord to grant him one last feat of strength. Samson is placed between two pillars in the temple and causes the whole building to collapse killing 3,000 Philistines and himself.

Wednesday • Matthew 23-25

The question found in Matthew 22:42 (Matt. 16:13), "What do you think about the Christ?" forms the basis for much of chapter 23. In verses 1-12 Jesus will warn the disciples of the doctrine of the Pharisees (Matt. 16:5-12) and in verses 13-36 he will pronounce a series of woes (condemnation) upon the scribes and Pharisees. In verses 2-3 "Moses' seat" refers to the stone seat in synagogues where the main teacher sat to teach. The Pharisees were only concerned with how they looked to others, and never were concerned about the condition of their heart. Jesus says they place burdens on people but will not help (v4), they only want to be seen and honored (v5-6), and they want the prestige of their positions (v7). In verses 8-10, Jesus is teaching that He is the only one who can sit in Moses' seat. The term "father" in verse 9 was a term ascribed to teachers in synagogues, and is not referencing biological fathers.

The woes can be seen as contrasts to the beatitudes which show the way to be pleasing to God. The woes describe a way of living that would not be pleasing to God. The woes in verses 13-36 concern the following: failure to see Jesus as Messiah (v13, Matt. 5:20), treatment of others (v14), leading people away from Christ (v15), twisting Scripture (v16-24), unbelief and self-righteousness (v25-28), and failure to recognize the prophets (v29-36). Jesus weeps over the city of Jerusalem where God revealed Himself to the people. Now they are known for being the city which rejects God and His prophets resulting in judgment (v37-39). Jesus walks away from the temple complex because of the unbelief of the Jews (Ez. 10:18).

Matthew 24 opens with Jesus and the disciples traveling to the Mount of Olives where He calls attention to the temple and its future destruction (Luke 21:20). This prompts the questions from the disciples in verse 3 concerning the destruction of the temple (which Jesus has already spoken of in verse 2). They also ask what will be the sign(s) when He comes again, and what will signal the end of the world. Much of what happens in chapter 24 fulfills two purposes within the context of Matthew. First, some of what is spoken concerns the destruction of the temple which took place in 70 AD. Second, there is also a future fulfillment. From the perspective of the disciples, all that Jesus spoke of is future fulfillment. The Mount of Olives is important in Scripture. It is where Jesus ascended to heaven (Acts 1:9-11), and where He will one day return (Zech. 14:4). The description of "birth pains" shows that these signs will become more frequent and will rise in intensity as the return of Christ approaches. The signs are: false christs (v5, 11), violence (v6-7), natural disasters (v7), religious persecution (v9), betrayal (v10), failure to love (v12), and worldwide evangelism (v14).

The abomination of desolation is spoken of here and three other times in Scripture (Dan. 9:27, 11:31, 12:11). Antiochus Epiphanes IV is the fulfillment of Daniel 11:21-35. He ravaged the temple and the Jews, while declaring to be a god. Most believe this reference is to a future Antichrist who will repeat the deeds of Antiochus, except on a much larger scale. In verses 16-20, Jesus is saying that when this happens you will need to flee immediately. Jesus describes this period as "great tribulation" and warns once more about false christs during this time (v21-28). Jesus describes His coming again in verses 29-31. He tells us that it will be characterized by cosmic disturbances (Isa. 13:10; Joel 2:31; 2 Pet. 3:7-12; Rev. 6:13-14). He also tells us that He will gather together all of His people from even the most remote parts of the earth. In the parable of the fig tree (v32-34), Jesus is teaching that when these things (signs) begin to happen they will know that His return is near. Verse 35 teaches the faithfulness and eternal value of God and of His Word (Luke 16:17; John 10:35). Jesus teaches in verse 36 (v43-44) that no one knows the time of His return.

In verses 37-42, Jesus compares the day of His return to the days of Noah. This is primarily an example of people living their lives and not heeding the warnings of His return (Noah warned of flood). Verses 43-44 emphasize being prepared for Christ's return. In verses 45-51 the faithful and evil servant are contrasted. The emphasis here is not so much on preparedness, but actual service before the return of the Lord.

Matthew 25 opens with a parable about being prepared for the return of Christ in verses 1-13. The five wise virgins were prepared for the coming of the bridegroom, while the five foolish virgins were not. Not only is the importance of being prepared taught in these verses, but also the importance of being watchful (v5) and being ready (v13). The parable of the talents continues the theme of preparedness, but also concentrates on performing one's duties while the Master is away (v14-30, 24:45-51). The talents in this story probably represent the opportunities to do the master's will while he is away. Some opportunities are great and some are small but the point is taking advantage of our opportunities and using what has been entrusted to us for the furtherance of the kingdom.

Matthew 25:31-46 is normally called the "judgment of the nations". Here Jesus divides the sheep (believers) from the goats (unbelievers). The works that characterize the sheep were works that were done from a heart transformed by God's gracious act of saving them (v34-40), while those who did not know Him performed no works (v41-45). This also fits well with James 2:14-26. Someone's work will demonstrate whether they have true faith or dead faith. Someone who has been truly converted will perform works (fruit). Only a good tree can bear good fruit (Matt. 7:16).

Thursday • Job 15-16

Eliphaz responds to Job's lengthy speech in chapters 13-14 with some pretty harsh words. In verses 1-6 Eliphaz again accuses Job of being full of hot air, but adds that Job is being dishonorable to God and deceitful with his words. Eliphaz accuses Job of doing this because there is sin in his heart. Eliphaz accuses Job of being arrogant in verses 7-13 by asking him if he was wise enough to sit in God's council. Verses 14-20 form the main point of Eliphaz's argument with Job-human beings are too sinful to stand before God, and the wicked always get the punishment they deserve (4:17-19). In verses 21-35, the point of contention between Job and Eliphaz becomes plain. Job believes that the wicked prosper, while Eliphaz believes the wicked suffer. Eliphaz tries to prove his point in verses 27-35 by telling Job that each person he describes gets what they deserve- including Job (15:21, 28, 29, 30 all describe what happened to Job).

Job responds to Eliphaz in chapter 16. In verses 1-5, Job believed that if the tables were turned he would have encouraged his friends. One thing to consider again is that when people are going through trials, sometimes the best thing we can do is be there and be silent. Just your presence is a powerful indicator of your love for the person. In verses 6-14 Job believes God has handed him over to the wicked, that he is God's target, and that he must be God's enemy. Job believes he will die before God vindicates him (v18, 22), and he continues to believe he has an advocate in heaven who will argue his case before God.

Friday • Micah

Micah ("Who is like the Lord?") is a contemporary of Hosea, Amos, and Isaiah according to verse 1 (Jer. 26:18). Micah is a prophet primarily to the southern kingdom of Judah, although he references the northern kingdom of Israel. Micah's message concerns the social injustice and religious corruption in Judah just as Hosea spoke to the northern kingdom of Israel. Both kingdoms were prospering economically at the time. Micah's message is composed of three cycles that target the sins of the people, their coming punishment, and hope for the future.

Micah 1:2-7 concerns the coming judgment upon Samaria (north) and Jerusalem (south) as God calls the nations to witness what He is about to do. This should have also served as a warning to the nations that if God is going to judge His own people for their sin, their judgment would be coming as well. Micah's reaction to the coming judgment is recorded in verses 8-9 where he compares the sins of Samaria and Judah to an incurable wound. The cities Micah mentions in verses 10-16 will experience the opposite of what their names mean. For example Shaphir means "beautiful" or "pleasant", but they will be reduced to shame and dishonor.

Micah 2:1-5 concerns the fall of Israel as whole because of their sins, which include taking advantage of the poor. Micah sees their judgment (captivity) as unavoidable. In verses 6-11 Micah condemns the false prophets for telling the true prophets not to prophesy (v6), treating women (widows) cruelly (v9), and for taking bribes (v11). Chapter 2 concludes the first cycle with hopes of a future restoration that probably refers to a future day beyond them coming back from captivity.

Micah 3:1-4 begins the second cycle which includes judgment upon the rulers of Israel. Micah uses graphic language to portray the leaders of Israel as exploiting the poor just as a person prepares an animal for eating. Micah turns to the religious leaders in verses 5-8 and compares their false message to the bite of a serpent (v5 "chew"), but Micah proclaims his message is "full of power by the Spirit of the Lord". In verses 9-12, Micah says the result of corrupt leaders and prophets is that the people commit acts of injustice which is primarily fueled by their greed.

Micah 4 begins the closing of the second cycle with the future restoration of the nation. In verses 1-8, Micah speaks of the future glory of Jerusalem as it becomes the center of God's work on earth. Micah mentions Babylon in verse 10, which will be the nation that carries Judah into captivity.

Micah 5:2-4 is a prophecy of a coming Ruler (Jesus) who will reign over His people (Matt. 2:6). The description of this Ruler is eternal in origin and can only be describing the first coming of the Lord Jesus Christ. He will lead His people to times of peace and deliver them from their enemies (v5-6). The future remnant of Israel will include Gentiles and no enemy will overpower them again (v7-9). After the victory over their enemies everything will be removed that caused His people to turn away from God (v10-15).

Micah 6:1-8 begins the third cycle as Micah lists the sins of the people. God wants to know what He has done to them to cause them to turn away from Him (v3). God recounts some of His past acts for them in verses 4-5, such as delivering them from the Egyptians and causing Balaam to bless instead of cursing them. In verses 6-7, Micah speaks on behalf of the people by asking how they can come before God. The one who comes to Him must act justly (social justice), love mercy (show kindness to others), and walk humbly with their God (fellowship with God). God passes judgment on them in verses 9-16 for their sins. They would become desolate and be brought to "ruin" (object of horror).

Micah 7:1-2 concerns the failure of the people to be godly, as few have remained faithful to God. In verses 3-6, Micah describes the judicial system as corrupt and only helping those who can offer bribes. The godly must have an attitude of trusting God to answer their prayers knowing that God will vindicate them (v7-10). The remaining verses in the chapter discuss the future kingdom of God. This includes the growth of the kingdom with the inclusion of the Gentiles (v11-13), their victory because of God's leadership over the nations (v14-17), and also because of who God is (v18-20).

Saturday • 1 Corinthians 1-2

Paul wrote 1 Corinthians between 54 and 56 AD. Paul founded the church there on his second missionary journey, and he stayed there over a year (Acts 18:1-11). Corinth was an important trade center with a population believed to be close to 700,000, including those who worked as slaves. Corinth was primarily known for three things. First, they were known for the Isthmian games that would resemble our modern day Olympic Games. Second, they were known for their immorality and drunkenness. Thirdly they were known for their temple to Aphrodite, where a thousand prostitutes served in the temple. Corinth had many cults in the city and many others were indulging in magic. An ancient proverb from their day states "Not many men can afford a trip to Corinth". What plagued the church in Corinth was their inability to separate themselves from the world. This led to a lack of unity and morality in the church.

In the opening of the letter, Paul begins to address the problems in Corinth. In verses 1-3 he reminds them that they are "sanctified" (set apart) in Christ, which emphasizes they are to live as God's holy people. He also reminds them that as God's people they should be united. In verses 4-9 Paul praises them for their spiritual gifts, especially in the areas of speaking and knowledge. Both of those things were highly thought of in Corinth. Paul will return to the topic of gifts later, because this too caused problems in the church. Notice also that Paul does not praise them in how they use the gifts, but praises God who gave them their gifts. In verses 10-17, Paul addresses the problem of division in the church and makes a plea for unity. They were divided into four separate groups with some claiming they were superior because Paul baptized them. Paul says that his primary purpose is not to baptize, but to preach the gospel.

The division in the church leads to his discussion about the preaching of the gospel in verses 18-31. Paul says that the message of the gospel is foolishness to lost people, but to saved people it is the power of God. The root of this discussion is human wisdom versus God's wisdom. Humans have a tendency to always think they are right, especially as opposed to God (Isa. 29:14; Prov. 14:12, 16:25). Salvation does not come through human wisdom, but from believing in Jesus. This message of Paul's (gospel, cross) was a stumbling block to the Jews, who we see in the Gospels repeatedly asking Jesus for a sign. The same message was foolishness to the Greeks (Gentiles), because they believed they were already wise. But, Paul says that God has chosen the weak and insignificant in the world to put to shame those who consider themselves wise (v26-31). Paul closes chapter in verses 30-31, teaching that salvation is all from God and that all the wisdom you would need is found in Him.

In 1 Corinthians 2:1-5 Paul shows that he did not come in his own power to preach the message, but that his power came from God. Paul did not use man's words, but his words came from God. He did not come using his own wisdom, but came to speak the wisdom of God. In essence Paul is saying his preaching was not because of his own speaking skill or his own intelligence, but that he came in the power of the Holy Spirit to preach the gospel. Paul is saying "there is nothing special about me, but the message I preach has the power".

Paul returns to the theme of wisdom in verses 6-16. Paul claims once again that the wisdom he spoke with only comes from God and that it had no human or worldly origin (v6-9). Men in their own wisdom crucified Jesus because they did not fully understand who He was (v8). While verse 9 is commonly used to describe thoughts about heaven, in its context it refers to the wisdom God has prepared for believers to receive from Him. Paul explains how to receive this wisdom in verse 10-it is through the Spirit of God. Only those who know Christ receive this wisdom, because only they have the Spirit of God living inside of them. Paul gives an example in verse 11 showing that only a man truly knows what is going on inside of his own mind (except God of course). He does this to show that only the Holy Spirit knows the wisdom of God. The Holy Spirit reveals this to man (v12-13). An unsaved person cannot receive this type of wisdom because they do not have the Holy Spirit living inside of them (v14). It is the Holy Spirit that helps believers discern things (v15) and guides us in the truth because we have the mind of Christ (v16).

Cover to Cover Challenge

Week 9

Sunday • Psalm 30-32

Welcome to week 9 of the *Cover to Cover Challenge*! Isaiah 55:11 states "So shall My word be that goes forth from My mouth; it shall not return to Me void, but it shall accomplish what I please, and it shall prosper in the thing for which I sent it." Through the *Cover to Cover Challenge* we are privileged to read the very words from the mouth of God. The Word will do just what Isaiah 55:11 says it will do. Keep praying for the Lord to be honored and glorified through this. As God's people, the greatest things any of us can do is be in the Word and pray for one another.

Psalm 30 is a psalm of thanksgiving that praises the Lord for answering prayer. In verses 1-3 the psalmist experiences the deliverance of the Lord. He is rejoicing that the Lord has delivered him from being near death, hearing his prayer, and not allowing the wicked to rejoice over him. With verses 4-7, the psalmist asks all the people to praise the Lord for forgiveness and restoration. The word "favor" means "renewal" of God's forgiveness, restoration, and blessing. In verses 8-12 the Lord is praised for His faithfulness because He has turned the psalmists crying into dancing, his mourning into joy, and his cries of death into a song of joy.

Psalm 31 is a psalm concerning God's goodness during times of trouble. In verses 1-5 David declares his trust in the Lord because He delivers him (v2), leads and guides him (v3), gives him strength (v4), and has redeemed him (v5). David has committed his life to the Lord in total trust (v5). In verses 6-8, David continues speaking about his trust in the Lord because He delivers him from troubles. What David is experiencing during this time is found in verses 9-13, as he expresses the anguish in his soul. His enemies' attacks have taken a toll on him. David feels like he is a dead man and feels that they slander him continually. David again expresses his trust in the Lord in verses 14-18. He gives his enemies over to the Lord, continues to love the Lord, and prays for the adversity to end. In verses 19-24, David thanks the Lord because He has heard and answered David's prayer for help. He wants all to know what the Lord has done for him, and for them to remember that the Lord will help them when adversity strikes.

Psalm 32 is a psalm of the blessings and joy of forgiveness. In this psalm most of the details are in groups of three. In verses 1-2 there are three words for sin followed by three words which detail forgiveness. Transgression (rebellion), sin (miss the mark), and iniquity (crooked) are all qualified by forgiven (removal of sin), covered (atoned for, not remembered), and does not count (justified). Verses 3-5 detail the experience of sin, which David confesses before the Lord with three different terms- acknowledged, have not hidden, and confess. After the confession of sin, God promises to protect those who seek Him (v6-7). We also see one more set of threes promises. God will tell us that He will instruct, teach, and guide those who belong to Him. Following the ways of the Lord is a choice of the individual (v9). The choice made determines whether one will experience adversity (v9) or the blessings of the Lord (v10).

Monday • Genesis 35-40

Jacob, at the Lord's request, returns to Bethel in Genesis 35:1-5. In verses 6-15, God changes Jacob's name to Israel. This signifies that he is no longer deceitful or struggling, as the name Jacob suggests. God also reminds Jacob that his lineage will include descendants and land, continuing the promises made to Abraham and Isaac. Rachel dies giving birth to Benjamin in Ephrath (which is Bethlehem), an important place in the future of Israel and humanity in general (Micah 5:2; Matt. 2:18). Simeon and Levi's conduct in chapter 34, and Reuben's in verse 22, pave the way for the stories of Judah and Joseph. Isaac's death is recorded in verses 27-29. His death fulfills the vow made between God and Jacob in 28:21. God vows to watch over him and return him to his father's house safely.

Genesis 36 records the genealogy of Esau, making note that Esau dwelt in Mount Seir and was known as the Edomites, who plagued Israel through the years. Genesis 37:1-11 begins the story of Joseph. Jacob's obvious favoritism of Joseph is clearly seen by his brothers, and is noted in the passage. This may result from his special love for Rachel (29:30). Joseph's dreams are another concern for the brothers as they are pictured as bowing down to him. In verses 12-18 Joseph's brothers begin the plot to kill him, but Reuben and Judah intervene and he is sold into slavery to the Ishmaelites (v19-36). What they did not know was that what they were planning would end up fulfilling Joseph's dreams, and be the fate they and their descendants would experience at the hand of the Egyptians.

Genesis 38 records the story of Judah and Tamar. When Judah married a Canaanite it caused the promise regarding the descendants of Abraham and Isaac to be unfulfillable. It is through the line of Judah that the Promised Seed would come, and Judah placed this in jeopardy due to his actions. Again, there is a story of twins (25:22), and Perez gained the right of the firstborn (Num.26:20).

Genesis 39:1-6 returns to the story of Joseph. He is living in Potiphar's house, in charge of all his household. The theme of Joseph's story is found in verse 2 as "the Lord was with Joseph and he prospered". This fulfills part of the Abrahamic covenant (12:3) which says that others will be blessed because of him and his descendants. In verses 7-23, the story of Joseph takes another tragic turn as he is accused falsely of trying to lie with Potiphar's wife. But, even in prison, Joseph found mercy and favor from the Lord. Genesis 40 records the story of the butler and the baker that Joseph meets in prison, and we see for the first time Joseph interpret dreams. God has him there for a particular purpose, and this paves the way for the story in chapter 41. Joseph will interpret Pharaoh's dreams, and it will be known that Joseph has the spirit of God (41:38).

Tuesday • Judges 17-21

Judges 17:1-6 begins the story of Micah and his idolatry. Micah had stolen a large amount of silver from his mother. When he returned it, his mother decided to turn her curse into a blessing. His mother made an idol for her son from only a portion of it, but she was now liable herself to be under God's curse (Deut.27:15). It is in this chapter where we will begin to read about the fact that there is no king in Israel. This will be mentioned in each of the following chapters. The reason this statement is made so often is to imply that if there had been a king, the events of chapters 17-21 may have never taken place (we will see later God had always desired to be their king). Israel's problem was the sin of elevating self. Micah hires a priest from the Levites and sets up his home as a shrine to earn God's blessing (v7-13).

In Judges 18:1-6 the Danites are looking for more land to take for their own when they come upon the Levite in Micah's home. He blesses them to continue their journey. In verses 7-10 they spy on the city of Laish and see that there is no line of defense against any incoming enemies. The Danites take all of Micah's possessions, including the young priest, and begin to lay siege on the city of Laish (v11-31). Micah's idols were set up there, and the city was renamed Dan after their ancestor. This gives us the backstory for the city of Dan, and details their descent into idolatry.

Judges 19 contains the story of the Levite and his concubine, which is probably one of the most tragic events of Israel's history. When his concubine commits adultery and goes back to her father's house, the Levite pursues her and stays many days (v1-11). They end up staying in Gibeah, which belongs to the tribe of Benjamin, with a resident of the city. In verses 22-28 we read about a scene reminiscent of Sodom and Gomorrah from Genesis 19. The Levite gives the men his concubine, they abused her all night, and she later dies. He cuts her into twelve pieces, and sends a piece to each of the twelve tribes of Israel. The term "perverted men" in verse 22 means "sons of Belial", and describes someone who is worthless and continually seeks to do evil. The events of this chapter are spoken of in Hosea 9:9 and 10:9.

The events in chapter 19 begin the war with the Benjamites in chapter 20. It is decided in verses 1-7 that the Gibeahites deserved to be punished for what they have done. In verses 8-18 all of the tribes of Israel rise up to become one against Gibeah and the Benjamites, because they would not take sides with the other tribes. In the first two battles the Benjamites prevailed over the children of Israel, killing 40,000 men (v19-28). After a time of offering sacrifices and fasting the Israelites won the third and decisive battle over the Benjamites, killing all but 600 of their men (v29-48). The word "whole" in verse 37 usually means "whole burnt offerings" and suggests the whole city became a burnt offering.

Judges 21:1-4 describe the concern over the survival of the tribe of Benjamin. The other tribes take a vow not to let their daughters intermarry with them. Jabesh Gilead did not participate in the war with Benjamin, so the men of the city were struck down to provide wives for 400 of the men of Benjamin (v5-15). The rest of the men stole wives from the festival in Shiloh (v16-22). Chapter 21 closes with a recap of the times of the judges (v23-25). It was a time of no king, and everyone did what was right in their own eyes.

Wednesday • Matthew 26-28

In Matthew 26:1-5 Jesus predicts His death for the fourth time, and we also learn that the religious leaders are plotting to kill Jesus. Remember that the Passover celebrates Israel's deliverance from Egyptian bondage and also what Jesus will do will deliver people from their sin. In Bethany, at the home of Simon the leper, Jesus is anointed for the second time (Luke 7:36-50) in preparation for His burial (v6-13). Judas agrees to betray Jesus for thirty pieces of silver (v14-16, Zech. 11:12). This is also the amount to be paid for a slave who is accidently killed by an ox in Exodus 21:32.

The disciples prepare the Passover meal to be eaten after sundown (v17-19). It is at this meal where Jesus announces that one among them will betray Him (v20-25). Jesus institutes the Lord's Supper in verses 26-30. Jesus knows that His sacrificial death is inaugurating a new covenant through the shedding of His blood. This new covenant will allow mankind to have their sins forgiven, and begin a relationship with God through Him

(Ex. 24:8; Zech. 9:11; Jer. 31:31-34). Jesus predicts that the disciples will all be scattered because of what will happen to Him (v31-32). Peter emphatically denies that he would do that to Jesus (v33).

Jesus prays in the garden of Gethsemane with all of His disciples. He takes Peter, James, and John to pray alongside Him, but they fall asleep (v36-46). The cup that Jesus prays to pass is not only a cup of suffering and death, but the cup of God's wrath. Jesus prays in agony over the upcoming events (Luke 22:43), but knows the Father's will must be done to provide access to the Father. Gethsemane means "oil press" which may be symbolism to show the pressure Jesus felt knowing what lay before Him. In verses 47-56, Jesus is arrested in the garden by a group of men who were led by Judas. The kiss was normally a mark of special honor. For Judas to betray Jesus in this way made his betrayal even more deceitful.

Jesus appears before the Sanhedrin in verses 57-68. After false witnesses speak, the high priest places Jesus under oath and asks Him if He is the Son of God. Jesus says that He is, and one day they will see Him coming in the clouds of heaven (Dan. 7:13). He is accused by the Jews of committing blasphemy, which is worthy of the death penalty (Lev. 24:16). In verses 69-75, Jesus' prediction of Peter's denial comes true as Peter lies and calls down curses upon himself. When Peter's denial is read in light of Matthew 10:32-33, you can see the reason why Peter wept bitterly.

The Jews, under Roman authority, could not put anyone to death. Instead they lead Jesus to Pilate and accused Him of treason or insurrection (Matt. 27:1-2). In verses 3-10 a remorseful (not repentant) Judas wants to return the thirty pieces of silver to the priests but they refuse to accept it. Judas hangs himself over the acts that he has committed against the One who was innocent of any wrongdoing. The quotation found here comes from Zechariah 11:12-13. The Zechariah passage is about a coming Shepherd-King that the people will reject (11:4-14). Matthew's use of the passage shows that Jesus is a suffering Messiah.

Jesus appears before Pilate, and agrees that He is the king of the Jews (v11-14). Jesus will take the place of Barabbas upon the crowd's request for Jesus to be crucified (v15-26). Pilate stresses the innocence of Jesus because he knew that the Jews were envious of Him. Verse 22 shows that the evil in the heart of the Jews results in a desire for Jesus to be crucified. Crucifixion was a Roman punishment. Most Jews would not even say the word crucifixion, much less want one of their own people to suffer that punishment. As a result Pilate turns Jesus over to be crucified. Jesus is scourged and mocked by the Roman soldiers (v26-31). In their day "scourge" meant to "flay someone to the bone".

In verses 32-50 Jesus is crucified. Crucifixion was only reserved for the worst criminals and for the lowest classes. The scourging alone would have been unbearable, but the agony of being crucified usually lasted for days. Many Old Testament Scriptures are fulfilled and alluded to during this time (Ps. 22:7, 8, 18; 69:12; 109:25; Lam. 2:15, Isa. 53:12). The ignorance of the religious leaders is shown in verses 41-44. They wanted Him to come down off the cross and save Himself, and then they would believe Him. If He came down from the cross there would be no salvation, no forgiveness, and no gospel to save others.

The darkness in verse 45 signifies judgment on the people due to their rejection of Jesus, and the judgment that has fallen upon Jesus in dying for the sins of the world. At the moment of Jesus' death a great earthquake happened, and the veil of the temple was torn into. Earthquakes in the Bible are God's attention-getters (Judg. 5:4; Ps. 114:7-8; Acts 16:26) and many times they occur in judgments of God (Joel 3:16; Nahum 1:5-6). The tearing of the veil shows that man now has access to God (v51). Many of the dead rose again to life (v52-53). The centurion's statement in verse 54 shows that even he knew Jesus must have been who He said He was.

Jesus is buried in Joseph's tomb, fulfilling Isaiah 53:9-12 (57-61). Most people who were crucified were never buried but were taken off the cross and left on the ground. Mark's gospel explains that Joseph was a member of the Sanhedrin. Luke explains that Joseph opposed the plot against Jesus, and John tells us that Joseph was a secret disciple of Jesus. In verses 62-66, the religious leaders take precautions concerning Jesus' prediction of rising again in three days by placing guards at the tomb and sealing it. They did not believe Jesus' words, but believed that the disciples may come and steal His body.

The women come to visit the tomb on Sunday morning in Matthew 28:1-8. After another earthquake, an angel rolls back the stone. The angel does not do this to let Jesus out, but to let them in to see that He had risen. On the way to tell the disciples the news of the resurrection, Jesus appears to the women and they worship Him (v9-10). In Matthew 28:11-15, Matthew tells us that the chief priests instructed the guards to lie and say that the disciples had stolen Jesus' body while they slept. It is believed that Roman guards who were caught sleeping would be punished by death.

In verses 16-20 Jesus appears to the disciples in Galilee just as He predicted. Here He gives the Great Commission to His disciples and to us today. Jesus had earlier sent the disciples out to the "house of Israel" and now He was sending them all over the world to spread the gospel. In the Great Commission Jesus tells us that He has been given "all authority", that we are to go to "all nations" making disciples, that we are to teach "all to obey" Jesus' words, and He promises to be with us "always" until He comes again.

Thursday • Job 17-18

Job 17 continues Job's response to Eliphaz from chapter 16 which we read last week. Job continues to defend his innocence in chapter 17. In verses 1-9, Job calls upon God to defend him because he is being mocked by his friends. Job wants God to promise to hear his case (v3). To Job, there were not many who believed that he was innocent. He also thought that those who would spit in his face believed they were doing God a favor (v6-9). In verses 10-16 Job again prays to die because of his situation, and makes a mockery of their advice.

In Job 18, Bildad speaks for the second time (ch.8). In verses 1-4 Bildad tells Job that he is speaking out of his grief, and not with reason like they speak to him. In verses 5-21 Bildad, as he did the first time he spoke, assumes that Job is suffering because of his sin. Bildad proceeds to tell Job of the terrible fate of the wicked, as he did in chapter 8. Bildad wants to be sure that Job understands that every wicked person gets what they deserve in this life for the wicked deeds they have done.

Friday • Isaiah 1-5

Isaiah ("the Lord is Salvation") was a contemporary or near contemporary of Micah as a prophet to Judah at the same time Amos and Hosea was to Israel. The opening verse places the ministry of Isaiah in the reigns of Uzziah, Jotham, Ahaz, and Hezekiah. Uzziah reigned for 52 years and it was during his reign that Judah grew economically, but declined even further spiritually. Under Uzziah's son Jotham Judah experienced growth, but there was still idolatry in the land. Ahaz made an alliance with Assyria during his reign which led to even more idolatry, and it was during his reign that Israel was taken into captivity. The context of Isaiah is much the same as that of the above mentioned prophets that we have already studied. Both Israel and Judah are prospering economically, but spiritually they are drifting further away from God. Isaiah is also known for his many prophecies such as the healing of Hezekiah, the Babylonian captivity, the prediction of Cyrus releasing Jews from captivity, and his prophecies concerning the Messiah. The book of Isaiah is also known as the "little Bible". The first 39 chapters deal with judgment for Israel's sins, and the final 27 chapters deal with hope and restoration. Tradition says that Isaiah died due to being sawn in half when Manasseh was king (Heb. 11:37).

Isaiah 1 opens with the time frame of Isaiah's ministry and a call for heaven and earth to give witness to the rebellion of Judah (v1-2). The rest of the chapter discusses the nations continued disobedience to God. In verses 3-9 God announces that even a donkey knows its master, but His people remain stubborn in committing sin. As a result the whole nation suffered like Sodom and Gomorrah. Because of their leaders, the nation had become just like Sodom. They were offensive to God, especially in their worship (v10-17). In verses 18-20, God offers them forgiveness if they would only come to Him and be obedient. Verses 19-20 relay the concept of coming to God in obedience (eat the good), or remaining disobedient (and be eaten). In verses 21-23, Isaiah again addresses the sins of the leaders and how it affected society. The hand that defeated Israel's enemies will now be turned against them because of their continual sin (v24-26). In verse 24 Isaiah uses three names for God. Lord means "master", Lord of Hosts means "supreme power", and Mighty One means "strength". After a brief hint of future restoration in verses 26-27, Isaiah returns to the destruction that is coming because of their idolatry (v28-31).

Isaiah 2:1-5 concerns the future and resembles Micah 4:1-3. One day all people will come to Zion. In Zion there will be peace, no more war, and they will receive teaching. The Day of the Lord, mentioned by many of the prophets we have read, is discussed in verses 6-22. The Day would come because of the people's refusal to separate from their sin, and because they sought the help of other nations instead of God and continued to worship idols (v6-11). In verses 12-19 the Lord will personally visit the prideful nation with His glory, power, and judgment and they would be humbled.. Instead of worshiping the idols they have made, they will worship the One who made them (v20-22).

In Isaiah 3:1-7 God rebukes Israel for putting too much trust in human leaders. In verses 8-12 God reminds them of their sins, pronounces that their nation and city will collapse, and tells them that they will be destroyed because of their rebellion. Isaiah again addresses the leadership of the people as they have been the cause of people being led into sin (v13-17). God will take away every item of luxury when He comes in judgment (v18-26). Babylonians removed hair and often branded those they took in as captives (v24). The destruction would be so severe that men will be hard to find (4:1).

Isaiah 4 concerns the restoration of Zion. While the Day of the Lord brings judgment, it also brings salvation as God cleanses His people. The reference to "Branch" in 4:2 is a reference to the Messiah (Jer. 23:5, 33:15; Zech. 3:8, 6:12). At that time, the glory over Jerusalem will be seen as a protective canopy. Canopies were used for royalty and also for wedding feasts.

In Isaiah 5:1-2 Isaiah plays the part of the best man in a wedding, singing a song for the groom to his bride. The vineyard is Israel, and God is the groom. He gave His vineyard everything it needed to be prosperous, but it only brought forth wild grapes. Because there is nothing but wild grapes, God pronounces judgment upon Israel for their sins (v3-7). Their sins include exploiting the poor (v8-10), excessive pleasure (v11-12), boasting of sin (v18-19), perverting right and wrong (v20), worldly wisdom (v21), and intoxication (v21-23). Just as they were consumed with excessive pleasure in verses 11-12, the grave will consume (enlarge) itself for them. In verses 24-30 God will judge them and His hand will smite them by sending the Assyrians to make war with them.

Saturday • 1 Corinthians 3-4

Paul will continue to address the Corinthians' lack of wisdom in chapter 3. He discusses the Corinthians' immaturity and divisiveness, tells them how to build on the right foundation, and tells the Corinthians to depend on God and not worldly wisdom. In verses 1-4 Paul addresses the Corinthians immaturity (v1-2), and divisiveness (v3-4), which go hand in hand. Spiritual immaturity displayed in believers will always lead to envy, strife, and divisions. The word "carnal" reflects worldliness in the lives of the believers.

In verses 5-9, Paul goes back to the discussion of 1:10-17 and the Corinthians following a particular leader. He uses the example of himself and Apollos to convey his point. They worked in unity, but only God made it all work. Paul explains that they are all workers together with the Lord, and no one is to be idolized. Each worker has their own work that benefits the body of Christ. Verse 9 emphasizes that every believer is in partnership with God in ministry.

Paul next discusses how workers should work together and build upon the right foundation, which is Christ (v10-17). Paul tells them that he laid the foundation (Christ) for which the Corinthians were to build on, but each individual was to be careful with what materials they used. The gold, silver, precious stones, wood, hay, and straw all represent the works of each worker that are built upon the foundation. The works done with the right motive will endure the fire of judgment and the individual will receive rewards. Works done with the wrong motive will be burned up, but the person will be saved. All this will happen when the Lord returns. In verses 16-17 the "you" is plural, so it refers to the whole body of Christ being a temple. Those who try to destroy the temple (church) by causing division (as the Corinthian's were) within the church would be destroyed themselves.

Paul explains to the Corinthians in verses 18-23 that their own wisdom is not sufficient for salvation or for building up the church (James 3:13-18). These verses are probably directed toward the leaders in the church who have deceived themselves into believing they could lead, teach, and build the church with their own wisdom. Paul quotes Job 5:12-13 in verse 19 to show that man's wisdom is no match for God's wisdom. In verse 20 he quotes Ps. 94:11 to show that the Lord knows all the useless thoughts of the world's so-called wise men. The point is no one has a right to boast because all they have been given comes from God, and those things that are given by God belong to all.

In 1 Corinthians 4:1-5, Paul explains that the workers are to be good stewards of the things revealed to them through God's Word. They are to demonstrate this by their faithfulness. The word used here for steward refers to a slave who had been placed over his master's estate (v1-2). God has entrusted believers with many things, and each believer will answer to the Master for what is done with them. From verse 3 it seems that the Corinthian leaders were judging Paul and placing themselves in a position over him (this is made clearer in v6-13). Paul knew that the only judgment that mattered to him was the Lord's (v4). It is when the Lord comes that all things will be brought to the light, and He will reveal the counsels (motive) of the heart (v5).

In verses 6-13, the picture of the Corinthians becomes clearer. They are boasting about being spiritually rich because of their spiritual gifts, their positions, and their cliques. Paul and the apostles were looked down upon by many of them. According to Paul in verse 6, they were "going beyond what is written" and becoming "puffed up". The term "differ" in verse 7 carries the same idea as "superior". Paul is asking "what makes you superior to someone else?" Anything they have has come from God, they did not achieve it themselves. Paul uses sarcasm in verses 8 and 10 to prove his point to them-even the apostles do not reign, but suffer terrible hardships at the hands of men. In their minds the Corinthian leaders had already reached a place where they no longer needed anything (v8). The phrase "wish you did reign" can be translated "wish you did reign but you do not".

In verse 9 Paul makes a sharp contrast between the leaders in Corinth and himself and the other apostles. While the Corinthian leaders believed they reigned, a spectacle was made out of Paul and the other apostles. The word for "spectacle" means to "publicly gaze", and possibly refers to Christians being paraded around the streets before they were condemned to die. Paul continues the contrast in verses 11-13. Paul and the other apostles went without necessities to proclaim the gospel, while those in Corinth believed they had everything they needed in themselves. In verse 13 Paul says that they also have been made like filth and were only fit to be thrown out (refuse). He also says they were useless (offscouring). Instead of trying to exalt themselves over each other because of certain gifts, they needed to see themselves for what they were and recognize how far they had moved away from the gospel that Paul taught them.

In verses 14-21, Paul warns the Corinthians about their actions based upon his position as their spiritual father, and challenges them to imitate him. Paul wanted them to know that he was not holding them to a higher standard or making unrealistic demands of them (v17). He also addresses those who are undermining his authority and tells them he would soon visit those who are arrogant and who are boasting of their great power (v19-20). He leaves them with two options-he will either come with a rod of discipline or in love with a gentle spirit (v21).

Cover to Cover
CHALLENGE

Week 10

Sunday • Psalm 33-35

Welcome to week 10 of the *Cover to Cover challenge*! We pray that the Holy Spirit is using His Word mightily in your life, in your family, and in your church. Jesus said in John 6:63 "It is the Spirit who gives life; the flesh profits nothing, the words that I speak to you are spirit, and they are life". It is through God's Word that we see what living truly should mean to Christians. We pray that through the readings this week the Lord will reveal this life to you and give you hope, encouragement, and strength.

Psalm 33 is another psalm praising God for being the Creator and Ruler over the earth. In verses 1-3, the psalmist encourages all of God's people to praise the Lord and sing to Him a "new song". In verses 4-5 God's Word is right (without deception, full of integrity), and His works are truth. These verses tell us that God is praised for His creative acts and His rule over man in verses 6-11. In verses 12-17 the psalmist deals once more with God's rule over man. It is He who sees the works of man, and all are accountable to Him. Another reason that people can praise the Lord is because of His unfailing love (mercy). God is to be praised because He helps, shields, and has an unfailing love for His people (v20-22).

Psalm 34 is a psalm of thanksgiving (v1-7), but is mostly made up of wisdom (v8-22). In verses 1-3, David calls upon all people to praise the Lord along with him. David's praise is constant, continual, and centered in the Lord. In verses 4-7, David teaches from his own experience with the Lord. The wise will "taste" and see that the Lord blesses His own, and that He provides for their every need (v8-10). In verses 11-14 David teaches about the fear of the Lord (Prov. 1:7). To fear the Lord is to submit yourself to the Lord and His instruction. In verses 15-22 David tells the results of those who fear the Lord. God watches over them (v15), He hears their cries (v16), He delivers them from trouble (v17,19), and He is near to them (v18).

Psalm 35 is a psalm of lament and vindication upon David's enemies. God is pictured in verses 1-10 as David's Counselor, Warrior, Deliverer, and Helper. David wants God to represent him in his case against those who have betrayed him. David wants God to judge his enemies with shame (military defeat), cause them to become like chaff (worthless), make dark and slippery paths for them (troubles), and bring them to ruin. In verses 11-18 David explains his betrayal by his enemies, whom he treated as friends by mourning for them and praying for them in their troubles. David returns to the theme of betrayal in verses 19-25. His enemies may have turned their backs on him, but David will trust in the Lord. In verses 26-28 David asks that God will allow his enemies to suffer the consequences of their actions.

COVER TO COVER CHALLENGE

Monday • Genesis 41-43

Genesis 41 continues the story of Joseph. Pharaoh has two dreams that no one in his kingdom can interpret (v1-8). The cupbearer finally remembers Joseph (v9-13). Even this is portrayed to be the sovereign hand of God working on Joseph's behalf. Joseph is brought out of prison to hear and interpret the dreams of Pharaoh (v14-36). Pharaoh's dreams reveal that there will be seven years of plenty and seven years of famine in the land of Egypt and beyond. God even gives Joseph a plan to provide for the people during the seven years of famine. Joseph is elevated to second in command of the whole kingdom and is married (v37-47). The gathering of grain during seven years of plenty was immeasurable (v46-49). Joseph has two sons during this time, Manasseh and Ephraim (v50-52). As the famine overtakes the land people from every country came to Egypt to buy grain (v53-57). Joseph's rise to power can only be attributed to the power of God and it paves the way for the events of the coming chapters.

Genesis 42 brings us to the land of Canaan where Jacob and the brothers are residing. Jacob sends the brothers to buy grain so they can survive the famine (v1-2). The narrator of the story now divides the sons into two groups-ten of Joseph's brothers and Benjamin (v3-13). Reuben and Judah will play important roles in the events that follow as they are the ones who pleaded to save Joseph's life when the others wanted to kill him. In verses 14-24, Joseph makes two plans to test his brothers. The first one is that one brother must return and bring the younger while the others are placed in prison. The second plan was that one brother should remain behind while all the others go get Benjamin. In verses 21-22 the brothers realize all of this maybe happening to them because of their treatment of Joseph. The brothers return home and tell Jacob all that has happened and they are again reminded of their deceitful plan to do away with Joseph.

In Genesis 43 the brothers make a second trip to Egypt to buy food. Judah reminds Jacob that they cannot come unless they bring Benjamin with them (v1-14). The brothers arrive in Egypt and are invited to a feast with Joseph (v15-25). The brothers are worried about being made slaves. They explain to the servant the events that happened when they left Egypt the first time. Verse 23 is one of the themes of the story of Joseph-"Your God and the God of your father has given you treasure". The chapter closes with Joseph and the brothers sharing a meal together (v26-34). The brothers are astonished at the turn of events. God was indeed showing them His treasure (v23) and His grace (v29).

Tuesday • Ruth

The book of Ruth has been called one of the most beautiful stories every written. Jewish tradition attributes the book of Ruth to Samuel, but there is no evidence in the book that identifies the writer. Ruth was a Moabite. They were one of the enemies of Israel throughout much of their history (Gen. 19:37). The setting of Ruth is during the time of the judges (1:1), and bridges the gap between judges to the rule of kings. Ruth's story shows that God was providentially orchestrating all events of the book-the famine, the deaths, Ruth gleaning in Boaz's field, his attraction to her, and their marriage. Ruth along with Tamar, Rahab, and Bathsheba are all found in the genealogy of Jesus. Boaz is a type of Christ who becomes Ruth's kinsman-redeemer.

Ruth 1:1-2 gives us the time period of the book and the details of the situation that caused them to leave Bethlehem and go to Moab. The situation gets much worse for the women of the story as both Naomi's husband and her sons die (v3-5). Her sons were married to Orpah and Ruth. It was a serious event for a woman to be left without her husband in a foreign country. Naomi wants to return to Bethlehem and insists her daughters-in-law return to their home as well so that they can find a husband (v5-13). Orpah follows Naomi's advice, but Ruth refuses to leave (v14-15). Ruth pledges to stay with Naomi and makes a commitment to her to stay until death parts them (v16-18). The people of Bethlehem were excited to see Naomi and Ruth return (v19). Naomi ("Pleasant") changes her name to Mara ("Bitter") to reflect her circumstances (v20). The chapter closes with a reference to the coming barley harvest and sets the stage for the rest of the story.

Ruth 2:1-3 introduces us to another main character in the story-Boaz. Boaz is a relative of Elimelech, and is a distinguished and honored person. The providential hand of God is working to provide for Ruth and Naomi. Boaz notices Ruth gleaning in the fields (v4-7), and makes great provisions for Ruth as she works (v8-17). He blessed Ruth for her loyalty to Naomi, shares the noon time meal with her, and tells his workers to let her gather from among the already gathered sheaves. In verses 17-23 Ruth tells Naomi of gleaning in Boaz's field. It is here that we learn that Boaz is qualified to be her kinsman-redeemer (*goel*) who, according to levirate law, could fulfill the duty of preserving the name of the dead by marrying Ruth.

In Ruth 3:1-5, Naomi asks Ruth if she can seek security and benefits for her through marriage. Naomi knew that Boaz was a near relative and could provide this for her. She instructs her to visit Boaz at the threshing floor and to do exactly as she says. Ruth carries out the instructions of Naomi in verses 6-13. Boaz agrees to be her kinsman-redeemer, but there is someone else who is a nearer kinsman then him. Boaz makes an oath to be her kinsman-redeemer if the other cannot fulfill the duty. Ruth returns to Naomi to tell her of what had happened the night before and Naomi wisely instructs Ruth to wait and see what happens (v14-18).

In Ruth 4:1-6 we see Boaz search out the nearest kinsman and call together witnesses for what will transpire. The near kinsman agrees to buy the land, but once he hears that he must marry Ruth he declines to serve as her kinsman-redeemer. With this forfeiture, Boaz can now become the kinsman-redeemer for Ruth and her family. In verses 7-12 the transaction of land is completed (removing of sandal symbolizes), and Ruth will become the wife of Boaz. Blessings of prosperity and are pronounced on Boaz and a blessing of fertility on Ruth. In verses 13-17 Ruth has a son which the women of the community name Obed ("Servant"), perhaps because he will take care of her in her old age. The book of Ruth closes with a genealogy linking Ruth with King David and the Messiah who is to come (v18-22).

Wednesday • Mark 1-2

The gospel of Mark was written sometime between 55 and 65 AD. Mark is the John Mark from the book of Acts (Acts 12:12, 25; 15:37-40), and is also mentioned by Peter (1 Pet. 5:13). The early church fathers report that Mark was a companion of Peter, and he is the likely source for Mark's gospel considering he was not one of the apostles. Mark's gospel was written primarily to a Gentile audience. The evidence for this lies in the gospel of Mark itself. He explained Jewish customs so that Gentile readers could understand them, and he translated Aramaic words for his audience. Mark places a heavy emphasis on the humanity of Jesus, on His suffering, and on His deeds. In regards to His humanity Mark explains that Jesus grew tired (4:38), that He was amazed (6:6), He was disappointed (8:12), He was displeased (10:14), He was angry (11:15-17), and He was sorrowful (14:34). About one-third of Mark's gospel focuses on the death of Jesus. Mark is showing his readers that the way of following Jesus involves faithful obedience, which may lead to suffering and even death. Mark also directly addresses those who are reading his gospel (2:10, 4:41, 7:19, and 13:37). This style invites the reader to respond to Jesus and become an active participant. Mark's gospel can be seen in two halves. First, from 1:1-8:26, Jesus' ministry in Galilee is covered. In 8:27-16:20 His journey from Jerusalem to the cross is covered.

Mark begins his gospel with the ministry of John the Baptist and the important role that he played in preparing the way for Jesus (v1-8). The message of repentance is centered in the gospel or good news- of the death, burial, and resurrection of Jesus Christ. John the Baptist's task is to pave the way for Jesus' ministry. He does this by preaching a message that calls for people to repent and turn back to God. The baptism and temptation of Jesus are covered briefly by Mark, but show that Jesus identifies with sinful man, that He is anointed for the ministry by the Spirit, and He also begins His many encounters with Satan in Mark's gospel (v9-13). Notice throughout the gospel of Mark how many times the word "immediately" is used. Jesus is constantly and consistently ministering and moving toward the cross. Jesus begins His ministry and preaching His message of repentance in verses 14-15.

Jesus calls the first four disciples, who leave everything to follow Him in verses 16-20. The first healing that Mark records is the casting out a demon on the Sabbath. This is a point of controversy between Jesus and Pharisees, but it also demonstrates the conflict between Jesus and Satan (v21-28). After healing Peter's mother-in-law (v29-31) many come to Jesus to be healed (v32-34). After a time of prayer (v35), Jesus expresses His desire to move on to other towns so He can preach the coming of the kingdom (v36-39). In verses 40-45 Jesus heals a leper. Leper's were not allowed near people, and they were required to shout "Unclean!" before anyone came near to them and became defiled. Notice that Jesus reaches out and touches the leper. Under Mosaic Law this would have made Jesus unclean.

Mark 2:1-12 begins with the story of Jesus healing the paralytic and forgiving his sins. This is also recorded in Matthew 9, and is one of the greatest miracles Jesus performed. It proves that Jesus has the power to forgive sins and to heal, which are two things only God can do. In verses 13-17 Jesus calls Levi (Matthew), and is charged with eating with sinners (v16). Tax collectors were hated by the Jews because they practiced extortion against their own people. Many would take as much as four times the amount required for taxes in order to keep some for themselves. Zacchaeus would be another example of a hated tax collector (Luke 19:1-10). This also demonstrates Jesus' mission: to seek and save that which is lost (Luke 19:10). Jesus, referencing their sickness (sin), knows these people need to experience the mercy of God and be healed of their sickness (sin). The Pharisees were so consumed with self and with religious formalism they could not see that they were sick.

The Messianic banquet theme is used in verses 18-22. God has always been the bridegroom, even in the OT (Isa. 54:5-6; Hosea 2:16-20), and Jesus is announcing that the time of the Messiah has come. While Jesus is with them they will rejoice over His coming and not fast. Verses 21-22 are a reference to the new and living way, introduced by Jesus, which could not be placed into the old wineskins of Judaism. The objection of the Pharisees in verses 23-28 was not because Jesus and His disciples were breaking the law (Deut. 23:25), but breaking the Pharisees tradition of the Sabbath regarding work. The Pharisees had 39 regulations that were meant to keep someone from breaking the Sabbath. Only their regulations caused the Sabbath to be a day of burdens instead of a day of rest. Jesus will explain to them that the day of rest was made for man to rest and worship God.

Thursday • Job 19-20

Job's reply to Bildad is in chapter 19 and can be divided into four stanzas. Job grows more weary of his friend's attacks on him in verses 1-5. He believes his friends were playing the role of God and had no right to interfere in his life (v4). Job still believes God has abandoned him and is attacking him (v6-12). Job, along with his friends, have a faulty perception of God. Job believed God was at war with him, and expresses this by vivid imagery.

In verses 13-20, Job blames God for his friends and family pushing him away and turning against him. Job does express faith that there is One who will vindicate him as the chapter closes (v21-29). Believing his friends are against him, and feeling as if he is near death, Job peers into the future where there is someone who will vindicate his cause. The Redeemer (*goel*) will plead his case for him. Job believed that even after his death he would live again to see his vindication. You have read Ruth this week, so you have a picture of the purpose of the *goel*, but the main responsibility is to redeem the lost inheritance of a deceased relative.

Zophar speaks for the last time in here in chapter 20. Zophar took Job's words personally (v1-3) and will again ask Job to consider the fate of the wicked. Zophar believed that the joy of the wicked would always be short lived and that it would end in death (v4-11). A wicked person's deeds are like food with a sweet taste that turns the stomach sour only to be vomited up (v12-19). In verses 20-28 Zophar states that once a wicked person is filled and there is nothing left to devour God will pour out his anger against them. The wicked believe they are getting away with their wickedness, but God makes them pay with their life. Zophar believes he is speaking on behalf of God, and condemns Job for his words against God and them (v29).

Friday • Isaiah 6-10

The great vision of the Lord seen by Isaiah is recorded in Isaiah 6. Uzziah's lengthy reign had come to an end, and God wanted Isaiah to see who the true King was. When Isaiah encountered God he saw his own sinfulness, and the sinfulness of the people (v5). If Isaiah is to be a prophet and minister of God's Word, then he will need to be cleansed (v6-7). In response to being cleansed, Isaiah answers God's call to go and speak to the people on behalf of God (v8). Isaiah's message would be rejected by the people. Isaiah 6:10 is quoted in each gospel (Matt. 13:14-15; Mark 4:10-12; Luke 8:10; John 12:39-41) and by Paul (Acts 28:26-27; Rom. 11:8), showing the rejection of God's Word by the people. Isaiah's message would be preached until the people were taken into captivity, and only a remnant would return (v11-13). The reference to "seed" links it to the promise given to Abraham (Gen. 12, 17).

Isaiah 7-9 will cover the subject of children with symbolic names. Chapter 7:1-9 opens with Rezin of Syria and Pekah of Israel coming to war against Ahaz and Judah. Isaiah and his son are sent to Ahaz to relay the message that their wicked plans will not come to pass. Isaiah's son's name, Shear-Jashub, has different meanings. It can mean "warning and hope" or "a remnant shall return". The Lord speaks to Ahaz personally beginning in verse 11. The Lord asked Ahaz if he would ask for a sign and he refuses. Ahaz's plan did not include God (v11-13). The sign of 7:14 is fulfilled fully in Jesus Christ (Matt. 1:21), and demonstrates God's complete control of the situation. In verses 17-25, the Lord speaks of the coming army of the Assyrians and the shame and defeat they will bring. He also speaks of the judgment of devastation on the land and its people, although a remnant will remain.

The birth of Maher-Shalal-Hash-Baz ("quick to plunder, swift to spoil") in 8:1-4 is a sign that the Assyrians would soon be coming to bring destruction before the child is old enough to speak. In verses 5-10 it is clear that Ahaz is going to trust in Assyria to deliver them and not God and they would suffer the judgment of God. It is both Judah and Israel that will suffer the consequences of their course of action (v11-18). Because they have rejected their stone (Rock) they will stumble, be smashed, snared, and seized (Matt. 21:44; Luke 2:34; Romans 9:33; 1 Pet. 2:8). Isaiah and his children have become a sign of the message of God to His people. Judgment would come because they sought answers from unholy sources instead of going to God's Word (v19-22).

The ending of chapter 8:19-22 continues the theme of judgment in 9:1-7. Even though the people have rejected the Lord's Words, He will give them light once more. The theme of children ends here in 9:6-7 as Isaiah prophesies of One to come. He will be wise, powerful, caring, and bring peace for His people. He will sit on the throne of David, and His kingdom will never end. Only Jesus could fulfill this prophecy. In verses 8-10:4 the Lord's judgment on the northern kingdom for its rebellion against the Him is described. God's judgment is for punishment, but also for restoration. Even though the leaders had led people astray, all must be punished. Even the fatherless and the widows would be punished . Isaiah shows that their wickedness had spread like a fire.

Isaiah 10:5-19 is about the judgment on Assyria. God uses the Assyrians to punish Israel. He will also punish the Assyrians and Judah as well with the Babylonians. Assyria is pictured as a tool in God's hands as He rules over the earth. In verses 20-34, the Lord delivers His remnant of the people of Israel. God will not completely destroy His people, but will continue with the promises He has made them (v22) and through His mighty power (note the names used of God in v21-23). The power that God used to judge them will be the same power that saves them (v24-27). The chapter closes with God punishing the coming Assyrians in verses 33-34.

Saturday • 1 Corinthians 5-6

In 1 Corinthians 5:1-13 Paul deals with immorality and sin inside the body of Christ. It may be that their thoughts of spiritual superiority also caused them to have loose morals. In verses 1-8 there is actually someone who has an immoral relationship with his mother (some believe step-mother). The Corinthians have done nothing to address the situation, and allow the person to continue in the fellowship of the church. Paul says in verses 2, 7, and 13 that they should purge the man from their church. Paul rebukes them for being arrogant and not mourning over this sin (v2). The word "mourn" is used for mourning for the dead. Paul instructs them to remove the person from their fellowship and to place them back out into the world in hopes that they will repent and be restored to fellowship (v4-5). The words "deliver such a one to Satan" is only used one other time in Scripture (1 Tim. 1:20). Many believe that doing this will result in the culprit repenting and being restored to fellowship with God and the church. Verses 6-8 address the effects that sin can have in a church and commands the church to purge it out. If the practicing sinner were allowed to stay in the church sin would spread throughout. To keep this from happening it is to be purged out (v7). Any sin can infect and spread throughout the church if it is not handled correctly. Before celebrating the Passover Jews would rid their homes of all yeast symbolizing the necessity of getting rid of sin (Ex. 12:15, 13:7).

In verses 9-13 Paul clears up something he had previously told the Corinthians concerning fellowship with those who practice sin inside and outside the church. The words "keep company" mean "to mix up yourself with". He was not speaking of people in the world who practice sin (v10). Paul was speaking to them about being around anyone in the body Christ who practices sin (v11). God is the judge of those who do not belong to the body of Christ (v12-13). It should also be pointed out that by saying this Paul is once again telling them that it is their responsibility to judge and discipline those who are inside the church, as stated in verses 1-8.

In 1 Corinthians 6:1-11 Paul deals with those inside the church who were suing one another. Like 1 Corinthians 5:1-8, this shows another instance where the Corinthian believers failed to do the right thing in the church. Paul encourages them to take these matters before qualified, wise Christians because they will one day judge the world and angels. What bothered Paul the most was they were taking these matters to secular authorities, and not settling them among their brothers and sisters in Christ. They were harming one another by practicing such things. Paul says they should be willing to suffer wrong rather than cheat fellow Christians (v7-8). Also, their acts of suing one another hurt the reputation of the whole church. Paul reminds them that when they act this way they are no better than unbelievers, which they once were (v9-11). Another point of concern was that they were taking their brothers to court and being judged by people who practice these things. He reminds them they have been "washed" (cleansed), "sanctified" (set apart), and "justified" (declared righteous) by God.

Paul returns to the subject of sexual immorality in verses 12-20. Verses 12-13 contain two phrases that many believe were said by the Corinthians to justify their behavior. The first is "all things are lawful for me". The second is "foods for the stomach and the stomach for the foods". Paul qualifies the two statements with his own additions. First, "all things are lawful for me" but all are not helpful (beneficial) to me. There are things that we can do but they will not benefit our walk with the Lord. Second, "I will not be brought under the power of any" shows that Paul will not allow it to be his master or to overpower him.

Many people in the church at Corinth believed that they could do what they wanted, and that sex was no different than eating food. They claimed it to be a natural process of the human body. The people in Corinth had grossly overestimated their freedom in Christ and had turned it into license. License is saying "Now that I am a believer I can do what I want". Paul will address this more in chapters 8-10. Paul refutes their argument by stating that their body is for the Lord's use (v14-15). Verses 16-17 form a contrast using the word "joined". The word means "to glue together". Our bodies are to be joined with the Lord, not with a harlot. In verse 18 Paul warns them to "flee" immorality because committing this sin is a sin against your own body. Paul compares their bodies to a temple where God dwells, and writes that they have no right to practice immorality because of this (v19). Paul also reminds them that they have been bought with a price (Christ's sacrifice) and they should use their bodies to glorify God (v20).

Cover to Cover Challenge

Week 11

Sunday • Psalm 36-38

Welcome to week 11 of the *Cover to Cover Challenge*! Psalm 119:50 says "This is my comfort in my affliction, for Your word has given me life". God's Word not only comforts us, but gives us life. Continue to pray for understanding as you read and study God's Word this week.

Psalm 36 is a wisdom psalm written by David. In verses 1-4, David sees the ways of the wicked and how they live. Their thoughts, speech, and actions reflect the wickedness that resides deep within themselves. In verses 5-6 David sees how God, in His wisdom, works through His mercy (loyal love), faithfulness, righteousness, and judgments (justice) throughout the earth. In contrast to the wicked, the godly put their trust in the Lord and He brings satisfaction to their lives by meeting their needs (v7-9). In verses 10-12 David prays for God to continue to pour out His love and righteousness to His people and he also prays for God's protection.

Psalm 37 is another wisdom psalm that looks at issues such as life, wisdom, reward, death, folly, and punishment in the lives of both the godly and the ungodly. In verses 1-2 we see the prosperity of the wicked, and a warning not to be jealous of their lives because they will soon fall. The godly are encouraged to trust (wait for Him to act), delight themselves in the Lord, and commit themselves to His ways (v3-6). In verses 7-11 we are warned not to look at the wicked and be angry, anxious, or jealous. The wicked prey upon the godly and take every opportunity to bring them down (v12-17). In verses 18-26 we see a series of contrasts between the blessings of the godly and the actions and coming destruction of the wicked. It is the Lord who establishes the godly, takes care of them, and they will never be forsaken. In verses 27-33 we read that the righteous love God and God loves His people. God will preserve His people while the wicked will be cut off (destroyed). In verses 34-40 the godly are encouraged to hope in the Lord, be obedient to Him, and have faith in God's justice. When the godly do this they will be exalted, be given an inheritance, be delivered and protected, and be crowned with salvation.

Psalm 38 is a prayer of reconciliation. Some believe David may have written this after his adultery with Bathsheba and the murder of Uriah. David is under the chastening hand of the Lord because of his sins, and no part of him has been left unaffected by it (v1-4). You will also notice from verses 5-12 that David is very specific about his suffering. It affects him physically, spiritually, mentally, and emotionally. David cries out to the Lord for help because he knows God is the one who can help him and forgive him (v13-16). David confesses his sin again and pleads with that his enemies do not overcome him during his time of suffering (v17-20). Feeling as if he is alienated from God (as we all do when we sin), David calls upon the Lord to be near to him during this time of need (v21-22).

WEEK 11

Monday • Genesis 44-47

In Genesis 44 we continue the story of Joseph and his brothers. They have once again come to buy food, and have enjoyed a feast with Joseph (ch. 43). Once more, Joseph will trick his brothers by having his cup placed in Benjamin's sack of grain. After having been caught, the brothers make a foolish vow that puts Benjamin's and their own livelihood in danger (v1-13). The evil done by the brothers has been a constant theme throughout these chapters. We also see the good that God has accomplished through it demonstrated by Joseph's schemes. The brothers become more aware of their guilt as the story unfolds (v14-34). Judah intercedes for Benjamin on his father's behalf and describes the grief it will cause him if they return without Benjamin.

Joseph reveals himself to his brothers in Genesis 45:1-8. It is reiterated that what they have intended to bring harm to Joseph, God worked it out for the good. The reason it happened was so Joseph could spare their lives, and bring them to Egypt so the family could survive (v1-8). Plans would be made by Joseph and Pharaoh to bring them all to Egypt, and they would dwell in the land of Goshen during the final five years of the famine (v9-28). It is a continuation of the blessings promised to Abraham and his descendants that was also given to Isaac and Jacob.

Jacob begins the long journey to Egypt, but stops in Beersheba to offer sacrifices to the Lord in Genesis 46:1-7. What the Lord did not allow Isaac to do (26:2), Jacob is allowed to do. He goes to Egypt in obedience to the Lord. The total number of those going to Egypt is 70. This represents the sons of Israel, just as the 70 nations in Genesis 10 represented the 70 nations descending from Adam (v8-27). Jacob and his family will settle in Goshen and have it all to themselves, because shepherds were an abomination to the Egyptians (v28-34).

It is because of Joseph's wisdom that the family of Jacob can rest securely in the land of Goshen (Gen. 47:1-12). Jacob blesses Pharaoh once again. This shows that God would bless those who blessed the descendants of Abraham God. Joseph's wisdom saved the life of his family, but in verses 13-27 we are reminded that it also saved Egypt and all its inhabitants (v13-27). Once the people's money runs out, Joseph exchanges grain for their land and for their lives. Jacob gives Joseph specific instructions to not bury him in Egypt, but to return his body to the Promised Land to be buried with his ancestors (v 28-31).

Tuesday • 1 Samuel 1-5

The books of 1 & 2 Samuel will cover 135 years of history after the time of the judges. Israel as a nation was failing morally and spiritually, and had plunged into anarchy. On top of this there is a corrupt priesthood, idolatry was rampant, and the judges were unjust. The book of Judges' repetitive statement that "Israel had no king" prepares the way for the reign of a king. Samuel, Saul, and David are the three most important figures in 1 Samuel. By the end of 2 Samuel, Israel will be the most powerful nation in the region.

In 1 Samuel 1:1-8 we are introduced to Hannah ("Grace"), the mother of Samuel ("Name of God"), who is barren. Elkanah (her husband) goes to the sanctuary to make sacrifices for his family, while Peninnah (his other wife) continually provokes Hannah because she is not able to have children. In verses 9-18 Hannah pours out her heart to the Lord, and makes a vow to the Lord that if He would give her a son she would give him back to the Lord for His service. The Lord remembers Hannah and she gives birth to Samuel and after he is weaned she will present him to the Lord (v19-28).

1 Samuel 2:1-11 records Hannah's song to the Lord. It bears a strong resemblance to Mary's song in Luke 1:46-55. Hannah rejoices in the Lord because He is holy and mighty. The song closes with a pronouncement of strength on the king which will initially apply to David, but be ultimately fulfilled in Christ. In verses 12-26, we meet Eli's

sons Hophni and Phinehas. They are described as wicked men who profane the sacrifices, and who are intimately involved with the women who serve in the tabernacle. The sons of Eli will be contrasted with Samuel, who will be a faithful priest to the Lord. Hannah is blessed by the Lord to have more children, and Samuel continues to grow in the Lord. In verses 27-36, a judgment is pronounced upon the house of Eli for their wickedness. The chopping off of the arm signals that Eli and his descendants will be judged by God.

1 Samuel 3:1-9 records the calling of Samuel to be a prophet. Special revelation was rare in the days of the judges. Samuel was open to serving God and hears the Lord calling but mistakens it as Eli's voice. After accepting the Lord's call, Samuel receives a word from the Lord confirming the judgment that is to fall on the house of Eli (v10-14) and recounts it to Eli the next morning (v15-18). It became evident to all in the land that God had called Samuel to be a prophet (v19-21).

In 1 Samuel 4 the judgment on the house of Eli comes to pass. After the Philistines attack the Israelites and defeat them, they bring in the Ark of the Covenant which they believed would ensure them victory (v1-3). Hophni and Phinehas bring the ark to battle, but the Israelites were defeated once more. Hophni and Phineas were both killed and the Ark of the Covenant is captured (v4-11). Upon hearing the news, Eli falls backward out of his chair and dies (v12-18), and his daughter-in-law also dies giving birth (v19-22). She names her son Ichabod, referring to the capture of the Ark of the Covenant.

The Philistines suffer greatly for stealing the Ark of the Covenant in chapter 5. In verses 1-5 the Philistine god Dagon is pictured as falling prostrate on the ground before the Ark not once but twice. A plague of tumors falls upon Ashdod, Gath, and Ekron because of the Ark. The Philistines gather together to send the Ark away from them, back to its own place.

Wednesday • Mark 3-4

Mark 3 begins the same way that Mark 2 ended, with controversy involving the Pharisees over the Sabbath. The Pharisees and other religious leaders kept a close eye on Jesus as He again heals on the Sabbath, breaking their traditions but not God's law. The hardness of their hearts angers Jesus, and we see the Herodians (backers of family of Herod) join in the plot to destroy Jesus (v1-6). Jesus withdraws from the crowds, yet many from the surrounding regions follow Him. They are only interested in His healing power (v7-12). Once again, Jesus silences the demons because it was not time to make Himself known fully to the people.

The names of the disciples are recorded in verses 13-19, along with their mission of preaching the good news, healing, and casting out demons. Thinking that He was going out of His mind, Jesus' family comes to possibly take Him back home to Nazareth (v20-22). Jesus is accused of casting out demons by the power of Beelzebub ("prince of demons"). Jesus' reply shows that He is not in cohorts with Satan because He is destroying Satan's work. This is evidenced by verse 27 in the binding the strong man (v23-27). Because of the hardness of their hearts they have rejected Christ (v28-30). Chapter 3 closes with a return to the story of Jesus' family coming to get Him. Jesus' true family are those who do the will of His Father (v31-35).

Mark 4 is dominated by the parables of Jesus. Taken from ordinary life, these stories are meant to convey moral or spiritual truths about the kingdom of God. Verses 1-9 cover the parable of the sower, and verses 13-20 explain it. Only one seed is received in good ground and produces fruit. In verse 9 "let him hear" means to hear something that requires a response. Going back to verses 10-12, Jesus explains the reason He speaks in parables the mysteries of the kingdom. Jesus speaks in parables to conceal the truth, but for some the parable will reveal it. He explains this by quoting Isaiah 6:9-10 where Israel had once before stopped listening to God. Jesus does explain these truths to the disciples in verses 33-34. Those who cannot see or hear are those who have already rejected Him in their heart. To some the parable of the lamp is a reference to Jesus being revealed, or the message of the gospel that needs to be preached. In verses 24-25, Jesus warns the people to listen closely to His Words because the one who heeds His Word will receive more truth.

Verses 26-29 illustrate the sovereign reign of God over His kingdom. He is the one who truly grows the kingdom. Verse 29 shows that God's kingdom will be ripe for harvest. This shows the theme of salvation and judgment. The parable of the mustard seed (v30-32) is concerned with the growth of the kingdom. This parable explains that the kingdom will start off small, but grow very large. Jesus begins to show His power over nature in verses 35-41 by rebuking the storm. Jesus also rebukes the disciples because of their lack of faith.

Thursday • Job 21-22

Now it is Job's turn to speak about the wicked and refute the claims of his friends in Job 21. Job asks his friends to be quiet and listen to his words (v1-6). In verses 7-16, and throughout many of the chapters, you can see that Job's friends believe the wicked suffer, while Job believes the wicked prosper. Zophar has said the wicked die prematurely (20:11), but according to Job they live a long life. Not only do they live a long life, but they seem to live in prosperity- all the while never caring about God (v7-13). Job felt that the wicked should be immediately punished, but life seemed to show a whole different picture (v17-21). Job sees continual injustice working in the world (v22-26), and challenges his friends to look around them and see if he was right about the wicked going unpunished in this life (v27-34).

Eliphaz the Temanite answers Job's claims in chapter 22. Eliphaz believed Job must have been a wicked man (v1-5). Eliphaz gives a hint that maybe Job cannot be vindicated (v5). He believes Job has committed many social injustices upon his fellow man, and is being punished for them (v6-11). In verses 12-20, Eliphaz uses Job's own words against him and portrays Job as a man who follows the ways of the ungodly. Eliphaz encourages Job to repent in verses 21-30. He encourages Job to repent and be at peace with God, to hear God's word and hide it in his heart, to return to God and do away with wickedness, and to delight in God rather than gold.

Friday • Isaiah 11-17

After judgment falls upon Assyria at the end of chapter 10, chapter 11 begins with the reign of the true Davidic King and the peace that ensues. The One to come will be from the line of Jesse, who will be equipped to do His work by the Spirit of the Lord (v1-2). He will be just in His judgment. He will not just be King over Israel, but the whole world (v3-5). Under His reign there will be a peace in all areas of life as nature is restored to its original condition (v6-9). All people will be brought together by the "Root of Jesse" coming from all over the earth, and He will make a way for them to come (v10-11, 15-16). The once divided nation of Israel will also be brought back together (v12-14).

Isaiah 12 is a hymn of praise that will be sung by the people when the day described in chapter 11 comes. One day God's name will be exalted throughout the whole earth. Many of the words expressed here are similar to the Song of Moses in Exodus 15. In a future day Israel will believe in the Lord and trust Him as Savior as He becomes the sole object of their praise. The song is a celebration of God's grace poured out upon His people.

While Babylon was a national power it was the Assyrians who were the main power. So what we see here in Isaiah 13 is the rise and fall of the Babylonian empire. In verses 1-5 the Babylonians are going to be the Lord's instrument in the destruction of Judah in a future day, just as the Assyrians will be for Israel (10:5). Fear would come upon the whole land as a result of the impending judgment (v6-8). In verses 9-13 we see this world power expand in judgment, but there are hints in these verses of it being a universal judgment. Isaiah returns to the theme of the destruction of Babylon in verses 14-16. The judgment on the Babylonians will come from the hands of the Medes at a future time (v17-22). The Medes would also conquer Nineveh, the capital of Assyria, but it would be the Medes and the Persians who would conquer Babylon.

Isaiah 14:1-3 concerns the nations of Israel being brought back from captivity to once again be the people of God. There will be a reversal of fortune for the king of Babylon in verses 4-21. The great kingdom and king of Babylon that enjoyed prosperity will be brought down to hell. Satan was the real ruler over Babylon so it should be of no surprise that Satan's characteristics are seen in the king of Babylon. Because of their sins Babylon (v22-23), Assyria (v24-27), and Philistia (v28-32) will be destroyed.

Isaiah 15-16 concerns the destruction of Moab, which is the descendants of Lot (Gen 19:30-38). They will be invaded and completely destroyed. The reference to the lion in verse 9 may be Assyria, considering Amos uses the lion to refer to Assyria in Amos 3:12. Moab was famous for its sheep so the rulers send lambs to Judah and seek refuge there (16:1-5). As with many of the nations the sin of Moab is pride (v6-7). Because of its sin, judgment would come and nothing of the land will be left (v8-12). Isaiah proclaims that this judgment would come within 3 years (v13-14).

The judgment of Syria and Israel (Ephraim) is in view in Isaiah 17. Bethel and Dan had apostate shrines setup, and you read the background of this in Judges 17-18. Israel and Syria also made alliances together so if one is to be judged both will be judged. Three occasions of "in that day" shows the decisiveness of the judgment to come will be thorough (v4-6). Some would repent (v7-8), but they would lose the land the Lord had given them (v9-11). God's judgments will also be decisive over His enemies (v12-14).

Saturday • 1 Corinthians 7-8

1 Corinthians 7 contains instructions on marriage within the community of believers at Corinth, which was known for its sexual immorality. In verses 1-2, Paul speaks on singleness (v1) and also speaks to the married (v2). Verses 2-4 teach that marriage should be monogamous, that one should give more than receive, and about the obligations that husbands and wives have toward one another. Some in Corinth may have been practicing celibacy within marriage, and Paul warns them not to deprive one another sexually because of their lack of self-control and the temptations of the devil (v5). Some are called to be married while others are not, but it is better to marry than burn with passion and commit immorality (v6-9).

In verses 10-16 Paul discusses divorce (Matt. 5:32, 19:3-9) and marriages that contain only one believing spouse. One spouse probably became a believer after marriage and this may have caused conflict within the home (2 Cor. 6:14-7:1). Paul adheres to Jesus' teaching on divorce and proposes that reconciliation be made in order to not destroy the marriage covenant. The believer is encouraged to remain married to the unbeliever if they will stay because it sanctifies the home, and also in hopes that the believer will influence the unbeliever to come to the Lord. Jesus and Paul both teach that reconciliation and restoration of the marriage bond is the best course of action. Death is not divorce, and Paul teaches that death also dissolves the marriage bond and the living partner is free to marry (1 Cor. 7:39).

In verses 17-24, Paul is teaching that all believers must live obediently to the Lord whether they are married or unmarried, Jew or Gentile, or slaves or free. One example Paul uses is circumcision (v18-19). Jews saw the uncircumcised as outside the covenant, and Gentiles saw circumcised Jews as despised. Another example is the slave and the free man. In Paul's day the slave could show other slaves how to live freely in the Christian life and the free man could show other free men how to become a slave to Christ (v21-23). It is obedience and our relationship with the Lord that matters most.

Paul addresses the unmarried and virgins in 25-40. Paul encourages them to remain as they are, whether married or single, because the time to do the Lord's work is short. Paul does note that those who are married are concerned for their spouses, while those who are unmarried have more time to devote to the Lord.

1 Corinthians 8 concerns the question about meat offered to idols, and centers on the subject of Christian liberty. It is believed that Corinth had 16 temples and shrines dedicated to pagan gods. The sacrifices would be divided between priest and the offerer, and the other would be burned up. Many times the priest would sell the meat in the meat market. So what was a believer to do? Paul says the believer's behavior in these matters is to be fueled by love because not all have knowledge (v1-3). The people in Corinth claimed to have knowledge. This led to them being prideful.

Paul knows that there is only one God and that other gods are nothing (v4-6). But, not everyone has that type of knowledge (v7). Believers with this knowledge can eat meat because all things are provided by God. Paul also gives a stern warning to those who are exercising their liberty by eating meat (v9-13). Their actions can cause a weak believer to stumble, and the believer will be guilty of sinning against their brother and against the Lord. Those who are weak do not believe it is right to eat the meat, and when they see a believer doing so it causes them to stumble in their own walk with the Lord. The "strong" believer with knowledge is then encouraging the "weak" believer to sin, destroying him spiritually (v11). Paul concludes that while he has this knowledge, out of love, he would never eat meat again if it caused his brother to stumble (v12).

Cover to Cover Challenge

Week 12

Sunday • Psalm 39-41

Welcome to week 12 of the *Cover to Cover Challenge*! Continue to pray for understanding of the Word. The psalmist writes "Let my cry come before You, O Lord; give me understanding according to Your word" (Psalm 119:169). Life presents us with many challenges, and it is in those times that we should seek the Lord's help through His Word. Let us pray together that we find those answers in the Word as we read it together each week.

Psalm 39 is a lament about life and its troubles and trials, but it also has elements of wisdom. In verses 1-3, David withholds from speaking (James 3:1-12) in front of the wicked in regards to the life they live and also in the midst of his own suffering. It may be that he sees that the wicked seem to prosper while he, a follower of the Lord, is suffering (v4-6). David inquires of the Lord about life, which he knows is short (v4-6). David knows that his hope is in the Lord, and he prays to be delivered from the ways of the foolish (v7-9). David knows that through his experiences in life he has learned the ways of the Lord (v10-11). In verses 12-13, David prays to be forgiven and for the Lord to deliver him from his present circumstances.

Psalm 40 can be divided into two parts. In the first part (v1-10), David gives thanks to God for a past situation in which God helped him. The second part (v11-17) addresses a current situation that David is in. Based upon God's past acts, David wants God to help him in the same way. In verses 1-3, David begins to recount the past situation that God had delivered him from. After placing his trust in the Lord, David knew it was the Lord that protected him and delivered him. In verses 6-8 David knows that the Lord was not pleased with formalities of sacrifice, but with those who are committed to do His will (Heb. 10:5-7; Rom. 12:1-2). David tells all about God's righteousness, faithfulness, love, and truth (v9-11). After confessing his sin (v12), David prays that God will come quickly to deliver him from his present situation. He prays for God's justice over his enemies through His acts of deliverance (v13-16). David closes out the psalm with a petition for the Lord to deliver him with no delay (v17).

Psalm 41 is mainly a psalm of thanksgiving for the blessings given by God to all those who do the Lord's will. Those who do the will of the Lord will be protected, delivered, and restored by Him (v1-3). David asks for the Lord to forgive him of his sin (v4). In verses 5-9 David discusses, at length, the hatred that his enemies have for him. They hate him even to the point they wish he would die. David's own friends, those he considered family, have turned against him (v9; John 13:18). But David trusts in the Lord to protect him (v10), and he has confidence in the Lord to deliver him in the midst of his adversities (v11-12). David closes out the psalm by noting that only the Lord is worthy to be praised (v13).

WEEK 12

Monday • Genesis 48-50

Some time has passed since the events of chapter 47 and the revealing of Joseph to his brothers. Here in chapter 48, Jacob will bless Joseph's sons Ephraim and Manasseh and include them into the family as if they are his own sons. In verses 1-4, Jacob recalls the blessing that he received from the Lord in Genesis 35:9-13. This blessing continues the theme of the blessing from Genesis 12 that Abraham received from God. Ephraim and Manasseh are counted as being Jacob's sons. They would become two of the most important tribes in the northern kingdom (v5-7). The younger son, Ephraim, will receive the blessing of the first-born. We continue to see the theme of Genesis- the sovereignty and grace of God-emphasized in these passages (v8-20).

Genesis 49:1-28 contains the blessings of the twelve sons of Jacob. Each of the twelve sons receive a blessing of future prosperity that is in accordance with God's blessing upon Abraham in chapter 12. Reuben, Simeon, and Levi are all disqualified from the blessing of the first-born because they each dishonored their father (Genesis 34-35). The tribe of Simeon disappears after the time of Joshua, and Levi becomes the priestly tribe (v1-8). Judah is pictured as the one who receives the blessing. According to Genesis 48:5, Joseph received the right of the first-born. Despite this, according to 1 Chronicles 5:2, it is Judah that was the strongest tribe. It is through the line of Judah that both King David and the Messiah would come from (v8-12). Dan is not mentioned in the listing of tribes in Revelation 7, and this may be because they led their own people into idolatry (Judges 13,18). Jacob announces his death and his desire to be buried at Machpelah with his ancestors in verses 29-33. Jacob's burial takes place in Genesis 50:1-14, and they carry his body back to Canaan to be buried. In verses 15-21, for the final time, we return to the story of Joseph and his brothers. He reassures them that what they meant for evil, God intended it for good. Joseph, being near death, asks to be buried in the Promised Land and his people agree but the story ends with him being buried in Egypt. Moses will be the one to remove Joseph's bones (Ex. 13:19), and Joshua will bury them in Shechem (Joshua 24:32).

Tuesday • 1 Samuel 6-10

The Ark of the Covenant was captured by the Philistines in chapter 4, and in chapter 5 we see how it affected the Philistines. In 1 Samuel 6:1-6, the Philistines seek their own priests to see what they should do with the ark. The Philistines were instructed to send the ark on its way, along with a trespass offering. In verses 7-12 they were instructed to take the calves from their mothers, and send them along with the trespass offering to Beth Shemesh ("Temple of the Sun god"). If the cart went straight to Beth Shemesh they would know it was the Lord who caused the plagues upon them. The cart arrived in Beth Shemesh, and the men there used the cart and the cows to make a sacrifice to the Lord (v13-19). Over 50,000 men were killed from looking into the ark, which was a sin (Num. 4:5,20; 2 Sam. 6:6-7). The ark is then sent to Kirjath Jearim where it would stay for the next 20 years until David restored it to its rightful place (v20-7:2).

Samuel begins to judge Israel in chapter 7:2. In verses 2-3, Samuel urges them to repent and turn from their idols so they can experience the deliverance of the Lord. The children of Israel put away their idols and confess their sins to the Lord (v4-6). As the Philistines prepare to come against Israel, the Israelites ask Samuel to intercede to the Lord on their behalf (v7-9). In verses 10-11 the Lord comes against the Philistines in response to Samuel's prayer and the repentance of the Israelites, and delivers them from the Philistines. Samuel sets up the Ebenezer stone ("Stone of help") to remind them that the Lord delivered them that day (v12-13). God restores the cities which the Philistines had taken to the Israelites, and Samuel will judge Israel all the days of his life (v14-17).

Israel's demand for a king is the theme of chapter 8. Ultimately God himself was their true King (Ex. 15:18; Num. 23:21; Deut. 33:5). With Samuel getting older, and the wickedness of his sons, the people of Israel ask Samuel for a king (v1-5). Samuel was not pleased with the request and begins to seek the Lord, Who told him that he is to obey the voice of the people (v6-8). Samuel is told to warn them of the oppressive regime of the king, and they would basically become the king's slaves (v9-18). In addition to this, the Lord would not hear them when they cry out because of the king they have chosen. The Israelites main purpose for wanting a king was so he could fight their battles for them, something the Lord had been doing for them all along (v19-22).

In 1 Samuel 9:1-2 we meet Israel's first king, Saul, who is from the tribe of Benjamin. Saul and his servant were looking for his father's donkeys, which leads to the divine encounter with Samuel (v3-14). In verses 15-24, we see Samuel's side of the divine encounter and what God had spoken to him about Saul. In verses 25-27 Samuel begins to prepare Saul to be the king of Israel and to hear a word from the Lord.

In 1 Samuel 10:1-8, Samuel anoints Saul to be the king of Israel and details three signs that would confirm the Lord's choice of him. The Spirit of the Lord comes upon Saul confirming him as the king of Israel (v9-16). Samuel gathers and addresses the people concerning the Lord's deliverance of them in the past, while also reminding them that they have rejected God as their King (v17-24). In verses 25-27 we see that Saul was a popular choice among some who were ready to serve him, while others despised him.

Wednesday • Mark 5-6

Mark 5 records the stories of 3 people who would have been considered ceremonially unclean and unable to come in contact with Jesus. They also serve as illustrations to show what happens when a seemingly hopeless situation meets the Son of God. In verses 1-20, Jesus will once again demonstrate His power over evil by casting out demons from a man who lived among the tombs. Even the demons know their rightful place before the Son of God and bow down to Him (v6-7, James 2:19). Jesus sends the demons into a herd of pigs. Unable to destroy the man, the demons instead destroy the pigs. The people of the area ask Jesus to leave because of the event. The man Jesus healed wants to go with Jesus, but He instructs him to go home and tell others what the Lord had done for him. As a result, there is a witness to Jesus' miraculous deed.

In verses 21-43 we see the two intertwining stories of Jairus' daughter and the woman with a hemorrhage. While Jesus is on the way to heal Jairus' daughter (v21-24), the woman with the hemorrhage only wants to touch the hem of His garment (which she does) and be made well. Jesus confronts the woman and assures her it is her faith that has made her well (v25-34). After Jairus is informed that his daughter has died, Jesus continues with Jairus to his home. Jesus is laughed at because He says she is only sleeping. Peter, James, John, and the girl's parents witness Jesus raising the young girl back to life. Jesus showed His power over nature in Mark 4:35-41, and here in Mark 5 showed that He also has power over life and death.

Mark 6 begins with Jesus being rejected in His hometown of Nazareth (v1-8). The unbelief of the people led to Him being unable to do many works there. In verses 7-13 Jesus sends out the disciples two by two to preach repentance, cast out demons, and heal the sick. During their mission, they were to trust God for all their needs. The story of the death of John the Baptist is recorded in verses 14-29. John the Baptist was in prison for standing for the truth to people (Herodians) who did not honor God's truth. From church history we know that the Herodian dynasty was filled with immorality and murder. It is also here that we learn many of the opinions of who people thought Jesus was. Because of his guilty conscience, Herod believed that Jesus was John the Baptist raised from the dead.

In verses 30-44 we find the feeding of the 5,000. We also see during this miracle that Jesus had compassion on the people because they were like "sheep without a shepherd". Jesus satisfies their hunger by providing for them and demonstrates His miraculous power once again. This, along with Jesus' other miracles, showed that He was able to meet needs. Often in Scripture a physical need is met in order to meet the greater spiritual need of an individual (Phil. 4:19). God's provision is always more than enough to meet our needs. Mark 6 closes with Jesus displaying His power over nature by walking on the water in the middle of a raging storm and by causing the storm to cease (v45-52). Many people believe chapters 4-6 all took place in one day of Jesus' life. If they did, there is no doubt that the disciples and Jesus were tired and weary. When Jesus was tired and weary He would pray to the Father. Mark summarizes the healings of Jesus in the area. If you notice, he adds in verse 56 that they believed if they could "touch the hem of His garment" they would be healed.

Thursday • Job 23-24

Job 23 is once again a reply to his friends but he is also pleading with God over his situation. In verses 1-7, Job is still wants a trial before God because of his situation and also because of his friends' accusations. Job wants to be vindicated, and still believes he is blameless before God. As a matter of fact, God used Job as an example of blamelessness in 1:8 and 2:3. In verses 8-12 Job did not feel the presence of God, and he did not hear God speaking to him. Job did not think that God was testing him to purge away sins, but to prove he was pure gold. Job's words in verses 13-17 show that Job believed God was sovereign. We all must trust in the sovereignty of God, especially when we do not understand why bad things happen.

Job continues his speech in chapter 24. In verses 1-17, Job continues to complain about the lack of justice being poured out upon the wicked for their wicked deeds. Job believed God should do this for everyone to see. Job saw injustice in many cases such as people carrying food yet going hungry, and people treading the winepress but going thirsty. Job simply believed God treated the godly and the godless alike, but the wicked will eventually be punished (v18-25).

Friday • Isaiah 18-24

Starting in Isaiah 13, we began reading about the judgment of the nations and of Israel. Isaiah 18 will continue that theme, with the judgment on the Ethiopians (Cush). Isaiah 18-20 concerns the judgment on the lands of Ethiopia and Egypt. They are trying to seize an alliance among all the nations to go against Assyria, and the whole world will know its fall (v1-3). In verses 4-6, the details of the judgment are fierce as they become the prey of other nations. In verse 7 they are presented as bringing gifts to Zion, which will become the religious center of the world.

Isaiah 19 describes the judgment upon Egypt. God will begin to do this by causing them to turn against one another, and eventually they will fall to the Assyrians (v1-4). Judgment will also come against their land as the Nile will be dried up, and their source of income will come to a halt (v5-10). The judgment of God will confound the wise of Egypt, rendering them helpless in the judgment that will come (v11-15). The Egyptians will fear the Lord and Judah (v16-17), which will lead to their repentance (v18-22). In a display of the grace of God, the hated Egyptians and Assyrians will stand side by side with Israel and worship the Lord (v23-25). Isaiah 20 is a dated prophecy of Isaiah, and is also an acted prophecy. The Assyrians come against Ashdod and take it because it was the center of the rebellion against the Assyrians. In verse 6, there is a warning for any who will put their trust in Egypt (especially Judah).

Isaiah 21 contains judgments upon Babylon, Edom, and Arabia with each falling at the hands of the Assyrians. The fall of Babylon would shatter the hopes of many nations hoping they could defeat the Assyrians (v1-10). The oracle concerning Edom may be a reference to the fall of the Assyrians (morning comes) and the rise of the Babylonians (also the night) in the future (v11-12). The Arabians also are no match for the fierce Assyrian army as they will flee hungry, thirsty, and exhausted from fighting with the Assyrians (v13-15). In verses 16-17 there is a time period directed to this prophecy and also assurance that it comes from the hand of the Lord (v16-17).

Isaiah 22:1-14 concerns the judgment on Jerusalem. The name "Valley of the Vision" may be because of all the prophetic visions that were received there and given to the people. The historical Day of the Lord in 2:6-22 would fall on Jerusalem in 586 BC at the hands of the Babylonians because the people chose to trust in human alliances rather than God. If the people would not choose to trust in God, they would experience His judgment. In verses 15-25 judgment turns from Jerusalem to Shebna, the steward of the king's palace (36:3, 11, 22, 37:2). God will show this proud man who has the real power, as God will take him out of his office and into another land. Eliakim will take over his office and become the "peg" (stability) of the kingdom.

In Isaiah 23, God judges the Phoenicians and its cities of Tyre, Cyprus, and Sidon. Tyre and Sidon were important ports for sea trade, but these and their cities would fall to the Assyrians. Their lavish trade and abundant sea ports caused a sense of complacency, but God is warning them that judgment is coming and they will not escape (v1-14). Tyre will once again flourish, but its purpose will be to supply the needs of the house of God in Jerusalem (v15-18).

Isaiah 24 pictures a universal judgment. This judgment will affect all people in society (v1-3). God will carry out this judgment based on the people's immoral acts (v4-6). This judgment will affect the whole world, even its plant life (v7-9). This judgment will bring to an end the existing human order of things (v10-13). The remnant that remains will praise the Lord with songs of thanksgiving (v14-16). There will be no escape from this judgment of God that will come upon the whole earth (v17-20). It will be so great even the heavens will be shaken (v21-23).

Saturday • 1 Corinthians 9-10

Continuing the theme of Christian liberty from chapter 8, Paul cites examples from life and uses himself as an example of Christian liberty. In verses 1-12, Paul gives the example of him forfeiting his rights as an apostle as exercising his Christian liberty. In doing this Paul is hoping the people of Corinth will adopt this practice in their own lives, especially as it concerns eating food offered to idols. Paul also takes this opportunity in verses 3-6 to criticize those who do not believe that he is an apostle because he exercises his Christian liberty. It is known from Scripture that Paul supported himself in ministry through tent making (Acts 18:2-3; 1 Cor. 4:12). In verses 7-14 Paul gives examples of the soldier, vineyard keeper, shepherd, and the ox (Deut. 25:4) showing that the worker is worthy of his wages. After establishing the principle that as apostles they could receive support from the church, in verses 15-18 Paul will say he has refused that right. In verses 15-18 Paul states that if he preaches voluntarily he has a reward, but if he does it for pay he is still fulfilling the commission given to him. Paul is basically saying his pay is to serve God without pay and the gospel gives him this right. Verses 19-23 detail the reasons why Paul chose to do this-to reach more people with the gospel.

In verses 19-23 Paul also used his Christian liberty to reach the Jews, Gentiles, and the weak with the gospel. In verse 19 Paul is saying that although he was free, he would become a slave to all in order to reach them with the gospel. Paul adapted himself to the group he was attempting to reach, but never broke God's law. This is exemplified in Paul's life in the circumcision of Timothy (Acts 16:1-3), in teaching the gospel to Gentiles (Acts 17), and in participating in purification rites (Acts 21:23-26). Paul uses the popular Isthmian games to prove his point about self-control in verses 24-27. Every person participating in these games trained for 10 months in order to come out a victor in the games. He brings his body under subjection in order to win the prize, but makes sure that he is living within the rules of the gospel so he does not become disqualified (disapproved).

Paul continues the theme of self-control in chapter 10. In verses 1-13 Paul uses examples from the Old Testament and their lack of self-control. Although they were miraculously delivered and had God's provision (v1-5), they still failed to exercise self-control and fell into disobedience and idolatry (5-10). All the events that happened and took place are to be examples to the Corinthians, as well as all believers (v6). Verse 7, with its quote from Exodus 32:6 warns against idolatry. Verse 8 refers to the incident at Baal Peor in Numbers 25. Verse 9 refers to Numbers 21:5-6 when the people tested God concerning food. Verse 10 is probably referring to Korah in Numbers 16. These function as a warning to the Corinthians and all Christians that temptation comes to all people, but God provides the way to escape it (v11-13). Verse 12 is a warning to those who are arrogant, proud, and who are overconfident in how they live their lives. Those who play with fire are sure to be burned.

Paul warns them of participating in pagan feasts and rituals in verses 14-22. Verse 14 is actually saying "keep running from idolatry". The Corinthians were seeing how close they could stay to the line and not cross it, while Paul is urging them to run as far as they can from it. Paul gives the example of the Lord's Supper to show them that they are in a relationship with the Lord (v16-17). It also shows that because of this relationship, believers should be in unity with one another. In verses 18-19 Paul is showing that sharing in food is establishing fellowship. So participating in pagan feasts means participating with demons, and this is a mistake the ancient Israelites made themselves (v20-22). In 10:23-11:1 Paul details principles for exercising Christian liberty. One principle that is very clear in this passage is that whatever the believer does is to be for the glory of God (v31). Believers should also be more concerned for someone else's well-being (v32) and seeing how we can exercise our liberty in order to lead someone to Christ (v33).

Cover to Cover Challenge

Week 13

Sunday • Psalm 42-44

Welcome to the *Cover to Cover Challenge* for week 13! Continue to pray that the Lord will work through His Word in the lives of those participating in the readings every week. Psalm 119:133 says "Direct my steps by Your word, and let no iniquity have dominion over me". Let's get started!

Psalm 42 is a song of lament. The psalmist is longing for God's presence during a time of intense trial. There is an escalation in the psalmist's desire as he longs (pants) for God's presence through verses 1-3. During this trial, the psalmist's opponents ask him where his God is. The psalmist goes back and forth between faith, doubt, and despair in verses 4-8, as he still clings to the hope that is within him. The psalmist realizes that God is his Rock despite the oppression of his enemies and their continual questioning of where his God is (v9-10). Verse 5 is again repeated in verse 11 as the psalmist reflects upon his situation, but still clings to his hope in God.

Psalm 43 is another song of lament, and some believe Psalm 42 and 43 originally formed one psalm. In verses 1-2 the psalmist prays for God to vindicate him against those who oppress him and again questions the absence of God's presence. He asks God to send out His light and truth in the midst of the darkness and lies that are being spoken (v3-4). Verse 5 is a repeat of Psalm 42:5,11 as he reflects upon his situation, clings to his hope in God, and praises Him.

Psalm 44 continues the theme of lament, and many believe this psalm is a lament on behalf of the nation of Israel. In verses 1-3, the psalmist recalls the past victories won by God on behalf of His people (especially during the times of Joshua). God is pictured as King and Commander of the victories won during the battles that took place as they took possession of the land (v4-8). Each individual is pictured as giving God praise for His acts on their behalf (v8). The triumphs of the past are interrupted by the lament of the present in verses 9-16. They are now shamed (v9), conquered and plundered (v10), scattered (v11), enslaved (v12), and their name has become disgraced among the nations (v13-16). In verses 17-22 the people claim innocence and proclaim that they have kept the covenant, they are devoted to the Lord, and they are not committing idolatry. The psalm closes with the people asking God to help them immediately, as they fall to the ground in prayer and ask God to rise up for them (v23-26). They do this based upon God's covenant love (mercies) for them.

WEEK 13

Monday • Exodus 1-5

The book of Exodus ("Departure" or "Exit") continues the story of the Israelites in Egypt. As with Genesis and the rest of the Torah, Moses is the author of the book of Exodus (17:14, 24:4; 34:4). The New Testament also affirms this position (Mark 12:26; Luke 2:22-23). God will begin to reveal more of Himself to the people through His justice, mercy, and holiness. You will see the beginning of the priesthood, the role of the prophet, and the covenant relationship between God and the people. Exodus is best known for three main themes: deliverance, salvation, and worship. It also forms the foundation for moral and ethical laws.

Exodus 1:1-7 is a record of the promises of God to Abraham, Isaac, and Jacob being fulfilled (Gen. 15:5, 22:17). God's people were truly multiplying in the land of Egypt during their 430 year stay. In verses 8-14 the Egyptians feared the children of Israel. They believed that the Israelites would one day ally with their enemies and overtake them, so they made them slaves. In verses 15-22 the midwives are given orders to kill all Hebrew male children, and they refused to do so. God rewards the midwives in defiance of the king's orders. Pharaoh then gives the order to all the people of Egypt to kill every male child born to the Hebrews. This chapter sets up the story of the birth of Moses and the events of the book of Exodus.

In Exodus 2:1-10 Moses ("Drew out of water") is born to Levite parents, placed in his own "little ark", saved by the Egyptian princess, and given back to his parents by divine providence. In verses 11-15, Moses kills an Egyptian for beating a Hebrew slave. When he realizes that what he has done is known, he flees to Midian because Pharaoh is seeking to kill him. In verses 16-22 Moses, who is in Midian, comes to the aide of the seven daughters of Reuel (Jethro). It is also at this point Moses takes Zipporah to be his wife and she bears him a son. When the king of Egypt dies, the children of Israel cry out for God to deliver them (v22-25). Notice that God hears, remembers, looks, and knows what is happening to the children of Israel.

In Exodus 3:1-10 the Angel of the Lord (preincarnate Christ) appears to Moses. The Angel of the Lord appears in the burning bush, but the bush itself is not consumed. Fire symbolizes God's powerful presence, but also His holiness (v5 is the first time holy is used in this way). It became holy because of the presence of God. This passage is the commissioning of Moses to lead the people of Israel out of Egypt and face Pharaoh. Moses felt insignificant to do this mighty task, but God assures him that He will be with him (v11-12). Moses asks God what His name is in case the people ask. The name "I AM" is Yahweh and means "to be" (v13-15). It also means "totality" and can be "I AM truly He who exists". Moses is to take the elders of the Hebrew families to meet Pharaoh. They are to ask Pharaoh if they can go for three days and make sacrifices to their God. Pharaoh will refuse (v16-19). God will deliver the Israelites from Egypt as prophesied by Joseph in Genesis 50:24. They come out with great possessions just as God told Abram in Genesis 15:14.

Moses offers up more excuses not to go to Pharaoh in chapter 4:1-17. God gives him three signs so the people will believe he is sent by God and the message is true. The first sign is a rod/serpent, the second sign is a leprous hand, and the third sign is water will be turned into blood. Moses complains that he does not speak well, but God promises to be "his mouth" for him as he speaks (v11-12). Moses angers God by asking Him to send someone else in verses 13-17. Moses' brother Aaron will go with him and be his spokesman, and God will teach them both what to say. Moses takes his family and heads to Egypt (v18-20). The Lord reminds Moses of what he is to do as he meets with Pharaoh in verses 21-23. God will harden Pharaoh's heart (4:21; 7:3; 9:12; 10:1, 20, 27; 11:10; 14:4, 8, 17) but Pharaoh will also harden his own heart (7:13, 14, 22; 8:15, 19, 32; 9:7, 34, 35; 13:15). Verses 24-26 can be confusing, but these verses are more than likely caused by the failure of Moses to circumcise his son which is a sign of the covenant. Zipporah has to do it because Moses did not (Gen. 17:10-14). In verses 27-31, Aaron and Moses finally meet and visit the elders of the Israelites who believe all the words spoken to them.

Moses and Aaron go to meet Pharaoh in Exodus 5:1-5, and just as God had said he refused to let the people go. In verses 5-14, Pharaoh had instructed his foremen to not provide straw for the Israelites to make bricks. This made their task even harder. The Hebrew foremen complain to Pharaoh about finding straw to make bricks, and Pharaoh accuses them of being lazy (v15-19). The Hebrew foreman also asks God to judge Moses and Aaron for being troublemakers and causing them to stink (abhorrent) to Pharaoh. Moses complains to God in verses 22-23. Moses wonders why God even sent him if He was not going to deliver them like He said He would.

Tuesday • 1 Samuel 11-15

In 1 Samuel 11:1-11 Saul defeats the Ammonites after they threaten the people of Jabesh Gilead. The putting out of the right eye was usually for violation of a previous covenant. Saul, filled with the Spirit of God, defeats the Ammonites by a surprise attack. In verses 12-15, Samuel makes plans to anoint Saul as king in Gilgal. Three significant events happen here between Samuel and Saul-Saul: is anointed king, Samuel rebukes Saul for not waiting on him (13:7-14), and Saul is rejected as king (15:10-26).

1 Samuel 12 continues the coronation of Saul as king. It also shows a transfer of leadership from Samuel to Saul (v1-2). In verses 3-5 Samuel contrasts his innocent behavior with his earlier warnings over the conditions under a king (1 Sam. 8). Samuel gives a brief history of Israel in verses 6-13, highlighting their decision and desire for an earthly king (8:19-20; 10:19; 12:12) when the Lord was their King. Samuel warns them of the blessing of obedience, and the cursings of disobedience in verses 14-15. The sign of rain in verses 16-18 is to show the people their own evil motives in asking for a king. In response, the people fear the Lord and Samuel and ask him to intervene for them (v19 notice it says "your" not "our" God). Samuel encourages the people to serve the Lord, not to serve idols and to live a life pleasing to God (v20-23). Samuel promises to continue to teach them and reminds them, once again to fear the Lord and not act wickedly (23-25).

1 Samuel 13:1-15 records the first signs of Saul's decline in his role as king. Philistine forces were gathering at Michmash, which led to mass defections of the Israelite army. Saul proceeds to make the sacrifice himself without waiting on Samuel as the Lord had commanded. His disobedience in chapter 13 and chapter 15 led to him being rejected as king by God. God would find someone who was "after His own heart". In verses 16-23, the Philistines begin to raid the depleted forces of Saul and Jonathan. The men of Israel had nothing to fight with because there was no blacksmith in Israel at the time.

In 1 Samuel 14:1-14, Jonathan and his armor bearer take the initiative to fight the Philistines. They believed the Lord would fight for Israel, and deliver them into their hand. In verses 15-23, confusion ensues in the Philistine camp (promised in Deut. 7:23 when they trust in the Lord). Saul and his men join the fight, along with those who had previously deserted the battle, as the Lord rescued Israel. Verses 24-30 set the stage for confrontation with his son Jonathan. This confrontation was due to an oath Saul placed over his men to not eat food during the day. Not aware of this oath, Jonathan eats honey found in the forest. No longer under oath, the men eat meat still containing blood which was forbidden under the law (Lev. 17:10-14). Saul seeks to absolve the men of their guilt and builds an altar to the Lord. The reference to it being his first altar probably refers to his lack of devotion to the Lord. The confrontation with Jonathan is found in verses 36-46. Here, he seeks the Lord's advice to continue fighting with the Philistines, but receives no answer. Knowing there must be sin in the camp, he finds out that Jonathan ate honey in the forest while under oath. Saul is prepared to take his son's life, but the troops intervene for Jonathan because he had fought alongside them with the Lord. In verses 47-52 we see Saul's genealogy and a reference to adding people to his troops in verse 52, which will include David.

In 1 Samuel 15:1-9, the Lord commands that Saul destroy the Amalekites for refusing to fear God (Deut. 25:18). Destroy (*herem*) means "do not spare" and literally means "to kill everything that breathes". After directing the Kenites to leave, Saul and the army battle the Amalekites, but spare the king and the best animals. In verses 10-21 Saul is renounced by Samuel for disobeying the Lord's command, and Saul tries to shift the blame to his troops. Saul has been rejected as king of Israel because he rejected the Lord's commands (v22-31). The tearing of Samuel's robe symbolizes the torn relationship between Samuel and Saul, and also Saul's kingship has been torn away from him.

Wednesday • Mark 7-8

At the beginning of chapter 7 we see confrontation between Jesus and the Pharisees regarding His teaching. The Pharisees believed that their tradition was on par with Scripture. Jesus clarifies the distinctions between their tradition and the actual words of God. Jesus labels them "hypocrites" because their worship is merely outward, and not from a desire of the heart to live a life pleasing to God. The Pharisees even abused the command to take care of their parents by legally excluding themselves from doing it (v10-13). Jesus goes on to explain that it is what comes from the heart that causes defilement (v14-23). The Pharisees hearts were evil and selfish, so therefore their deeds are evil and selfish. There are still Pharisees among the church today. People hold on to traditions rather than clinging to and obeying the Word of God. It is easier for people to obey their own traditions than to obey God's Word, and this may be due to their unconverted hearts.

In verses 24-30 Jesus heals a Gentile woman's daughter. This is also within the same territory that Elijah performed miracles for a Gentile widow (1 Kgs 17). The point of the story is that Jesus initially came to Israel, so the Israelites get fed first. The woman understands, claiming that all she wants is the crumbs that fall from the master's table. This demonstrates her faith. In verses 31-37 Jesus heals a man who is blind and mute, again in Gentile territory. Verse 33 shows that Jesus communicated to the man what He was going to do. The words of verse 37 echo Genesis 1:31, "God saw all that He had made, and it was very good".

Jesus performs another miracle in Gentile territory by feeding the 4,000 in Mark 8:1-10. One of the main themes in verses 1-21 is a failure to understand the miracles that Jesus did. The Pharisees come to dispute with Jesus, once again asking Him to perform a sign in verses 11-12. The signs He has been performing testify to who He is, and they demonstrate that the Messiah and His kingdom are here. Jesus warns the disciples of the doctrine and teachings (leaven) of the Pharisees and Sadducees in verses 13-21. He also shows the side effects of false doctrine and rebukes them for their lack of faith in feeding the 5,000 and 4,000. Leaven probably does not just stand for sin. It would also include the type of thinking and attitudes of the Pharisees and the Herodians that they display in Scripture. They are both worldly groups, hypocrites, and both seek things of the world.

In verses 22-26, Jesus heals the blind man in Bethsaida. This healing is only recorded in Mark. The opening of the man's eyes foretells the opening of Peter's spiritual eyes to see Jesus for who He is-The Messiah (v27-30). In verses 31-33 Jesus predicts His death for the first time, which also signals the movement toward Jerusalem and the cross. Jesus rebukes Peter for his words, trying to get Jesus to avoid the cross just as Satan did at the beginning of His ministry (Matt. 4:8-10). True followers of Jesus must deny self and take up one's cross to become a follower of Jesus (v34-38). This is the first of three occasions that Jesus explains to the disciples the cost of discipleship (9:31,10:33). These actions demonstrate that Jesus, not self, is at the center of someone's life. Denying Jesus may help one survive physically, but eternally they will be lost. Before believers receive a crown they must first bear the cross.

Thursday • Job 25-26

Job 25 is the last we hear from Job's three friends. Bildad knows that God is exalted and that he shows His power on the earth. But Bildad's God is inaccessible, especially to someone like Job, who he viewed as hopeless. Man is like a maggot or a worm to God. In chapter 26, Job rebukes Bildad's claims. In verses 1-4, Job again claims his friends have been no help-especially the recent words of Bildad. In the rest of this chapter, Job will proclaim how mighty and majestic God is. In verses 5-6 God is omniscient, and no one can be hid from the eyes of God (Ps. 139:7-10). Job boasts of God's omnipotence in verses 7-8 and His kingship in verse 9. God also is the ruler of the night and the day (v11). In verses 12-13, God is also the ruler over creation and nature. Job ends in verse 14 with a declaration that even all the things he has described are just a tiny glimpse of the power of God.

Friday • Isaiah 25-30

After the themes of judgment on the nations, in the next few chapters, Isaiah will be comprised of songs of praise and salvation to God. The focus of the songs and praise is on God's great acts, and also God's faithfulness. Isaiah 25-27 can be pictured as taking place in history, but most of these verses portray the future as God rules and reigns over the earth. In Isaiah 25:1-5, God is praised for being the refuge and shelter over His people (Deut. 33:27). God prepares a great feast for His people in verses 6-8. Paul quotes the first part of verse 8 in 1 Corinthians 15:54 when he speaks of the resurrection. Verse 9 praises the Lord for a completed salvation. In verses 10-12, God's hand is pictured on Zion pouring out blessing while His feet tread on Moab in judgment.

Isaiah 26 can be divided into three parts: praise (v1-6), prayer (v7-18), and prophecy (v19-21). In verses 1-6 praise is given to God because He is the One who gives strength and peace to His people while also providing salvation for them. The righteous nation is made up of people who have trusted in the Lord for salvation. Judgment falls upon the prideful city in verses 5-6 and the people of God are seen trampling over it, sharing in the victory. The righteous and the wicked are contrasted in verses 7-11 as the righteous learn from God, while the wicked will not learn. After this contrast Isaiah speaks about God's dealings with Israel (those who learn from God), and the other nations' (who do not learn from God) destruction. In verses 16-18 the people will one day come to God in great distress because of foreign oppression. It will be only through the Lord's Servant (52:13-53:12) that the salvation they long for will be accomplished. In verses 19-21 prophecy is spoken about the resurrection (v19), the coming exile of the people (v20), and future judgment (v21).

In the opening of chapter 27, God is pictured as a mighty warrior bringing judgment (v1). In verses 2-6 God is pictured as taking care of His vineyard (Israel; Isa. 5) by caring and tending for its needs. In verse 6 this plant is seen as filling the whole earth with its fruit (Gen. 49:22). In verses 7-11 God is going to punish His people to bring them to a place of repentance by removing them from the land. The Assyrians and the Babylonians would both invade from the east. In verse 12, the whole nation will be brought back together after it is purified during the time of exile. One day people (especially Gentiles) will come to Jerusalem to worship the Lord.

Isaiah 28 is directed toward the northern kingdom of Israel (Ephraim). In verses 1-4 the Assyrians are pictured as a coming storm that will come upon them suddenly. Verses 5-6 may refer to the last days, but in Isaiah's context the people will look to the Lord for strength. In verses 7-8, the leaders of the people are pictured as being drunk and cannot provide spiritual guidance to the people. In verses 9-15 judgment is coming because they did not heed the words of the Lord and respond in faith. Their unwillingness to listen and going their own way, along with their sin has turned the words of the Lord into meaningless words (v10, 13). If they would listen to the Lord

He would be a sanctuary for them. If they refuse to listen, He would be a stone of stumbling that they would fall over (v16-19). The people have made their choice and soon the Assyrians would devastate Israel, and later the Babylonians would destroy Judah (v20-22). Isaiah offers a bit of wisdom in verses 23-29 on listening to the Lord. The agricultural references represent God's dealing with the people differently at different times (Heb. 1:1-3).

Isaiah 29 concerns the judgment on Jerusalem (Ariel), or Judah, which is the southern kingdom. In verses 1-4 the people delighted in their feasts and believed all was well between them and God, but He was about to come in judgment. Those God sends to judge Jerusalem will overtake the city, but also be punished themselves (v5-8). Isaiah's ministry of speaking to people who would not hear is seen in verses 9-12 (Isa. 6:9-10). Neither the people who could read or could not would heed the words of the prophet (spiritually blind). Not only were the spiritually blind but they had become "religious" but had no relationship (v13-16). These conditions will be no more one day in the future as people will hear and see the words of the Lord (v17-21). The Lord will bring His people back to the land as they become aware of how holy God is and of His goodness toward them (v22-24).

Isaiah 30:1-5 returns to the theme of Judah making alliances with foreign nations against Assyria instead of trusting in the Lord to deliver them and because of their continual sin. The people sought an alliance with Egypt, but even Egypt would be no match for them (v6-7). The people no longer wanted to hear the words of the Lord, but only what they wanted to hear. Because of this, Isaiah was told to write the prophecy down (v8-11). Their trust in foreign powers would be their downfall, and judgment would come swiftly and would be thorough (v12-14). God had promised in the past (Lev. 26:7-8) victories for obedience and defeat for disobedience, but the people were unwilling to trust in the Lord when given another opportunity (v15-18). Verses 19-26 speaks of a time after the exile when God will pour out grace upon His people. They will once again hear and respond to the Word of God, and He will bring healing to them. Assyria will be judged in verses 27-33. This judgment is pictured as a powerful fire, overflowing waters, sieve of judgment, and a horse led to destruction.

Saturday • 1 Corinthians 11-12

In 1 Corinthians 11:2-16 Paul addresses the covering of women's heads. This was a custom in Corinth. Some believe Paul is actually speaking of a veil, while others believe he is speaking of a woman's hair. An adulterous woman would leave her hair down, and if accused and found guilty would have her head shaved. Whether it is a veil or hair, the same principles emerge from the text. Paul is speaking about the functions of the person as opposed to their worth. Both males and females are equipped to serve the Lord, but each function differently in their unique roles. Paul, while addressing customs in Corinth, is giving timeless principles to you and me.

In verses 17-34, Paul continues to address issues that occur when they gather to worship. Here he addresses their observance of the Lord's Supper. In verse 17 Paul tells them that when they come together to celebrate Lord's Supper they are doing more harm than good. It appears there was a great divide in the church between the rich and poor (v18-19). They were making a mockery of the Lord's Supper through their behavior, which led to disunity in the church (v19-22). Worse yet, they had lost the true meaning of the Lord's Supper and needed to be reminded that it was about the sacrifice of Christ (v23-36). Paul sternly warns them that they should examine themselves so that they would not be guilty of profaning the Lord's Supper (v27-34). Celebrating the Lord's Supper is a special time for believers and for the church to remember all that Christ has done for believers.

In 1 Corinthians 12:1-11 Paul addresses another cause of disunity and division in the church-spiritual gifts. Paul wanted them to know and understand the gifts that had been given to them by the Holy Spirit (v1). Before they knew Christ they were "carried away" (led like a prisoner) by the idols they worshiped (Read Ps. 115:1-8). No true believer would say Christ is cursed, and no one can say that Jesus is Lord unless they are true believers and have the Holy Spirit (v3). Paul writes that the gifts are many (v4), there are many ways to use them (v5), and it is God who works through them (v6). The purpose of spiritual gifts was meant to bring unity and to help the church function, not to be a source of strife and division (v7). Each gift is given by the Holy Spirit to build up the body, not to tear it down.

In the last section of the chapter, Paul uses the human body as an example to emphasize the importance of each church member and their use of spiritual gifts (v12-31). While there is diversity in the body, with many having different gifts and services, this is what produces true unity in the church. If the church doesn't work together, we all become less effective in ministering with our gifts (v14-17). Every gift is important to the body of Christ and we should not want gifts that others have, but use the gifts that God has given us to bring glory to Him. Without each person using his or her gifts, we all become ineffective (v18-21). No matter the amount of giftedness or abilities the body of Christ is to be in unity supporting and loving one another (v22-26). All true believers are a part of the body, and none are excluded (v27). God has also given the church many gifts to use within the body (v28), but not all have the same gifts (v29-30). The gifts and their use caused much division within the church at Corinth, which is why Paul in the next chapter will show them "a more excellent way".

Cover to Cover CHALLENGE

Week 14

Sunday • Psalm 45-47

Welcome to week 14 of the *Cover to Cover Challenge*! 1 Peter 2:2 says "As newborn babes, desire the pure milk of the word, that you may grow thereby." Many books have been written on the subject of Christian growth. Here Peter prescribes one way to truly grow: to cultivate a desire to be in God's Word. I hope that has happened in your heart during the first 13 weeks of the *Cover to Cover Challenge*. Continue to pray for understanding and pray for each other as we continue reading the Word of God together.

Psalm 45 is a royal psalm that is believed to have been sung at a royal couple's wedding. This psalm will describe the bridegroom in verses 2-9, and the bride in verses 10-15. In this psalm we can see Jesus (bridegroom) being married to His bride (people of God). After the skillful writer pays honor to the king, he describes the bridegroom (v2-9). His speech is wise and showered with grace (v2). He will be prosperous because He rules with truth, humility, and righteousness (v3-5). His rule will be forever, and it will be established throughout all the earth (v6-7). Because of His righteous rule, His kingdom will be blessed by God (v8-9). The bride is to be loyal, submissive, and worship the King (v10-12). The bride wears the finest of clothing, and she and her companions are filled with gladness and rejoicing for her marriage to the King (v13-15). The psalm concludes with one more look at the King and the blessing of being married to Him (v16-17).

Psalm 46 is praise for the presence of God. You may recognize some of it from the song "A Mighty Fortress is Our God". In verses 1-3 the theme is God's protection. Here, He is pictured as being a shelter (refuge) for His people. In this shelter there is no fear despite what circumstances may come. The theme of verses 4-7 is God's presence. Again despite what circumstances may come, God has assured His people that His presence is there with them. In verses 8-11, God's preeminence (power, authority) is on display. Once again, despite the circumstances, God is still in control.

Psalm 47 praises the King for His rule over all the earth. In verses 1-2, the people are encouraged to clap their hands and shout because of the power of the great King. The reason they are doing this is because of God's past acts on their behalf. These acts include subduing the nations and giving them an inheritance (v3-4). The King also reigns victorious, and the people are once again encouraged to sing praises to His name (v5-6). In verses 7-9, the King's universal reign over all the earth is proclaimed whether other nations acknowledge it or not.

COVER TO COVER CHALLENGE

Monday • Exodus 6-8

Moses and Aaron have appeared before Pharaoh and have been denied their request. This brought judgment from Pharaoh down upon the children of Israel in order to make their life harder. Moses complains to God about why He even sent him, and why He didn't deliver His people. In Exodus 6:1-8 God answers Moses' question. In the passage, God affirms to Moses that "I am the Lord" on four separate occasions. The promises made to Abraham, Isaac, and Jacob would soon become reality to Moses and the children of Israel. In verses 6-8 there are three promises of redemption (bring you out, free you, redeem you), two promises that they will be His people (take you as My own, I will be your God), and two promises of land (bring you into the land, give it to you). Moses again goes to the children of Israel, but they do not listen because they are discouraged (anguish of spirit) and are still in bondage (v9-12). The genealogy list in verses 14-27 shows that God choosing Moses had nothing to do with who he was, but simply because God chose him to deliver Israel.

In Exodus 7:1-5, the Lord directs Moses and Aaron to once again return to Pharaoh and ask him to let the people go. It is during these plagues that the people of Israel and Egypt would know the great I AM (Yahweh). In verses 6-13 Moses and Aaron appear before Pharaoh and perform the sign, only to see the magicians of Egypt duplicate their sign. God proved He was greater when Aaron's rod swallowed the Egyptians' rods. The first plague is turning the waters of Egypt into blood and is found in verses 14-25. Despite the horrors of this plague, Pharaoh still refused to let the children of Israel go and his heart grew harder still.

Exodus 8:1-15 records the second plague of frogs on the land of Egypt. Pharaoh does acknowledge the power of the Lord, and says he will let the people go if the frogs go away. Moses intercedes and the frogs die, but Pharaoh refuses to let them go and his heart grows harder still. The third plague of lice (gnats) is recorded in verses 16-19. This one could not be duplicated by the magicians, and they do acknowledge it was the hand of God. The fourth plague is the plague of flies and is found in verses 20-32. Still, Pharaoh hardens his heart and goes back on his word to let them go and sacrifice. In the fourth, fifth, seventh, ninth, and tenth plagues the Egyptians are the only ones harmed by the plagues, while the children of Israel are not. The innocent are not affected, only the guilty.

Exodus 9:1-7 continues with the fifth plague on the cattle of the land. All of the Egyptian cattle died, but none of the children of Israel's did. The sixth plague of boils is the first time that human life was in danger, but still Pharaoh will not let the people go (v8-12). The seventh plague of hail is seen in verses 13-35 and reveals even more purposes for the plagues. The people would know that there is only one God, know there is none like Him, and His name would be known in all the earth as a result of the plagues (v14-15). Pharaoh again hardens his heart even after admitting he had sinned.

Tuesday • 1 Samuel 16-20

1 Samuel 16 marks the middle of 1 Samuel, and can be split into two passages. In verses 1-13 Samuel is sent to anoint David as king, and he receives the Spirit of the Lord. In verses 14-23, we see the Spirit of the Lord depart from Saul. Samuel goes to Bethlehem to anoint one of Jesse's sons as king (v1-5). Samuel is impressed by Eliab's appearance, but it is the Lord who looks upon the heart. None of the sons who are present are chosen (v6-10). The youngest son of Jesse, David, is anointed with oil and receives the Spirit of the Lord. It can probably be assumed that the spirit that torments Saul in verses 14-23 is the same spirit that causes Saul so many mental and psychological problems. His servants, perceiving that a spirit is bothering him, call for one of Jesse's sons to play the harp. David is described in verses 18-19 in eloquent terms that are fit for a king.

1 Samuel 17 is about David versus Goliath which takes place in the Valley of Elah. The Philistine giant is twice called a champion and is over 9 feet tall, while David is a small shepherd with only a sling. The Israelite army is afraid and petrified of Goliath, who came out twice a day for forty days to taunt them. Upon hearing Goliath speak, David becomes angered instead of afraid. He is angered over Goliath defying God, and he offers to slay the Philistine giant just as he had the lion and the bear. David had experienced the deliverance of the Lord in those situations and was sure that he would again. Goliath is not just fighting David, but David's God. David kills Goliath with only a sling and one small stone, and the Philistines flee knowing who the only true God is.

In 1 Samuel 18, Saul's hatred for David will only increase. In verses 1-4, David and Saul's son Jonathan make a covenant of friendship with one another that is symbolized by Jonathan giving David his robe. David's continued success as a warrior is brought out as David is praised more than Saul for his victories in battle (v5-8). Saul becomes paranoid about David. He tries to kill him personally, and also by sending him out to fight the Philistines on numerous occasions (v9-19). Saul's actions only tighten the bond between David and the people. David is offered both daughters of Saul, but one is given away to another man while David has to fight the Philistines for the other (v20-26). It becomes apparent to Saul that the Lord is with David, and he would remain David's enemy for the rest of his life (v27-30).

In 1 Samuel 19, David begins his life as a fugitive on the run from Saul. Saul even goes as far as asking Jonathan and his men to kill David as Jonathan pleads for David's life (v1-7). David once again fights and prevails over the Philistines, angering Saul once again (v8-10). Some believe verses 11-17 are the setting for Psalm 59, but it is not certain. Saul once again tries to kill David with a spear. David flees for his life, and Michal helps him escape (v11-17). Saul sends men to capture David, but the Lord spoils their plans (v18-24). Saul setting aside his robe is symbolic of his rule, showing that he is not fit to be king.

David and Jonathan's friendship is highlighted in chapter 20. Before the events of this chapter are over, Jonathan will see the true intentions of Saul for David. David comes up with a simple plan during the New Moon festival to explain his absence. Saul's reaction would show Jonathan and David his true intentions. Based upon the earlier covenant they had made with one another, Jonathan assures David that he would tell him if his father wanted to hurt David. After the confrontation with his father, Jonathan sees that the true intentions of Saul were to kill David. Saul, in his anger, even tried to kill his own son. Apart from a brief encounter later on, this will be the last time David and Jonathan see one another.

Wednesday • Mark 9-10

Mark 9:1-13 begins with the transfiguration of Jesus before Peter, James, and John. The word "transfigured" means that something on the inside becomes visible from the outside, or that there is an outward change that comes from within. Most believe these three disciples saw Jesus in all His glory upon the mountain. Clouds, when spoken of in Scripture, point to the presence of God (Ex. 13:21-22, 40:34-38). Moses and Elijah also appear. This represented the law and the prophets which foretold of the coming of the Messiah. Moses spoke of Christ (Deut. 18:15, Luke 24:37, John 1:45) and Elijah represented the prophets whom spoke of His coming. Luke tells us they were discussing Jesus' death (Luke 9:31). The reference to Elijah having already come regards John the Baptist (Matt. 17:13) who pointed people to Christ and confronted sin.

The last instance of casting out a demon in Mark's gospel is found in verses 14-29. It seems that while Jesus and the other disciples were on the mountain, this event had taken place. Why were the disciples unable to cast the demon out? It was due to their own lack of faith. This was demonstrated by the conversation between Jesus and the father of the boy. The question is not whether or not Jesus could do it, but whether or not he believed that Jesus could. Every believer probably has experienced a moment like the father in the story. There is nothing wrong with asking God to help our unbelief.

In verses 30-32 Jesus predicts His death for a second time. In verses 33-37 the disciples had been arguing over who would the greatest in the kingdom. Their self-centered attitude is contrasted with Jesus' statement of His coming death and resurrection. True greatness is sacrificing self through serving others. Matthew helps bring this principle to light. In Matthew 18:4 Jesus says "Whoever humbles himself like this child, he is the greatest in the kingdom of heaven".

In verses 38-41, another person is casting out demons in Jesus' name. The casting out of demons is an act of God, so the man must have been a believer in Christ. Verse 41 relates that every good deed will have its own reward (Matt. 25:31-46). Mark 9:42-50 corresponds with Matthew 5:29-30. What is added in Mark is "their worm does not die, and the fire is not quenched" when describing the torments of hell. The Old Testament context of Isaiah 66:24 will help explain this. Isaiah 66:24 is a reference to what will happen to those who have rebelled against God. The term "gehenna" is the final place for the wicked (lake of fire). Gehenna refers to the Valley of Hinnom just outside of Jerusalem where in the Old Testament children were sacrificed to Molech. In Jesus' day it was a garbage dump that was constantly burning.

In Mark 10:1-12, Jesus teaches on the subject of divorce. It is word for word in its similarity to Matthew 19. The Pharisees once again ask Jesus a question about divorce which was designed to trap Him. This inquiry is from the Jewish male perspective which gave no dignity to the woman. The Pharisees refer to Deuteronomy 24:1-4 and the writing of divorcement given by Moses, but they misinterpret it as a command. Many Jewish men believed they could divorce for any reason. Jesus corrects their flawed view of marriage and divorce by citing Genesis 1:27 and Genesis 2:24. Jesus, within this context, teaches that the only reason for divorce is adultery. In verses 13-16 Jesus uses the example of children to convey the response of anyone who wants to enter the kingdom of God-it must be by faith. The story of the rich young ruler who was unwilling to separate himself from his riches to follow Christ is found in verses 17-27 (Matt. 6:24; Matt. 19:16-22). Jewish leaders believed if a man was rich he was blessed by God and was surely going to heaven. Jesus teaches the opposite (v23-26) in the previous passage in verses 13-16. Jesus tells the man that there is one thing he lacked (needed). Outwardly the man had everything but he was missing something on the inside. His riches were keeping him from making a true heartfelt commitment to God. It is sad that "things" (possessions, wealth, social standing) will keep people from placing their faith in Christ. The simple truth here is that salvation is impossible without Jesus.

In verses 28-31 Jesus teaches His disciples about their place in the kingdom and the reward they will receive. The rich young ruler would not give up his riches so it is natural that the disciples who had given up everything to follow Jesus would contemplate their place in the kingdom. They had given up everything to follow Jesus and to spread the gospel. Not everyone is rewarded in this life, but all who are obedient will be rewarded in heaven. After He predicted His death for the third time (v32-34), Jesus teaches again about serving others in response to James and John wanting to sit by Jesus' side in the kingdom (v35-45). Cup (Isa. 51:17, Ps. 23:5) and baptism (Ps. 69:15) were Old Testament symbols of suffering. Jesus is asking them "Are you willing to suffer the way I am going to suffer?" They will suffer, not for the sin of the world, but for being followers of Christ. Verses 32-45 also cover Jesus' two main themes as His death approaches: to prepare the disciples for His death, and to prepare them to be without His physical presence. The healing of blind Bartimaeus is the final miracle before the passion week in Mark's gospel (v46-52).

Thursday • Job 27-28

In chapter 27, Job continues his speech from the previous chapter where he rebuked his friend's assessment of him and spoke of the power of God. Here in chapter 27 Job defends himself in verses 1-12, and speaks about the punishment of the wicked in verses 13-23. In verses 1-6, Job makes an oath to proclaim his innocence before his friends. Job once again addresses his friends and asks God to turn their accusations against him upon their own head (v7-10). Verses 11-12 introduce Job's discourse in verses 13-23 that tells that the wicked deserve God's wrath. Job paints a very grim picture of the fate of the wicked in this life.

Job 28 is a speech about wisdom. Wisdom must be searched for (v1-11), wisdom has a surpassing value (v12-19), and wisdom is found only in being submitted to God (v20-28). Job describes the search for wisdom with illustrations from ancient mining practices (v1-11). The main point of using these illustrations is found in verses 12-14. Even if these places could be searched out completely, wisdom would not be found there. In verses 15-19 the surpassing value of wisdom is shown through the many mentions of precious gems and metals. Job stresses that only God knows where wisdom is, and only He possesses it. It was there at creation (Prov. 3:18-19) and we must look to Him for it (v28). From the New Testament we also learn that wisdom is found in Christ (Eph.3:8-10; Col. 2:2-3).

Friday • Isaiah 31-37

God pronounced a woe upon Judah for seeking an alliance with Egypt instead of turning to Him for help in Isaiah 31. Judah was actually showing that they trusted in Egypt more than they did God. By doing this, both would fall (v1-3). If they would turn to the Lord of Hosts, He would defend them and make them the object of His special care (v4-5). The Lord calls upon the people to return to Him and rebuke their idol worship in verses 6-7. The battle spoken of in verses 8-9 is recorded in 2 Kings 18 & 19, and mentioned again in Isaiah 36 & 37.

Isaiah 32 concerns the conditions in the messianic reign (v1-8), warnings of judgment (v9-15), and the blessedness of God's rule (v16-20). The scene in verses 1-8 shows the passing away of human government, and the reign of Messiah and His government. When government is righteous it offers protection for the people. Under His rule the leaders will rule justly as opposed to the leadership Judah was currently experiencing. If the leaders are blind (not following the Lord), the people will be blind also (Matt. 15:14). From the examples of Israel and Judah we see that a nation gets the leader it deserves. In verses 9-14 the sin of complacency is in view, and the women are called to mourn over the land. The land will bear no fruit because of the judgment of God. In verses 15-20 we read that judgment will turn to blessing where justice prevails, righteousness rules, and peace spreads throughout the kingdom.

Isaiah 33 opens up with a woe pronounced on the Assyrian army (v1). The people of Judah cry out for the Lord to help as the enemy approaches (v2-4). After a doxology of praise in verses 5-6, the whole land is in mourning because of their current condition (v7-9). The Lord calls out to the whole world to see what He is going to do to the Assyrian army in judgment (v10-16). The deliverance from the Assyrian army moves Isaiah to picture the Messiah sitting on His throne where God will dwell with His people forever (v17-24). Verse 22 covers the three periods of Israel's history. This shows that the Lord has always been their Judge, Lawgiver, and King.

In Isaiah 34 God pronounces judgment on all the nations of the world, especially Edom which was not spoken about in the judgment speeches in chapters 13-23. Divine retribution is coming upon the nations that do not follow the Lord (v1-4). Edom was one of the great enemies of Israel, and God chooses them to personify the destruction that will come upon the nations (v5-7). It will be desolate as the judgment of God is complete, and just for how the nations dealt with Him and His people (v8-15). In verses 16-17 God tells them to search the book (probably Isaiah's scroll) and see if what He has said comes to pass. Scripture testifies of God's truth and His faithfulness to it.

Isaiah 35 fits many contexts. Its words picture the return from exile, describe the coming Messianic kingdom, and verses 5-6 describe the ministry of Jesus the Messiah (Luke 7:18-23). All of these describe the blessings of God's people in each of those periods.

Isaiah 36-39 contains the story of the Lord delivering Judah from the hands of Assyria. Hezekiah is faced with a decision to trust in Egypt or the Lord. You will notice in chapter 36 the representative of Assyria who speaks with Hezekiah's men is very brash and confident of their upcoming victory. It would be useless, according to the representative of Assyria, to trust in Egypt (v6), the Lord (v7), or Hezekiah (v14-19) against them. Upon hearing the news, Hezekiah goes to the temple to pray and sends for Isaiah (37:1-2). Isaiah tells them not to be afraid of Assyria (v3-7). Hezekiah receives a letter from the king of Assyria with more threats concerning trusting in the Lord (v8-13). Hezekiah prays to the Lord to deliver them so all the world will know that He is Lord (v14-20). Isaiah prophesies about the Lord delivering His people (v21-25) and about the judgment upon Assyria (v26-29). The sign in verses 30-32 relates to the Lord delivering Judah from Assyria. The Lord Himself repeats the prophecy of deliverance for Judah which shows His faithfulness to protect His people (v33-35). The Angel of the Lord (preincarnate Christ) kills 185,000 Assyrian soldiers, and they retreat back to Nineveh fulfilling the words of Isaiah and the Lord (v36-37). Verse 38 is proof that Judah's God is the only true God, while all others are powerless.

Saturday • 1 Corinthians 13-14

In 1 Corinthians 12 Paul instructed them on the importance of gifts, which divided them because of their lack of love in using them. Here in chapter 13, Paul is stating that the right use of gifts includes using them in love toward one another. No matter how great the gifts may seem to be, if they are not used in love they are useless (v1-3). The gift of tongues is useless without love (v1), prophecy and faith are useless without love (v2), and living a sacrificial lifestyle is useless without love (v3). The personality of love is brought out by referencing what love does, and what love does not do (v4-8). Here is another way to read the verses. In verse 4 we read that "love is not short-tempered (suffers long) and is good to others (kind even when treated badly), love does not get jealous (envy), love does not boast in itself (parade itself), and love is not proud (puffed up)". Verse 5 says "love is not dishonorable (behave rudely), it does not act selfishly (seek its own), it is not easily angered (provoked), and it keeps no record of wrongs (thinks no evil)". Verse 6 says "love does not rejoice in evil of any kind (iniquity), but rejoices in the truth". Verse 7 tells us that love "always protects (bears all things), and always trusts (believes all things)". The permanence of love is that it will always be practiced, and it is the greatest gift of all (v8b-13). We are to pursue love by loving the Lord and loving others (by using our gifts) because this is who God is-love (14:1a).

1 Corinthians 14 can be titled "the pursuit of love". Now that they know about their gifts (ch.12) and how to administer them (ch.13), Paul now calls them to pursue love through the use of their gifts. Paul focuses on the gift that was abused in Corinth-the gift of tongues. It is probable that those who had the gift of tongues in Corinth believed themselves to be superior to those who could not, considering the depth Paul goes in order to deal with it. When gifts are used in the right manner they should bring unity to the church, not division as they have done. Paul argues in this chapter that the gift of prophecy is preferred over tongues because it builds up the church (v1-5). In verse 1 Paul wants them to pursue (chase persistently) the love he describes in chapter 13.

This type of love will keep them from abusing spiritual gifts. For most of this chapter Paul will also contrast the gift of tongues with prophecy. Prophecy is to be desired because it edifies (strengthens), exhorts (encourages), and comforts (v3). Speaking in tongues does edify the one speaking but prophecy edifies the whole church (v4). Prophecy is superior to tongues if tongues are not interpreted (v5).

In verses 6-19, Paul addresses the situation of tongue speaking in the church at Corinth. These verses make it plain that tongues must be interpreted or there is no edifying of believers. Just picture trying to understand someone speaking French when you do not speak it or understand it in anyway. There can be no communication because there is no understanding. Tongues only edify when they are interpreted, but the people at Corinth only used them to boast about themselves (addressed in v20-25). Paul tells them to use what gifts build up the church (v12, 19). In verses 20-25 we read that tongues are a sign for unbelievers, but prophecy is for all. Prophesy brings conviction and builds up, while an uninterpreted tongue brings confusion.

In verses 26-40, Paul gives guidelines for using tongues and prophecy in times of worship. He highlights the importance of being able to understand and edify one another. Their times of worship were disorderly and brought confusion into the church because of their abuse of the gifts. Each part of the service (list in v26) is to be regulated and done in order starting with tongues (v27-28) and prophecy (v28-31). The theme here is order and edification. It must be orderly for anyone to be edified (built up), or otherwise it will end up confusing all (v32-33). A true prophet will acknowledge that what Paul says is from the Lord, but if they do not they should not be recognized (v37-38). In closing Paul again addresses that he preferred prophesy to be done in the worship service, but not to the point that tongues would be neglected (v39-40).

Cover to Cover Challenge

Week 15

Sunday • Psalm 48-50

Welcome to week 15 of the *Cover to Cover Challenge*! We pray you are enjoying the Bible study plan and being in God's Word together. Continue to pray for understanding and for the Holy Spirit to move in your life, your family, your church, and our nation. 2 Chronicles 7:14 says "If My people who are called by My name will humble themselves, and pray and seek My face, and turn from their wicked ways, then I will hear from heaven, and will forgive their sin and heal their land". While we as a nation are not ancient Israel, I believe the principles prescribed here are still the same. If God's people get right with Him and begin to live for Him, God will move in miraculous ways for His people. Reading God's Word together and praying together will take us in that direction.

Psalm 48 is a psalm that celebrates the presence of God with His people in the city of Zion. God is pictured in verses 1-3 as powerful and glorious, while His people enjoy His presence and protection over them. Because of God's presence their enemies went away in fear (v4-7), and in verses 8-11 the people of God think upon His ways and acknowledge that all things belong to Him. In verses 12-14, the people are invited to walk around Zion and see the protection of God over His people.

Psalm 49 is a psalm of wisdom. In verses 1-4, the psalmist invites everyone to listen to godly wisdom because it is available to all people. Verses 5-6 show the foolishness of trusting in wealth or material possessions in the face of death and adversities of life (v7-12). Death is the equalizer for all, whether rich or poor. The rich who have cared for themselves in this life will die, but those who are righteous will be victorious over death (v13-14). This happens not because they are rich, but because of their insensitivity toward God. The godly are those who are wise, and God rescues them from death (v15). Death bestows no favor to the rich, and if he is not wise he will perish just like an animal that dies (v16-20).

Psalm 50 concerns God being the judge of all people, but especially His covenant people. In verses 1-6 God calls all of His covenant people together for judgment, and calls heaven and earth to be a witness. God did not need the offerings of His people unless they were in true honor of His name because everything already belongs to Him (v7-15). We have and will continue to see these verses play out in the historical books and prophetic books of the Old Testament. In verses 16-21 God warns the wicked of rejecting His instructions and partaking with others who commit evil. Those who reject God have no other way of deliverance except to come to Him in repentance and faith (v22-23).

WEEK 15

Monday • Exodus 10-13

Exodus 10 contains the 8th and 9th plagues concerning locusts and darkness. In the plague of locusts (v1-20) there are two more added reasons why these events are taking place. The first is so future generations can see the miraculous hand of God. The second is to bring people to faith in the Lord. During this plague, even Pharaoh's officials questioned his answers to Moses and Aaron and encouraged him to let the people go which of course he does not. The ninth plague of darkness is unannounced like the 3rd and 6th plagues, and Pharaoh has had enough. He tells Moses and Aaron not to come see him again, and if they try it will be punishable by death.

Exodus 11 must have happened before they were told to go away from Pharaoh's presence. The Lord instructs Moses to prepare the people for the last plague, which will be the death of the firstborn in Egypt. In this plague the Lord Himself will go out.

Exodus 12 is the institution of the Passover. In verses 1-13, preparations were to be made to celebrate. The lamb was to be one year old because it was taking the place of Israel's firstborn, the bitter herbs were a reminder of the bitter years of service to the Egyptians, and the unleavened bread was to reflect the hurriedness of their escape from Egypt as well as the pure and clean heart needed to celebrate. Verses 14-20 add more specific preparations as this would become a feast they would keep throughout their years. Two new instructions are listed in verses 21-23 regarding applying the blood to the doorframe and stating that no one was to leave the house until morning. In verses 24-28 they are instructed on how to tell their children the significance of this event. We see them do just as the Lord commanded them to. This is a change from what we have been reading about the Israelite's obedience later in their history. The death of the firstborn and release of the Israelites occurs in verses 29-36, just as God had said (11:1). The Israelites leave with a mixed multitude which probably includes some Egyptians or other mixed races among them (v37-39). Verses 40-42 sum up the Israelite stay in Egypt as 430 years. Verses 43-51 contain more Passover regulations pertaining to who can and cannot participate.

In Exodus 13 the setting aside of the firstborn and the celebration of the Feast of Unleavened Bread is recorded in verses 1-16. The firstborn males from human and animals were to be dedicated and set apart for the Lord's use. In explaining this to later generations, notice in verse 8 how personal it is to be told-this is what the Lord did for me. The journey toward the Red Sea begins in verses 17-22. Now, the Israelites would have a visible symbol of the presence of God with them wherever they went. From 14:19 and 22:20-22 it seems the pillar was the Angel of the Lord.

Tuesday • 1 Samuel 21-25

In 1 Samuel 21 we see that David is fleeing from the presence of Saul, who is seeking to kill him. David travels to Nob, where Ahimelech gives him bread and a sword (v1-9). Jesus speaks of David eating the showbread in the temple (Matt. 12:1-8). Jesus is teaching that human needs take precedence over ceremonial law. Doeg the Edomite is introduced here, and he will play a larger role in chapter 22. In verses 10-15 David appears before Achish king of Gath pretending to be mad, and flees to a cave in Adullam.

1 Samuel 22:1-5 David is met by family and friends in Adullam. Bound together by adverse circumstances, David becomes the leader of over 400 men and entreats the king of Moab to allow his parents to stay there (David had Moabite blood in him) while he goes to the forest of Hereth. After learning where David is from Doeg, Saul (completely paranoid by this time) sends for Ahimelech and his family whom he accuses of conspiring with David (v6-23). Saul commands his officers to kill Ahimelech and the priests but they do not. Doeg steps in and

not only does he kill the priests, but goes to Nob and kills all but Abiathar. Abiathar will be David's priest the rest of his life, and both are now fugitives from Saul.

David delivers the people of Keilah from the hands of the Philistines in 1 Samuel 23:1-13. You will notice a contrast in this chapter that shows how David always seeks the Lord's guidance, and Saul always seeks human help in searching for David. Saul even believes the Lord had delivered David into his hand when he heard of David being in Keilah (v7). David continually seeks the Lord, and moves from place to place away from Saul and his army. Jonathan, Saul's son, comes to encourage David in the Wilderness of Ziph and to assure him that his father will not touch him (v. 14-23). In verses 24-29, David and his men are delivered from Saul as the Philistines begin to attack Israelite territory while David flees to En Gedi.

In 1 Samuel 24:1-7 Saul pursues David to En Gedi, and both end up in the same cave. David had opportunity to kill Saul, and was even encouraged by his men to do so, but would not harm the Lord's anointed. You can see from the previous chapter, the distinctive differences between Saul and David. In verses 8-15 David calls out to Saul. He assures Saul he would never harm him and that there is no reason Saul should be hunting him down. David asks the Lord to deliver him from Saul. In verses 16-22 Saul speaks to David and even contrasts his actions with those of David. Saul also knows that the kingdom is to be David's.

In 1 Samuel 25 Samuel dies and is mourned over by all the Israelites (v1). The rest of the chapter concerns the story of Nabal ("Fool") and his wife Abigail ("My Father is Joy"). Here, there is also a contrast between the evil of Nabal and the goodness of Abigail. This sets her up to be a perfect match for David at the end of the story. David sends men to ask for supplies from Nabal. He declines to help, and also insults David in his speech (v4-13). Upon hearing their servants recount how Nabal treated David's men, Abigail prepares the supplies David needs for his men while he prepares to go to war with Nabal (v14-19). Abigail sends her servants ahead with the supplies and follows after to meet David (v20-31). Abigail submits herself to David ("my master" and "your servant"), which is another contrast between her and Nabal's attitude toward David. She takes on Nabal's guilt and references Nabal as a "wicked man", "fool", and to "pay no attention to him" while asking David's forgiveness. Abigail does not want David to do anything that may keep him from ascending to the throne. David accepts her gift and acknowledges that God has used her to keep him from avenging himself to Nabal (v32-35). Upon telling Nabal about the gifts and supplies she has given David, Nabal's heart turns to stone and the Lord kills him ten days later (v36-38). In verses 39-44 David takes Abigail to be his wife, and we learn he has also married Ahinoam.

Wednesday • Mark 11-12

In Mark 11:1-11 Jesus enters Jerusalem fulfilling Zechariah 9:9, which refers to the Messiah. In verses 9-10 the shouts of Hosanna (save, deliver), and Son of David (Messiah) are shouts of praise and adoration for Jesus. The hope of the people following Jesus was that this would be the time that He would announce Himself as king over Israel. The cursing of the fig tree in verses 12-14 fits into the narrative of cleansing the temple in verses 15-19 and Jesus teaching on prayer in verses 20-24. When Jesus cleanses the temple He uses Isaiah 56:7 and Jeremiah 7:11 to condemn the practices that were taking place at the temple. They were not using the temple to be a witness to the nations, but to take advantage of the people just as the ancient Israelites had done. The cursing of the fig tree is an acted parable related to cleansing the temple, which shows His disgust with them (v12-14, 20-24). It also teaches the importance of having faith when you pray. For prayers to be effective they must be with faith, and there must be forgiveness for others also (v25-26). There are other aspects of prayer taught here. At the end of verse 15 the disciples heard Jesus curse the fig tree. In verse 21 it says that Peter remembered that Jesus cursed the fig tree. One of the keys to a powerful prayer life is remembering God's faithfulness in answering past prayers.

Answered prayers also increase our faith (v22). Prayer is also to be without doubt (v23). Both the cleansing of the temple and the cursing of the fig tree demonstrate divine judgment. The question of Jesus' authority was designed to trap Him (v27-32). Jesus turns the table by asking them a question concerning John the Baptist. If they answered "from heaven" they had to believe John and his claims about Jesus.

Mark 12:1-12 records the parable of the wicked vinedressers. The landowner is God, the vineyard is Israel, the servants are the prophets, and the son is Jesus. This is a reference to Isaiah 5:1-7, where God calls out the Israelites for their sin and rejection of Him. In verses 13-17, Jesus discusses the proper attitude toward government and God. Again, it was designed to trap Him with His words. Proper submission should be made to both, but when Caesar desires what belongs to God, God's people must obey God (Acts 4:19; Rom. 13:1-7; 1 Pet. 2:13-17). In each instance they try to trap Him, but Jesus turns the trap back on them. The Sadducees (who do not believe in a resurrection) try once again to trap Jesus with His own words in verses 18-27. This account was concerning a woman who had no children and married seven brothers. Jesus corrects their beliefs by explaining that they do not understand God's power or His Word.

It would be the scribes (mostly Pharisees) turn, in verses 28-34, to try and trap Him. In response to their question, Jesus quotes Deut. 6:5 and Lev. 19:18, and gives the highest praise for loving God and loving one another (Matt. 22:34-40). In verses 35-37, Jesus explains that He is the Son of David and the Son of God by quoting Psalm 110:1. He is identifying Himself here as the Messiah. In verses 38-40 Jesus condemns the scribes for being outwardly religious but inwardly they have no relationship with God at all. In contrast to the religious leaders of the day, the story of the widow's mites shows true faith and devotion to the Lord (v41-44). It is believed that the priests who were in the temple would listen to the money hit the trumpet shaped cylinders and celebrate over those who gave a lot of money. The widow gave two small copper coins that may have hardly made a sound at all. While others gave from their own abundant finances, this poor widow gave all she had. This passage also teaches that no good deed goes unnoticed by God.

Thursday • Job 29-30

In Job 29, Job recounts his life before tragedy struck. Job begins to look back upon the days with blessing of God and family (v1-6). From verses 7-11 we see that Job must have enjoyed a prominent seat in his city, as the actions described show an elder within the city. In verses 12-17 Job describes his ministering to the poor, widows, blind and lame, how he opposed the wicked, and how he was a defender for those who had no one to defend them. Verses 18-20 form a contrast between the life he once had, with the life he is living now. In verses 21-25 Job goes back to the theme of verses 7-11 where people sought his counsel, approval, and leadership.

Job 30 portrays the reversal of chapter 29. The words "but now" in verses 1, 9, and 16 contrast chapter 30 with chapter 29. At one time the most highly respected waited for his words, but now the lowest of society mock him and treat him poorly (v1-10). Job feels while he is in the middle of his affliction everyone has come against him to make him even more miserable (v11-15). To make matters worse not only have people come against him (v1-15), but now God has come against him (v16-23). Job believes God has removed His blessing from him and that God doesn't even answer him. Job believed God was working against him and that the only way out was death. In verses 24-31 Job places himself in the position of those whom he previously helped. He feels that all the help he once gave is missing from his life now that he is in the same position.

Friday • Isaiah 38-42

Isaiah 38 concerns Hezekiah who is the king of Judah, and his illness. You can read more about Hezekiah in 2 Kings 20 and 2 Chronicles 29-32. At the time of his illness he had no heir to the throne. Upon hearing of his death from Isaiah, Hezekiah cries out to the Lord, and the Lord adds 15 years to Hezekiah's life (v1-5). God also promises to deliver them from the Assyrians, and gives Hezekiah a sign that He will do this (v6-8). The sign represents Hezekiah's coming death and God giving him more years. In verses 9-14 Hezekiah recalls his life during his sickness, while verses 15-20 recall God answering his prayer and giving him a longer life to live. From this experience Hezekiah showed gratitude for the Lord in healing him, but especially as it pertains to the forgiveness of his sins.

Isaiah 39 paves the way for the chapters that follow, and also closes the first part of Isaiah (ch.1-39) and its theme of judgment. The chapters that follow will be concerned with the future and the Servant of the Lord. In a little over 100 years, Babylon will carry Judah into captivity. Hezekiah's actions were foolish, but he probably had hopes of making Babylon their ally.

Isaiah 40:1-11 pertains to a future day when His people will need comfort in coming out of exile from Babylon (v1-2). Verses 3-5 refer back to 35:8-10 and the highway referenced by Isaiah as the exiles return to the land. In verses 6-8, God and His Word are pictured as unchanging. God will lead them from Babylon, and once again be their God (v9-11). God is described as a Shepherd and Creator in verses 12-17, and as Sovereign in verses 21-24. The foolishness of idolatry is referenced in verses 18-20, and 25-26 as people worshiped creation instead of their Creator. In verses 27-31 God is urging His people to exchange their weakness in their captivity for His strength that is to come and to return to the Promised Land.

Isaiah 41 displays the sovereignty and power of God over His people and of all the nations (v1-4). Verse 2 also contains what many believe to be the first reference to Cyrus ("who raised up one from the east?"), who would give the decree for the Israelites to return to their own land. While the nations make more idols to calm their fears (v5-7), it is God who will be the comfort of His people (v8-10). God again calls them to not be fearful as it is He who will make them His people once again (v11-16). God promises to provide for their needs as they return home from exile (v17-20). God calls out the idols of the nations and their failure to be able to predict the future in verses 21-24 in order to prove they are not gods at all. In response to this, God makes a prediction of the future of the coming of Cyrus in verses 25-29 to show He is the only True God.

Isaiah 42 begins the theme of the servant. Many believe the servant is Israel while others believe it is Jesus. Here in chapter 42:1-4 Jesus' ministry is presented, while verses 5-9 demonstrate that it is with God's help He has the power in doing His will. Jesus' prime purpose was to provide salvation for all people. In verses 10-13 the Servant will be praised for His work- even in places where there are not many people such as the islands, deserts, and mountain tops (v10-13). In verses 14-17 we read that when the exile is over, God will remove all obstacles in front of His people (Isa. 40:3-4). But, we also read that right now the people are still blind and deaf in their sin (v18-20). Not only are they blind and deaf but they have become plunder for other people (v21-25).

Saturday • 1 Corinthians 15-16

Paul now turns to the subject of the resurrection in chapter 15. In verses 1-11, you will find 8 eyewitnesses of the Lord's resurrection. They are: (1) an individual's own faith, (2) the church present in Corinth, (3) Scripture, (4) Peter, (5) the Twelve, (6) the 500 people, (7) James, and (8) Paul. Apparently some in Corinth believed there was no resurrection (v12-19). Paul argues that if Christ has not risen then preaching, their own faith, and Paul's own words are useless. Without a resurrection believers are still in their sin, and those who have already died have perished. He also stresses that the hope we have in Christ is not only for this life here on earth, but that there is a life to come (v19). Paul argues in verses 20-28 that because Jesus was raised from the dead, all who believe in Him will be also raised. These verses are also similar to Romans 5 where the concept that Jesus is the second Adam is more fully developed. Because of Adam's sin we are all sinners, but because of Christ's resurrection believers will be resurrected. The consequences of not believing in the resurrection are dealt with in verses 29-34. Paul does not approve of, or promote baptism for the dead in verse 29. He is simply asking why they do it if there is no resurrection. In verses 30-32, Paul argues that if there is no resurrection there should be no reason why they are suffering such hardships. Paul quotes one of their own poets in verse 33 in order to show that those who are teaching that there is no resurrection are corrupting all those who are around them. Paul tells them in verse 34 that denying the resurrection leads to living immoral lives. They should be ashamed, because there are people among them who do not even know Christ.

Paul discusses the nature of the resurrected body in verses 35-49, and the transformation of it in verses 50-58. Verse 36 is important. The term "made alive" means that God is the one who gives life when it dies. Jesus said in John 12:24 "Most assuredly, I say to you, unless a grain of wheat falls into the ground and dies, it remains alone; but if it dies, it produces much fruit". Paul uses the analogies of a seed, a body, and celestial bodies to demonstrate that God can take a perishable body and make it imperishable (v37-41). Verses 42-44 form a series of contrast between the natural body and its state when it is resurrected. He uses the analogy of Adam and Christ to distinguish between the natural and the spiritual body in verses 45-49. The natural body cannot inherit the kingdom of God, so it must be changed (v50-58). This change will happen whether one is alive or dead at the return of Christ. It will result in all believers receiving a new body, it will be instant and complete, and all believers will experience victory over death because of the resurrection. Because of the resurrection of Christ and our own to come, believers are to be steadfast (settled), immovable (firm grip), and always abounding (growing, continuing) in the Lord's work knowing that it is not useless (v58).

Paul's closing remarks in 16:1-4 concern a collection for the saints who were suffering in Jerusalem, probably because of famine or persecution. Paul also details his agenda in verses 5-12 as it concerns his own travel, as well as the travel of Timothy and Apollos. In verses 13-18, Paul gives more instructions to the church at Corinth on how to conduct themselves among one another. Verse 13 can be read as "Make a determined effort to be on guard, stand firm in the faith, act as men of courage, and be made strong." To correct the problems at Corinth, the leadership of the church would need exactly that. Paul closes out the letter with an *anathema* (curse) on those who do not believe in the Lord and a *maranatha* which means "O Lord come".

Cover to Cover CHALLENGE

Week 16

Sunday • Psalm 51-53

Welcome to week 16 of the *Cover to Cover Challenge*! Let us continue to pray that our eyes will be opened to the truth of God's Word, that the Holy Spirit will move in our lives, and for the Lord Jesus to get the glory and honor from it. We read last week the words of Isaiah the prophet and he said "The grass withers, the flower fades, but the word of our God stands forever".

Psalm 51 is probably a psalm we all know, and have even experienced in our own lives. The superscription says this was written after David had committed sin with Bathsheba. In verses 1-2 we see David cry out to God for what he has done. In verses 3-6 David confesses his sin, and in verses 7-9 he seeks a cleansing from his sin. Verses 10-13 contain David's desire for God to create in him a clean heart and to restore the joy of his salvation. In this passage, David desires also to tell others about the Lord. David asks the Lord to consecrate him in his life moving forward so he can be the vessel he is appointed to be. David asks the Lord to be good to the people of Jerusalem, and not let the people suffer consequences because of his sin.

Psalm 52 is a contrast between the godly and the ungodly. The superscription on this one relates to a story we read last week concerning David and Doeg (1 Sam. 22:17-23). In verses 1-2, it is the wicked who deceive and destroy through their words and deeds. Verses 3-4 add to the description of the wicked. It is through their lips they pervert and corrupt what is right. In verse 5 we see that God will judge the wicked and that they will be uprooted from the land of the living. In verses 6-7, the righteous see the judgment of God on the wicked and fear the Lord. In contrast to the Lord uprooting the wicked, the righteous are like a green olive tree enjoying the presence of God in verses 8-9.

Psalm 53 is similar to Psalm 14. It also concerns God's triumph over the wicked. In verse 1 the "fool" is someone who acts independently of God. Here, David describes the fool as being corrupt, performing detestable acts in defiance of God, and as being incapable of doing good. In verses 2-3, David describes God looking down to earth to see if anyone is seeking Him. God sees that all have turned away (Rom. 3:10-12). In verses 4-6, there is a reversal of circumstances as the enemy who was once attacking is now fearful and defeated. It was shameful to not bury the dead and have their bones scattered over the earth.

WEEK 16

Monday • Exodus 14-18

The Israelites have been delivered from the bondage of the Egyptians, and now they enter the wilderness directed by the pillar of cloud by day and pillar of fire at night. In verses 1-4, the Lord advises them which route to take so He could show His power once more. Pharaoh and the Egyptian army decide to follow after the Israelites, supposing God is done fighting for them (v5-12). Upon hearing the Israelites complaints Moses instructs them to (1) Not be afraid, (2) Stand still, and (3) See the deliverance of the Lord (v13-14). The Lord commands Moses to stretch out the rod over the sea, and it will divide so they can pass through, to escape the Egyptians in verses 15-18. The Angel of the Lord gives light so the Israelites can pass through while casting darkness on the Egyptians so they cannot see (v19-20). The Lord drives back the waters and the miracle of the Red Sea begins to take place (v21-22). Pharaoh and the Egyptian army begin to follow after the Israelites, but the Lord causes confusion among them and causes their chariot wheels to jam (v23-28). Just when the Egyptians were ready to turn around, the Lord causes the sea to come together again and none of the Egyptians survive. The Lord delivered Israel that day, and they saw the powerful hand of God (v29-31).

Exodus 15:1-21 contains the song of Moses after the Lord delivered them from the Egyptians. It is a song of victory that displays God's power as it recounts the Red Sea story. In verses 22-27, the people complain to Moses about not having any water to drink at Marah. Here the water is bitter, but the Lord "showed" (means "to teach") Moses a tree which would make the waters sweet. This was done in order to test the Israelites. Moses pronounces a blessing for obedience and cursings for disobedience.

Exodus 16 shows that God miraculously feeds the people quail and bread from heaven. In Exodus 16:1-3 we see that it has been one month since they have left Egypt and the people are complaining because they have no food. God would bring them food, but it would also be a test for the children of Israel (v5-6). Moses instructs the people so they will know that when they complain they are complaining against God (v 6-8). The provision of the food was so Israel would know that the Lord is God (v9-12). In verses 13-18, God does provide quail in the evening and manna in the morning. Instructions were given on how to gather the manna, and even in this task people disobeyed Moses. (v19-21). They were instructed to gather twice as much on the 6th day because they would rest on the Sabbath, and there would be no gathering (v22-31). The Israelites would eat manna for the next 40 years, and a portion of it would later be placed in the Ark of the Covenant (v32-36).

Once again, the people complain about not having any water to drink in Exodus 17:1-7. Moses takes the complaint to the Lord and believes the people are ready to kill him. It is quite telling that after all the Israelites had experienced at the hands of the Lord that they would ask, "Is the Lord among us or not?" In verses 8-16 Joshua defeats the Amalekites, who are the first to attack Israel. The name "The Lord is my Banner" shows that the victory did not belong to anyone but the Lord.

Moses is reunited with his wife, children, and father-in-law Jethro in Exodus 18:1-5. Moses tells Jethro everything the Lord has done for them, beginning with leaving Egypt (v6-8). This causes Jethro to praise the Lord, and he offers a burnt offering and fellowship offering before the Lord (v9-12). Jethro offers Moses advice on delegating some leadership responsibilities to others so he would not have to do it all alone (v13-23). The qualifications listed in verse 21 include men who are capable of doing the job, who fear God, and who are truthful men. Jethro's advice proved to work, and Moses benefited from his instructions.

COVER TO COVER CHALLENGE

Tuesday • 1 Samuel 26-31

1 Samuel 26 is the last time David and Saul will be confronted with one another. Verses 1-5 give us the setting for this final confrontation, as David goes to inspect Saul's camp while they are sleeping (v12). Abishai agrees to go with David to the camp where they see Saul asleep with a spear by his head (v6-12). Abishai wants to kill Saul, but David once again will not allow anyone to harm the "Lord's anointed". After taking the spear and water jug, David calls out to Abner (v13-16). In his speech, David affirms his innocence of any wrongdoing and wonders why Saul the king is coming out against someone as insignificant (flea) as David (v17-20). Saul acknowledges his sin and David offers to return the spear (symbol of death), but not the water jug (symbol of life) in verses 21-25.

In 1 Samuel 27:1-4, David flees to the land of the Philistines with the hopes that Saul will stop pursuing him. Not wanting to live in the city with the king, Achish gives David the city of Ziklag where he will live for 16 months (v5-7). David deceives the king as he had earlier in 21:12-15. Achish believes David is fighting on his behalf, but he is really fighting the enemies of Israel. Achish believes David's actions have turned the Israelites against David, and that David will be his servant forever (v8-12).

1 Samuel 28 begins with Achish telling David he will fight alongside of him against Israel, to which David replies "he will see soon what he can do" (v1-2). The scene now shifts back to Saul as he consults the witch at En Dor. Saul, being fearful of the coming battle with the Philistines, consults the Lord for an answer but does not receive one (v3-6). Disguising himself, Saul decides to consult a medium which is forbidden by the Lord (Deut. 18:1,14). Saul swears an oath to the Lord that she will not be punished, which coincidently is the last time he uses the Lord's name. Surprised herself to see Samuel, Saul ask Samuel what he should do about the approaching Philistines and he receives an answer he does not want to hear (v15-19). David will be king and Saul, along with his sons, will die the next day recalling Samuel's words in 1 Samuel 12:25. Saul is now fearful because of Samuel's words and falls to the ground (v20-25).

1 Samuel 29 is rather short, and tells how David is sent back to Ziklag and avoids fighting his fellow Israelites. The Philistine commanders do not trust David, fearing he may turn against them. David returns to Ziklag to find the city had been raided by the Amalekites in 1 Samuel 30:1-3. After a time of weeping, the men want to take David's life because of what has happened (v4-8). David consults the Lord about pursuing the Amalekites, and God says He will win the victory and recover all that was lost. In verses 9-20, David and his men meet an Egyptian slave of the Amalekites in a field who takes them to the camp. David and his men emerge victorious and recover all that was taken. After a confrontation between David's men over the spoil (v21-25), David sends some of it to the elders in Judah where it is used to help people of many cities (v26-31).

1 Samuel ends in chapter 31 with the death of Saul and three of his sons. In verses 1-7, the word "fell" is used three times to show the completeness of the Philistine victory. Saul, and his armor-bearer kill themselves on the battlefield. The next day the Philistines come through and desecrate the body of Saul and his sons, and place his armor in the temple of their god (v8-13). The men of Jabesh Gilead, whom Saul had rescued from the Ammonites (11:1-11), retrieve their bodies and give them proper burial. Saul's story is tragic, and his life is epitomized by the verses in 1 Chronicles 10:13-14-"Saul died because he was unfaithful to the Lord, he did not keep the word of the Lord and even consulted a medium for guidance, and did not inquire of the Lord…so the Lord put him to death and turned the kingdom over to David son of Jesse".

WEEK 16

Wednesday • Mark 13-14

Mark 13 begins with Jesus and the disciples traveling to the Mount of Olives where He calls attention to the temple and its future destruction (Matt. 24:1-3, Luke 21:20). This prompts the questions of the disciples in verse 4 that concern the destruction of the temple (which Jesus has already spoken of in verse 2). They also want to know what the sign(s) will be when He comes again. According to Matthew 24, these signs will become more frequent and rise in intensity as the return of Christ approaches. The signs are: false christs, violence, natural disasters, religious persecution, betrayal, failure to love, and worldwide evangelism. The abomination of desolation is spoken of here and three other times in Scripture (Dan. 9:27, 11:31, 12:11). Antiochus Epiphanes IV is the fulfillment of Daniel 11:21-35. He ravaged the temple and the Jews, while declaring himself to be a god. Most believe this reference is to a future Antichrist who will repeat the deeds of Antiochus, except on a much larger scale. In verses 14-20, Jesus is saying that when this happens you will need to flee immediately. Jesus describes this period as "great tribulation" and warns once more about false christs during this time (v21-23).

In verses 24-27 Jesus describes His coming again. He tells us that it will be characterized by cosmic disturbances (Isa. 13:10; Joel 2:31; 2 Pet. 3:7-12; Rev. 6:13-14), and He tells where He will gather together all of His people. In the parable of the fig tree (v28-31), Jesus is teaching that when these things (signs) begin to happen they will know His return is near. Verse 31 teaches the faithfulness and eternal value of God and His Word (Luke 16:17; John 10:35). Jesus teaches in verse 32 that no one knows the time of His return, which is a warning to those in our day who think they know. In verses 33-37 Jesus encourages His followers to keep watching because they do not know the time of His return.

In Mark 14:1-2 we read that the religious leaders are plotting to have Jesus killed two days before the Passover and the Feast of Unleavened Bread. In Bethany, at the home of Simon the leper, Jesus is anointed for the second time (Luke 7:36-50) in preparation for His burial. This is to be contrasted with the actions of the religious leaders and Judas (v3-9). In verses 10-11 Judas agrees to betray Jesus for thirty pieces of silver (Zech. 11:12). This is also the amount to be paid for a slave who is accidently killed by an ox in Exodus 21:32. The disciples prepare the Passover meal to be eaten after sundown (v12-17). It is at this meal where Jesus announces that one among them will betray Him (v18-21). Jesus institutes the Lord's Supper in verses 22-26. Jesus knows that His sacrificial death is inaugurating a new covenant through the shedding of His blood. This new covenant will allow mankind to have their sins forgiven, and begin a relationship with God through Him (Ex. 24:8; Zech. 9:11; Jer. 31:31-34).

In verses 27-31 Jesus predicts that the disciples will all be scattered because of what will happen to Him. Peter emphatically denies that he would do that to Jesus (v31), but Jesus says "before the rooster crows you will deny (disown) Me three times" (v30). Jesus prays in the garden of Gethsemane with all of His disciples. He takes Peter, James, and John to pray alongside Him, but they fall asleep (v32-42). The cup that Jesus prays to pass is not only a cup of suffering and death, but the cup of God's wrath. In verses 43-50, Jesus is arrested in the garden by a group of men who were led by Judas. Mark is the only gospel writer to include verses 51-52. Tradition says this person may have been Mark but no one knows for certain. Jesus appears before the Sanhedrin in verses 53-65. After false witnesses report, the high priest places Jesus under oath and asks Him if He is the Son of God. Jesus says that He is, and one day they will see Him coming in the clouds of heaven. He is accused by the Jews of committing blasphemy, which is worthy of the death penalty (Lev. 24:16). In verses 66-72, Jesus' prediction of Peter's denial comes true as Peter lies and calls down curses upon himself.

Thursday • Job 31-32

Job closes out his testimony as he specifically calls out sins, and asks God to punish him for them if he is guilty of them. Verses 1-4 serve as an introduction to the speech. In verses 5-8 Job says he has never been guilty of falsehood, deceit, or evil deeds. Job also defends himself from being guilty of committing sins such as adultery in verses 9-12. Job even treated the servants in his home well (v13-15). In verses 16-23 Job did all he could to help the poor, widows, and the fatherless. Although he was rich, Job did not boast or trust in material things (v24-28). The sin Job is denying in verses 29-34 is hypocrisy. Job is confident he is innocent of any of these charges as he closes out his defense (v35-37). Job even calls out for his land to be a witness of his good deeds (v38-40).

Elihu enters the picture in Job 32, and will continue to speak until chapter 37. Elihu is a young man who waits for his turn to speak to Job. In verses 1-5, we see he is angry at Job for justifying himself and angry at his friends because they do not refute Job's answers. The counselor's arguments do not impress him. Wisdom, according to Elihu, may be given to the young if God gives it and the old may not receive it (v6-14). He does agree to argue a different case than what the friends did. In verses 15-22, Elihu says he is literally bursting at the seams to speak to Job and also vows to be impartial in his speech.

Friday • Isaiah 43-48

Isaiah 43 is linked with chapter 42, where the consequences of Israel's refusal to obey God were called into question. Here Isaiah 43 says that they will experience God as their Redeemer, showing the special relationship between God and His people. In verses 1-7 the exodus is spoken of from the sense that Israel could trust in the Lord to deliver them as He had in the past and to bring them back to the land after the exile. In verses 8-13 we see that it is the Lord alone who foretells the future, and He alone is God. Because He is their Redeemer, Babylon will be judged (v14-15). In verses 16-21 God will make a way for them to return just as He had made a way for them out of Egypt (v16-21). The past deliverances of the Lord on behalf of His people should have led them to sacrifice to Him, but the only thing He received was their sin. The people are guilty, and would suffer destruction by His hand (v22-28).

Isaiah 44 is a contrast of God with the uselessness of idols. The contrast begins with Jacob ("Deceiver") and the name Jehurun ("Upright One"), showing that the people are the object of God's judgment, but also receive His grace. Only the Lord is God, sovereign over history, and able to predict the future (v6-8). In verses 9-20 an idol maker is pictured as being as useless as his idol. We also see the blinding effects of idolatry (v9-20). Unlike the idols, God will blot out their many sins and provide forgiveness for them when they return to Him (v21-23). God promises His people that He plans on rebuilding the land, and only He can do this (v24-28). His people will be brought back by a foreigner (Cyrus), who will make it possible for them to rebuild the land.

Isaiah 45:1-7 continues to tell us about Cyrus, who would enjoy victories over his enemies which was for the sake of Israel. In verses 8-10 it is God who will bring righteousness and save His people, even by the hand of a pagan king. Cyrus will come just as the Lord predicted to set His people free (v11-13), and even pagan people will acknowledge the Lord is God (v14). In verses 15-17, the foreign people will put away their idols and participate in the salvation of the Lord. When the Lord speaks like He did in creation, His word is true and helps people know who He is (v18-19). God gives one last challenge to those who still have not come to Him-only He has told them all of this beforehand (v20-21). It is clear from verses 22-25 that God is calling them to salvation. Not all will be saved, but all will acknowledge Him as Lord (Phil. 2:9-11).

Isaiah 45 ended with all bowing down before the Lord, and in chapter 46 the gods of Babylon will bow down to the true God (v1-2). The Babylonians will carry their gods away on their backs, but it is the Lord who carries His people and rescues them (v3-4). The gods of the Babylonians cannot hear, speak, or save but the Lord can (v5-7).The Lord now calls His people to remember His past deliverances of them and His relationship with them (v8-13).

In Isaiah 46 the gods of the Babylonians fall, and in chapter 47 so will their nation. In verses 1-4 Babylon is pictured as a beggar, slave, and a fugitive. Its treatment of Israel is another reason for their judgment in verses 5-7. Babylon will become like a widow with no chance for children because of her sins, but especially her sorcery (v8-11). There will be no hope for Babylon to be delivered. Even their famed astrologers cannot save them (v12-15).

In Isaiah 48:1-6 God calls upon His people to listen to His words because while they have "leaned" on the Lord, many have never fully trusted in Him. Some even going as far as attributing His acts to other gods. The new things they have heard are about Cyrus and the coming servant of the Lord (v6-11). God did not tell them before because they would not believe it. God calls them to listen once again as He speaks of Himself and Cyrus (v12-16). Most attribute verse 16 to the coming Servant of the Lord. God laments over His people in verses 17-19. Verse 20 is about the return from exile, while verse 21 refers to the past and the exodus. In verse 22, there is a final declaration over the fate of the wicked.

Saturday • 2 Corinthians 1-3

2 Corinthians was probably written soon after the writing of 1 Corinthians, and can be dated between 55-56 AD. There are two simple reasons for the letter. Paul writes to praise them, and Paul writes to condemn them. Paul is glad for the positive response of the first letter, he continues to encourage them about the offering to be taken up, and he wants to prepare them for his soon coming.

In 2 Corinthians 1:1-7, Paul writes to encourage the believers at Corinth during a time of intense suffering. Paul related to them that he too has suffered (4:7-12, 11:23-29), but it is the Lord who delivered him from it (v8-11). Along with verse 6 in this passage, it also is proof that some of the things believers endure in this life (hardships) are so that we can help others who go through the same thing. Paul defends himself against accusations that he behaved poorly while in Corinth (v12-14). These accusations continue in the next passage because he had changed his travel plans (v15-17). To the Corinthian believers, it was as if he was speaking out of both sides of his mouth (v18). So in these verses Paul explains himself, because if they questioned his integrity they may also question the gospel he preached to them. This gives Paul an open door to speak about the message of Christ, in whom all the promises of God are answered "Yes" (v19-20). We know His promises are true because He has given us His Spirit as a guarantee (v21-22). What Paul will say in verses 1:23-2:2 is that he cancelled his visit so that he would not have to make two visits.

In 2 Corinthians 2:3-4 Paul wrote them a letter so they would know that he loved them. In verses 5-11 Paul addresses an issue where someone was punished for wrongdoing. Paul says this was done to restore and bring about forgiveness so the person would not be overcome with sorrow (v6-7). The people at Corinth should reaffirm their love for him by encouraging him and forgiving him (v7-10). Forgiving the person and restoring them would also keep Satan from using the situation to his advantage (v11). Paul adds, in verses 12-13, another reason his plans changed-the Lord opened up a door for him to preach in Troas. In verses 14-17, Paul speaks about the privilege of being servants of Christ. The word "triumph" in verse 14 shows that God leads Paul (and believers) as victorious soldiers. In verse 17 Paul says that he did not "peddle" the word of God. This word means to trade in. Paul is saying he never tampered with God's word and never used it for his own personal gain.

2 Corinthians 3:1-3 shows us that some in Corinth were questioning Paul's credentials as an apostle. Letters of recommendation were usually carried by travelling preachers to show that they were approved to preach. Paul writes that he did not need a letter of recommendation. The Corinthians themselves served as his letter of recommendation, because he was the apostle who brought the gospel to them. The Holy Spirit, living inside of the believers in Corinth, was proof of this. In verses 4-6 Paul says that he was divinely equipped and commissioned to preach the gospel. In verse 6 the "letter" represents the Old Covenant, and the "Spirit" represents the New Covenant which gives life. The reason the "letter" (Old Covenant) kills is because no one could satisfy its demands. It placed all people under condemnation, although it now points to Christ (Gal. 3:24). Under the New Covenant, enabled by the Holy Spirit, believers' sins are forgiven and remembered no more. In addition to this, the Spirit enables believers to live a godly life.

In 2 Corinthians 3:7-11 Paul argues that if Moses' face shone when he came down with the law, then the glory of the New Covenant must even be more glorious (Ex. 34:29-32). These verses from Exodus describe Moses coming down from the mountain with the two tablets and with his face shining. In these verses Paul shows that the ministry of the Spirit in the New Covenant is more glorious than the Old Covenant because: it is greater in glory (v7-8), it gives righteousness to those who believe (v9), and because it is permanent (v11).

In verses 12-18, Paul adds the theme of veiling and unveiling, using Exodus 34:33-35 as background information. Just as Moses' face was veiled, the Israelites still have a veil today when they read the Old Testament. One has to turn to the Lord for the veil to be taken away (v16). Living in the Spirit, under the New Covenant, gives liberty. This is in contrast to the Old Covenant that represents bondage to the law. Romans 8:1 clearly teaches that "There is therefore now no condemnation to those who are in Christ Jesus, who do not walk according to the flesh, but according to the Spirit". In verse 18 Paul is saying that all Christians reflect the glory of the Lord with unveiled faces, displaying outwardly the character of Christ.

Cover to Cover Challenge

Week 17

Sunday • Psalm 54-56

Welcome to week 17 of the *Cover to Cover Challenge*! 2 Timothy 3:16-17 says "All Scripture is given by inspiration of God, and is profitable for doctrine, for reproof, for correction, for instruction in righteousness, that the man of God may be complete, thoroughly equipped for every good work". All the words of the Bible are breathed out by God and are for our benefit. Every time we read it, it speaks. Think on that this week as you read. Keep praying for understanding, and for the Lord to be glorified!

Psalm 54, like Psalm 52, pertains to David's escape from Saul. We read this passage a couple of weeks ago (1 Samuel 23). In verses 1-2, David asks God to protect and rescue him from those who have come against him. In the passage, verse 3 would refer to the Ziphites who told Saul where David was. The term "stranger" refers to those who do not have a covenant with God. In verses 4-5, David expresses trust in the Lord because David knows God is faithful to His Word. The last two verses focus on David being thankful to the Lord for delivering him.

Psalm 55 is a prayer of lament. David once again finds himself being threatened by enemies, and they are causing him to suffer (v1-3). In verses 4-8, David expresses that he wants to escape his present situation and the great pain it is causing him. David turns to the Lord in verses 9-15 and cries out for justice, when all he can see is injustice. David learns it is a close friend who is betraying him (v12-14). The situation drives David to pray and have his prayer answered (v16-19). While the Lord is faithful, David knows his enemies are not (v20-21). In verses 22-23, David assures those who trust in the Lord that God will protect them and judge the wicked.

Psalm 56 is another lament written by David regarding suffering because of his enemies. In verses 1-2, David says that he is under constant affliction from his enemies. In spite of his suffering David trusts in the Lord, because he knows the Lord will deliver him (v3-4). His enemies twist his words and scheme against him, but David knows that the Lord has heard his prayer (v5-9). David knows that trusting in the Lord means that he does not have to fear any mortal man (v10-11). David thanks the Lord for delivering him, because He is faithful to His promises (v12-13).

Monday • Exodus 19-22

It has been 3 months since the Lord had delivered them from the bondage in Egypt. The Lord, speaking through Moses gives instructions to the children of Israel in chapter 19. In verses 1-8 we read how the Lord has brought His people out of Egypt, and sustained them on the eagles' wings. This symbolizes His compassion, protection, and strength over them. If they obey the covenant He has made with them they would become His special people (distinct), a kingdom of priests, and a holy nation (mediators of grace). In verses 9-25 the Israelites are told that God will descend upon Mount Sinai. They are to prepare themselves by washing their clothes, staying away from the mountain, and abstaining from sexual relations. These outward acts would show the inner desire of each person to meet with God. Those who did not obey would be punished by death.

Exodus 20:1-17 contains the Ten Commandments. The purpose of the law is to show the sinfulness of man and to show the need of a mediator. Moses would be the mediator for the children of Israel (v18-21), then the priests. All of this pointed to the coming of Jesus who would be the Mediator for all mankind. In verses 22-26 God warns Moses not to make an idol of God to worship, and not to use tools to make an altar. This was probably said so they would not make an idol out of it.

Exodus 21:1-11 is the laws pertaining to servants. They are to be set free, becoming citizens again unless the servant wants to stay with his master. In that case, the relationship became permanent. Verses 12-17 contain a list of offenses that require the death penalty, while making a distinction between accidental and premeditated offenses. In verses 18-32 five examples of bodily injuries are given, along with instructions on how to punish the offender and recompense the owner. Verses 33-36 discuss laws pertaining to property damage that results from being negligent, which is continued into chapter 22.

Exodus 22:1-4 discusses theft of property. Each of these laws, going all the way to verse 15 make proper restitution to the owner. Each of these laws contains principles we can still use today. The laws listed in verses 16-27 cover different people groups in society. As throughout the Old Testament, God shows that special care must be taken of the poor, widows, and orphans. Verses 28-31 pertain to man's relationship with God. God reminds them once more that they are to be "holy men", separated for His use.

Tuesday • 2 Samuel 1-5

2 Samuel will discuss the rise of David to kingship of Israel. 2 Samuel begins the way 1 Samuel ends- with the death of Saul. In verses 1-16, the story of the death of Saul is recounted by an Amalekite who claims to have finished killing Saul upon his request. If the Amalekite was the son of an alien, he would have known not to touch the Lord's anointed king. This is something even David did not do, even though he had every opportunity to. In the "Song of the Bow" David laments over the death of Saul and Jonathan.

In 2 Samuel 2:1-7, David seeks the Lord's help on what to do next. The Lord wants him to move to Hebron with his two wives and his army of men. It is here David is anointed king of Judah, and he blesses the people of Jabesh Gilead for their loyalty to Saul. Saul's commander Abner makes Ishbosheth ("Man of shame"), Saul's son king of Israel while David reigns over Judah. After a brief contest between Abner's men and Joab's men (v12-17, v18-32) Asahel (Joab's brother) dies at the hands of Abner. But, it is David's army that is about to gain the upper hand.

2 Samuel 3:1 portrays the outcome of the war which will take place over the next two chapters. In verses 2-5 David's family grows and Amnon, Absalom, and Adonijah will all be prominent figures in 2 Samuel. After the accusation by Ishbosheth, Abner, who has a strong hand over the kingdom, vows to help make David king

over all of Israel (v6-11). Messengers of Abner and David meet to arrange a meeting between David and Abner (v12-16). David asks for his wife Michal, given to him by Saul, to return to him. David does this to strengthen his claim to the throne. Meanwhile, Abner convinces the Benjamites that it is time to make David ruler over all of Israel, and comes to an agreement with David to do so (v17-21). David sends Abner away in peace, angering Joab (v22-30). Joab sends for Abner to return where he kills him, avenging his brother's death. David proclaims innocence of his kingdom, and that the guilt of killing Abner will fall on Joab and his household. David and all of Israel weep over the death of Abner (v31-39).

In 2 Samuel 4:1-7 Ishbosheth is killed by two of his own men, and we are introduced to Mephibosheth-who is Jonathan's son. Mephibosheth is disqualified from ruling Israel because of his youth and his lameness. The two men bring Ishbosheth's head to David, and claim to have done this in the name of the Lord in vengeance for David (v8-12). David, swearing an oath, holds them accountable for taking Ishbosheth's life. They too will die just as the Amalekite who brought David news of the death of Saul and Jonathan.

In 2 Samuel 5:1-5, David is anointed king over all of Israel. The elders of Israel give 3 reasons why they have come to David to make him king-David's kinship, David's a warrior, and David's choosing by the Lord. In verses 6-12, David defeats the Jebusites in battle and makes Jerusalem, or the "city of David" his new home. David acknowledges it is the Lord who gave him victories in battle and fought for him (v10). More children are born to David in Jerusalem as we see the first mention of Solomon's name. In verses 17-25 the Philistines attack David twice, to no avail as it is the Lord who fights on behalf of David and His people. Notice in verses 19 and 23 that David asks the Lord what he should do.

Wednesday • Mark 15-16

Jesus appeared before the Sanhedrin at the end of Mark 14, and now He appears before Pilate in Mark 15:1-5. While they charged Him with blasphemy before the Sanhedrin and before Pilate they will accuse Him of being a threat to Caesar's throne. Pilate would try to take advantage of the custom of releasing a prisoner before Passover to Jesus' favor, but the people choose Barabbas instead (v6-15). Barabbas name means "son of the father" or could mean "son of the great one". In any case even the name of Barabbas even points toward the divinity of Jesus. This passage also shows that Jesus died as a substitute for man.

In verses 16-20, the soldiers mock Jesus after they have scourged Him. The Romans hated the Jews, so you can imagine the pain they inflicted upon Him. Simon helps Jesus carry the cross to be crucified, and He is nailed to the cross (v21-26). The scene at the cross in verses 27-32 shows that those who should have understood who He was were mocking Him. Their cries for Him to come down from the cross and save Himself show their unbelief. Jesus' sole mission was to stay there and save others, it was never to save Himself. Jesus being crucified with two other criminals also demonstrates that He was taking Barabbas' place. It is a picture of the innocent dying for the guilty, or the just dying for the unjust. It also fulfills Isaiah 53:12, showing that the events of the cross were ordained by God. Because of our sin being laid upon Him, Jesus is forsaken by God and dies upon the cross of Calvary (v33-37). The supernatural darkness during this time is fitting for those who rejected "the light of the world". Some commentators see a fulfillment in the verses of Amos 8:9 which is a prophecy about the sun going down at noon in judgment. From events surrounding His death, a Roman centurion claims that Jesus is the Son of God (v38-41). Joseph of Arimathea asks for the body of Jesus so He can be properly buried in a tomb (v42-47).

Mark 16:1-8 records the resurrection of Jesus. The resurrection is the central doctrine that we, as believers, must trust in. Mary Magdalene sees the risen Jesus, but the disciples did not believe her when she told them (v9-11). The two disciples that He appears to in verses 12-13 could be the disciples who are on the road to

Emmaus (Luke 24:13-35). Jesus appears to the eleven disciples, and rebukes them for their unbelief in verse 14. In verses 15-18 Jesus gives them the Great Commission to preach the gospel everywhere they go, and signs that will accompany the preaching of the gospel. Verses 19-20 record Jesus' ascension and the disciples' obedience to the commission of the Lord.

Thursday • Job 33-34

In Job 33:1-7 Elihu speaks to Job by name, something his earlier counselors never did, and encourages Job to listen to his words. Elihu conveys much of the same response as Job's friends, but does not accuse Job of being wicked. In verses 8-22, Elihu believes that God's purposes cannot be understood by humanity. Elihu believed God does communicate with man, and that He does this through dreams and illness. In verses 23-30, Elihu appeals to God's mercy and grace. Elihu, in verses 31-33, encourages Job once again to listen and offers to teach him wisdom.

In Job 34, Elihu continues his speech by calling upon all to hear his words and how good they were. Elihu does seem to be angry at Job for justifying himself and not God (v5-9). Beginning with verse 10, Elihu claims that God only does what is right and can do no wrong. God is not accountable to Job (v13-15), nor is any human God's judge (v16-20). Job did complain that God was delaying his justification, but Elihu believes that God does not have to and can remain silent (v21-30). Elihu believed that Job was being tested because Job's behavior was wicked and because of the many words he had spoken against God (v31-37).

Friday • Isaiah 49-53

Isaiah 49:1-7 contains the second Servant Song which portrays Jesus' ministry and that here extends to the nations. Jesus' ministry is for Israel and they will despise Him, but He will be honored by God. The song of Simeon in Luke 2:32 refers to verse 6 and verse 7. It speaks plainly that He will be rejected by the nation. As the people of Israel return from exile in verses 8-12, the Lord will take care of them abundantly. Verses 13-21 deal with the discouragement of the people when they return from exile, as the Lord assures them He has not forgotten them. In verses 22-23 other nations will see how special Israel is. Verses 24-26 may refer to the Lord's previous deliverance of the Israelites from Egypt, where God made Himself known to them and the Egyptians. God will do the same when they return from exile.

Isaiah 50 contains the third Servant Song (v4-9). The illustrations of divorce and debt give details about how Israel pictured their relationship with the Lord during the exile (v1-3). They believe the Lord is done with them, so He sent them away. It is their unbelief that sent them away to exile. While the Israelites did not respond to God's Word through His prophets, the coming Servant will (v4-9). God's Servant will wait, and hear God when He speaks. The Servant will even offer His body for the cause of God. In verses 10-11 is a call to repent. It contains the illustration of coming out of darkness to walk in the light given by the Lord's Servant.

God calls upon all who fear Him to wait for their deliverance from exile in verses 1-3. Just as God made a covenant with Abraham and was faithful to it, His faithfulness also applies to those in exile. In verses 4-8 it is God who works on behalf of His people with justice, righteousness, and salvation which endures forever. God's power had been made known in the past, especially in delivering them from Egypt, and should give the people confidence that God will act on behalf of His people again (v9-11). God rebukes the people for their lack of faith, but He is going to make Himself known to them (v12-16). Through the exile God has judged His people (v17-20), but it will also be God who comforts them as they experience His mercy while their enemies drink the cup of His wrath (v21-23).

Isaiah 52:1-2 concerns Jerusalem as it becomes, once again, the glorious city of God. In verses 3-6 Babylon will be added to Egypt and Assyria as nations that oppressed Israel as God delivered His people from their hand. Verses 7-10 show that it is God who will bless His people and deliver them from exile. God promises that He will protect His people as they leave Babylon, as the call to depart goes out (v11-12).

Isaiah 52:13- 53:12 contains the fourth Servant Song, and is probably the most familiar one to everyone. In verses 52:13-15, we see the Suffering Servant who will cause many to be speechless by His ministry. He will also be the Sorrowful Servant in 53:1-3, who will be rejected and experience much grief. In verses 4-6, He will be the Smitten Servant punished for the sins of the people. He will also be the Silent Servant who will not open His mouth, although He is innocent of any sin (v7-9). In verses 10-12, He is the Submissive Servant who submits Himself to the Father's plan to redeem mankind.

Saturday • 2 Corinthians 4-5

In 2 Corinthians 4:1-6, Paul continues to defend his ministry against those who have opposed him. As we know from Scripture, Paul met many obstacles during his ministry. Because he knew his ministry was from the Lord, as explained in chapter 3, he did not lose heart (v1). The word "handling" in verse 2 means to tamper with. It was used in Paul's day to refer to the diluting of wine. What Paul is saying is that he did not water down the gospel. Paul preached the gospel to all men. If any did not understand him, it was Satan who had blinded the minds of those who do not believe (v3-4). Also it is worth mentioning that every place Satan is spoken of in 2 Corinthians, he is hindering the work of God. Paul did not promote himself, but the gospel, and he became a servant of those in Corinth (v5-6). It is also interesting in light of Paul's own testimony (Acts), how he describes those who are lost as "blind" and how the "light of the gospel" can shine on them.

In verses 7-15, Paul discusses the trials and rewards of serving the Lord. His ministry was one of suffering, but it was beneficial to others as he boldly preached the gospel and brought people into the kingdom (v7-12). Verse 7 is a testimony for each believer. All believers are earthen vessels (no value) with a treasure (gospel). The power to live a godly life or witness to people is not in us but in the treasure that lives in us. Each of the statements in verses 8-9 serve to illustrate this point. For example, "we are hard pressed on every side" speaks of the trials of Paul and of each believer. But in spite of this ("yet not crushed") the power of God keeps believers from being crushed. Verses 10-12 also serve to illustrate this point. Believers, especially Paul, were continually in danger of dying for the sake of Jesus and the gospel (Matt. 16:24). Verses 13-15 explain that despite the trials and the sufferings Paul has experienced he still lives by faith. It is comforting to Paul to know that if he were to lose his life for the sake of the gospel that he would be raised, along with the Corinthians, and ushered into the presence of Jesus. In verses 16-18, Paul once more discusses the suffering he has endured through his ministry, as many in Corinth may have been experiencing suffering as well. Paul did not want them to lose heart (v16) or focus on things of this world (v17), but to focus on eternity (v18).

Paul comforted the Corinthians in the face of persecution and hostility in the previous chapter but, there must also be an acknowledgement that those things could also mean death (5:1-10). Paul assures them that upon their death they will receive a new body because the Holy Spirit is a guarantee of that taking place (v5). Faith in Christ also assures the believer that at death they will be with the Lord (v6, 8). In view of these truths, Paul says that we should live our lives to be pleasing to God because we all will appear before Him to give an account of our lives (v9-10). Regarding the subject of judgment, Paul examines his own motives for service in verses 11-15. The motive of ministry for any person should be the love of Christ, which compels us to serve and be a witness to others. This is Paul's subject in verses 16-21. Those who have been reconciled are a new creation in Christ, and have also been given the ministry of reconciliation to preach to others. We are ambassadors of Christ, who became sin for us so that we could partake of His righteousness (v21).

To end this chapter I want to outline verses 14-21 again in light of Paul's ministry and how it relates to our own walk with the Lord. In verses 14 and15 Paul describes his motivation for his ministry. His motivation was that he loved Jesus, and he knew that Jesus died for all. In verses 16 and17 Paul describes his mindset for his ministry. In verse 16 Paul is saying that he views people based on whether or not they have a relationship with Christ. Verses 18 and 19 show Paul describing his ministry as one of reconciliation. He is to preach the gospel so that others can be reconciled to God. In verse 20 Paul describes the goal of his mission is to preach the gospel to others. Verse 21 is Paul's message. Paul's message was Jesus Christ, who became a substitute and sacrifice for our sin.

Cover to Cover CHALLENGE

Week 18

Sunday • Psalm 57-59

Welcome to week 18 of the *Cover to Cover Challenge*! I pray your studying is going well and that the Lord is revealing Himself to you through His Word. Romans 12:2 says "Do not be conformed to this world, but be transformed by the renewing of your mind, that you may prove what is that good and acceptable and perfect will of God". We live with the temptation to be like the world and to go along with its ideals. Paul tells us we need to renew our minds, and two of the best ways are reading the Word and prayer. The *Cover to Cover Challenge* will help us renew our minds so we may know what God's will is for our lives by studying Scripture and praying.

Psalm 57 is similar to Psalm 56 in that it is a song of lament and that it portrays trust in the Lord to deliver. According to the superscription, David wrote this when fleeing from Saul. In verses 1-5 David is being pursued by Saul, and persecuted unjustly as he prays for God's protection and seeks refuge with the Lord. In verse 6 David prays that those pursuing him would fall into their own pit they have laid out for him. In verses 7-11, David sings a song of praise for the mercy the Lord has shown him during this trial.

Psalm 58 is an imprecatory psalm where David calls for God to judge the wicked for their wickedness. In verses 1-2, David says that the wicked are unjust because their hearts are wicked. The wicked have gone astray from the Lord and are deceiving (v3). David compares their wickedness to a snake that can no longer be charmed. David is saying that they have become insensitive to God (v4-5). Through three analogies David prays for God to avenge the wicked, and that they will perish (v6-8). David knows God is going to address the wicked (v9) and that will cause the righteous to rejoice over God's justice and vindication (v10-11).

Psalm 59 is another psalm of lament as David is being pursued by his enemies. In verses 1-3, David prays for God to deliver him from those who are seeking his life. David proclaims his innocence and reliance on the Lord to help him during this time (v4-5). The wicked cause chaos and speak arrogantly, but it is God who will have the last laugh (v6-8). In verses 9-10 David will wait on the Lord because he knows God is stronger than his enemies. In verses 11-13 David prays that the Lord will make Himself known through judgment on his enemies. When God moves it will bring confidence to the people of God, and tell the nations that the Lord is Lord over all the earth. Although the wicked will return, David will rejoice in the Lord because of His mercy upon him (v14-17).

Monday • Exodus 23-26

The commandments continue in Exodus 23. In verses 1-9, the main focus is on justice. God warns not to slander, being partial in judgment, and not to accept bribes. God once again reminds them of their treatment of strangers (aliens), because they were once strangers in Egypt. Sabbath rest for land and for workers is prescribed in verses 10-12. Verse 13 is a warning against idolatry. The three great feasts are mentioned in verses 14-19. The Feast of Unleavened Bread was to remember the Exodus, the Feasts of Harvest (Weeks) was to remember the giving of the Law, and the Feasts of Ingathering (Tabernacles) was to remember the wilderness wanderings. In the closing passage of the chapter the Israelites are promised that the Angel of the Lord (preincarnate Christ) would be with them, and if they obeyed Him they would enjoy the protection of the Lord and have great success. One of the main arguments that this is Jesus is in verses 20-22 in that He forgives sin, and only God can forgive sin.

In Exodus 24:1-8, Moses gives the people all of the commandments of the Lord and they agree to obey the Lord. Here we also read that Moses wrote down everything that the Lord had said, and it is called the Book of the Covenant. In verses 9-18 Moses, Aaron, Nadab, Abihu, and 70 of the elders of Israel go up the mountain and see a form of God and the floors of heaven. The three symbols of God's glory are present in this chapter- cloud, fire, and the voice of God. Moses goes up the mountain and stays 40 days and nights where it is believed he received the instructions of chapters 25-31.

The final 16 chapters focus on the worship of God. Chapters 32-34 focus on the golden calf episode, and are a contrast between true worship of God and the false worship that is portrayed there. Exodus 25:1-9 concerns the collection of the materials (14) that will be used to build the Tabernacle. It was to be a sanctuary ("holy place"), and it was a pattern (model or type) of the real thing. The word tabernacle appears for the first time. God would come and dwell with His people. In verses 10-22 are the instructions for building the Ark of the Testimony, and the Ten Commandments were to be placed inside. The mercy seat would be the place of atonement. The word behind "mercy seat" and "atonement" literally means "to ransom or deliver by a substitute". In verses 23-30 are the instructions for the Table for the Showbread which would be in the Holy Place. Twelve loaves of bread would be placed on it, reminding Israel that they were under the protection of God. It would also be the bread the priests served and pointed to the future Bread that would come down from heaven. In verses 31-40 are the instructions for the Golden Lampstand which was patterned after an almond tree.

Exodus 26:1-14 details the two sets of curtains for the Tabernacle which would be dyed many different colors. The curtains made of goat hair were a reminder of the daily sin offerings (Num. 28:15), and to remind them of their cleansing from sin (Lev. 16). The ram's skins recalls the sacrifice made for consecrating the priests (Lev. 8) which was dyed red because they were set apart by the blood. The frame of the Tabernacle is discussed in verses 15-30. What is interesting about this is that it fit on 40 silver bases. The silver is described in 30:11-16, as atonement money so you could say that the foundation of the Tabernacle rested on redemption. In verses 31-35 the veil separating the Holy Place from the Most Holy Place is described. This is the curtain that was torn in two, showing that believers now have permanent access to God (Matt. 27:51). The screen described in verses 36-37 was an entrance curtain dividing the two inner rooms.

Tuesday • 2 Samuel 6-11

Now that David is king and has defeated the Philistines handedly, he wants to bring the Ark of the Covenant to Jerusalem. The Ark has not been mentioned since 1 Samuel 7, where it was left at Kiriath Jearim at the home of Abinadab (2 Sam. 6:1-5). Upon the Ark returning, Uzzah touches the Ark because he thought it was falling and is struck dead by the Lord (v6-11). Three reasons why this may have happened are- he touched the Ark, they were transporting it on a cart and not carrying it, and he is not a Kohathite Levite (Num. 4:15). This causes David to be angry, but yet fearful of the Lord. The ark is taken to the home of Obed-Edom where it stays for 3 months, and the Lord blesses his home. David decides to bring the Ark on to Jerusalem and they sacrifice bulls and calves every six steps they make (v12-19). Seeing David dance before the Lord, Michal becomes disgusted with David and scolds him for his actions (v20-23). David says that he is more concerned about what the Lord thinks about him. Michal, the daughter of Saul, dies without having any children.

The Davidic Covenant is the focus of 2 Samuel 7:1-17. The chapter begins with David's desire to build a house for the Lord (v1-3). Nathan the prophet enters the story of David as the Lord reveals to him that David will not build the house, but his son will. David would not be able to build the temple because he was busy defeating his enemies (1 Kgs. 5:3) and because he had shed blood (1 Chron. 22:8). In verses 8-11a God promises David three things-He will make David's name great, He will provide a place for Israel, and He will give David rest. In verses 11b-17 God promises that David's throne, kingdom, and dynasty will last forever. This promise is fulfilled in Jesus. In verses 18-29, David goes into the tent for the Ark and thanks the Lord for the promises He has made concerning his house. God's greatness to David and Israel is expressed in this prayer because God has redeemed them, made a name for Himself, and He performed great wonders on behalf of His people.

2 Samuel 8 records more of David's victories over Israel's enemies, and his subduing of them into servanthood in his kingdom. David's rule up to that point is characterized as doing what is "just and right" in verse 15. The story of Mephibosheth, Jonathan's son, is recorded in 2 Samuel 9. David does this because of the relationship he had with Jonathan and the covenant they had made together (1 Sam. 18:3 20:12-15). David's kindness to Mephibosheth shows David's heart, as he still cares for the house of Saul.

David's kindness is refuted by the new king of Ammon in 2 Samuel 10:1-6. Hanun, the new king, humiliated David's messengers and the people knew this would anger David against them. The Ammonites hire a large army to help fight on their behalf, and both eventually retreat from David's army in verses 6-14. In verses 15-19, the Syrian led army regroups but is defeated by the Israelites. The Ammonite army is also defeated, as recorded in 2 Samuel 12:26-31.

2 Samuel 11 contains the tragic story of David and Bathsheba. David should have been out fighting with his men, but he stayed home instead (v1). Verse 4 makes it clear that she was not pregnant before David sent for her. David desperately tries three times to cover up his sin in verses 6-17. In David's conversations with Uriah it can be seen that Uriah is more honorable than David, and that he is an innocent man. David devises a plan that will place Uriah in a heated battle where he will be killed. Deuteronomy 27:24 says "Cursed is the man who kills his neighbor secretly". David's actions will have severe consequences. In verses 18-27 David hears the news of Uriah's death and shows no signs of remorse.

Wednesday • Luke 1-2

Luke is the only writer of the New Testament that is a Gentile. Luke is the author of the gospel that bears his name, and also the book of Acts. Both of these books mention Theophilus ("Lover of God") as being the beneficiary of Luke's work. While Paul wrote more books than Luke, Luke's gospel and the book of Acts make him the biggest contributor to the New Testament. Luke wrote his gospel in the early 60's AD, and formed it from the accounts of eyewitnesses during his investigation of Jesus' ministry (1:1-4). It is primarily written for a

Gentile audience. In many cases Luke writes about Jesus' compassion for the downtrodden of society, especially Gentiles. Beginning at Luke 9:51 and covering the next 10 chapters most of the material is unique only to Luke.

In Luke 1:1-4 Luke has investigated Jesus' ministry for Theophilus ("Lover of God") in order to have an accurate and thorough account of what has taken place. Luke was not an eyewitness himself, but sought the help of others who saw and experienced firsthand Jesus' life and ministry. Luke starts his gospel by detailing the announcement of the birth of John the Baptist, who would prepare the way for Jesus (v5-25). Zacharias was a priest and Elizabeth was from a priestly family, and both were righteous and blameless before God (v5-6). There is no specific age mentioned, but they were past the age of having a child. In addition, Elizabeth had been barren her whole life (v7). It was a great privilege to burn the incense in the temple and most priests would serve their whole life and never get the opportunity to do so (v8-10). While at the altar of incense, Zacharias receives a heavenly visitor (v11-12). The angel tells Zacharias that his prayer has been heard and Elizabeth will give birth to a son who he is to name John (v13). Verses 14-17 tell about the impact of the ministry of John the Baptist. He would bring joy and gladness, he would be great in God's eyes, he would refrain from drinking, he would be filled with the Holy Spirit, and he would turn many people back to the Lord. His ministry would be like Elijah's, as he prepares people for the coming of the Lord. Because Zacharias did not believe the angel's message he was mute until the time of John's birth (v18-20). Zacharias finishes his service in the temple and Elizabeth is five months pregnant (v21-25). Being barren was seen as a punishment from God, but Elizabeth would no longer have to hear the reproach of people.

In verses 26-38, Gabriel comes to Mary from the very presence of God to announce the birth of the coming Savior. Mary was chosen by God to give birth to the Savior of the world. Luke uses the term "highly favored". It can be translated "greatly graced", and is the same word used in Ephesians for all believers. Mary is a receiver of grace, not a giver of grace. The child is described in verses 31-33. His name will be Jesus ("Jehovah is salvation"), He will be great (sinless, perfection), He will be the Son of the Highest (Son of God), He will inherit the throne of David (2 Sam. 7 fulfillment), He will reign over the house of Jacob (Messiah), and His kingdom will never end (eternal). Verses 34-36 cover the conception. What Mary heard was humanly impossible, but she also knew that with God nothing is impossible (v37). Mary wanted God's will to be done in her life and obediently gave herself totally to God (v38).

Mary's servant heart is revealed both in verse 38, and in her song in verses 46-56, which she sings while visiting her cousin Elizabeth (v39-45) who is pregnant with John the Baptist. Mary's song is a call to praise, and displays her heart of worship. She takes the proper stance of worship-lowers self to magnify God. In verses 46-49 Mary praises God for His goodness toward her, but also for providing her a Savior. Verses 50-55 show Mary praising God for His mercy and love (v50), His power (v51), His justice (v52), His goodness (v53), and His salvation (v55). In verses 57-66 John the Baptist is born, and Zachariah's tongue is loosed to sing his song of praise in verses 67-80. Zachariah's song addresses God's redemption of man (v66-70, Eph. 1:7, Titus 2:14), God's rescuing of His people (v71-75), and God's revealing of Himself through Jesus (v76-79).

In Luke 2:1-7 Jesus is born, and Luke is the only gospel writer who links this event with world history. The announcement of the birth of Jesus is given by the angels to shepherds tending sheep in the field (v8-20). The announcement uses three names for Jesus-Savior (deliverer, rescuer), Christ (anointed one), and Lord (one who brings salvation). Jesus will reconcile people to God (v14). The shepherds were actually the first to tell others about the good news of the birth of the Savior of the world (v17). 2 Corinthians 5:12-21 says that the message of reconciliation has been given to all believers to tell to others. Mary and Joseph bring Jesus to the temple to be circumcised and dedicated to the Lord (v21-24).

In verses 25-32, Simeon ("God has heard") praises God for doing what He had promised. Simeon, As well as many Jewish people, were waiting for the "Consolation of Israel". This was a prayer that Jewish people prayed asking God to send the Messiah to rescue them (v25). Salvation would be offered to all, including the Gentiles (v32). Every person's eternal destiny is based on whether or not they believe in Jesus (v34). One day in the future Jesus will give His life for each person and even Mary will suffer the pain of losing her Son (v34-35). Anna, a devout follower of God, praises God for providing redemption for His people through Jesus (v36-38). Mary and Joseph return to Nazareth and Jesus grows physically, becomes strong spiritually, is filled with wisdom, and God's grace (favor) was on him (v39-40). In verses 41-52, we read the only story that refers to Jesus' childhood. Twelve was the age that young boys were thought to start becoming men. Even then people were amazed at His understanding. The central point of the story is Jesus would always be about His Father's business throughout His life (v49).

Thursday • Job 35-36

Elihu continues to speak to Job in chapter 35. In verses 1-3 Elihu is telling Job that he is inconsistent, claiming God would vindicate him, but also that God was the one bringing him harm. In verses 4-8, Elihu continues to address Job's inconsistent speech by saying that Job's righteousness or unrighteousness only affected himself. Elihu's argument for this is that God is not indifferent to people, but that people are indifferent to God. People want God to help them, but they are not interested in honoring Him (v9-11). Human arrogance and pride keeps God from answering the calls of man for help (v12-13). God's silence to Job reveals what kind of person Job is (v14-15), and the words Job has spoken are without knowledge of God (v16). We must remember in Elihu's speeches he is not defending Job, but defending God against Job and his friend's view of Him.

In Job 36:1-4, Elihu claims to speak perfect words because they come from God. Verse 5 proclaims that God's power will assure His purposes are accomplished. Elihu will build the rest of his argument on this verse. This argument is probably aimed at Job's speech about the suffering of the righteous and the prosperity of the wicked. In verses 6-14, Elihu relates that at times God uses "cords of affliction" to reach the hearts of people to get their attention. In verses 15-16 Elihu agrees that at times the righteous do suffer, but only because they have strayed from the Lord. Elihu also rebukes Job for being unjust and not using his wealth wisely (v17-21). In verses 22-26, Elihu continues to praise God for His great power. Elihu is telling Job that he should concentrate on God's power rather than God's seemingly injustice toward him. In verses 27-33 Elihu praises God for His power, and gives an example of His power over nature in the rain cycle.

Friday • Isaiah 54-61

The work of the Servant of the Lord is accomplished, and Isaiah 54:1-10 is a hymn of praise welcoming in a new age. The proper response to the work of the Servant of the Lord is to praise the Lord like a barren woman who brings forth a child. While suffering as a widow during the exile, the intent of verses 4-8 is for the people to focus on God and His grace. Just as God promised never to flood the earth, God promises His loyal love to His people in verses 9-10. In verses 11-15 God will protect and bless His people, they will learn of Him through His instruction, and Jerusalem will once again be a place of peace but will still have enemies. Even those who come against them are under the sovereign hand of God (v16-17).

Isaiah 55 is about the grace of God. In verses 1-5 we see a picture of someone who sells water, which was popular in Babylon where the exiles are. It is God who calls out to them to partake of the waters of salvation He offers. Paul quotes this in Acts 13:34 in reference to Jesus and His resurrection. This call to repentance is urgent and needs to be heeded before it is too late (v6-7). Verses 8-13 tie together the themes of the passage. God's grace comes through His Word and offers repentance to all those who hear it. His Word always accomplishes its purposes.

Isaiah 56-66 concerns the people who are back in the land after the exile. When they return, the land is a place of corruption and devastation which we will see in the rest of this chapter and those that follow. In verses 1-8 the proselyte and eunuchs are addressed because they were prohibited in the past from worshiping (Deut. 23:1-8). Faithfulness to the Lord is expressed here in keeping the Sabbath. God is saying if anyone is faithful to Me, they will have a place to come and worship. The Court of Gentiles in Jesus' day envisioned this. It is from there Jesus drove out the moneychangers, and quotes verse 7 in this passage. In verses 9-12, God addresses the wicked leaders of Israel who feed off the sheep instead of leading them.

In Isaiah 57-59 the people are condemned for their spiritual adultery (57), hypocritical fasting (58), and injustice (59). In all of these chapters their prayers are not being answered because of these particular sins. The condemnation of the leaders and the people is the concern of Isaiah 57:1-10. The people had given themselves to other gods. God likens the people to adulterers and prostitutes for following other gods. The people had forgotten God and feared other gods, but those who trust in the Lord will inherit the land (v11-13). In verses 14-21, God's anger and grace are revealed in the midst of human rebellion. Those who continue in their sin will experience His anger, while those who realize they are "crushed and bowed low" will experience His grace.

In Isaiah 58 God addresses the people's empty spiritual lives by illustrating their observance of fasting. They would fast, but for the wrong reasons (v1-5). They showed outward obedience, but their hearts were far from the true reason for fasting (v6-9). Fasting should have led to them being more concerned for those less fortunate than them. These concerns should have been a normal pattern of life for God's people (v10-12). What the people were missing was that their fasting should have been done because they loved God, which would have led to them loving the people around them (v14-15).

In Isaiah 59, God addresses their social injustices. The people had become unjust even down to the most basic needs such as food and clothing (v1-8). Morally speaking they had reached the lowest level as evidenced by these sins. In verses 9-11 the people face the consequences of their sin, and it is then they see that their sins are against the Lord (v12-15a). In 15b-18, God's wrath is made known against sin and He will repay them for each one. God's wrath against sin will result in people from all over the world fearing Him (v19-21).

Isaiah 60 speaks of the future glory of Zion that will shine with the glory of God as nations and kings come there to worship (v1-3). As God's glory resonates through the city, all peoples will come there to worship the Lord (v4-9). At one time the gates of Jerusalem were always shut due to their enemies, but they are now open wide for all to come (v10-12). Foreign nations that were once their enemies shall supply the needs of the city (v13-22). Peace and righteousness will be found there (v17). Verses 19-21 form much of the background for Revelation 21-22.

Isaiah 61:1-2 is quoted by Jesus at the beginning of His ministry. Jesus stopped short of the day of vengeance because this will apply to His Second Coming, not His first. Anointed by the Spirit of the Lord, He ministers to the poor, brokenhearted, captives, and prisoners. All of these apply physically and spiritually. Because of His ministry, the people will exchange their sorrow for joy. In verses 4-9 the land will be restored to God's people because according to His covenant, it belongs to them. Verses 10-11 may be the city of Zion speaking expressing its joy in the Lord.

Saturday • 2 Corinthians 6-8

2 Corinthians 6:1-13 continues the theme from chapter 5 regarding being ambassadors of the kingdom, and the ministry of reconciliation that the Lord has given to His people. When reading the passage Paul's

hardships in ministry shine through, as well as his commitment to the cause of Christ. Paul could have listed many accomplishments supporting his ministry, but the hardships were proof that he truly was an ambassador of Christ who was seeking to reconcile people to Him. Verse 2 quotes Isaiah 49:8 concerning the return of the exiles from captivity. By quoting this verse Paul is saying that if the day the exiles returned is *a* day of salvation, then what God has done through Christ in reconciling the world to Himself is *the* day of salvation. In verses 4-5 Paul offers proof that his ministry that it is in Christ. In verse 5 a "tumult" is a civil disorder of which Paul suffered through on numerous occasions (Acts 13:50, 14:19, 16:19, 19:29). Verses 6-7 are the moral integrity of his ministry, which describe the characteristics of his ministry. Verse 7 will probably remind you of Ephesians 6 and the armor of God and may refer to spiritual warfare. Most believe verses 8-10 describe Paul's ministry in terms of how others viewed him and what Christ thought of him. For example, in verse 10 "sorrowful" would describe what others saw when they looked at him during his sufferings. But "yet always rejoicing" is something Paul could do because he knew Christ despite all of his hardships.

In verses 14-16, Paul warns of forming close relationships that may lead the Corinthians to compromise their faith. For the people in Corinth this was probably a warning not only for marriage, but also to not participate in their pagan rituals. The reason for this is because as Christians they belonged totally to God. Believers are the temple of the living God, and we are His sons and daughters (v17-18). In 1 Corinthians 3:16-17 all Christians were called "temples" of God and in 1 Corinthians 6:16-20 each individual Christian is spoken of as being a "temple" of God. Verse 16 is a reference to Ezekiel 37:26-27 and is referenced again in Revelation 21:3. God was present in the tabernacle and temple in the Old Testament, but in the New Covenant God dwells within His people. Verses 17-18 are taken from Isaiah 52:11 which was an appeal for the Jewish exiles to leave the paganism of Babylon and return to Jerusalem. By quoting these verses, Paul is warning those in Corinth to stay away from being involved with pagan worship because they are the temple of God. 2 Corinthians 7:1 belongs here also. Paul is warning Christians to avoid every possible source of defilement in their lives.

In 2 Corinthians 7:2-16, Paul speaks of his joy over their repentance. In verse 2 "open your hearts to us" can be translated "make room for us in your hearts." Paul viewed his relationship with the people at Corinth as his friends, even though they attacked his integrity as an apostle (v3-4). Titus brought great news to Paul that the Corinthians had repented and longed to see Paul again (v5-7). This repentance was due to a letter that Paul had written them (v8-12). Paul does say he regretted writing the letter, but after he found out from the report of Titus that it produced repentance Paul was overjoyed. Verse 10 demonstrates the difference between repentance and remorse. Godly sorrow leads to repentance and salvation, while worldly sorrow produces death. An example of godly grief would be Paul in Acts 9, and an example of remorse would be Judas in Matthew 27:3-5. Upon hearing this good news of their repentance, Paul praises them for their obedience (v13-16).

Paul had previously instructed the people of Corinth to begin setting aside an offering to be collected (1 Corinthians 16:1-4). In an effort to get them to resume their offering for the Jewish Christians in Judea, Paul gives them an example from the Macedonians (Philippi & Thessalonica) in 2 Corinthians 8:1-7. The churches of this area gave during times of affliction, and they gave out of their own poverty (v1-2). Paul also tells us they gave above their means (v3), they wanted to give (v3), and they gave themselves to the Lord (v5). In verse 7 Paul appeals to the people of Corinth to excel in giving, just as they excel in other things. Giving to others will provide them with an opportunity to show their love to others (1 Cor. 13).

In verses 8-12 Paul cites the example of Christ and His sacrificial giving up of all things so that others could have salvation. His gift of salvation was driven by love. The people in Corinth were advised to complete the taking up of the offering to give to those in Judea (v10-11). They also were to give out of what they had and it would be acceptable to God (v12). Paul stresses in verses 13-15 that giving is not meant to be a burden, but an equal sharing among them so that all may have. Paul cites Exodus 16:18, which is from the story of God giving them manna to eat, to show that each person's needs were met. No one had too much, and no one lacked any food.

In verses 16-24 Paul gives the credentials for Titus and two other men (v18, 22) that qualified them to receive the offering at Corinth. The offering taken up was to be for the glory of God and was to demonstrate the Corinthians good hearts (v19). One thing of note about the offering is that you had Gentile churches taking up an offering for a Jewish congregation. Any animosity that existed between the two groups could be reconciled with the giving of the offering. In verse 24 Paul encourages the Corinthians to give out of their love for Christ and their love for fellow brothers and sisters in Christ.

Cover to Cover Challenge

Week 19

Sunday • Psalm 60-65

Welcome to week 19 of the *Cover to Cover Challenge*! Let us continue to pray that God gives each of us understanding of His Word and that He alone will get the honor, glory, and praise for everything that comes from our study of the Word. May we all agree with the psalmist when he says "My soul keeps Your testimonies, and I love them exceedingly".

Psalm 60 is a national lament representing the nation of Israel. This may refer to 2 Samuel 8:13. In this psalm David expresses that with all of the adversity surrounding them that the people should look to God and be revived (v1-3). David is confident victory will come and the Lord will deliver them (v4-5). God answers the prayer in verses 6-8, as His sovereignty over the nations is displayed. The psalm closes with David still looking to God for victory over their enemies (v9-12).

Psalm 61 is an individual lament as David displays his longing for God. In verses 1-2 David seeks protection from an enemy, but David feels as if he is far away from the Lord. God has always been David's refuge and strong tower from his enemies (v3-4). He also knows that God hears his prayers, and remains true to the promises He has made to His people (v5). In verses 6-8 David prays for God's protection, a long reign, and he will praise the name of the Lord forever.

Psalm 62 is a psalm of confidence in the Lord. David expresses in verses 1-2 that God is all he needs for protection. David's enemies have come against him, and seek his ruin and destruction (v3-4). In facing this adversity, David trusts solely in God alone for his protection (v5-7). David gives a warning to all that they should not trust in anything but the Lord, in verses 8-10. In verses 11-12 David trusts in the Lord's power and His mercy (love), and all will receive their reward according to what they have trusted in.

Psalm 63 is another psalm of lament. In verse 1 David describes his longing for God as a thirsty person desires a drink. From past experience, David knows where to meet with God and to praise Him (v2-3). David praises the Lord because it is from the Lord all of his blessings come from (v4-5). In verses 6-8, David remembers all of the great things the Lord has done for him and continually seeks protection from God. These verses also express James 4:7-8, that we are to draw close to God and He will draw closer to us. God will vindicate David against those who seek his life, while David rejoices in what God has done (v9-11).

Psalm 64 is also a lament, and expresses divine retribution on behalf of the godly against the wicked. David prays for the Lord to hear his prayer, and asks the Lord to protect him from his enemies (v1-6). These enemies of David are rebellious, work iniquity, and lurk in secret to harm David. Their schemes are designed against

David, but ultimately against God. It is God who will vindicate David (v7-9). As the wicked ambushed David, the wicked will come under the ambush of God. In verse 10, David encourages the godly to trust in the Lord during times of adversity.

Psalm 65 is a song of thanksgiving, calling on all of God's people to thank Him for His presence and His rule over the earth. In verses 1-3, God is to be praised for His salvation provided for His people. In verse 4 God is to be praised for His goodness toward those who believe in Him. In verses 5-8 God is praised for His acts in creation and His control of history. In verses 9-13, God is praised because of His giving water to the earth to replenish and restore it.

Monday • Exodus 27-30

Exodus 27 continues the discussion of the articles of the Tabernacle. In chapter 27:1-8 we read about the altar of burnt offering. This is the largest piece and would be 7 ½ ft. by 4 1/2 ft. In verses 9-19 is the description of the courtyard of the Tabernacle. It was 150 ft. long and 75 ft. wide. There are four purposes for this: (1) to prevent people approaching, (2) keep out wild animals, (3) to separate the holy presence of God from the world, and (4) with its one gate it was the only way to approach God. Verses 20-21 deal with the oil for the lampstand that would burn continually and the setting aside of Aaron with his sons to be priests of God.

Exodus 28:1-5 discusses the making of the garments for the priesthood. In verses 6-14 we read that the ephod would have the 12 tribes of Israel engraved on it, representing all of Israel. The breastplate would have four rows of three stones, also with the names of the tribes of Israel engraved upon them. The Urim and Thummim (lights and perfections) would also be on the breastplate. These were used to determine the will of God in times of crisis (Num. 27:21). The sleeveless blue robe described in 31:5 was to be worn under the ephod. The bells upon the hem assured the people that the high priest had not died in the Holy Place. The gold plate was to be placed upon the turban, and would go from ear to ear (v36-39). Verses 40-43 describe the attire of the ordinary priests, and introduce the next chapter on consecrating Aaron and his sons.

In Exodus 29:1-9, Aaron and his sons are set aside to be priests. Notice the sacrifices are without defect, and without leaven. Aaron and his sons were also to be washed, symbolizing the removal of uncleanness from sin. In verses 10-14, a bull was brought as a sin offering for Aaron and his son's sins. One of the rams would be offered to the Lord completely (v15-18). Upon sacrificing the second ram its blood was to be applied to the right ear (to hear the Word of God), to the right thumb (hands would do the work of the Lord), and the right big toe (walk of the priests would be an example to the people). This ram would also help serve for the wave offering. The direction of the wave offering was not back and forth, but to the altar and back toward the priest. This symbolized it being given to God, and received back for its use (v22-26). Parts of the ram were to be given back to the priest (v27-28). The garments were to be passed down for future priests (v29-30). The breast and thigh from the second ram were to be cooked and eaten by Aaron and his sons, with leftovers being burned (v31-34). The bull offering for sin was to be done for seven days so the altar would be holy (v35-37). The daily offerings are discussed in verses 38-42, while verses 43-46 highlight the importance of the consecrating service and that God would dwell among the people.

The altar of incense in Exodus 30:1-10 symbolized continual intercession before God. Failure to burn the incense would lead to desecration of the altar. The ransom (atonement-means to deliver or redeem by substitute) money in verses 11-16 was to be taken during a census of those twenty years old and older. The bronze laver in verses 17-21 was for the priest to wash before they made an offering of fire before the Lord. The oil and incense were to consecrate the furniture pieces (v22-38). Both the oil and incense were unique, and if anyone duplicated it for their own use they were to be excommunicated from the people.

Tuesday • 2 Samuel 12-16

In 2 Samuel 12, we learn the consequences of David's sin with Bathsheba and the murder of her husband. Through Nathan the prophet and his parable, David is accused of his sins against the Lord. In the parable David is the rich man, Uriah is the poor man, and Bathsheba is the ewe lamb (v1-10). David repents of his sin and is forgiven, but the consequences will be tragic (v11-14). Not only will the son die (v15-23), but his family is about to be torn apart. Solomon ("God is peace") is born in verses 24-25, and the Lord gives him another name Jedidiah ("Loved by the Lord"). In verses 26-31 Joab, with David's help, defeats the Ammonites.

2 Samuel 13 begins the adversity that will come upon David's house. In verses 1-22, David's oldest son Amnon is in love with his sister Tamar. With help from Jonadab, Amnon devises a plan to be alone with his sister and rapes her. She goes to stay with her brother Absalom, and remains unmarried and childless (desolate). While David is angry, he is guilty of a similar sin. After two years Absalom devises a plan to murder Amnon, which removes the oldest son of David from succeeding to the throne (v23-33). David hears that all of his sons are dead, but Jonadab tells David that only Amnon is dead. It could be probable that Absalom and Jonadab had from the beginning planned all of these events to get rid of the oldest son. How would Jonadab know only Amnon was dead? Absalom flees to Geshur to the home of Talmai, his grandfather on his mother's side, in verses 34-39 (3:3).

2 Samuel 14 is about Absalom's return to Jerusalem from exile. In verses 1-20, Joab devises a plan to get Absalom back to Jerusalem. Joab will use a woman from Tekoa who tells a story of blood vengeance against her son. He was responsible for murdering her other son. The story is used to get David to see that Absalom should be welcomed home. David perceives that Joab is behind this. He agrees to let Absalom come to his house after three years away, but David still does not want to see him (v21-24). Absalom is described as handsome and is noted for his hair, which will be part of his downfall (18:9-15). Two more years pass before Absalom, after getting Joab's attention, gets an audience with the king (v25-33).

In 2 Samuel 15:1-6 Absalom constructs a plan to become king of Israel. He suggests that he should be the one to judge the cases of the people who come from Israel to have their cases heard. Absalom basically tells each person what they want to hear. After four years (not forty), Absalom sends messengers throughout the kingdom to declare him king at the sound of a trumpet (v7-12). In an ironic twist, David is now the one fleeing Jerusalem (v13-18). After Ittai declares his devotion to David (v19-23), he commands Zadok and Abiathar to carry the Ark back to Jerusalem and remain there along with their sons (v24-31). David learns that Ahithophel ("My brother is foolishness") is behind the plot to take the throne. David sends Hushai back to confuse Ahithophel's counsel to Absalom and to work with Zadok and Abiathar in bringing news to David (v32-37).

In 2 Samuel 16:1-4 Mephibosheth's servant Ziba has supplies for David and his people. Mephibosheth has stayed behind, believing the kingdom will be restored to him and his family. Shimei, who belonged to the house of Saul, meets David along the way (v5-14). He curses and throws stones and dirt at David, but David does not retaliate. Shimei will pay for what he did (1 Kgs. 2:8-9). Hushai declares his loyalty to Absalom in verses 15-19, in compliance with David's advice. Absalom depends upon the advice of Ahithophel as one who has spoken with God (v20-23).

Wednesday • Luke 3-4

Luke 3:1-6 is the beginning of the ministry of John the Baptist. Each gospel clearly identifies John as the one sent by God to prepare the way for Jesus. Luke links world history with biblical history by providing dates for those reigning at the time. In verse 2 shows that the Word of God came to John the Baptist while he was in the wilderness. John's calling to preach God's Word follows that of all the Old Testament prophets before him of which he will be last. John preached a message of repentance and baptism was the sign that they had done this (v3). To the Jew this was a cause of concern because the only ones who were baptized were Gentile converts. Gentiles were baptized because the Jews viewed the Gentiles as unclean. John's message and ministry showed that Jew and Gentile alike needed repentance. His ministry is spoken of as someone preparing the way for the coming of royalty according to Isaiah 40:3-5 (v4-6). Within the context of Isaiah these verses depict the return of the Israelites from captivity.

In verses 7-20 his message is one of repentance, which will also be Jesus' message as well. Verses 7-9 are about judgment. John the Baptist makes it clear that being Abraham's descendants will not save them. The image of the "ax is laid to the root of the trees" shows that judgment is imminent for each person. John the Baptist also shows that true repentance involves bearing fruit. Individuals who hear the message must repent or experience the judgment of God. He addresses three groups of people-people in general, tax collectors, and soldiers (v10-14). Each group asks what they must do in response to the message John the Baptist has preached. They want to know how they should live their life. In verses 15-18 John the Baptist makes it clear that he is not the Messiah and does this in two ways. First, there is Someone else coming who is mightier than him. Second, He will baptize you with the Holy Spirit and fire. The reference to Holy Spirit and fire may mean some will hear the message of repentance and be saved and receive the Holy Spirit while others will reject the message with fire symbolizing their judgment. Verses 19-20 give the reason why John the Baptist is put in prison. Jesus is baptized, and we have another example of the Trinity being in one place at one time (v21-22). Luke's genealogy shows that Jesus is around 30 years old, a descendant of David, goes back to Adam to show He identifies with all of humanity, and ends with a declaration that He is the Son of God (23-38). This genealogy also shows that all of humanity is dependent upon Jesus for salvation because there is no other name under heaven by which man can be saved (Acts 4:12).

Luke 4 records the temptation of Jesus in verses 1-13. These verses also give believers a glimpse of spiritual warfare and a strategy to defeat temptation when they come. Jesus was filled with the Spirit for the time of temptation He was about to endure (v1). It is important that believers be filled with the Spirit during these times. Jesus was also dependent on God and His Word during times of temptation (v4, 8, 12). With each temptation Jesus responded with God's Word to defeat the attack of the devil. Some also see in these temptations a parallel with the apostle John's lust of the eyes, lust of the flesh, and the pride of life in 1 John 2. Jesus was hungry so Satan tempted Him to turn stones into bread (v3-4). In verses 5-8 Satan tempts Jesus with ruling over the world. Some do not see how Satan could do this because it was not his to give. Scripture does say that Satan rules over this world (John 12:31, 14:30. 16:11, Rev. 13:2). In verses 9-12 Satan tempts Jesus to throw Himself off the temple because He knows God will save Him. This temptation also shows that Satan knows Scripture but twists it to fit his own agenda. But all of the temptations were designed to get Jesus not to trust God and be dependent on Him. It also shows the power of God's Word, and its effectiveness for us to use in our own lives in defeating temptation. Just as the Spirit led Jesus into the wilderness, it led Him to begin His ministry at Galilee (v14-15).

Luke is the only gospel that records the first sermon of Jesus where He is rejected by His hometown (v16-30). Jesus, in quoting Isaiah 61:1,2 is showing what His ministry will be and sets the tone for what Luke will record in his gospel. By quoting these verses from Isaiah Jesus was also identifying Himself as the Messiah which the verses speak of. In verses 24-30 the Jews are angry at Jesus because of the two stories He referenced to them. In both stories God's prophets performed miraculous deeds for Gentiles. They were so angry that they attempted to throw Jesus off a cliff. Jesus' authority over demonic forces is recorded in verses 31-37. The stories of demon possession prove James 2:19 to be correct. The people are amazed at His teaching. Jesus also shows His power over sickness by healing Peter's mother-in-law of a fever (v38-39). Once His fame had gone out, people brought those who were sick and possessed and He healed them (v40-41). Jesus moves through other cities and preaches repentance (v42-43).

Thursday • Job 37-38

Elihu continues his speech from the end of chapter 36:1-13 when he was discussing God's power in the realm of nature. It is God who sends the rain, thunder, lightning, and snow. Just as God's ways in nature are a mystery, so is God's providence. God sends the storm for punishment, for love of His people, and for His own pleasure. In verses 14-20, Elihu asks Job to think about the position he has been portraying in his speeches. Even after the storm, God displays His majesty as the skies become clear and the sun shines (v21-24).

In Job 38, God begins to speak to Job out of the whirlwind. Job will not hear a reason for his suffering, but he will learn that God had not abandoned him. Job needed to learn about God, and God will show Job who He is by taking him on a journey through creation (v1-3). Job had spoken against God and how he managed the universe, so God puts him in his place by asking him the question "Surely you know" (v4-7). We could probably say that God is asking Job "Where were you when I …?" God controls the sea (v8-11), the morning and dawn (v12-15), things Job could not see (v16-18), and the light and darkness (v19-21). God has the power and authority, and displays it as He wants (v22-30). In verses 31-38 God controls the weather and the stars, and puts them in their place for His own purpose. He even supplies the food for the wild animals that are in need (v39-41).

Friday • Isaiah 62-66

In Isaiah 62:1-7, Isaiah prays that the vision of Jerusalem that he has seen from the Lord will soon come. The whole world will come to Jerusalem to see her. The reference to a new name symbolizes her following the Lord (v4, 12). God will give them watchmen to proclaim His Word, and to pray for them. In verses 8-9, God makes an oath that their enemies will no longer plunder them because they will be a righteous people. All obstacles will be removed out of their way so they can return to Jerusalem (v10-11). The fulfillment of this event is shown in verse 12 by the different names they will be known by.

Isaiah 63:1-6 may be the watchmen on the wall who sees the Lord coming from Edom with His clothes dripping with crimson from judging Edom. In Revelation 19:11-16, the Lord Jesus will return in the same way. What is a day of judgment for some, will be a day of redemption for others. Isaiah 63:7 through the end of chapter 64 is a psalm of praise and lament on behalf of the people. Verses 7-10 portray a picture of God as a hurting father knowing that His children have rebelled against Him. The background of these verses and verses 11-14 is against the backdrop of the exodus. Beginning with verse 15 through 19, the people cry out for mercy. In this prayer, Isaiah recalls that through his ministry the people would continue to sin and their hearts hardened. In 64:1-7, the background shifts from the exodus to God revealing Himself at Sinai. Just as God came down to the mountain, Isaiah is praying for the Lord to come down now. In these verses sin is presented as continual, defiling, and destructive-creating a barrier between the people and the Lord. In verses 8-12 the analogy of the potter and the clay is used to present God as sovereign over His people, as the people are dependent on the mercy of God as their Father.

Many people believe that chapters 65-66 are the answer to the prayer of chapter 64. In 65:1-5 God is pictured as holding out His hands of love all day, but the people only responded with rejection. Their acts of disobedience are paganism, necromancy, and disregarding God's law. Paul uses verses 1-2 in reference to the Gentiles in Romans 10:20-21. God must, and will repay them for their sin (v6-7). In verses 8-10 there is a remnant that will be spared, as well as those who will suffer judgment for their disobedience (v11-12). God's people will enjoy His fellowship, but those who disobey will become a byword and be cursed by God (v13-16). Verses 17-25 contain future promises even from our day. God will create not only a new heavens and a new earth, but the whole order of the way we live will be transformed. The greatest of these will be that God will dwell with His people. Verse 25 may also be an allusion to Jesus' defeat of Satan, and not just a living condition during this time period.

Isaiah 66:1-4 may refer to empty religious practices of God's people. In chapter 65 they offered pagan sacrifices, but here they offer sacrifices with no reverence for God. God calls on those who believe in Him to rejoice, because He will repay His enemies (v5-7). In verses 7-11 we read a warning to prepare for the many people who will be coming to Jerusalem (54:1-3). The nations who will come are no longer coming to conquer, but to be at peace with them (v12-16). Those who worship the Lord will go to other nations and proclaim God to them (v17-21). In verses 22-24 God guarantees all the promises He has made to His people, and states that all will come to worship Him.

Saturday • 2 Corinthians 9-10

In chapter 9 Paul continues the theme of preparing and giving an offering. In this chapter Paul explains what giving truly is. According to verses 1-5, giving should be done to meet needs of others. The Christians in Judea had a need, and the churches in Macedonia and Corinth were encouraged to meet that need. Paul also likens giving to sowing in verse 6. Giving can result in the giver being blessed. In verse 7 we see that giving should be done with an attitude of rejoicing (Prov. 22:8). Verse 8 shows that it is by God's grace believers are able to give and to perform good works. In other words, God blesses you so that you can be a blessing to others. Paul quotes Psalm 111:9 in verse 9. This psalm celebrates the blessings of God to His people. Giving is also a form of trusting, as seen in verses 10-11. Giving displays one's trust in the Lord. In verse 12 we read that giving results in people giving thanks to God. Giving should be a part of every Christian's life so that everyone can benefit from this blessing. Giving also glorifies God according to verse 13. Glorifying God is what all believers should do when they perform good works. Finally in verse 14 we see that giving results in prayer. Those in Judea who received the gift would pray for those who gave it. Verse 15 gives praise to God for His "indescribable gift". What is God's "indescribable gift"? It is none other than Jesus Christ.

. In 10:1-6 Paul presents spiritual warfare as a military battle where one must invade enemy territory to stop the advancement of evil. This bondage that Paul speaks of is like a castle holding its prisoners, who must be set free. There were probably people in Corinth who not only opposed Paul, but also to the gospel message that he preached. Spiritual warfare cannot be won through human means. It can only be defeated through the divine power granted to believers (Eph. 6:10-20).

In an effort to condemn Paul, some at Corinth taught that Paul was not even really an apostle (v7-8) and that he was only trying to intimidate them through a letter because his physical presence was weak (v9-11). Paul shows his humility in verses 12-18. Unlike the false teachers at Corinth who compared themselves to one another, Paul refused to. Paul chose only to boast in the gospel that he preached and the Lord that he served, and he did not care what others said about him.

Cover to Cover Challenge

Week 20

Sunday • Psalm 66-68

Welcome to week 20 of the *Cover to Cover Challenge*! Continue to pray for all of those who are reading God's Word together through the week. Also, that the Lord be honored and glorified. Psalm 119:33 says "Teach me, O Lord, the way of Your statutes, and I shall keep it to the end".

Psalm 66 can be divided into two separate parts. In verses 1-12 the psalmist instructs all the earth to praise the Lord for His rule and reign, while verses 13-20 are personal thanksgivings from the author of the psalm. In verses 1-4, the whole earth is called to give glory for God's power and His glory that is revealed through His works. An example of His work is the deliverance from Egypt, which is referred to in verses 5-7. This deliverance also comes daily to those who follow the Lord as He refines them during trials and sufferings (v8-12). The psalmist turns from how the Lord delivered the nation, to how the Lord has delivered him (v13-20). Verses 18-19 are a great reminder that we need to keep our lives pure in order for our prayers to be heard.

Psalm 67 is a psalm of blessing. In verses 1-3, the psalmist asks for God's grace (mercy) to be shown to them so that people will know His ways-resulting in praise. This blessing will draw the nations to know God and will result in them praising the Lord (v4-5). In the Old Testament, God's desire for Israel was exactly this. He would bless them, and they would praise Him. They would be a light to the Gentiles, in order for them to come to know the Lord. The final two verses depict a time when both Jews and Gentiles will be blessed by the Lord and praise Him.

Psalm 68 speaks of the goodness of God, but also pictures Him as a warrior coming to deliver His people. In verses 1-3 God is pictured as a warrior, coming to scatter the enemy as the righteous rejoice. God is to be praised because He delivers those who are oppressed (v4-6). The Canaanites worshiped Baal, (who they believed rode upon the clouds) but it is the Lord who "rides in the heavens" and delivers His people. The example of the exodus is given to show the deliverance of the Lord (v7-10). The Lord defeated the enemies of Israel, and they fled before Him (v11-14). Mount Bashan is small in comparison to Mount Sinai, and envies her because God chose to dwell in Sinai and protect His people (v15-18). The deliverance of the Lord brings praise as He has protected His people (v19-20). While they are protected by God, He assures them once again that He will avenge them against their enemies (v21-23). Verses 24-27 describe a victory procession led by the Lord, and a song of victory sung by the people of Israel. In verses 28-31 the people call upon God to show His power against their enemies who oppress them. The psalm closes with a hymn of triumph as the Lord's rule is pictured as extending to the highest heaven (v32-35). The people praise Him because God is the one where their strength comes from.

COVER TO COVER CHALLENGE

Monday • Exodus 31-35

Exodus 31 describes those who would be in charge of building the tabernacle and its components (v1-11). Verses 12-17 are a reminder of being obedient in keeping the Sabbath days because it is a sign of the covenant between them and God. Verse 18 signifies the end of the forty days where Moses was on the mountain with God.

Exodus 32 contains the great contrast between how they were to worship the Lord and how they were not. Another contrast in the story is the presence of God on the mountain and the presence of sin in the desert. The people request Aaron to make them a god to worship in the absence of Moses (v1-4). This is a good example of how if we are not in constant communion with God through prayer and Bible study, we will also make ourselves a god to worship. And, as can be seen in verses 5-6, once this happens we will indulge in sin. God reveals to Moses that the people had sinned against Him (v7-10). The word "corrupt" means "to go to destruction". Moses pleads with God on behalf of the people through the special relationship the Lord has with them, on behalf of God's own name, and His promises to the patriarchs (v11-14). Moses comes down from the mountain to see the corrupt worship of the people. He breaks the two tablets made by God, symbolizing the people's breaking of the covenant (v15-20). Aaron offers many excuses in the presence of Moses (v21-24), and because of the people's lack of restraint 3,000 people died (v25-29). Moses goes back up to the mountain to intercede on behalf of the Israelites (v30-35).

In Exodus 33:1-6, God instructs Moses and the people to depart and begin moving toward the Promised Land. It is here that God reveals to them that He will not go with them because they are a stubborn people. The people remove their jewelry as a sign of mourning over hearing this. In verses 7-11 the tabernacle of meeting is the place Moses met with the Lord to worship and inquire from Him. The pillar of cloud showed that the Lord was there speaking to Moses. Moses asks the Lord to "show me your way", and for His "grace" (v12-14). The Lord responds by telling Moses that He will go with them. In verses 15-23 Moses ask the Lord if he can see His glory, and God grants his request but he cannot see God's face.

In Exodus 34:1-9 God instructs Moses to prepare two new stones and come up to Him on the mountain so He can write the law on them. It is here the Lord reveals Himself to Moses, and Moses once again asks the Lord to go with them even though they are a stubborn people. The covenant is renewed in the rest of the chapter, with stipulations on how the Israelites were to live. In verses 10-17 they are warned not to make a covenant with any foreigners, not to worship other gods, or make any god to worship. Verses 18-26 go back over previous commands of the Lord from 23:14-19. Moses' face shined because he spent time with God (v29-35). People can still tell today if you spend time with God.

Exodus 35:1-3 is a reminder for the people that before they begin work on the tabernacle they need to honor the Sabbath. In verses 4-9 the people are asked to give an offering to the Lord for the materials to build the tabernacle and its furniture. Verses 10-19 cover all the previous mentioned furniture. In verses 20-29 the people bring their offerings, and the people depart to begin work on the tabernacle. Verses 30-36:1 serve as reminders of Bezalel and Aholiab, who will lead the construction of the tabernacle and its furnishings.

Tuesday • 2 Samuel 17-20

2 Samuel 17:1-4 is a continuation of the instructions given by Ahithophel to Absalom from last week's readings. Ahithophel plans to kill David and bring back those who are with him. Remember, Hushai is there to inform David and to confuse the plans of Ahithophel. Hushai does succeed in frustrating Ahithophel's advice

as Absalom decides to follow Hushai's plan instead (v5-14). Hushai's plan will also give him time to get word to David, through Jonathan and Ahimaaz the sons of Zadok and Abiathar of what is happening next (v15-16). After nearly being caught, Jonathan and Ahimaaz get word to David (v17-22). Ahithophel knows Hushai's plan will not defeat David, and that David will come and avenge his enemies. This results in Ahithophel killing himself (v23). David goes to Mahanaim where he and the people are refreshed by three of his friends (v24-29).

In 2 Samuel 18:1-5, David prepares his troops for battle against Absalom and his army. He asks that they deal gently with his son. Verses 6-8 prepare the way for how Absalom will get caught in a tree and be killed by Joab and his troops (v9-18). With the death of Absalom, David has now lost three sons as a result of his sin with Bathsheba. Ahimaaz and a Cushite run to tell David the news of victory, but only the Cushite knows that Absalom is dead (v19-32). David mourns over his son in private and wishes it were him instead.

The victory of David's army over Absalom's army is turned into a time of mourning for Absalom in 2 Samuel 19:1-4. Joab interprets David's mourning as a sign that David would trade their victory and the lives of his army for the life of Absalom (v5-8). He encourages David to address the people or they may no longer be loyal to him. In verses 9-15, David replaces Joab with Amasa as the leader of the army. The men of Judah want to bring back David as king. Shimei is forgiven for his earlier disrespect for David (16:5-14) in verses 16-23. Mephibosheth is also forgiven for not fleeing with David from Absalom (v24-30). Barzillai is rewarded for helping David while he was in Mahanaim (v31-39). The men of Israel complain to the men of Judah because they were not included in the procession to return David as king (v40-43). This foreshadows the future division of the kingdom.

This dysfunction leads to the story of Sheba in 2 Samuel 20. Sheba, who is from the northern tribes (men of Israel), urges them to desert David (v1-2). David orders Amasa and his army to pursue Sheba, because he may cause more trouble than Absalom (v3-7). Joab takes this time to take advantage of Amasa and kill him (v8-13). Joab then pursues Sheba to Abel, and begins to take over the city wall (v14-15). A woman from the city rebukes Joab because their city is a city of peace (v16-19). Joab asks for Sheba to be handed over to them and they would stop with their siege of the city. The people of Abel kill Sheba and throw his head over the city wall, and Joab and his army retreat from the city (v20-22). Verses 23-26 give a list of David's new officials who will reside in his court.

Wednesday • Luke 5-6

Luke 5:1-11 records the miracle of the great catch of fish. For all of Peter's failings in Scripture here is an example that Peter knew he was in the presence of God realizing his own sinfulness (v8). In verse 10 the word "catch" means to catch alive. Peter, as all of apostles Jesus called, will leave behind the greatest catch of fish they have ever seen and their whole livelihood to follow Jesus. Jesus heals a man with leprosy in verses 12-16 by the touch of His hand (which was forbidden). Leviticus 14 contains the guidelines for a healed leper presenting themselves to the priest. Since Jesus' fame had spread (v15), for the first time in Luke, we see the Pharisees and teachers of the law get involved in verses 17-26. Mark tells us that four men brought the paralytic to Jesus to be healed. In one of the greatest miracles in the Bible, Jesus proves that He not only has the power to heal the paralytic but He also has the power to forgive sins. This miracle should have told them that God was in their midst, because even they knew only God could forgive sin.

In verses 27-32 the calling of Matthew (Levi) the tax collector is recorded. Tax collectors were some of the most hated people in society. They were also targeted by the Zealots and many of them were killed by the Zealots to show their defiance with Rome. Matthew invites his friends to a meal with Jesus (v29). The scribes and Pharisees complain to the disciples about the company they were with but it will be Jesus who answers the question (v30). Jesus came to call sinners to repent not the righteous. The irony here is that the Pharisees already saw themselves a righteous and needed no repentance. His message would mean nothing to someone who believed they were not sick with sin. In verses 33-39 God has always been the bridegroom, even in the OT (Isa. 54:5-6; Hosea 2:16-20), and Jesus is announcing that the time of the Messiah has come. In regards to fasting, the Pharisees only fasted to make themselves look holy. The disciples of John fasted in mourning over sin, but Jesus' disciples did not need to fast because the Bridegroom was with them. Verses 36-39 are a reference to the new and living way introduced by Jesus, which could not be placed into the old wineskins of Judaism. People would be reluctant to leave the old for the new.

In Luke 6:1-11 we read about two confrontations over the Sabbath (v1-5, 6-11). The Pharisees had their own traditions about Sabbath-keeping and work. This is how the Pharisees viewed the action by Jesus and the apostles. Plucking the grain would be reaping, rubbing it in their hands was threshing, throwing away the husks was winnowing, and eating the grain showed they prepared a meal. All four of these broke the Pharisees tradition of Sabbath keeping. He uses the example of David from 1 Samuel 21:1-6 and Numbers 28:9-10. Verses 6-11 record the healing of the man with the withered hand. For the Pharisee healing was only allowed when someone's life was in danger. Verse 5 is the key verse: the One who is greater than the temple was here, Jesus is the Lord of the Sabbath. From this point forward, the Pharisees will be even more opposed to Jesus (v11). Jesus is shown to be in prayer all day before choosing the twelve apostles. Other lists of the apostles are in Matthew 10, Mark 3, and Acts 1. This shows how vital prayer should be in our own lives (v12-16). Jesus heals many of their diseases and unclean spirits in verses 17-19.

Instead of the Sermon on the Mount, here in Luke it is called the Sermon on the Plain from verse 17 (v20-26). Luke's version of the Beatitudes is shorter, and also contains woes. The Beatitudes and the woes show a reversal of fortunes. Compare verse 20 to verse 24, and you will see the difference. Luke's gospel contains many reversals of fortune, such as Luke 16:19-31. Verses 27-36, with its theme of love, show how the disciple of Christ loves even when they are mistreated. They are to love their enemies, do good to those who hate them, bless those who curse them, and give to others. Verse 31 is the key to the passage. You treat others how you want to be treated. In verses 37-42 Jesus warns about being critical of others when we ourselves have sin, and when we may be doing the same thing we condemn others for. Verses 43-45 remind the reader that a disciple will look like his Master in the fruit that they bear. Matthew 7:18 says "A good tree cannot bear bad fruit, nor can a bad tree bear good fruit". Verses 46-49 show the firm foundation of those who are obedient to the teachings of the Lord. It also bears a strong resemblance to James 1:22 "But be doers of the word, and not hearers only, deceiving yourselves."

Thursday • Job 39-40

Job 39 continues God's speech directed at Job, which began in chapter 38. Reminder: God is showing Job how He manages the universe, and here in chapter 39- His creatures in nature. God puts him in his place by asking him the question "Surely you know". We could probably say that God is asking Job "Where were you when I …?" The format of questions stops at verse 13. Through each of these references to animals, God is showing Job that not only did He create them, but He sustains them and directs their paths.

After Job gets the tour of God's creation and learns how God sustains them, God turns it over to Job to speak (v1-2). Job responds with exclamations of his unworthiness. The one who accused God of being against him is now speechless to say a word (v3-5). God's second speech will continue until the end of chapter 41. In verse 6, God will again ask Job questions. In verses 6-14 Job is faced with the fact that God is God, and he is not. It is God who creates and sustains the universe, and God also defines the moral order of the universe. No human being can compare to God. Job needed to learn to trust God and rest in Him. In verses 15-24 God created the behemoth (means beast par excellence), and there was no other beast that compared to him in its power, yet God took care of it and provided for it. If God could take care of such a large and powerful beast, could He not also take care of Job?

Friday • Nahum

Nahum ("Comfort") is the prophet chosen by God to deliver a message of judgment against Nineveh, the capital of Assyria. It is the Assyrians who took the northern kingdom captive in 722 BC. Most believe Nahum was written during the reign of Manasseh, but because there are no kings mentioned, it is difficult to tell. The only clue is found in 3:8-10 and is the fall of No Amon (Thebes), which occurred in 663 BC. Assyria is still at the height of its power when Nahum proclaims its doom. Just a hundred years before, Nineveh repented at the preaching of Jonah. Assyria will finally fall at the hands of Babylon in 612 BC. This would be God's judgment upon the Assyrians for their oppression and cruelty toward Israel, and a comfort to Judah who still remained.

Nahum 1:1-6 describes God's justice as He pours out His wrath through manifestations of His power upon those who turn against Him. God is good, but those who devise evil plans against Him must be punished (v7-11). Many believe the enemy in verse 11 is Sennacherib. He was the most powerful and destructive leader in Assyria and was threatening the southern kingdom of Judah. You read of his fall in Isaiah 37. A reversal of fortunes takes place in verses 12-15. The Assyrians who are safe will be cut down, and the ones they are trying to cut down will be safe.

Nahum 2:1 refers to the Assyrians because they will be attacked and defeated soon (Babylonians), while verse 2 refers to the restoration of God's people. Verses 3-4 describe the attack against Nineveh as its defenses fall and those captured become slaves (v6-10). Verses 11-12 mock the Assyrians who had once terrorized the land. In verse 13, the hand of justice against the Assyrians belongs to the Lord. The one who preyed on others will be cut off by the One who defends His people (v13).

Nahum 3 begins another description of Nineveh's fall. Not only is there a woe pronounced against them (v1), Nineveh will be overwhelmed by those who come against them (v2-3). Assyria is pictured in verse 4 as being full of prostitution and sorcery that lures people in in order to enslave them. God will repay all of their violence with violence as He overthrows the city (v5-6). This judgment will be complete and final (v7). It wasn't until the late 1800's that any evidence of Nineveh was found. The third description of Nineveh's fall is in verses 8-11. When the Nile overflowed it allowed the Babylonians to come in and destroy Nineveh. Verses 12-14 continue the theme of Nineveh's fall with the fourth description of it. The people of Nineveh are described with the characteristics of locusts in verses 15-17. As they devoured one another and their enemies, they would be devoured from within and without. Assyria also suffered through failed leadership, which helped bring the nation down. (v18-19).

Saturday • 2 Corinthians 11-13

Paul shows deep concern for the Corinthians in chapter 11. He is worried that they may actually be deceived by those in Corinth who are turning them against him. If they could succeed in turning the Corinthians against Paul, then they may believe a different gospel if it is preached to them (v1-4). Paul believes that some in Corinth are in danger of being led astray, just as Eve was led by the serpent to disbelieve God's word in Genesis 3:1-7. Notice in verse 4 that Paul describes the three areas in which they could be deceived, and may have already been deceived: preaching of another Jesus, a different spirit, and a different gospel (Gal. 1:6-9). In the full passage (v1-15) Paul mentions the serpent (v3), Satan (v14), and demons (v15). It was Satan who was behind the attacks on Paul and who was putting out false doctrine in hopes of deceiving people. Paul's argument in verses 13-15 goes along with verses 1-4. Paul compares Satan being transformed into an angel of light to those in Corinth who are preaching a different Jesus, who are being deceived by another spirit, and who are preaching a different gospel. In verses 7-12 Paul defends, once again, his right not to take money from them for preaching the gospel.

Those in Corinth who have come against Paul boast about their accomplishments or about their knowledge in spiritual things (v16-21). Paul could have boasted about many things (miraculous conversions, starting churches, getting revelation from the Lord), but instead Paul boasted in his weaknesses and all of the trials he went through (v22-33). Why? Because it proved he was a true apostle who was fully dedicated to the people at Corinth. It also showed how mightily Christ worked through him.

Paul continues his boasting about the trials he had suffered in chapter 12, and also the revelations and visions he had received from the Lord (v1). Paul received many visions and revelations of and from the Lord (Acts 9, 16:9-10, 18:9-11, Gal. 1:12, Eph. 3:3-5, 1 Cor. 2:9-10, 1 Thess. 4:15). In verses 2-6, one of his trials led to him experiencing heaven. Many believe this may have occurred in Lystra when Paul was stoned (Acts 14:8-20). In verses 7-10 he spoke of a "thorn in the flesh" that humbled him, that kept him from being prideful, and that produced obedience in his life. This trial also led to him realizing that the Lord was all he needed; it gave an opportunity for the Lord to show His power, and it gave glory to the Lord. Paul was disappointed that the faithful in Corinth had not defended him, because they knew he was an apostle sent from the Lord (v11-13). Paul would lay his life on the line for the people in Corinth because he loved them, even though he did not receive the same love back from them (v14-15). He was also disappointed because they were questioning his motives (v16-19). Paul wanted to visit them, but he was fearful of what he would find taking place there when he came (v20-21).

Paul loves the people of Corinth so he confronts them over their behavior (2 Corinthians 13:1-10). Most of this letter shows Paul defending himself, but here he is warning them that all they have done before God. In verse 2 Paul warns them that when he comes again he will take disciplinary action if he needs to. For those who were wondering about Paul's apostleship and accusing him of not being an apostle, Paul says they will see the power of Christ work through him when he visits them again (v3-4). Paul also warns them that instead of examining him, they should be examining themselves to see if they are really believers (v5). Even though Paul warns them sternly over these things he still prays for them to not sin and do what is right (v6-7). Paul does this because the truth of the gospel should be proclaimed (v8). The whole purpose of Paul's letter is so that when he comes he will not have to use the authority that he has in Christ (v10). Paul closes the letter with encouragement for them to keep striving toward the goal of being like Christ, and for instructions to pursue unity in their relationships with one another (v11-13).

Cover to Cover Challenge

Week 21

Sunday • Psalm 69-71

Welcome to week 21 of the *Cover to Cover Challenge*! I pray that the *Cover to Cover Challenge* has been a blessing to you so far. Matthew 1:21 says, "And she will bring forth a Son, and you will call His name Jesus, for He will save His people from their sins". Be thankful for a risen Savior!

Psalm 69 contains elements of an imprecatory (calling down a curse) and a lament. Because of its references in the New Testament, it is also Messianic. Out of adversity from his enemies, David cries out for the Lord to help him (v1-4). From verses 5-12 it seems that David is experiencing this adversity because of his service to God (and the God he serves), which in turn causes his enemies to disgrace him. David prays for the Lord to deliver him in verses 13-18 as the floodwaters, the deep, and the pit seem to be overtaking him. God knows everything there is to know about David and his situation (v19-21). David looked for human help, but there was none. Verses 22-28 form the imprecatory part of the psalm. This is where David calls down a curse on his enemies. David is saying "what they have done to me be done to them". Verse 29 transitions the psalm from a lament to a hymn of praise that is seen in verses 30-36.

Psalm 70 is a rewording of the prayer in Psalm 40:13-17. The word "hasten" is added to Psalm 70 at both the beginning and the end of the psalm. David prays for God's justice over his enemies through His acts of deliverance (v1-4, v13-16). David closes out the psalm with a petition for the Lord to deliver him with no delay (v5, v17).

Psalm 71 is an individual lament with thanksgiving. In verses 1-4, David prays that the Lord will deliver him from his present situation. David has complete trust in the Lord. He trusts the Lord because He has delivered and protected him his whole life (v5-8). David prays for the Lord not to abandon him in his old age, and to be vindicated from his enemies (v9-13). He understands that the Lord is his only hope (v14-18). Because of this, David wants to share the works of God with the next generation. It is through past troubles that David has learned who God is (v19-21). Each time he was brought low the Lord revived him. David is going to declare the faithfulness of the Lord to all, through songs of praises (v22-24).

Monday • Exodus 36-38

Last week at the end of chapter 35, the people brought offerings to begin the work of the Tabernacle. In 36:1-7 we see the generosity of the people in bringing their offerings, as they had more than enough. The people begin to build the Tabernacle and its furniture over the next couple chapters. Bezalel is specifically mentioned, building the holiest of the furniture in 37:1-9. In 38:21-31 is the inventory of all the materials. According to the half-shekel each man over 20 was to give, some estimate the population of Israel at this time to be close to 2 million.

Tuesday • 2 Samuel 21-24

In 2 Samuel 21:1-4 a famine has struck the land of Israel because of Saul's bloody reign. David hands over seven of Saul's descendants to make restitution for what Saul had done to their people. Mephibosheth is spared because of the oath between David and Jonathan. David retrieves the bones of Saul and Jonathan, and buries them with Saul's seven descendants in the tomb of Saul's father Kish. Verses 15-22 record four battles with the Philistines, four giants of the land were killed.

2 Samuel 22 is Psalm 18, with just a few variations in the wording. In verses 1-3, David declares who God is to him. God is his strength, rock, fortress, and deliverer. Because of who God is David trusts (v4) and calls upon Him (v4) to deliver him from his enemies. In verses 5-7, David describes the situation he is in with strong language that refers to his death. David declares how God is going to help him in verses 8-16. God will move heaven and earth to help David, and no one can oppose Him. In verses 17-20, God delivers David from his enemies. In verses 21-25 David declares his faithfulness to God, and in verses 26-31 David speaks of God's faithfulness to him. David discusses the Lord's goodness to those who belong to Him in verses 32-37, and tells how He helps them. In verses 38-44 David claims victory over his enemies because of the strength God had given him, and in verses 45-47 David declares the results of the victory God had given him. In verses 48-51, David reflects on what God has done for him and the deliverance he has experienced by the Lord's hand.

2 Samuel 23:1-7 are not David's last words, but like a last will and testament. David knew that it was the Lord who gave him words to speak. He also knew that any king must be just (righteous) and fear the Lord. If a king would do these things, he would be beneficial like sunlight and rain. David acknowledges the covenant God has made with his house concerning his rule. Verses 8-39 list David's mighty men (strong and courageous).

In 2 Samuel 24:1-9 David, probably motivated by pride, angers the Lord by ordering a census of the people to enlarge his military capability. In verses 10-17 David realizes he has sinned against the Lord, and confesses his sin. The prophet Gad is sent by the Lord to give him three choices of which to pick from. David loses 70,000 fighting men to the plague. Upon seeing the Angel of the Lord (preincarnate Christ), David once again confesses his sin and shows his love for the people by asking that the judgment fall upon him instead. David is instructed in verses 18-25 to build an altar at the threshing floor of Araunah the Jebusite. It is here the Lord hears his prayer and the plague is withdrawn from Israel.

Wednesday • Luke 7-8

In Luke 7:1-10, Jesus meets the centurion who has a servant who is sick. This Gentile is praised for his great faith (v9), which was demonstrated by his belief that Jesus could just speak the word and his servant be healed. Scripture only speaks of Jesus as being "marveled" twice. Once is here at this man's faith and the other at the unbelief of those in His hometown of Nazareth. Thus far, Jesus has healed many people of disease and cast out demons. Here in verses 11-17, Jesus raises a widow's son back to life. This is the only time this story is recorded in Scripture. The widow would have been all alone in the world and no one to provide for her. Jesus' compassion can be seen in this story. Notice the reaction of the people in verses 16-17. They were fearful (awed) and they also glorified God. The phrase "God has visited His people" occurs in the Old Testament and is often associated with blessing (Ruth 1:6, 1 Sam. 2:21).

In verses 18-35, we see John the Baptist sending two of his disciples to question Jesus concerning Him being the Messiah, and we see Jesus' response. Jesus assures them that He is fulfilling the mission God had sent for Him to do (Isa. 61:1-2). Jesus affirms that He is the Coming One through His miracles, His teachings, and His mission. In verses 24-30, Jesus speaks of the greatness of John the Baptist. John the Baptist was not unstable or weak, but walked in the ways of an OT prophet who called people to repentance and prepared the way for Jesus. Verses 31-35 characterize the generation that rejects Jesus and John the Baptist. Wisdom, especially in the book of Proverbs is directly related to righteous living. In verses 36-50 we can see two reactions to Jesus. One from a hardened Pharisee who did not see himself as a sinner, and the second from an immoral woman who knew she was a sinner. This story reflects the fruit of someone who does not believe and the fruit of someone who does. In the parable, what Jesus tells the Pharisee brings out the forgiveness aspect. The one who had been forgiven bore fruit, and showed it through acts of love.

Luke 8:1-3 shows the prominent role that women played in supporting Jesus and His ministry, in a society that did not have much respect for them. The parable of the sower is recorded in verses 3-8, and its explanation is found in verses 11-15. In one soil the seed never penetrates but is snatched away by Satan (v12), in another soil the seed doesn't take root because of trials (v13), and in a third type of soil the seed is choked out by caring for the world (v14). Only one is received in good ground and produces fruit (v15). In verses 9-10, Jesus speaks in parables to conceal the truth by quoting Isaiah 6:9-10. Those who cannot see or hear are those who have already rejected Him in their heart. Jesus warns the people in verses 16-18 to pay attention to His words. Those who are listening will be given more, while those who fail to listen will have what they have been given taken away. In verses 19-21 Jesus tells the people that the true members of His family are all of those who hear His words and obey them.

For the first time in Luke's gospel, Jesus shows His power over nature in calming the storm (v22-25). In verses 26-39, Jesus will once again demonstrate His power over evil by casting out demons from a man who lived among the tombs. Jesus sends the demons into a herd of pigs. Unable to destroy the man, the demons destroy the pigs. The people of the area ask Jesus to leave because of the event. The man who Jesus healed wants to go with Jesus, but He instructs him to go home and tell them what the Lord had done for him. In verses 40-56 we see the two intertwining stories of Jairus' daughter, and the woman with a hemorrhage. While Jesus is on the way to heal Jairus' daughter (v40-42), the woman with the hemorrhage only wants to touch the hem of His garment (which she does) and be made well. Jesus confronts the woman and assures her it is her faith that has made her well (v43-48). After Jairus is informed that his daughter has died, Jesus continues with Jairus to his home. Jesus is laughed at because He says she is only sleeping. Peter, James, John, and the girl's parents witness Jesus raising the young girl back to life.

Thursday • Job 41-42

God moves from His description of the behemoth at the end of chapter 40, to describing Leviathan in chapter 41. God uses both of these illustrations to point out that Job had no hope of controlling those things, but God does (v1-9). God is sovereign and is in control of all things.

In 42:1-2 we see that Job understood the purpose of God's speeches. God is in control, and what He wants to bring to pass will take place. Job also admits that he did not know everything about God (v3-4). Job repents of his words where he questioned God's justice and His ways (v5-6). Job's "friends" have not spoken what is right about God either (v7-9). They are to make sacrifices and have Job to pray for them so their sin can be forgiven. Job is restored with twice as much as he had before his trial, with the exception of sons and daughters (v10-17). His daughters were the most beautiful in the land, and Job lives long enough to see four generations. God saw Job through all of the calamity he went through.

Friday • Zephaniah

Zephaniah ("The Lord hides") was written during the time of Josiah (1:1), probably before the reform under Josiah in 2 Kings 22-23. Zephaniah also had a royal background, which would have given him an audience with the king. His message concerned the Day of the Lord. Zephaniah speaks of the nearness of the "Day of the Lord", and urges people to seek the Lord.

In Zephaniah 1:1-3, Zephaniah describes the "Day of the Lord" as God's wrath against the sin and rebellion of the nations. His wrath was also against His own people in Judah because of their disobedience, rejection of Him, and idolatry. Verses 4-13 describe the "Day of the Lord" as coming on Judah and Jerusalem at the hands of the Babylonians. The judgment will be severe ("great"), because of their sin, and there would be no escape from His wrath (v14-18).

A call to repentance begins chapter 2. In verses 1-3, the people are urged to gather together and seek the Lord. Repentance would result in people seeking justice, righteousness, and humility. In other words, good works would follow true repentance. The land of the Philistines will be judged and become desolate for a time, until the remnant of Judah would return (v4-7). Another enemy of Israel will be judged in verses 8-11. Moab and Ammon are likened to Sodom and Gomorrah, in that they were destroyed because of their pride. Cush (Ethiopia) will be destroyed in verse 12, along with Assyria (Nineveh) in verses 13-15.

Zephaniah returns to the topic of Judah in verses 1-8 with three new charges: (1) they did not obey God, (2) they did not trust in the Lord, and (3) they did not draw near to God. This affected all levels of their leadership, and went down to the people. What God had done to other nations, He would now do to His own people. Even after this judgment there would come a day of joy. In verses 9-10 the scattered people would return, and verses 11-13 detail a restoration of the people. Verses 14-20 picture the rejoicing of the people as they return, in the future, from exile.

Saturday • Romans 1-2

The apostle Paul wrote the book of Romans in 57-58 AD. Around three years after writing to the Romans, Paul would be imprisoned in Rome for two years following a trial and an appeal to Caesar. His primary purpose in writing was to teach about salvation to a people who had never had apostolic instruction, and also to unite the Jewish and Gentile Christians living there. His ministry grew out of his desire for the gospel to spread westward. Romans 1-11 contain doctrine, while chapters 12-16 contain application of the doctrine in the lives of people.

In Romans 1:1-7 Paul introduces himself to the Christians in Rome by explaining who he is, and the truth about Jesus Christ. In verses 8-15, Paul tells them of his plans to visit them and preach the gospel there. Paul is thankful for the Christians at Rome. He constantly prays for them and wants to be of service to them (v8-10). Paul's greatest desire is to preach the gospel to those in Rome (v15). Verses 16-17 are the purpose statement of the book of Romans. Paul will expound on this theme throughout the book of Romans: salvation is for the Jew and for the Gentile. Paul quotes Habakkuk 2:4 to show that he has faith in God and His word. In the context of Habakkuk, this verse shows that wickedness will not win and that those who are righteous will be vindicated. It is only those who have been declared righteous (justified) by faith that will live.

In verses 18-32 Paul will show the lost state of mankind (especially Gentiles). Verse 18 declares that God does/will pour out His wrath on those who oppose Him. God has done this in the past through the Flood, the Red Sea, and through men such as Nebuchadnezzar. This shows that they know God (conscious and creation), but do not acknowledge Him as God (v 19-21). Verse 22 can be seen in Psalm 14:1 "The fool has said in his heart, there is no God". All of mankind worships something. If not God they will chose an idol to worship, as shown in Exodus 32 (v23). This begins the dark and dangerous road down the path of a life lived apart from God (v24-28).

In verses 24, 26, 28 "God gave them over" to do as they want. In verse 24 it is to their "lusts of their hearts". The term "lust" means a diseased soul. It also can be described as wanting something that God hates. These people know God's standards, and are guilty of rejecting them in favor of a lie (v25). This lust grows progressively worse in verses 26-27. The term "vile passions" refers to something the soul lust for or craves. In verse 27 the term "lust" means to bait the hook. This is shown in the text to be the sin of homosexuality, but it also fits James 1:12-16 as it describes temptation. This verse also shows that sin has a "built in" consequence (penalty) that will be paid unless the person repents and turns to Christ. Verse 28 contains the final "God gave them over". The word "knowledge" means clear knowledge. No one can say they do not have evidence of God. The "debased mind" is God abandoning the person to their sin, and its consequences have their way with the person. Paul also includes a long list of sins in verses 29-31 that describe the behavior of people who are separated from God. Verse 32 had a severe verdict for those who practice these sins. It also has a severe warning for those who approve of such things, even if they do not participate in them.

In Romans 2 Paul addresses the Jews and shows that they too are lost apart from Christ. In verses 1-16, Paul addresses the Jews who agree with Paul's assessment of the Gentiles found in 1:18-32. Jews believed they were "better" than Gentiles, so Paul now has his sights set on them. Paul is arguing that if the Jew's can see the sin and hopelessness of the Gentiles, they should be able to see it in themselves. They are in the same predicament as the Gentiles because they are guilty of the same sins (v1-5). Just because they are Jews does not mean they will be spared from experiencing God's wrath (v6-11). God sees both Jew and Gentile alike-they both need to be saved and the law cannot do it. Both Jew and Gentile will also experience the judgment of God. God does not respect one over the other (v6,12-16, Prov. 24:12, Rom. 14:12).

In verses 17-20 Paul addresses the advantages of being a Jew (having the law) only to expose them, in verses 21-24, for their inconsistent lives. In verses 25-29 Paul brings up circumcision, which symbolized the relationship between God and His people. Circumcision was no good to the Jew who did not keep the law. It was not circumcision that truly set them apart, but the circumcision of the heart (obedience). Verses 17-29, as a whole, also reflect the responsibility of the Jews to not only keep the law, but to keep the law in order that others may know God (v24). It was always (still is) God's intent that His people be obedient so that others could come to faith in Him.

Cover to Cover Challenge

Week 22

Sunday • Psalm 72-74

Welcome to week 22 of the *Cover to Cover Challenge*! Continue to pray for one another as we read and study God's Word together. Pray that our eyes will be opened, and that we all will be obedient to the Word of God. Lamentations 3:22-24 says "Through the Lord's mercies we are not consumed, because His compassions fail not. They are new every morning; great is Your faithfulness. The Lord is my portion, says my soul, therefore I hope in Him!"

Psalm 72 is a royal psalm where prayer is made on behalf of the king. Solomon is the author of this psalm and of Psalm 127. In verses 1-4, justice and righteousness are repeated qualities needed for a king to rule justly. The result of a king who rules justly is peace, especially for the oppressed. Verses 5-7 are another result of the reign of a king who rules with justice and righteousness-they influence for generations to come. The king's influence will also spread to other lands, including those who are enemies (v8-11). The psalmist notes once more the concern of the king for the needy and the poor in verses 12-14. Prayers are to be made for the king (v15), others will be blessed because of his reign (v16), and a king like this will be remembered and blessed (v16). The king's blessed reign can only be attributed to the Lord (v18-19).

Psalm 73 is a lament, but is best seen as a wisdom psalm as the psalmist responds to evil and injustice in the world. The psalmist observes the wicked and realizes he has become envious of their life, even though he knows God is good to all of Israel (v1-3). In verses 4-9, he records his observations. They are strong, healthy, and worry-free. But, they are also proud, insensitive, and self-centered. The psalmist believes they are not held accountable for their actions, and even become wealthier and have an easier life (v10-12). It even gets to the point for the psalmist where he wonders if doing right is worth it because he is suffering (v13-14). It is not until he sees from God's perspective, that he truly understands the end for the wicked (v15-17). It is the wicked who will meet a bitter end (v18-20). The psalmist realizes he wasted much time being grieved and acting foolishly (v21-22). He knows God has, and will always be with him (v23-26). The psalm ends with a contrast of the fate of the wicked (v27), and the one who puts their trust in God (v28).

Psalm 74 was probably written after they were carried into exile in 586 BC, after the destruction of the temple. This is a community lament, representing all people as they mourn over their loss. In verses 1-3, the psalmist asks God to remember the people He has redeemed (exodus), and not be angry with them. The Babylonians, who are still God's enemy, destroy the city and the temple in verses 4-8. They do not know how long this will last, but ask if God will let His name be reproached (v9-10). The psalmist urges God to use His powerful right hand to defeat the Babylonians in verse 11. God is the only source of salvation (v12), and His creative power shows that (v13-17). In verses 18-23 the psalmist knows that the Lord will protect His people. Even though the enemy is now having its way with them, this terrible time will not last forever.

Monday • Exodus 39-40

Exodus 39:1-31 records the making of the garments for the priesthood: the ephod, breastplate, and other garments they will wear. In verses 32-43 the work is completed, just as the Lord commanded through Moses. This shows the obedience of the people to the Lord and to Moses.

Exodus 40 contains the arrangement and setting up of the Tabernacle. According to verse 17 this is their second year in the wilderness, so the Tabernacle took less than 6 months to build. Aaron and his sons were anointed for the priesthood in verses 12-16, while verses 17-33 record the actual placing of the furniture in the Tabernacle. In verses 34-38, the glory of the Lord fills the Tabernacle. He was now living among His people to lead and guide them.

Tuesday • 1 Chronicles 1-2

1 and 2 Chronicles were written after the return from exile. 1 Chronicles begins with Adam, and 2 Chronicles ends with the decree of Cyrus for the Jews to return home. While the author is not named, Jewish tradition says Ezra is the author of the Chronicles (Ezra 7:1-6). It is obvious it is written by someone from the priesthood who had details about worship and the temple. 1 Chronicles 1-9 is full of genealogies, and is there to remind the people of God's promises to each generation and of how He fulfilled them. These promises will include-the land, the nation, the Davidic king, the Levitical priests, the temple, and how to worship the Lord. The people are returning to a land and a people that will be drastically different than what they have ever known. So, the Chronicler is reminding the people of their past to give them a hope for their future. 1 and 2 Chronicles are also unique in that around 55% of the book material is not found in any other book. You could pair up 1 Chronicles with 2 Samuel and 2 Chronicles with 1 and 2 Kings in what each book covers. 1 Chronicles focuses on David and shows hope for a future Messiah to come. 2 Chronicles will focus only on the southern kingdom of Judah and show that when the king was obedient to the Lord the people prospered, but when the king rebelled against the Lord the kingdom faltered. The main themes of the book are-obedience brings blessing, disobedience brings judgment, and there is hope for the future. The first 9 chapters are genealogies. I know you are looking forward to reading them (sarcasm).

1 Chronicles 1 will have familiar names for everyone. Just think of the promises associated with these listed in chapter 1. The promises given to Adam, Enoch, Noah, Abraham, and Isaac had an impact on those coming from exile, and even to us today. God made promises to each of these individuals. Those promises were fulfilled and would be fulfilled as they pertained to a promised Messiah to come.

1 Chronicles 2 focuses on Israel (Jacob) and his descendants. The focus here will quickly move to Judah and his descendants, and will show you the importance of Genesis 38. If Genesis 38 does not happen, this genealogy does not happen. We have already read about Ruth and Boaz. What if Boaz refused to be her kinsman-redeemer? Then there is no David. You see the genealogies are important because it reminds them of promises made and fulfilled. What God had done for them in the past gave them faith in the present, and hope for the future.

Wednesday • Luke 9-10

In Luke 9:1-6 Jesus sends the twelve out on their first mission. Verse 1 describes their ministry, and verse 2 describes their message. In verses 7-9 we meet Herod, whom had beheaded John in prison. Even he was intrigued by the stories he had heard about Jesus. In verses 10-17 we find the feeding of the 5,000. Jesus satisfies their hunger by providing for them and meeting their needs, and He demonstrates His miraculous power once again. It is revealed to Peter, not by signs or wonders, but from the Father Himself who Jesus is (v18-20). This, along with Jesus' prediction of His death and resurrection in verses 21-22, always marks a turning point in the Gospels as Jesus begins His journey to Jerusalem to be crucified. In verses 23-26 we see the characteristics of being one of His disciples. A true disciple of Christ will give up his own desires to follow God's will for his life.

Luke 9:27-36 records the transfiguration of Jesus before Peter, James, and John. The word "transfigured" means that something on the inside becomes visible from the outside, or there is an outward change that comes from within. Most believe these three disciples saw Jesus in all His glory upon the mountain. Moses and Elijah also appear, representing the law and the prophets which foretold of the coming of Messiah. Jesus rebukes His disciples for their lack of faith in verses 37-42, and for their failure to be able to cast out a demon. In verses 43-45 Jesus predicts His death a second time. Jesus uses a little child to teach about how one must come to Him in verses 46-48. Jesus warns that the one who comes to Him must come in humility and faith like a child in order to participate in the kingdom. In verses 49-50, another person is casting out demons in Jesus' name. The casting out of demons is an act of God, so the man must have been a believer in Christ. Jesus rebukes James and John for their attitude against a village of Samaritans because He did not come to destroy, but to save (v51-56). The cost of discipleship is outlined in verses 57-62. Following Jesus requires commitment, sacrifice, making Jesus a priority, and serving.

Luke 10:1-12 is the only recording of the sending out of the 70. It mirrors the instruction given in Matthew 10 to the disciples, with the exception that they are sent to every city. The number 70 also is equivalent to the table of nations found in Genesis 10. Some believe this illustrates that the gospel is for the whole world. Each of them was to depend on God for their sustenance (v4). God's judgment is based upon the people's acceptance or refusal of the message (v12-16). The judgment of Sodom and Gomorrah will be nothing compared to what will happen to those who reject Jesus. In verses 17-20, the 70 return with joy over the power they have in Jesus' name. Verse 18 may refer to the original fall of Satan, or the results of the 70 being sent out. But, Jesus tells them to rejoice because their names are written in heaven (v20). Jesus thanks God for the people whom God revealed His will to, and tells the disciples they are blessed to see the things they see (v21-24).

The story of the Good Samaritan is in verses 25-37. The journey from Jerusalem to Jericho was about 17 miles and the road descends about 3,000 feet. It was a place known for thieves and robbers to hide. Jesus' story would have shocked the lawyer who was asking the question, because the priest and the Levite passed the man by and it was the Samaritan who helped him. A Samaritan as the hero in the story would have angered the Jews. The point of the story was that the Samaritan had compassion and showed kindness to the man who was suffering. The question the lawyer asked was "who is my neighbor?" Now the lawyer must ask himself "to whom am I neighbor?" Verses 38-42 record Jesus' visit with Martha and Mary which only Luke records. It is a great reminder that serving is good, but priority should be given to sitting at Jesus' feet to learn.

WEEK 22

Thursday • Song of Solomon 1-4

This book is a love song that praises the purity of marriage and romance, including the sexual intimacy between a husband and wife within the bonds of marriage. Many people make an allegory out of it and believe it is solely about God's love for His people. Some even interpret it as Solomon (a Jew) taking a Gentile (Shulamite girl) to show that one day God include the Gentiles in the future building of His church. I believe the book should be taken at face value and not allegorical. We know God loves His people, and that God often chooses the marriage covenant to depict His love for His people. I believe the book shows their courtship, the early days of marriage, and them maturing together after they are married. The literal title of the book is Song of Songs, which means greatest of all songs.

Song of Solomon 1-3:5 describe the courtship between Solomon and the Shulamite. It is clear from 1:2-4 that the Shulamite girl expresses her desire for him. In verses 5-7 her beauty is described and she wonders where he is, because she does not want to be without him. Solomon (the Beloved) invites her to come look for him, and he describes her beauty as incomparable (v8-11). In verses 1:12-2:6, their attraction to each other grows as they continue to describe one another's physical beauty. Verse 7 marks an end to the first unit, and is a warning that intimacy is between only those who are married. In 2:8-17 the Shulamite is waiting on her beloved to come and see her. In 3:1-4 she cannot find her beloved, and goes out to try and find him. She longs to see him and be with him, because their love for one another is great. Verse 5 repeats the warning from 2:7 that intimacy is only for those within the bonds of marriage. In verses 3:6-11 the royal wedding procession is described and they are finally joined together as husband and wife. Just from the first four chapters of the Song of Solomon you can see that the sanctity of marriage between one man and one woman is upheld and praised.

Friday • Habakkuk

Habakkuk ("One who embraces") prophesied during the last days of the southern kingdom (Judah). Habakkuk is unique because he did not speak from God to the people, but from the people to God. Habakkuk is distressed over the sins of the people and asks God when He will intervene. He will not enjoy God's answer. His prophecy may have been written shortly after the death of Josiah. This would reflect the coming defeat of the Assyrians by the Babylonians (Chaldeans) and soon coming defeat of Judah.

In 1:1-4 Habakkuk asks God to intervene because the people have become corrupt from the top down. God's answer is not what Habakkuk expects to hear. In verses 5-11 we read that God is going to send the Chaldeans to judge Judah. The Chaldeans were rising up as a strong military power. They were noted for their mighty army, which caused destruction everywhere they went. Habakkuk wondered- why God would use such a cruel people to punish His people, who were more righteous than them? (v12-2:1). God's answer came in verses 2-4. The Chaldeans are coming at the time appointed by Him. The theme verse of Habakkuk is verse 4. The proud are not right with God, but those who have faith in God act justly just as God is just. God will punish the Chaldeans but His people must trust in His judgments. In verses 5-18 God will punish the Chaldeans for their many sins. They are guilty of greed (v6-8), corruptness (v9-11), violence (v12-14), immoral behavior (v15-17), and idolatry (v18-19). In 3:1-7 Habakkuk praises God for His plan in delivering Israel in the past. In verses 8-15, he praises God for bringing salvation to His people. Verse 13 is looking to the future, when Jesus would come and secure salvation for His people. Fear comes over Habakkuk in verse 16, because he knows that the punishment of Judah is coming. Habakkuk closes with praise for the Lord. Even though all things will be gone, Habakkuk will still praise the Lord because He is the God of his salvation (v17-19).

Saturday • Romans 3-4

In the first two chapters Paul described the fate of all people, whether Jew or Gentile, who are apart from Christ. Both are sinful, and both need salvation that is found only in Jesus Christ. Here in 3:1-8, Paul describes that there were benefits to being Jewish. Paul describes that they were given the words of God first even though they were unfaithful to it. Their unfaithfulness showed that they needed a Savior. What is also being taught here is that the unfaithfulness of man cannot stop God's good purposes. No matter how much we may fail God, God never fails.

In verses 9-20, Paul shows once again that both Jew and Gentile are guilty before God. The law could not save no matter how much one may believe they "keep" the law. Paul may have quoted these verses to show that even though the Jews were blessed to receive the words of God they did not obey them. If a case were to be made, the Jew is worse off because they are the ones who received the words of God first and failed to obey. All of these verses show the universal lostness of humanity. All people need Jesus, whether they are Jews or Gentiles. This also proves the need for missions. Unless someone hears the gospel, there is no hope for them to be saved.

In verses 21-26, Paul now presents the answer to the problem of sin for Jews and Gentiles-Jesus. All people come short of the glory of God, whether Jew or Gentile. In verse 25 the term "propitiation" is the equivalent of the Hebrew term for mercy seat. In simple terms it is a place where sins are atoned for. It also carries the meaning of deflecting or averting God's wrath. Jesus did that for us when He died upon the cross for the sins of mankind. Jesus died for all, and He is the one who can save both Jew and Gentile alike (v27-31). Man is not saved by the law, but only through faith alone in Christ alone and only Christ should get glory for it (v28).

In Romans 4:1-4 Paul shows by the example of Abraham that faith, not law keeping, justifies a person before God. Abraham's works and obedience were a result of his faith in God. A good summary of what God believed about Abraham can be found in Genesis 26:5. In verses 5-8, Paul uses the example of David. David simply acknowledged his guilt, and by faith depended on the mercy of God to be forgiven. With this quote from the Psalms, Paul has quoted from each section of the Hebrew Bible (Prophets, Law, and Writings) to demonstrate that in order to be righteous one must have faith in God. Man has always been justified by faith. Paul returns to Abraham to further prove his point about faith. Abraham placed faith in God even before the command to circumcise was given (v9-12, Gen. 17:10-14). Circumcision only served as an external symbol of what had already taken place when Abraham placed his faith in God. Even God's promise that He would make Abraham the father of many nations (before the birth of Isaac) was not through the law, but believed by faith (v13-25). As a matter of fact, the law would not come until 430 years later (Gal. 3:17). All who place their faith in Jesus Christ receive justification just as Abraham did (v23-25). Paul's point in this chapter is that Abraham's justification and blessings were based upon his faith in God. They were not earned in any other way, especially through the law.

Cover to Cover Challenge

Week 23

Sunday • Psalm 75-77

Welcome to week 23 of the *Cover to Cover Challenge*! Continue to pray for understanding of the Word and for the Lord to receive all the honor, glory, and praise from it. The psalmist writes "Your hands have made me and fashioned me, give me understanding, that I may learn Your commandments" (Ps. 119:73).

Psalm 75 is a psalm of thanksgiving. The context of the psalm is that the Lord watches over Israel and judges its enemies. The psalmist thanks the Lord for His works which mean His presence is among them (v1). In verses 2-3 God is speaking as judge of all the earth. God warns the wicked because they are arrogant and they resist His rule (v4-6). The sovereign hand of God is pictured in verses 7-8 as the wicked will drink of the cup of His wrath. While the wicked must drink from the cup, the psalmist chooses to praise the Lord (v9). Verse 10 seems to shift back to the voice of God. In righteous judgment He cuts of the wicked, but exalts the righteous.

Psalm 76 is a hymn of victory celebrating God's past victories on behalf of His people. In verses 1-3, the psalmist reflects upon God delivering Israel from their enemies. After a description of God in verse 4, the psalmist turns to a display of God's wrath against their enemies in verses 5-6 and the fear it produces among them. In verses 7-9 we read that God is to be feared over the whole earth because of His judgment. Even when people stand against God, He always wins the victory over them (v10). Those who understand the fear of the Lord pay their vows, and offer gifts to the Lord (v11-12).

Psalm 77 is a psalm of lament that reflects upon God's works, and eventually turns into a psalm that celebrates them. The psalmist is in a state of misery and distress (v1-3). This leads to inability to sleep, but the psalmist remembers how God has helped him in the past (v4-6). He asks "Where is God now?" and "Is God going to help me now?" (v7-9). The psalmist turns back to past memories of how God had helped (v10-12). The psalmist reflects upon the exodus in verses 13-20, which was the greatest deliverance of His people recorded in the Old Testament. If God delivered them, then the psalmist knew God would lead them now.

Monday • Leviticus 1-5

Leviticus is primarily about proper worship and instructions for the priests. The material here was given before Israel's wilderness wanderings. Chapters 1-7 deal with the offerings for the bronze altar. Consecration of the priests and tabernacle worship are the focus of chapters 8-10. The cleanliness laws are located in chapters 11-15, and chapter 16 is about the Day of Atonement. Chapters 17-27 emphasize the moral code, or sometimes called the Holiness Code. Chapter 27 gives regulations concerning property. Themes dealt with in this book are sin, sacrifice, and cleanness.

Leviticus 1 concerns the burnt offering. This is a voluntary and personal offering not for specific sin, but for the state of sinfulness. The purpose of this offering is to make atonement for the sin of the offerer, and also helps the offerer focus on God's righteousness. Bulls (v3-9), sheep and goats (v10-13), and birds (v14-17) could be offered.

Leviticus 2 concerns the grain offering. These offerings (grain, olive oil) were a great sacrifice, because they could not grow crops in the desert. It showed they had to depend upon God for more. The Israelites were told to do the grain offering after the burnt offering, because then their sin was atoned for. All of this offering was not burned, and what remained was given to the priests. The purpose of this offering was worship. The salt added to the offering in verses 11-13 may have been to remind Israel of their covenant with God.

Leviticus 3 concerns the peace or fellowship offering. This offering was made on top of the burnt offering (v5). Its main focus was the peace the Israelites had with God. It is also called the fellowship offering, because of the meal that would be shared together. The priests would receive what remained from this offering as well.

Leviticus 4 concerns the sin offering. There was no sacrifice for intentional sin. These offerings were to be made immediately after the knowledge of sin is present (v14,23,28). This chapter is outlined by categories of people. Priests (v3-12), community sin (v13-21), leadership sins (v22-26), and individual's sin (v27-35). Chapters 4-6 will emphasize the result of the process-forgiveness. This offering is explained further in chapters 5 and 6.

Leviticus 5:1-13 deals further with the sin offering by naming specific sins. There is a provision made in verses 7 and 11 for the poor. Not everyone could afford the offering, but everyone was given the opportunity to experience forgiveness (God's grace). Verses 14-19 concern the guilt offering. Atonement could be found in this offering, but restitution was still necessary for what the person did or did not do.

Tuesday • 1 Chronicles 3-4

Judah's line continues to be traced through chapters 3-4. King David's line is traced in chapter 3. While no human king would ever sit on the throne after returning from exile (Jer. 22:30), David's line continued to have an important role to play- especially the future Messiah who was to come.

The genealogy in 4:1-23 of the family of Judah is found nowhere else in Scripture. It is included because the future Messiah was to come from the tribe of Judah. Verses 24-43 concern the line of Simeon. It is here we see that Simeon's descendants defeated the rest of the Amalekites to obtain more land.

Wednesday • Luke 11-12

In Luke 11:1-13, Jesus teaches His disciples how to pray. Verses 1-4 teach them what to pray, verses 5-8 teach persistence in prayer, and verses 9-13 continue to teach on persistence and also dependence upon God to answer prayer. Jesus heals a demon possessed man in verses 14-23, and it gives an opportunity for the Pharisees to accuse Jesus of healing with Satan's power. Jesus Himself said He did this by the "finger of God." This means that God's kingdom had come near them. If anyone should have been able to recognize God and His kingdom it should have been the religious leaders of the day. Their own blindness, caused by their hard selfish hearts, would not allow them to see that Jesus was God. By casting out the demon Jesus showed them that He is the one who binds the strong man. In verses 24-26, Jesus explains that one cannot remain neutral about Him. A decision must be made. In verses 27-28 Jesus emphasizes obedience to God's Word. Jesus speaks again to this generation concerning signs in verses 29-32. They are always asking Him to perform a sign to prove who He is and prove His authority. Jesus uses three examples from the Old Testament and two have to do with the same story. The first example is Jonah as a sign to the Ninevites. Jonah being inside the great fish for three days was a sign to the Ninevites. Jesus rising again after being buried three days will be a sign to them. Second, the queen of the South (Sheba) came from a distant land to hear Solomon's wisdom. The people of the present generation do not even believe Jesus and He is greater than Solomon. Third, the people of Nineveh repented at the preaching of Jonah. The people of the present will not repent, and One greater than Jonah is preaching to them. On a side note the queen of Sheba and the Ninevites were both Gentiles.

In verses 33-36 Jesus is urging those hearing His words to believe in Him. He does this by contrasting the image of the eye. Either your eye is "pure" or it is "evil", depending on whether you believe in Him or not. An example of those with an evil eye is found in verses 37-54, where Jesus pronounces woes upon the Pharisees in the home of a Pharisee. The Pharisees would wash their hands before they ate, not for hygienic purposes but so they would be ceremonially clean. This washing represented removing defilement from contact with a sinful world. They are more concerned with how they appear to look to others than with their own soul or the souls of others. The first woe is in verse 42. Here, Jesus is denouncing them for holding to their own law instead of practicing justice and loving God. The second woe concerns sitting in places of honor and to be greeted in the markets (v43). They loved to be held in high esteem and honored by others. In the third woe Jesus is teaching that they make people unclean by their way of living and what they teach (v44). In verses 46 Jesus pronounces woes against lawyers who were mostly Pharisees. Here the fourth woe is against their traditions (their interpretation of the law) which made it unbearable upon the people nor would they even try to help them. The fifth woe in verse 47 concerns the lawyers following in the footsteps of their ancestors. Their ancestors killed God's prophets and they were burying them. The final woe of verse 52 demonstrates that the religious leaders had taken away the ability to understand God's Word. Not only have they done this, but they do not even know Him themselves and they keep others from knowing Him also.

In Luke 12:1-3 Jesus teaches on hypocrisy, using the Pharisees as an example. Accountability and judgment are also included, because all will give an answer for their words. The antidote for hypocrisy is to fear God (v4-7). How does someone demonstrate that they fear God? They confess Christ before all (v8-12). The parable of the rich fool addresses attachment to material things over the things of God (v13-21). The man in the parable assumed he would live a long life and enjoy his riches. He does not use any of it to help others or to further God's kingdom because he is only concerned with himself. Like some even today, the man believed the future was all under his control. Little did the man know that he would be meeting God that night to give an account of his life. The phrase in verse 20 "your soul will be required of you" in the Greek literally reads "God requires your soul". The antidote to worry and greed (treasuring material things) is found in verses 22-34. We are to "seek first the kingdom of God and His righteousness". Doing this puts our worrying and our pursuit of worldly things into perspective.

In verses 35-48 Jesus teaches about being ready for His coming. It not only teaches readiness, but encourages His people to always be faithful in what they have been called to do because no one knows the time of His return. Verses 47-48 teach about judgment on those who knew His will and on those who did not. In verses 49-53, those who hear Jesus' teaching must make a choice whether to believe in Him or not. The choice will cause division. Jesus is trying to get the people's attention, in verses 54-56, about the urgency of making a decision before it is too late. Verses 57-59 urge the people to take advantage of their situation. They are hearing the Son of God speak the very words that can give them life.

Thursday • Song of Solomon 5-8

Chapters 5 and 6 show the maturing of a married couple. In chapter 5 she misses an opportunity to see her beloved (v2-8). In verses 9-16 she describes the physical features of her beloved. This is followed by a description of the Shulamite in 6:1-10, and verses 11-13 describe their longing to see one another. The depth of their love for one another is described in chapter 7. In verses 1-9 the beloved describes his bride, while in verses 9-8:3 the bride is speaking to her husband. In verse 8:4 there is another warning that intimacy is reserved for within the bonds of marriage. Verses 8:5-7 show the strength of their love for one another, and the seal of the marriage vows. Verses 8-14 show the ongoing love between Solomon (Beloved) and the Shulamite.

Friday • Ezekiel 1-7

Ezekiel ("God will strengthen") was a priest called by God to be a prophet to the people being taken to Babylon. His name shows that the people will not listen to his message. With Ezekiel in Babylon, Daniel serving in the royal court, and Jeremiah prophesying in Jerusalem the Lord's word was being sent out and His works were on display. Ezekiel was one of the ones carried into exile with King Jehoiachin. Ezekiel is known for its visions, and the prophet himself acting out or symbolizing the words he spoke.

Ezekiel 1:1-3 opens the book with the date, where he was at the time of his calling, and his circumstances. His first vision will be of God and of the cherubim around the throne. In verses 4-14 he sees the cherubim (10:15,20) and describes them in detail. They moved rapidly like lightning in the midst of what looked like coals of fire. After describing what looked like wheels that moved with the cherubim (v15-21), Ezekiel describes what from other Scriptures would be heaven (Ex.19, 1 Kgs. 6, Isa. 6, Dan. 10, Rev. 4). This will be the backdrop for the judgments announced by Ezekiel. Ezekiel sees the One sitting on the throne surrounded by fire.

In Ezekiel 2 the One sitting on the throne speaks to Ezekiel, calling him the "son of man". This title is to remind Ezekiel that he is dependent upon God for his message and his power to deliver the message. Jesus was given this same name to emphasize His humanity and His dependence upon the Lord. In verses 3-5, Ezekiel will be sent to the children of Israel who have rebelled (hard-hearted) against the Lord. God commands him not to be afraid, but to be faithful in proclaiming the message (v6-7). Starting with verse 2:8-3:3 Ezekiel eats the scroll, showing his acceptance of the word of the Lord. These words will be filled with funeral songs, mourning, and lamentations to the people of Israel. It would have been easier to preach to a people who could not understand, but Ezekiel is sent with the word of the Lord to preach to the people (v4-9). Ezekiel was to receive the words of the Lord and go and speak it to the people (v10-11). The Spirit carries him away, as he contemplates the message he is to carry a rebellious people (v12-15). The period of 7 days is equal to the time period of mourning for the dead, and the length of time for a priest's consecration. Ezekiel is made a watchman over the house of Israel in verses 16-21. The watchman stood on the wall of the city to warn of any coming threat. He was to warn the wicked, as well as the righteous, to turn from their wicked ways or die. In verses 22-27, Ezekiel sees another vision of the Lord. Ezekiel would be unable to speak unless the Lord opened his mouth to give him words to say. Normally a prophet would go out among the people, but here the people will come to Ezekiel for the message.

Chapters 4-24 contain message and symbolic acts to warn the people of Judah that judgment was coming. Chapters 4-7 concern Jerusalem (ch. 4), the people going into exile (ch. 5), and they could not escape it through their own effort (ch. 6-7). Ezekiel is commanded to act out warnings to the people in verses 1-3. Ezekiel would play a "wargame" while prophesying against Jerusalem. During this time, Ezekiel would lay on his left side for

390 days bearing the punishment for Israel's sins. He would lay on his right side bearing the guilt of Judah's sins for 40 days (v4-8). Ezekiel would live on a strict diet during this time as well. (v9-17). This was symbolic of the coming captivity and the famine that would come with it. The unclean manner of preparing the food showed that the captives would eat defiled foods in a foreign land.

In Ezekiel 5:1-4, Ezekiel is told to shave his head and beard which is a picture of defilement, humiliation, and is forbidden by the law for a priest (Deut. 14:1). This symbolized the people who were no longer holy to the Lord, but were defiled. The hair symbolized the people and their fate. Verses 5-7 are a judgment speech by the Lord against the people for rebelling against Him. In verses 8-17, the judgments of the Mosaic Covenant would become realized. A third will die from disease and famine, a third would die by the sword, and a third would be scattered among the nations.

In Ezekiel 6:1-7 Ezekiel is told to prophesy to the surrounding mountains, hills, and valleys and pronounce judgment on their pagan rituals. The only way to escape the judgment of God for their idol worship was to turn from their wicked ways and follow the Lord, which some will do (v8-10). In verses 11-14 Ezekiel is either told to show joy over their judgment, or anger because of their sin. Four times in this chapter (v7, 10, 13, 14) God tells Ezekiel to remind the people that the purpose of this judgment is to restore the people so they will have a knowledge of God.

Ezekiel 7:1-13 contains 4 prophetic speeches against Israel and its coming judgment. Verses 1-4 speak of the extent of the judgment for their wickedness. In verses 5-9, the surprise and horror of the judgment is announced. Verses 10-11 speak of the imminence of the judgment and that the day had arrived. Verses 12-13 speak of the permanency and suddenness of the judgment. In verses 14-27, the reaction of the judgment is recorded by Ezekiel. Disease, hunger, and the sword would kill many. Any that escaped would be humiliated and ashamed at what had happened (v14-18). It is the people's own idolatry and wickedness that had led to the judgment (v19). They had profaned the temple by making idols out of its ornaments (v20-22), so they would be taken captive in chains as the Babylonians destroyed their city (v23-24). People will run to the prophet, priest, and elder for help but none will be found (v25-27).

Saturday • Romans 5-6

Paul will now begin to speak of the benefits of knowing Christ in Romans 5. In verses 1-5 one of the benefits of having peace *with* God is having the peace *of* God. All of our trials and tribulations produce in us perseverance, character, and hope. Believers also receive the love of God, which is poured into their hearts. Another benefit of knowing Christ is to know that we will be saved from wrath because of Jesus' death on our behalf (v6-11). Jesus has reconciled (go from enemy to friend) us to God. The first eleven verses also carry a theme of rejoicing. Verse 2 says that believers are to rejoice in the hope of the glory of God. All believers should be committed to bring glory to God through times of anguish or times of joy. Verse 3 demonstrates that believers can also rejoice in the middle of suffering. It is in times of suffering that endurance, character, and hope are produced. Verse 11 says that believers are to rejoice in God through Jesus Christ. It is because of the sacrifice of Jesus that believers can know God and have a relationship with Him. That is something to rejoice about and be thankful for.

Paul presents the basis of all these benefits as being that Jesus' death overturned the negative effects of Adam's fall (v12-21). Just as sin came on all men for Adam's sin, all can be made righteous because of Jesus' sacrifice and can be justified before Him. Through Adam's disobedience came death, but through Christ all can be made righteous by placing faith in Him. Isaiah 53:11 says "by his knowledge shall the righteous one, My servant (Jesus), make many to be accounted righteous; and he shall bear their iniquities." This is what Jesus did in reversing the curse. Verses 13-14 show the role of the law. The law served to show that sin is sin. It brought it out into the open to be seen. Though sin had existed since the fall, the law points it out.

Another benefit of knowing Christ (Romans 6:1-14) is that sin's power over us has been broken once and for all. The main point here is that believers have a new nature and the Holy Spirit within to help them live. Our old nature is still present, and is capable of sinning, but we do not have to be slaves to it. A picture of this can be seen from Paul's hometown of Tarsus. Someone guilty of murder there would have the person they killed attached to them for punishment. When the dead corpse began to deteriorate it would also do the same to the convicted murderer. The same principle applies here. If believers continue to carry around the old self, it will gradually deteriorate and take over the new if we are not careful. This is why the old self must stay dead, and believers must live their new life in Christ through the Holy Spirit. Believers no longer have to give in to, and be slaves to sin. This passage warns believers to not continue in sin (v2) because they have died to it (v3-5). All believers have been released from the grips of sin (v6-10) and it should no longer rule over them (v11-14). No believer has to be a slave to sin, but rather a slave to Christ, and this is the subject of verses 15-23.

Verse 3 also shows the importance of baptism in a believer's life. Baptism does not save, but it is an essential element in experiencing Christ. First, it identifies the believer with Christ. Jesus was baptized (Matt. 3:13-17) and also commanded His disciples and those who followed Him to be baptized (Matt. 28:19). Second, Paul also shows here in verse 3 that baptism showed that their old life came to an end and a new one in Christ began. It also demonstrated that they were buried with Christ. The old self was dead, and they were raised a new creature. Thirdly, it is an evangelistic opportunity for others to hear the gospel. Finally, it is also a testimony. It lets others know the decision that you have made to believe in Jesus, that you are saved, and that you are going to heaven. If you are reading this and have never been baptized, I would personally encourage you to do that. It will be a blessing because you are being obedient to the Lord, and it will allow others to know that you are saved.

Paul explains in verses 15-23 that experiencing God's grace is not permission to live any way we want. Experiencing God's grace should lead to living for Christ, and the way He would have us to live. Jesus said in Matthew 6:24 "No man can serve two masters: for either he will hate the one, and love the other; or else he will hold to the one, and despise the other. You cannot serve God and mammon". Here in these verses Paul echoes this principle that Jesus spoke of. A person is either a slave to sin which leads to death (v16, 19, 20, 21, 23), or a slave to obedience and righteousness (v16, 17, 18, 22, 23). True repentance will lead to a change of masters and a changed life.

Cover to Cover Challenge

Week 24

Sunday • Psalm 78

Welcome to week 24 of the *Cover to Cover Challenge*! Continue to pray for understanding and that the Holy Spirit will teach each person participating in the *Cover to Cover Challenge*. Jesus said in John 14:26, "The Helper, the Holy Spirit, whom the Father will send in My name, He will teach you all things, and bring to your remembrance all things that I said to you". The greatest teacher that each believer has is the Holy Spirit dwelling in us.

Psalm 78 is a wisdom psalm that reminds the reader of God's faithfulness by recalling past events. It also serves as a reminder for future generations that God is faithful (v1-4). Verse 2 is used by Matthew (13:35) to refer to Jesus' teaching in parables. The psalmist uses the example of the exodus to recall not only God's faithfulness, but the people's response to the works of God on their behalf. In verses 5-7 the purpose of the psalm is seen. The people are to place their hope in God, not forget His works, and not be like their fathers who were unfaithful to God. Verses 8-12 show the many ways they were unfaithful, including the unfaithfulness of one whole tribe (Ephraim). God performed many miracles on behalf of His people (v13-16), but their response was to keep sinning and rebelling against Him (v17-20). This made God angry (v21-22). Despite their rebellion, God still provided for His people (v23-29). Even then, the people continued to sin, and God's wrath was moved against them (v30-33). When God displayed His wrath against them the people returned to Him, but this did not last long (v34-41). Even in wrath, God had mercy upon them. The Israelites in the wilderness should have learned a valuable lesson from the Egyptians during the exodus (v42-51). Rebelling against God brings wrath, but in obedience the Great Shepherd led the sheep to the Promised Land (v52-55). Verses 56-64 may be referring to the time of the judges when the Israelites repeatedly worshiped idols. Even in the Promised Land the people forsook God to follow other gods. God, in His sovereign plan, rose up the tribe of Judah and David to change the direction of the nation (v65-72). David's reign was the high point of Israel's history, and was a lesson of faithfulness to be passed on to future generations.

Monday • Leviticus 6-9

Chapter 6 is a continuation of the guilt offering from 5:14-19. Atonement could be found in this offering, but restitution was still necessary for what the person did or did not do. This shows that a sin against one was a sin against both the entire community and against God (v1-7). Restitution had to be made before there could be forgiveness. Verses 8-13 concern the burnt offering. They were to make sure the sacrifice was completely consumed by not allowing the fire to go out. Verses 14-23 concern the grain offering and what to do with the leftovers. Verses 24-30 relate to the sin offering and the holiness of it. The sin offering was sacred and not to be taken lightly.

Leviticus 7:1-10 gives more rules concerning the guilt offering, with the focus on keeping it holy. Only the priest could eat the meat and cooked grain of this offering. Verses 11-38 pertain to the peace offering. If the offering was one of thanksgiving, both unleavened and leavened cakes were to be offered. What was left of the animal sacrifice was given to the offerer to enjoy a meal that symbolized peace with God and others. If it was a thanksgiving offering it was to be eaten that day, or the next day if it was a vow. Anyone who was unclean or had touched anything unclean could not eat the meal because they would be cut off from the people. This warning applied also to anyone who ate the fat or blood of any sacrificed animals. Being cut off from the people meant loss of one's identity and covenant relationship.

Leviticus 8 is the ordination of Aaron and his sons into the priesthood. Aaron and his sons are chosen by God to be priests in verses 1-4. In verses 5-13 Aaron and his sons were symbolically purified through baths, while the oil symbolized their divine anointing. In verses 14-36 the sacrifices were made to consecrate Aaron and his sons as priests. The second ram (v24) symbolizes how the priest should hear God's voice, do righteous deeds, and walk in God's ways. Aaron and his sons partake in a ceremonial meal and the ordination is finished 7 days later, after they show their obedience to the Lord. This detailed ordination showed that the worship of God is very serious.

In Leviticus 9, Aaron and his sons officially take over as priests for the nation of Israel. In verses 1-14 Moses instructs Aaron to make sacrifice for himself and to educate the people about what they are to do. Aaron makes a sin offering and burnt offering for himself and his family. In verses 15-24 Aaron makes a sin, burnt, grain, and peace offering on behalf of the people. The purpose for this is to make the people ready for God to reveal Himself to the people.

Tuesday • 1 Chronicles 5-6

The families of Reuben, Gad, and Manasseh are given in chapter 5. These three lived on the east side of the Jordan River. In verses 18-22 they win the victory over their enemies because they trusted in the Lord, but we also see their tragic fall. Because of their unfaithfulness, they would be the first to fall to the Assyrians.

In 1 Chronicles 6 the family of Levi is the focus. For those coming back from captivity it would have been important to know if they were descendants of Levi, in order for them to work in the temple to be built. The Gershonites, Kohathites, and Merarites will be mentioned quite often in 1 Chronicles because it identifies those who could serve in specific tasks. The Gershonites were responsible for the fabrics of the tabernacle, coverings, tents, clothes, curtains, and cords. The Kohathites were to care for the Ark of the Covenant and all related furnishings. The Merarites took care of the boards, sockets, walls, and floors. The descendants of Aaron would be the priestly line. The 48 cities mentioned were for Levites to minister in, and ensured that no person would be more than a day's journey from a Levitical city which had a priest.

Wednesday • Luke 13-14

Jesus issues a call to repentance in Luke 13:1-9. Two examples of people physically losing their lives are given. Jesus uses these examples to show them that all people are sinners; all people need to repent, and to emphasize the urgency of their situation. Verses 6-9 focus on God's grace and mercy in giving more time to repent of their sinfulness. If there is no repentance, all that is left is rejection. It should be noted that the opportunity to repent will not last forever (2 Pet. 3:8-10).

The story of Jesus healing the woman on the Sabbath is unique to Luke (v10-17). This story shows the arrogance and pride of those who opposed Jesus, and it clarifies Jesus' example of the fig tree in verses 6-9. In verse 15 Jesus calls the ruler of the synagogue a hypocrite. The word was used in Jesus' day for actors. The man is a hypocrite because he would take care of his animals on the Sabbath but rebuke a healing on the Sabbath. Also we learn that this woman's sickness was caused by Satan. We know from 1 John 3:8 that Jesus came to destroy the works of the devil. Notice in verse 17 the results of the miracle. All those who opposed the miracle were put to shame while the others rejoiced. The parable of the mustard seed (v18-19) teaches the growth of the kingdom of God, and the parable of the leaven (v20-21) teaches the influence and transforming power of the gospel.

In verses 22-30 Jesus teaches the way into the kingdom (v24), the urgency of making the decision to believe in Him (v25-28), and that people from all over the world will be a part of His kingdom (v29-30). This story also teaches one of Luke's themes of reversal. Jesus is teaching those who oppose Him and who also think they are already in the Kingdom, that they will be excluded if they do not repent and believe in Him. They also will see the Gentiles included in the Kingdom while they are left out. In verses 31-33, Jesus shows that God's plan for Him will not be changed by human circumstances. Jesus would continue His ministry until God's appointed time for it to be over. The word "fox" that Jesus used to describe Herod was used to describe someone who was cunning or sly, but it was also used to call someone insignificant or worthless. He also foretells His resurrection in these verses. Jesus weeps over the city of Jerusalem where God revealed Himself to the people. Now they are known for being the city which rejects God and His prophets (v34-35).

Luke 14:1-6 opens with Jesus healing a man on the Sabbath in the home of a leader of the Pharisees. This reveals, once again, the heart of the Pharisees and the love, mercy, and compassion of Jesus. This leads to Jesus teaching about honor in verses 7-14 and condemning them of their pride and arrogance. The humble person will end up where he should and receive the honor he is due. The parable of the great supper also shows the urgency of responding to the invitation of salvation (v15-24). Jesus is still at the home of the Pharisee, so it is highly probable that it is a Pharisee who says "Blessed is he who shall eat bread in the kingdom of God!". Two invitations were given in Jesus' day for a great banquet. One would be similar to our RSVP today and would be given months ahead. The next invitation was the announcement that the banquet was ready. No one declined the first invitation, when the second invitation was given people began to make excuses of why they could not come. This portion is aimed at the Pharisees who will not be a part of the banquet which is going to take place. Others are invited to the banquet and accept the invitation. Those who were invited first will not receive further invitations. As Paul mentions in 2 Corinthians 5:14-21, those who are in God's kingdom should persuade (v23, compel) people to be a part of the kingdom, before it is too late.

In verses 25-35 through chapter 18, Luke focuses on the demands of discipleship. In these verses we see the characteristics of being one of His disciples. In verse 26 Jesus is not teaching that believers should hate their loved ones. Jesus is teaching that the love they have for their earthly loved ones should look like hate when compared to the love they have for Him. Devotion to Christ is to be first above all others. Paul explains this principle in 1 Corinthians 7:32-33. Becoming a true disciple also means bearing one's cross (v27) and counting the cost (v28-32). A true disciple of Christ will also give up his own desires to follow God's will for his life (v33).

Thursday • Proverbs 1

Most know that Proverbs is associated with wisdom. Wisdom in Proverbs is shown to be the skill of living by using knowledge. Wisdom will help people say the right thing, and do the right thing at the right time. Solomon is attributed authorship of most of the proverbs. 1 Kings 4:32 tells us that he wrote over 3,000. The main focus of the book is to provide wisdom, that when applied will lead to a godly life. Wisdom is presented as priceless and to be treasured. Wisdom affects all areas of life-attitude, behavior, and relationships. The first 9 chapters focus on a father giving advice to his son so that he can obtain wisdom. The young man has a choice. He can either follow wisdom, or choose the way of folly. The second part begins in chapter 10 and focus on short observations, warnings, and encouragement. The definition of a proverb is a short saying that combines knowledge with action. Proverbs can also be described as applying divine principles to life situations. If anyone wants to be wise, seek wisdom in the book of Proverbs.

The main purpose of the book of Proverbs is found in verses 1-7, with the focus being on verse 7. If someone is to obtain wisdom it begins with reverencing God. On the other hand, the fool despises wisdom and instruction. Verses 8-19 are a warning to avoid a sinful lifestyle (v10-14), and an encouragement to follow wisdom (v15-18). At the end of these comparisons there will be a conclusion as to how the ones who chose wickedness turn out, and it usually involves their own sin being turned back on them (v19). Wisdom calls out to the simple (young, naïve), the scorner (ridicules) and the fool (morally insensitive) in verses 20-33 challenging them to turn to wisdom. Verses 24-32 show the consequences of turning from wisdom, and verse 33 shows those who chose to listen to wisdom.

Friday • Ezekiel 8-13

Chapters 8-11 are one vision received by Ezekiel. This occurred while he was still lying on his right side bearing the sins of Judah (4:6). The main purpose of the vision was to show the reason for the coming judgment. This whole vision is to contrast the glory of God and the wickedness of the leadership of the nation for falling into idolatry (v1-6). The north gate is the gate where the altar of sacrifice is located. After being told to dig through a hole in the wall, Ezekiel sees the leaders worshipping idols in secret (v7-12)-see Romans 1:23. They believed that God did not see them and that He was no longer with them. In verses 13-14 Ezekiel observes women weeping for Tammuz which was also known as Adonis and Aphrodite by name. In verses 15-16 Ezekiel observes 25 men worshipping the sun. The chapter closes with God declaring judgment on Judah for their idolatry (v17-18).

In Ezekiel 9:1-4 the Lord calls on the men who will execute the judgment in Jerusalem. The man with the inkhorn was to mark all of those who had genuine remorse and concern for the sins of the people. In verses 5-8 the judgment begins to take place. They were not to spare anyone who did not have the mark of God on them. Ezekiel pleads with God to spare the people. In verses 9-11, God tells Ezekiel that the wickedness of the people is great because they have denied Him.

In Ezekiel 10:1-7 the man in linen who had the inkhorn is instructed to take coals of fire from the cherubim and pour them out in judgment on the city, perhaps to purify it. The cherubim in verses 8-17 and 20-22 are the same as described in chapter 1. Cherubim are presented in the Old Testament as guardians (Gen. 3:24) and worshippers on the mercy seat (Ex. 25:18-20). One of the main themes of Ezekiel is the departure and return of God's glory. God's glory leaves the temple in verse 18 and goes to the east gate. Earlier Scriptures said that if the people strayed from God's ways, His glory would depart from them (Deut. 31:17, Hosea 9:12).

In Ezekiel 11:1-4 Ezekiel is brought to the East Gate and sees 25 men led by Jaazaniah and Pelatiah. They had given the people evil counsel, and had led them into sin. Verse 3 is basically saying that Jerusalem is the pot (security), and the people the meat (safe from harm). Ezekiel prophesies to the leaders that their sin was not hidden from God (v4-6). In God's judgment, these leaders would be placed outside the pot (Jerusalem) and slain (v7-12). Proof that Ezekiel's words were from God is the death of Pelatiah in verse 13. Verses 14-21 contain the first mention of a future restoration. Even though they are in exile, God will still be with them. One day He would regather them, restore to them the land, cleanse the land, and fulfill a new covenant with them (Jer. 31:31-34, Ez. 36:26-27). In verses 22-25 God's glory departs to the mountains, and Ezekiel shares his vision with those in exile with him.

In chapters 12-19, Ezekiel will counter the people's rejection of his warnings. In chapter 12 the people reason that judgment would not come in their lifetime. In chapter 13 the people say that Ezekiel is only one prophet of many, so why should they listen to him. Chapter 14 is about the corrupt leaders, and if judgment is coming it should only fall on them. Chapters 15-16 show the people believed that God would not judge them because they belonged to Him. In chapter 17 the people believed God would not judge them for their ancestor's sins. In chapter 18 the people believed that if judgment was coming it would not be stopped, even if they repented. Finally in chapter 19 the people believe Zedekiah (the king) could be trusted, and that he would stop the Babylonians. In 12:1-7 Ezekiel would continue to act as a sign to the people. In these verses he is acting out the process of going into exile, showing that there would be more exiles to come and they would not be going back anytime soon. Ezekiel would explain his sign to them in verses 8-16, which would also include Zedekiah (the prince). Zedekiah would be carried away into captivity, see his sons killed, and be blinded and killed in Babylon (2Kgs. 25:5,7; Jer. 39:6-7). The sign in verses 17-20 was to show the fear that would come on Jerusalem and Judah when their cities were destroyed and ruined. This would allow the people to see that God was faithful to His promises. The people's problem, as mentioned earlier, was they did not believe any of Ezekiel's words and that what he said would not happen (v21-28). God's response in verses 26-28 was that judgment will no longer be delayed.

Ezekiel 13 condemns the false prophets who prophesied peace when there was no peace. In verses 1-7 we see that the foolish prophets relied upon their own selfish hearts and did not seek God. The word "foolish" in the Old Testament meant someone who was spiritually and morally insensitive. These foolish prophets could not stand in the gap for the people because of their sinfulness. The prophets would be cut off from among the people and allowed to come back (v8-16). Those foolish prophets who helped people repair their walls would see the walls torn down, and their own lives torn down with them. The women who were false prophets would also come under the judgment of God (v17-23). These women led people into their sin and caused many people to die. Not only this, but they also encouraged those who were already wicked to continue in their ways.

Saturday • Romans 7-8

Paul continues to deal with the issue of our sinful nature in Romans 7. In verses 1-6, Paul uses the example of marriage. Just as death breaks the marriage vow, believing in Christ breaks our "marriage" to sin. The one who has believed in Christ is delivered from the law, and is now led by the Spirit in their union with Christ. This new marriage bond with Christ is to bear fruit for God (v4). Also, it is good to remember Paul's background as he discusses the law. He was once a Pharisee who tried to live by the law (v5-6). His devotion to the law led him to persecute the church (Gal. 1:13-14, Phil. 3:6). Paul knew what it was like to try to live by the law, and now he knows what it is to be led by the Spirit.

In verses 7-12 Paul argues for the benefits of the law. The law pointed out that Paul, and each of us, are sinful people (v7). The law also shows that the judgment of God on sin is death (v9-10). In verse 11, the law shows that sin is deceitful in its character. The law also shows believers that the law is holy, just, and good. These are each characteristics of God (v12). Salvation has never come from keeping the law. Only salvation found through faith alone and in Christ alone can provide salvation, which Paul explains in verses 13-25.

Even after salvation, there is an ongoing battle with sin that rages in each believer. This is because of the sinfulness of our flesh (v13-25). Many people interpret this in different ways. Some believe Paul is writing about his pre-converted life and that he is showing his struggles with keeping the law and sin. In my own personal opinion through my study, Paul is talking about his current life and his own struggle with sin. There are two reasons for this. One, verses 7-13 are written in past tense and verses 14-25 are written in the present tense. Second, these verses describe the life that each believer lives today. Even though one is born again and has the Holy Spirit, there is still a struggle with sin. Paul is describing the struggle that takes place when a believer tries to defeat sin on their own. The only victory over this kind of life is found in Christ.

Romans 8 is considered by many to be the greatest chapter in all of Scripture. In this chapter Paul is showing another benefit of salvation which is living in the power of the Holy Spirit. In this chapter alone, the Holy Spirit is mentioned 19 times. In verses 1-4 Jesus' death is the basis for our deliverance from sin. Upon placing our faith in Him, believers receive the Holy Spirit. In verses 5-11 it is by the power of the Holy Spirit that we can have true freedom from the power of sin in our lives. It is those who walk according to the Spirit, and not the flesh that are under no condemnation (v1) and who fulfill the law (v4-5). Those who live their life in the flesh only live for their fleshly desires. The result of their life is death, and they cannot be pleasing to God (v6-8). Verse 9 makes it clear that if you do not have the Holy Spirit, then you do not belong to Christ. Those who have the Spirit are dead to their old life (v10) and will one day be resurrected, just as Christ was (v11).

Since we are still living in the flesh, we need the Holy Spirit to help us put to death the deeds of the flesh (v12-17). If we live our lives according to the Spirit, then we will have assurance in knowing that we are the children of God and heirs of Christ. These verses also serve as an assurance of salvation. Do you live according to the Spirit? Do you follow the leadership of the Holy Spirit? While we find assurance of our salvation in the pages of Scripture and through prayer, obedience is the key to assurance. Living according to the Spirit and following the Spirit both require obedience.

In verses 18-25 Paul contrasts the present suffering of this life (probably our daily battle with sin) with the future glory that awaits. The term "earnest expectation" in verse 19 pictures someone leaning forward in interest (redemption of our bodies, looking forward to eternity). It is in these things that we have hope, and we eagerly await for them to come to pass (v24-25). In verses 26-27 it is the Holy Spirit that intercedes for us when we pray, especially when we do not know what to pray. Verses 28-30 speak of God's love for His people that goes back to eternity past, brings us all the way to the present, and continues into to the future. Coupled with the preceding verses on prayer, it should be a focus in our prayer lives on how we can bring glory to God. God works all things out for the good in a believer's life so that we can be conformed into the image of His Son. Some interpret this verse to mean that life will be easy and comfortable for them. That is not what Paul is saying. Paul has already mentioned the suffering of believers many times in Romans.

In verses 31-39 we learn that nothing can separate us from the love of Christ. We win life's victories through Christ. Here, Paul also shows what God has done on behalf of believers. First, God is for us. He is on our side throughout life (v31). Second, God gave His own Son for each of us. Jesus died in our place for our sin (v32). Third, God has justified us (declared not guilty). Believers will not stand guilty before God for their sin (v33). Fourth, Jesus makes intercession not only for our salvation but in our prayers (v35, Heb. 7:25). Fifth He has made us conquerors. There is nothing that enters our live as believers, that through Christ, we cannot overcome (1 John 5:4). Finally, nothing will ever separate us from God's love (35-39).

Cover to Cover Challenge

Week 25

Sunday • Psalm 79-82

Welcome to week 25 of the *Cover to Cover Challenge*! Continue to pray for understanding as we study the Word of God, and pray for the Lord to be honored and glorified. Psalm 111:1-2 says "Praise the Lord! I will praise the Lord with my whole heart, in the assembly of the upright and in the congregation…The works of the Lord are great, studied by all who have pleasure in them".

Psalm 79 is a lament representing the nation of Israel during the time of Jerusalem's fall and during the exile of the Israelites. In verses 1-4 the writer of the psalm focuses on the devastation caused by their enemies, who had no regard for God or His people. The question of verse 5 comes from those who are left after the devastation. The psalmist cries out for God's justice (v6-7), forgiveness (v8), and deliverance from their enemies and their sin (v9). The psalmist poses another question in verse 10 in light of the devastation their enemies have caused. "Why isn't God dealing with our enemies?" Again, the psalmist cries out for justice and for God to deliver them from their present situation (v10-11). The "sevenfold" refers to God repaying their enemy for what they have done to God's people (v12). In verse 13 the people praise God, knowing He will deliver them in the future.

Psalm 80 is another lament. It probably refers to the last days of the northern kingdom with the mention of the three tribes in verse 2. The main focus of this psalm is for God to restore them by forgiving their sins and by driving out the enemy (v1-3). Similar to Psalm 79, the psalmist knows God is angry with His people over their sin (v4-7). Instead of experiencing God's grace, they are oppressed and ridiculed by their enemies. Israel is the vine of verses 8-13 (Isa. 5:1-7). The psalm closes with another appeal for God to deliver and restore them (v14-19).

Psalm 81 was probably sung during the Feast of Tabernacles, which followed the Day of Atonement. This psalm served as an invitation for the people to reflect on God's past acts and the hope for the future that they had in Him. This background fits the context of verses 1-5. It was during the Feast of Tabernacles that the people were to proclaim the acts of the Lord in salvation, beginning with the exodus from Egypt. The exodus is referenced in verses 6-7 as God delivered them from their burdens. The people were to listen to the Lord and obey His commandments (v8-10). Israel, however, rebelled against the Lord and did not submit to Him (v11-12). God calls upon His people to listen (v13). If they would obey, He would deliver them from their enemies and supply all of their needs (v14-16).

Psalm 82 shows that God is the great judge and that all powers are subject to Him. Verses 1-2 may refer to "gods" of other nations, or the judges and kings of Israel who were supposed to represent the Lord and protect the people as God would. If it is the latter, it was the leadership of Israel that were being unjust to the very ones they were supposed to protect (v3-4). Their rule has become evil and unjust (v5). Because they rule unjustly over the people, they will die (v6-7). Because of the unjust rulers the psalmist asks for God to be the judge over the whole earth (v8).

Monday • Leviticus 10-13

Leviticus 10:1-5 begins with Nadab and Abihu being consumed with fire from the Lord. This happens because they offered strange fire before the Lord because they are intoxicated (v9). Moses intercedes so that Aaron and his other sons do not become unclean because of their mourning (v6-11). God speaks directly to Aaron in verses 8-11 concerning his sons. He makes a distinction between what is holy and what is common. In verses 12-15 further instruction are given by Moses concerning the offerings. Verses 16-18 give explanation for why the sin offering was not eaten. Aaron believed (because of what has happened) eating the offering would have been inappropriate, so it was totally burned.

Leviticus 11 begins the third section of the book, and concerns what is clean and unclean. Leviticus 11 focuses on food. The animals are separated into categories of land, water, and flying creatures. For a land animal to be clean it must have a split hoof and chew its cud (v1-8). Animals that lived in the water must have fins and scales (v9-12). The list for birds includes those that could not be eaten (v13-23). These birds are the ones that eat other animals or feed off what is already dead. Touching an unclean animal that is dead made the person unclean. Eating a clean animal without going through the proper procedure also made the person unclean (v24-47). Becoming unclean was solved in these cases by water and lasted until the evening. Only what is clean can become holy, which explains verses 44-45. What is unclean could not approach God, and this restricted fellowship among the people.

Leviticus 12 covers women who have given birth and their rite of purification. It is not known for certain why the uncleanness doubles if the woman gives birth to a girl. In any case, a burnt offering and a sin offering are to be done before she can be clean again.

Leviticus 13 deals with leprous skin and clothing. All of the skin ailments that we read about here are not what we know as leprosy today, but more than likely are skin infections (v1-23). All people who had such skin problems were to go to the priest to be checked. If the priest was unsure, the person would be isolated and checked again to see whether or not they were clean or unclean. Any person who was found to have an infectious disease was placed outside the camp and had to announce to anyone approaching that they were unclean to keep it from spreading. These rules also applied to clothing. If it spread upon the clothes they were to be burned.

Tuesday • 1 Chronicles 7-10

1 Chronicles 7 records the genealogies of six of Jacob's sons. Naphtali only gets a single verse. In the line of Ephraim, Joshua only has his name mentioned and nothing about his leading the Israelites into the Promised Land is recorded here. Manasseh's line mentions Zelophehad, whose story is recorded in Number 27:1-11. He only had daughters, so they go to Moses because the law made no provision for inheritances for families with no sons.

1 Chronicles 8 traces the family history of Saul who is from the tribe of Benjamin. If you remember, Saul said that he was from the smallest tribe and from the least significant tribe within it. This sets the stage for the opening story in 1 Chronicles of the death of Saul.

One thing that needs to be remembered is that when this book was written, the people were already coming back from exile into the land. The first people to go back were the religious leaders (9:2). It is obvious from chapter 9 that someone knowledgeable of the priesthood and the temple functions wrote the book because of the attention to detail given in these areas. The priests, Levites, and gatekeepers are specifically mentioned as having returned. Gatekeepers were assigned the task of opening and closing the temple gates, and allowing people in or keeping them out.

1 Chronicles 10 recounts the last days of Saul and his reign. There are three reasons the author gives for Saul's reign coming to an end (v13-14). First, Saul is unfaithful to God. In 1 Samuel 15, Samuel had instructed Saul to wipe out the Amalekites but he does not. Second, Saul did not keep the word of the Lord. Saul did not wait for Samuel to sacrifice to the Lord, he instead took it upon himself to do it (1 Sam. 13:5-14). Third, Saul failed to seek the Lord. When Saul no longer receives help from the Lord after the death of Samuel he consults a medium, where he also learns of his coming death (1 Sam. 28:4-25).

Wednesday • Luke 15-16

Luke 15-19 focus on the social outcasts of their day and Jesus' concern for them. The whole context of chapter 15 can be seen in the first two verses. Notice who drew near to hear Jesus (tax collectors and sinners), and notice who was complaining (Pharisees and scribes). The tax collectors and sinners were social outcasts who normally had no opportunity to hear God's Word. The Pharisees and scribes were the supposed experts in God's Word. The following parables show the joy of sinners coming to God in repentance. The point of the lost sheep (v3-7) and the lost coin (v8-10) is to show Jesus seeking and receiving sinners with joy.

The parable of the lost son in verses 11-32 teaches valuable lessons to all those who were hearing the parables (v1-2). Notice from the very beginning the point of the parable is the contrast of two sons (v11). Many believe the younger son asking for his inheritance indicates that he was saying his family was dead to him (v12). The younger son wasted all of his inheritance on reckless living and had nothing left (v13). The famine also added to the difficulty of having no money (v14). For a Jew feeding the swine was about as low as you could get (v15-16). Sometimes God has to put us in the pig pen to open our eyes (v17). It is at this point the son confesses his sin (v18-19, 21). He knew he needed to go home first to God, and then home to his father. In Jesus' day an elderly father would never have ran toward his son in compassion (v20). Giving the son the best robe, the signet ring, and sandals demonstrated the father's forgiveness and compassion (v22-23). The joy expressed over the lost sheep and coin is also expressed when the lost son comes home (v24). The added element here is the older son (v25-32). He would represent the Pharisees and scribes and their attitude toward those who are coming to Jesus for repentance. Just like the older son, the Pharisees could not comprehend the meaning of forgiveness, so there is no joy.

Luke 16 concerns material possessions being valued over eternity. The point of Jesus speaking these parables is found in verse 14. We read here that the Pharisees were lovers of money (material possessions). Luke 16:1-9 is one of the most difficult parables to interpret. If the focus is on material possessions, then it becomes much easier to see the point. The dishonest manager shrewdly uses his position to secure his future by discounting the outstanding accounts of his master's debtors. The master, in turn, praises him for this act. Jesus praises him, not for his dishonesty, but for his shrewdness. He is preparing himself for his master's judgment against him for wasting his goods. Jesus was urging His followers to be shrewd (wise), with respect to eternal matters. In verses 10-13 Jesus teaches that faithfulness in temporary things will lead to one being faithful in eternal things. No one can serve two masters (money/God). In verses 14-18 Jesus contrasts the greed of the Pharisees with the faithfulness He just spoke of in the previous verses. They did not value what He valued (v15) and they interpreted the law incorrectly (v16-17). An example of that is their view on divorce (v18).

The story of the rich man and Lazarus ("God has helped") closes chapter 16 and is unique to Luke (v19-31). Psalm 121:1-2 reflects Lazarus' name. This story also represents the great reversal. The rich man lived a life of comfort with his riches, but he was apart from God. Lazarus, the beggar, lived a life of torment but he knew God. In the afterlife, the reversal happens. Lazarus experiences comfort while the rich man is tormented. The rich man did not go to hell because he was rich, but because he valued his riches over God. Hell will be a place of heightened awareness (v23,24), a place of extreme agony (v23-25, 28), a place of the blackest darkness (Matt. 8:12; Jude 13), a place of eternal weeping (Luke 13:28), a place of eternal separation (v26), and a place of no hope (v26). This story also shows that there is a permanent separation in the afterlife (v26). There is no second chance beyond death to believe in Jesus. Everyone is going to live forever, but where you spend it depends upon your relationship with Jesus Christ.

Thursday • Proverbs 2-3

Proverbs 2 is mainly about the value of wisdom. In verses 1-3 the father is urging his son to be wise. He is declaring what wisdom is, and what it can do for him. The son can discover wisdom in verses 4-5 by searching for it. Verses 6-9 pertain to the dawning of wisdom. When one seeks wisdom, it comes from God who is the source of wisdom. The word "walk" in verse 7 refers to someone's way of life, character, and conduct. The word "path" means a well-worn path, referring to a way that is often traveled on. Verses 10-11 show that wisdom provides discretion for the one who has it. Wisdom will also help someone be delivered from the evil man (v12-15) and from the immoral woman (v16-19). In verses 20-22, the father urges the son to make a decision to follow wisdom.

In Proverbs 3 the father is guiding his son to choose wisdom. In verses 1-4 the father outlines benefits of following wisdom-it will add life to your years (quality) and years to your life (length), peace, love (mercy), faithfulness (truth), and favor with God and man. Verses 5-6 are some of the most well-known Scriptures in Proverbs. I will insert the meanings of the words into these two verses- "Trust (rely on for help and protection) in the Lord with all your heart, and lean not (do not rely on yourself for help and protection) on your own understanding, in all your ways (character, conduct, choices) acknowledge (to know, submit to) Him, and He shall direct your path (smooth and straight path)". Someone who possesses wisdom will also give their best to the Lord in honor of Him (v9-10). Verses 11-12 are about what God does to keep someone from sinning, and to bring them up in His ways (training). In verses 13-18 the values of wisdom are listed-it brings happiness (v13) and it is priceless to have (v14-15). Wisdom also leads to a long life (v16), riches and honor (v16), peace (v17), and fullness of life (v18). Verses 19-20 show that God is wise and uses wisdom, so we also should desire to have wisdom ourselves. In verses 21-26 other benefits of wisdom are listed-it adds meaning to life (v22), provides safety (v23), calms fears (v24,25), provides pleasant sleep (v24), and gives assurance the Lord will be by your side (v26). Wisdom will also guide you to do good (v27-28) and keep you from sinning (v29-31). Verses 32-35 show a contrast between those who are wise and those who fail to follow wisdom, going their own way.

WEEK 25

Friday • Ezekiel 14-18

Ezekiel will continue to counter the people's rejection of his warnings all the way through chapter 19. Here, in chapter 14, the people believe that if the leaders are corrupt then judgment will only fall on them. In Ezekiel 14:1-11 some of the leadership of Israel comes to Ezekiel to inquire of the Lord, while following idols in their hearts (v1-3). This had also led the nation to be unfaithful to God and placed them in their present situation. God response comes in three parts (v4-11). First, He would give the elders of Israel over to their idols. Second, for those who refused to repent, He would begin to enforce the cursings of the covenant. Thirdly, the false prophets who spoke to the leaders and the people would be punished. In verses 12-23 it is personal repentance that is called for. This is illustrated by God using Noah, Daniel, and Job as examples. Even these three men would only deliver themselves and not another person, even from their own family, when judgment comes. God, by His grace, will spare a remnant (v21-23).

In Ezekiel 15 the people believed God would not judge them because they belonged to Him. The parable is designed to show that the vine (Israel) was useless for anything except to bear fruit, which they did not do. After having been put into the fire (exile) because of her unfaithfulness, the only value she has left is to be fuel for the fire.

Ezekiel 16 covers the history of Israel as a nation. The people are still convinced that because they are God's people He will not punish them. In verses 1-5 the birth of the city is spoken of. As the nation grew the Lord provided, loved, and cared for her (v6-14). In verses 15-31 the nation began to indulge in idolatry and became a harlot. They used the very gifts God had given them to make idols to worship with other nations. They were not just harlots, but adulterous wives (v31-34). For all of this they would be judged. The very nations that they committed adultery with would come against them (v35-43). In verses 44-48 Jerusalem, Sodom, and Samaria are compared. They all became perverted by paganism, but Jerusalem was the worst of them all (v49-52). Judgment was coming because of this (v53-58). In verses 59-63 we read that the Lord will still be faithful to His covenant that He has made to them. This will remind them of their sinful past, but also show them that God is faithful to His word.

In chapter 17, Ezekiel counters the argument that God would not judge them for their ancestors' sins. Ezekiel responds that they will be judged because of their own sin. The background for this chapter is found in 2 Kings 24:8-20, 2 Chronicles 36:9-13, Jeremiah 37, and Jeremiah 52:1-7. Verses 3-4 go with verses 11-12. The eagle is Babylon, and Lebanon stands for Jerusalem. This refers to Nebuchadnezzar's attack on Jerusalem and his carrying King Jehoiachin to Babylon. Verses 5-6 go with verses 13-14. Nebuchadnezzar had set up Zedekiah as king, and Judah was in subjection to Babylon. Verses 7-8 go with verse 15. The second eagle is Egypt, which influenced Zedekiah to rebel against Babylon. So, each eagle represents a ruler who was used as an instrument to punish Judah. Verses 9-10 go with verses 16-21. The consequences for Jerusalem, "the vine", would be terrible. Babylon would pull up its roots and cut off its fruit and it would wither because Jerusalem sought an alliance with Egypt. In verses 22-24 God is pictured as taking one of the twigs and planting it on a high mountain. This shows that God will restore His people and restore them to their land.

In Ezekiel 18 the people believed that if judgment was truly coming it would not be stopped, even if they repented. This is shown by the proverb used in verse 2. This proverb shows that what the father does affects his children. The people most likely believed that righteousness and wickedness were hereditary so there was no reason to change their ways. The Lord's response to this is in verses 3-4. Each person lives or dies according to their own actions and each person bears responsibility for their self. God uses three illustrations to prove that an individual is responsible to God. Verses 5-9 demonstrate a righteous person, verses 10-13 demonstrate an unrighteous son who had a righteous father, and verses 14-18 demonstrate that an unrighteous man may not have an unrighteous son. All of this is explained even further in verses 19-32. The simple fact is each individual has a responsibility to choose whether or not to follow God's ways. In the final verses of the chapter God pleads with them as individuals to repent of their sin.

Saturday • Romans 9-10

Romans 9-11 concern the Jews and their continuing part in God's plan. In Romans 9:1-5 Paul shares his burden over his people for their lack of faith in Christ. Paul says that if it would save his people, he would gladly be accursed from Christ for their sake (v3). In verses 6-13 Paul argues that God will keep His promises to those who truly are of Israel. The "true Israel" are those who are not only descendants of Abraham (Gal. 3:7- all believers are the spiritual seed of Abraham), but those who have embraced Christ. These are the children of promise, like Isaac, who are chosen by God.

In verses 14-19 Paul uses the example of Pharaoh to demonstrate that God is free to show mercy on whomever He wishes. God is the potter, and Israel is the clay (v20-21). Both vessels of wrath and vessels of honor deserve condemnation. By His grace, salvation is offered to all both Jew and Gentile (v22-24). Passages from Hosea show the inclusion of the Gentiles, and passages from Isaiah show the exclusion of the Jews (v25-29). In the plan of God, Gentiles were provided righteousness before they even looked for it. Jews, on the other hand tried to be righteous by the works of the law apart from faith therefore they stumbled over the stumbling stone (v30-33).

The Jew's pursuit of righteousness by works is continued into chapter 10. In verses 1-4 Paul shows that the Jews were zealous for God through works and not by believing in Christ. Paul knows this from his own experiences in pursuing God the same way (Phil. 3:6, Gal. 1:13-14). The law demands perfection if one is to try and live by it (v5). By believing in Jesus, who fulfilled the law, all believers are justified before God. Verses 6-8 show that Jesus is near and can be known through faith. These verses come from Deuteronomy 30:11-14 and are a part of Moses' farewell discourse. Most believe that Moses' words anticipate the future new covenant. Paul also covers this in verses 9-10, showing the necessity of faith in order to be saved. Only Christ satisfied the demands of the law, paid for their sins, and bore their punishment. Each person who calls upon the Lord will be saved, whether they are a Jew or a Gentile (v11-13).

How can this come about? God sends people out to preach the gospel so that it can be heard, although not all will believe (v14-17). Paul makes it clear in verse 18 that the Jewish people all had heard and understood the words of God, but were found to be disobedient to it (v21). Verses 19-21 also portray the Gentiles as turning to God in order to provoke Israel to jealousy.

Cover to Cover CHALLENGE

Week 26

Sunday • Psalm 83-86

Welcome to week 26 of the *Cover to Cover Challenge*! As always pray that the Lord be honored and glorified through this study and pray for understanding of God's Word. Psalm 119:133 says "Direct my steps according to Your word, and let no iniquity have dominion over me".

Psalm 83 is a lament which represents all of Israel crying out to God for deliverance from their enemies (v1). Verses 2-4 describe the enemies of Israel, who are making themselves ready to attack. The enemies described are not only formed against Israel, but against God (v5-8). The psalmist asks God to judge them, as He did His enemies in the past (v9-12). God's judgment upon their enemies is so that they will know who the Lord is (v13-18).

In Psalm 84 the psalmist expresses a longing to be closer to God. The psalmist loves and longs to be in the presence of God (v1-4). Verses 5-7 may describe people coming to celebrate the feasts, or the ones coming back from exile. The main focus here is a blessing for all who trust in the strength of the Lord. The psalmist asks God to hear his prayer for the king in verses 8-9. In verses 10-11 the psalmist declares that he would rather be a doorkeeper in the house of God than to be thriving anywhere else apart from God's presence. Verse 12 closes with another blessing for those who place their trust in God.

Psalm 85 is another lament representing all of Israel, asking for God to deliver them. This psalm probably reflects the conditions of the exiles returning to the land. Here the psalmist reflects upon their past in verses 1-3, and also on how God has forgiven them and brought them back to the land. In verses 4-9 the psalmist speaks of their present situation. The people long to be restored, to be revived, and to once again experience the relationship they had with the Lord in the past. Verses 10-13 describe their future where God's loyal love (mercy), faithfulness (truth), righteousness, and peace dwell in them and with them again.

Psalm 86 is another lament by David as he pleads for God to show him mercy during his time of need. In verses 1-5 David calls upon God to hear his prayer. Because David knows that God is good, forgiving, and loving (mercy) he has full trust in the Lord to answer his prayer (v6-7). Verses 8-10 are a hymn of praise for God's goodness and uniqueness because He alone is God. David asks for God to help him walk in His ways as he waits on God's deliverance (v11-13). In verses 14-17 David cries out to be delivered from his enemies, and prays for the Lord to have mercy upon him and give him strength.

Monday • Leviticus 14-16

Leviticus 13 dealt with skin problems and mildew and how to detect them. Leviticus 14 deals with the cleansing process. Those found with skin ailments were sent outside the camp so others could not catch the disease (v1-8). If the person was found to be healed after a week then there was a cleansing ceremony. After the cleansing there would be another seven days of examination that included shaving and the guilt, sin, burnt, and grain offerings (v9-32). Verses 33-57 deal with mildew in the home and the purification process. The cleansing ritual is the same for the home as with a person who is unclean. Any affected stones were taken outside the camp and disposed of.

Leviticus 15 deals with clean and unclean discharges. Verses 1-12 deal with an unclean discharge and verses 13-15 the purification process. Verses 19-32 deal with female discharges and the purification process.

Leviticus 16 introduces the Day of Atonement. From the opening verses of chapter 16 this was given to Moses after Aaron's sons offered profane fire before the Lord (v1). These instructions were given to prepare Aaron to enter the Holy of Holies. The instructions included a sin offering and burnt offering for himself and his family (v2-5). The two goats included in the sacrifice were very significant (v6-19). One would be sacrificed as a sin offering for the people, while the other symbolically took on the sins of the people and would be sent away. This takes place in verses 20-34. The people participated in this day by resting and becoming humble before God (v31).

Tuesday • 1 Chronicles 11-15

1 Chronicles 11-12 document David's rise to the throne and his mighty men along with his army. The anointing of David in verses 1-3 is the third anointing of David, and was sealed with a covenant before the Lord and all the leaders. Verses 4-9 show David taking Jerusalem for himself. The recording of David's mighty men in the rest of the chapter is here because of the role these men played in the rise of David's kingship and in his taking Jerusalem (v10-47). The men in 1 Chronicles 12:1-7 supported David before he was made king over all of Israel, and were from Saul's tribe of Benjamin. Those listed in verses 8-15 are from the tribe of Gad and probably joined him much earlier than the Benjamites. The Holy Spirit led Amasai and his army to join David's army in verses 16-18. Those from Manasseh joined David just before the death of Saul (v19-22). Verses 23-40 show those who came to Hebron to turn the kingdom over to David and brings us back to 11:1-3.

1 Chronicles 13 describes the journey to retrieve the Ark from Kirjath Jerim. This would show those coming back from exile that there should be a desire to seek and to worship God. The action of Uzza, and his death would show that the people needed to conform to God's standards in order to worship Him. The blessing upon the house of Obed-Edom would show God's blessing upon those who do.

1 Chronicles 14 records David's victories over the Philistines. In verses 1-7 the king of Tyre sent David supplies, and it is then David knew that the Lord had made him king over Israel. David wins two victories over the Philistine army in verses 8-17. What is to be noticed here is that David consulted God before each battle and that he obeyed.

1 Chronicles 15 concerns bringing the Ark back from the home of Obed-Edom to Jerusalem in the way prescribed by God (v1-15). This would prevent another tragedy like Uzza's. Verses 4-11 show all the major clans that assisted in worship. Their genealogies were recorded earlier in 1 Chronicles. Additional help was needed to sing and play instruments and their names are recorded in verses 17-24. Verses 24-29 show the elaborate celebration of bringing the Ark to Jerusalem. This part is also recorded in 2 Samuel 6 where it is said Michal, because of her actions, would have no children.

Wednesday • Luke 17-18

Luke 17:1-4 deals with people being stumbling blocks to others and the subject of forgiveness. The word "offenses" can be translated temptations or hindrances. The thought behind the word is bait in the trap. Verses 3-4 do not just teach forgiveness, but that forgiveness is to be habitual. The teaching in verses 5-10 is about having faith (v5-6) and being a servant to others (v7-10). In the world, someone's success may be used to gain an advantage over people. But in Jesus' kingdom, success is becoming a servant to all. Verses 11-19 are unique to Luke and demonstrate the faith of a Gentile (theme in Luke's gospel). The story implies that the other nine were Jews. Jesus told them to go and show themselves to the priest just as a healed leper would according to Leviticus 14. Jesus was putting their faith to the test by having them go to the priest like they were already clean. This also demonstrates the need to be grateful when God blesses.

In verses 20-37 the coming of the kingdom of God is discussed. When Jesus speaks in verses 20-21 it is the Pharisees asking about the kingdom. In verses 22-29 Jesus begins to speak about the kingdom to His disciples. God's kingdom was already with them, but its full consummation would come at a future day that is likened to the days of Noah and of Lot. Both Noah and Lot knew judgment was coming and both did what was necessary to save themselves and their family. This is why Jesus warns them to remember Lot's wife (v32). As she was being carried to safety she stopped because she did not want to leave her old life behind. She represents someone who came close to being delivered but never received it. Jesus' coming will be sudden, so people are to be prepared for it when it comes (v30-37).

Luke 18:1-8 teaches the importance of prayer in someone's life. Prayer is something that believers should be passionate about (v1), it should be made a priority in our lives (v3), and we should be persistent in it (v5). Verses 9-14 show the proper attitude of someone in prayer by contrasting the prayers of a Pharisee and a tax collector. What the Pharisee said about himself was true, but he demonstrated the wrong attitude to have in prayer. His prayer was "me" centered. The tax collector was one of the most hated professions of Jesus' day but his prayer was centered on God and his need for Him. The humility of the tax collector is again demonstrated in verses 15-17 with the example of a child. One must approach God with humility to come into the kingdom. It was also a common practice in Jesus' day to bring children to be blessed by a rabbi. In Matthew's account the parents brought the children to Jesus so that He could pray for them.

In verses 18-30 Jesus teaches how one cannot enter the kingdom with the story of the rich young ruler. The question he asks Jesus reveals that he believed there was some way for him to earn eternal life. If you will notice, in verses 18-19, Jesus reveals Himself to be God to the young man. In verse 18 he calls Jesus "Good teacher" and in verse 19 Jesus responds with "no one is good but One, that is God". The implication is that Jesus is God. The rich young ruler was unwilling to give up his riches. His failure to enter the kingdom was not because he was rich but because he would rather have riches than to have God (v24-27). Jesus assures the disciples that anyone who sacrifices for His kingdom will receive a reward (v28-30). In verses 31-34 He predicts it for the third time, this time adding His resurrection. The healing of the blind man is the last miracle in Luke's gospel before Jesus enters Jerusalem (v35-43). It demonstrates the faith of the blind man in Jesus, his Messiah.

Thursday • Proverbs 4

In verses 1-9 the father gives instructions on how to acquire wisdom. In order to gain wisdom, someone must pay attention to it (v1), not let go of it (v2), retain it (v4), keep it (v4), get it (v5), not forget it or turn away (v5), and love it (v6). Wisdom should be the principal thing (first choice) in our lives. Verses 10-19 show the blessings of wisdom-length of life (v10), guidance to the right path (v11-13), and avoidance of the wrong paths (v14-19). Verses 20-27 show the care of wisdom. The father shows the care of wisdom by showing how wisdom protects through the physical attributes of a human body. Wisdom will care for what you see, speak, and every issue that flows from the heart (Prov. 4:23).

Friday • Ezekiel 19-23

In chapter 19 Ezekiel continues to answer those who reject his warnings. The objection in chapter 19 is that the people believe the king can actually stop the Babylonians from invading. This chapter is actually a funeral song for Judah's rulers. Ezekiel uses the imagery of a lioness (Israel) and her cubs (kings). The first cub is Jehoahaz (2 Kgs. 23:31-34, 2 Chron. 36:1-4) and the second is Jehoiachin (2 Kgs. 24:8-17, 2 Chron. 36:8-10). The vine imagery in verses 10-14 also represents Israel. These verses show Israel's growth with its many branches (kings), its fall, and being transplanted in a desert place (exile).

Eleven months have passed since Ezekiel's last messages. It will be apparent over the next few chapters that the exiles still had hope of deliverance. His messages in chapters 20-23 are a response to this. Israel's history has always been one of rebellion and the time for judgment had come. In verses 1-9 Ezekiel outlines the beginning of the nation of Israel to show that they have rebelled against God by not getting rid of their idols. Verses 10-17 outline the Israelites' rebellion in the wilderness, and verses 18-26 pertain to the next generation after them who also rebelled. Notice also verses 9, 14, and 22. God did not want His name profaned before the Gentiles by His chosen people. The great sins of Israel were blasphemy and unfaithfulness (v27-29). The reason Ezekiel goes through the history of Israel's rebellion is to tell the present day elders that they are no different than their ancestors (v30-44). In spite of this, God would bring them back and restore them once again. Verses 45-49 describe the judgment God will pour out.

Ezekiel 21 continues the judgment from chapter 20:45-49. The fire from verses 45-49 becomes a sword (Nebuchadnezzar, v18-22) in 21:1-7. The devastating effects of the judgment are found in verses 6-7. Ezekiel is to weep for the sword of judgment that was against Judah (v8-17). Judah's sins were known, and the land would be taken (v18-27). The Ammonites would be judged, but not at the same time as Judah (v28-32). The Ammonites would mock Judah and actually help the Babylonians carry the Israelites away.

In Ezekiel 22:1-16 Israel's sins are made known to the people. Jerusalem had become a city of bloodshed due to its rulers (v6). God's judgment on them would result in exile, cleansing of their sin, and their defilement before the nations. In verses 17-22 Israel is shown to be worthless dross that would be melted again by God's wrath. Judah had become dross because of the failure of their leaders (priests, princes, prophets) to be godly. God found no one to stand in the gap for those being mistreated, so He is going to pour out His wrath in judgment (v29-31).

Ezekiel describes two sisters in chapter 23. Oholah is also known as Samaria, Israel, or the northern kingdom. Oholibah is Jerusalem, Judah, or the southern kingdom. Both of these formed the nation of Israel before it was divided into the two kingdoms (v1-4). Oholah (Samaria) made alliances with Assyria and tried to be like them, committing spiritual adultery against the Lord. The Assyrians took them captive in 722 BC. Oholibah (Judah) may have believed they were safe from judgment. In verses 11-21 Ezekiel says that God is even angrier with them because they continued to commit spiritual adultery even after they saw what happened to the northern kingdom. Just as in the northern kingdom, the people of Judah will be judged by those they have committed spiritual adultery with (v22-35). Both sisters will be judged for their spiritual adultery (v36-45). The punishment would be severe for their spiritual adultery (v46-48).

Saturday • Romans 11-12

In Romans 9, Paul argues that in God's sovereign plan He chose the Jews for Himself. In Romans 10, Paul shows how God dealt with Israel's failure to receive Christ. In Romans 11:1-10 Paul argues that God is not done with Israel, and that He still has a plan for them. To show that God is not done with Israel, Paul uses himself (v1), as well as Elijah (v2-4), as an example. The example of Elijah proves that God will not allow His own people to be completely done away with, and that He will always leave a remnant. Verses 5-6 show that this is part of God's plan, and it is solely by grace. Verses 7-10 deal with the hard hearts of the Jewish people caused by their rejection of God. The word "stupor" means "to sting" and primarily refers to the numb feeling associated with it. Because of their persistent unbelief, the Jewish people had become numb to the words of God. This is also seen in many places in both the Old Testament (Isaiah 6:9-10, 29:10, Deuteronomy 29:4) and in the Gospels (Matt. 13:14-15, Mark 4:12, Luke 8:10, John12:40).

In verses 11-24 Paul demonstrates that Israel's rejection of her Messiah has brought salvation to the Gentiles (v11), who are grafted in to the olive tree (v15-20). It was a common practice in Paul's day to spur growth by grafting in part of a wild olive tree to an olive tree that was not producing as it should. So the grafting in of the wild olive tree (Gentiles) should have provoked Israel to jealousy and should have been a factor in them returning to God (v14). Verses 18-22 are a warning to Gentiles to not be arrogant against the Jewish people because of their place in salvation history. What happened to the Jews could happen to them also. Verses 23-24 show that Jewish people will be saved and grafted in again.

In verses 25-32 Paul discusses the future salvation of Israel. God's mercy that has been shown to the disobedient Gentiles will one day be shown to disobedient Israel. Disobedience by both groups led to God showing His mercy, and both groups must believe in Jesus to be saved. The statement made in verse 26 that "all Israel will be saved" must not be taken that every single Jew will be saved. For example America is spoken of as a Christian nation, but not all are Christians. Whether Jew or Gentile, you must believe in Jesus to be saved. In verses 33-36 Paul closes with praise to God for His wisdom and His ways.

The first 11 chapters of Romans were doctrinal. Now Paul turns to the practical in chapter 12. In verses 1-2 Paul shows how a Christian must live their lives for God. We are to surrender ourselves to God, be willing to give God our all, all because of what He has done for us. We are not to let the world mold and shape us, but be transformed (inwardly) through the renewing our minds (Bible study, prayer, worship, evangelism, etc…) so we will know the will of God for our lives. In verses 3-8 Paul deals with the diversity of our spiritual gifts that actually bring unity to the body (1 Cor. 12). Believers existing in unity and using their spiritual giftedness will produce three things. First, this will produce a community of believers that are united in faith in Jesus Christ. Second, it will produce cohesiveness. Believers will work together to perform God's will. Third, unity will be contagious. Other believers will join in and begin to use their gifts as well. It will also be contagious for those who do not know Christ. It will serve as a catalyst to draw them to Jesus when they see a community of believers working together for the good of others.

The exhortation in verses 9-21 apply to all Christians. They also are very similar to the teachings of Jesus, especially in the Sermon on the Mount (Matt. 5-7). Verses 9-13 primarily relate to treatment of fellow Christians. In verse 9 "without hypocrisy" can be translated as "sincere" or "genuine". Verses 14-21 primarily relate to relationships with those outside the church. Christians should not behave or treat one another as unbelievers do. Their behavior is described to be so different that it serves to draw people to Christ.

Cover to Cover Challenge

Week 27

Sunday • Psalm 87-88

Welcome to week 27 of the *Cover to Cover Challenge*! Keep praying for the Lord to be honored and glorified, pray for understanding as we read God's Word, and pray for the Holy Spirit to work in each heart that is participating. Psalm 119:73 says "Your hands have made me and fashioned me, give me understanding, that I may learn Your commandments".

Psalm 87 focuses on Zion (Jerusalem) as God's city. Among all of the cities in Israel (Jacob), Zion stands out because of the presence of God (v1-3). Verses 4-6 mention many enemies of Israel that are granted citizenship because they have acknowledged the Lord. In verse 7, the music of these nations will sing of the blessings (springs) that come from God.

Psalm 88 is a lament in which the psalmist experiences extreme sorrow and is seeking the Lord for deliverance. In the midst of suffering the psalmist cries out to God in prayer, asking for help (v1-2). The psalmist feels as if his life is slipping away from him and that God is nowhere to be found (v3-5). He feels like God has placed him in the lowest pit, away from all of his friends as he continually pleads with Him about his suffering (v6-12). The psalmist expresses that he still prays to God about his suffering each morning, even though he feels like God is distant (v13-14). In verses 15-18 the psalmist ties together all of his feelings he has expressed throughout the psalm. In these verses he is still pleading with God for deliverance.

Monday • Leviticus 17-20

Leviticus 17 concludes the sacrificial process, with its focus on the sacredness of blood. Any animal that was to be slaughtered had to be offered to God as a sacrifice, otherwise it was considered blood shed (v1-9). A peace offering was to be done before voluntarily slaughtering and eating an animal. No one living in Israel could eat the blood of any sacrifice (v10-16). Blood is equated with life and atonement, so any person who ate blood would be cut off from the people.

Beginning in Leviticus 18, the Lord begins to lay out practical guidelines for the Israelites to follow in order to live as a holy people. This chapter focuses on relationships. In verses 1-5 God reminds them of their covenant relationship they had with Him because they had a tendency to mimic the culture around them (Egypt, Canaan).

The boundaries listed in verses 6-23 function to separate sex from religious worship, which the pagan cultures around them practiced. Verses 24-30 show the consequences of failing to meet the standards that God sets forth for His people. The land God was giving them was a blessing, and those who violated God's law would be expelled from the land.

Leviticus 19 continues with instructions on how to practice holiness. This chapter focuses on loving God and loving others. In verses 1-8, Moses gathered the people together and reminds them of earlier laws God has given. Verses 9-18 focus on loving one's neighbor which includes the vulnerable, Israelites, foreigners, and their enemies. In verses 19-37 they were reminded about having right relationships, not mixing with other cultures, practicing compassion, and being fair in their dealings with others.

Leviticus 20 outlines sins from the previous chapter and lists their punishments. Verses 1-6 show God and the people condemning people who are guilty. They are even warned of closing their eyes to the sins of others. In verses 7-21 the relational sins from chapter 18 are repeated, and a penalty for them is prescribed. The penalties are: being cut off from the people, being burned, barrenness, and death. God urges the people to follow His laws (v22-27). If they disobeyed they would lose the land, if they obeyed they would continue to experience God's blessing.

Tuesday • 1 Chronicles 16-21

After bringing the Ark back to Jerusalem in chapter 15, it will now be placed in the Tabernacle in chapter 16. The placing of the Ark will be accompanied by a time of worship (v1-6). David's song of thanksgiving in verses 8-36 matches three psalms. Verses 8-22 correspond with Psalm 105:1-15, verses 23-33 with Psalm 96, and verses 34-36 with Psalm 106:1, 47-48. The theme of Psalm 105 (v8-22) is remembering God's past acts that demonstrate His faithfulness. Psalm 96 (v23-33) focuses on is the Lord's reign over all the earth. Psalm 106 (v34-36) contrasts God's faithfulness with Israel's unfaithfulness to the Lord. In verses 37-42, David institutes daily worship at the Ark with Abiathar leading the way.

1 Chronicles 17 corresponds to 2 Samuel 7, which records the Davidic Covenant. In verses 1-6 David expresses a desire to build a temple for the Ark. Through Nathan the prophet, God tells David that he will not build Him a house (v7-15). Instead, God will build David a kingdom (dynasty). Solomon will be the one to construct the temple at a later time. This also points forward to Christ. It is in Christ that David's kingdom will never end. In verses 16-27, David praises the Lord for showing him grace and for establishing his kingdom.

1 Chronicles 18 corresponds with 2 Samuel 8 in recording David's victories over their enemies. In verses 1-13 we see that these victories covered every direction as the Lord expanded David's kingdom. This would provide encouragement for those coming from exile because God gave David victory wherever he went. Verses 14-17 show those who served alongside David in his administration.

In 1 Chronicles 19:1-2 David sends men to comfort Hanun over the death of his father, Nahash, who was king of the Ammonites (descendants of Lot). Hanun receives bad advice from his counselors, and humiliates the men David has sent (v3-5). After word gets back to David and the Ammonites realize they have done wrong, they hire men from Syria to help them fight (v6-9). The Israelites divide into two forces led by Joab and Abishai to fight the Ammonites and the Syrians (v10-13). The Syrians are defeated and become David's servants (v16-19).

1 Chronicles 20:1-2 gives background information to 2 Samuel 11. It is during this battle that David stays home and commits adultery with Bathsheba, and her husband Uriah is killed. Rabbah is taken by Joab, and all of the cities of Ammon fall under David's reign (v1-3). Verses 4-8 record the killing of three more giants, showing that David's faith in the Lord inspired many to do the same.

In 1 Chronicles 21:1-7 David, probably motivated by pride, angers the Lord by ordering a census of the people to enlarge his military capability. In verse 8 David realizes he has sinned against the Lord, and confesses his sin. The prophet Gad is sent by the Lord to give him three choices of which to pick from (v9-16). David loses 70,000 fighting men to the plague. Upon seeing the angel of the Lord (preincarnate Christ), David once again confesses his sin and shows his love for the people by asking that the judgment fall upon him instead (v17). David is instructed in verses 18-30 to build an altar at the threshing floor of Ornan the Jebusite. It is here the Lord hears his prayer and the plague is withdrawn from Israel.

Wednesday • Luke 19-20

In Luke 19:1-10 Zacchaeus the tax collector meets Jesus. A different term is used for tax collector in this story. Most believe Zacchaeus was the chief tax collector who oversaw the operations in the area. This endeavor would have made him very rich. The story shows the change that believing in Jesus has on a person. Zacchaeus changed after he met Jesus. This is demonstrated by his giving to the poor and repaying those he had taken from. Zacchaeus would have been a real life illustration of the lost sheep and the lost coin from Luke 15. In the parable of the minas in verses 11-27, those given the minas (3 months wages) were to put them to use and be wise stewards of their resources. Some compare this to Matthew 25 and the parable of the talents, but these are two different parables Jesus told. Most believe this one in Luke is about a believer living out their faith because all receive the same amount. In the end there are only two groups of people. The ones who made wise use of what was given them and the ones who did not. The ones who make good use of what is given them will get more. Some believe this parable also teaches an interval of time between Jesus' first coming and His second coming.

In verses 28-40 Jesus enters Jerusalem, fulfilling Zechariah 9:9, which refers to the Messiah. The people's shouts of praise and adoration for Jesus angered the Pharisees. The nations' rejection of Him would result in their judgment (v41-44). In verses 45-48 Jesus cleanses the temple of those who tried to profit from the people. Jesus directly confronts the wickedness being done in the temple courts. God's house is meant to be a house of prayer.

In Luke 20:1-8 the chief priests, scribes, and Pharisees question Jesus' authority. Jesus turns the table by asking them a question concerning John the Baptist. If they answered "from heaven", they had to believe John and his claims about Jesus. Verses 9-19 record the parable of the wicked vinedressers. The landowner is God, the vineyard is Israel, the servants are the prophets, and the son is Jesus. This is a reference to Isaiah 5:1-7, where God calls out the Israelites for their sin and rejection of Him. The chief priests and scribes begin to find a way to lay hands on Him. Verses 20-26 show the religious leaders still trying to trap Him by asking questions. Jesus discusses the proper attitude toward government and God. Again, it was designed to trap Him with His words. Proper submission should be made to both, but when Caesar desires what belongs to God, God's people must obey God (Acts 4:19; Rom. 13:1-7; 1 Pet. 2:13-17).

The Sadducees try once again to trap Jesus with His own words in verses 27-40, concerning a woman who had no children and who had married seven brothers. This is the only time the Sadducees are mentioned in Luke's gospel. Jesus corrects their beliefs by explaining that they do not understand God's power or His Word. In verses 41-44, Jesus explains that He is the Son of David and the Son of God by quoting Psalm 110:1. In verses 45-47 Jesus gave a warning against the scribes. The long robes they wore were a sign of distinction for them. The meetings in the market places show that they wanted to be called rabbi or other names of importance. The devouring of widows shows their lack of care for widows. Their prayers were known more for their length than their depth because they did not know God. The scribes only wanted to look good before the people, but cared nothing for how they looked to God.

Thursday • Proverbs 5-6

In Proverbs 5 the father warns the son about immorality. In verses 1-6 the father warns the son about the bitterness (symbol of suffering) of immorality. The "immoral woman" in verse 3 is someone who is outside the covenant of God. He warns the son that following her path will lead to his death. In verses 7-14 the father explains the loss of immorality. Going down this path will lead to loss of life and possessions, resulting in total ruin. In verses 15-20 the father warns the son of the pollution of immorality, and guides him to be "enraptured" (captivated) with his wife at home and not the immoral woman. Verses 21-23 warn of the bondage of immorality. This destructive behavior will lead to him being "caught in the cords of his sin".

Proverbs 6 contains warnings of things that will ruin you. In verses 1-5 the father's warning pertains to finances. If finances are not handled correctly it will bring misery and lead to uncontrollable circumstances. Laziness is the subject of verses 6-11. Here, the father urges the son to be prepared and to provide for himself and others by using the example of the ant. In verses 12-15 the father warns of following the ways of the wicked man. Verses 16-19 list the seven deadly sins-proud look (arrogance), lying tongue (deceitful, deceptive), shedding innocent blood, heart that devises wicked plans (plots evil), feet that run to evil (destroy what they cannot have), false witness (perjury), and sowing discord among the brethren (break unity). In verses 20-23 the son is warned again about listening to the wisdom of his parents, and the protection that it brings. Verses 24-35 warn again about following the adulterous woman. The consequences of immorality will make one poor spiritually, mentally, physically, and emotionally.

Friday • Ezekiel 24-29

Throughout the past few chapters Ezekiel has answered each argument the Israelites had against the coming judgment, and proclaimed the coming judgment against them. In the coming chapters (25-33), he will proclaim judgment on the nations for coming against Judah. Here in chapter 24, the judgment against Judah begins. From verses 1-2 we see that it has been 2 years and five months since Ezekiel last prophesied (20:1). This day would become a memorial day in Israel's history that would be remembered by an annual fast (Zech. 8:19). In verses 3-8 the boiling pot is Jerusalem, and the meat represents the people who will be judged for their sin. Verses 9-14 explain that the meat will be boiled until only bones remained, then it will be removed (exile). Then, the empty pot would be heated until its filthiness was removed. This shows Jerusalem being purified and cleansed. In verses 15-24 Ezekiel's wife dies and he is told not to mourn for her. This was to be a sign to the people that they too would not mourn over the destruction of Jerusalem and the death of their children, because their judgment had been foretold.

Ezekiel 25:1-7 proclaims judgment upon Ammon for being joyful over the destruction of Judah. Even Ammon's destruction is so that they will know who the Lord is. Each of these judgments fulfills Genesis 12:3, whether a nation blessed or cursed Israel. Moab and Seir would suffer the same fate as the Ammonites so they would know the Lord (v8-11). Edom is judged for taking vengeance against Judah, and joining Ammon and Moab in mocking them (35:1-36:15). The purpose of their judgment is not so they can know the Lord, but that they will know His vengeance. In verses 15-17 the Philistines would be judged for their vengeful attitude and actions against Judah.

The city and king of Tyre will be the subject of the next 3 chapters. Tyre was a prominent city both politically and religiously. Their judgment was for rejoicing at Jerusalem's fall so they could take the plunder of the city (v1-14). The "waves" of judgment would come from the Babylonians, and later the Persians. In verses 15-18 the cities and nations that fell under Tyre's rule would be frightened over their fall and sing a funeral song (lamentation). Tyre's fall would mean she would never exist again (v19-21).

Ezekiel 27 is a funeral song for Tyre. It fell because of its pride and conceit (v1-3). The destruction of Tyre is compared to a wrecking of a ship (v4-11). Verses 12-24 show the wealth of its goods and its trade with many nations. Its pride, coupled with its enormous wealth, would cause the "ship" to be destroyed by the sea (nations). The nations disown Tyre, which would help lead to its destruction.

Ezekiel 28 is a judgment and funeral song for the king of Tyre. The king's wisdom led him to be prideful and believe he was a god (v1-5). God's judgment would bring him to a disgraceful death at the hands of foreigners (v6-10). The funeral song in verses 11-19 (in its context) applies to the king of Tyre. It may also function to describe Satan and his fall because of his pride (Isa. 14:11-21). Verses 20-23 describe the judgment upon Sidon (a sister city of Tyre), and verse 24 summarizes all of the judgments on Israel's enemies. The future (even from our day) restoration of Israel is described in verses 25-26.

Ezekiel 29 begins a series of judgments against Egypt. In verses 1-16 Egypt will fall because of her pride, just as Tyre did. The Egyptians failed to support Judah as they should have (v1-7). Both Egypt and pharaoh would fall, and they would be scattered for forty years at the hands of the Babylonians (v8-16). Egypt would always be a lowly and weak nation. Verses 17-21 provide proof that Ezekiel's prophecy came true 17 years later.

Saturday • Romans 13-14

Paul spoke on a believer's relationship with fellow believers and all people in Romans 12:9-21. He now turns to a believer's relationship with the government in Romans 13:1-7. At this time in Rome Nero, who was probably one of the most ruthless leaders, is on the throne. In this passage, Paul lays the groundwork that all people should obey the government because it has been ordained by God (v1, Jer. 29:7). The government is supposed to protect its citizens, punish those who disobey, and restrain evil in society (v2-4). Because God is the higher authority, the calling for each believer is to obey God rather than men (Acts 5:28-29, Matt. 22:21). When the government enacts a law that is contrary to God's Word, believers are to obey God's Word. In verses 8-10 Paul teaches that loving one another fulfills the law. Love is listed first in the fruit of the Spirit (Gal. 5:22), love will endure forever (1 Cor. 13), and love also describes God (1 John 4:16). Love is to be the distinguishing quality in us that draws people to Christ.

In verses 11-14 Paul again encourages people to obey the government and to love others, because of the time they live in. The time of Christ's coming is not known, but each day that passes it becomes nearer than before. So, Paul is encouraging them to live like Christ and to live for Christ. In light of this passage and the times we live in, I would encourage people to know a few things. First, I would encourage you to know your Bible. Secondly, I would encourage you to know your nation's history. Despite what others claim our nation was founded upon Judeo-Christian values and much of our laws come from Scripture. Thirdly, I would encourage you to pray for each other and our nation's leaders (1 Tim. 2:1-2). Pray for revival to sweep through our nation. Fourthly, I would encourage you to stand for the truth. Finally, be discerning. 1 Thessalonians 5:21 says "Examine everything carefully, holdfast to that which is good". Jesus himself said to "Be wise as serpents and harmless as doves" (Matt. 10:16).

Romans 14 discusses issues that divided the Gentiles and Jews in Rome. Two of these issues were dietary laws and the observance of special days. Paul had dealt with the issue of "weak" versus "strong" in Corinth concerning the issue of eating meat offered to idols (1 Corinthians 8-10, 1 Tim. 4:4-5). The worry here is the strong causing the weak to stumble, and the weak sitting in judgment of the strong. In verses 1-12 Paul is warning them not to sit in judgment of one another. What is important is that each person not violates his own conscious when it comes to dietary laws and the observance of special days. These principles apply to us today as well, and cover a variety of issues. But if someone is walking in love they will not harm another person in this way (1 Cor. 8:11-12). As believers there really is no need for things of this nature to be allowed to cause division. Each person will stand before the Lord and give an account of their life (v9-12).

Paul further develops his argument in verses 13-23 from the perspective of the "strong" causing the "weak" to stumble. Paul's law of love from 13:8-10 applies here as well (1 Cor. 13). His main concern is that all believers pursue things that bring peace and build up others (v19). No one should force their beliefs or way of life on another person. For example there are many people who will not go to a restaurant that serves alcohol. This is their own personal choice and if they go against their own conscious they are sinning (v23). In this case the one who believes it is ok to go should, in love, relinquish their right to go and choose another place in order not to harm the other person.

Cover to Cover Challenge

Week 28

Sunday • Psalm 89

Welcome to week 28 of the *Cover to Cover Challenge*! Continue to pray for understanding of the Word and for the Lord to be honored and glorified. Proverbs 10:17 says "He who keeps instruction is in the way of life, but he who refuses correction goes astray".

Psalm 89 begins with praise to God (v1-37) and ends with a lament (v38-52). The context may be God's loyal love (mercy) and faithfulness to David in establishing a covenant with him (v1-4). Even those in the heavens praise God for His wonders and faithfulness (v5-8). God also rules over all of the earth because He created and controls it (v9-13). His rule is one of righteousness, justice, love (mercy), and truth which is a blessing to the people (v14-18). In verses 19-37, the subject is the covenant God made with David. God chose David, and it is God who empowers him to reign as king (v19-25). David is not just a servant of God but is a son, just as all kings who serve after David will be if they obey (v26-29). If they rebel, then punishment will follow (v30-32). Although they may disobey, God will not stop loving His people because God will never break His covenant (v33-37). Here in verse 38, the mood of the psalm changes to a lament. God has removed His hand of protection and is punishing them for their sin. For these reasons it seems to the psalmist that God has forsaken and forgotten the covenant He had made with David (v38-45). The psalmist asks God to show the great love that He had sworn to David, and to move on behalf of His people before it is too late (v46-52).

Monday • Leviticus 21-23

Leviticus 17-20 concerned the holiness of the people and how they were to remain pure. Leviticus 21-22 concerns the holiness of the priests and how they were to avoid being defiled. Verses 1-9 cover mourning over the dead (only close relatives) and marriage for the priests. The high priest had even stricter standards. He could not mourn at all or even leave the tabernacle to participate in a burial. Also, the high priest must marry a virgin from his own people (v10-15). No one who descended from Aaron with a physical defect could participate in the sacrificial offerings (v16-24).

Leviticus 22 continues the commands for the priests on how to not become defiled. Verses 1-9 concern the rules of cleanness from chapters 11-15, regarding touching something that would make them unclean. Additional instructions are given in verses 10-16 on how to handle the food left over from the offerings (ch. 2-7). In verses 17-33 additional regulations are given for sacrificial offerings (ch. 1-7). The one offering the sacrifice must be without defect, and also the animal being offered must be without defect.

Leviticus 23 pertains to the feasts and special days set aside by the Lord to remind the Israelites of how He had helped them throughout their history. Verses 1-3 deal with the Sabbath ("Rest") as a day set apart by God for rest and worship. The Passover celebrates their deliverance from Egypt and birth as a nation, and the Feast of Unleavened Bread celebrates them being God's people (v4-8). The Feast of Firstfruits reminds the people of their hope and future blessings from God (v9-14). The Feast of Weeks (Pentecost) celebrates the giving of the law (v15-22). The Feast of Trumpets (Rosh Hashanah) is a reminder that the Day of Atonement (v26-32) is coming, and provides a time of reflection on their relationship with God (v23-25). To remind the coming generations of their deliverance from Egypt, the Israelites celebrate the Feast of Tabernacles (v33-43).

Tuesday • 1 Chronicles 22-25

If the exiles coming back to Jerusalem were to be encouraged to build a temple recounting David's preparations for Solomon to build would have done that (v1-5). Verses 6-16 recount a conversation between David and Solomon to build the temple. David, being a man of war, would not be allowed to build it. Solomon ("Peace") experienced peace in all the land. Also notice in verse 12 that David prayed that the Lord would give Solomon wisdom and understanding. Solomon could not do this alone, but would need the help of all-especially the leaders (v17-19).

1 Chronicles 23-26 concern the Levitical organization. The system David set up provided a way to continually maintain worship before the Lord. Here in 1 Chronicles 23, David numbers the Levites and finds 38,000 to serve in the temple. They are separated into temple workers, judges, officials, gatekeepers, and musicians (v1-6). They are further divided into three groups, with each having specific duties to perform (v7-23). The official priests come from the Kohathites, who are descendants of Aaron (v24-32). Because this work is so great, David lowers the age requirement from 30 to 20.

1 Chronicles 24:1-19 is the organization of the priests. The author mentions Nadab and Abihu to show the seriousness of ministering before the Lord and its responsibilities. A total of 24 families are found to serve. These priests will work in two week shifts, with most families serving once a year. Most believe the list in verses 20-31 would have served as assistants to the priests.

1 Chronicles 25 shows the organization of the musicians. Asaph, Heman, and Jeduthun are names you are familiar with through reading the psalms. Each of them are called seers-Heman (25:5), Asaph (29:30), and Jeduthun (35:15). This is because their music spoke of the mighty works of God. Between the three men there were 24 sons matching the division of the priests, with each having 12 members for a total of 288 people.

Wednesday • Luke 21-22

After warning the disciples of the greed of the scribes, Jesus turns to an example of the humility and great faith of the widow in Luke 21:1-4. Most of Luke 21 corresponds to both Matthew 24 and Mark 13 and is focused on the end times. These chapters serve as a warning and as an encouragement to persevere during the difficult time that lies ahead. It contains warnings to not follow false teachers (v8), not be afraid of wars and persecution when they arrive (v9-10), warnings of disturbances on earth and in the heavens (v11), persecution (v12), and calls them to persevere (v19). These warnings applied to the coming destruction of Jerusalem in 70 AD, but also are a reference to a day that is to come (v20-24).

All of these events and signs point toward the coming of Jesus (v25-28). Using the image of the fig tree Jesus is teaching that the signs are to be heeded because these events will come to pass (v29-33). Verse 33 also shows the inerrancy and infallibility of God's Word (Ps. 119:89). It is important that God's people are watching and praying for what lies ahead (v34-38). This day that Jesus speaks of will come suddenly to those who belong to the world.

Luke 22:1-6 details the plot to kill Jesus, Judas' role in that plot, and the one (Satan) who was ultimately behind the evil. Judas, according to Matthew, was motivated by his own greed (Matt. 26:14-16). At the command of Jesus the disciples make plans to celebrate the Passover, which celebrated their deliverance from Egypt and focused on redemption (v7-13). Jesus institutes the Lord's Supper in verses 14-20. The main point of celebrating the Lord's Supper is to focus on Jesus. It contains a past look at His sacrificial death, a present look within ourselves, and a look into the future focusing on His return. Afterwards Jesus announces that the one who will betray Him is among them, and the disciples begin to wonder which one it is (v21-23). Immediately the disciples argue over which one of them is the greatest (v24-30). Jesus urges them to follow His example of being a humble servant. Jesus predicts Peter's denial in verses 31-34, but also his return where he is told to strengthen them when he does. Verse 35 refers back to chapter 10, when Jesus sent them out and provided for their every need. In verses 36-38 Jesus is preparing them for the time of His arrest and betrayal.

In verses 39-46 Jesus' agony over His coming crucifixion is told. Jesus is also teaching His disciples about the importance of prayer and not giving in to temptation. During the betrayal of Judas in verses 47-53, Luke is the only one who records the healing of the man who had his ear cut off. Verse 52 shows that all leaders of society were represented at Jesus' betrayal-chief priests (religious), captains of the temple (military), and elders (political). Peter's denial takes place in verses 54-62. Jesus is mocked and beaten in verses 63-65 and goes to trial before the Sanhedrin in verses 66-71, where Jesus claims to be the Son of God.

Thursday • Proverbs 7

Proverbs 5-6 warned of the consequences of following the ways of the immoral woman instead of wisdom. Proverbs 7 gives a clear warning to avoid her ways. Proverbs 7:1-5 is a call to preserve wisdom and make it your most prized possession (apple of your eye). In verses 6-9 the young man who lacks common sense (devoid of understanding) passes by (intentionally) to the immoral woman's house. Verses 10-12 describe her as being dressed provocatively to draw the young man in. Her plan for the young man is shown in verses 13-20. The way of the immoral woman is persuasive in verses 21-23, and the consequences of his actions were severe. The father calls again for his son to pay attention to his words, because to follow her is to follow the way of death (v24-27).

Friday • Ezekiel 30-33

Ezekiel 30 continues with the judgments upon Egypt one of Israel's enemies. In this chapter Egypt will be destroyed by the hands of Nebuchadnezzar, king of Babylon. Not only would Egypt fall, but all those who supported her will as well. In the midst of judgment there will be grace and mercy shown because it is through judgment the Egyptians would learn that He is the Lord (v8, v26).

In Ezekiel 31 the fall of Egypt is compared to the fall of Assyria, which was probably the greatest nation up until the time it fell. In verses 1-9 the cedar (Assyria) had many nations (birds and beasts) at its control. Because of its greatness Assyria became proud, and would be defeated by the ruler of the nations (Nebuchadnezzar, v10-18). The comparison between Assyria and Egypt shows that if Assyria can be brought down, then Egypt also will because it was not as powerful as Assyria.

Ezekiel 32:1-16 is a funeral song for Egypt and Pharaoh. The nations who sing this song will stand by amazed that Egypt has fallen. Verses 11-16 make it clear that it will fall at the hands of the Babylonians. Verses 17-32 conclude the judgment speeches against the nations. Ezekiel is told to cry out for the Egyptians because they would descend into the pit of death just as other nations before them.

Ezekiel 33:1-11 is about the watchman and his message. For Ezekiel, he faithfully proclaimed the Lord's message to the people. It was their own responsibility in how they responded to it. Verses 12-20 show some of the responses. The main focus is for the people to turn to the Lord before it is too late. With the fall of Jerusalem, God opens Ezekiel's mouth for the first time in seven and half years (v21-22). In verses 23-29 the Judean remnant believed the land to be theirs. Because of their sin the land would not be theirs but would become desolate. Many would die because of the sword, disease, and to wild animals. Ezekiel had faithfully warned the people, but they had failed to heed his warnings (v30-33). They had become a people who honored God with their lips but whose hearts were far from the Lord (Isa. 29:13).

Saturday • Romans 15-16

Romans 15:1-13 continues the strong/weak argument. In verses 1-6 Paul uses Jesus as an example of self-denial. Jesus put our interests ahead of His own when He died for our sin (Phil. 2:5-8). We should be willing to do without so that others may not be offended but most importantly so that the body of Christ can be built up (2 Cor. 8:9). Also in quoting Psalm 69:9 Paul shows that what Jesus did for us in accordance with the will of God. It is God's will that believers be in unity.

In verses 7-13 Paul again uses the example of Jesus to show that they should accept one another, just as Jesus had accepted them. Both the "weak" and the "strong" should be willing to accept one another. Also, this points to the Jew/Gentile relationship. Each of the Old Testament quotes confirm the inclusion of the Gentiles in God's plan, and because of that both should accept one another (Col. 3:11).

In verses 14-21 Paul speaks about the ministry that God has given him, and how he has ministered to others. Paul had a deep desire to share Christ with people who had never heard the good news of salvation, which is found only in Christ. It should be pointed out that Paul preached the whole counsel of God when he preached (v19). Paul's future plans were to visit the Roman church as he made his way to Spain after delivering an offering to the church at Jerusalem (v22-29). Paul asks for prayer as he travels to Jerusalem. This would have been hostile territory for Paul because he was a marked man (v30-33).

In Romans 16:1-16, Paul commends many of the people who had helped him in his ministry that had made their way to Rome. For the time they lived in many, if not all, were risking their life to work with Paul and to share the gospel. These twenty-six names coming from five households represent people from all of society. In verses 17-20, Paul warns of false teachers who cause division among believers. From the book of Acts we see many false teachers following Paul and causing division everywhere he went. The word for "division" means "works of the flesh" and "offenses" means "obstacles". Both can harm and lead a body of believers into discord and disunity. After sharing greetings from those with him in verses 21-24, Paul closes the letter with a doxology of praise (v25-27).

Cover to Cover Challenge

Week 29

Sunday • Psalm 90-92

Welcome to week 29 of the *Cover to Cover Challenge*! Continue to pray for our understanding of the Word of God, that the presence of the Holy Spirit will be made known, and for the Lord to be honored and glorified through the *Cover to Cover Challenge*. 1 Chronicles 29:11 "Yours, O Lord, is the greatness, the power and the glory, the victory and the majesty; for all that is in heaven and in earth is Yours; Yours is the kingdom, O Lord, and You are exalted as head over all".

Psalm 90 is attributed to Moses and concerns God being the Creator and Ruler of the universe. In verses 1-2 God is pictured as being the refuge of His people from everlasting to everlasting. Compared to the everlasting God, man's life is like a watch in the night (v3-6). Because of our sinfulness, God's anger and wrath are shown as expressions of His judgment (v7-10). Moses asks God to teach man to number his days because this shows the contrast between humanity and God (v11-12). In verses 13-16 Moses prays to be restored to God's favor, that He will restore joy to him, and for God's continual blessing.

Psalm 91 is a wisdom psalm. In verses 1-2 the psalmist invites all to make the dwelling place of God their home so that He can provide protection for them. The Lord's protection extends to all situations-whether it is day or night, and in both seen and unseen dangers (v3-8). The psalmist has personally experienced the protection of God (v9-10). God's protection is seen once more in verses 11-13 in the many ways He delivers them. Verses 14-16 are a salvation speech by God Himself which shows that those who place their trust in Him will be delivered and protected.

Psalm 92 begins with a hymn of praise (v1-4) and ends with thanksgiving (v5-15). Verses 1-5 form a praise to God because of His works that He does on behalf of men. He does these things because of His love and faithfulness. His work on behalf of man will be rejected by some, while others will praise Him for it (v6-8). Those who reject God will be judged (v9-11), but those who trust in the Lord will flourish (v12-15).

Monday • Leviticus 24-27

Leviticus 24 deals with the care for the lamps and bread of the tabernacle, and with the punishment for someone who blasphemes God. Due to the thickness of the curtains, the lamps would need to be continually burning (v1-4). Verses 5-9 address the changing out of the showbread. In verses 10-16 we read that the punishment for blaspheming God was death by stoning (v10-16). As with the earlier laws, the punishment must fit the crime (v17-23).

Leviticus 25 concerns the Sabbath Year and the Year of Jubilee, and how they pertain to the land (v1-34) and to people (v35-55). The Sabbath Year, as it applied to the land, provided many benefits (v1-7). It provided for the poor since anyone was allowed to eat of it, and it would provide a chance at a new beginning for people. The Year of Jubilee celebrated freedom and liberation from bondage after the Day of Atonement (v8-34). Fellow Israelite slaves were to be released, and the land was to be restored to its original owner. Verses 35-55 dealt with the poor. Verses 35-38 deal with someone who needed money. No interest was to be charged. Verses 39-46 deal with someone in poverty who sells himself to a fellow Israelite. Verses 47-55 deal with someone in extreme poverty who sells himself to a stranger in the land.

Leviticus 26 outlines the blessings (v1-13) and the cursings (v14-39) that are determined by their obedience and disobedience. The results of obedience are peace, prosperity, and the presence of God. The cursings that disobedience would bring are the opposite of obedience (v14-39). Instead of peace they would have fear and insecurity, instead of prospering they would be brought to poverty, and instead of God's presence they would be separated. All of the cursings would come to pass during their exile. Many believe the years of captivity correspond with each time they failed to keep the Year of Jubilee. In verses 40-46 God shows His faithfulness in keeping His covenant with Israel even though they may disobey Him.

The vows of Leviticus 27 are voluntary promises that offer a particular gift to God whether it be people (v1-8), animals (v9-13), or property (v14-25). Nothing that already belonged to God was to be offered (v26, 30-33). The system set up here discouraged vows that could not be kept based upon their valuation. If someone wanted to go back on a vow there was a penalty to be paid. Each of these are voluntary acts of worship, and some say they are offerings done out of love and not law.

Tuesday • 1 Chronicles 26-29

1 Chronicles 26 continues David's organization of worship. The gatekeepers were temple guards, and the treasurers were responsible for the upkeep of the sanctuary (v1-26). Verses 29-32 describe those placed in positions of judgment. Moses was the first to give the Levites the responsibility to teach the Word and to apply it to situations for interpretation (Deut. 33:10). This chapter concludes the organization of worship (ch.23-26).

1 Chronicles 27 details three other areas of David's kingdom. In verses 1-15 David organizes his military into 12 corps. Each had its own general and 24 skilled chiefs who were active for one month each year. Verses 16-24 show the tribal organization of the 12 tribes, where they lived, and their overseeing officers. Verses 25-34 conclude the civil authorities, which includes executives and overseers of David's property.

1 Chronicles 28-29 can be considered the last instructions of David. David encourages the people and Solomon in building the temple for the Lord and in following Him (v1-10). David gives them the plans for building the temple that he had received from the Lord, and provided the materials to build (v11-19). With the same words of encouragement given to Moses and Joshua, David again encourages his son in leading the task of building the temple (v20-21). Knowing the youth and inexperience of his son, David turns to the nation and its leadership to help Solomon build the temple (v1-5). The people gave abundantly to help build it (v6-9). David praises the Lord for what He had done for David and for the nation of Israel (v10-22). Solomon is crowned king over all of Israel (v23-25). 1 Chronicles closes with the death of David and a summary of his reign (v26-30).

Wednesday • Luke 23-24

After appearing before the Sanhedrin in Luke 22:66-71, Jesus appears before Pilate (v1-5). The Sanhedrin accuses Him of blasphemy, but before Pilate He is accused of inciting the people. Luke is the only one who records Jesus' appearance before Herod in verses 6-12. As will be seen in verses 13-25, neither Pilate (3x) or Herod find anything wrong to accuse Jesus of. Verses 21-25 show, in detail, the action of the crowd and their demand to have Jesus crucified. On His way to be crucified, Luke records the recruitment of Simon to help carry the cross and His conversation with the women (v26-31). Luke is the only gospel writer to record the conversation with the women. Jesus does not want them to weep for Him, but wants them to weep for themselves and their children. Jesus is warning them of a day that will come upon them in the future. Jesus may have been warning them of the future destruction of Jerusalem in 70 AD, but it also fits a day in the future from today (Rev. 6:16).

In verses 32-38 Luke is the only gospel writer that records Jesus' prayer of forgiveness for those who are crucifying Him. Verses 39-43 show two distinct reactions to Jesus from the two criminals who are crucified with Him. While one criminal went along with the crowd and religious leaders and blasphemed Jesus, the other began to have a change of heart. This criminal expresses Godly fear, admits his guilt, and calls Him Lord. He placed his faith in the Lord and was saved. At Jesus' death, darkness overcame the land and the veil of the temple was torn in two. This showed that by His death all men had access to God (v44-49). Even the centurion saw the innocence of Jesus. Joseph of Arimathea asks for the body of Jesus and places it in the tomb (v50-56).

Luke 24:1-12 records the Resurrection of Jesus. Although the disciples had been told by Jesus that this event would take place, they still did not believe what had happened. The story of the two men walking to Emmaus is unique to Luke (v13-35). This takes place the same day as the resurrection (v13). As they were walking and discussing what has transpired over the last three days Jesus joins them but they do not know it is Him (v14-16). The men recount what had happened to Jesus in Jerusalem over the past few days (v17-24). Their failure to believe was rooted in their failure to understand the Scriptures (v25-26). Jesus explained to them, from the Old Testament, all the things that concerned His death, burial, and resurrection (v27). After they had stopped their journey Jesus joined them for a meal (v28-29). When Jesus broke bread they realized it was Jesus, but He disappeared before their eyes (v31). Verse 32 shows the impact of what Jesus shared with them on the road. As the two travelers report the news to the disciples and others, Jesus appears in the room among them (v33-43). In verses 44-49 Jesus gives the disciples understanding of the Scriptures and the Great Commission. Luke closes his gospel and opens the book of Acts with the ascension of Jesus (v50-53).

Thursday • Proverbs 8-9

Wisdom speaks for the first time since Proverbs 1:20-33 in chapter 8. In verses 1-3 wisdom cries loudly to show that she is available. Wisdom is for all whether they are simple, prudent, or a fool (v4-11). Verses 12-21 show the attractiveness of wisdom and the reasons why people would want wisdom. Verses 22-31 record the appeal of wisdom. Wisdom has an announcement in verses 32-36. There is a blessing for those who hear and obey wisdom, while those who reject wisdom will end up with death.

Proverbs 9 is about the banquet (v1-6) and the burial (v13-18). Wisdom called out to the simple, the scorner, and the fool in 1:22. In 8:5 wisdom called out to the simple and the fool. Here in chapter 9, only the simple receive an invitation to listen to wisdom. This may show that the scorner and the fool have rejected their final invitation. In verses 1-6 wisdom calls out to the simple to dine on the luxuries that it offers. Wisdom is offered to many and their response to it shows the direction of their life (v7-12). Wisdom is shown in these verses to offer many benefits for those who choose to go the way of wisdom. For those who reject it there is a burial (v13-18). These verses show the way of folly that ends in death.

Friday • Ezekiel 34-37

One of the main reasons that Israel fell into sin and was led astray from God was because of its leadership. Ezekiel 34 addresses the false shepherds of Israel. In verses 1-6 the leaders of Israel are shown to only care for themselves and not the people. Instead of feeding the flock, they fed on the flock and allowed them to fall prey to other nations (v7-10). In verses 11-16 God will rescue, gather, and care for the flock. The shepherds who only cared for themselves would be judged (v17-24). God will appoint a true Shepherd, the Messiah, to care for the people. The covenant of peace in verses 25-31 shows that God will remove all foreign nations from the land, they will enjoy blessings from the land, Israel will dwell in security, and they will realize they are God's people. The peace covenant will be the subject of chapters 35-39.

In Ezekiel 35 Mount Seir (Edom) is judged for its treatment of Israel. Here, it probably represents all the nations that have come against Israel. Edom was always hostile toward Israel, and at many times helped other nations attack Israel. Because they loved to shed blood, God would bring the same to them (v1-9). Edom wanted to control both Israel and Judah and had spoken proudly against God (v10-15). Because of this judgment the land of Edom would become desolate forever, and they would know that He is the Lord.

Ezekiel 36:1-15 is a judgment speech to the nations that serves as an encouragement to Israel. God will cause shame to all nations that have come against Israel. God will gather His people back into the land and remove the nations that have oppressed them. In verses 16-21 Ezekiel gives two reasons why Israel was removed from the land-bloodshed and idolatry. In gathering the people back to their land, God would show the nations that He was the only true God. Verses 22-32 describe the restoration of Israel. God would regather His people, cleanse them from their sin, give them His Spirit to follow His ways, and return Israel to the land. Once Israel returns to the land its land will produce abundantly, the city will be rebuilt, and people will know that the Lord had done it.

The vision of the dry bones in Ezekiel 37:1-14 is the rebirth of the nation of Israel. The once dead nation will be brought back to life. In verses 15-28 Ezekiel uses a symbolic act to show that the once divided kingdoms of Israel and Judah will be reunited when God brings them back into the land. They will never again be divided and they will be led by the Messiah.

Saturday • Ephesians 1-3

Ephesians is known as a prison epistle along with Philippians, Colossians, and Philemon. Paul left Priscilla and Aquila there on his second missionary journey (Acts 18) before he returned again and stayed three years with them (Acts 19). Ephesus is an important city and is best known for its temple of Diana, which is one of the Seven Wonders of the World. It was an important city in all areas of life and was a hub to the surrounding communities. The first three chapters are doctrinal and the last three are practical, focusing on Christian behavior. The letter primarily gives instruction on how to maintain unity in the church and also details all the blessings we receive because of Christ.

After greeting those in Ephesus (v1-2) Paul, in verses 3-14, begins to draw upon the spiritual blessings we have in Christ. These verses are one long sentence in Greek and they introduce the themes that follow. Paul makes it very clear that the origin of every blessing we receive and enjoy comes from the Father (v3).We have been chosen by God, adopted as sons, redeemed, He has made known to us His will, we have an inheritance, and He has given us His Holy Spirit. There is also high praise for Jesus in these first 14 verses. Jesus is mentioned 15 times in these verses and the words "in Christ" or "in Him" are used 11 times. The assurance of all these blessings comes through believers by the Holy Spirit (v13-14). The Holy Spirit is described as a promise, a seal, and a guarantee. The Holy Spirit was promised to be given through OT prophets and Jesus to all those who believe. Believers are sealed by the Holy Spirit which shows that all believers are under the ownership and authority of God. The Holy Spirit is also a guarantee or a "down payment" that there is more to come in the future for believers.

Verses 15-23 are a prayer that Paul prayed for the church at Ephesus. Paul prayed that they would grow in their understanding (put into practice) of Jesus in verses 17-18. In verse 18 "the hope of His calling" can be applied in many ways. First, all believers are called to be like Christ. Second, all believers are also called to holiness. Third, all believers are called to minister. There is always a reason and purpose God calls each believer. Verse 18 also speaks of "His inheritance in the saints". These would include seeing God, fellowship with God, a body like His, and heaven. In verses 19-23 Paul also prays that they will know the greatness of God's power. God's power can be seen in many ways, but Paul gives three examples. In verse 20 God's power can be seen in the resurrection of Jesus. In verses 20-22 God's power can be seen in Jesus being at His right hand and all things being put under Him, including the powers of evil. In verses 22-23 God's power can be seen in Jesus being head of the church.

In Ephesians 2:1-10 Paul addresses the theme of redemption and how, through Christ, God gives man new life. Paul's thought from the end of chapter 1 is transferred to all believers in chapter 2. One simple outline to the passage is that verses 1-3 describe what all believers were before Christ. Verses 4-9 describe what God has done for all believers. Verse 10 describes what all believers are now. In verse 1 Paul describes that all believers were once dead in trespasses (wrong path) and sin (miss the mark). Paul takes this description further in verse 2. All believers once lived their lives according to the course of this world (values and attitudes), according to the prince and power of the air (Satan), and were sons of disobedience (characterized by disobedience). In verse 3 Paul says that all believers once lived according to the lust of their flesh (fallen nature) and were children of wrath (John 3:18). In verses 4-9 Paul proceeds to tell what God has done for us. By God's mercy, love, and grace, even when we were lost in sin, He saved us. Salvation is a work of God and there is not anything any believer has done to earn or buy it. What believers are now is God's workmanship. The word for workmanship means "something made or crafted". God created each believer to do good works, not to be saved by them (v10).

In verses 11-18 the theme is reconciliation. God desired that all people be united and be in unity in the church. In verses 11-13 Paul reminds the Gentiles that at one time they were alienated from Christ and from the commonwealth of Israel, and that they were strangers to the covenants of promise. At that time they also had no hope and were without God in the world. Why would Paul want them to remember who they once were? Because if they remember who they once were, they will remember the greatness of God's grace toward them in Christ. In verses 14-18 Paul goes on to speak specifically of what Christ has done. Jesus, who is our peace, is the peacemaker between man and God and also between Jew and Gentile. Paul uses the analogy of a building to show that we are all united in Christ and that the Gentiles are no longer aliens (v19-22). They are now members of God's family (v19) and also a part of God's building (v20-22).

In Ephesians 3:1-7 Paul speaks of a mystery, or something that has previously been unrevealed. The word "mystery" means a truth that was hidden from human knowledge but now has been revealed by God. Here the mystery is the plan for the Gentiles to be included in the church, which God was revealing to the apostles and the prophets. By God's grace Paul became a minister to the Gentiles. Paul's mission was to make Christ known to the Gentiles, which had always been in the plan of God (v8-13). Paul's name means "little. In verse 8 when he says "less than the least of all the saints" Paul is saying "I am littler than the littlest of all Christians". This shows Paul's humility regarding being given the ministry to preach Christ to the Gentiles.

In verses 14-21 Paul prays a second time for the church at Ephesus. He prays that they would be strengthened by the Holy Spirit (v16), that they would lead a Christ-centered life (v17), that they would lead a life of love (v17), that they would understand the love of Christ (v18-19), and that they would be filled (consumed with) with God (v19). The word "dwell" in verse 17 means to settle down or to take up a permanent residence. The Holy Spirit of God takes up a permanent residence in each believer's heart. Verses 20-21 show God's answer to Paul's prayer for the church. This answer should also help each believer in their own prayer life. First, it is helpful to realize that God is able. God can do anything we ask and God can do anything we think. Second, God can do more than what we ask or think. There are no limits to what God can do. Third, we should remember that it is according to the power that works in us that our prayers are answered. Ephesians 1:19-20 describes this as resurrection power. That resurrection power is shown to work here in our prayers, and it also lives in and is available to every believer.

Cover to Cover Challenge

Week 30

Sunday • Psalm 93-95

Welcome to week 30 of the *Cover to Cover Challenge*! Continue to pray that the Lord be honored and glorified through our study, and for understanding of His Word. John 8:31-32 says "Then Jesus said to those Jews who believed Him, if you abide in My word, you are My disciples indeed…and you shall know the truth, and the truth will set you free".

Psalm 93 is about the Lord's reign over the earth. Because the Lord rules and reigns over the earth by His strength, nothing can cause it to be moved. The "waters" in verses 3-4 represent the nations. No nation or nations can overthrow God's reign. God's testimonies and His presence (holiness) are forever.

Psalm 94 is a national lament (v1-15) and an individual lament (v16-23) that shows the Lord as judge over all the earth. In verses 1-2 the psalmist calls out to God to respond to the evil that has been done by those who are proud. Verses 3-7 describe the words and works of the proud, or those who believe that God does not see or pay attention (understand) to what they are saying and doing. The psalmist rebukes the wicked for their foolish acts and words because the Lord knows all (v8-11). Those who follow the Lord's words are blessed, relieved (rest), not abandoned, or forsaken (v12-15). Beginning in verse 16 the psalm takes on a personal tone. The psalmist personally experienced the proud coming against him, but it was the Lord who brought him comfort (v16-21).

Psalm 95 is a call to worship the Lord as Creator. Verses 1-2 are a call to worship. This call is given for the people to thank God because He provides their security and protection. Verses 3-7 praise God because He is sovereign, in control, and the Creator. Verses 8-11 are a call to be obedient to the Lord. The psalmist recalls two instances from the wilderness wanderings: at Meribah (rebellion) and Massah (tested) the Lord was grieved (disgusted) with the people.

Monday • Numbers 1-2

The book of Numbers gets its name from the two censuses taken of the nation of Israel at the beginning and end of the book. This book covers the forty years the Israelites wandered in the wilderness, beginning with the judgment that fell on the first generation and continuing to the second generation who would see God's promises come true. Numbers also shows that despite the people often rebelling against God, He will keep the covenant and provide for His people. Exodus shows Israel moving from Egypt to the early days of Sinai. Numbers covers the wilderness wanderings up until they arrive at Moab. Deuteronomy begins with Moab and covers their preparations as they enter into Canaan.

The primary function of the census is to see who can go into battle as soldiers (v1-4). The census is taken by tribe with each leader of the tribe listed (v5-16). The results of the census are listed in verses 17-46, and show a total of 603,550 who can go into battle. The Levites are not to be numbered because they are instructed to care for the tabernacle and its furnishings. They will be responsible for protecting it, setting it up, and taking it down (v47-57). Their main role is to lead worship. Numbers 2 describes the organization of the camp. All tribes would camp around the tabernacle, which would be in the center surrounded by the Levites. Ephraim, Manasseh, and Benjamin would be on the west. Judah, Issachar, and Zebulun would camp on the east. Naphtali, Asher, and Dan would camp to the north. Gad, Simeon, and Reuben would camp to the south.

Tuesday • 2 Chronicles 1-6

1 and 2 Chronicles were written after the return from exile. 1 Chronicles begins with Adam, and 2 Chronicles ends with the decree of Cyrus for the Jews to return home. While the author is not named, Jewish tradition says Ezra is the author of the Chronicles (Ezra 7:1-6). It is obvious it is written by someone from the priesthood who had details about worship and the temple. The Chronicler is reminding the people of their past in order to give them a hope for their future. 1 and 2 Chronicles are also unique in that around 55% of the book material is not found in any other book. You could pair up 1 Chronicles with 2 Samuel, and 2 Chronicles with 1 and 2 Kings in what each book covers. 1 Chronicles focuses on David and shows hope for a future Messiah to come. 2 Chronicles will focus only on the southern kingdom of Judah. It shows that when the king was obedient to the Lord the people prospered, but when the king rebelled against the Lord the kingdom faltered. The main themes of the book are-obedience brings blessing, disobedience brings judgment, and there is hope for the future.

2 Chronicles 1 highlights God's promises to David as Solomon ascends to the throne. The main focus of this chapter is Solomon asking God for wisdom so he can lead the people (v10). David had previously prayed this for his son (1 Chron. 22:12). Because Solomon asked for wisdom, God gave Solomon great honor and wealth. Silver and gold became as common as stones in Solomon's kingdom (v15).

In 2 Chronicles 2, Solomon begins to make preparations to build the temple. The 153,600 workmen come from those who are aliens in Israel (v2, 17-18). Solomon also seeks the help of Hiram, king of Tyre, to provide laborers and materials to build the temple (v3-10). In this letter Solomon praises God before he asks the king of Tyre for anything. Hiram grants Solomon's request and also sends Huram, who is a Hebrew and Phoenician (v11-16). This would allow him to communicate with all the workers constructing the temple. His knowledge in working is presented like Bezalel who was the master builder of the Mosaic tabernacle (Ex. 31:2-5).

2 Chronicles 3-4 describe the construction and materials used in the temple. Verses 1-2 show that the temple was built on Mount Moriah (Abraham/Isaac Gen. 22) which was also the place where David had an encounter with God (1 Chron. 21:18-22:1). Also, notice the construction did not begin until the fourth year of Solomon's reign, which shows the planning and preparation needed to build the temple. The temple would measure 105 feet x 35 feet. The larger room in verse 5 would correspond to the Holy Place of the tabernacle. The wingspan of the two large cherubim in the Most Holy Place would have been 35 feet (v10-13). The pillars were named Jachin and Boaz and symbolized the sustaining power of God. The bronze altar was about 30 feet square and close to 15 feet high (4:1). The Sea of cast bronze was used by the priests for washing, and showed that purity was needed

for those who would approach God (v2). There was only one table and golden lampstand in the tabernacle, but the temple would have ten of each (v7-8). Verses 11-18 give a summary of what Huram built for the temple.

2 Chronicles 5 begins to describe the events of the temple's dedication. Solomon gathered all of the elders of Israel together to bring the Ark of the Covenant into the temple (v1-10). The temple on Mount Moriah would now be the place where God would dwell with His people. This is symbolized as the shekinah cloud filled the temple (v11-14). 2 Chronicles 6:1-11 show Solomon blessing the people and praising the Lord for His faithfulness to His promises to David concerning the building of the temple. Solomon would now stand upon an elevated platform before God and all the people and offer a prayer to God (v12-42). Solomon also asks God to hear and answer the prayers that come from the temple (v19-21). There are seven situations in which Solomon specifically asks God to intervene- (1) swearing an oath in the temple, (2) defeat or exile by an enemy, (3) lack of rain, (4) disease, (5) hearing foreigners who come to pray, (6) during times of war, and (7) in captivity caused by sin.

Wednesday • John 1-3

The Apostle John is the author of the gospel of John. It is believed to have been written sometime between 85-95 AD. The purpose of John's writing can be found in John 20:30-31. He wrote it as an apologetic (to convince people Jesus is the Son of God), and to be evangelistic (for people to believe in Jesus). After reading Matthew, Mark, and Luke you have probably noticed many of the stories about Jesus are repeated. John is different. Only around 8% of John can be found in Matthew, Mark, and Luke. John is clearly a unique gospel. John presents Jesus as the Lamb of God, Messiah, King of Israel, Son of God, and Son of Man in the first chapter alone. The seven sign miracles, along with the seven "I AM" statements truly present Jesus as God. You can divide John up this way as you read: John 1-12 is called the Book of Signs, with its focus on the miracles. John 13-21 is called the Book of Glory, with its focus on Jesus' last moments with the disciples as He goes to the cross. John also offers the most extensive teaching on the Holy Spirit in all of Scripture.

John 1:1-18 is probably some of the deepest teaching in all of Scripture. John takes us back to the beginning, even before Genesis 1:1, with the first three verses of his gospel. It teaches that before there was anything Jesus existed, He existed with God, and that He was God (Col. 1:15-20, Heb. 1:1-4). Jesus truly was the life (salvation) and the light of men (v4, John 5:26,8:12). His light shined in darkness and the darkness could not overcome it (v5, Isa. 9:2). The word "comprehend" or "overcome" has many other meanings. It can also mean to accept or to receive. In this case it would mean that those in darkness did not receive the light of Jesus. Verse 9 describes Jesus as the "true Light". The word "true" means something that is authentic and complete. This shows that Jesus is the true (and only) source of spiritual life and light. Verse 10 points toward Jesus coming into the world that He created, yet the world refusing to know Him. The word "know" in this verse means a willful knowledge. People knew all they needed to know so that they could make the decision to accept or reject Him. The tense of verse 11 in the phrase "did not receive Him" means a decisive act of rejection. With these two verses together the people had all the knowledge they needed, but yet they still rejected Him. In verse 12 those who accept Him are those who believe in Him. Salvation does not come because your family is Christian (not of blood). Salvation does not come by personal desire, such as keeping rules or trying to be good (will of the flesh). Salvation does not come by following a man-made religion or making your own way to God (will of man). The only way anyone will experience salvation is through Jesus Christ (but God).

Verses 6-8 and 19-28 focus on the ministry of John the Baptist. John would be the first prophet sent by God in over 400 years. Notice he did not want anyone to believe he was the Messiah, but always pointed to Jesus who was the true Messiah (witness=testify). Being a witness entails commitment to what you are witnessing about.

His sole purpose was to point people to the Lamb of God (v29-34). In John's gospel there are many witnesses who testify to Jesus being the Messiah. Along with John the Baptist they are Jesus and His works/words, Moses and the Scriptures (5:39, 46), the Father (5:32,36,37, 8:28), the Holy Spirit (ch.14-16), the disciples (15:27), the Samaritan woman (4:39), the crowd (12:17), and the apostle John (19:35, 21:24). John the Baptist even points his own disciples to follow Jesus in verses 35-42. Andrew, in John's gospel, is always bringing people to Jesus (6:8, 12:22). In verses 43-51 the number of Jesus' disciples continues to grow with the addition of Philip and Nathanael. Jesus also demonstrates His omniscience by telling Nathanael that He saw him under the fig tree. Verse 51 shows that Jesus and the Father are in direct communication with one another.

Chapters 2-4 of John begin what is called the Cana cycle. In the Cana cycle the theme is believing. In John 2:1-12 Jesus turns water into wine at the wedding in Cana, which is the first sign miracle out of seven in the gospel of John. A wedding was a major social event for a community in Jesus' day. The failure to have enough wine would have not only been an embarrassment to the family, but could have also resulted in a lawsuit. This miracle points to Jesus being the Son of God, and also shows that the disciples believed in Him (v11). The word John uses for signs is a supernatural act that shows who Jesus is. As was the case for the disciples, these signs are so that people can see who He is and believe in Him.

The context of John clearly points out that this temple cleansing is at the beginning of Jesus' ministry; while those in Matthew, Mark, and Luke are at the end of His ministry (v13-22). The temple cleansing shows that the religious leaders were exploiting the people, that God wants His house to be a place of prayer, and that God wants all people to come to Him. This temple cleansing took place on the Passover which celebrated Israel's deliverance from Egypt. The exploitation of the people is done through the selling of the animals at an inflated price and the exchange of money needed in order to purchase the animals (usually 10-25%). Instead of leading people to worship God, events like the Passover became a way to take advantage of people. Verses 18-22 are a reference to the death, burial, and resurrection of Jesus. The temple was the center of each Jew's religious identity and was where worship took place. Because of this, Jesus is telling them they should worship Him as opposed to the temple. Verses 23-25 are important because they show that Jesus is the discerner of hearts. These verses lead the way for John 3-4, where He meets Nicodemus and the woman at the well.

John 3 is probably the most well-known chapter, and contains the most famous verse in all of Scripture. In verses 1-8 Jesus teaches Nicodemus that it is necessary for one to be born-again (born from above) to enter into the kingdom. Most believe that Nicodemus was a member of the Sanhedrin and that his coming to Jesus at night may represent the state of his heart. As believers we should be careful not to read into this with our modern terminology. Jesus would have spoken to Nicodemus in a way he could have understood. The water and the Spirit are symbolic of the spiritual renewal and cleansing from Ezekiel 36:25-27 (v5). This can only be accomplished by believing in Jesus as Lord. Jesus teaches the way to do this in verses 14-16. Nicodemus would have clearly understood verse 14 for two reasons. First, he would clearly know the story of Moses lifting up the serpent in the wilderness (Num. 21). Second, the term "lifted up" was used in Jesus day as a euphemism for being placed on the cross. This makes faith the key of verse 14. Just as those people who looked at the serpent lifted up on the pole had faith, we must look to Him and have faith when He is on the cross. People who choose not to believe are already judged because they fail to have faith in Jesus (v17-21).

Verses 22-36 show the transition from John the Baptist's ministry to Jesus ministry. John admits that Jesus' ministry must increase and his must decrease. John gives many reasons in verses 29-36 as to why Jesus is to increase. What John the Baptist speaks in verse 36 sums up the conversation Jesus had with Nicodemus. Those who believe in Jesus have everlasting life right now, which will be fully realized in the future. Those who do not believe abide in God's wrath right now and it will also be realized in the future.

COVER TO COVER CHALLENGE

Thursday • Proverbs 10

Proverbs chapter 10 begins the section where many of the verses are standalone verses. At times there are common themes found among them, although they may not be in a particular order. Verses 1-5 can be seen to teach the wise versus the foolish children. A family can flourish if the children follow wisdom, but it also shows that if the children become lazy or live a life of crime it will fall apart. In verses 6-11 you will find a contrast between a righteous person and a wicked person. In verse 6 the wicked can be known by their deceitful speech, while the righteous are known by God's favor being on their lives. Verse 7 shows that a wicked person will be remembered as such, which will ultimately end in his name being forgotten. The righteous will be remembered and continue to be blessed. In verse 8 the wicked person is known for foolish talking, while a righteous person will be teachable. Verse 9 teaches that a person's sin will eventually become known, while the righteous walk with integrity. In verse 10 the wicked are shown as being deceptive and the righteous as peacemakers. In verse 11 the wicked cover up their wickedness with their words while the righteous words offer life. Verses 12-17 show how righteousness looks lived out in contrast to the wicked. Verses 18-21 talk about the tongue. It will be destructive in a wicked person and positive in a godly person. Verses 22-25 discuss the stability of life for the righteous against the wicked. In verse 26 laziness becomes the topic of discussion. Verses 27-30 discuss again the stable life of the righteous and verses 31-32 discusses the tongue again.

Friday • Ezekiel 38-43

Ezekiel 38-39 go together and describe a final attempt by foreign nations to possess the land of Israel. God will defend Israel because He is faithful to the covenant He has made with them. The setting according to Ezekiel will be in the latter years (v8,16). Magog and Meshech are names from the descendants of Japheth (Gen. 10). Many nations will come against Israel. God is pictured here as placing "hooks into their jaws" to bring them into the land (v3). The purpose of this battle is so the nations will know that He is God (v16). God will judge the nations who come against Israel (v17-23). The judgment and defeat of the armies will be by way of an earthquake, confusion among the soldiers, disease, and cosmic disturbances.

In Ezekiel 39:1-8 God will use the defeat of Gog to show that He is the only true God. It will take Israel 7 years to burn all the weapons of the invading army (v9-10). It would take 7 months, to bury the dead from the battle (v11-16). Verses 17-20 show that the result of the great battle was a sacrifice to God and He invites all the beasts of the earth to feast upon them. Verses 21-29 confirm God's promises to give the land to Israel. If the nations viewed Israel's God as weak for removing them from the land, they would not any longer. The nations as well as Israel would now know that God is the only true God.

Ezekiel 40-48 is a vision given to Ezekiel 13 years after the message he gave in 33:21-39:29. What we see here in these chapters is still future from our day. No temple has existed the way Ezekiel describes this one in chapters 40-42. This would especially refer to the river which flows from it in Ezekiel 47. Even the procedure for worship is different in chapters 43-46. The purpose of this temple is for God to dwell among His people and it will reflect God's holiness.

In chapters 40-42 Ezekiel is given a vision of a future temple. Here, a divine messenger will guide him through the temple complex beginning on the outside and working their way inward. The highlight of your reading this week will be Ezekiel 43:1-12. In these verses Ezekiel sees God's glory return. It would come from the east, enter by the east gate, and it will completely fill the temple causing all the land to be filled with God's glory.

Saturday • Ephesians 4-6

Paul will now turn from the doctrinal teaching of the previous three chapters to discussing the application of those doctrines in chapters 4-6. Paul teaches about the unity that should exist in the church in verses 1-6 by using the unity in the Trinity as an example. The calling of verse 1 is the call to salvation. Paul is encouraging them to do everything possible to stay true to the Christian life. In verses 2-3 Paul gives the characteristics of the Christian life. In verse 2 "lowliness" means to be humble while recognizing the worth of others. Also in verse 2 we see "gentleness" (strength under control), "longsuffering" (patience with difficult people), and "bearing" (to tolerate in peace) listed as characteristics that a Christian should display. When all believers live this type of life the result will be unity and peace within the body of Christ (v3). Verses 4-6 show the unity in the Godhead, which is to exist within the church.

In verses 7-16 Paul teaches the diversity of the church regarding the gifts given to us by the Holy Spirit. These gifts are to be used in equipping other believers to minister, in serving fellow believers, and for building up the body of Christ (v12). Doing these things will produce unity, knowledge, and maturity within the body of Christ (v13). They also will aid in keeping people from false teachers and false doctrine (v14) while teaching the truth of the gospel in love (v15). Verse 16 gives a picture of what the body of Christ will look like with all of these parts function together as one.

In verses 17-24 Paul warns the Ephesians to put off (strip away) the old man and put on the new man (saved). Paul tells them not to live their life aimlessly (futility) like their fellow Gentiles who do not know Christ (v17). In verses 18-19 Paul gives them characteristics of how lost people live their lives. Verse 20 states that if you know Christ those will not be the characteristics of your life. Paul says in verses 21-22 that if you know Christ you will strip away (put off) the old man who craves evil (deceitful lusts). Believers should be continually renewing their minds and living their lives as the new man which was created by God (v23-24). In verses 25-32 Paul gives additional instructions on how to live the Christian life. Verses 25-27 warn against lying and being consumed with anger because it gives the devil opportunity to attack. Verse 28 warns against stealing and praises hard work. Verse 29 warns against corrupt (rotten) words but praises speech that builds people up. Verse 30 warns against grieving (offending) the Holy Spirit. Verse 31 lists more attitudes that the believer is to avoid-bitterness (grudge filled attitude), wrath (wild rages), anger (deep seated), clamor (loss of control), evil speaking (slander), and malice (evil). Verse 32 praises kindness, being tenderhearted (compassionate), and forgiveness.

In order for the Ephesians to live life as the new man created by Christ after salvation they would need to imitate God (5:1). In verses 1-14 Paul is teaching that because they know Christ and they have the Holy Spirit they can live for Christ in their attitudes, characteristics, and they can be obedient. They should be known as people of love (v2), people who give thanks (v4), people who are not easily deceived (v6), people who do not associate with evil (v7,11-14), and people who walk in the light bearing fruit (v8-9).

In verses 15-17 Paul teaches them about living wisely. In verse 15 Paul warns them to walk carefully (circumspectly). This leads to verse 16 and "redeeming the time". Most translate this "make the most of your time". No one knows how much, or how little time they have. Verse 18 warns against drunkenness. Here the warning is to not be under the influence of alcohol but under the influence of the Holy Spirit. The word "dissipation" means wild and uncontrolled actions. Those who are under the influence of alcohol cannot control their actions, but those under the influence of the Holy Spirit are under the control of the Holy Spirit. Verse 19 teaches that fellowship and worship go together. Notice in the first part of the verse it says believers are to speak to one another this way. Verse 20 is also a part of worship. Believers should thank God for His many blessings given to them. Verse 21 shows that submissiveness is also a part of relationships in the Christian life.

Verses 22-33 give instructions on the marriage relationship. Husbands and wives are to love one another and seek a relationship through the Lord that exemplifies the relationship that Christ has with the church. Submission is the key here, and in all relationships. There is a mutual submission in marriage. A wife will submit to her husband and the husband is to love his wife and seek the best for her. In this passage the husband is told to love his wife on three separate occasions (v25, 28, 33). His love is to be like Christ's love, a sacrificial love that would do anything for his wife. Many wonder why the wife is not told to love her husband. Submission is an act of love.

Ephesians 6:1-3 continues with instructions on relationships, this time focusing on the relationship between parents and their children. It is the parent's responsibility to raise their children in the Lord through their words and their actions. Children must also honor their parents. The Fifth Commandment, found in Exodus 20:12, says to "Honor your father and your mother, that your days may be long upon the land which the Lord your God is giving you". Verses 5-9 concern the Christians relationship with bondservants. Bondservants had very few rights in Paul's day, but in the church they were to be treated fairly and with love.

In verses 10-20 Paul teaches about the armor of God. This armor is to protect the Christian in our daily battles with the kingdom of darkness. Just as each piece of armor was important to the Roman soldier, each piece of the armor of God is important for the Christian. In verse 10, Paul encourages each believer to be "strong in the Lord" (position) and "in the power of His might" (power). Position involves knowing the Lord as Savior. The word "power" means to be endowed power. It is power that God has given you. Ephesians 1:19-20 and Ephesians 3:20 describe this as resurrection power. The armor is designed to help each believer stand against the schemes (wiles) of the devil. These include temptation, deception, discouragement, fear, and sin. Verse 12 tells us that the battle that each believer faces is not against our fellow man, but against demonic forces. The word "wrestle" means to throw down and brings to mind a picture of face to face conflict. The armor is also designed to help each believer resist and oppose (withstand) during spiritual warfare. Verses 14-17 describe each piece of defensive armor. Many see only one offensive weapon (sword=Word of God), but prayer (v19) should be an important part of spiritual warfare. Paul, who is writing from Rome, sends greetings from the Christians there to their brothers and sisters in Ephesus (v21-24).

Cover to Cover Challenge

Week 31

Sunday • Psalm 96-102

Welcome to week 31 of the *Cover to Cover Challenge*! Continue to pray for one another as we read and study God's Word together. Pray that our eyes will be opened, that the Lord will be honored and glorified, and that we all will be obedient to the Word of God. Psalm 115:1 says "Not unto us, O Lord, not unto us, but to Your name give glory, because of Your mercy, because of Your truth".

Psalm 96 is another psalm about the Lord's rule over the earth. In verses 1-3 the psalmist urges all His people to sing to the Lord a new song pertaining to salvation. Through His splendor, majesty, strength, and glory the Lord shows that He is the only true God who is worthy to be praised (v4-6). The families on earth are called to worship the Lord and to bring an offering to Him (v7-9). Verses 10-13 show that the Lord is coming to judge the earth in righteousness and truth, and for this reason the earth should rejoice.

Psalm 97 is about the Lord's rule over the earth. In verses 1-6 the whole earth is to rejoice at the Lord's presence. Verses 7-9 serve as a warning for those who are worshiping idols to turn to the Lord, and it shows that He is the only true God. In verses 10-12 the benefits of loving and following the Lord are shown. Those who love the Lord are preserved by the Lord, delivered by the Lord, and experience His righteousness and gladness.

Psalm 98 is another psalm praising the universal rule of the Lord. In verses 1-3 the Lord has made known His salvation, revealed His righteousness, and has been merciful and faithful. Because of these things the whole earth has seen the salvation of the Lord and is called upon to rejoice in the Lord (v4-6). Even creation rejoices at the coming of the Lord (v7-9).

Psalm 99 is also a psalm about the Lord ruling over the earth. This psalm will highlight the holiness of God (v3, 5, 9). The people of the earth are to tremble and shake at the very presence of God and exalt Him (v1-3). His rule will be governed by justice, equity (truth), and righteousness (v4-5). Verses 6-8 display God's goodness to His people by His answering the prayers of Moses, Aaron, and Samuel, and by showing mighty His works and forgiveness. Because of these things, the people are called upon to exalt the Lord (v9).

Psalm 100 praises God for who He is and His goodness toward His people. All the earth is called upon to praise the Lord, serve Him, and to come and be in His presence (v1-2). God's people confess (know) He is the only true God, and He watches over His people (v3). Verses 4-5 are a call to give thanks because of His goodness, covenant love (mercy), and faithfulness (truth).

Psalm 101 is a royal psalm written by David which shows his commitment or faithfulness to the Lord. In verses 1-2 David will praise the Lord for His love (mercy) and justice. He shows his faithfulness to the Lord by living a blameless (perfect) life. As king over Israel, David promises to keep evil away from himself and out of his kingdom (v3-5, 7-8). Only those who are faithful and live blameless (perfect) lives will David have serve in his kingdom (v6).

Psalm 102 is a lament that shows the suffering and discipline that comes with sin. It may have been written close to the end of Israel's exile. The psalmist cries out for God to hear his prayer and answer it quickly (v1-2). In verses 3-11 the psalmist speaks about his terrible suffering that he is experiencing. He is full of anxiety, depression, and cannot sleep. Despite his condition, he recalls the goodness of the Lord (v12-22). God will continue to show mercy, favor, and forgiveness to His people and will restore them. The psalmist records another lament over his own life and its shortness, and contrasts it with the Lord remaining forever (v23-28).

Monday • Numbers 3-4

In Numbers 3 & 4 the Levites are to care for the tabernacle. The census taken in chapter 3 deals with males age one month and above, while the one in chapter 4 deals with ages 30-50 and can who can presently serve in the moving of the tabernacle. After listing the sons of Aaron in verses 1-4, the remainder of the chapter deals with organization of the Levites through Aaron's three sons (v5-20). The descendants of Gershon will care for the curtains and coverings (v21-26). The descendants of Kohath will care for the furniture and utensils (v27-32). The descendants of the Merari will care for the boards and bars (v33-38). Verses 40-51 discuss the substitution of the Levites for the firstborn sons and cattle.

Numbers 4 goes deeper into the duties of each of the three sons of Levi. After taking down the tabernacle and covering all of its furnishings the Kohathites would carry them (v1-20). They were not placed in wagons or on animals. The Gershonites would carry the curtains of the tabernacle (v21-28). The Merarites would have carried the poles and tent pegs (all very heavy) of the tabernacle (v29-33). In verses 34-39 the census is summarized and lists the number of the ones serving as 8,580. Taking down the tabernacle to be moved was serious and was not taken lightly. This showed the Lord honor, but most importantly it emphasized His holiness.

Tuesday • 2 Chronicles 7-12

In 2 Chronicles 7:1-11 Solomon dedicates the temple, and the glory of the Lord entered in to it. From the dates given, this dedication service coincided with the Feast of Tabernacles and the Day of Atonement. Many people would have made their way to Jerusalem to celebrate during this time. The Lord appears to Solomon and affirms the earlier prayer of Solomon that He will hear the prayers offered in the temple (v12-15). If they were to experience God's blessing they would have to stop sinning, turn from their proud lives and wicked ways, and then God would hear, forgive, and heal their land. Verses 17-22 are the blessings and cursings of being obedient or disobedient. If Ezra wrote 2 Chronicles, he is showing the people why they went into exile (v22).

2 Chronicles 8 corresponds to 1 Kings 9 and shows Solomon's many successful achievements. This chapter outlines his civil and military achievements (v1-6), the organization of his work force (v7-10), his public worship (v11-16), and expansion his commercial activities (v17-18).

In 2 Chronicles 9:1-12 the queen of Sheba, known for its gold and spices, pays a visit to Solomon. Even she recognized the greatness and love of God toward His people and was specifically impressed by Solomon's great wisdom. In verses 13-28 Solomon's great wealth is described. Solomon dies in verses 29-31, and his son Rehoboam reigns in his place. The writer of 2 Chronicles never brings up Solomon's idolatry, polygamy, or the latter years of his reign which led to the kingdom faltering.

From chapters 10 through 36, the focus begins to shift toward the kingdom of Judah after the split of the kingdom. 2 Chronicles 10 shows the revolt of the people under Rehoboam. God had already spoken through Ahijah the prophet to Jeroboam that the kingdom would be divided because of Solomon's idolatry (1 Kgs. 11:29-33). This is also shown by 10:15 and 11:1-4. 2 Chronicles 11:5-12 shows the cities Rehoboam built up to defend Judah. In verses 13-17 Jeroboam would not allow the Levites to serve as priests, but set up idols instead. This led to the Levites and those who truly sought the Lord to move to Judah, which only strengthened them. Verses 18-23 show the family of Rehoboam and his intent to make Abijah the future king.

2 Chronicles 12 begins the history of the rulers over the southern kingdom of Judah. In discussing the kings of Judah the writer of the Chronicles is teaching some valuable lessons-do not compromise with the world, do not disregard God's law, and do not commit idolatry. Rehoboam was guilty of forsaking the law of God (v1-2). For his sin, the Egyptians took all of the fortified cities (v3-4) and the treasures of the house of the Lord (v9). Shemaiah the prophet tells them why this has happened to them and the leaders of Israel repent, but they will still be servants of Egypt (v5-8). It wasn't until Rehoboam humbled himself that the Lord's wrath was turned away (v10-12). Rehoboam would reign for 17 years over Judah, but he is known for doing evil in the sight of the Lord because he did not seek the Lord (v13-16).

Wednesday • John 4-5

John 4:1-26 covers the story of the woman at the well in Sychar in Samaria. Normally a Jewish person would have no contact with the Samaritans, especially a woman from Samaria. During Jesus' discussion with her, He broke down the ethnic (Jew/Samaritan), religious, and moral barriers that existed between Himself and the woman. It is a perfect story demonstrating a conversation with a lost person.

In verses 1-7 He breaks down the ethnic barrier by asking her for water. In verse 10 He led the conversation to spiritual matters. Throughout the whole conversation He listens intently to every word she said and offered a response. In verses 15-17 Jesus showed her it was sin that separated her from God, even while she tried to divert the conversation another way (v20). Finally, Jesus reveals Himself to her as the Messiah (v26-27). Jesus explained the importance of working in the harvest to His disciples in verses 27-38. He even explained to them that this work is fully satisfying (v33-34). Because of the woman's testimony and Jesus' own teaching, many of the Samaritans believed in Him (v39-42). In verses 43-45 Jesus goes to Galilee, and after seeing the works He did in Jerusalem they gladly receive him. In Cana He heals a nobleman's son without the boy being present (v46-54). John 2-4 was known as the Cana cycle where we see many believe in Him.

John 5-11 is the Festival cycle because the Jewish feasts are the setting. We will begin to see conflict and rejection in 5:1-15 with conflict over the Sabbath. In verses 1-15, Jesus heals a man who had laid by the pool in Bethesda ("House of Mercy") waiting to be put into the water to be healed. The Jewish leaders' interpretation of the law believed that Jesus could not heal on the Sabbath, but neither could the man carry his bed. They were so blinded by their legalism that they missed the miracle that the Lord had performed. Another reason they sought to kill Jesus was because He spoke of God being His Father, which would be considered blasphemy by the religious leaders (v16-23). The Jews believed that only God can heal, only God can give life, and that only God could raise the dead. Jesus will do each of these before them, but yet they will still not believe in Him.

In this passage, Jesus also shows His perfect obedience and He continues the Father's work. The religious leaders' failure to honor Jesus meant that they did not honor the Father either. The main theme of verses 24-30, and one of the main themes of John, is Jesus giving eternal life to those who are spiritually dead (1:4; 3:15-16; 4:14; 5:39-40; 6:27,33,35,40,47-48,51,54; 8:12; 10:10, 28;11:25; 14:6; 17:2-3; 20:31). In verse 25 the phrase "those who hear will live" is speaking of those who heard and believed. Only those will be raised to live eternally with God. Those who do not believe in Jesus will also live forever but be separated from God (v26-30). In verses 31-47 Jesus speaks of the witnesses to Him and His mission. These witnesses include John the Baptist (v33-35), His own works (v36), the Father (v37-38), and the Scriptures (v39). Those who do not believe refuse the fourfold witness of verses 31-47.

Thursday • Proverbs 11-12

Proverbs 11:1-3 shows that God hates fraud, and warns of pride and dishonesty. Righteousness is a main theme throughout the chapter, especially as it concerns deliverance (v4, 6, 8-9, 21). Righteousness also causes a city to rejoice (v10), get a reward (v18, 31), leads to life (v19), and they will flourish (v28, 30). Other instructions include surrounding yourself with godly wisdom (v14), beauty without character is like fancy jewelry on a pig (v22), and wickedness affects all those in the home (v29).

Proverbs 12:1-4 is about a good man who loves the discipline of the Lord, obtains favor from the Lord, does not go the way of wickedness, and his wife becomes his crown. Verses 5-7 are about the righteous standing secure in the world because they stand in the righteousness of God. Verses 9-15 teach about having a humble work ethic in life. Verses 16-22 contrast the fool with the wise, and teach the value of truth and the recklessness of lying. Verses 23-28 show the life of wisdom. The wise are slow to speak, value hard work, do not lead others astray, and value good words.

Friday • Ezekiel 44-48

In Ezekiel 44:1-16 God would give regulations concerning those who could and could not serve as priests in the temple. Only those from the Aaronic line were to serve in the temple (Num. 3:10). The Levites would no longer serve as priests before the Lord because they had went away from the Lord and led the nation into sin. Only the descendants of Zadok would perform the priestly duties because they had remained faithful to the Lord. Verses 17-31 contain regulations for the priests who served. These regulations would allow the priests to teach the differences between holy and unholy. Most people are intrigued about the prince in verses 1-3. The designation "prince" is used at least 14 times in chapters 44–47. He is most likely not Jesus because he has to offer sacrifices for his own sin (45:22) and has sons (46:16-18). Also he will not perform duties of the priest, but Jesus as Messiah will (Ps. 110:4; Zech. 6:12, 13). In addition to this, he will also worship the Lord (46:2). Many believe he will be an administrator who represents King Jesus during this time.

Ezekiel 45:1-8 concerns a section of land set aside for the priests and the sanctuary. It is divided into areas for the Zadokian priests, the Most Holy Place, the Levites, an area for the prince, and a section that belongs to Israel. The leaders of this new era were not to cause violence and oppress the people, but were to be just in all of their ways with the people (v9-12). The offerings given by the people to the prince will provide for public sacrifices (v13-17). There will also be a continuation of Passover, Feast of Unleavened Bread, and the Feast of Tabernacles (v18-25). Although the Day of Atonement is not mentioned, there is a new feast celebrated in verses 18-20 with an emphasis on holiness.

Ezekiel 46:1-15 discusses the Sabbath and New Moon (v1-8), appointed feast days (v9-11), voluntary offerings (v12), and daily sacrifices (v13-15). It is the prince who will set the example for the people to follow. Verses 16-18 deal with the regulations concerning the gifts given by the prince to his sons and his servants. Verses 19-24 describe the kitchens where the priests would prepare the guilt and sin offerings, where they cooked the grain offerings, and where they ate all the offerings.

In Ezekiel 47:1-12 the river flowing from the temple to the Dead Sea transforms it into fresh water that can now support life. Trees on the banks of the river provide food and the leaves for healing. Verses 13-23 deal with the division of the land. Joseph is given two portions that fulfill the promise by Jacob to Joseph (Gen. 48:5-6, 22; 49:22-26). In Ezekiel 48, the division of the land continues among the 12 tribes. The portion of Judah mentioned in verses 8-22 has already been described in 45:1-8 and is the area for Zadokian priests, Levites, the city, and the prince. The gates of the city show it to be 6 miles around (v30-35). It is to be called Yahweh Shammah ("The Lord is There"). The glory of God has returned, and at this point each covenant God has made with Israel is fulfilled.

Saturday • Philippians 1-2

Philippians, Ephesians, Colossians, and Philemon were all written during Paul's imprisonment in Rome. Philippi was the first city in Macedonia where Paul established a church during his second missionary journey (Acts 16:12-40). It was here that Lydia was converted, and it is likely that the church met in her home. It was also in Philippi that Paul and Silas were placed in prison and beaten after casting out a demon from a possessed girl (Acts 16:16-24). After an earthquake released them from prison, the Philippian jailer received Christ (Acts 16:25-34). Paul wrote to them to thank them for their gift they had given him, to update them about his current situation, to encourage them to be in unity, and to warn them of false teachers.

In Philippians 1:1-11 Paul thanks the church for their gift to him in support of his ministry, and offers a prayer for the people at Philippi. Paul prays for the people at Philippi in verses 9-11. In verse 9 he prays for their love to continue to grow (abound), he prays for them to know God's Word (knowledge), and he prays for them to be able to apply God's Word (discernment). In verse 10 he prays that they will be able to approve (determine what is best) the things that are excellent (valuable), and that they will be sincere (know true from false) and without offense (blameless) until the Lord returns. Most believe the "fruits of righteousness" is the fruit of the Spirit. So Paul is praying that the fruit of the Spirit fill up their lives. In verses 12-19 Paul knew that his imprisonment would mean the gospel would be spread. Everyone in the palace knew Paul was there because of the gospel. His imprisonment gave him the opportunity to tell people about Jesus that he may have never had an audience with otherwise. Many people preach Christ with good and bad motives, but Paul was grateful that the gospel was being preached.

In verses 19-26 Paul knew that whether he lived or died the Lord would be magnified. If he continued to live it would be for Christ, and if he died he would go and be with Christ which was far better. When Paul said in verse 23 that he was "hard-pressed between the two" these are the two things he is speaking of. Paul's view of life was that as long as he was on this earth he was going to give all he had to the Lord and the ministry He had given him. Paul was able to live his life this way because by knowing Christ Paul knew that at death he would be with Him. Paul knew that if he were to keep living he would bear fruit (v22) and to continue to preach and teach to people (v24). In verses 27-30 Paul begins to express the theme of unity in the church (v27), and address the persecution they are suffering (v28-30). The preaching of the gospel may lead to suffering.

Philippians 2:1-11 is one of the greatest passages in all of Scripture. In verses 1-4 Paul is teaching the Philippians how to achieve unity and in verses 5-8 he gives them the example of Christ. In verse 1 Paul is basically saying that because believers share these qualities with Christ, they should also share them with one another in their pursuit of verses 2-4. In verse 2 Paul teaches unity, in verse 3 humility, and in verse 4 selflessness. Verse 5 is what is called a hinge verse, which points to verses 1-4 and verses 6-8. In verse 5 the phrase "Let this mind be in you" can actually be read "Let this attitude be in you". In verses 6-8 Paul shows that Jesus possessed those three qualities. Unity is described in verse 6, humility in verses 7-8, and selflessness in verse 8. The Philippians, and all believers, are being urged in this passage to develop these characteristics for themselves. One day all of heaven and earth will bow before Him and acknowledge Him as Lord (v9-11).

Verses 12-18 are an encouragement to the Philippians to live out their salvation because it is God who is working in them and through them (v12-13). They are not to grumble and argue, but must live out their salvation for others to see in order to bring light to the dark world around them (v15). The key to them doing this is "holding fast the word of life". They must hold on to God's Word in order to live out the Christian life. Paul was happy to live out his life in this way, and if needed he was willing to give his life for Christ (v17, Rom. 12:1-2).

Paul wanted the Philippians to rejoice with him (v18). Paul's plan was to send Timothy to them when he found out what his fate in prison would be (v19-24). From this short passage it can be seen that Paul and Timothy shared a unique relationship. This passage also shows how Timothy imitated Paul. Timothy cared for other believers (v20), he sought God's will (v21), he had a proven character (v22), and he was willing to give his life for the gospel (v23). Epaphroditus was to carry the letter he was writing to Philippi and minister to the people there (v25-30). From this passage it can be seen that Paul and Epaphroditus also had a unique relationship. Paul said they were brothers, fellow workers, and fellow soldiers (v25). Paul wants the people of Philippi to receive him when he comes and honor (esteem) him because of the work he does for Christ (v29-30).

Cover to Cover CHALLENGE

Week 32

Sunday • Psalm 103-104

Welcome to week 22 of the *Cover to Cover Challenge*! Continue to pray for one another as we read and study God's Word together. Pray that our eyes will be opened, and that we all will be obedient to the Word of God. John 15:4 says "Abide in Me, and I in you as the branch cannot bear fruit of itself, unless it abides in the vine, neither can you, unless you abide in Me".

Psalm 103 is a psalm of thanksgiving written by David to promote praise to the Lord (v1-2). The term "all that is within me" represents the whole person. The benefits are listed in verses 3-5: forgiveness of sin, recovery from sickness, deliverance from death, lovingkindness and mercy, and food to sustain life. Verses 6-19 contain the attributes of God that His people experience. God blesses His people with: righteousness and justice, mercy and grace, forgiveness of sin, and compassion. Verses 20-22 are a call to praise for those who serve the Lord- whether in heaven or on earth to bless the Lord.

Psalm 104 is a psalm of praise to God for His rule over creation. In verses 1-2 the psalmist describes the Lord's clothing as splendor, majesty, and light. The psalmist moves to the creative acts of God from the heavens (v3-4) to laying the foundations of the earth separating the waters from the mountains (v5-9). The abundance of water gives life for all of the surrounding grass, trees, and animals (v10-18). God also designed the night and the day, in which the beasts of the field and humans find their way of life (v19-23). Creation shows the works and wisdom of God (v24-26). God sustains the whole earth and all of its inhabitants (v27-32). It is in all of this that the psalmist praises God for His work in creation and sustaining each one by His hand (v33-35).

Monday • Numbers 5-6

With the Israelites preparing to move, they must purify themselves here in Numbers 5. This chapter will cover physical (v1-4), moral (v5-10), and marital impurities (v11-31). Those who have a skin disease, discharge, or have contact with a dead body are to be cleansed (v1-5). All wrongs were to be made right by restitution in verses 5-10. This would be done by adding 20% to the value of what was lost. If the family had no one to take the restitution, it went to the priest. This process also left no excuse for not making wrongs right again.

The process of marital purity is odd for us to read in our culture. What this process did was place the woman before God to determine whether she was innocent or guilty.

Numbers 6:1-20 outline the vow of the Nazirite. There are three stipulations of the Nazirite vow: abstaining from wine and strong drink (v3-4), not touching anything that has died (v6-8), and not cutting the hair (v5). The term "Nazirite" in Hebrew means vow and crown. This may mean that the long hair functions as a crown and evidence of the vow taken.

Tuesday • 2 Chronicles 13-19

In 2 Chronicles 13 Rehoboam's son Abijah rules over Judah for three years (v1-2). The Chronciler highlights the split of the kingdom and the bravery of Abijah in fighting a war with Jeroboam and the northern kingdom. It was God who won the battle for Judah over the northern kingdom because they "relied on the Lord God". While Abijah is noted for his bravery, 1 Kings 15:3-5 does say that "his heart was not fully devoted to the Lord".

After the death of Abijah, his son Asa would reign in his place. 2 Chronicles 14-16 shows that Asa, at least up to this point, was the most godly of the men who reigned over Judah. 2 Chronicles 14:1-8 show that the first ten years of his reign were peaceful, and that he removed all of the pagan gods from the area. In verses 9-15 Zerah the Ethiopian attacks them with an army of one million men. Asa cries out to the Lord, who gives them the victory. The reform of Asa in chapter 15 was more thorough and complete than the first. After the preaching of Azariah the prophet, Asa removed the idols and restored the altar of the Lord (v1-9). They would enter a covenant with the Lord where they would seek the Lord and follow Him in faith and obedience so they would experience peace (v10-19). 2 Chronicles 16 records the ending of Asa's reign as king of Judah. Baasha (king of Israel) came against him in verses 1-9, but instead of relying on the Lord he made a treaty with Ben-Hadad (king of Syria) instead. Hanani the seer confronts Asa and he has him put in prison and Asa began to oppress the people (v9-10). Even during the time of a serious illness Asa did not seek the Lord. He died in the forty-first year of his reign.

In 2 Chronicles 17 Jehoshaphat, son of Asa, begins to reign over Judah. Jehoshaphat walked in the ways of David and sought the Lord (v1-5). Jehoshaphat also removed the pagan idols from the land and instructed the religious leaders of his day to go throughout the cities and teach them the Book of the Law (v6-9). The removal of the pagan idols and the teaching from the Book of the Law caused the fear of the Lord to fall on the surrounding areas (v10-19). Jehoshaphat became a powerful ruler in the area because of this. 2 Chronicles 18 shows the alliance made between Jehoshaphat and Ahab of the northern kingdom (v1). Jehoshaphat's son Jehoram marries Athaliah, the daughter of Ahab and Jezebel. This alliance is probably because of the Assyrians, as they become a growing threat to both Israel and Judah. The goal here for Ahab is for Jehoshaphat and Judah to help them regain Ramoth-Gilead from the Syrians. Jehoshaphat wants to seek the Lord, but Ahab has only false prophets (v3-6). Ahab calls for someone to get Micaiah, a prophet he despises, so he can also ask the Lord if they should go to battle with the Syrians (v7-12). Once Micaiah prophesies of Ahab's coming death, he dismisses it as evil (v13-17). Ahab's life shows that once someone dismisses the truth they open themselves up to lies (v18-22). Zedekiah, the false prophet, contradicts what the Lord has said through Micaiah and they take him to prison to be punished (v23-27). Jehoshaphat follows Ahab into battle who disguises himself as he goes into battle (v28-29). Jehoshaphat nearly loses his life in battle and Ahab-just as the Lord-said did lose his life (v30-34). In 2 Chronicles 19:1-3 Jehu the son of Hanani, who had earlier warned Asa not to enter in an alliance with a foreign king rebukes Jehoshaphat for putting himself in position to be led astray. In his absence the people of Judah go astray, and another reform is put into place (v4-11). Amariah will be over those judging religious matters, and Zebadiah over civil matters.

Wednesday • John 6-7

John 6:1-14 records the feeding of the 5,000, which is the only miracle recorded in all four Gospels. The multitudes are still sign followers and not Savior followers (v2). It is also the second of three Passovers mentioned by John. This helps date the length of Jesus' ministry (v4). Matthew (14:21) tells us that the number 5,000 did not include women and children and Mark (6:39-40) tells us that they all sat in groups of hundreds and fifties. Jesus fed them with the young boy's five barley loaves and two fish (v9). This miracle reveals His compassion, His provision, His power. Jesus walking on the sea shows His power over nature (v15-21). At this point in Jesus' ministry the people are about to make Him king (v15-18). The people of His day believed the Messiah would come and take Jerusalem back from the Romans and that they would rule the world under the Messiah's leadership. Jesus' mission was not to take Jerusalem back from the Romans, but to come and provide man a way to God. The feeding of the 5,000 gives Jesus an opportunity to tell them that He is the true bread from heaven (v22-40). The true bread is not the bread Moses gave, but Jesus Himself. The ones who partake of this Bread will never hunger or thirst (v35-36). In this passage, Jesus emphasizes that one must believe in Him in order to have eternal life. Many of them only followed Him because of the food He provided and did not believe in Him (v26, 36).

Jesus' teaching gives the Jewish leaders an opportunity to question His claims of coming down from heaven (v41-59). Verse 44 emphasizes the role of the Father and of the Holy Spirit in salvation. Salvation is never accomplished apart from the drawing power of the Holy Spirit. In verses 46-48 Jesus emphasizes His heavenly origin and again tells them that He is the bread of life. Because of the hardness of their hearts they do not understand what Jesus is saying here and in verses 53-56. In verses 60-71, many of those who follow Jesus choose to walk away. Peter knew that Jesus spoke the words that give eternal life, and he believed that Jesus was the Christ (v68-69). John introduces us to Judas, who would be the betrayer of Jesus (v71).

John 7 pictures Jesus as a rejected Messiah. In verses 1-9 He is rejected by His own brothers, the crowds at the feast (v10-31), and the religious leaders (v45-53). This chapter also records many of the opinions people had about Jesus (v10-12, 20, 25-27, 31, 40-44, 45-52). Some believe He was a good man, and some thought He was deceiving everyone. Others believed He had a demon and some even called Him a prophet. One thing is certain, Scripture teaches that He was sent by God to die for the sins of the world and people must believe in Him for eternal life. Another theme of this chapter is "His hour had not yet come". Each and every second of His life was according to the plan of God and doing His will.

From chapter 6 to chapter 7 about 6 months have passed because we have gone from Passover to the Feast of Tabernacles. This feast was for remembering the wilderness wanderings, and booths were set up all over the city. In Jesus' day the feast became a time of expectation and hope that the Messiah would appear and rescue them from the Romans. During the Feast of Tabernacles lamps and torches were lit to remember God's leading of the people at night by a pillar of fire (Ex. 13:21). It also featured a water pouring ceremony during the first 6 days where the priests would draw water and carry it to the temple and to the altar while singing the Hallel Psalms (113-118). On the last day of the Feast a golden flagon was filled with water from the pool of Siloam by the High priest and carried to the temple. As they carried it to through the Water Gate the shofar was blown. This was known as the trumpet of joy. As this was taking place, the choir would sing the Hallel Psalms. Once they reached Psalm 118 they would shake a lulab (palm with myrtle twigs attached) and would raise a piece of fruit giving thanks for the harvest. The water that was poured out symbolized two things. First, it was a giving of thanks for providing water during the exodus. Second, it symbolized the pouring out of the Spirit in the last days. With this background read verses 37-39. Jesus very clearly told them that He was the Messiah. In verses 45-52 Jesus is rejected by the Jewish leaders.

Thursday • Proverbs 13

Proverbs 13:1-3 returns to the topic of the mouth pertaining to the wise/wicked son (v1), good words (v2), and those who guard their mouths (v3). Work ethic is the topic of verse 4 and verses 5-6 is about walking with integrity. Verses 7-11 deal with the subject of wealth. Someone may appear to be rich, but really have nothing that matters (v7). In verses 9-11 it is the person who pursues wisdom who gains a reward better than riches. Verses 12-19 show how to receive the tree of life which is symbolic of an abundant life. The person who wants this kind of life must practice obedience, learn from wise people, and not act rashly. Verses 20-21 give advice on how to choose friends wisely, and verses 22-25 show a wise family who provides for their future.

Friday • Jeremiah 1-5

Jeremiah ("The Lord Exalts or Establishes") prophesied to Judah through the reigns of five kings beginning with Josiah. Jeremiah's messages appeal to the people of Judah to repent, warn that God would send an invader to punish them, and tell that the judgment was coming for their sin. Judah fell into idol worship, worshiping Molech and the queen of heaven. It is also during Jeremiah's time that Assyria fell to the Babylonians, who would soon invade Judah. Jeremiah is the only prophet who shared his personal feelings as he preached God's message to the people. Jeremiah struggled over the sins of the people and their lack of repentance, earning him the name "the weeping prophet". Jeremiah also had more opposition than any other Old Testament prophet.

Jeremiah 1:1-3 introduces us to Jeremiah and the length of his prophetic ministry. He began his prophetic ministry five years before Josiah's reforms (2 Kgs. 22-23). The names of Jehoahaz and Jehoichin among the kings are probably omitted because their reigns only lasted about three months each. In verses 4-10 Jeremiah recalls his calling from the Lord to be a prophet. God "knew" (approved) him before he was ever born, and had set him apart to proclaim the word of God. Jeremiah would be opposed during his ministry, but the promise of God's presence would provide him boldness and the faith to succeed. Verse 10 shows that the purpose of Jeremiah's ministry was destructive and constructive. The vision of the almond tree shows that the time of Judah's judgment is near (v11-12), while the boiling pot shows that the judgment is coming from the north (v13-15). The reason for the judgment is their idolatry (v16). Jeremiah would have been encouraged throughout his ministry with the words of verses 17-19.

In Jeremiah 2:1-8, Jeremiah recalls the love God had for them in delivering them from Egypt. Jeremiah will go on and contrast God's love for them with the people presently falling away from the Lord. They have broken the marriage covenant by going after idols, which led them to become like the idols they worshipped-worthless. In verses 9-19 Jeremiah brings specific charges against the people for their idolatry. While they rejected God and the truth, they also became servants to Assyria and Egypt by following their gods who could not help them. Verses 20-28 deal specifically with immorality that is associated with idolatry. The people had become so wicked that they had forgotten God and could teach wicked women how to seduce. Their idolatry and immorality led to oppression of the poor and needy, which is a sign of spiritual decline.

In Jeremiah 3:1-5, Judah is pictured as an adulterous wife who refuses to be ashamed of her idolatry and immorality. God even withheld much needed rain for crops to get them to repent, but even that did not work. In verses 6-10 the exile of the northern kingdom of Israel was to be a warning to Judah so they would not suffer the same fate. Judah was actually worse than Israel because they had the lesson of Israel to go by, but refused to heed it. In verses 11-18, Jeremiah calls to the northern kingdom of Israel to repent with a promise of restoration.

God will give them godly shepherds and He will dwell among them. In this restoration, both nations will be united once again. Verses 19-25 show the people repenting over their sin before God.

Jeremiah 4:1-4 is another call to repentance. Jeremiah encourages them to repent through the metaphors of plowing their hearts and circumcising their hard hearts. In verses 5-18 the Babylonians are pictured as being on their way to invade and destroy all that is in the land. This judgment will not separate the good and bad, but will take everything in its path away. Verses 19-22 show the pain Jeremiah suffers from knowing the coming judgment upon Judah. The judgment is pictured in verses 23-26 as being like creation, but in reverse. The destruction will be bad, but the Lord will not completely destroy everything (v27-31).

Jeremiah 5:1-9 shows the search for one righteous person in all the land. While there can be a case made for men like Jeremiah and Josiah, the land was so corrupt that even men like this were the exception and not the norm. The people also lied about God because they believed He would not send judgment on them, and they rejected His word through the prophets (v10-13). What the people of Judah accused the prophets of is what we would call "blowing hot air". In response, God says He will use Jeremiah's words as a fire as he addresses the nation about the coming judgment (v14-19). Because they worshipped other gods in the Lord's land they will serve foreign leaders in a foreign land (exile). Jeremiah shows that the people of Judah have become like the idols they serve and are in rebellion against God (v20-31).

Saturday • Philippians 3-4

Paul warns the people of Philippi about the Judaizers in 3:1-4. The Judaizers believed that one must believe in Christ, but that they also must keep the law and be circumcised. It was a works based system, and in his warning Paul explains that all anyone needs is Christ. Paul details the specifics of his identity before he met Christ in verses 4-6. Paul was from the tribe of Benjamin which was Israel's elite line. He was a pure Hebrew, he was driven by the traditions of the Pharisees, he was full of zeal, and according to their way of life he was blameless as it pertained to the law. These things Paul said did not compare to knowing Jesus as Lord (v7-11). What Paul once thought gave him an advantage over others, he now counted as loss (v7). Paul knew that nothing compared to knowing Jesus Christ as Lord (v8). Paul's life was a pursuit to know Christ (intimate fellowship), to know the power of His resurrection (Eph. 1:19-20), to know the fellowship of His sufferings (price of obedience), and to be conformed to His death (die to self/live for God). You could also read this as being justified (v9), being sanctified (v10), and being glorified (v11).

In verses 12-16, Paul sums up the earlier passage by saying that his goal was to be like Christ. Verse 12 shows that Paul was in continual pursuit of becoming what Christ wanted him to be. In verses 13-14 Paul shows that although he was still short of that goal, he would keep pressing forward until he reached the goal. In verses 17-21 Paul encourages them to follow his example and the example of others who follow Christ. He also encourages them to be on guard for those who are enemies of the cross of Christ. In verse 18 Paul warns them that there are some who are enemies of the cross and in verse 19 he gives a few details about them. They will be eternally lost (end is destruction), they worship self (god is their belly), what they glory in should they should be ashamed of, and they only think of earthly things.

In Philippians 4:2-9 Paul encourages the Philippians to be in unity. In verse 2 Paul urges two ladies in Philippi to settle their differences with one another. Paul also urges the church to help those who have labored with Paul in spreading the gospel (v3). A church united in the gospel should be a church that is united in helping one another when a need arises. Also, a united church should rejoice in the Lord (v4). All believers should rejoice over what the Lord is doing in their life and in their church. In verse 5 Paul encourages them to let their gentleness (forbearance) be made known to all. Gentleness or forbearance is accepting people the way they are. He is not talking about letting unrepentant people join the church. Paul is referring to believers. Each believer is different, and he is urging them to accept one another just the way they are. In verses 6-7 instead of worrying, Paul instructs them to go to God in prayer. When they pray God will set His peace around them to guard their hearts and minds. Verses 8-9 also help combat the anxieties and worries believers have. The phrase "meditate on these things" at the end of verse 8 means to ponder and to ascribe worth to. What Paul is saying is instead of pondering and giving the highest value to anxieties and worries we should give highest value to the things that are true, noble, just, pure, lovely, of good report, virtuous, and praiseworthy.

Paul commends them for the gift they had sent to him during his time of need (v10-20). During this time Paul had learned to be content in his circumstances because it was Christ who strengthened him (v11-13). Verse 13 is a well-known and favorite verse of many. What Paul is saying is that there is no circumstance that could have entered Paul's life that would be too big for God to handle. Paul prayed that just as they have met his need, God would meet their needs as well (v14-20). Being generous not only meets the needs of the recipient, but may lead to your own need being met (reap what you sow).

Cover to Cover Challenge

Week 33

Sunday • Psalm 105

Welcome to week 33 of the *Cover to Cover Challenge*! Continue to pray that the Lord be honored and glorified through our study, that the Holy Spirit will move in each of our lives, and for understanding of His Word. 2 Thessalonians 3:3 says "But the Lord is faithful, who will establish you and guard you from the evil one".

Psalm 105 is a hymn of praise for the Lord's faithfulness to Israel. In verses 1-6 the psalmist calls upon God's people to give thanks to the Lord, to make known His deeds, to sing, to seek the Lord, and to remember His works for them. Verses 7-11 recall God's faithfulness to Abraham and the covenant He had made with their ancestors. In verses 12-15 it was the protective hand of the Lord that delivered them from their enemies as they journeyed to the land of Canaan. God's providence can also be seen in the lives of Joseph and Jacob, as God protected and cared for them in Egypt (v16-23). Through Moses and Aaron, God delivered His people from being in bondage to the Egyptians (v24-36). God blessed them with possessions and gave them food and water as they needed because He was faithful to the promises He had made to them (v37-45).

Monday • Numbers 7-8

Numbers 7-9 describes the dedication of the tabernacle. Numbers 7 is the second longest chapter in the Bible. It describes the 12 day festival and the bringing of gifts to be used in the tabernacle. Moses accepts the offerings from the leaders of the tribes, which are 6 covered carts and 12 oxen (v2-11). These are given to the sons of Gershon and Merari to help carry the tabernacle. The tribes all offer the same gifts, although they are listed separately (v12-83). In verses 84-89 there is a summary of the gifts.

Numbers 8 records what God spoke to Moses when he went into the tabernacle. Verses 1-4 are instructions for the lampstands. The lampstand shows that God is the giver of life and it also shines down on the showbread, symbolizing God's daily provision. In verses 5-26 the Levites are ceremonially purified through washing by water, shaving their hair, washing their clothes, and offering various offerings. Through this, God is showing the Israelites what it is like to be separated for His service.

COVER TO COVER CHALLENGE

Tuesday • 2 Chronicles 20-25

2 Chronicles 20 records the war that was won by worship. The people of Ammon, Moab, and Mount Seir come against Jehoshaphat and Judah (v1-2). Jehoshaphat proclaims a fast through all of Judah and sought help from the Lord (v3-5). Jehoshaphat prays to God and recalls the promise that God had made to hear the prayers of the people (v6-13). Jehoshaphat knew that without the Lord's help there was no way they could win the battle. Jahaziel, led by the Spirit of the Lord, prophesies that the Lord is going to fight the battle for them (v14-17). In response to the answered prayer the people, led by Jehoshaphat, praised the Lord (v18-21). After the Lord had won the battle, they renamed the valley the Valley of Blessing because of the spoil the Lord had given them. They returned to praise the Lord (v22-30). Jehoshaphat reigned for 25 years and did what was right in the sight of the Lord (v31-32). Two instances tarnish his reign. First, there were still places of pagan worship in the land and second, he made an alliance with Ahaziah the king of Israel.

In 2 Chronicles 21, Jehoshaphat's son Jehoram takes over as king of Judah. Jehoram is married to Athaliah, who is the daughter of Israel's wicked king, Ahab. He reigned 8 years in Judah and was not mourned over when he died (v20). He is known for murdering his brothers and the princes of the kingdom (v4), for doing evil in the sight of the Lord (v5-6), and because he built pagan worship sites in Judah (v11). The reason God did not destroy David's dynasty is because of the covenant He had made with David (v7). Edom, the Philistines, and the Arabians all revolted during his reign. They defeated him while carrying away his wives and children, except for Jehoahaz (v16-17). Because of his extreme wickedness, Elijah prophesied that he would die of an incurable intestinal disease (v12-15, 18-19).

In 2 Chronicles 22, Ahaziah the son of Jehoram begins his one year reign as king of Judah. Because of the influence of his mother and of the house of Ahab, Ahaziah did evil in the sight of the Lord (v1-4). Ahaziah would enter an alliance with Jehoram (Joram) king of Israel to fight against the Syrians (v5-6). This alliance would cost him his life, as Jehu is sent to destroy the whole house of Ahab (v7-9). The full account is in 2 Kings 9. Athaliah would make herself queen and kill her own grandchildren to secure the throne (v10-12). She would reign for 6 years and attempt to lead Judah in the Baal worship after her mother Jezebel. Jehoshabeath (wife of Jehoiada the high priest), Ahaziah's sister (2 Kgs. 11:2), would rescue Joash, the son of Ahaziah from the slaughter. 2 Chronicles 23 continues the story of Athaliah and her death in a plan made by Jehoiada the high priest. Joash is placed upon the throne where they make a covenant to be the Lord's people.

2 Chronicles 24 contains the story of Joash, who reigned for 40 years over Judah. Joash only did what was right in the eyes of the Lord while Jehoiada was alive (v1-3). It was during this time the temple was repaired (v4-14). After the death of Jehoiada the high priest, Joash and other leaders began to worship idols (v15-18). They were warned by prophets and Zechariah the son of Jehoiada but they refused to listen, and even had Zechariah killed (v19-22). Because of these acts by Joash, the Syrians would defeat them in battle and even his own servants would turn against him (v23-28).

In 2 Chronicles 25:1-4 Amaziah reigns for 29 years over Judah. His first act was to execute those who murdered his father the king. Amaziah did what was right in the eyes of the Lord, but not with a loyal (wholeheartedly) heart. 2 Kings 14:4 says that he allowed the pagan worship places to remain as well. Before the war against Edom, Amaziah hired some from the tribe of Ephraim (Israel) to fight with him, but a prophet warned him not to let them go because the Lord was not with Israel (v5-9). This shows that Amaziah did not fully trust in the Lord and angered the Ephraimites that he had sent away (v10-13). After defeating the Edomites Amaziah begins to worship their gods, which angers the Lord (v14-16). Amaziah king of Judah and Jehoash king of Israel go to war against one another and Israel prevails (v17-24). Amaziah dies in Lachish while fleeing Jerusalem (v25-28).

Wednesday • John 8-9

In John 8:1-11 we see the scribes and Pharisees testing Jesus after catching a woman committing adultery. If he objected to stoning her He would be opposing the law, but if He agreed with them He may not be looked upon as being compassionate toward sinners. In His reply in verse 7 Jesus took side with the law, but His reply also included the guilt of her accusers. Most people want to know what Jesus wrote on the ground. While no one knows for sure, some have said Jeremiah 17:13 or Exodus 23:1. The story shows Jesus' love and compassion for sinners. John 8:12-30 takes place during the Feast of Tabernacles, which commemorates God leading the Israelites through the wilderness and their recommitment to Him. During this ceremony four very large candelabras were lit. This would light up the whole courtyard. It is against this backdrop that Jesus says "I am the light of the world". In doing this Jesus was identifying Himself as the source of life, especially eternal life (Ps. 27:1).

Verses 31-36 teach that being obedient to the truth of God's Word is a clear sign of a true disciple of Christ. Those who believe are set free from bondage to sin. The Pharisees, who were trusting in being descendants of Abraham, were still slaves to sin. Jesus' explanation goes on through verses 37-47. Both Jesus and the Pharisees claim God as their Father. Jesus' words and His works show them who His Father is. The Pharisees' words and works show who their father is-the devil. They are murderers and liars just like him. Once the argument turns for the worst for the Pharisees, they begin to insult Jesus (v48-59). Abraham did rejoice knowing that Jesus was coming and that God would fulfill all His promises (v56; Heb. 11:13). When Jesus says "I am" He is saying He is God. This is what angered the Pharisees and made them want to stone Him.

John 9 records the story of the man born blind. It was believed by many Jews that sin caused blindness and other sicknesses. While this can be true, it is not true in all cases. The reason this man was born blind was so that the work of God could be performed in his life (v1-5). This miracle is unique because it involved healing someone who had the condition from birth. It also fulfills Scripture that point toward Jesus being the Messiah (Isa. 42:7). Not only was the miracle unique, but the way Jesus healed the man was as well (v6-12). If it was still during the Feast of Tabernacles it was even more significant. It was during this time the pool of Siloam became synonymous with God's blessing and looked forward to the coming of Messiah. The man is brought before the Pharisees and questioned over how he received his sight (13-17). Being unconvinced, they also sent for his parents to make sure it was their son (18-23). The Pharisees question the young man again, and eventually he is excommunicated (v24-34). The word used here for excommunicated also has the added meaning of being placed under a curse. This always resulted in being cut off from people both religiously and socially. In verses 35-41 Jesus meets the man whom He had healed of his blindness and he believes in Jesus and worships Him. Verses 40-41 show that there is no cure for people who reject the only cure there is. Proverbs 26:12 says "Do you see a man wise in his own eyes? There is more hope for a fool than for him".

Thursday • Proverbs 14

Proverbs 14:1-17 continues with the path of the wise and the path of the fool(ish). These can be seen in how a woman makes her home (v1), in one's work (v4,23-24), the use of the mouth (v3,5-7), having ones heart right with the Lord (v8-14), and making decisions (v15-17). Those who really seek to honor God will have honor for themselves (v18-19). Showing kindness toward others no matter their standing in society will result in the blessing of God (v20-22). Verse 25 is an encouragement to tell the truth at all times, and verses 26-28 teach that those who fear God will be secure. In verses 28-35 there is wisdom for those in leadership positions, especially leaders in the government. Leaders must know they need the people (v28), need patience (v29-30), should care for the poor (v31), should avoid wickedness (v32), should walk in fear of the Lord, should be moral (v34), and should surround himself with wise counsel (v35).

Friday • Jeremiah 6-10

In Jeremiah 6:1-5, the invaders from the north (Babylonians) are pictured as being on their way to destroy Judah. The Babylonians were known to have a desire to destroy. When they captured their enemies they were known to burn them alive in a furnace, impale them on poles, and flay people's skin while they were alive. Because of Judah's sin the Babylonians will be God's judgment on them (v6-8). The vine (Judah) will be gleaned completely because they have refused to listen to God (v9-15). God's wrath will be poured out on all ages, but especially the prophets and the priests who were responsible for leading the people astray by being unfaithful to the covenant with God, for not listening to the warnings of the true prophets, and for rejecting the law (v16-21). Jeremiah describes the coming Babylonian army and the people of Judah are struck with fear (v22-30).

Jeremiah 7 is believed to be Jeremiah's first sermon. Here at the gate of the temple, Jeremiah would begin to experience opposition from the people because of the words he spoke to them. His message was simple-repent. The people had begun to believe that God would not bring destruction on the temple (v1-7). This led the people to believe that they could live like they wanted, but remain safe because of the temple (v8-11). Jeremiah is warned not to intercede for the people, who were worshiping the "queen of heaven", because God would not hear his prayer (v16-20). Because of their lack of obedience and godliness the Lord wanted none of their sacrifices (v21-26). Once again, God tells Jeremiah that the people will not hear him or obey his word (v27-28). God condemns the sacrifice of their children to Molech in the Valley of Hinnom. This later became known as Gehenna which Jesus used as a description of hell (Mark 9:43-48). The ground where they worshipped Molech would become the place of their judgment and their burial (v29-34).

Jeremiah 8:1-3 continues with the destruction of Judah because of their sin. Their kings and leaders will be exhumed to be put to further shame. In verses 4-7 the people of Judah are compared to a war horse going into battle because they give no thought to the consequences of their sin and they will not repent. Much of the blame lay on the priests and the prophets who proclaimed a false message to the people and led them astray (v8-13). God's judgment was coming and when it arrived there would be nothing left (v14-17). In verses 18-22, Jeremiah mourns over the spiritual state of his people. They have been given every opportunity to repent but fail to do so.

In Jeremiah 9:1-2 Jeremiah continues to mourn. He is mourning for the people because of the results of the coming judgment, but also for their refusal to repent. In verses 3-9 Jeremiah shows that their descent into idolatry led to corrupt morals in society. People became liars, deceitful, and oppressed the poor and needy. They did not know God, but now they did not want to know Him at all. Their sin would lead to complete destruction of the land (v10-16), and all in the land will mourn over it (v17-22). The people of Judah had trusted in their own wisdom, strength, and riches and they had failed to know God (v23-24). Now they would be exiled among the nations (v25-26).

Jeremiah 10:1-5 is a warning not to worship the gods of other nations. Jeremiah even describes the stages of making an idol to show it is worthless. In verses 6-16 Jeremiah contrasts the worthless idols with God and His power. Verse 11 was written in Aramaic, which was the language of many in that day. It was written that way so that everyone would know why Judah was being punished. In verses 17-22 the exile is coming, and Jerusalem is pictured as a mother with no children or home. Jeremiah prays that Judah will not suffer more than it can bear (v23-25).

Saturday • Colossians 1-2

Colossians was written by Paul while he was in prison in Rome. It also belongs to a group of letters written by Paul around 60-62 AD which are called the Prison Epistles (Ephesians, Philippians, Philemon). Paul wrote to warn them not to go back to their former lives and to refute false teaching. The false teaching in Colossae was probably a mixture of Judaism, paganism, and Christianity (in name only). There was a great emphasis placed on circumcision, dietary laws, and the observance of holy days. It is believed to be similar to Gnosticism, which teaches that salvation is not through faith but knowledge. This is why Paul focuses on teaching them about the person and work of Christ, how to live in Christ, and relationships.

In Colossians 1:1-8 Paul gives thanks for their faith in Christ (v4), for their love for all believers (v4), for the hope that awaits them (all believers) in heaven (v5), for bearing fruit (v6), and for the ministry of Epaphras who brought the gospel to them (v7). In verses 9-14 Paul prays for the believers at Colossae to be able to discern the will of God so they can be pleasing to Him (v9-10). He also prays that they will bear fruit (v10), they will continue to grow spiritually (v10), that they will experience the strength of God in their lives (v11), and that they will give thanks to God (v12). Thanks are to be given because we share in the inheritance with Christ, because He has rescued us from darkness, because He has redeemed us, and because He has forgiven (sent away) our sins (v12-14). Another way to see verses 9-14 is that believers should seek to live a life that is filled with the Word (v9), that is worthy (v10), fruitful (v10), maturing (v10), spiritually strong (v11), and that is thankful (v12).

Paul in verses 15-18 shows that Jesus is God (v15), that He is the Creator (v15-17), and that He is the head of the church (v18). Many scholars believe that verses 15-18 or verses 15-20 comprise one of the earliest Christian hymns. Early hymn writers wrote these not only for worship, but so Scripture could be easily memorized. Paul shows that Jesus is supreme overall, not only because of His position but because of His work of reconciling sinners to God through His death on the cross (v19-23). In verses 24-29 Paul tells them that the sufferings he has gone through for Christ benefited the people and the church at Colossae (v24). Paul preached the gospel and received the word of God to speak to others that was once a mystery (v25-26). Part of that mystery revealed was Christ living in each believer (v27). It is through this ministry given to him by God that he proclaims the gospel message (v28-29).

In Colossians 2:1-5 Paul shows great concern for the people in Colossae because they needed to remain true to the Lord and walk in His ways (v6-7). Paul wanted to encourage them, to show them love of Christ, and to give them a more complete understanding of God the Father and Jesus Christ (v2-3). Paul did not want them to be deceived by the false teachers and doctrine that they had been exposed to (v4). Even though Paul was not physically there, he wanted them to continue to walk in the truth they had received (v5-6). The truth they had believed was to be the foundation for and the cause of their growth (v7). Paul warns them of the false teaching that was infesting the church (v8) and points them to the truth about Christ and His supreme position (v9-10).

Because of Christ's supreme position He is also able to meet every need, especially as it pertains to salvation (v11-15). Because of who He is and what we have from Him, any other belief must be wrong. Back in verse 8 Paul warned of "philosophy and empty deceit" and describes it in three ways. First, Paul says it was "according to the tradition of men". Whatever this was it was man's attempt at truth as opposed to God's truth. Second, Paul says it is also "according to the basic principles of the world". In Jewish thought "basic principles" refers to supernatural beings that people thought ruled the world. Considering Paul mentions angels in verses 18-19 this may be what he is referring to. Third, Paul says it was "not according to Christ". Whatever was being taught was not divine truth from God. Any false religion or teaching will have these qualities present. Paul confronts the false teaching of many in the next few verses. In verses 16-17 he confronts legalism, in verses 18-19 he confronts those who worship angels, and in verses 20-23 he confronts man-made rules which supposedly earn favor with God.

Cover to Cover Challenge

Week 34

Sunday • Psalm 106

Welcome to week 34 of the *Cover to Cover Challenge*! Continue to pray for one another as we read and study God's Word together. Pray that our eyes will be opened, and that we all will be obedient to the Word of God. 2 Kings 6:16-17 says "Do not fear, for those who are with us are more than those who are with them…and Elisha prayed, and said, Lord, I pray, open his eyes that he may see…then the Lord opened the eyes of the young man, and he saw. And behold the mountain was full of horses and chariots of fire all around Elisha".

Psalm 106 details the history of Israel. The focus is on God's goodness to His people and their continual rebellion and unbelief. After opening with thankful praise to the Lord (v1-3) the psalmist turns to God's salvation (v4-5). The psalmist gives the example of their deliverance from Egypt in verses 6-12 (Ex. 13:17-14:31). Notice in verse 6 that the psalmist is identifying his generation with their ancestors when it comes to their sinfulness. God saves not because of anything we have done, but because of His own name sake. Verses 13-15 concern their grumbling about not having any food (Num. 11:4-34). Verses 16-18 describe the rebellion of Korah, Dathan, and Abiram against the leadership of Moses and Aaron (Num. 16). The golden calf of Exodus 32 is the subject of verses 19-23. Moses "stood in the breach" showing that Moses was willing to give his own life to save Israel. In verses 24-27 the generation that complained against the Lord was not allowed to enter the Promised Land (Num. 13-14). Verses 28-31 show the Israelites worshipping Baal and the heroics of Phinehas in stopping the plague (Num. 25). Even Moses in Numbers 20:2-13 disobeyed the command of the Lord and was not allowed to enter the Promised Land (v32-33). Even after they enter the Promised Land of Canaan they rebelled against the Lord by committing idolatry repeatedly (v34-46). The psalmist knows that only the Lord can deliver them and restore them (v47), and only He is worthy to be praised (v48).

Monday • Numbers 9-10

Numbers 9:1-14 marks the second year of their deliverance from Egypt. God instructs them to keep the Passover which celebrates their deliverance from Egypt. Verses 15-23 describe the cloud by day and pillar of fire by night. This was the presence of the Lord, which led them in the wilderness. It served as a daily reminder that God was always with them.

Numbers 10:1-10 describes the two silver trumpets. They were to be blown to gather the people, as a signal to begin to move, to signal a time of war, and to mark the celebrations of the feasts. In verse 11 the Israelites begin to move for the first time and settle in Paran (v12). Verses 13-28 give a detailed account of the order in which they would leave. Moses talks to his brother-in-law Hobab, who also goes with them (v29-32). Verse 35 can be seen as a prayer for protection as they move through the wilderness. Verse 36 may be a prayer of fellowship.

Tuesday • 2 Chronicles 26-31

2 Chronicles 26 concerns the reign of Uzziah who reigned 52 years in Judah. In verses 1-15 Uzziah faithfully followed the Lord, and when he did the Lord blessed him and the land (v5). They were able to defeat many of their enemies with the Lord's help, and he was able to rebuild much of what had been destroyed. His disobedience is recorded in verses 16-23. Uzziah became prideful and went into the temple to burn incense to the Lord, which was something only the priests were able to do. God struck him with leprosy and he was a leper the rest of his life. 2 Chronicles 27 details the reign of Jotham who reigned 16 years in Judah. Although not much is said about him, he did follow the Lord and was blessed with victories over the Ammonites. In 2 Chronicles 28, Jotham's son Ahaz reigns in Judah for 16 years. He did not follow the Lord. Instead he followed the ways of the kings of Israel, worshiping other gods (v1-4). Because of this the Syrians and Israel defeated them in battle (v5-8). In verses 9-15 the prophet Obed confronts the Israelites who have taken captives from Judah, and warns them to return them to their land or they will suffer the wrath of the Lord. After being defeated by Syria and Israel, Judah suffers even more defeat at the hands of the Edomites and the Philistines (v16-21). Ahaz believed the gods of the Syrians won the battle for them and he began to worship their gods, defiling the temple, and the altars in the temple (v22-27).

In 2 Chronicles 29 Hezekiah, Ahaz's son, reigns in Judah for 29 years. He did what was right in the sight of the Lord, and began to cleanse the land from the idolatry of his father Ahaz (v1-3). 2 Kings 18:5 says that there was no king like him before or after him in Judah. The cleansing of the land began with the consecration of the Levites and the priests (v4-14). Next they were to cleanse the temple, repair it, and purify it (v15-19). There was also a ceremony of rededication of the sanctuary and the altar (v20-30). After this, all the people were encouraged to bring their sacrifices to the Lord (v31-36).

2 Chronicles 30 records the celebration of Passover, which may not have been celebrated since the time of Solomon (v26). Hezekiah even sent letters to Israel to come and celebrate the Passover with them. Most laughed at them but some did come from Asher, Manasseh, and Zebulun (v1-11). Passover celebrated their deliverance from Egypt, and the Feast of Unleavened Bread reminded them to be separated from sin (v12-16). Hezekiah's heart is revealed when he prayed for God to forgive those who had not cleansed themselves (v17-20). God blessed the celebration of the Passover and the feast of Unleavened Bread, and the people rejoiced together (v21-27).

In 2 Chronicles 31 Hezekiah begins his reforms to get rid of the pagan altars in the land (v1). Even those from Israel participated in this as they helped remove the pagan altars before returning home. In verses 2-19 Hezekiah begins to ensure that the priests and the Levites are supported for their work in the temple through the offerings of the people. 2 Kings 18 records that the brazen serpent God instructed Moses to build was being worshiped, and it is during Hezekiah's reforms that it was destroyed. Verses 20-21 say that Hezekiah prospered because he did what was good, right, and true before the Lord.

Wednesday • John 10-11

In John 10:1-21 Jesus proclaims that He is the Good Shepherd (v11) and that He is the Door (v7,9). By using these illustrations Jesus is saying that all of the sheep are His, He watches over them, and the only way to be a sheep is to go through Him. The thieves, robbers, and hireling represent the Jewish leaders of the day and only want to steal, kill, and destroy the sheep. Remember that in John 8, Jesus said the religious leaders of the day were like their father the devil so they have taken on his characteristics. Jesus is the Good Shepherd (Ps. 23), who lays down His life for the sheep (Ps. 22), and will one day come again for His sheep (Ps. 24). This chapter also shows that Jesus died as a substitute for all the sheep (v11, 15, 17, 18).

In verses 22-30 after opposition by the religious leaders, Jesus relates His relationship with His sheep even further. In these verses Jesus teaches that His sheep hear (the word means to hear, understand and obey) His voice, as opposed to the religious leaders who do not hear because they are not His sheep. Jesus gives His sheep eternal life, they will never perish, and no one can take them out of His hand (v29, security). The religious leaders again attempt to stone Jesus but He escapes out of their hand (v31-39). In this passage Jesus is asking them to look at His works so they can know who He is, but they refuse. Jesus is basically telling them to judge the tree by its fruit (Matt. 7:15-20). Jesus is bearing good fruit for all to see. If the fruit is good the tree is also good. The witness of John the Baptist leads people to believe that Jesus is the Messiah (v40-42).

John 11 is probably one of your (and mine) favorite chapters in all of Scripture. The raising of Lazarus is truly a miracle that only God can do. The miracles of Jesus glorify God, deepen the faith of the disciples (and ours), and were a sign to others to believe in Jesus. The opening of the chapter sets the stage for the raising of Lazarus. Verses 1-5 tell us about the family, and of Lazarus' sickness. As Jesus tells the disciples about Lazarus' sickness the debate begins about returning to Judea (v6-10). The last time they were in Judea they wanted to stone Jesus (10:31-32). In verses 11-16 the discussion returns to the health of Lazarus. Jesus reveals to them that Lazarus is not just sick, but that he has died. The statement by Thomas in verse 16 reveals that he should not be known solely as "doubting Thomas". Here he is willing to go and die with Jesus.

The next verses show Jesus and His disciples returning to Bethany to the home of Lazarus where Jesus will have conversations with Martha (v17-27) and Mary (v28-37). One of the most interesting things is that Jesus waited four days because the Jews believed the spirit of a person stayed around the body three days (v17). Both sisters knew Jesus and saw Him work miracles. But both sisters insist that if Jesus had been present Lazarus would not have died (v21,32). In the conversation with Martha, Jesus tells her that her brother will rise again (v23). Martha understood this would happen at some point in the future. (v24). Jesus taught the resurrection as a fact (John 5:21, 25-29; 6:39-40, 44, 54) in the New Testament, as well as the Old Testament (Job 19:25-27, Ps. 16:10, Dan. 12:2). Verses 25-26 are some of the greatest in all of Scripture. They teach that Jesus has the power to resurrect us and give us life (eternal), but also that He is those things.

Verse 35 pictures Jesus weeping. The word used here is different than the normal words for crying or weeping. This word pictures someone who is silently weeping or someone standing there with tears rolling down their cheeks. In Scripture Jesus weeps over the Jew's failure to believe in Him (Matt. 23:37-39), when He prays for the disciples (John 17:9-26), and over His coming death and the disciples' weakness (Matt. 26:37-41, Luke 22:40-46). Jesus is probably weeping here for many reasons: over the death of Lazarus, the effects of sin, and possibly a failure by the disciples and others over not believing that He could raise Lazarus (v37). In verses 38-44 Jesus prays to the Father and raises Lazarus from the dead.

In verses 45-57 we learn of the plot of the Pharisees and other religious leaders to have Jesus killed. Verse 48 gives two reasons for this. First, is jealousy over Jesus. They knew if they continued to let Jesus minister everyone will believe in Him. This would cause others to look away from them and toward Jesus. Second, they also knew the Romans would take away their place (positions) and their nation. If this happened they would lose their power over the people, which they craved. In this passage we also see Caiaphas plan to have Jesus killed. The third Passover mentioned in John's gospel is mentioned in verse 55 (2:13, 6:4). This is how most come to believe that Jesus had a ministry that lasted 3 years.

Thursday • Proverbs 15

Proverbs 15:1-17 has much to say about the words we use and the condition of the heart. Those who follow wisdom speak with gentleness, truth, give good advice, and speak words that are pleasing to God (v1-8). These people are also characterized by their heart, which follows righteousness (v9). Those who do not follow wisdom will suffer the consequences of their actions (v10-11) and they also will not seek wise counsel (v12). Hell and Destruction in verse 11 can be translated death and destruction. The heart is the focal point of verses 13-17. Following wisdom, experiencing the fear and love of the Lord, and seeking knowledge make a merry heart. Verses 18-32 show a contrast between someone who follows wisdom and others who choose to follow folly. Anger (v18), laziness (v19), parental relationships (v20), joy, (v21,30), taking advice (v22, 31-32), words (v23,28), being cautious (v24), protection (v25), intentions (v26), greed (v27), and prayer (v29). In verse 33 we are reminded that it is the fear of the Lord where wisdom begins.

Friday • Jeremiah 11-16

In Jeremiah 11:1-13, Jeremiah warns the people of the consequences of breaking the covenant. In verses 1-3 he reminded them of the curse that would be associated with breaking the covenant. All God wanted was an obedient people that would enjoy fellowship with Him (v4-5). Despite the warnings of the prophets, the people continued to rebel against God (v6-8) and were determined to follow the ways of their ancestors (v9-13). Jeremiah is also instructed not to intercede for the people because He would not hear their cries (v14-15). God had desired for the nation to be a green olive tree, but because of their sinfulness they had become fruitless and ready for destruction (v16-17). God reveals to Jeremiah there was a plot in his hometown of Anathoth to take his life (v18-23). All the ones who seek his life will be punished by the coming judgment.

In Jeremiah 12 Jeremiah poses the question about the prosperity of the wicked. Why do the wicked seem to prosper? Jeremiah contrasts his life with the lives of the wicked (v1-4). Jeremiah again asks the Lord to deal with those who oppose him and give them what they deserve. The Lord tells Jeremiah that what he endured from his own people at Anathoth would be nothing compared to what he would go through in the future (v5-6). In the future Jeremiah would not even be able to trust his own family. In verses 7-13 God speaks about Judah's punishment as if it is already being fulfilled. Although those who punish Judah will experience punishment themselves (v14-17), if they will turn to the Lord as the Israelites turned to their foreign gods, God would take them in and they would be His people.

The story of the linen sash in Jeremiah 13:1-11 shows that Israel was once pure, but had become worthless because of their persistent idolatry. Because of their sin the people would suffer and drink the wine of God's wrath (v12-14). Kings, priests, false prophets, and the people would suffer the wrath of God because they would not listen when the Lord asked them to repent (v15-17). The warning to the king would not be heeded (v18-19).

Judah will go in to captivity and be shamed (v20-27). They are so engulfed with sin that if they were to repent it would be like a leopard changing its spots.

Jeremiah 14:1-6 concerns the many droughts the land had been experiencing. Drought was one of the curses for disobeying the covenant (Deut. 28:23-24). It was so severe that even the animals would no longer care for their offspring. In verses 7-9 the people admit they are sinful and pray that the Lord will not forsake them. They were hoping that because God had been their deliverer before He would be again. The Lord explains to them that the reason they are being punished is because of their persistent sin (v10-12). Because they had rejected Him and followed after other gods, He would reject them. He would be sending the sword, famine, and pestilence. Jeremiah pleads on behalf of the people that it is the false prophets who have led the people astray by preaching a message exactly opposite of Jeremiah's (v13-16). Jeremiah grieves over the condition of Judah (v17-18). The people of Judah once again plead with God on the basis of God's reputation on the earth, the temple, and the covenant (v19-22). They know He is the only one who can help them.

In Jeremiah 15:1-9 the people continue in their sin and will not repent. God would not even answer Moses or Samuel if they interceded on their behalf. The nation will have to answer for their sin which finds its prime example from the reign of Manasseh. Jeremiah complains to God because of what he is suffering through, but God promises to strengthen him and to vindicate him before his enemies (v10-11, 15-18). Because of their sin Judah will be exiled from the land (v12-14) but Jeremiah is to remain strong, trust in God, and remain faithful (v19-21).

In Jeremiah 16:1-9 Jeremiah is told he cannot marry nor have a family because of the impending judgment on Judah. The people will ask Jeremiah why they are being punished (v10-13). It is because of their ancestors' sin and their own sin which is much worse. God will bring the people back into their land that He had given them (v14-15), but before they can be restored they must pay for their sin and there would be nowhere they could hide (v16-18). In a future day all nations will come and worship before God (v19-20). It will be through the coming judgment that all will know that He is God (v21).

Saturday • Colossians 3-4

After warning the people of Colossae to stay away from false teachings in chapter 2, Paul instructs them on how to live their life in Christ here in chapter 3. Paul tells them that the only way they can live a victorious Christian life is to live a resurrected life (v1-4). In verses 1-2 we see that Paul wants them to have the right focus. They are to focus on things found above, and not on earthly things. In verses 3-4 Paul wants them to know that they have the right source. In these first four verses alone, Jesus is mentioned five times. Jesus is the right source. They are to put to death their old worldly ways of living and live out the resurrected life that Christ has given them (v5-11). He does this by saying that sin is to be put to death (v5-7), that sin is to be put away (v8), and that sin is to be stopped (v9). The old man is to be done away with so that the new man, who is made in the image of Christ, can live (v10-11).

The victorious Christian life is one to be lived out in love for others (v12-14). Once we have the right focus and are grounded in the right source, we will begin to have the right values. Paul tells the Colossians that when they have these values they will have a heart of compassion (tender mercies), goodness (kindness), humility, meekness (willing to suffer insults), longsuffering (endurance), forgiveness, and love which holds all these values together. Verses 15-17 speak of the right lifestyle. They will live a Christ led life, which consists of peace and brings unity to the body (v15). They will also let the Word of God make its home in them. They will teach it to others and have a lifestyle that worships God (v16). It will be a victorious Christian life because everything they do will be in the name of the Lord Jesus (v17). Living this kind of life will also affect their relationships with their spouses (v18-19), children (v20-21), and servants (v22-25, 4:1).

In chapter 4 Paul urges the people to be devoted to prayer (v2). The word "vigilant" means to watch or to be on alert. Prayers were also to be offered with thanksgiving. It is through prayer that believers thank God for the many blessings He bestows on us and for the grace that they have received. Being thankful also acknowledges that God is working in a believer's life. Paul has two specific requests as the believers at Colossae pray. First, he asks that the people pray for doors to be opened so they could share the gospel (v3). Second, Paul asks that they pray that he can make the gospel clear for those who hear (v4). In verses 5-6 Paul cautions them that they should live their lives and use their words wisely in front of those who are unbelievers. Paul encourages the church at Colossae to welcome Tychicus so that he could inform them of Paul's circumstances and so that he could also encourage them (v7-8). Onesimus is the servant of Philemon who had run away (v9). In verses 10-15 Paul sends greetings from those who are with him and in closing he gives instructions for the letter to be read by Laodiceans (v16-18).

Cover to Cover CHALLENGE

Week 35

Sunday • Psalm 107

Welcome to week 35 of the *Cover to Cover Challenge*! Keep praying for the Lord to be honored and glorified, pray for understanding as we read God's Word, and pray for the Holy Spirit to work in each heart that is participating. 1 Corinthians 1:18 says "For the message of the cross is foolishness to those who are perishing, but to us who are being saved it is the power of God".

Psalm 107 is a psalm of thanksgiving and wisdom. It shows God's faithfulness and love toward His people. After a call to give thanks to the Lord (v1-3) the psalmist will list reasons to give thanks (v4-32) and reasons to praise (v33-43). Within the thanksgiving portion of the psalm, (v4-32) the psalmist paints four pictures to show God's faithfulness and each follow a pattern. There will be a dilemma to be delivered from, a cry for help, a deliverance from the circumstances, a call to give thanks, and a reversal of circumstances. Verses 4-9 show a wanderer in the desert, verses 10-16 show someone who is a prisoner, verses 17-22 show someone who is sick, and verses 23-32 show someone who is caught in a storm. In the praise section (v33-43) God is shown to have the power to change circumstances. The wicked who settle on good land may find it useless (v33-34), and those who follow God may find their useless land become fruitful (v35-42). Those who are wise will see how the Lord is faithful to His people (v43).

Monday • Number 11-13

In Numbers 11:1-3 the people begin to complain because they have no meat. This angers the Lord, who sends fire among them. Moses intercedes for them but they continue to complain, this time about the manna (v4-9). As a result of all of the complaining, Moses expresses his displeasure with the people and with God (v10-15). God will answer both problems that Moses approached Him with (v16-35). God will appoint 70 elders to help Moses lead and He will send quail for the people to eat.. There were quail for 12-15 miles all around the camp. Ten homers could be as much as 65 bushels of quail. God struck those who had gathered too much out of their greed. Joshua is also introduced in this chapter (v28).

In Numbers 12 Miriam and Aaron begin to complain about Moses' leadership after he marries the Ethiopian woman (v1-3). This chapter also describes Moses as humble, a prophet, and as faithful to the Lord. God calls all three siblings for a meeting in which He describes Moses' commission as leader (v4-8). The Lord is angry with Aaron and Miriam, and she is struck with leprosy (v9-10). Aaron asks forgiveness, submits to Moses' leadership, and pleads with him to intercede for Miriam (v11-13). Miriam must go through the purification process and be outside the camp for seven days (v14-16).

Numbers 13 contains the story of the spies being sent to Canaan to check out the land. Moses chooses a leader from each tribe to evaluate the land, the people, and the cities (v1-20). After 40 days the spies return to give their report (v21-24). The majority of the spies do not want to enter Canaan because they believe there is no way they can conquer the inhabitants of the land (v25-33).

Tuesday • 2 Chronicles 32-36

After Hezekiah's reforms (ch. 31), Sennacherib king of Assyria makes plans to come against Jerusalem in 2 Chronicles 32. In verses 1-5, Hezekiah takes steps to prepare for war against the king of Assyria. Hezekiah gathers the troops together to encourage them by letting them know it is the Lord who fights for them (v6-8). In verses 9-19 Sennacherib sends his servants to warn Hezekiah and the people of Judah that their God would not be able to deliver them from the hands of the Assyrians. Both Hezekiah and Isaiah pray for God to deliver them from the hands of the Assyrians (v20-23), and God sends an angel to defeat the Assyrians (2 Kgs. 19). Hezekiah is healed of an illness (2 Kgs. 20) and becomes proud, but he humbles himself before the Lord pours out His wrath upon Judah (v24-26). Verses 27-31 describe Hezekiah's wealth that he had been blessed with. 2 Kings 18-20 and Isaiah 36-39 also record the story of Hezekiah (v32-33).

2 Chronicles 33 records the reign of Manasseh. He had the longest reign of any king and was responsible for the final destruction of the kingdom of Judah (2 Kgs. 23:26, Jer. 15:4). He did evil in the sight of the Lord by worshipping other gods and rebuilding the high places and altars at which to worship them (v1-10). But after being carried away to Babylon, Manasseh repented and humbles himself before the Lord and took away the foreign gods from among them (v11-17). After his death, his son Amon would reign in his place for 2 years before his own servants killed him (v18-25). His son Josiah will reign in his place.

2 Chronicles 34 records the reign of Josiah who would be the last good king in Judah. Josiah's reign lasted 31 years, and he performed the most complete reforms of the kingdom. A more detailed account is found in 2 Kings 22-23. During the earliest stages of the reform Josiah cleansed Judah and Jerusalem (v1-7). While repairing the temple Hilkiah finds the book of the law and gives it to Josiah who immediately repents and seeks the Lord (v8-21). Huldah the prophetess tells Josiah of the coming judgment but, because he had humbled himself before the Lord Josiah will not see it happen (v22-28). Josiah gathers all the people to hear the Word of God and to make a covenant with Him to walk in His ways (v29-33).

2 Chronicles 35 continues the story of Josiah. Josiah and the people of Judah celebrate the Passover and the Feast of Unleavened Bread (v1-19). There had not been a Passover celebrated that met God's standard since the days of Samuel. Josiah dies going to battle against Necho king of Egypt (v20-27).

The final chapter of 2 Chronicles records the reigns of the last kings of Judah, their going into exile, and the decree to return to rebuild Jerusalem. Jehoahaz did evil in the sight of the Lord (2 Kgs. 30:32) and reigns for only 3 months before he is carried to Egypt and his brother Jehoiakim reigns in his place (v1-4). Jehoiakim reigns 11 years and he also did evil in the sight of the Lord and he is carried to Babylon by Nebuchadnezzar (v5-8). Jehoiachin will also be carried away to Babylon after reigning only 3 months and 10 days (v9-10). Zedekiah would be the last king of Judah. He reigned for 11 years and did evil in the sight of the Lord (v11-14). After not heeding the warnings of God through the prophets, Judah is carried away to Babylon for judgment (v15-16). The ruthless Babylonians would conquer Judah and devastate the land (v17-21). 2 Chronicles closes with the decree of Cyrus for the people to come back to Judah and rebuild the temple (v22-23).

Wednesday • John 12-13

In John 12:1-8 is the story of Mary anointing Jesus. In their culture a woman letting down her hair was seen as indecent and shameful, as was touching someone's feet. Not even a Jewish slave was allowed to do this. Mary was not ashamed of Jesus (Mark 8:38). Judas again appears and reveals his true character. In his gospel John describes Judas as a devil (6:70), a receiver of Satan (13:27), a son of perdition (17:12), and a unforgivable betrayer (18:5). In verses 9-11 there is also a plot to kill Lazarus. As long as Lazarus lived there was proof that Jesus was who He said He was, and proof of the miracle He performed. Jesus enters Jerusalem riding on a donkey (sign of peace), fulfilling Zechariah 9:9 (v12-19). The proclamation by the Pharisees that "the world has gone after Him" is affirmed in verses 20-22 as the Greeks (Gentiles) want to see Jesus. Jesus proclaims that His hour has now come to be glorified, showing that His death will bring about salvation for all who believe in Him (v23-26). Jesus also says that He came to glorify His Father through His death, and is confirmed by the voice of God (v27-33). The term "lifted up" was used by Jews to refer to dying on the cross. In verses 34-36, Jesus urges those who are following Him to believe in Him. Those who chose not to believe are presented by John to fulfill Isaiah 6:9-10 and 53:1 (v37-41). Continual disobedience hardens the heart and leads to people being condemned by their own choices. In verses 42-50 Jesus reiterates the call to believe in Him. This passage contains many of the themes in the first 12 chapters of John-believe in Jesus, Jesus is the One sent from God, and He is the Light.

John 13-21 is also known as the "Book of Glory" because Jesus is on His way to the cross. In verse 1, two themes of John's gospel merge. First, as John 12:23 had already announced His time had come to be glorified. Second, is His love. John says that He "loved His own" and that He loved them "to the end". Jesus' love is perfect and complete and He will show this by accomplishing salvation. Romans 5:8 perfectly captures what is being shown here in John.

In John 13:1-17 Jesus washes the disciples' feet. By this act, Jesus is communicating to the disciples the love He has for them and His own humility. They would need both in leading the church, and Jesus sets the example (1 John 2:6). The washing of the feet was set aside for non-Jewish slaves. In verses 18-30 Judas is revealed to be the betrayer of Jesus. The quote from Psalm 41:9 used in verse 18 is interesting. David wrote the psalm after he was betrayed by Ahithopel. Ahithopel would hang himself just as Judas would (2 Sam. 16:20-22, 17:23). To be given a piece of bread at the meal was a place of honor. Some say that this was Jesus' final act of love toward Judas. When Jesus tells Judas to "do it quickly" it shows that Jesus is in control of the situation (John 10:18). Jesus gives the new commandment to love one another as He had loved them. By doing this, people will know that they belong to Him (v31-35). One of the other themes of these chapters is following Jesus where He is going. In verses 36-38 Jesus tells Peter that he cannot come now, but will later. He told the Pharisees they could not come at all (8:21). Jesus is going to heaven, and through Him is the only way to get there (14:6).

Thursday • Proverbs 16

The proverbs in chapter 16 begin to shift from righteous and unrighteous behavior, toward having the values of righteous behavior. In verses 1-3 we are reminded that even though we may plan things out in our life, ultimately it is God who is in control of them. Even wicked evil people are under His sovereign hand (v4-5). God, who is full of mercy and truth, has provided atonement for those who fear Him (v6). Those who turn to Him will even see changes in the people around them and experience less opposition (v7). These same people will also understand that having very little in this world and remaining righteous is more beneficial than having much, but having no justice (v8). Verse 9 is a reminder that the Lord is sovereign over His people and their plans. Verses 10-15 apply to people in leadership positions. A leader must remember that what he speaks must be wise because he represents others (v10), he must be just in his dealings (v11), he should be committed to righteousness (v12-13), and it is better to obey than to experience His wrath (v14-15). Possessing wisdom is better than having riches because it will help you stay clear from evil (v16-17). Those who do take pride in their riches will fall (v18). Those who are humble (v19), follow words of wisdom (v20,21), increase in wisdom (v21), have understanding (v23), and give wise instruction (v24). Verse 25 serves as a warning not to follow the way you want to go, but to follow after wisdom that leads to God. Work is honorable and it provides food for those who are hungry (v26). Verses 27-30 show that the ungodly, perverse, and violent man brings harm to themselves and others. Verse 31 teaches that a wise person who lives a life of righteousness will have a quality life. Verse 32 is teaching about controlling one's anger and self-control in life. In verse 33 we are reminded again that God is in control of all things.

Friday • Jeremiah 17-22

Jeremiah 17:1-13 shows the deceitful and wicked heart of man. In verses 1-4 the people's sin of idolatry became so engraved in their life they would lose everything to their enemies. In verses 5-6 there is a curse pronounced on those who depend upon man, and in verses 7-8 there is a blessing for those who rely upon God. The heart is the most deceitful and wicked place, and only the Lord knows it and the ways of man (v9-10). Those who trusted in riches will soon lose them (v11). Only the Lord is to be trusted, and those who do not will soon be written in the dust (v12-13). Jeremiah prays and asks the Lord to vindicate him because of his enemies (v14-18). Up until this point, Jeremiah's prophecies have not been fulfilled so the people are taunting him. Jeremiah is instructed to go stand in the gate and preach a message encouraging them to practice the right keeping of the Sabbath (v19-27). The Sabbath shows that they recognize God as Creator, which would be a witness against idolatry.

Jeremiah 18:1-11 is known for the potter and the clay. God will use this illustration to show how He deals with all of humanity. The main point that is made is the power the potter has over the clay. Just as the potter remade the clay to conform to his purpose, God will continue to mold the nation until it has conformed to His plan. If they refused to repent (and they do), God would send them into exile. They are guilty of forsaking God and following their false prophets, false priests, and false gods (v12-17). They had turned their backs on God, so He will turn His back to them. In verses 18-23 the leaders of Judah plan to get rid of Jeremiah. They said they have their own priest to instruct them, their own elders to counsel them, and their own prophets to give them the word so they had no need for Jeremiah.In Jeremiah 19 Jeremiah performs another symbolic act. God instructs him to buy a clay jar and carry the elders and priests to the Valley of Hinnom, where they had sacrificed their children to Molech. Here, Jeremiah condemns them for their idolatry and refusal to repent. The valley will be known as the Valley of Slaughter because of what God will do there. The destruction will be devastating. Just like the breaking of the clay jar, it will be irreversible because they have refused to repent.

Jeremiah 20:1-6 shows the consequences suffered by Jeremiah for his message in chapter 19. Pashhur was the main priest responsible for maintaining order in the temple. He beat Jeremiah and had him placed in stocks. Stocks enclosed your neck, arms, and legs so you would be doubled over. Upon Jeremiah's release he gave Pashhur

("Ease") a new name- Magor-Missabib ("Terror on Every Side"). Because he opposed God's Word, he would be exiled to Babylon and die there. In verses 7-10, Jeremiah expresses his feelings concerning his prophetic ministry. He was continually being mocked and laughed at because what he was saying was not coming true (yet). Jeremiah wanted to quit, but could not hold in the words God had given him. He called upon the Lord to vindicate him because of those who had come against him (v11-13). Jeremiah even cursed the day he was born (v14-18).

In Jeremiah 21:1-10, Zedekiah has rebelled against Nebuchadnezzar and seeks a word from the Lord. Jeremiah has a word from the Lord for Zedekiah (v3-7), for the people (v8-10), and for the Davidic line (v11-14). The people should expect no help from the Lord because He will be the one fighting against them. Zedekiah will see his own sons die, and then have his eyes put out before he goes to Babylon. Jeremiah advised the people to surrender and not fight against the Babylonians (v8-10). The Lord called on the house of David (the king) to do what is right (v11-12). The people believed no one could come against them because of God's protection (v13-14). But, because they have disobeyed, it is God who is coming against them.

In Jeremiah 22:1-9 the current king Jehoiakim is instructed to make executing justice his primary responsibility. He was to correct the current situation of oppressing those who were less fortunate in society. Jeremiah tells the people in verses 10-12 not to mourn for Josiah, but to mourn for Jehoahaz (Shallum) who was exiled from the land by Neco and died in exile (2 Kgs. 23:34). Jehoiakim was the exact opposite of his father Josiah, and he was in conflict with Jeremiah and his message (v13-23). Because of his covetousness and his violence, Jehoiakim would not be mourned over when he died and his body would be left for the beasts of the filed to devour. Coniah is Jehoiachin, the son of Jehoiakim and only reigned 3 months (v24-30). He and his mother would go into exile and die in Babylon (2 Kgs. 24:8).

Saturday • Philemon

Philemon is the last of the prison epistles written by Paul (60-62 AD). Philemon was a member of the church at Colossae (Col. 4:9) and Onesimus was his slave. Onesimus stole from Philemon (v18) and fled to Rome, where he met Paul and was saved. Paul knew the relationship between Philemon and Onesimus had to be made right. Often, a runaway slave was beaten to death if found. Paul sends Onesimus back to Philemon with this letter as Tychicus brings the letter to the church at Colossae.

After the normal greeting for an ancient letter (v1-3), Paul addresses Philemon. In verses 4-7 Paul says that Philemon loved the Lord, he loved the saints, and that he shares his faith with others. In verse 6 the word "share" means to share all of life. Philemon must have been an important part of the church at Colossae, not only because he shared his faith, but also because he must have been a benevolent man (v7). In verses 8-16 Paul, out of love for Philemon and Onesimus, begins his plea on Onesimus' behalf. Paul could command Philemon to take Onesimus back, but Paul appeals to him on the basis of love (v7-8). Verse 11 is a play on words and is talking about Onesimus whose name means "useful". It could be read this way "Useful was once useless to you, but now (after his conversion) is useful to you and me". Because of Onesimus' conversion he was no longer just a slave, but a brother to Philemon (v16).

In verses 17-22 Paul told Philemon that if Onesimus owes you anything, put that on my account. In verse 19 Paul reminds Philemon that he was once in Onesimus' shoes. He also owed a debt he could not pay, which was paid for by someone else- Jesus (salvation). This is called the doctrine of imputation. Christ took our sins and added them to His account, so that when we believe in Him we could take His righteousness and add it to our account.

Cover to Cover Challenge

Week 36

Sunday • Psalm 108-109

Welcome to week 36 of the *Cover to Cover Challenge*! Continue to pray for our understanding of the Word of God, that the presence of the Holy Spirit will be made known, and for the Lord to be honored and glorified through the *Cover to Cover Challenge*. 1 Timothy 1:15 says "This is a faithful saying and worthy of all acceptance, that Christ Jesus came into the world to save sinners of whom I am chief".

Psalm 108 is composed of two parts which come from Psalm 57:7-11 and 60:5-12. Verses 1-5 come from Psalm 57:7-11. Psalm 57 is a song of lament and it portrays trust in the Lord to deliver. In verses 1-5 (v7-11), David sings a song of praise for the mercy the Lord has shown him during a trial he has been through. Psalm 60:5-12 also presents God as delivering His people, especially the nation of Israel. David is confident the Lord will deliver them (v6). God answers the prayer in verses 7-9, as His sovereignty over the nations is displayed. The psalm closes with David still looking to God for victory over their enemies (v10-13).

Psalm 109 is an imprecatory and lament. Imprecatory psalms are when David calls down judgments upon those who oppress God's people. After inviting the people to praise God (v1), David accuses his enemies of speaking against him from a wicked heart (v2-5). In verses 6-8 David prays that his enemies will have an evil person accuse them like they have accused David. In verses 9-11 he prays that his enemies' family will have no comfort or support and that they will lose their possessions. And, while they are in this state of helplessness, David prays that no one will be there to help them (v12-13). Finally, David prays in verses 14-15 that their whole family's names be blotted out. In verses 16-20 David prays that all the wicked acts and words that they have spoken against others will come back on them. Because of what his enemies have done to him, David prays for the Lord to deliver and help him in his present situation (v21-29). In verses 30-31, David praises the Lord for being the protector of His people.

Monday • Numbers 14-16

In chapter 14, the people of Israel will complain against Moses and Aaron for bringing them out to die (v1-10). Joshua and Caleb attempt to persuade the people to enter the land, but they refuse and even want to stone them for what they have said. The land was already theirs, but the people refused to believe what the Lord had spoken to them. In verses 11-19 Moses intercedes for the people for rebelling against God. Their lack of faith has severe consequences: all those 20 and older, except for Joshua and Caleb, will wander in the wilderness for 40 years until that generation died (v20-35). The spies who were sent out and brought back a bad report all died from the plague (v36-38). Although it is too late, the people try to take the land for themselves and are defeated by the Amalekites and the Canaanites (v39-45).

Numbers 15 is the first set of instructions given to the people after they are told they will wander in the desert for 40 years. These instructions cover establishing worship (v1-16). Verses 3-10 describe various offerings and sacrifices that are included in Leviticus 1-7. Foreigners were also allowed to participate in worship (v14-16). When they arrived in the land they were to give God the firstfruits out of gratitude (v17-21). Unintentional sin is the subject of verses 22-29. Intentional sin is dealt with in verses 30-31, with an example given in verses 32-36 of what would happen to someone who defied the Lord. The tassels with the blue cord woven into the corner of their garments would remind the people of their needed obedience to God (v37-41).

In Numbers 16, Korah and 250 other men rebel against the leadership of Moses and Aaron. They claim to have a special relationship with God, which has made them arrogant (v1-7). Moses rebukes them for what they are doing because it is God they are rebelling against, not Moses and Aaron (v8-11). Moses wants to speak with Dathan and Abiram but they refuse to listen to Moses (v12-15). God was going to consume the whole congregation of people until Moses and Aaron intercede on behalf of those who are not involved with the sin of Korah and the others (v16-24). Just as Moses announces the ground opens up and swallows all the 250 men and their families who rebelled (v25-35). The censers of those who rebelled were to be used to make a plate on the altar to remind them of what had happened (v36-40). The people complain once again to Moses and Aaron over what had happened to those who had rebelled (v41-45). God sends a plague that kills 14,700 people, while Aaron intercedes for them and the plague stops (v46-50).

Tuesday • 1 Kings 1-4

1 and 2 Kings combined tell the story of the kings in Israel and Judah, along with the stories of a few of the well-known prophets. Some believe Jeremiah wrote these books, but no one knows for certain who the author is. What is known is the author is going to tell the history of Israel to show why the exile came. Here are some main themes for 1 & 2 Kings- First, both Israel and Judah are judged because they have rejected God's law. Second, the words of the prophets come to pass because they have true words from the Lord. Third, God is sovereign and in control over all nations.

1 Kings 1 concerns the rise of Solomon to the throne and Adonijah's (David's oldest son) plot to take it from him. In verses 1-10 David is shown to be feeble and unable to rule well. Joab and Abiathar, who were once loyal to David, also become part of the plot to let Adonijah have the throne. After hearing of the plot of Adonijah, Bathsheba and Nathan appeal to David to publicly make Solomon king (v11-31). Upon hearing this David instructs Benaiah, Zadok, and Nathan to take Solomon to Gihon to anoint him as king (v32-40). Solomon being upon David's mule showed the public that this anointing had David's blessing. Jonathan reports to Adonijah that Solomon has been anointed king and was well received by the public (v41-53). This put an end to Adonijah's plot.

In 1 Kings 2:1-12 David gives Solomon some last instructions concerning his walk with God and on how to handle some people from his past. Joab, the sons of Barzillai, and Shimei must be dealt with. Adonijah still has not given up on trying to become king (v13-25). He asks Bathsheba to ask Solomon if he may take Abishag for a wife. She would have been regarded as David's wife even though she was only his nurse. This would have given him a way to try and get the throne from Solomon. David orders Benaiah to execute Adonijah and this ends the threat. Abiathar was sent to his home town and was removed from the priesthood, even though he deserved to die for betraying David and God's will (v26-27). Abiathar's removal fulfills God's Word to Eli in 1 Samuel 2:30-33. Joab is also executed for his role in the plot (v28-34). This allows Benaiah to take his place and Zadok to be high priest (v35). Shimei is the one who cursed David as he fled from Absalom but even he disobeys his own oath and is executed by Solomon, giving Solomon a time of peace upon the throne (v36-46).

In 1 Kings 3:1-3 Solomon marries Pharaoh's daughter to form an alliance with Egypt. He also worshiped at the high places because there was no temple built yet. Up to this point Solomon loves the Lord and walks in His ways. In verses 4-15 God appears to Solomon in a dream. God offered Solomon anything he wanted and he wisely requests wisdom to rule and to do justice. Because he had asked for this, God also gave him wealth and honor. God also reminds Solomon that he must walk in His ways. In verses 16-28 Solomon's wisdom is put on display in settling an argument between two mothers.

1 Kings 4:1-19 shows the organization of Solomon's kingdom. Verses 2-6 list chief administrators, and verses 7-19 list the district governors. In verses 20-28, the growth of the kingdom is noted as it became peaceful and prosperous. Verses 29-34 reveal the wisdom of Solomon. He was blessed by God to have insight into different areas. He had so much wisdom that other nations would send people to learn from him.

Wednesday • John 14-17

John 14-17 are unique, and only found in John's gospel. These chapters contain some of the first teachings on the Holy Spirit and what He will come to do in, and for believers. It also prepares the disciples for the days they will be without Jesus' physical presence with them. In John 14:1-6 Jesus clearly lays out the way to go where He is going, and also promises to return for them (and all believers) one day. These verses also show the picture of a groom preparing to come for His bride. When two people were to be married, the groom would go build onto his father's house and at an unspecified time return to claim his bride. John 14:6 is an example of exclusivism. This is the teaching that Jesus is the only Savior and faith in Him is necessary for salvation (Acts 4:12, 1 Tim. 2:5, 1 John 5:12). Jesus' words and works revealed the Father to them (v7-11). Those who believe in Jesus will do greater works (future mission of the church in proclaiming the gospel) and will also have their prayers heard and answered (v12-14). The greater works are only possible because of the finished work of Christ.

In verses 15-18 Jesus promises to send the Holy Spirit to help all believers. The word for Helper is *parakletos* and shows a picture of someone coming alongside another for help. The Holy Spirit will come and dwell within each believer but the world will not receive the Holy Spirit because they do not believe in Jesus. In verses 19-24 Jesus again expresses that those who love Him will obey His words. They also will live forever because He lives. Verses 20-21 teach that believers are in Christ (Rom. 8:1, 1 Cor. 1:30) and also that Christ is in believers (Rom. 8:10, Gal. 2:20). In verses 25-31 the Holy Spirit is mentioned again in teaching believers what Jesus' words mean, and in reminding them of the words He has spoken. John 2:19-22 is an example of them being reminded of Jesus' words. Verses 27-29 speak about the peace of God. True peace only comes through knowing Christ (Rom. 5:1, Isa. 26:3). They are to let this peace calm them when their hearts are troubled.

In John 15:1-8 contains the final "I AM" statement from the Lord. The key term in this passage is abiding (v4-7, 9, and 10). No Christian can bear fruit or do anything apart from the Lord. Bearing fruit is spiritual qualities (Gal. 5:22-23). In verses 9-17 we are told to abide in His love. From John's gospel there can be seen a "circle of love". The Father loves the Son (3:35, 17:23), the Son loves the Father (10:17, 14:31), the Son loves believers and they are to love and obey Him (13:34, 14:15). Loving the Son means being loved by the Father (14:21, 17:23), believers are to love one another (13:34, 15:12). The way to abide in His love is to obey His commandments. Jesus also warns them in verses 18-27 of the coming hatred they will experience from the world because they have hated Him. When you are not following the world, or its ways, the world will hate you. When you follow the world, the world will not hate you. In verses 26-27 we learn two more functions of the Holy Spirit. First, He will testify of Jesus by proclaiming the truth about Him. Second, He will enable believers to be a witness for Jesus.

In John 16:1-4, the help of the Holy Spirit enabling believers to be a witness will be needed because of coming persecution. Being put out of the synagogue would mean they would be cut off from the religious, social, and economic aspects of Jewish society. This is what happened in John 9 with the man born blind. Persecution would also include losing their lives. An example of this would be Saul persecuting Christians and the stoning of Stephen (Acts 7). In verses 5-14 we see even more functions of the Holy Spirit. The word convict in verse 8 means "to cause to see". One of the main functions of the Holy Spirit is that He causes the world to see its sin (v8-9). The word for "sin" used here means to miss the mark, and primarily refers to unbelief.

The Holy Spirit will also cause the world to see the righteousness of Christ and their unrighteousness (v8,10). Jesus is the standard of righteousness, and apart from Christ no one meets that standard (Rom. 3:10, 3:23, and 6:23). The Holy Spirit will also cause the world to see its judgment because those without Christ are already condemned (v8,11). This phrase is in the perfect tense in the Greek and means has been judged, and continues in a state of judgment (John 3:18). The Holy Spirit will guide believers toward the truth (v13). The Holy Spirit will always point believers toward the truth. The Holy Spirit will reveal things to come (v13) and will also glorify Jesus (v14). He does this by indwelling believers, teaching believers, reminding believers, testifying of Jesus, and enabling believers to witness, convicting the world, guiding believers, and revealing the Word to believers.

In verses 16-24 Jesus comforts the disciples concerning His coming death and resurrection. This will cause them to be filled with sorrow, but the world will be filled with joy (v20). Once Jesus is resurrected, their sorrow will turn to joy (v22). In verses 25-33 Jesus tells them of the Father's love, warns them of their coming defection, and promises them peace for what lies ahead. The word "peace" here means a satisfied life based on being in relationship with God. The word "overcome" means victory. This is written in what is called the proleptic sense which shows the victory has already been won.

John 17 records Jesus' prayer of intercession for Himself (v1-5), for the disciples (v6-19), and for all believers (v20-26). This is the longest prayer recorded of Jesus and displays His work as our Great High Priest who lives to make intercession for us (Heb. 7:25). Jesus prays in verses 1-5 that what He has done, and is about to do, will glorify God the Father. He has brought glory to the Father through His birth (Luke 2:14), His teaching (Matt. 5:16), His miracles (Matt. 9:8), His obedience (John 6:38), and will through His death and resurrection (John 12:23-28). His ministry and life have been about leading people to know Him and the Father (v2-3). In verses 6-19 Jesus prays for the disciples to have unity (v11), protection from Satan (v12), joy (v13), and to be sanctified by God's Word (v17). Jesus prays this for the disciples because the world is going to hate them (v14).

Jesus prays for all believers in verses 20-26. He prays that they will also have unity (v21), know the love of God (v23), and that they will spread the gospel message (v18,22-24). Philippians 2:2 says "Fulfill my joy by being like-minded, having the same love, being of one accord, of one mind". Believers who have the same love, and are united in Spirit, and all share the same purpose in advancing God's kingdom. It is the visible unity and love of the church that forms the foundation of evangelism and demonstrated to the world that Christ changes lives. In verse 24 Jesus prays that all believers will be with Him in heaven, where they can see His glory.

Thursday • Proverbs 17-18

Proverbs 17:1 teaches that it is better to have little but have peace, as opposed to having much but having a life filled with strife. Verse 2 is teaching that following wisdom can overcome disadvantages in life. Verse 3 is teaching that the Lord will allow adversity in someone's life to test their heart. Verse 4 serves as a warning to those who speak and listen to lies and gossip. Verse 5 is also a warning to not glory in someone else's misfortune. Verse 6 is teaching the importance of family. Verse 7 is teaching that a person of honor will not tell lies. Verse 8 shows that those who give are prosperous in what they do. Verses 9-13 go together with the main point coming in verse 11. Verses 9 teaches about forgiveness, and verse 13 teaches about retaliation. Verses 10 and 12 teach about the behavior of the fool. For both of these pairs, justice will be carried out (v11). Verses 14-19 are done much the same way. Verse 14 and 19 teach about strife or fighting. What do people experience strife over? Injustice (v15), use of money (v16,18), and adversity (relationships,v17). Verse 20 shows that those who practice deceit will have a life of trouble. Verse 21and 25 teaches that the son or daughter who fails to follow wisdom brings sorrow to their parents. Verse 22 is teaching that the key to a happy life is to have a merry heart. The New Testament teaches that those who know Christ can experience joy in all circumstances. Verses 23, 24, and 26 warn about perverting justice. Verses 27-28 are teaching wise use of the tongue.

Proverbs 18:1-3 teach that a fool will not listen to wisdom and will not remain silent. He will always want his own way and bring shame. In contrast, the person who has wisdom will know when and what to speak (v4). In verses 5-8 the focus is on evil speech and those who love to hear it. Verses 9-12 teach about security. Being lazy leads to insecurity (v9), God is the only true place of security (v10), riches do offer security but it is not to be depended upon (v11), and those who are arrogant will destroy themselves (v12). Verse 13 is about someone who is unwilling to listen to wisdom, and verse 14 is teaching about having the proper attitude. In verse 15 those who already possess wisdom will continue to seek it. Verses 16-19 are about administering justice and warn against making decisions in a hurry and settling disputes wisely. Verse 20 teaches that one must bear the consequences of their words. With words you can speak life or death. There is power in the tongue (James 3:1-12). Verse 22 teaches that a man who has a wife has received a blessing from God. Verse 23 may concern the rich taking advantage of the poor, while verse 24 teaches that a faithful friend will be there in times of trouble.

Friday • Jeremiah 23-27

In Jeremiah 23:1-8 God pronounces a woe upon the leaders (shepherds) of Judah, which would include civil and religious leaders. They had destroyed and scattered God's flock, but He would regather them one day from all the places they have been scattered- like a true shepherd. He would replace the false shepherd with true faithful shepherds. Verses 5-6 are about the coming of Jesus the Messiah. He will be the "Branch" and will also be called "The Lord Our Righteousness". He will reign as King, and His kingdom will be known for justice and righteousness. He will rule over a united kingdom, bring salvation, and rule with peace and security. This restoration will surpass anything the nation had experienced in the past. The rest of the chapter (v9-40) is for condemning the false prophets.. Instead of drawing people to God, the prophets and the priests only led people away from Him (v9-12). While the northern kingdom prophets listened to Baal, the prophets of Judah were misusing God's own name which hardened the hearts of the people to repent (v13-15). These false prophets gave false prophecy, which led to the people having a false hope (v16-22). In verses 23-32 God's Word is pictured to be like a fire- purifying and consuming evil, and also like a powerful hammer- crushing the hardness of hearts to bring repentance. The false prophets claimed to have an oracle (burden) from the Lord, but the Lord said that they had become a burden to Him and He would punish them by forgetting them (v33-40).

Jeremiah 24 concerns the two baskets of figs, each representing a group of people. The basket of good figs that were carried off to Babylon would experience future prosperity, be restored to the land, and turn to the Lord (v1-7). The group represented by the bad figs would be Zedekiah, and those left behind who would be scattered and hardened by their own failure to repent and continue down the path of unrepentance (v8-10).

Jeremiah 25 is about the rejection of the prophets God had sent, the coming exile, and the judgment of the nations including Babylon. In verses 1-7 Israel is shown to continually reject the prophets God had sent to warn them. Jeremiah's ministry has lasted 23 years with Zephaniah and Habakkuk warning Judah of what was to come. The Babylonians would be coming because of their disobedience, and they would go into exile 70 years (v8-11). Babylon would also be punished for its sin at a later time (v12-14,26). In verses 15-29 the cup of God's wrath (through the Babylonians) would fall down upon every nation mentioned (v15-29). God's judgment is also pictured as a lion and a judge ruling over a lawsuit making judgment (v30-33). In verses 34-38 Jeremiah tells the shepherds of Judah to weep and wail for what is about to come to them.

Some people believe Jeremiah 26 goes with Jeremiah 7 where Jeremiah preaches at the temple. Jeremiah 26 would give the results of what he preached in chapter 7. In verses 1-3 Jeremiah is told to go to the temple's outer court and say what God had given him to say. He emphasizes that they must obey God if the coming punishment was to be avoided (v4-6). False prophets had been telling the people they would experience peace and nothing would harm them. In verses 7-11 Jeremiah is arrested and accused of blasphemy, which is punishable by death (Deut. 18:20). With the civil authorities present, Jeremiah defends himself in verses 12-15. Jeremiah is released by the civil authorities because they knew he was what he claimed to be-God's prophet (v16-19). Verses 20-24 show that not all of God's prophets escaped death. Urijah was killed for preaching the same message.

Jeremiah 27 is about the sign of the yoke. The yoke symbolizes submission, service, and captivity. In this Jeremiah is encouraging Judah and all the nations named to not try to remove the yoke of the Babylonians, but to submit to them because it is God's will (v1-11). King Zedekiah of Judah is warned specifically not to revolt against Babylon, which is something they were already planning to do with the nations mentioned in verse 3 (v12-15). The priests and the people are also warned in verses 16-22 not to listen to the false prophets and revolt against Babylon.

Saturday • 1 Timothy 1-3

1&2 Timothy, along with Titus, make up what are called the Pastoral Epistles. These were written by Paul, probably between 63-66 AD to Timothy and Titus as they led the churches in Ephesus and Crete. Paul had probably led Timothy to Christ during his first missionary journey in Lystra (Acts 14). On his second missionary journey Paul chooses Timothy to come with him (Acts 16). This letter was written from Macedonia to Timothy to help him deal with false teachers, church life and organization, and to encourage Timothy in his task of leading the church. There was a strong presence of false teaching in Ephesus due to the cult of Artemis (Diana), the worship of the emperor, and the Judaizers (Galatians).

1 Timothy 1:1-2 contains the customary greeting of an ancient letter. In verses 3-11 Paul addresses the issue of false teachers. Verses 3-7 are proof that when someone chooses not to follow sound doctrine their life will be affected and changed. Wrong doctrine will always produce wrong living. As the evidence in verse 3 points out, there must have already been false teachers in Ephesus who were straying from sound doctrine. The term "charge" is a military term which means to pass commands from one to another. The doctrine that some held

in Ephesus caused disputes (controversy) within the church (v4). Paul is writing to Timothy in order to correct this error. He is also writing to show Timothy how he is to command others (v5). First, it is to be done with love that comes from a pure heart. This is a person's morality and their character. Second, it is to be done in good conscience. The word for conscience here means to know right from wrong. Third, it is to be done in sincere faith. This means real or genuine faith. Those who have turned away from sound doctrine have strayed (missed the mark) and turned aside (turned off course) to idle talk (meaningless talk). Verse 7 may offer a clue that it is the Judaizers whom Paul is referring to. These are those who caused Paul trouble in Galatia. The false teachers were apparently misusing the law (v8-11). The law functions to point people to Christ, and obedience to it is impossible.

Paul gives a brief part of his own testimony in verses 12-17 to show Timothy that if Christ could save and use him, He could reach those false teachers as well. In verse 12 the word "enabled" literally means to give strength. Paul knew his ministry was given to him by God and that he could not do it in his own power. You can read Paul's testimony in Acts 9, 22, 26, Galatians 1-2, Philippians 3, and here in 1 Timothy 1. It is because of God's exceedingly abundant grace (superabundant) that we are saved (v14). Paul ends his testimony about his life before Christ by saying that he is the chief (worst of) sinner. Paul also considered himself to be the "least of the apostles (1 Cor. 15:9) and the "least of the saints" (Eph. 3:8). It is because of God's mercy that Paul, and all believers are saved (v16). In verses 18-20 Paul encourages Timothy once more for the battle he is facing within the church. Timothy is involved in spiritual warfare in Ephesus (v18, Eph. 6:10-20). The word "rejected" means a violent and deliberate rejection of faith in Christ (v19). Hymenaeus and Alexander are mentioned again in 2 Timothy.

In 1 Timothy 2:1-4 Paul teaches that the most important thing that Timothy and all believers can do is pray, especially for those who are in leadership positions. This is done so that they can live a life of peace (v2). In verses 5-7 Paul presents that the only way they can be saved is through Christ. Paul's list of different types of prayer covers general and specific prayers, intercession, and thanksgiving. Another way to remember this is the acronym A.C.T.S. "A" stands for adoration (praise), "C" for confession of sin, "T" for thanksgiving, and "S" for supplication, which includes intercession. Verse 8 serves as a reminder to pray with unity in the body of Christ and with faith. From these verses it can be seen that prayer is to be done by individuals, in groups, and especially by the church at large.

In verses 9-15 Paul addresses the women in Ephesus. Women played a prominent role in the pagan religions, often serving as temple prostitutes. Paul is warning Timothy to tell them they should dress with modesty and have self-control over their appearance so they will not call attention to themselves or be a distraction. These verses also function as a deterrent for false teachers from the pagan religions, because many were women. If a woman was not allowed to teach in Ephesus then it prevented false teachers from leading people astray. Paul's main concern is that women live a godly life (v10).

1 Timothy 3:1-7 lists the qualifications of a pastor, and verses 8-13 for the deacon. Acts 6:3 also gives characteristics to go by when choosing leadership in the church. In verse 1 the first "desire" means to set your heart on something. It also describes external acts of striving forward. These may include prayer, bible study, and seminary training. The second "desire" expresses a strong desire. This word also describes an inward act. These types of desires brought together form a decisive "call" to hold the office of an bishop (overseer). It would be similar to Jeremiah experiencing fire in his bones to preach, or Paul feeling the necessity to preach the gospel. Timothy would need to surround himself with men with these characteristics to help him lead the church. No one should have to lead alone, nor without godly council. Verses 14-16 give another reason why Paul wrote to Timothy. It is vital that the people know how to live and conduct themselves in God's house. Verse 16 was probably an ancient hymn sung by the early church, and taught important doctrine.

Cover to Cover CHALLENGE

Week 37

Sunday • Psalm 110-112

Welcome to week 37 of the *Cover to Cover Challenge*! Continue to pray for all of those who are reading God's Word together through the week. Also pray that the Lord be honored and glorified. Psalm 100:4 says "Enter into His gates with thanksgiving, and into His courts with praise, be thankful to Him, and bless His name.

Psalm 110 is a royal and messianic psalm. Jesus applies this psalm to Himself in Matthew 22:41-45 and it is quoted many times in the New Testament (Mark 12:35-37; Acts 2:34-35; Hebrews 1:13, 5:6, 7:17-21). Making an enemy your "footstool" comes from the ancient custom of the winning king of the battle placing his foot on the neck of the losing king (v1). The Messiah will also have a kingdom that is strong and growing (v2) and will have many supporters (v3). The Messiah will also be a priest after the order of Melchizedek which shows His priesthood to be of a higher order and eternal in length (v4). He will also overcome His enemies and rule while judging the nations (v5-7).

Psalm 111 is a wisdom psalm that celebrates the works of the Lord. In verses 1-3 the psalmist invites all to praise God because of His works. These "honorable and glorious" works are to be studied as they reveal the characteristics of God. In verses 4-9 the psalmist encourages the people to remember all of the great works of the Lord. The giving of food and the covenant shows that God is gracious and compassionate, as well as faithful. Because of His great works the people should respond with fear of the Lord that will result in them gaining wisdom (v10).

Psalm 112 is also a wisdom psalm that shows a contrast between the righteous and the wicked. In verses 1-3 those who fear the Lord are blessed with descendants, wealth, and honor. Even when hard times come (darkness), they are given light to endure in their way (v4, 6-8). Those who fear the Lord are also concerned with those in need and they are just in their dealings with them (v5). In contrast, the wicked will be filled with anger and jealousy when the Lord rewards the righteous (v10).

Monday • Numbers 17-21

Numbers 17 is going to affirm the rule of Moses and Aaron. In verses 1-7 Moses instructs the leader of each tribe to bring a rod to be placed before the Lord. Each rod was to have their tribe name on it. The staff that sprouts leaves will be the one whom God has chosen to lead. The next day Moses finds that Aaron's rod not only sprouted leaves but it also had buds, blossoms, and had produced almonds (v8-13). This supernatural act done by God led to the almond branch becoming a symbol of life. Numbers 18-19 will teach the people about how they can approach God

Numbers 18 lays out the functions of the Levites in how they are to serve Aaron and his sons. In verses 1-7 the priestly roles are reiterated from Numbers 3-4. The priests can keep some of the offerings from the people, and they are divided into two categories (v8-19). The most holy offerings are the grain, sin, and guilt offerings. The other category is the firstfruits and the firstborn offerings, which are to be treated as special gifts from God and returned to Him. The tribute from the people of Israel is a gift from God for the priestly families (v19). The Levites will not receive any land because God is their inheritance (v20-24). In verses 25-32 the Levites are responsible to tithe to God out of the tithes they receive for their work. They are to give the very best of what is given to them.

Numbers 19 deals with the purification process for those who touch dead bodies. This would be needed because of the many deaths the children of Israel will experience over the next 40 years. In verses 1-13 the red heifer ritual is described. Its blood is to be mixed with cedar wood, hyssop, and scarlet. These are the same ingredients for sprinkling lepers in Leviticus 14:4-7. Eleazar is chosen instead of the high priest because the one who performs this task will be unclean until evening. Verses 14-22 explain those who need to be sprinkled with the mixture.

Numbers 20 is one of the saddest chapters in the life of the Israelites. Miriam dies in verse 1, and the people are still complaining against Moses and Aaron (v2-13). God instructs Moses to take the rod, call Israel together, and speak to the rock to get water. Instead of speaking, Moses strikes the rock twice disobeying God's command. Moses and Aaron are also guilty of not believing what God said. Because of these two acts, neither Aaron nor Moses will enter the Promised Land. Moses asks permission twice from the Edomites to pass through their land but they refuse (v14-21). In verses 22-29 Aaron dies, passing on the responsibilities of high priest to his son.

In Numbers 21:1-3 the king of Arad attacks the Israelites and takes some of them captive. God enables them to destroy them and their cities. The Israelites begin to grumble again and the Lord sends fiery serpents to punish them (v4-9). God instructs Moses to make a fiery brass serpent and place it on a pole. Everyone who looks upon it will be healed. This is done to teach the Israelites faith and obedience. This is the last time Israel will complain about not having food and wanting to go back to Egypt. In verses 10-20 God provides them a place to find water and to camp. The song in verses 17-18 is a song praising God for His goodness to them. Israel seeks permission from king Sihon to pass through the land of the Amorites, but they refuse to let them pass and go to war with them (v21-32). The Israelites defeat them which fulfills Genesis 15:16. In verses 33-35 they defeat Og king of Bashan because the Lord had delivered him into their hands.

Tuesday • 1 Kings 5-8

1 Kings 5-8 covers the building and dedication of the temple. 1 Kings 5 details the preparations (v1-12) and workforce (v13-18) behind the building of the temple. In verses 1-12 we read about the relationship between Solomon and Hiram the king of Tyre. Verse 12 serves to show that Solomon organized all of this endeavor by using the wisdom God had given him.

In 1 Kings 6 the temple building project begins in the 4th year of Solomon's reign (v1). 2 Chronicles 3:1 states that Mount Moriah is where the temple is built. Verses 2-10 give the dimensions of the outer structure of the temple and the materials used in building it. In verses 12-13 God reminds Solomon that for him to experience His blessing he had to walk as his father David walked before the Lord. The key here is obedience to God's Word. The highlight of the inner structure (v15-35) is the Most Holy Place, or the Holiest of Holies, where the Ark of the Covenant would dwell. From start to finish the building of the temple took 7 years (v37-38).

1 Kings 7:1-12 describes all the other buildings that made up one large complex within the courtyard. Huram was hired to do all the work because God had given him wisdom in working with precious metals (v13-14; 2 Chron. 2:14). Verses 15-22 describe the two bronze pillars named Jachin ("He Established") and Boaz ("By Him He Is Mighty"). The bronze Sea (v23-26), and the ten basins with their stands were also built by Huram (v27-39). Verses 40-47 contain a list that summarizes all of Huram's work. All of the golden furnishings within the temple are described in verses 48-50. Solomon also brought all of David's gifts into the treasury that he dedicated to the Lord (v51).

In 1 Kings 8:1-13 the Ark of the Covenant is moved into the Most Holy Place. The completion of the temple showed that God's presence would be among them and that He would be their God. In verses 14-21 Solomon addresses all who are gathered together to dedicate the temple. God has fulfilled His promise to David by Solomon becoming king and by allowing him to build a house for the Lord. Solomon's prayer in verses 22-53 concerns 7 specific requests that God hear the prayers of the people regarding: (1) oaths brought before the Lord, (2) forgiveness after being defeated by the enemy, (3) drought brought on by the sins of the people, (4) economic disruptions caused by famine and plagues, (5) that the Gentiles would desire to know God, (6) that God would hear the prayers of those who had no access to the temple, and (7) when the people sin against God He would hear their prayers. After praying Solomon addresses the crowd once more in verses 54-61; asking the Lord to always be with them, never forsake them, and to remember His people so others can know Him. In verses 62-66 all of Israel joins Solomon in sacrificing to the Lord.

Wednesday • John 18-19

John 18-19 is John's story of the crucifixion. There are two points that John will be making, which are also themes found earlier in John. First, Jesus is King (1:49; 12:13; 19:19), and Jesus is the Lamb of God (1:29,36; 19:14,31). In verses 1-11 Jesus is betrayed by Judas. Mark 14:45 tells us that Judas betrayed Jesus with a kiss. This gesture was only done between close friends to demonstrate how much you loved the other person. Verses 4 and 8 show that Jesus was voluntarily giving up His life to provide salvation (John 10:17-18). In verse 6 the power of Jesus was put on display, but this verse also shows His willingness to go with them to be crucified. Also in verse 10 we learn Malchus is the one whom Peter cut off his ear. Luke 22:51 records that Jesus healed the man's ear, which also provided another demonstration of His miraculous power.

Jesus is brought before Annas in verses 12-14 and is questioned by him in verses 19-24. Jesus had three Jewish trials: here before Annas, before Caiaphas in Matthew 26:57-68, and the next morning in Luke 22:66-71. Jesus also would have three civil trials: before Pilate (Luke 23:1-5), before Herod (Luke 23:6-12), and Pilate again (Luke 23:13-25). Verses 15-18 and 25-27 deal with Peter's denial of Jesus (Luke 22:61). Jesus appears before Pilate in verses 28-38. The Jewish leaders were about to crucify an innocent Jesus, but would not go into the Praetorium because they would be defiled and not able to celebrate the Passover. This shows the true state of their heart. In verses 39-40 Jesus takes Barabbas' place as he is released. Here in John and in Mark we read that Barabbas is a robber, and Luke adds that he was a murderer. Barabbas' name means "son of the father". The true Son of the Father is going to take his place and be crucified.

In John 19:1-4 Jesus is taken and scourged, and for the second time Pilate finds no fault in Him. In verses 5-16 the Jews want Jesus crucified, and for the third and final time Pilate finds no fault in Him. Jesus is being charged with blasphemy by the Jews and insurrection for making Himself to be a king. Pilate could find no way to release Him, even though he believed Jesus was innocent. Remember Pilate also had this warning from his wife "Have nothing to do with that just Man, for I have suffered many things today in a dream because of Him" (Matt. 27:19). The Israelites/Jews had always rejected God as being their King (1 Sam. 8:4-9, Judg. 8:23). The mention of the Preparation Day in verse 14 is the day the lambs would be slaughtered to prepare for Passover.

Jesus is crucified in verses 17-24, and He gives responsibility of caring for His mother to John in verses 25-27. Golgotha was just outside of Jerusalem and offerings for sin were made outside the camp (Ex. 29:14, Heb. 13:11-12). The title placed on the cross above Jesus would have been a jab at the Jews (v19). The Jews hated Jesus, Nazareth was looked down upon by the Jews, and calling Jesus their King would have been repulsive to them as well. In verses 28-30 Jesus dies upon the cross of Calvary. The term "It is finished!" means "paid in full". When it is coupled with the tense of the phrase it means paid in full, never to be done again. In verses 31-37 Jesus is shown to be the true Passover Lamb, and none of His bones were broken (Ex. 12:10). Joseph and Nicodemus take down the body of Jesus and bury Him in the tomb (v38-42).

Thursday • Proverbs 19

Verse 1 is teaching that honesty and integrity should be pursued in life. Verse 2 serves as a warning against being impulsive. In verse 3 there is a warning for those who follow their own way but blame God when it goes wrong. Verse 4 is teaching that true friendship does not care whether one is rich or poor. The "friends" of the rich may not be friends at all. Verses 5 and 9 warn against speaking lies. Verse 6 may also serve as a warning to people in power about choosing their friends wisely. Just the opposite of the rich, the poor have no friends (v7). This is thought to be an encouragement to them to find their well-being in God. Verse 8 serves as an encouragement to keep seeking wisdom. Verse 10 is teaching that neither the fool nor the servant are ready to rule because of their lack of self-control. Verse 11 shows that a wise man has self-control. This is essential for a leader, because the power of a leader can be used for the wrong reasons (v12). Issues with family relationships can cause harm within the home (v13). That is why it is important to seek wisdom when pursuing a wife (spouse,14). Laziness causes many problems in someone's life (v15). Obedience to God's Word can mean life or death (v16), this can be taught at home by the parents through discipline (v18). Verse 17 teaches compassion and being generous to those less fortunate. Verse 19 warns against those who cannot control their emotions. In verses 20-23 wisdom comes from fearing the Lord, which also can be described as listening to and obeying His commandments. The one who does will find themselves in God's will (v21), will be content (v22), and will not experience trouble (v23). Verse 24 is another warning about laziness. Correct a scoffer and he will not listen to you, but correct a wise person and he will learn from it (v25). Verse 26 shows the outcome for those who fail to discipline their children. Verse 27 is a warning for those who have stopped listening to wisdom. Those who are worthless witnesses (liars) will be judged and punished (v29).

COVER TO COVER CHALLENGE

Friday • Jeremiah 28-31

Last week in Jeremiah 27, Jeremiah used the symbol of the yoke to portray the coming domination of Babylon over the nations. Here in Jeremiah 28 Hananiah, a false prophet, will speak a different message than what Jeremiah has spoken. In verses 1-4 Hananiah claimed that God was going to break the yoke of the Babylonians, bring back the captives and the vessels, and bring Jehoiachin back from exile. Jeremiah answers in verses 5-9 with an appeal to past prophets and directions for how to tell a true prophet from a false one-their prophecy will come true. Hananiah responds by taking the yoke off Jeremiah and breaking it (v10-11). The Lord speaks to Jeremiah in verses 12-14 concerning the yoke. Now the people will suffer even more which is symbolized by the iron yoke. Hananiah in his false prophecy was teaching rebellion against the Lord. Because of his false message Hananiah would die within two months (v15-17).

In chapter 29 Jeremiah is going to send a letter to those who have been taken captive to Babylon (v1-3). In verses 4-9 Jeremiah tells the people who have been carried away that they should live normal lives while they are in Babylon so they would enjoy peace. He also warns them to beware of false prophets. Jeremiah also reminds them that the exile will be 70 years in length, but that God would not forget them. This gave them hope for the future (v10-14). Picking back up the theme of false prophets, Jeremiah tells the captives that their false prophecies will be shown as lies (v15-19). In verses 20-23 Jeremiah warns them about Ahab and Zedekiah, who are both false prophets. Shemaiah sends a letter from Babylon to Zephaniah to silence Jeremiah in verses 24-28. Jeremiah sends a letter to the exiles telling them Shemaiah's fate for being a false prophet-he would have no descendants, and he would not live to see God blessing His people (v29-32).

Jeremiah 30-33 is called "The Book of Consolation". These prophecies were given during the final siege on Jerusalem (33:1) and tell the future of the nation of Israel. Israel will not perish but experience a permanent situation in the land, the Gentiles will come to know the Lord, a New Covenant is given, and a King from the line of David will rule over them. Many of these prophecies await a future day from our own time. In Jeremiah 30:1-3 Jeremiah is commanded to write these prophecies in a book. Verses 4-7 refer to the "time of Jacob's trouble" which is the future "Day of the Lord". It is future because the deliverance is both physical and spiritual which has not happened to this day. When this takes place Israel will not be enslaved by another nation ever again. They will be free when the Messiah (Jesus) reigns as king. They will enjoy peace, freedom, and they will be regathered to their land (v8-11). Although she will suffer judgment, God will heal their wounds and avenge them against their enemies (v12-17). In verses 18-22 the nation is shown to experience the blessings of God. In verses 23-24 Jeremiah does remind the people that it is through judgment God will redeem them.

Jeremiah 31:1-6 primarily deals with the restoration of the northern kingdom (Ephraim). The whole nation will eventually return from exile and none will be excluded (v7-14). Israel will be redeemed, they will rejoice, and they will be restored. The picture of Rachel weeping for those who are in exile (v15) is overcome by the Lord's promise in verses 16-17 that her children are coming back from exile. They have expressed sorrow for their sins, and they realize they need to repent in order to be restored (v18-22). Jeremiah once more foretells of the promising future of those returning from captivity which brings him joy (v23-26). The land will also be restored and renewed (v27-30). The New Covenant and its effects are the focus of the rest of the chapter. The main focus of verses 31-32 is that the previous covenant will be no more because it was broken by His people. The New Covenant will be one that cannot be broken. The people will enjoy the fullness of the Spirit (v33), fellowship with the Father (v34), forgiveness of sins (v34), faithfulness of God (v35—37), and a future glory (v38-40).

Saturday • 1 Timothy 4-6

In 1 Timothy 4:1-5 Paul again deals with false teachers. In verse 1 the term "expressly" means clearly. Those who depart will "give heed" to deceiving spirits and doctrines of demons. This means they will follow and give their allegiance to them. They are desensitized ("seared") to the truth and they are "branded" by how they live and teach (v2). This conveys that they have become hardened to the truth of the gospel. Verse 3 shows two areas where false teachers will deceive others. The first area of deception is seen in the forbidding of marriage. Marriage was the first institution that God blessed man with, so we know it is ordained by Him (Gen. 2:24). The second area of deception is abstaining from certain foods. The example of Peter in Acts 10:9-16, Paul's words in 1 Corinthians 10:30-31, and this passage show that all food is good.

In verses 6-11 Paul tells Timothy to remind the people of what he has been taught and of Paul instructions in this letter. The main theme of these verses is godliness. The word "nourish" means something necessary for growth. The only way to be like Christ is to grow in godliness (spiritual disciplines-prayer, bible study, worship, service, fellowship, evangelism). These things are profitable now, and for the life to come (v8, eternity). Timothy is instructed in verses 12-16 to be an example in every part of his life to those he is leading, but especially as it pertains to the Word of God (v13).

1 Timothy 5:1-2 is about relationships with men and women in the church and how Timothy is to treat them. Verses 3-8 deal with widows and how their own family has first priority in taking care of them (v4, 16), and then the church. Some of the characteristics Paul mentions of a true widow are is that she is in need, is all alone, is someone who trusts in God, and is someone who prays. Verse 6 is probably a reference to widows who have used immoral means to make a living. Paul also instructs Timothy on the guidelines for widowhood, and who is to be accepted and who is not (v9-16).

Verses 17-25 may refer to the selection of elders in the church. It probably includes those who are pastors, deacons, and any other leadership role in the church. These verses teach us that those who preach or teach are worthy of double honor if they rule well (v17-18). They also discuss accusations made against an elder (v19), those who are practicing sin (v20), favoritism (v21), making someone an elder before they are ready (v22), and staying pure (v22). Verses 24-25 concern judgment based upon someone's fruit, whether it be sinful (v24) or good (v25).

1 Timothy 6:1-2 is about the relationship between a servant and their master. Paul again returns to the topic of false teachers in verses 3-5. In verse 4 the word "obsessed" means to be sick, or to become diseased. If allowed in the church, false teachers would cause havoc through their teaching and behavior. The term "destitute" can mean someone who knew the truth but has rejected it (v5). Verses 6-7 may function as a deterrent for Timothy to not follow the way of false teachers. Pastors, evangelists, and preachers are not to use their ministry for the sake of getting rich. Their sole desire for preaching should be for the glory of God, not to seek glory for themselves. The false teachers (or anyone) who desire to be rich (love of money) only fall into a trap laid by themselves (v9). This pursuit will cause them to stray from the faith (v10), destroy their lives, and send them to hell (v9).

In verses 11-16 Paul encourages Timothy to run from sin (v11), pursue godliness (v11), fight the good fight of faith (stand up for what is right, v12), and to remind himself of who (Jesus) he is faithful to in ministry (v13-15). Paul instructs Timothy to warn the rich not to trust in their riches, but to trust in the Lord and perform good works (v17-20). Paul closes the letter with one last warning to guard himself (and the Word) and to avoid false teachers and their teaching (v20-21).

Cover to Cover Challenge

Week 38

Sunday • Psalm 113-115

Welcome to week 38 of the *Cover to Cover Challenge*! Continue to pray for our understanding of the Word of God, that the presence of the Holy Spirit will be made known, and for the Lord to be honored and glorified through the *Cover to Cover Challenge*. Psalm 116:1-2 says "I love the Lord, because He has heard my voice and my supplications. Because He has inclined His ear to me, therefore I will call upon Him as long as I live".

Psalm 113 is a psalm of praise. In verses 1-3, the psalmist wants all of those who know the Lord to praise Him forever. In praising the Lord's name they are to remember the works of the Lord. In verses 4-6 God is shown to meet the needs of His people. There is no God like the Lord. Verses 7-9 show God delivering those in need. They are no longer social outcasts, but in a seat of prominence.

Psalm 114 is also a psalm of praise. In verses 1-2 God called the nation out of Egypt to be His special people. The psalmist calls on nature as a witness that God had chosen them as His own special people and to make them a nation (v3-6). Verses 7-8 show that only the Lord is God, and He makes His presence known among the people.

Psalm 115 is a psalm of confidence in the Lord. In verses 1-3 the psalmist makes it clear that God deserves glory because of His mercy and truth. Furthermore God is in control of all things. In contrast, the idols the nations serve are worthless-just like those who worship them (v4-8). The nation of Israel is called to trust in the Lord (v9-11). He is the one who will be their help and their shield. He also blesses those who trust in Him with fruitfulness, even in the midst of adversity (v12-15). God sovereignly rules over every created thing (v16), and the people are called upon to praise the Lord (v17-18).

Monday • Numbers 22-25

Numbers 22-24 contains the story of Balaam who was hired by Balak the king of the Moabites to curse Israel after they had moved into his territory (22:1-21). Other Scriptures also do not portray Balaam in a positive way (Deut. 23:4-5; 2 Peter 2:15; Jude 11; Revelation 2:14). Balaam does agree to go, but he will only speak what the Lord tells him. So why did the Angel of the Lord (preincarnate Christ) appear to be stopping him from going in verses 22-35? The most probable answer is Balaam was not going to do what God had asked, and that is to speak only the words the Lord would give him. Balaam was going to Balak to do what he asked because he was greedy for money (Jude 11). You will also notice as the story begins everything will happen in sets of three's. The donkey avoids the Angel of the Lord three times, Balaam strikes the donkey three times, there are three sets of sacrifices, and three meetings with God. Each of Balaam's blessings confirm promises in the Abrahamic Covenant. In the first prophecy in 23:7-10, the blessing is that the people will be multiplied as the dust of the earth. In the second prophecy in 23:18-24, the blessing is that with God by their side Israel will be mighty. In the third prophecy in 24:3-9 Israel will devour their enemies, inherit the land (Canaan), and those who bless them will be blessed and those who curse them will be cursed. In the fourth and final prophecy in 24:15-19, a king will come and defeat Israel's enemies. This prophecy is twofold. First it will apply to David and second it will apply to Jesus, who is the ultimate fulfillment of the prophecy. This prophecy also describes the future destruction of the leaders who are present: Amalek, Kain, Asshur, and Eber (24:20-24).

In Numbers 25:1-3 the women of Moab seduce the men of Israel to worship Baal. God commands the leaders to kill all of the men who have committed these horrible acts, which demonstrate how serious God takes sin (v4-5). Phinehas, the grandson of Aaron, kills Zimri the Israelite and Cozbi the Midianite for their sin against God. This also stops a plague, in which 24,000 lose their lives (v6-15). God orders Moses to attack the Midianites because they have led the Israelites into idolatry and immorality (v16-18). In Numbers 31:8, 16 it is shown that Balaam counseled the women to do this to Israel.

Tuesday • 1 Kings 9-13

After the dedication of the temple in chapter 8, God appears to Solomon a second time and answers his prayer in 1 Kings 9:1-3. This corresponds to 2 Chronicles 7 which has a longer and more detailed account. Verses 4-5 describe the responsibility of Solomon and each king thereafter to be obedient to the Lord. In verses 6-9 the consequences of disobedience by the king are outlined. Two catastrophic results come from disobedience. First, the people would go into exile and second, the temple would be destroyed. Verses 10-14 relate a business transaction between Solomon and Hiram of Tyre (2 Chronicles 8).Solomon expanded and rebuilt cities, which strengthened the nation in verses 15-24. Solomon also led the people in sacrificing to the Lord (v25), and continued to trade by sea with other nations (v26-28).

In 1 Kings 10:1-13 the queen of Sheba, known for its gold and spices, pays a visit to Solomon. Even she recognized the greatness and love of God toward His people and was specifically impressed by Solomon's great wisdom. In verses 14-29 Solomon's great wealth is described. It is mentioned many times in this chapter the wisdom which God gave Solomon and many came from afar to hear it.

1 Kings 11:1-13 shows the tragic downfall of Solomon's reign. In marrying many wives Solomon disobeyed the command of the Lord, which led to him worshiping the gods of his wives (Deut. 17:16-17; Ex. 34:12-17). Because Solomon did not keep the covenant God would take the kingdom out of his hands, but not in his lifetime. Another issue arose out of his disobedience-enemies. Hadad the Edomite (v14-22), Rezon of Damascus (v23-25), and Jeroboam (v26-40) all became a thorn in Solomon's side during the latter part of his reign. Through the prophet Ahijah, Jeroboam is told of the coming split of the kingdom and his reign over ten tribes of Israel, which would become the northern kingdom. Solomon dies after he has ruled over all of Israel 40 years (v41-43).

1 Kings 12:1-16 shows the revolt of the people under Rehoboam. This occurs after he refuses to lighten the burden of the people according to the advice given to him by the elders. After Adoram is stoned by the people, Rehoboam flees and Jeroboam is made king over the ten tribes of Israel (v17-20). Rehoboam is going to lead the tribe of Judah and Benjamin into battle against the other ten tribes but, Shemaiah warns them not to because what has happened is from the Lord (v21-24). In verses 25-33 Jeroboam builds two worship centers, one in Dan

and one in Bethel, each with a golden calf so the people will not travel to Jerusalem to worship. Because of this, many of the Levites return to Judah to worship (2 Chron. 11:13-17).

1 Kings 13 contains the story of the unnamed man of God who had come from Judah to warn Jeroboam of his false religion. The man of God prophesied that a man named Josiah would one day burn the bones of Jeroboam's priests on the altar (2 Kgs. 23:15-20). A sign was given assuring Jeroboam this would take place: the altar would be split apart and its ashes poured out. Jeroboam, in anger, pointed his hand at the prophet giving orders for him to be captured and instantly his hand became withered (v4-6). Instantly the altar was split in two, and the ashes were poured out. Jeroboam asks the man of God to pray for him to restore his withered hand, and he does. Jeroboam invites the man of God to his home, but he refuses because the Lord had given him specific instruction to not eat or drink and to not go back the way he came (v7-10). In verses 11-22 a prophet from Bethel catches up to the man of God and explains to him that an angel told him to come and dine with him and the man of God goes, disobeying God's known command to him. In verses 23-32, as soon as the man of God leaves he is killed by a lion and his body is brought back by the old prophet who mourns over him and buries him. None of these events affect Jeroboam. He continues to defy God, which will bring the northern kingdom to ruin (v33-34).

Wednesday • John 20-21

John 20:1-18 contains the story of the Resurrection. There are many proofs for the resurrection of Jesus. First would be the miraculous moving of the stone from the tomb. Second, each gospel, although written by different authors at different times, speaks of the tomb being empty. John offers the most convincing proof of this in verses 6-8. Third, is the appearance of Jesus to Mary Magdalene. Women were not viewed as credible witnesses in Jesus' day. Fourth, the appearances of Jesus included people hearing, seeing, and touching Jesus. Fifth, the disciples were transformed after they received the Holy Spirit at Pentecost. Sixth, the resurrection became the main theme of sermons that were preached. Seventh, there was never a body produced that would disprove the resurrection (Matt. 28:11). Eighth is the early church suffering persecution, but never denying the resurrection of Jesus. Ninth, is the conversion of Paul. Even skeptics accept that the conversion of Paul was miraculous.

Verses 19-23 are John's Great Commission statement (Matt. 28:16-20; Mark 16:14-18; Luke 24:46-49). In verses 24-29 Thomas receives proof from Jesus Himself that it is truly Him and resurrected. The blessing of verse 29 would apply to most Christians. Verses 30-31 are the purpose statement of John's gospel. It was written to prove that Jesus is the Son of God, and so that people would believe in Him.

In John 21:1-14 Jesus meets seven of the disciples on the Sea of Tiberias for breakfast. The scene in verses 5-14, with the fire of coals, is much like the scene where Peter denied Jesus earlier in John's gospel. This sets the stage for the restoration of Peter in verses 15-19. When Jesus asks Peter "Do you love Me more than these?" He is not asking Peter if he loves Jesus more than the disciples who are present, although they may be included. Jesus is asking Peter if he loves Him more than his boat, nets, fish, fishing business, and the other disciples. One thing that should be noted from each gospel is that the disciples never catch any fish without the help of Jesus (15:5). Most are intrigued by the specific number of fish and its significance. It is believed there were 153 different species of fish in the Sea of Tiberias. Jesus may have been teaching that now they would be fishers of men and would "catch" people, representing all different groups (Rev. 7:9-10). John 21:18 also foretells Peter's death by crucifixion ("stretch out your hands"). Peter would die some thirty years later at the hand of Nero being crucified upside down. Many people believed the apostle John would not die until Jesus returned. The closing verses of John refute that belief. Also, they serve as a reminder for each of us that we are responsible for how devoted we are to Christ (v20-25).

Thursday • Proverbs 20-21

Proverbs 20:1 teaches that it is wise to avoid strong drink because it can lead to deception. Only someone who is unwise would bring destruction on himself by provoking the king (v2). Verse 3 is saying that a wise man will avoid strife, but a fool will meddle and cause it. A lazy person will use any excuse to avoid work and will be in need (v4). Verse 5 teaches that a wise man will seek godly wisdom from others who have it. Verse 6 may be teaching that most people believe they are good from their own perspective, but very few are faithful. Verse 7 teaches that a godly wise man will have integrity, and it will be a blessing to his children. Verse 8 teaches that a righteous king sees the evil done in his kingdom and does away with it. No human can do verse 9. Only God can cleanse from sin. Verses 10 and 23 refer to cheating in buying and selling. In verse 11 even a child is known by their works which reveal their character. God created the ear to hear His word, the eye to see His works (v12). Those who are lazy will find themselves in poverty, but those who awake to work will be satisfied (v13). Verse 14 is about being dishonest in buying an item. Verse 15 is teaching that those who speak wisdom are worth more than precious gems. Verse 16 teaches about taking collateral from someone before you lend to them because you never know the poor decisions they will make. Things gotten through deceit will end up causing more harm than good (v17). Verse 18 teaches that wise people seek the counsel of others before beginning something new. Verse 19 is a warning about those who gossip. If you reveal anything to them they will tell others. Verse 20 is a warning not to dishonor your father and mother. Verse 21 is teaching that wealth gotten through dishonest ways will eventually be a curse and not a blessing. Verse 22 is a warning not to repay someone when they have caused you harm, but to wait on the Lord. Verse 24 is teaching that a man must follow God to understand where he is going. Verse 25 involves making a vow to the Lord to give something and not give it. A wise king will deal justly with the wicked and destroy them (v26). It is the spirit of man that the Holy Spirit uses to search his heart (v27). The king must reign in mercy and truth for his throne to be secure (v28). Being strong is the main attribute of the young, while wisdom is for those who are mature (v29). Physical discipline can keep someone from evil (v30).

Proverbs 21:1 teaches that the King's heart is in the hand of the Lord to do as He wishes. Verse 2 teaches that God is the one who knows the motive of a person's heart. Verse 3 teaches that being just and making right decisions is better than sacrifice. A proud look and heart and the deeds of the wicked are all sin (v4). Verse 5 is teaching that being hard working and diligent will cause a person to prosper. A person who gets rich by lying will not be satisfied (v6). When the wicked rob someone they are destroying themselves (v7). In verse 8 the guilty walks in perversity, but the pure person walks in purity. Verses 9 and 19 are similar. A man would be happier living on his roof or in the desert than to live with a nagging wife. The wicked man loves to do evil, even to his neighbor (v10). Someone who is a scorner will not learn from his punishment, but the wise will (v11). Verse 12 teaches that a wise man will not follow the ways of the wicked. Retribution is the theme of verse 13. Those who do not help the poor will not be helped themselves. Verse 14 is teaching the wise use of gifts. In verse 15 justice is performed by those who are just, but those who love injustice will be destroyed. A person who does not listen to wisdom will find himself among the dead (v16). In verse 17 being self-indulging is warned against because it leads to poverty. In times of judgment God often destroys the wicked and delivers the righteous (v18). Verse 20 concerns the wise use of money. Some store it up while others spend it quickly. The person who lives a righteous life, showing mercy to others, will have life, righteousness, and honor for himself (v21). Verse 22 is teaching that wisdom is better than having physical strength. Verse 23 is another warning about wise use of the tongue. Verse 24 shows how to identify a scorner. Verses 25-26 go together and warn against laziness. The wicked person's sacrifice is an abomination to the Lord because it is brought with the wrong motive (v27). A false witness will perish, but a true witness will only speak what he has heard (v28). Verse 29 teaches that the wicked will follow their own way. Verse 30 teaches that nothing will work if it is against God and His will. Verse 31 teaches not to rely on human strength but upon God.

Friday • Jeremiah 32-36

In Jeremiah 32 the context is the final siege on Jerusalem by the Babylonians. Zedekiah throws Jeremiah in prison because he believes Jeremiah is going to defect to the Babylonians (v1-5, 37:11-16). While in prison Jeremiah purchases a field at the Lord's command (v6-8). The purchase of the land was meant to be an encouragement for the people regarding their future return despite their current situation. Jeremiah purchasing the land is the only biblical account of a purchase of this type (v9-15). Jeremiah prays in verses 16-25 and recites God's goodness to the people of Israel, despite their continual disobedience to Him. God answers Jeremiah's prayer in verses 26-35, using the same language Jeremiah used in his prayer. In this prayer He tells Jeremiah that the people's sin caused Him to judge His people. The Lord also promises a regathering of the people and their restoration, highlighted by the New Covenant He is making with the people (v36-44).

Jeremiah 33 closes the "Book of Consolation". The main theme of this chapter is the restoration of Jerusalem. Jeremiah is still in prison and receives another word from the Lord (v1-3). What God is about to reveal to Jeremiah is unknowable to humans unless God reveals it to them. Jerusalem's fall is certain and any effort to stop it will fail, Jerusalem is to be destroyed (v4-5). The Lord promises that one day in the future they will once again prosper (v6-13). The promises in verses 14-22 are ultimately fulfilled in Christ; because it is only through Him righteousness can become reality. He also assures them that the covenant He has made with them cannot be broken (v23-26).

In Jeremiah 34:1-7, Zedekiah is warned to surrender to the king of Babylon because fighting against them would not change anything. He would meet Nebuchadnezzar face to face, be blinded, taken to Babylon, and die there (52:11; Ez. 12:13). In verses 8-11 Zedekiah makes a covenant with the people to set the Hebrew slaves free which was to be done every 7th year (Ex. 21:1-11). They did set them free, but ordered them to return to being slaves. In verses 12-16 God reminds them of their former bondage to Egypt and how their ancestors had disobeyed in this area. Because they have done this the Lord will set them free from His protective hand (v17-22).

The faithfulness of the Rechabites in Jeremiah 35 is to serve as a lesson to the people of Judah about obeying the commands of the Lord. This episode happened during the time of Jehoiakim, about 15-20 years before the siege on Jerusalem. These are the lessons taught from the story. First, the Recahbites obeyed Jonadab, while Judah would not obey God. Second, Jonadab only gave his instructions once, while God repeatedly reminded the Israelites and they still disobeyed. Third, their loyalty to Jonadab's command is rewarded while the people of Judah will be punished for their disobedience.

In Jeremiah 36:1-8 Jeremiah is told to write down the messages he has received from the Lord. The purpose of this is so all the people could hear and hopefully repent. Jeremiah cannot go to the temple, so Baruch will go and read them to the people (v9-10), the officials (v11-19), and to Jehoiakim (v20-26). Jehoiakim was not interested, but cut the Word and tossed it into the fire. In verses 27-28, 32 Jeremiah is told to rewrite the scroll. Jehoiakim is prophesied to go into exile and die, and not one of his descendants will sit on the throne (v29-31).

Saturday • Titus

1 &2 Timothy, along with Titus, make up what are called the Pastoral Epistles. These were written by Paul, probably between 63-66 AD, to Timothy and Titus as they led the churches in Ephesus and Crete. Titus is the shortest of the Pastoral Epistles. Titus went with Paul to Galatia and took up the offering for the Judean church in 2 Corinthians 7-8. Titus was in Crete which was an established church, while Timothy was in Ephesus at a new church. Paul writes to Titus to encourage him, to organize the church, to address false teachers, and to address their conduct.

After Paul's greeting in verses 1-4, he instructs Titus on how to discern who should serve as elders and overseers in the church (v5-9).The words "set in order" actually mean to straighten out. While the church in Crete had been in existence longer than Ephesus, both churches needed to appoint godly leaders to the church. Most of these characteristics are the same as 1 Timothy 3. In verse 9 there are further qualifications as they pertain to the Word of God. First, the leader must hold firmly to the Word of God. He must clearly and with conviction stay true to the Word of God. Second, the leader must be able to use the Word of God to encourage others. This would involve encouraging believers who are weak, encouraging believers to minister, and encouraging believers to practice spiritual disciplines. Third, the leader must be able to use the Word of God to convict. In the last part of this verse it means to counter those who are preaching false doctrine. Each leader must be able to refute those who are preaching another doctrine, another Jesus, or from another spirit (2 Cor. 11:4).

In verses 10-16 Paul addresses false teachers. From verse 10 we can see that the false teachers were probably Judaizers. Judaizers taught a works based salvation in addition to believing in Christ. These false teachers share three qualities. They are insubordinate (rebellious), they are idle talkers (empty headed), and they are deceivers (v10). Paul tells Titus that these false teachers must be stopped from teaching their false doctrine (v11). The Cretans (Titus is in Crete) had a reputation of being liars, evil, and lazy just like those in Corinth had a reputation of being immoral (v12-13). The false teachers taught Jewish myths and the words of men, not the true Word of God (v14). Teaching false doctrine had caused them to ruin others, and ruined themselves in the process (v15). While these false teachers professed to know Christ, it can be seen through their deeds they did not (v16). They are abominable (disgusting), disobedient, and disqualified (useless, no value).

In Titus 2:1 Paul instructs Titus to speak sound (healthy) doctrine, which would combat the false teachers. Verses 2-10 deal with relationships within the church. Each group is to have these characteristics "so the Word of God will not be blasphemed" (v5). In verse 2 the older men are to be sober (knowing what has real value), reverent (honorable), temperate (self-control), sound in faith (healthy faith), love, and patience (perseverance). In verse 3 the older women are to be reverent in behavior (honorable), not slanderers (use evil words), not given to much wine, and teachers of good (excellent) things. The older women are to admonish (train) the younger women to love their husbands and children, to be discreet (sound judgment), to be chaste (moral purity), to be homemakers, to be good (kindness), and to be obedient to their husbands (v4-5). In verses 6-8 the older men and Titus are to teach the younger men to be sober-minded (sound judgment) and how to be a good example. As it pertains to doctrine they are to have integrity (live according to Word), reverence (serious, mature), incorruptibility (dignified), and sound speech (healthy, worthy).

In verses 11-13 Paul teaches that we are saved from the penalty of sin, saved from the power of sin, and one day we will be saved from the presence of sin at the coming of Christ. Knowing that Christ could return at any moment should produce in us a desire to live a holy life. Verses 14-15 give the foundation of living the Christian life: Jesus sacrificed Himself to redeem us from sin.

Titus 3 may function to explain the behavior of believers to those who are not a part of the church (unsaved). The type of people believers should be in verses 1-2 is contrasted with who they once were in verse 3. Lost people do not know what it is like to be saved, but saved people know what it is like to be lost. In verses 4-8 Paul explains how we were changed: God provided salvation for us in Jesus Christ. This to be the motivation for living the Christian life in front of others so that they too can be saved. Good works are profitable for all men because the good works you perform reap benefits for you and others may see them and be saved.

In verses 9-11 Paul instructs Titus to address false teaching by rejecting the one speaking it. The word "warped" means to become perverted from another source (which would be Satan). Paul closes the letter with further instructions for the church. In verse 14 he urges Titus to help the church maintain (be devoted to) good works, to meet urgent (necessary) needs, and not be unfruitful (useless), and their teaching (v20-21).

Cover to Cover Challenge

Week 39

Sunday • Psalm 116-118

Welcome to week 39 of the *Cover to Cover Challenge*! I pray that the Holy Spirit is teaching you great and mighty things from the Word of God. There is nothing greater that any of us can do than to be in the Word of God, and allow the Lord to speak to us through it. Continue to pray for the Lord to use this for His glory, and to work in the lives of all those participating.

Psalm 116 is a psalm of thanksgiving. The psalmist is thanking God for delivering him from a terrible situation. In verses 1-2 the psalmist expresses his love for the Lord because it is the Lord who hears and answers prayer. Either death is near or his life feels like death, but it is the Lord who has delivered him from it. The psalmist offers his thanks to the Lord for the deliverance He provided (v3-7). Only God can deliver from death and tears (sorrow), and only God can keep someone from falling, and from being afflicted (v8-11). In response to God's deliverance, the psalmist will pay his vows to the Lord even though it is impossible to repay the Lord (v12-14). There may be times the Lord's deliverance of His servants is by the way of death, and even then they are precious in His sight (v15-16). The psalmist again offers his thanks to the Lord. He will continue to call on the Lord and pay his vows.

Psalm 117 is a psalm of praise and is the shortest psalm. This psalm calls on the Gentiles (nations) to praise the Lord for His mercy (loyal love) and truth (faithfulness) which endures forever.

Psalm 118 is a psalm of thanks to be sung by the community and by individuals. In verses 1-4 all people are called upon to give thanks to the Lord because "His mercy (loyal love) endures forever". In verses 5-21 the psalmist recounts God's goodness to him in a form of thanksgiving. In verses 6-7 the psalmist knows the Lord's presence is with him through all circumstances in life. He knew only to trust in the Lord (v8-9). Through all of his troubles and trials, the psalmist knew that it was the Lord who kept him from falling (v10-14). Because the Lord delivered him, all the people are called upon to rejoice (v15-16). The psalmist's life now will be dedicated to declaring how good God has been to him (v17-18). He declares that he will enter the presence of the Lord, praising Him because He answered his prayer (v19-21). Verses 22-26 are messianic and point toward Jesus. Verses 25-26 refer to Jesus' triumphal entry into Jerusalem ("save now"=Hosanna). The people demonstrate their thanks to the Lord by bringing sacrifices and praising the Lord (v27-29).

Monday • Numbers 26-29

In Numbers 26 preparations are made for entering the Promised Land. Moses and Eleazar are to take a census of the people 20 years old and up (v1-2). The census (v3-51) confirms God's promise in giving the land, confirms that the land is big enough for them, confirms they will have to fight for it, and confirms God's faithfulness to them. In total there are 601,730 men. In verses 52-56 the land is to be divided by lot. The Levites are numbered separately because they will not inherit land nor fight in the battles (v57-62). With the exception of Moses, Joshua, and Caleb none are left from the original census (v63-65).

Numbers 27:1-11 covers the laws of inheritance. The daughters of Zelophehad approach Moses because their father had no sons. They would be left without any inheritance and their father's name would not be remembered. Moses takes the case to the Lord, who allows the daughters to receive the inheritance (v5-8). Verses 9-11 contain the rules for the succession of the inheritance. In verses 12-23 the Lord commands Moses to go up on Mount Abarim to view the land He is giving to them. Moses requests that God place a new leader over them who will care for them and be their leader. Joshua is chosen by the Lord to be their new leader, and is commissioned before Eleazar and the children of Israel.

Numbers 28 & 29 concern the various offerings to be made to the Lord when they enter the land. The daily offering (v1-8), Sabbath offering (v9-10), New Moon offering (v11-15), Passover (v16-25), and the Feast of Weeks (v26-31) are discussed in chapter 28. Chapter 29 covers the offerings on the first day of the seventh month (v1-6), Day of Atonement (v7-11). Feast of Tabernacles (v12-38), and the eighth day offering (v35-38). All of this is done so there is not a time or season that is not in some way associated with worshiping the Lord. It encouraged the people to make worship a part of their daily lives, gave them opportunity to be obedient to the Lord, provided forgiveness of sins, and gave them days of rest to focus on the Lord.

Tuesday • 1 Kings 14-18

In 1 Kings 14:1-18 we see the fate of Jeroboam and his kingdom. After his son falls ill he sends his wife to Ahijah the prophet to see what will happen to the child (v1-4). God had already spoken to Ahijah and told him Jeroboam's wife would be coming (v5-6). In verses 7-16 Ahijah gives nothing but bad news concerning Jeroboam, his kingdom, and his child. Because of Jeroboam's sin and because he led the nation to sin, his dynasty will be cut off and one day all of Israel (northern kingdom) would be scattered. Added to all of this would be the death of their child. Ahijah's words came true in verses 17-18, and Jeroboam dies leaving his son Nadab to reign in his place (v19-20). Verses 21-31 concern Rehoboam and the southern kingdom of Judah. He also allowed paganism to be practiced in the land, and according to 2 Chronicles 12 he had stopped following the Lord. God allowed the Egyptians to overrun them and if not for the prophet Shemaiah and the repentance of Rehoboam, they may have been totally destroyed. His son Abijah (Abijam) will reign in his place.

In 1 Kings 15:1-8 Abijam becomes king of Judah, but reigns only 3 years. Although he was not faithful to the Lord, the Lord would remain faithful to the promises He made to David. During his reign there was continual war with the northern kingdom. Asa could be called the first "good" king to reign over Judah (v9-24). Asa removed the idols from the land, strengthened the military of Judah during his reign, and also removed Maachah from being queen. Asa's downfall would be making an alliance with Ben-Hadad of Syria after Baasha and the northern kingdom took the city of Ramah to cut off the trade routes. Ben-Hadad would attack the northern kingdom so Judah could retake Ramah. Verses 25-32 explain how Baasha came to the throne by murdering

Nadab (Jeroboam's son) and how he killed every descendent of Jeroboam, fulfilling Ahijah's prophecy (14:9-16). Baasha would reign 24 years, doing evil in the sight of the Lord (16:1-7). Baasha and his descendants would also suffer the same fate as Jeroboam, as told by Jehu the prophet. Baasha's son Elah would reign in his place for 2 years until Zimri murdered him and killed all of his descendants (v8-14). Zimri would reign only 7 days after the people found out he had killed Elah (v15-20). Omri would be made king of Israel, and Zimri burned the king of Tirzah's house down upon himself and died. After a 4 year struggle with Tibni, Omri becomes the sole king of Israel for 12 years (v21-28). He is responsible for building Samaria as the new capital of the northern kingdom, but spiritually he was worse than any king before him. Ahab the son of Omri becomes king over Israel and reigns 22 years (v29-34). His wife Jezebel led him into worshiping Baal. He also built a temple for Baal in Samaria, and led the people into worshiping it. He also instructed Hiel to rebuild Jericho, which was cursed by Joshua (Joshua 6:26).

1 Kings 17 introduces us to Elijah the prophet who was sent to the northern kingdom to speak against Ahab and the people of Israel. Elijah announces a drought on the land because of Ahab and his leadership (v1-7,19). God sends Elijah away because his absence would be a testimony to the people of God's displeasure. God would take care of Elijah through the drought in miraculous ways (ravens fed him). In verses 8-16 Elijah is sent to Zarephath of Sidon (Jezebel's home and Gentile), to the home of a widow with a son. God would honor her faith with the miracle of the flour and oil, and also provide for Elijah. In verses 17-24 the widow's son becomes ill and dies. Through Elijah's prayer the Lord brings the boy back to life.

In 1 Kings 18:1-15 Elijah has been in Zarephath for 3 years, and is told by the Lord to go to Ahab and tell him rain is coming. Obadiah and Ahab together go on a search to find food for the animals. Along the way Elijah meets Obadiah and requests that he tell Ahab he wants to meet him. This conversation takes place in verses 17-19. Ahab believes the drought is because of Elijah believing he has angered Baal, who has withheld the rain (v17). Elijah wants the people of Israel gathered together, along with the prophets of Baal on Mount Carmel. Mount Carmel is believed to have been a stronghold of Baal. Today it is known as El Muhraka which means "place of burning". In verses 20-24 Elijah confronts the people to choose between the Lord and Baal, but the people do not answer. Elijah proposes a contest between himself and the prophets of Baal to see who the true God is by building an altar and performing a sacrifice. In verses 25-29 the prophets of Baal have the first opportunity, but nothing happens. In verses 30-35 Elijah rebuilds the altar, digs a trench around it, and pours water on it three times. In verses 36-37 Elijah prays for God to make Himself known, that the people would know Him, and repent. In verses 38-39 God consumes the sacrifice, and the people respond with worship of God. The prophets of Baal are taken and executed (v40). Elijah persistently prays for rain and it does come (v41-46).

Wednesday • Acts 1-2

Luke is the only writer of the New Testament that is a Gentile. Luke is the author of the gospel that bears his name, and also the book of Acts. Both of these books mention Theophilus ("Lover of God") as being the beneficiary of Luke's work. Luke wrote his gospel in the early 60's AD, and formed it from the accounts of eyewitnesses during his investigation of Jesus' ministry (Luke 1:1-4; Acts 1:1-3). This same description will fit the book of Acts. In the book of Acts there will be times Luke uses the terms "we" or "us" because he is present. Historians also agree that the gospel of Luke and the book of Acts may have circulated together because they share the same author. Acts shows the history of the early church, the coming of the Holy Spirit, the progress of the gospel, highlights of Peter and Paul's ministries, and opposition to the church. Its main focus is the gospel message and the mission Jesus relates to the disciples and to us today (Acts 1:8).

In Acts 1:1-3 Luke refers to his previous work (gospel of Luke), Jesus' ascension, the fact that Jesus was resurrected, and that He talked with the disciples for 40 days. In verses 4-8 the disciples are still looking for Jesus to set up His kingdom in that present time. It is here that Jesus reminds them of the coming of the Holy Spirit and gives them the mission to spread the gospel throughout the world. Acts 1:8 is the purpose statement for the book and also serves as an outline of the spread of the gospel: first to Jerusalem (ch.1-7), then Samaria (ch.8-12), and then to the ends of the earth (ch.13-28). Jesus ascends back to heaven in verses 9-11, and the angels remind them that He is coming again the same way He left (Zech. 14:4). Verses 12-14 show the unity of the early band of believers as they all gathered together to pray. This group included Mary the mother of Jesus and His brothers.

In verses 15-26 Matthias is chosen by lot to replace Judas (Prov. 16:33). Notice that it is Peter who is leading the group (v15). The main purpose of this meeting was to choose a replacement for Judas. Psalm 69:25 is quoted in reference to Judas' betrayal and Psalm 109:8 shows the necessity of someone filling his place. In verses 21-22 one of the requirements for replacing Judas and becoming an apostle was being a witness to Jesus' ministry, especially the resurrection. After a prayer for divine intervention, lots are cast and Matthias is chosen to be one of the twelve apostles. According to 1 Chronicles 26:13 marked stones were placed in a jar and shaken out. Whichever stone fell out was seen to be determined by God.

Acts 2:1-4 records the coming of the promised Holy Spirit on the Day of Pentecost. The word "filled" means there would be more "fillings" to come, as you will see throughout Acts. Verses 5-13 record the confusion of the crowd, but also the miracle of each person hearing the gospel in their own language. The list of nations represents people from all over the known world who can carry the gospel back to their people. Verses 14-35 contain the first sermon preached by Peter. The words "raised his voice" show that Peter's sermon was the words of a man filled with the Holy Spirit (v14). Peter's sermon announces that the age of fulfillment had arrived (v14-21; Joel 2:28-32). This shows that the Messianic age was at hand, and that even at this early time humanity was living in the last days of history. Peter would use the closing verse of the passage from Joel (verse 21 here) to preach about how someone can be saved. Next, Peter gives an account of the ministry, death, and resurrection of Jesus (v22-24, 29-33). This is the main point of Peter's sermon. He is pointing people to Christ for salvation and the death, burial, and resurrection is key. Peter also cites the Old Testament scriptures which Jesus fulfilled (v25-28, 34-35). After the sermon Peter gives a call to repent (v36-39). The promise of salvation is for them, their children, the Gentiles, and all people whom God calls.

In verses 40-47 the growth of the early church is recorded along with their daily practices. In verse 42 "continued steadfastly" means to remain and never leave. The apostles' doctrine (teaching) consisted of the instructions that they received from Jesus and later revelation from Him. Fellowship means "oneness": they shared the same purpose, heart, and mind. Breaking of bread is the Lord's Supper, and they prayed for each other and those who would believe. Three characteristics comprised the early church. First, they were united (v44), they praised God (v47), and they multiplied (v47). Verses 40-47 show ten signs of a healthy church. Verse 42 contains four practices of the early church: apostles doctrine (1), fellowship (2), breaking of bread (3), and prayer (4). Verse 43 has two more characteristics: they lived in fear and awe (5) and they were Spirit-filled (6). Verse 45 shows unity (7) and verse 46 shows the priority they placed in being together (8). Verse 47 shows that they did worship (9) and they were evangelistic (10).

Thursday • Proverbs 22

Proverbs 22:1 is teaching that it is better to have a good reputation than to be rich. Verse 2 is teaching that all men are created equal before God. In verse 3 the wise (prudent) man sees evil coming and stays away from it. Verse 4 teaches that those who are humble and fear the Lord are rewarded. Verse 5 serves as a warning not to go the way of the perverse man. Verse 6 is an encouragement to raise a child the right way because it will always be with them. Verse 7 serves as a warning not to owe anyone money. Verse 8 teaches that those who live lives of sin will reap trouble. Verse 9 teaches that those who help the poor will be blessed themselves. Verse 10 teaches that in order to avoid contention, strife, and reproach one is to stay clear and avoid the scoffer. Verse 11 can be exemplified by people such as Joseph and Daniel who found favor in foreign lands because of their pure hearts. Verse 12 is teaching that God places high value on the truth. Verse 13 is the lame excuse of a lazy man to avoid work. Those who give in to the immoral woman will suffer consequences (v14). Verse 15 is teaching the discipline of children in order to correct them. Those who take advantage of the poor in order to get rich and those who give to the rich to get richer will one day be poor (v16).

Most believe verses 17-21 are an introduction to a new section of proverbs not written by Solomon. This section ends at the end of chapter 24. In verses 17-21 there is an encouragement to heed the writer's words of wisdom, because they have come from God. Verses 22-23 are a warning not to oppress or afflict the poor, because it is the Lord who will fight for them. Verses 24-25 teach us to avoid those who are angry and furious because we will fall into a trap and be like them. Verses 26-27 are a warning not to be responsible for others debts because it may leave you in poverty. Removing ancient landmarks refers to the stealing of someone's property (v28). Verse 29 teaches that a man who is good at what he does will be recognized.

Friday • Jeremiah 37-43

In Jeremiah 37:1-5, Zedekiah breaks his pledge to Babylon and the Egyptians come to their aid. Zedekiah also asks Jeremiah to pray, hoping the Lord has changed His mind and the Babylonian invasion will not happen. Soon after this the Babylonians would return and destroy Jerusalem. Jeremiah told Zedekiah that the Lord has not changed His mind, but tells him the Babylonians were still coming (v6-10). In verses 11-21 Jeremiah is arrested and charged with treason when he went to take care of the property he had bought. Zedekiah again seeks out Jeremiah. The message for the king from God has not changed, although Zedekiah did reverse the charge of treason.

In Jeremiah 38:1-4, Jeremiah is charged with treason and weakening the morale of the troops by some high ranking officials. They throw Jeremiah into the dungeon (mire, full of waste), which would result in his death if left there. Ebed-Melech told Zedekiah what was done to Jeremiah, and he rescues him from the dungeon (v9-13). Verses 14-28 record the last meeting between Zedekiah and Jeremiah. Zedekiah hears the same message he has all along: surrender and live or resist and suffer. Zedekiah's decision would affect not only himself, but his family, and Judah.

Jeremiah 39:1-3 records the fall of Jerusalem after the final siege, which lasted 18 months. Zedekiah's fate because of his decisions is recorded in verses 4-8. The Babylonians kill Zedekiah's sons and noblemen, burn down his houses, and put out his eyes as they carry him away to Babylon. The rest of the people were also carried away to Babylon, leaving only the poorest behind (v9-10). Jeremiah is released by the Babylonians, and Gedaliah is appointed governor of Judah (v11-14). Ebed-Melech is rewarded for rescuing Jeremiah and for trusting in the Lord.

In Jeremiah 40:1-6, after his release, Jeremiah is given a choice to go to Babylon or to remain with Gedaliah. Notice the words of Nebuzaradan in verses 2-3. It is the words Jeremiah has spoken all along that would take place. After hearing of Gedaliah being made governor, many of the Jews who had fled return to Judah (v7-12). Gedaliah was doing what he could to lead the people left behind to a normal way of life. But, some believed Gedaliah to be a traitor of the people. In verses 13-16 Gedaliah is warned that a man named Ishmael (who is from David's line) has been sent by Baalis king of Ammon to assassinate him. Johanan offers to take the life of Ishmael, but Gedaliah warns him not to.

In the opening verses (v1-3) of Jeremiah 41, Gedaliah is assassinated by Ishmael after he only pretended to be friends with them. In verses 4-10 Ishmael also massacres some pilgrims who had come to bring offerings to the now destroyed temple. Putting them in the cistern would have polluted the water supply in Mizpah. Ishmael will carry the remnant of the people who are left to Ammon in order to evade punishment, to find help from Baalis who was behind the plot, and possibly to sell them to the Ammonites. Johanan overtakes Ishmael before he makes it too far, and the remnant of people return with him to the land (v11-15). Johanan is now determined to flee to Egypt for safety from the Babylonians (v16-18).

In Jeremiah 42:1-6 Johanan and the remnant of people go to Jeremiah so he can ask God whether or not they should go. It will be shown later (v17) that they only wanted confirmation for their decision to go to Egypt and had no intention of ever listening to the Lord. After a period of ten days, Jeremiah receives an answer from the Lord (v7-22). The Lord wants them to stay in the land of Judah and live, and not go to Egypt. They would not be safe in Egypt. If they disobey the Lord and go, He would bring on them the very disasters they are fleeing from.

In Jeremiah 43:1-7 Johanan and all the other prideful men are determined to go to Egypt. They accuse Jeremiah of lying to them, and Baruch of conspiring against them so the Babylonians can kill them or carry them away captive. What is ironic is that they flee to Egypt, which is the exact place God had set them free from 900 years earlier. God instructs Jeremiah to hide large stones in the mortar of the brick near Pharaoh's house because this would be the place Nebuchadnezzar would set up his throne (v8-13). God would punish the Egyptians for their idolatry, and Johanan and the remnant from Judah would suffer along with them.

Saturday • 2 Timothy 1-2

2 Timothy is the last of the Pastoral Epistles and the last letter written by Paul, probably in 65-67 AD. Paul is in prison, having been arrested during the time of Nero's persecution of Christians. In this letter Paul continues to encourage Timothy to remain faithful to his calling, to continue to preach sound doctrine, to avoid the errors of false doctrine/teachers, and to put faith in the Word of God and preach it.

In 2 Timothy 1:1-7 Paul instructs Timothy to continue to "stir up" (v6, keep the fire alive) the gifts God has given him. Timothy may have grown discouraged by his stay in Ephesus and the persecution from the false teachers. God did not give this "fear" (means to flee from battle) to Timothy; but has given him power (Eph. 1:18-20), love, and a sound mind (ability to know what is best). Paul assures Timothy not to be afraid of being persecuted for preaching the gospel because he was in prison for the same thing (v8-12). It is believed verses 9-10 may have been part of an early hymn sang by Christians. In verse 9, it is God who saved and called both Timothy and Paul as well as all believers. This calling is not because of anything believers have done but because it fulfills God's own purposes and grace. It is through the revealing of Jesus (first coming) that death has been destroyed and salvation has come through the gospel. (v10). It is because of this God had chosen Paul to be a preacher, an apostle, and a teacher. It is because of Paul's calling to preach and proclaim the gospel that he suffers. In spite of his sufferings, Paul knew with certainty Whom he had believed in (v12). The word "commit" means to make a deposit, and is referencing all that Paul had done for Christ.

In verses 13-18, Paul also encourages Timothy to remain loyal to the gospel ("that good thing" v14). The word "pattern" in verse 13 refers to Paul's teaching. Timothy is not only to teach it, but follow it for his own life. Paul was in the middle of a trial as people in Asia were turning away from him (v15). The words "turned away" means to desert. The fact that he mentions two by name probably means that they were the two most responsible for them deserting Paul. In verses 16-18 Paul praises Onesiphorus for his kindness and generosity in contrast with those from Asia who deserted him. Onesiphorus often refreshed (brace up) Paul and was not ashamed of his chain (v16).

In 2 Timothy 2:1-13 Paul continues to encourage Timothy. He encourages him to overcome, to be committed to Christ (v1), and to continue to teach others (v2). Paul cites three examples of enduring hard times: the soldier (v3-4), the athlete (v5), and the farmer (v6). Enduring the hard times is difficult, but it happens so that others can hear the gospel (v10). The example of the soldier will remind you of Ephesians 6:10-20. It is necessary that each Christian wear the armor of God because when hard times do come Satan will take advantage of them. The example of the athlete displays the sacrifice and discipline needed to overcome when hard times come. The example of the farmer is a reminder of when hard times come to be patient and also to work through those hard times.

In verses 14-26 Paul tells Timothy to remind the church not to argue over useless things because there is nothing good to gain from them and they lead to more ungodliness (v14,16). They also should give maximum effort ("be diligent") in proclaiming the truth in order to counter false teaching (v15). If they do not stand against the false teaching it will spread like "cancer" within the body of Christ (v17). The word used for "cancer" here means something that spreads rapidly and overtakes life. Paul shows that the false teachers have strayed (abandoned) from the truth and have overthrown (cause to fall) the faith of some (v18). Despite the false teachings and their teachers, the Lord knows those who belong to Him and those people should pursue holiness and not sin (v19). In verses 20-21 Paul encourages them to cleanse themselves and be vessels of honor who can be used of God. In verses 22-26 Paul explains to Timothy how people are to be vessels of honor. In verses 25-26 he is especially concerned with those who oppose the truth of the gospel. Paul wants the false doctrine corrected so they can repent and turn to God.

In verses 16-18 Paul also addresses false teaching and its teachers. These false teachers have "strayed" (abandoned) from the truth and cause others to be "overthrown" (destroyed). Most believe the "solid foundation" referenced in verse 19 is the church built upon Christ, and verses 20-21 refer to 1 Corinthians 3:10-15 and their works. Verses 22-24 contain characteristics to be both pursued and avoided in the lives of believers. The reason these are to be pursued and avoided is so those who are in "opposition" (unbelievers) may repent and turn to Christ for salvation.

Cover to Cover Challenge

Week 40

Sunday • Psalm 119:1-40

Welcome to week 40 of the *Cover to Cover Challenge*! Let us continue to pray that our eyes will be opened to the truth of God's Word, that the Holy Spirit will move in our lives, and for the Lord Jesus to get the glory and honor from it. Psalm 119:34 says "Give me understanding and I shall keep Your law; indeed, I shall observe it with my whole heart".

Psalm 119 is a wisdom psalm that concerns the Word of God. In fact many call it the "Word of God" psalm. It is also an acrostic psalm. Each set of 8 verses begins with a letter from the Hebrew alphabet (22), equaling 176 verses. Out of these 176 verses only 5 do not make reference to God's Word. There are also 8 different words used in the psalm for God's Word: (1) law (*torah*) means instruction or to point the way, (2) word (*dabar*) focuses on the spoken truth Of God's Word, (3) laws (*mishpatim*) is the verbal or written word that is to be obeyed, (4) statutes (*edoth*) is oftentimes a warning for those in covenant with Lord, (5) commands (*mitswah*) is a specific instruction from God's Word, (6) decrees (*huqqim*) means engraved and to be valid for all time, (7) precepts (*piqqudim*) is an expression of God's will to be obeyed by those in covenant with Him, (8) word (*imrah*) refers to the certainty of God's Word coming to pass. In verses 1-8 there is a double blessing for those who live according to the Word of God and for those who seek God with their whole heart. Those who are blessed do not practice sin, (v3) but praise the Lord (7). The set of verses in 9-16 are under the Hebrew consonant *beth* which means "house or home". You can see these verses show how to make your heart a home for God's Word (v11). Hiding God's Word in your heart will help you live a godly life (v9), keep you from wandering from God (v10), keep you open to receiving God's Word (v12), help you speak God's Word to others (v13), give you a heart that rejoices (v14), help you understand God's ways (v15), and find pleasure (v16). In verses 17-24 the psalmist wants to have close fellowship with the Lord through His Word. His desire is to be obedient by submitting himself to the Word of God. Meditating is the reading, reflecting, and responding to God's Word. In verses 25-32 the psalmist seeks God's deliverance through a trial or sickness (v25). He has opened his heart to the Lord and His Word (v26) and seeks to understand it (v27). It is through God's Word he can be revived and strengthened (v28). The psalmist wants his life to be anchored (cling) to the Word of God (v31) and he wants to be devoted to the Lord (v32). In verses 33-40 the psalmist wants to be taught and wants to understand God's Word so that he can live a godly life (v33-35, 40). He longs to walk down the path God desires for him, and not one of sin (v36-39).

Monday • Numbers 30-33

Numbers 30 concerns the taking of vows (oaths). An oath went above what was required by the law. Those who make vows are obligated to fulfill them (v1-2). A woman's father (v3-5) or husband (v6-16) can annul, or make void, any vow made by the woman. Also, see Matthew 5:33-37 for more on this issue.

In Numbers 31:1-6 the people of Israel are called to go to war with the Midianites because they have led some of Israel into idolatry and immorality (Num. 25). Verses 7-12 record the victory won over the Midianites as they killed every male, the five kings of Midian along with Balaam, captured the women and children, got the Midianite livestock, and burned their cities. In verses 13-24 Moses is angry that they returned with the Midianite women because they are the ones who led them to commit idolatry and immorality. The actions of these verses shows that God takes sin seriously and that God takes offense with those who try to hinder His people, His plan, and His purposes. In verses 25-47 God commands them to divide what was taken in the war among those who fought, and among the children of Israel. Not one of the Israelites are killed and they present to the Lord a memorial offering of thanksgiving in gold to celebrate (v48-54).

In Numbers 32:1-6 the tribes of Gad and Reuben want to live in the land just before entering the land of Canaan. Moses rejects their proposal in verses 6-15. Moses views this as being selfish, discouraging, unfaithful to God's plan, and sees them as following in the footsteps of their ancestors. In verses 16-19 the two tribes add to their request. Now they will help them fight and receive their inheritance in the land of Canaan and then return to the land they seek. Moses agrees with this plan in verses 20-27, noting that if they disobey they will be sinning against God. Moses informs the other leaders in verses 28-30 of the plan to give the tribes of Gad and Reuben the land after they have fought alongside of them. He also makes plans to give them land in Canaan if they disobey their word. Moses gives Gad, Reuben, and half tribe of Manasseh the land of the Transjordan (v31-41).

Numbers 33:1-4 would serve as a review of the goodness of God and how He delivered them time and again during their wanderings in the wilderness. God commanded Moses to write these things down because the generation entering the land of Canaan would need to be reminded of these things. If God delivered them from Egypt He would surely deliver them as they enter the Promised Land. Verses 5-15 would cover the deliverance from Egypt and times of testing. Verses 16-36 would remind them of their grumbling and rejection of God's will. Verses 37-49 would be a reminder that even their leaders rebelled against God. In verses 50-56 God commands Moses for them to take the land and destroy them and their false gods, and if they did not they would lead them astray from God. It is evident from these verses that God desired for them to be separated from the world.

Tuesday • 1 Kings 19-22

After the victory on Mount Carmel in 1 Kings 18, things take a drastic turn for Elijah in chapter 19. Ahab tells Jezebel all the things that Elijah had done, and she basically threatens Elijah that within a day she would take his life (v1-3). Jezebel was no ordinary woman. She was evil to the core, and eventually would cause both the northern and southern kingdoms to fail spiritually and morally. Elijah went south to Beersheba, which was over 90 miles away (v4-9). He wanted to be alone and he wanted to die. Eventually he ends up after 40 days at Mount Sinai. The Hebrew actually says in verse 9 "the cave". Many believe Elijah may have been in the cleft of the rock where God revealed Himself to Moses (Ex. 33:21-23). God reveals Himself to Elijah there as well (v9-18). God gives Elijah three tasks to perform: (1) he was to anoint Hazael a king of Syria, (2) Jehu was to be anointed king of Israel; (3) he was to commission Elisha as his successor. In verses 19-21 Elijah throws his mantle on Elisha which symbolizes his call to be a prophet. Elisha does have a final meal with his family, using his own plowing equipment to cook the meat. This shows that Elisha is leaving his old life behind and will now serve as God's prophet.

1 Kings 20 records the battle between Ahab and Ben-Hadad king of Syria. Coming against a weakened Israel; Ben-Hadad demands to have Ahab's silver, gold, wives, and children (v1-6). After Ahab agrees, Ben-Hadad then asks to have anything he finds of value in the Ahab's palace. Ahab refuses this demand and Ben-Hadad threatens to destroy Israel (v7-12). A prophet then tells Ahab that if he would send the leaders of the provinces to lead the attack they would win the victory (v13-14). Ahab listens to the prophet and they do defeat the Syrian army easily (v15-21). The prophet returns and warns Ahab to strengthen his army because the Syrians would be returning (v22-25). Israel's army wins the victory once again over the Syrians, just as God had promised (v26-31). This leads the Syrians to approach Ahab to have mercy on them, and Ahab makes a treaty with them (v32-34). Ahab did this because of the growing Assyrian threat which also shows he still trusted in men, rather than trusting in God. By another prophet's symbolic actions, Ahab is told that he will pay with his own life for making a treaty with Ben-Hadad because God had appointed him for destruction (v35-43).

In 1 Kings 21:1-5 Ahab desires to have Naboth's vineyard that is located close to the king's palace. Naboth declines to let Ahab have or to buy the field (Lev. 25:23-28). Jezebel questions Ahab as to why he is sad and he tells her of Naboth's refusal to let him have the vineyard (v6-8). She then devises a wicked plan to get the vineyard for Ahab. The proclaimed fast would have been one for the people's sin and to avoid the judgment of God (v9-10). There they would accuse Naboth of blasphemy against God and the king, which was punishable by death (Deut. 13:10-11, 17:5). In verses 11-16 the conspiracy is carried out and Ahab immediately takes possession of the property. 2 Kings 9:26 also says that Naboth's sons were killed so there would be no claim on the land. Elijah confronts Ahab and pronounces God's judgment on him, Jezebel, and his kingdom (v17-24). Verses 25-26 testify that Ahab was the most wicked of all the Israelite kings. Ahab does humble himself in verses 27-29 so God will delay the judgment on his kingdom. Even though Ahab humbles himself here, there is no proof it was true repentance because he still continued in his idolatrous ways.

In 1 Kings 22:1-5 Ahab summons Jehoshaphat (his brother-in-law) king of Judah to join him in battle to retake Ramoth Gilead. Jehoshaphat agrees, but wants to hear what the Lord says about going into battle. In verses 6-14 Ahab calls 400 of his own prophets, who all agree that they should go to battle. But, Jehoshaphat wants to hear from a prophet of the Lord so they send for Micaiah whom Ahab hates. Micaiah, speaking true words from the Lord, gives them two visions (v15-23). The first shows Israel as scattered sheep with no shepherd. The second shows a scene from heaven where a lying spirit is sent to the prophets of Ahab to get him to go to battle and die. Micaiah's words get him placed in prison (v26-28). Despite the warning, Jehoshaphat (who nearly dies) goes to war with Ahab (v29-33). Ahab disguises himself but is killed in battle, fulfilling Micaiah's prophecy. Just as Elijah had predicted earlier, the dogs do lick up Ahab's blood (v37-40). Verses 41-50 briefly cover the reign of Jehoshaphat, which is covered in more detail in 2 Chronicles 17-21. Jehoshaphat was a good king and his son Jehoram married Ahab's daughter Athaliah. Ahaziah, Ahab's son, reigns in Israel and just like his father did evil in the sight of the Lord.

Wednesday • Acts 3-4

In Acts 3-5 the persecution of the church will grow worse, beginning with the Jewish leaders. The miracle recorded in Acts 3:1-10 was accomplished through Peter and John and shows the continuing power of Jesus' ministry through His disciples. It is also similar to Jesus healing the paralytic in Luke 5:17-26. The "ninth hour" was 3 in the afternoon and was also the time of the Tamid which was one of the two sacrifices held daily in the temple. After being healed, the lame man would be allowed to worship God in the temple for the first time in his life (Isa. 35:6).

The miracle would also give Peter an opportunity to preach the gospel to the gathered crowd (v11-26). Peter's sermon describes Jesus as the Holy and Righteous One, the Prince of Life, the prophet like Moses, and His Servant Jesus. Peter's sermon is similar to the one at Pentecost. Peter announces that the age of fulfillment had arrived, gives an account of the ministry, death, and resurrection of Jesus, cites the Old Testament scriptures which Jesus fulfilled, and is a call to repent.

In Acts 4:1-4 the captain of the temple and the Sadducees are angry over the preaching of Peter and John so they arrest them. The captain of the temple would have been over the temple police and the Sadducees did not believe in any resurrection. Despite the continual persecution the church had grown to over 5,000 people. In verses 5-12 Peter gets another opportunity to preach the gospel, this time to the religious leaders of the day. The former high priest, the current high priest, and the future high priest are all going to hear the gospel (v6). The word "whole" in verse 10 means "healing" and "to save." The lame man was healed of his infirmity and also forgiven of his sin. Peter answers the question asked in verse 7 here in verse 12. There is no other name under heaven that saves. It is only through Jesus that someone can be born again (John 14:6).

In verses 13-22 Peter and John are told by the religious leaders to speak no more in the name of Jesus. Verses 19-20 show that along with Peter and John, but each Christian has a divine duty to speak and stand for the gospel. It also shows the sense of urgency that the early church had to proclaim it. Peter and John return to tell what had happened to them (v23-31). These verses show that persecution brought more unity to the church and they needed the Lord's strength to carry on their witness. The word for "Lord" in verse 24 is unique. It means "absolute master" and shows that the disciples knew that the Lord was in control of all things and that all things happen according to His plan (v28). The prayer for boldness includes three things: (1) freedom to speak, (2) courage in the face of threats, (3) and the ability to speak plainly. Their prayer was answered immediately as they each were filled with the Holy Spirit. Verses 32-36 show the unity of the church, the power they preached with, and the grace God bestowed on them. This passage also introduces us to Barnabas, who will play a significant role in the church.

Thursday • Proverbs 23

Proverbs 23:1-3 is a warning to have self-control, especially as it pertains to wants versus needs. In verses 4-5 there is a warning not to waste your life on pursuing riches because it can disappear. Life is to be lived in pursuit of God. The "miser" of verses 6-8 is someone who has an evil eye. The picture here is someone who gives gifts to people so they will be obligated to them in the future to do as they please. Verse 9 is a warning not to speak wisdom to those who will never listen to it. Verses 10-11 teach that it is not wise to take advantage of those who are less fortunate because it is God who fights for them. Verses 12-16 teach that if a man is to be wise he needs to open his heart and ears to wisdom (God's Word). This wisdom is to be given to our children, even in discipline. When our children receive this wisdom it brings joy. Verses 17-18 warn of going the way of sinners, but show that we should follow the ways of the Lord because there is a life to come. Verses 19-21 teach that by following wisdom (God) we will avoid the path of sinners. In verses 22-25 children should listen to the wisdom of their parents and hold on to it and never forget it. Verses 26-28 are encouragement to follow wisdom and not the unfaithful ways of the harlot. In verses 29-35 there is a warning to avoid drunkenness. It will only bring sorrow, contentions (fighting), complaints (loose tongue), and wounds (physical ailments).

Friday • Jeremiah 44-48

Chronologically, Jeremiah 44 is Jeremiah's last message. It is for those who went to Egypt despite the Lord's warning not to go. God was punishing the nation for their sins, but especially that of idolatry. Now they have went to Egypt and continued in it, so Jeremiah is rebuking them for it (v1-10). In verses 11-14 Jeremiah warns them of the coming punishment that will come upon them in Egypt. The people's response is that they will keep on in their idolatry (v15-19). The people are claiming that worshiping the queen of heaven brought them more benefits than God ever did. Jeremiah tells the people that God will punish them for their idolatry, and that they have given up the right to call upon God's name (v20-28). God gives them a sign to know that His words will come to pass-Egypt will fall to Babylon (v29-30).

Jeremiah 45 is a short message from God to Baruch for encouragement. Just like Jeremiah, Baruch was concerned over the sins of the people and the coming fall of the nation (v1-3). The Lord tells Baruch that He is concerned over the well-being of His people and that Baruch's life would be spared (v4-5).

With the exception of Jeremiah 52 the rest of the chapters will prophesy judgment on the nations and restoration for Israel. Jeremiah 46 is the prophecy of the defeat of Egypt by the Babylonians. Verses 1-6 show the Egyptians preparation for battle, and verses 7-12 show their defeat at the hands of the Babylonians. Egypt will never be the same after this defeat, even to this day. Nebuchadnezzar is shown in verses 13-19 as coming into Egypt and the Lord instructs them to prepare to go into captivity themselves. Egypt will be like fattened calves ready to slaughter when the Babylonians come to defeat them, but the Lord does promise they will be restored in the future (v20-26). Verses 27-28 are a promise to the Israelites who are in captivity that they will be restored.

Jeremiah 48 is the judgment on Moab. Verses 1-10 is a list of the many cities of Moab that will be destroyed because of their materialism (v7), idolatry (v7), treatment of Israel (v20-28), and pride (v29). The only way they would be able to escape judgment would be is if they could fly (v9). Chemosh, Moab's chief god, would not be able to help them escape this judgment (v11-19). Their destruction would be so thorough that the nations will mourn for them. Moab was known for its vineyards. The joy of harvesting the vineyards would be replaced by lamentations as the people mourned (v29-39). Even Jeremiah will mourn for Moab. Moab will be helpless as the Babylonians invade, and there will be no escape (v40-47).

Saturday • 2 Timothy 3-4

In 2 Timothy 3:1-9 Paul continues to warn Timothy of false teachers. False teachers will not only teach false doctrine, but will lead false lives. Some false teachers may not be recognizable by their words, but could be recognized by the life they live. In verse 1 Paul outlines the period of these false teachers and describes them as perilous times. The word "perilous" describes an infected wound. In verses 2-5 Paul warns him of their personality, and in verses 6-9 he warns Timothy of the pattern they follow. Most of the personality traits are easily understood but here is an explanation of some of the terms you read in the text. Boasting is claiming a greatness they do not possess (v2). The word used for "unholy" is used of someone who satisfies their desires no matter what they are (v2). The word used for "unforgiving" means refuse to change (v3). It is someone determined to have their own way regardless of the consequences, even if it destroys them. The word "brutal" means someone who attacks and is used to describe the attack of a wild beast on its prey. The word "headstrong" means someone who is careless (v4). The word "haughty" means conceited. This is someone who cannot see outside the world they live in. One of the most dangerous things about these false teachers is that they "have a form of godliness" (v5). They will look godly and may even sound godly, but they are not. Paul cautions Timothy and tells him to "turn away" from them (v5). The words "turn away" is spoken in the middle voice in Greek and means make yourself turn away.

In verse 8 Paul gives three descriptions of these false teachers. First, they resist the truth. These false teachers will not place themselves under the authority of the truth of the gospel. Second, they are men of corrupt minds. The word used here is also used in Romans 1 and speaks of having a depraved mind. It is a mind that is useless and if it remains in that condition is unalterable. Third, they are disapproved concerning the faith. It means they do not pass the test and they are disqualified, being unfit for usefulness.

Paul again encourages and comforts Timothy in verses 10-15, but also warns that persecutions will come to all of those who follow Christ, especially from false teachers. To combat false teaching Timothy would not only need to live a godly life, but he would need to know God's Word (v16). All scripture is inspired (breathed out) by God. God's Word is profitable, or in other words it can meet all the needs of God's people. It is good for doctrine (teaching, instruction), reproof (rebuke or convict), correction (restoration), and instruction in righteousness (growth in the Christian). Knowing God's Word will result in each believer being complete (capable, literally "in good shape") for anything they are called to do.

In 2 Timothy 4 Paul reminds Timothy of his service to the church in verses 1-2 and 5. Timothy is to take his call seriously and be prepared to preach the truth of God's Word. Paul not only reminds Timothy of his service to the church, but also of the season he is living in verses 3-4. They were living in a time (just like us) where people did not want to hear God's Word. Paul gives Timothy four things that should characterize his ministry during this season. First, he tells Timothy to be watchful in all things. The word for watchful means to be levelheaded. Second, he tells Timothy to endure afflictions. Because Timothy is a preacher of the truth he will suffer at the hands of those who oppose him. Third, he tells Timothy to do the work of an evangelist. Timothy is to tell the lost of the saving message of the gospel of Jesus Christ. Fourth, he tells Timothy to fulfill his ministry. Timothy is to do what God has called him to do-be a faithful preacher of the gospel and to lead the church in Ephesus.

Verses 6-8 could be called Paul's Last Will and Testament. Paul is ready to die if it is the Lord's will because he has endured, by faith, in his walk with the Lord and he knew a reward awaited him on that day. In verse 6 the word "departure" has many different meanings. First, it means to rest from work. Second, it can mean to be set free. Third, it can mean move on. Fourth, it is used of ships moving from one harbor to the next. In verses 9-16 Paul asks Timothy to come and requests four things: Timothy to come quickly, his cloak, his study books, and his scrolls. Paul also notes that Demas and some of his Roman friends have deserted him. Despite those who have left him, Paul notes that it was the Lord who stood with him and gave him strength (v17-18).

Cover to Cover Challenge

Week 41

Sunday • Psalm 119:41-80

Welcome to week 41 of the *Cover to Cover Challenge*! Continue to pray for understanding and that the Holy Spirit will teach each person participating in the *Cover to Cover Challenge*. Psalm 119:66 "Teach me good judgment and knowledge, for I believe Your commandments".

In Psalm 119:41-48 the psalmist wants to experience God's mercies (loyal love) and salvation through His word. He also wants to experience God's deliverance from his enemies through His word. The psalmist also promises to be loyal to the Lord, even to the point of standing before kings and proclaiming the Word of God. In verses 49-56 the psalmist says that God's Word has given him hope and life in the midst of his trial. He knows the Lord will be true to His promises. Seeing the lives of the proud led him to be more loyal to the Lord. He shows this by being angry with those who rebel against God. In verses 57-64 the psalmist is making a deeper commitment to be obedient to God's Word. Even if the Lord were to delay, the psalmist will stay true to God's Word. He pays attention to God's Word and is a friend to all who keep it. In verses 65-72 the psalmist was disciplined by the Lord through some type of trial. He thanks God for this because through this experience he now remains faithful to God's Word and longs for God to teach it to him. Verses 73-80 also have the theme of affliction. The psalmist understands that the reason God made him is to know Him through His Word. It is in the middle of his affliction and through God's Word that he experiences the mercies of God. Even though it seems his affliction is not over the psalmist continues to trust in God.

Monday • Numbers 34-36

Numbers 34:1-12 concerns the distribution of the land. God will distribute the land before they take it, showing that it is theirs. As you have already read, they will never occupy all of the land because of their failure to drive out their enemies. In verses 13-15 the tribes of Reuben, Gad, and the half tribe of Manasseh have already received their inheritance of land and are not included in receiving the land in Canaan. Eleazar, Joshua, and one leader from each tribe are appointed to divide the land (v16-29).

In Numbers 35:1-8 the Levites are given a part of each tribe's inheritance. They do not receive any land because they are to dedicate themselves to the worship of God. Out of the 48 cities set apart for them, 6 are to be cities of refuge (v9-34). These are for those who kill someone accidently so he can go to the city of refuge for protection until he can have a trial. If he is guilty he must stay in the city of refuge until the death of the high priest. The victim's family is not allowed to bring them harm while they are in the city of refuge. But, if he leaves the city of refuge, the avenger is allowed to take their life. The person who commits deliberate murder is not allowed a place of refuge, but is to be put to death by the avenger (family member of one who died). For the trial there must be more than one witness to the crime for someone to be convicted. If found guilty they must surrender their life, and the avenger must be the one who puts them to death.

Numbers 36 concerns the inheritance of the daughters of Zelophehad (Num. 27:1-11). Their father had no sons so they inherited their father's portion. Here, the issue is if they marry someone from another tribe will they lose their land. To address the issue God says they must marry within their own tribe so the land will remain with it. If not, people would begin to intermarry between the tribes just to gain more land. This command given by God ensures the generations that follow will receive the land given to their families. One of the main themes of Numbers is obedience and it ends with the daughters of Zelophehad marrying within their own tribe obeying the word from God.

Tuesday • 2 Kings 1-5

1 and 2 Kings combined tell the story of the kings in Israel and Judah, along with the stories of a few of the well-known prophets. Some believe Jeremiah wrote these books, but no one knows for certain who the author is. What is known is that the author is going to tell the history of Israel to show why the exile came. Here are some main themes for 1 & 2 Kings- First, both Israel and Judah are judged because they have rejected God's law. Second, the words of the prophets come to pass because they have received true words from the Lord. Third, God is sovereign and in control over all nations. Here in 2 Kings we continue the story of the kings of Israel and Judah.

In 2 Kings 1:1-4, Ahab's son Ahaziah is the king of Israel. He has fallen and suffered a serious injury and wants to know if he will live so he asks Baal-Zebub the god of Ahab and Jezebel. The angel of the Lord (preincarnate Christ) tells Elijah to meet them on the way to tell them that Ahaziah will die for inquiring Baal-Zebub. In verses 5-8 the men return to tell Ahaziah the words of Elijah. In verses 9-12 he sends two groups of 50 to get Elijah, but they are killed by fire from heaven. Another group is sent, but this captain and his men plead for their lives and ask Elijah to come and see the king (v13-14). The angel of the Lord tells Elijah to go and personally speak His message to the king and he does die (v15-18). With no son to reign Jehoram, his brother, will reign in his place.

In 2 Kings 2 Elijah is taken to heaven, and Elisha will become the prophet of God to Israel. Elijah knew this was about to take place (v1). Elijah and Elisha travel to Bethel, Jericho, and to the Jordan River. In traveling from city to city, Elijah asks Elisha to stay but he refuses (v2-6). This may be a test for Elisha to see if he is dedicated to God and to Elijah and the prophetic office. When they reach the Jordan River, Elijah parts its waters with his mantle and they cross on dry ground as 50 other men watch (v7-8). Elijah wants to know what he can do for Elisha before he goes and Elisha responds by wanting a double portion of Elijah's spirit (v9-10). If this is to happen it is in God's hands. Elijah is taken to heaven in a chariot of fire in a whirlwind (v11-12). Elisha does receive a double portion of Elijah's spirit as he takes up Elijah's mantle and parts the Jordan River (v13-14). The 50 who saw the miracle now know that Elisha is the prophet to Israel (v15-18). Verses 19-25 record two miracles of Elisha. The first is the healing of the waters of Jericho, which had been cursed by Joshua (Joshua 6:26). The second occurs in Bethel, where the youth are killed by two bears after they mock Elisha and blaspheme God.

2 Kings 3 concerns a war with the Moabites who have refused to give tribute to Israel since the death of Ahab (v1-5). These verses also show that Jehoram continued in Ahab's ways and led the people in sinning against God.

Jehoram also asks Jehoshaphat king of Judah to go to war with him while also joining forces with the Edomites (v6-9). As usual, Jehoshaphat wants to inquire to the Lord about the battle and for the need of water for the troops (v10-14; 1 Kgs. 22:7). They go to Elisha who rebukes Jehoram but agrees to go to the Lord for Jehoshphat. After calling for a musician, Elisha prays and the Lord gives an answer: they must dig ditches for water and the Lord will give them victory over the Moabites (v15-19). The next morning the Moabites mistake the water for blood, supposing the approaching army had begun to fight one another (v20-25). The Moabites are defeated and their cities destroyed. The king of Moab even sacrifices his own son to appease his god (v26-27).

2 Kings 4-7 are the center of the Elisha cycle (Ch. 2-13) in 2 Kings. In verses 1-7 the widow of a prophet is in desperate need to pay her creditors before they take her sons into slavery (Ex. 21:1-4). The small flask of oil she does have fills all of the empty vessels she gathers from her neighbors. She is able to use it to pay off her debt and to provide for her sons. In verses 8-37 Elisha raises the Shunammite woman's son. They had taken special care of Elisha providing him meals and a place to stay (v8-14). In response Elisha prophesies that she will have a son the next year because they were childless (v15-28). The son grows ill and dies, and the Shunammite woman immediately goes to Mt. Carmel where Elisha is staying. Gehazi, Elisha's servant, lays his staff on the boy but there is no response (v29-30). Elisha and the mother return to the home where the boy is and Elisha, through symbolic action, revives the boy (v31-37). In verses 38-41 Elisha makes a poisoned stew safe to eat, and in verses 42-44 he multiplies a few small loaves into a meal that even has some left over.

In 2 Kings 5:1-7 we meet Namaan the Syrian who has leprosy. A captured Israelite girl informs him of a prophet in Israel who can cure Namaan's leprosy. In verses 8-14 Elisha hears of Namaan's condition and sends word back to the king of Israel that God was still at work in Israel. Elisha sends Gehazi to meet Namaan with a cure: dip 7 times in the Jordan River and you will be healed. This angers Namaan because he was expecting a great display of Elisha's power. He decides to go and is instantly healed. In verses 15-19 Namaan returns to offer gifts to Elisha but he refuses to accept them. In verses 20-27 Gehazi the servant of Elisha goes after Namaan, lies about a need, and gets some of the gifts from Namaan. When confronted by Elisha, Gehazi lies again to cover up his scheme. His punishment for lying is getting the leprosy that once plagued Namaan.

Wednesday • Acts 5-6

Acts 5:1-11 is the story of Ananias and Sapphira. It is an illustration of giving into temptation to sin and of sin being conceived (James 1:12-16). They had sold land, but had lied about the selling price and they had kept some for themselves. The word "kept back" in verse means to embezzle or to pilfer. Ananias was keeping money for himself that rightfully belonged to the church. Most people were buried on the same day they died, but the burial of Ananias was rather quick (v7). People were buried quickly for one of three reasons-unusual circumstances, suicide, or a believed judgment of God. This incident in the early church also shows how serious God takes sin. This is the first time the word "church" is used to describe the community of believers. The result was that people both in the church and outside the church feared God (v11). Verses 12-16 show the continued ministry of the apostles who were performing signs and wonders. These verses also identified the church with Jesus' ministry and confirmed the gospel. During this time the church was growing daily (v14). The rest of the chapter shows that the apostles spoke for God (v17-21), stood for God (v22-32), and suffered for God (v33-42) in the midst of growing persecution.

In verses 17-21 the apostles are arrested again for preaching the gospel, but are miraculously set free. Standing before the high priest and the Sanhedrin, the apostles boldly proclaim the gospel to them and proclaim their allegiance to Jesus (v22-32). Do not forget that these are the same people who crucified Jesus even though they witnessed His many miracles and heard His life changing words. The high priest and the Sanhedrin were plotting to kill the apostles like they did Jesus (v33-42). Gamaliel offers the Sanhedrin wise advice: if this movement is from men it will come to nothing, but if it is of God you will not stop it. The disciples were beaten and let go but were rejoicing that they were worthy enough to suffer for the Lord. 1 Peter 4:13 says "But rejoice to the extent that you partake of Christ's sufferings, that when His glory is revealed, you may also be glad with exceeding joy".

Acts 6 shows the expansion of the church, and introduces Stephen, who will become the first martyr of the church. In verses 1-7 there was a dispute between the Hebrews and Hellenists (Jews who lived as Greeks) over the treatment of widows. Out of this came the appointment of 7 deacons who would help meet the needs of the church. These men were to have a good reputation (be trusted by the people), be full of the Holy Spirit (believers), and have wisdom (ability to make wise choices). The laying on of hands functions as bestowing a blessing, identification, conferring authority, and commissioning for service. Notice in verse 7 the result of the decision. The word of God spread, the number of disciples grew, and many of the priests were also saved. Verse 7 is also the first of what many call progress reports of the church. The others are in 9:31, 12:24, 16:5, 19:20, and 28:31.

In verses 8-15 we are introduced to Stephen and the plot against him. Stephen is said to be full of faith and the Holy Spirit and did many signs among the people (v8). The Synagogue of the Freedmen were Greek-speaking Jews who were former slaves that were set free by their owners (v9). Verse 10 reminds me of Luke 12:11-12 "Now when they bring you to the synagogues and magistrates and authorities, do not worry about how or what you should answer, or what you should say. For the Holy Spirit will teach you in that very hour what you ought to say." They accuse him of blasphemy against Moses and God (v11). Stephen's testimony thus far mirrors that of Jesus being falsely accused (v12-14). He will go to trial before the Sanhedrin in chapter 7.

Thursday • Proverbs 24

Proverbs 24:1-2 warns against following the ways of evil men or having a desire to be like them. Verses 3-4 may refer to a person's character, which is built by collecting and using wisdom. A person who is wise will seek wisdom from others before making decisions (v5-6). Foolish people do not practice wisdom; therefore they have none to offer (v7). The person who works and speaks evil will be known for their evil (v8-9). How we react in times of adversity reveals our true strength (v10). Failure to help those who are perishing (spiritually or physically) displeases God (v11-12). Verses 13-14 are an encouragement to keep practicing and seeking wisdom. Verses 15-16 are a warning for the wicked not to come against the righteous. Verses 17-18 are warnings not to rejoice, even when our enemy suffers. Verses 19-20 are another warning not to envy those who are wicked in their prosperity. Verses 21-22 serve as a reminder to fear God and that those who are in leadership positions are there because they have been placed there by God (Rom. 13). Verses 23-26 serve as a warning to administer proper judgment based upon facts, not someone's stature. Verse 27 is instructions on being prepared before taking on any task. Verses 28-29 warn against witnessing against our neighbor without a cause, slandering our neighbor, and repaying evil for evil. Verses 30-34 warn against laziness because it brings a person to poverty.

Friday • Jeremiah 49-50

Jeremiah 49 continues with the judgment of the nations who will experience God's wrath because of their idolatry and their treatment of Israel. In verses 1-6 the Ammonites, who are descendants of Lot, will suffer destruction at the hands of Nebuchadnezzar. From these verses they had taken control of land that belonged to the tribe of Gad, but destruction would drive them away. This took place around 5 years after the final siege on Jerusalem, but they will be restored. The prophecy against Edom is similar to Obadiah (v7-22). The Edomites are descendants of Esau and have been in conflict with Israel for centuries. According to Obadiah, the Edomites are guilty of rejoicing at Israel's tragedies and of their own pride (Ob. 3). There is no promise of restoration for them. In verses 23-27 we see that Damascus will be destroyed and verses 28-33 state that Kedar and Hezor will be as well. In verses 34-39 the Elamites will be judged. They were famous for their skilled archers and while they are to be destroyed, there is a promise of restoration for them.

Jeremiah 50 begins the prophecy against Babylon and their future destruction. This will be the longest and most detailed prophecy against any nation. Even though Nebuchadnezzar and Babylon are God's judgment against the nations, they too must suffer judgment from God because of their sin. In verses 1-3 Babylon's doom is pictured as having already taken place by a nation from the north (Medo-Perisa). Their false gods (Bel, Merodach) will not be able to save them. Verses 4-10 are a call for God's people to leave the area before the destruction of Babylon and be joined to the Lord. In verses 11-16, the destruction of Babylon is because of their harsh treatment of Israel. Babylon's enemies are called to destroy them. Verses 17-20 show the suffering of Israel at the hands of the Babylonians and Assyrians, and their coming restoration to the land. The most important aspect here is they will have their sins forgiven. Verses 21-28 picture Babylon as hammering the nations, but they will now be hammered themselves by their enemies. The fall of the proud Babylonians will be thorough and complete (v29-32). In verses 33-39 Israel's Redeemer will come to their aid and fight against the Babylonians. Cyrus will lead the Medo-Persians, at the appointed time, to destroy Babylon just like Sodom and Gomorrah were destroyed (v40-46).

Saturday • 1 Peter 1-2

1 &2 Peter were written in the early 60's AD, shortly before his martyrdom. Peter was one of the first disciples called by Jesus, one of the inner three disciples (James, John), and would eventually become the leader of the 12 disciples. Peter wrote from "Babylon" (5:13, Rome) to Christians who were suffering for their faith. Peter writes to encourage them in the midst of their persecution, and challenges them to continue to live for the Lord in the midst of people who do not know God. Peter's letter can be divided into three sections, each beginning with "dear friends" (1:3, 2:11, 4:13).

In 1 Peter 1:1-2 Peter reminds those Christians scattered throughout the region that they are the elect of God, they are being sanctified by the Spirit, and that they should be obedient to Jesus-even in the middle of their suffering. Verses 3-9 remind them that their belief in Jesus gives them hope (v3), an inheritance (v4), and salvation (v5). Verse 6 shows that they are to rejoice in their hope, their inheritance, and their salvation even though they are experiencing suffering at the present time. Peter explains to them in verse 7 that their faith is purified through these times of suffering (Isa. 48:10). Verses 8-9 refer to their personal relationship with the Lord is as what they are to rejoice in. These verses are in the present tense in the Greek signifying something that is continuous and daily. The salvation they experience was preached by the prophets, and even angels desire to look into it (v10-12).

Peter encourages them to live a life of hope (v13-14). The phrase "gird up the loins of your mind" refers to being spiritually alert. In verse 14 Peter is encouraging them not to return to their old way of living before they were saved. In verses 15-16 Peter also encourages them to live a life of holiness. Instead of returning to their old way of living Peter encourages them to live a holy life. Holiness is not just being separated from evil, but also includes a life dedicated to holiness. They are to live their whole life in this way. In verses 17-21 Peter encourages them to live a life that honors the Lord because they have been redeemed by His blood (v17-21).

In verses 22-25 Peter instructs them to also live a life of love. The basis of this love is one found in the Word of God. Verses 22-23 say that they had been purified and born again by the Word. The words "living" and "abiding" show that God's Word is powerful (Heb. 4:12) and permanent. The quote from Isaiah 40:6-8 stresses the faithfulness of God, which stands behind His Word and also reflects permanence.

Cover to Cover Challenge

Week 42

Sunday • Psalm 119:81-120

Welcome to week 42 of the *Cover to Cover Challenge*! Continue to pray that the Lord be honored and glorified through our study, and for understanding of His Word. Psalm 119:81 says "My soul faints for Your salvation, but I hope in Your word".

In Psalm 119:81-88 the psalmist is being persecuted by his enemies without a cause. He ponders when God will come and comfort him during this difficult time. It is through God's Word that he knows the promises of God's salvation and comfort, and he submits himself to them. In verses 89-96 the psalmist understands God stands behind His Word. Even in his trials he delights in God's Word because in them he knows that he belongs to God. As his trials continue, he continually seeks God through His Word because it is God alone who sustains him. In verses 97-104 the psalmist is in love with the Word of God. He meditates on it (read, reflect, respond), and is obedient to it. God's Word is sweeter than honey to him. In verses 105-112 the psalmist knows that God's Word keeps him from the path of the wicked and the traps they lay for him. Even in the middle of affliction he has not strayed from the Word, but keeps his heart turned toward God's promises. In verses 113-120 the psalmist describes the ways of the wicked in contrast to those of the righteous. The psalmist makes it clear that he hates the ways of wicked, but loves God's Word. It is through God's Word he understands that God protects, sustains, upholds him, and gives him hope. Judgment will come upon the wicked, and the Lord will destroy them.

Monday • Deuteronomy 1-3

Moses is the author of the book of Deuteronomy (1:1, 5, 9, 5:1, 27:8; 29:2, 31:1, 30). Jesus confirms this (Matthew 19:7-8) as well as Peter (Acts 3:22), Stephen (Acts 7:37-38), and Paul (Romans 10:19). Joshua more than likely added 32:48-34:12 to the book after Moses' death. Deuteronomy means "second law". In it Moses goes over and expands on the laws God has already given Israel, while also calling them to renew the covenant. Deuteronomy records Moses' last words as they prepare to enter Canaan after 40 years of wandering in the wilderness. You will notice that the words "Hear O Israel" and "Be careful to do" are repeated often. These words show that Israel is to be obedient to what the Lord has asked them to do. Deuteronomy will be like Moses' commentary on the events that have transpired thus far.

Deuteronomy 1:1-5 gives the historical and geographical setting of the time that Moses speaks again to the children of Israel. Notice this is the 40th year, and in two short months they will be entering the land of Canaan for the first time. The main purpose is renewing the covenant before entering the land. In verses 6-8 Moses reminds the people of the faithfulness of God to the promises He has made. Abraham's descendants did become as numerous as the stars in the sky (Gen. 15:5). Moses understood that he could not lead the people by himself so others were appointed to help him with the task (v9-18). Verses 19-33 record Israel's refusal to enter the land of Canaan 38 years prior. In disobeying God's command to take the land the real issue of the people was revealed- they lacked faith in God (v32). For punishment God refuses to let that generation enter the Promised Land except for Caleb and Joshua, who would be allowed to enter because they had faith in the Lord's promises (v34-46).

Deuteronomy 2 begins the journey into the wilderness. Verses 1-23 show the care that God had for the people who lived in the region of Seir. He had provided for them just as He has provided for the Israelites during their journey. Two other things are pointed out in these verses. First, in verses 14-16, it is noted that the entire generation had perished in the wilderness at this point. Second, it is God who will drive out the nations before them and who is giving them the land (v21-22). In verses 24-37 the Israelites' interactions with people will change. They will go to war, especially when others deny peaceful relationships with them. Verses 30-37 record the first victory over Sihon, destroying all within their path. The Hebrew word for "destroy" in verse 34 means dedicated for destruction. It speaks of something which stands in the way of God's work.

In Deuteronomy 3:1-11 God instructs the Israelites to defeat and destroy Og and the people of Bashan. In verse 6 the word "destroyed" again means devoted to destruction. Verses 12-23 detail the allotment of land given to Reuben, Gad, and the half tribe of Manasseh east of the Jordan River because they had many livestock. They still must fight with their fellow Israelites until they receive their inheritance. Verses 24-29 record the prayer of Moses pleading with God to let him enter the Promised Land. God would not allow Moses to enter because this showed the people of Israel the seriousness of the consequences for being disobedient.

Most of us will read these chapters and wonder why God had them destroy the men, women, and children in Heshbon and Bashan. First, we must understand no person is innocent. All stand guilty before God. Second, these battles fulfilled Scripture. In Genesis 15:16 it was told to Abraham by God that Israel would live in bondage in Egypt for 400 years because the sins of the Amorites were not yet full. The Amorites had been given time to repent. Third, it kept the people of Israel from adopting their pagan rituals and gods. As we read at the beginning of the *Cover to Cover Challenge* in Joshua and Judges, the Israelites do fail to drive out all of the people and they do become corrupt and adopt their pagan practices.

Tuesday • 2 Kings 6-10

2 Kings 6:1-7 records the miracle of the floating ax head that was being used to build a larger building for the prophets. In verses 8-23 the Syrians hope to invade Israel, but Elisha warns Joram king of Israel of their plans. The king of Syria sends an army to Dothan to take Elisha. The Lord reveals to Elisha's servant that the army on their side outnumbered those of the enemy in an answer to Elisha's prayer. The men are struck with blindness, led to Samaria, and discover when their eyes are opened they are prisoners of Joram. Elisha instructs Joram to feed them and send them back, and for a time this ended the Syrian threat. In verses 24-29 yet another invasion by Syria is recorded, this one during a time of famine. The famine was so bad that people were reverting to cannibalism. Joram blames the famine on Elisha and seeks to have him killed (v30-33). In 7:1 Elisha prophesies relief from the famine, but is mocked by the kings officer (v2). Elisha replies that the servant will see the prophecy take place but will not eat of it. The prophecy will begin to be fulfilled by 4 leprous men who would discover

the Syrian camp had been abandoned because God intervened (v3-7). The 4 lepers decide they should tell the king, and Joram sends officers to the camp. They find the camp abandoned, just as it had been reported (v8-15). Elisha's prophecy was fulfilled, and the officer who mocked him was trampled to death (v16-20).

In 2 Kings 8:1-16 Elisha warns the Shunammite woman to flee Israel because there is a famine coming that will last for 7 years. After the famine is passed, the Shunammite woman returns to reclaim her land. By God's providence Elisha's former servant Gehazi has an audience with the king who wants to hear stories about Elisha. Gehazi is there to verify her claim and the Shunammite woman has her request granted. In verses 7-15 Ben-Hadad king of Syria is ill and sends Hazael to ask Elisha if he will recover from his sickness. In 1 Kings 19:15-17 Elijah was told he would anoint Hazael, but this would now fall to Elisha. From the words of Elisha he knows the king of Syria would recover, but also reveals he knows Hazael's plans to kill Ben-Hadad. In verses 16-24, Jehoram son of Jehoshaphat becomes king of Judah. He did evil in the sight of the Lord, in large part because he had married Ahab's daughter. Jehoram as recorded in 2 Chronicles 21, would kill all of his brothers and would later die from an incurable bowel disease. The only reason God did not destroy Judah is because of the covenant he made with David. Jehoram's son Ahaziah would become the next king of Judah. He also would do evil in the sight of the Lord, following the ways of Ahab (v25-29). He would go to war with Joram king of Israel against Hazael the king of Syria.

In 2 Kings 9:1-3 Elisha calls one of his servants to go and anoint Jehu king. The anointing of Jehu as king serves two purposes. First, he was to kill all of the descendants of Ahab. Second, this served to avenge for all of the blood of those who were faithful to God (v4-10). Jehu tells his troops that he has been anointed king and immediately they go to Jezreel to find Joram (v11-16, Jehoram). The watchman warns Joram that Jehu is coming (v17-21). Joram sends two messengers, but both join forces with Jehu. Joram and Ahaziah both meet Jehu at the field of Naboth, whom Jezebel had murdered so Ahab could have his vineyard. Jehu kills Joram and leaves his body in Naboth's field, fulfilling the words of Elijah (v 25-29; 1 Kgs. 21:19-24). Next Jehu confronts Jezebel (v30-34). Jehu calls out to see if anyone will stand with him, and two eunuchs throw Jezebel out of the window killing her. When they return to bury her, because she was the daughter of a king, they find that the rest of Elijah's prophecy had been fulfilled (v35-37; 1 Kgs. 21:23).

After the deaths of the two kings and of Jezebel, Jehu will begin to remove the rest of the descendants of Ahab beginning with Ahab's sons in 2 Kings 10:1-8. In verses 9-11 Jehu addresses the people. He orders the execution of any who remain of Ahab's descendants in Jezreel and any officials, aides, or friends. In verses 12-14, Jehu meets the brothers of Ahaziah king of Judah and executes them as well. Remember the house of Joram and Ahaziah are all directly related to Ahab. In verses 15-17 Jehu meets Jehonadab the Recabite and invites him to come with him to see his "zeal for the Lord". The Recabites are in Jeremiah 35, and God uses them as an example of obedience to their ancestor's instrcutions (Jehonadab). In verses 18-24, Jehu tricks the worshipers of Baal to gather together for a sacrifice. Once they begin to worship Baal, Jehu sends 80 men in to kill them and destroys the temple (v25-27). While Jehu rid Israel of Baal worship and was blessed by God to have descendants to sit on the throne for 4 generations, he did not walk in the ways of the Lord (v28-36). Israel continued to worship the golden calves at Dan and Bethel. Because of this, the Lord allowed Hazael to conquer some of the land of Israel. Jehu dies after reigning 28 years and his son Jehoahaz will reign in his place.

Wednesday • Acts 7-8

At the end of Acts 6, Stephen is being accused of blasphemy by a mob of people because he was preaching the gospel. In Acts 7 Stephen's speech demonstrates that God has always risen up deliverers for His people, only for them to be rejected. One other theme that Stephen shows in this history of Israel is their rejection of God, His revelation to them, and their turn to idolatry. Stephen also shows that the way God has worked in the past He is still working today. God sent Jesus to be their deliverer, but they refuse. In rejecting Jesus, they showed that they did "always resist the Holy Spirit" (Isa. 63:10). The term "stiff-necked" gives a picture of an animal throwing off their master's yoke. Stephen is stoned for his stand for the gospel of Jesus Christ and becomes the first martyr of the church. Also, the only time Jesus is pictured as standing in Scripture is found in verse 56. In verses 59-60 Stephen demonstrate the actions of Jesus when He died upon the cross (Luke 23:34, 46).

Acts 8:1-3 begins the persecution of the church in Jerusalem. There are also more details given about Saul. We see here that he agreed with them stoning Stephen and played a role in persecuting the church. Beginning here in 8:4-8, the gospel will spread to Samaria through the preaching of Philip and the miracles that were done there. In verses 9-25 we are introduced to Simon the sorcerer. While verse 13 says that he believed, he was not a true believer at this point. In fact he may have never become one, because Scripture does not record his conversion. After seeing more miracles when the Holy Spirit came to the Samaritans, Simon tries to buy the power of the Holy Spirit. If he was a true believer, why had he not already received the Holy Spirit? Peter also tells him that he and his money will perish in verse 21, and in verse 22 he tells him to repent because his heart is not right with God. Verse 22 reveals that his motive ("thought of your heart") for wanting to receive the Holy Spirit was not right. Peter reveals in verse 23 that Simon was "poisoned (root of) with bitterness" and was "bound (chained) by iniquity."

In verses 26-40 Philip (one of the original deacons) meets the Ethiopian eunuch. This passage teaches many of the same truths found in Luke 15-something is lost, sought, found, and there is rejoicing. It is clearly seen that the Holy Spirit was working in this situation because He was at work with Philip and the Ethiopian eunuch. Philip was obedient to the Lord's call on his life to leave a fruitful ministry in Samaria and go to where the Lord was calling him to go. The Ethiopian eunuch was reading Isaiah 53 at the time he encountered Philip on the road. Several verses come to mind when reading about the Ethiopian eunuch. Jeremiah 29:13 says "And you will seek Me and find Me, when you search for Me with all your heart." Jesus says in John 5:39 "You search the Scriptures, for in them you think you have eternal life; and these are they which testify of Me." One in particular that would have spoken to the eunuch is found in Isaiah 56 that speaks of a eunuch's name not being cut off from God's kingdom. As with any witnessing opportunity it was the Holy Spirit that guided Philip (v29). He asked the eunuch questions to gauge where he was spiritually (v30). Philip then presents the gospel to him (v35-37).

Thursday • Proverbs 25

In Proverbs 25 we once again return to the proverbs written by Solomon (v1). Verses 2-3 teach that a leader should search out the will of God, but just like God, there are things the leader needs not to reveal. In verses 4-5 the removal of dross purifies silver, just as the removal of the wicked from places of power does. Verses 6-7 echo some of Jesus' parables. It is better to take a low seat and be asked to move higher, than to take a high seat and be asked to move lower. Verses 8-10 teach that it is better to talk through a problem than to sue over it. Verses 11-12 teach that the right words spoken at the right time to the right person are beneficial. Verse 13 is teaching that a faithful person brings refreshment to the soul. Verse 14 teaches that there is no benefit from someone who boasts of false things (Jude 12, false teachers). Verse 15 teaches that persistence and kind words will break through resistance. Verse 16 is teaching self-control and moderation. Good things can be harmful if we over indulge in them. Verse 17 is another way of saying "don't wear out your welcome". Verse 18 teaches that a lying tongue can bring destruction. Verse 19 teaches that placing your faith in someone who is unfaithful is disappointing and painful. Verse 20 is teaching that we should be considerate of our words toward those who are experiencing grief. Verses 21-22 are quoted by Paul in Romans 12:20. We are to give good when someone gives us evil. Verse 23 teaches that those who slander cause others to be angry. Verse 24 is saying that a man is better off living on the roof than in a mansion with a woman who causes trouble. Verse 25 is a good missionary verse. Good news (gospel) from a far country is refreshing to the soul. Verse 26 is teaching that a godly man who fails before those who are lost brings harm to his witness. Verse 27 teaches that it is not good to think too highly of yourself or be self-centered. Verse 28 teaches that those who have no self-control will let anything into their life.

Friday • Jeremiah 51-52

Jeremiah 51 continues the prophecy of the judgment of Babylon. The Babylonians will be attacked and no one will be spared (v1-4). This judgment is based upon their harsh treatment of Judah and for destroying the temple (v5-14). In verses 15-23 we see that the idols of the Babylonians are no match for God. Verses 20-23 refer to Cyrus the leader of the Medes, who will conquer and destroy Babylon. In verses 24-26 Babylon is pictured as never being rebuilt. The once powerful nation will be brought to nothing. Verses 27-33 are a call to the nations to fight against Babylon. The people mentioned would fight along with Cyrus and his army to defeat Babylon. The god of Babylon, Bel, and the wall surrounding its kingdom will fall and the nation will be no more (v34-44). In verses 45-48 God warns His people once again to flee the coming destruction of Babylon. Babylon's destruction is certain (v49-53) and will be complete as waves of troops overrun them (v54-58). Seraiah's symbolic act showed the people that Babylon would fall (v59-64).

Jeremiah 52:1-11 gives an account of how Jerusalem falls. This event is recorded fourtimes in Scripture (2 Kgs 25, 2 Chron. 36:11-21, Jer. 39:1-14, Jer. 52). Zedekiah is captured, his sons and princes are killed, and Zedekiah is taken to Babylon after having his eyes put out. In verses 12-27 the Babylonians destroy the temple and all of the houses in Jerusalem by burning them with fire. All of the sacred vessels in the temple are carried to Babylon as well. Verses 28-30 record the deportations of the Israelites to Babylon. Jehoiachin is released from prison in the 37th year of captivity and is treated fairly by Evil-Merodach, Nebuchadnezzar's son (v31-34). This shows that God did not forget the Davidic line during the exile.

Saturday • 1 Peter 3-5

1 Peter 3:1-7 addresses wives and husbands. The woman is to live her life in obedience to her husband even if he does not know the Lord, because through her behavior she may lead him to Christ (v1-2). Verses 3-6 show that a woman's true beauty is not in how she adorns herself outwardly, but in the woman she is inwardly. How can a woman show her inward beauty? The word Peter uses for "gentle" in verse 4 is only used in Scripture three times, with two of them used to describe Jesus. The word means not insistent on one's own rights or not selfish. Her inward beauty is also shown through her obedience to her husband, and Peter gives the example in verse 6 of Sarah obeying Abraham. Husbands are told to honor their wives so that their prayers will not be hindered (v7). Even though the man has been given greater authority within marriage, their wife is still equal to them in eternal importance. Both the man and wife are "heirs together of the grace of life".

In verses 8-12 Peter encourages all Christians to be of one mind, to be full of sympathy, to love one another, to be tender hearted, and to have humble minds in the face of persecution instead of repaying with evil. The quotation from Psalm 34:12-16 shows that Peter's principle in verses 8-9 has a Scriptural backing. Those who do not repay evil for evil in the face of persecution will be blessed. During times of suffering believers need to be submitted to Christ, prepared to share the gospel, have the attitude of Christ, and be living for Christ (v13-17). The quote from Isaiah 8:12-13 served as a warning not to fear what faithless people fear. But here, Peter uses it to encourage believers not to be afraid when they suffer persecution for righteousness' sake. Peter cites the sufferings of Christ as our primary example for enduring suffering (v18-22). Jesus, who was just, suffered unjustly at the hands of sinful man in order that sinful man could have a way to God.

In 1 Peter 4:1-6 we read that because Christ has suffered for all believers they should not live the way they lived when they did not know Christ. In verse 3 Peter is saying that they should not even want to live according to who they once were and indulge in the sins of their past. Those sins include lewdness (no moral restraint), lusts (sinful desires), drunkenness, revelries (wild immorality), drinking parties, and abominable idolatries (lawless worship). Those who do not know God are surprised ("strange") that believers no longer participate in these sins (v4). Peter adds in verse 5 that judgment is coming for those who live apart from God and indulge in those sins.

In verses 7-11 Peter encourages them that because they are living in the last days they should be of sound mind and alert in their prayers (v7), have a fervent (maximum effort) love for each other (v8), be hospitable (meet needs) to one another (v9), and be good stewards with what God has given them. The person who speaks whether preaching, teaching, or any speaking should do so according to Scripture (v11). The person who ministers (serves) should do so as God has given them the ability.

Just as Jesus warned the disciples' that suffering would come to them, Peter warns them (the church) that they should not be surprised that they will suffer (v12-19). This should bring them joy and show them that they are blessed because they are the children of God (v13-14). If they suffer because they do wrong it would be just, but if they are suffering for being a believer they should not be ashamed (v15-16). Peter also warns that judgment will begin at the house of God (v17-18). In Ezekiel 9 and Malachi 3:1-3, the Lord's judgment began at the temple. God's goal in this is to purify the church and to cleanse believers of their sin (1 Cor. 11:32, Heb. 12:7-8).

In 1 Peter 5 Peter encourages the elders (v1-4), the younger men (v5-11), and the church (v5-11) in the midst of their persecution. The elders are told to care for the flock of which they have been given by the Chief Shepherd (Christ). The beginning of verse 2 can actually be read "Shepherd the sheep of God". Peter warns the shepherd of the church to avoid three things. First, do not shepherd the church out of "compulsion" (obligation). This means doing it with the attitude of "someone has to do it so it might as well be me". Second, do not shepherd the church for "dishonest gain." This means someone should not use the office of shepherd for greedy or selfish motives. In Scripture this often portrayed by false teachers in pursuit for money. Instead of doing it for dishonest gain it should be done "eagerly". This word means to do something with a desire to do the work. Third, do not shepherd the church to "lord over others". This phrase means to use the office of shepherd to oppress others or to be their master. The shepherd is not to lift himself up over others, but is to edify (build up) the flock. The shepherd is to be an example to the flock (1 Tim. 4:12-16).

The younger people, along with the church, are to submit themselves in humility to the leadership of the shepherd and the elders who serve (v5-6). Within this passage Peter warns them to have self-control and to be on alert because the devil is seeking to devour them (v8). The word "resist" in verse 9 paints a picture of someone taking a stand, fully armed and ready for battle (Eph. 6:10-20). So in verses 8-9 Peter is encouraging believers to stay awake, stay in control, stand up, and stand firm against the devil. Peter closes his letter with a reference to "Babylon" (v13). Many believe this is another name for Rome. Nero's persecution of Christians may have already begun or was about to take place.

Cover to Cover Challenge

Week 43

Sunday • Psalm 119:121-152

Welcome to week 43 of the *Cover to Cover Challenge*! Psalm 119:125 says "I am Your servant, give me understanding, that I may know Your testimonies". What an encouragement to each of us as we continue to study the Word of God together! Let us keep praying for the Lord to be glorified, and for the Lord to speak to each of us as we seek His face.

In Psalm 119:121-128 the psalmist longs to be delivered from the proud, who oppress him. He loves God's Word and proclaims that it is more valuable than the purest gold. The psalmist also believes what God's Word says to be the truth. In verses 129-136 the psalmist states the many benefits of God's words. They give light and understanding (v130), they give direction to avoid sin (v133), they relieve oppression (v134), and they teach us (v135). The psalmist is also brokenhearted over those who do not keep God's Word. In verses 137-144 the psalmist knows that God is righteous, upright (trustworthy), and faithful even in his adversity. As the psalmist's adversity increases, so does his dedication to God's Word. It is in it that he finds delight in the middle of difficult circumstances. In verses 145-152 the psalmist cries out continually through the night for God to hear and to deliver him from the wicked. He meditates on God's Word, because it is there that he finds hope in his trials.

Monday • Deuteronomy 4-6

In Deuteronomy 4:1-8, Moses speaks about the importance of obedience. Obedience does not earn salvation, but does give people wisdom and understanding and it brings blessings to the people. They were to teach God's law to their children because of the benefits associated with knowing and obeying it (v9-13). Moses also warns them of keeping themselves from idols (v15-31). They were not to make anything to worship, or worship anything God had made. Worshiping idols would (and did) lead to them losing their land. Only those who look to God and repent will experience the blessings of God. In verses 32-40, Moses speaks about the works of God throughout the history of Israel. He does this so the people of Israel will learn from the past as they enter Canaan. In verses 41-49 Moses established cities of refuge on the eastern side of the Jordan River.

In Deuteronomy 5:1-5 Moses speaks to this generation of Israelites the same way the original hearers heard it. They did not just inherit the covenant; it was specifically for them as well. The Ten Commandments can be seen as a summary of the entire law of God because every law given by God is an expression of these (v6-22). In verses 23-33 Moses recalls the scene at Mount Sinai where the law had been given. The people feared (awe) God and asked Moses to intervene for them. This type of fear (awe) is reverencing God because of who He is. God commends them for fearing Him because they should always have this type of fear (awe) before God. With this type of fear the people should respond in obedience.

After recounting the previous generations' experience with God to the generation present in chapter 5, Moses will now speak to the current generation about the future generation in chapter 6. In verses 1-9 the parents are to teach their children about God and their relationship with Him (v4-5). Parents must be intentional about passing on their faith to their children and teach it to them until it is understood. In every context of life parents can teach their children lessons about loving God. In verses 10-25 the parents are told themselves to keep walking with God and not be disobedient. They are to trust the Lord in and with everything. With each generation to come they will be able to tell how God had blessed them and watched over them.

Tuesday • 2 Kings 11-15

In 2 Kings 11:1-3, after the death of Ahaziah, Athaliah (daughter of Jezebel) his mother reigned over Judah after killing all the heirs (her grandchildren). Jehosheba the wife of the high priest Jehoiada hid Ahaziah's son Joash so he would not be killed. After six years, Jehoiada makes a plan to anoint Joash king of Judah and to kill Athaliah (v4-12). In verses 13-16 Athaliah is killed by the sword, and Joash is crowned king of Judah. In verses 17-21, Jehoiada led the king and the people to be allegiant to God and to the Davidic line. The temple to Baal was destroyed and the high priest of Baal, Mattan was killed.

2 Kings 12 continues the story of Joash. In verses 1-6 he makes preparations to fund the repairing of the temple. After 23 years the task still had not been completed, so Joash commanded a chest be set aside for the collection of an offering to fund the repairs (v7-16). Soon there was plenty of money and workers began the work to repair the temple. In verses 17-21 Hazael the Syrian king came to make war on Jerusalem. Joash takes the royal treasury and gives it to Hazael as payment and avoids the war. What 2 Kings 12 does not tell is that after the death of Jehoiada the high priest, Joash began to worship other gods (2 Chron.24). This is the reason Hazael and the Syrians came against Israel.

In 2 Kings 13:1-9 Jehoahaz becomes king of Israel. Because he walked in the ways of Jeroboam, God allowed Hazael the king of Syria to trouble him during all of his reign. He did seek the Lord during this conflict and God showed Israel mercy. After his death, his son Jehoash reigns in Israel for 16 years (v10-25). When hearing of Elisha's coming death, Jehoash goes to visit him. Through symbolic actions, Elisha predicts the coming victories over the Syrians. In verses 20-21 a dead man is lowered into Elisha's grave and when he comes in contact with his bones is restored to life.

2 Kings 14:1-7 records the beginning of the reign of Amaziah as king of Judah as he defeats the Edomites. 2 Chronicles 25 records that while he did win the victory over the Edomites, he also began to worship their gods. After winning this victory Amaziah, in his pride, goes to war with Jehoash king of Israel (v8-22). Amaziah and Judah would be defeated by Jehoash and Israel in this battle as God was showing Amaziah and Judah not to trust in foreign gods. In verses 23-29 Jeroboam II would reign in Israel for 41 years. It is during his reign that God showed them mercy and restored the land back to them that they had lost as predicted by Jonah. This shows that even though people are unfaithful to God, He will never be unfaithful to His word.

2 Kings 15:1-7 records the reign of Uzziah (Azariah) as king of Judah. Uzziah would later become prideful and attempt to make an offering to the Lord that only the priest could do. In this incident Uzziah is stricken with

leprosy and dies (2 Chron. 26). In verses 8-12 Zechariah becomes the 4th descendant of Jehu to rule, fulfilling the promise to Jehu in 10:30. Zechariah is killed by Shallum who reigns for only one month (v13-16). Menahem kills Shallum and reigns in Israel for 10 years (v17-22). It is during Menahem's reign that Israel becomes a vassal state coming under the rule of Assyria. Pekahiah his son would begin to reign in his place for two years before he is murdered by Pekah (v23-26). It is under the reign of Pekah that Israel begins to really suffer at the hands of the Assyrians. Pekah is killed by Hoshea who reigns in his place. In verses 32-38 Jotham the son of Uzziah reigns in Judah. 2 Chronicles 27 records that Judah prospered economically under his reign but continued to falter spiritually.

Wednesday • Acts 9-10

Acts 9:1-9 records the conversion of Saul (Paul). He also tells more of his testimony in Acts 22:3-16 and 26:4-18, which fulfills Jesus' words in Acts 9:15-16. Paul was completely opposed to the followers of Jesus and would carry them to prison. There is no doubt from this passage that the Lord had been speaking to Paul, but at that time he would not listen to the Lord's call. Ananias is sent by the Lord to pray for Paul (v10-19). Most people never pay attention to Ananias in this story. He listened to God (v10) and even though he did make excuses not to go (v13-14), he was eventually obedient to what the Lord had for him to do (v17-19). Ananias played a pivotal role in the conversion of Paul. The words in Acts 9:15-16 will be fulfilled throughout his ministry. Paul began to preach about Jesus, and the Jews even began to find a way to kill him (v20-25). In verse 22 the word "confound" means to put together. Paul was able to put together an argument from the Old Testament proving that Jesus was their Messiah and Savior.

With many afraid of Paul, Barnabas helped Paul in a time when many believed he was still plotting against the church (v26-30). Verse 31 is referred to as a "church report" and gives the status of the church. Verses 32-35 record a healing by Peter of a man who was bedridden and paralyzed, which led many in the area to be saved. Peter raises Dorcas back to life in verses 36-43. The raising of Dorcas resembles both Luke 5:17-26 and 8:41-56, showing that the Holy Spirit is working through the church and is in continuity with Jesus and His ministry. Dorcas is described as a woman who was "full of good works and charitable deeds" (v36-37). She was a great supporter of the church and made clothing for the women (v39). For Peter the journey to Joppa from Lydda would have taken him about 3 hours (v38). The similarities between this story and the raising of Jairus' daughter are striking.

Acts 10 records the gospel coming to the Gentiles. In verses 1-8 a man named Cornelius receives a vision from God for him to send for Peter. The description of Cornelius is of one whom they call a God fearer. He had fully accepted Judaism, but had not been circumcised. The next day Peter also receives a vision from the Lord (v9-16). In the vision of the sheet, God is teaching Peter that the Gentiles (all people) are to be viewed as clean. Peter preached the first sermon to the Jews in Acts 2, welcomed the Samaritans in Acts 8, and preaches to the Gentiles here in Acts 10. The band of Cornelius's men arrives to ask Peter to come to them (v17-23).

In verses 24-33 Peter and Cornelius both share their stories of how God has spoken to them over the past few days. Peter's message makes it clear to the Gentiles that everyone is a sinner, everyone needs salvation, everyone needs forgiveness, and that it all comes through Jesus Christ (v34-48). One difference between Peter's earlier sermons and this one is his audience. Prior to this this many of his sermons were to the Jews, which is why he includes many Old Testament Scriptures to show that Jesus is the Messiah. Here he is preaching to Gentiles. This is also the reason he begins this sermon differently (v34-35). Notice he appeals to them with the fact that God shows no partiality or that God is not a respecter of persons. Peter was taught this by God with the vision of the sheet (v9-16). God's plan of salvation will be preached to all people, not just to the Jews. Verses 44-48 serve to confirm the Gentiles receiving the Holy Spirit. This demonstration of the Spirit by the hand of God would prove that the Gentiles and Jews alike were recipients of God's grace.

Thursday • Proverbs 26-27

Proverbs 26 generally covers the four types of people who do not pursue wisdom. Verses 1-12 speak of the fool. The fool in proverbs does not seek wisdom nor will they heed it when it is offered. In verses 1-3 the fool never deserves honor, and when he does something foolish wisdom should be given him in return (v4-5). No one should put confidence in a fool (v6), and in verses 7-9 it is suggested not to even offer them wisdom because they will not listen to it. Verses 10-12 suggest that nothing is to be expected of the fool because they will keep doing the same thing over and over again (v10-11). The only thing worse than being a fool is being a person filled with pride (v12). Verses 13-16 describe the lazy person. The lazy person makes excuses (v13), chooses sleep over work (v14), is too lazy to feed himself (v15), and is prideful (v16). Verses 17-22 describe the madman. This is someone who meddles in others business and stirs up trouble (v17). They also keep their lies hidden by claiming only to be joking (v18-19). They stir up trouble among others by gossiping (v20-21) and love to keep pouring gas on the fire (v22). Verses 23-28 describe the hypocrite. These verses would also fit the Pharisees of the New Testament whom Jesus described as hypocrites. They speak words that seem good, but behind them is wickedness (v23). With words they try to hide the true motive of their hearts (v24-25). They will lie but be exposed for what they really are in front of all (v26).

Proverbs 27 speaks about right and wrong attitudes. Being prideful of what you will do in the future or being prideful in yourself is dangerous (v1-2). Being resentful (v3) and being envious (v4) are also warned about. Verses 5-6 are an encouragement to have friends who are willing to tell you the truth. Verses 7-8 describe the attitude one's words can be taken with depending on their situation. Verses 9-10 describe the joy over having friends who give wise counsel. In verse 11 Solomon is encouraging his son to be obedient to his words. Those who are wise avoid trouble (v12), avoid being taking advantage of (v13), and say the right thing at the right time (v14). The wise son will also avoid marrying a rebellious wife (v15-16). Verse 17 shows the advantages of having godly parents, friendships, and mentors in one's life. Verse 18 is an encouragement to be faithful to your master. Someone's outward behavior is a good indicator of their heart (v19). Ecclesiastes teaches verse 20. If a man could have the whole world in his heart he still would not be satisfied. Only a relationship with God brings satisfaction. Verse 21 is teaching that how a person responds to praise reveals his character. Verse 22 says that once a person commits themselves to being a fool it is nearly impossible to remove the foolishness from them. Verses 23-28 teach that we are to be diligent in caring for the resources God has given us by being good stewards of it.

Friday • Lamentations

Lamentations was written shortly after the fall of Judah by Jeremiah. Jerusalem has been destroyed and the people have been taken away captive by the Babylonians. The author of Lamentations is writing as he sees all of this unfold. God is punishing His people for their unfaithfulness and now they are experiencing great suffering. Lamentations means "loud cries" and is associated with funeral songs. But, even in the midst of the suffering and sorrow, there is hope in God.

In Lamentations 1:1-7 the author describes the many losses they have suffered from their enemies. The author does acknowledge that all of it has happened because of their sin (v5). In verses 8-11 he describes the feelings of those who were in Jerusalem. They feel shame and defilement over their sin that has caused this to happen (v8-9). God's punishment of their sin has a purpose (v12-17). It was so they would turn back to Him. In verses 18-22 the people know that they have sinned against God, and they do cry out to God for mercy (v18-22).

Lamentations 2:1-10 describes God's anger over the sins of Judah. God is personally mentioned in these verses 40 times, showing that He was the one bringing judgment on the people. In verses 11-13 the author is mourning over the state of Judah and the people. It is so devastating that he has no words to offer. The destruction of Judah also shows that the false prophets' prophecies were false (v14-17). In verses 18-22 the people are told to mourn over what is taking place because of their sin. After Jerusalem was destroyed women ate their children, priests were killed in the temple, and people were lying dead in the street.

Lamentations 3:1-18 paints a picture of utter hopelessness for Jerusalem and the people. It is in the middle of all the suffering and mourning that God's mercy, compassion, faithfulness shines through (v19-30). In verses 31-39 there is also a reminder that God is in control during times of sorrow and affliction. The punishment on Judah however did produce repentance as they ask for God's forgiveness (v40-66). Even though they are still suffering (v43-49) they are assured God will soon bring them relief (v48-51). Verses 52-63 seem to supply proof that Jeremiah is the author of Lamentations (Jer. 38:6-13). Just as God rescued him from this situation God will also rescue the people (v64-66).

In Lamentations 4 the author paints a before/after picture of Jerusalem. The people who were once cherished as gold had become like pottery (v1-2). Jerusalem is even said to be worse off than Sodom (v6). People of royalty who once had it all were covered in filth and roaming the streets (v3-5, 7-8). The cause of their punishment came from false religious and political leaders who did not know God or trust in Him (v13-20). Even in this there is a glimmer of hope. The Edomites who rejoiced over Jerusalem's downfall would be punished (v21) and the punishment of Judah would end (v22).

The book of Lamentations closes with a prayer for God to be merciful to His people. In verses 1-10 the author describes the conditions during the time of his prayer. They have lost their inheritance, been exiled, and are starving. The six groups of people in verses 11-13 show that the judgment of God affected everyone. There is no longer any joy among the people (v14-18). Who can help them heal? God is the only One who can help them (v19-22). The author prays that God will restore them and turn their hearts back to Him.

Saturday • 2 Peter

2 Peter was written to encourage the people to grow in their understanding of the Christian life and to practice it (2 Peter 3:18). Peter also writes to warn them of false teachers who have risen up since he last wrote to them (2 Peter 2:1-3). Some have noticed that 1 Peter deals with problems that arise from the outside which try to get into the church while 2 Peter deals with problems that arise from within the church.

In 2 Peter 1:1-11, Peter asks them to keep growing and maturing in the Christian life so they will bear fruit. The foundation of living a fruitful life is in verses 3-4. It is through knowledge of God and Jesus Christ and His promises to all believers that salvation has come. It is through faith in Christ that the fruitful life can begin (v5). Peter then begins to add things needed to live a fruitful life beginning with verse 5. To faith is added virtue (goodness, moral excellence), to virtue is knowledge (of God), to knowledge self-control, to self-control perseverance (endurance), to perseverance godliness (living godly life), to godliness brotherly kindness (love between believers), and to brotherly kindness love. Having these will produce fruit in a believer's life (v8). In verses 12-15 it seems Peter is writing with a sense of urgency, knowing that his death is quickly approaching. In verse 15 Peter may be referring to his writing this letter as the reminder they will have after his death.

In verses 16-21 Peter urges them to follow God's Word because it was spoken to them by the Holy Spirit. Peter notes in verse 16 that they were eyewitnesses to Jesus. Verse 18 reveals that Peter has in mind the time he, James, and John saw Jesus transformed before them on the mountain (Matt. 17). According to verse 19, Peter uses this example to show his readers that his experience on the mountain confirms the prophetic words he has been giving them. It is the truth of God that God gave to the prophets as they were moved by the Holy Spirit (v20-21). Because it has come from God through the prophets, Peter tells them they should "heed" (pay attention) to it. Peter knows it is through the Word of God that they must keep maturing and heeding God's word to combat the false teachers which is the subject of chapter 2.

2 Peter 2 is a warning against false teachers and bears a strong resemblance to the book of Jude. It covers the destructive doctrines of false teachers (v1-3), the doom of false teachers (v4-11), the depravity of false teachers (v12-17), and the deception of false teachers (v18-22). The teaching of the false teachers is denying the redemptive sacrifice of the Lord Jesus Christ (v1). Peter says that many will follow them because of their deceptive words (v2-3). Judgment will come upon them because they have blasphemed God. Matthew 10:33 says "Whoever denies Me before men, I also will deny before My Father in heaven".

In verses 4-11 Peter presents their actions and their judgment with examples from the Old Testament. Using the generation of Noah and Sodom and Gomarrah, Peter tells of the certain judgment that awaits them. Another prevailing theme not often seen in these verses is the deliverance of the godly. Both Noah and Lot were saved from judgment while those who opposed God received the judgment due to them. Some do not believe Peter could describe Lot as righteous. While Lot lived in Sodom he did show kindness to the angels when they visited him, even protecting them from a violent mob. Genesis 18:25 will give you a clue as to why Lot was not judged along with Sodom and Gomorrah.

In verses 12-17 Peter relates the depravity of false teachers. In verses 12-13 the false teachers will be destroyed and receive the judgment that is due for their sin. It is clear from verses 13-14 that these false teachers indulge themselves in immorality to the point that they cannot even stop from sinning. Verse 14 also adds that they have a heart that is covetous (greedy) and that they are accursed children (under a curse). Verse 15 says that they have "forsaken the right way". It literally reads "they have forsaken the straight way". There is only one way to God (John 14:6).

In verses 18-22 Peter shows the deceptions the false teachers use. In verse 18 the issue is with new converts to Christianity. New converts, as seen even in our day, are prey for those who promote false teaching. This is done through their words and also their deeds of sin. Verse 19 shows that while they believe they are free to live how they want, they are actually slaves to their depraved way of thinking and living. Verses 20-22 relate to the recent converts discussed above. If they give in to the seducing of the false teachers they will be worse off than before their conversion. How can they be worse off? Because many of those who have been exposed to the Christian faith then reject it are unlikely to return again. It also shows that they were not truly converted to begin with. 1 John 2:19 "They went out from us, but they were not of us; for if they had been of us, they would no doubt have continued with us: but they went out, that they might be made manifest that they were not all of us."

In 2 Peter 3:1-9 Peter reminds them to remember the words of the Lord and of His prophets warning them of the coming of false teachers. Peter has already spoken of some of the teachings that the false teachers promoted (2:1). Another subject that the false teachers attacked was the second coming of Christ (v4). This is similar to Ezekiel prophesying the coming judgment of God and the people mocking him because it had not happened yet (Ez. 12:22). It may be that the false teachers believed that if Christ was not coming then there would be no future judgment. They could live like they want to live with no consequences, because as far as they believed God was no longer active in the world. Peter reminds them in verses 5-7 that God is still at work in the world, just as when He created it. The reference to the flood in verse 6 also points toward judgment spoken of in verse 7. While God pledged not to destroy the world with water ever again (Gen. 9:11-17), God will destroy it with fire. Verse 8 is probably an allusion to Psalm 90:4 which compares the eternal God with the temporary state of humanity. Just because God is delaying His coming does not mean He will not come. There is a reason God is delaying His coming. Peter cites the reason for the delay in the Lord's coming as the salvation of people (v9).

In verses 10-13 Peter describes the coming of the Lord (v10-11), and the coming judgment (v12-13). Peter emphasizes that the Lord "will come" (v10). His coming will be like a thief in the night (Matt. 24:42-44, 1 Thess. 5:2, Rev. 3:3, 16:15). This is the focal point of this verse. Peter is saying the Lord will absolutely and most certainly come. Because the Lord is coming believers should strive to live holy lives (v11). Believers then can look forward to the day of His coming (v12). Peter also reminds them that when this takes place there will be a new heaven and a new earth where only those who are righteous (believer) will live (v13). In verses 14-18 Peter encourages them to be on alert for false teachers who teach false doctrines and to continue to grow in their faith.

Cover to Cover
CHALLENGE

Week 44

Sunday • Psalm 119:153-176

Welcome to week 44 of the *Cover to Cover Challenge*! Continue to pray for understanding as we study the Word of God, and pray for the Lord to be honored and glorified. Psalm 119:162 says "I rejoice at Your word as one who finds great treasure".

In Psalm 119:153-160 the psalmist is not only seeking to be delivered but is seeking for the Lord to revive him. He knows this can only be accomplished through God and His Word. He pleads for God to defend him against the wicked who do not seek His Word while the psalmist loves it. The psalmist is still being persecuted in verses 161-168. His comfort is in God's Word for which he praises God seven times a day. He obeys God's Word because through it he has peace. In verses 169-176 the psalmist is still broken over his situation which has yet to be resolved. He prays for God to give him understanding, and for deliverance. He pledges to God that he will remain committed to His Word and will praise the Lord when his deliverance comes.

Monday • Deuteronomy 7-9

In Deuteronomy 7:1-11 Moses makes it clear to the people of Israel that God had chosen them to be His own special people. This choosing was not because they deserved it, but was based on the love the Lord had for them. Because they were chosen by God, they should be obedient to what the Lord had instructed them to do. Verses 12-15 contain a promise of blessing for those who are obedient to the Lord. God would bless them and cause them to be successful in every aspect if they would remain faithful to His word. In verses 16-26 the wicked nations will suffer defeat, also based upon them remaining obedient and faithful to the Lord. They were to destroy the nations given over to them by the Lord so they would not fall into idolatry.

In Deuteronomy 8, Moses is reminding the people of Israel not to forget what the Lord has done for them (v1-2). Although they had been disobedient and grumbled against the Lord, He had remained faithful to His promises to them and provided for their needs (v3-5). The people of Israel's response should be to obey the Lord (v6-8). God was blessing them with a land of their own (v7-9), and Moses warns them that when God causes them to prosper not to become arrogant and forget God (v10-14). It is only because of God's faithfulness they endured the 40 years of wandering (v15-18). The people of Israel must make every effort to remember what God had done for them (Deut. 6). If they rebel against the Lord they will be punished, just like the nations the Lord drove out before them (v19-20).

In Deuteronomy 8 the Israelites were to remember what God had done for them, and here in chapter 9 they will need to remember what their fathers had done in the wilderness. In verses 1-3 Moses tells the people they will be successful in defeating the Anakites because the Lord will fight for them. It is because of the Anakites they did not enter Canaan 40 years earlier (Num. 13:26-33). In verses 4-6 Moses ensures them that they are not receiving the land because of their righteousness, but because of the other nations' unrighteousness and God's faithfulness to His covenant. The people of Israel are stubborn and do not deserve the land. In verses 7-29 Moses reminds them of the golden calf (Ex. 32), along with three other instances where the people of Israel doubted God and complained about what He did give them (Taberah Num.11:1-3; Massah Ex. 17, Kibroth Hattaavah Num.11-4-35). At the end of the passage, Moses reminds them that they also failed to enter the land of Canaan earlier because their fear was greater than their trust in God.

Tuesday • 2 Kings 16-20

2 Kings 16 concerns Ahaz, who ruled over Judah for 16 years. His reign is known for three things. First, he is known for following the ways of the kings of Israel, sacrificing his own son to Molech (v1-4). Second, was the war with Rezin king of Syria and Pekah the king of Israel (v5-9). What reasons that lie behind this are uncertain, but it gave opportunity for God to deal with the apostasy of Israel and Judah at the same time. These events are also recorded in Isaiah 7. It is through Isaiah, God assures Ahaz that his enemies will fall. Because Ahaz depended on the Assyrians, Judah would become a vassal state to the Assyrians. Third, Ahaz is known for changing the religious practices of Judah. In verses 10-20 he orders Urijah to build an altar patterned after the Assyrians altar, and rearranges the temple furnishings. 2 Chronicles 28 records that Ahaz closed the temple, and all worship was offered at the new altar, showing further his declining spiritual condition.

2 Kings 17 records the fall of Israel under the reign of Hoshea, who ruled for 9 years. His attempt to break away from Assyria was unsuccessful and he was carried away captive, along with Israel (v1-6). The reason for their captivity was they had sinned against the Lord and had begun to worship the idols and gods of the nations, something that God warned them not to do (v7-12). They had also ignored God's prophets, Gods word, and God Himself- becoming slaves to sin (v13-18). The captivity of Israel would also serve as a lesson to Judah (v19-23). Assyria sent many other nations to live in Israel and to occupy the land (v24-28). The northern kingdom of Israel would become a scene of false religions, all because Israel chose not to follow God (v29-41).

2 Kings 18-20 is the story of Hezekiah, who ruled over Judah for 29 years. In 18:1-8 Hezekiah's character is of one who trusts the Lord, is faithful to the Lord, and obeys the Lord. Hezekiah's reforms involved rededicating the temple and reinstituting the Passover celebration (2 Chron. 30). In verses 9-12, we are also told of the captivity of Israel because of their disobedience to God during the 4th year of Hezekiah's reign. Verses 13-16 speak of Hezekiah's submission to Assyria in paying tribute to them. In verses 17-25 the king of Assyria sent a delegation to meet with Hezekiah's men. These men warn Hezekiah not to trust in his military, his alliance with Egypt, or the Lord. In verses 26-37 the men from Assyria warn all the people not to trust in Hezekiah or the Lord to deliver them from the Assyrian army. None of the other nations they had conquered, or their gods, could stop the king of Assyria. After hearing the words spoken by the Assyrian delegation, Hezekiah mourns over the situation (19:2). Hezekiah believed they were being punished for their sin (v3). Hezekiah sends them to Isaiah so he can pray for the nation (v4-5). Through Isaiah, God sends a message to Hezekiah not to be afraid of the Assyrians (v5-7). Once more the Rabshakeh (chief captain) of the Assyrians returns to threaten Hezekiah to not trust in the Lord to deliver them

because no god of any of the other nations had been able to (v8-13). Beginning in verse 14, Hezekiah cries out to the Lord for deliverance from the Assyrian army. In his prayer, Hezekiah affirms that God is the only God and is also the Creator of all things. Hezekiah prays that through God's deliverance of His people others will know that He is the Lord. God hears Hezekiah's prayer and sends Isaiah with an answer. Sennacherib, who is the king of Assyria, will answer for his pride and arrogance against the Lord (v21-28). God will also give Hezekiah a sign that He will deliver His people (v29-31) and there will not even be a battle to be fought (v32-34). In verses 35-37 the angel of the Lord (preincarnate Christ) kills 185,000 of the Assyrian army, and later Sennacherib's sons would kill him as well.

2 Kings 20 tells the story of Hezekiah's sickness, healing, and the miraculous sign God gave him as proof. Isaiah tells Hezekiah to get his house in order because he is going to die (v1). In verses 2-3 Hezekiah pours his heart out to the Lord, reminding the Lord of his devotion and faithfulness to His ways. The Lord answers his prayer before Isaiah leaves. God will add 15 years to his life as he would recover from his sickness (v4-7). The moving of the sun's shadow backwards was a clear sign to Hezekiah that his prayer had been answered (v8-11). Verses 12-21 record the foolishness of Hezekiah in showing the king of Babylon all of the treasures Judah possessed. He is confronted by Isaiah over his decision. Isaiah prophesies that one day the Babylonians would invade them and carry the people away along with the treasures.

Wednesday • Acts 11-12

In Acts 11:1-18, Peter returns to Jerusalem with news of the Gentiles coming to faith in Christ. He recaps his experience from Acts 10 to the Jews he was speaking with. Up to this point in church history, Christianity was considered a movement within Judaism. Many Jews would proclaim that these new Gentile Christians should become circumcised and obey the Jewish dietary laws as a Jewish proselyte would. This will become a point of contention settled by the Jerusalem Council in Acts 15. Paul would also write a letter to the Galatians concerning this same thought. Notice in verse 16, Peter recalls the words Jesus had spoken to them. Up until this point the church was primarily Jewish, so it was vital they had proof that God was also moving among the Gentiles.

The church continues to grow and move toward Antioch because of the persecution mentioned in Acts 7-8. It is believed that Antioch had a population somewhere between 500,000-800,000 people. Verses 19-21 show the church being established and the beginning of their outreach. Verses 22-24 show that the church in Antioch was endorsed by the Jerusalem church through the sending of Barnabas. Barnabas plays a crucial role in the church, and the description of him in verses 23-24 is spoken of no other person in Acts. He is also the first to reach out to Saul (Paul) and give him opportunity to minister. They stay and preach for a year in Antioch, where believers are first called Christians (v25-26). A prophet by the name of Agabus predicts a famine (46-47 AD), and the church in Antioch prepares to collect an offering for the church in Judea (v27-30). Agabus will also appear again in Acts 21:10-11, prophesying the arrest of Paul.

In Acts 12:1-4 the church continues to be persecuted, this time by Herod. James the brother of John is the first apostle to die, and it is also during this time that they arrest Peter and place him in prison during the Feast of Unleavened Bread. Herod would not put Peter to death during these days because this would anger the Jews. Verses 5-19 tell the miraculous story of the release of Peter from prison the night before his trial, after which he probably would have been killed. Verse 5 says that the church was in constant prayer for Peter and verse 7 records the answer to their prayer. Verses 12-15 have often caught people's attention. Why did they say she was seeing Peter's angel? Jews believed that each person had a guardian angel and that angel appeared after their death. The James who is mentioned in verse 17 is the Lord's brother who became one of the leaders in the early church (Gal. 2:9). The killing of the guards proved Herod's plan for Peter. If a Roman guard allowed their prisoner to escape they suffered the penalty the escaped prisoner would have suffered. In verses 20-24 the people of Tyre and Sidon pay a visit to Herod because he is angry with them. Herod wanted to be worshiped as God, and here he actually accepted the people's worship. Because he accepted God's glory for himself, the Lord killed him. As a result of Herod's death the word of God continued to spread. Evil men like Herod may chain the men who preach the gospel, but the word of God can never be chained.

Thursday • Proverbs 28

Proverbs 28:1 states that those who are righteous will be given boldness to stand up to anything especially the wicked. Verse 2 says that when a leader has wisdom the nation and his rule will last. You can see this proverb come to life in the descriptions we have been reading about the northern and southern kingdoms. Many believe verse 3 goes with verse 2, as the result of leaders who do not have wisdom. Poverty can become so bad that even the poor prey on one another. Verse 4 is teaching that those who do not keep God's law praise the wicked, but those who do will stand up for what is right. Verse 5 teaches that those who are evil are spiritually blind, but those who seek God have understanding in all things. Verse 6 is teaching that it is better to have integrity than to be rich. Verse 7 speaks about the wise son who keeps God's law. Verse 8 is teaching that if a man gains money by unjust means, God will make sure that money goes to someone who will give it to the poor. Verse 9 is teaching that if a person refuses to hear God's law then his prayers will certainly not be heard. Verse 10 says that those who purposely cause people to stumble will be destroyed (Matt. 18:6). Verse 11 teaches that the poor but wise man can see through the plans of the rich self-centered man. Verse 12 is much like verse 2. When the righteous rule there is rejoicing, but when the wicked rules men hide. Verse 13 teaches that those who confess their sins will receive mercy. Verse 14 is teaching that those who have fear of the Lord will be happy, but those who harden their hearts will keep falling deeper into sin. Verses 15-16 are also like verses 2 and 12, speaking about the type of rulers who rule over people. Verse 17 is teaching the judgment of the wicked. Verse 18 teaches that those who walk according to God will be delivered, but those walk crookedly will fall suddenly. Verse 19 is teaching the advantages of hard work versus those who are lazy and will not work. Verse 20 is teaching that those who faithfully work will be blessed, but those who pursue riches through unjust ways will be guilty. Verse 21 teaches not to be a respecter of persons. Verse 22 is teaching that a person who chases after riches will be poor. Verse 23 teaches that it is better to rebuke someone when they do wrong than to flatter them and approve of their ways. Verse 24 teaches that a person who despises their parents is likened to someone who only destroys. Verse 25 is teaching that a proud person is always fighting, but those who trust in God will have their needs met. Verse 26 teaches that people should not trust in their own heart, but rely on God's wisdom. Verse 27 teaches that people should help the poor, not ignore them. Verse 28 is like verses 2, 12, 15-16. It concerns leadership that is wicked or righteous.

Friday • Daniel 1-6

Daniel ("God is My Judge") covers the entire period of the Babylonian exile. Daniel is the author of the book that bears his name (8:1, 9:2, 10:2). Jesus also accepted Daniel as the author of the book (Matt. 24:15). Daniel is also mentioned by Ezekiel as being righteous (14:14, 20; 28:3). Ezekiel, Habakkuk, Jeremiah, and Zephaniah also prophesied during the time of Daniel. Daniel would become God's spokesperson during this time to the Jewish and the Gentile world, proclaiming God's present and future plans. This book is also unique in that it was written in two languages. Chapters 1 and 8-12 are written in Hebrew and the primary subject is God's special plans for His people. Chapters 2-7 were written in Aramaic, which was the common language of the day. These chapters cover the Babylonian and Persian empires. Daniel was taken into captivity during the first siege on Jerusalem in 605 BC, and Ezekiel in the second siege in 597 BC. Daniel probably wrote the book in 526-535 BC. One of the main purposes for the book of Daniel is for those in exile to see that God was sovereign and still in control. The time of Daniel is known as one of the periods in history where God supernaturally intervened to accomplish His purposes (Dan. 1-6). The others are during creation, during the time of Moses, the times of Elijah and Elisha, Jesus and the apostles, and a future day when Jesus comes again. Another theme in Daniel is how to live for God in a society where God's people are in the minority. The power of prayer is also another theme.

Daniel 1:1-2 gives the context of the first deportation of the Jews to Babylon. Even in the first two verses, Daniel is sure to point out that God was in control of the whole situation. Nebuchadnezzar took the most promising and gifted Israelites. They gave them new names, and taught them the way of the Babylonians (v3-7). Daniel, Hananiah, Mishael, and Azariah became Balteshazzar, Shadrach, Meshach, and Abed-Nego. Their first test of remaining true to the Lord involved declining the king's food, which was probably sacrificed to idols, only wanting vegetables and water (v8-16). After a period of testing, Daniel and his friends were more nourished than those who ate the king's food. God blessed the four young men with knowledge, skill, and wisdom (v17). Daniel could also interpret dreams, much like Joseph in Egypt, another godly man in a foreign land. Nebuchadnezzar approved of them and gave them a prominent place in his kingdom (v18-20). Verse 21 helps date the book of Daniel as the first year of Cyrus, which would have been when the Jews went back to Jerusalem.

In Daniel 2:1-13 Nebuchadnezzar demands that the dream he has had be interpreted so he asks his own wise men to tell him. The catch is they must not only interpret the dream, but also tell the content of the dream he had before interpreting it. When the wise men are unable to do so Nebuchadnezzar gives a decree for all the wise men to be killed including Daniel and his friends. Arioch, the captain of the king's guard, tells Daniel of Nebuchadnezzar's decree (v14-23). Daniel asks for time so he may find out the dream and its interpretation. Daniel and his three friends pray to the Lord for the answer, and the king's dream is revealed to Daniel. Daniel praises the Lord for His wisdom and power in revealing the dream and its interpretation. In verses 24-35 Daniel reveals the dream, and in verses 36-47 interprets it. The dream is of a giant statue that represents Nebuchadnezzar's kingdom and the future kingdoms of the world. The golden head is Nebuchadnezzar's kingdom, the silver is Medo-Perisa, the bronze is Greece, the iron is Rome, and the feet of iron and clay is a mixed kingdom. The rock cut from the mountain that smashes the statue is God's kingdom (Dan. 7). Because Daniel was able to interpret the dream, he received a prominent standing in Babylon along with his friends (v48-49).

Daniel 3:1-18 concerns Shadrach, Meshach, and Abed-Nego being thrown in the fiery furnace for not bowing down to worship Nebuchadnezzar's golden image. Just as they did earlier, they chose to make a stand and be faithful to the Lord whether they were delivered or not. In verses 19-23 Nebuchadnezzar orders the furnace to be made hotter and throws them into the fiery furnace. Verses 24-27 reveal that the three men were not even harmed by the fire, but that there was a fourth man (Jesus) walking among the fire with them who had delivered them. Nebuchadnezzar praises the God of Shadrach, Meshach, and Abed-Nego and promotes them in the kingdom (v28-30).

Daniel 4 is the story of Nebuchadnezzar's insanity because of his pride. This is written in the form of a decree by Nebuchadnezzar after he had experienced insanity (v1-7). Once again the wise men were unable to interpret the dream, and Nebuchadnezzar calls upon Daniel. In verses 8-18 the dream of the great tree is described. The tree will be judged by God and for seven years suffer as a beast of the field. In verses 19-27 Daniel interprets the dream to be Nebuchadnezzar who would lose his rule and his sanity and live like wild beasts in the field, but after a time be restored to his throne. After one year the dream comes to fulfillment. As you can see Nebuchadnezzar was judged because of his pride, never realizing it was God who had given him his kingdom (v28-33). After the seven years passed Nebuchadnezzar praises God, realizes God's kingdom will never end, and acknowledges that he, as well as humanity, is nothing before a sovereign God.

In Daniel 5:1-4, Belshazzar is having a great feast using the sacred vessels taken from the temple in Jerusalem. Then appeared a hand writing on the wall about Belshazzar's doom (v5-9). With the wise men unable to interpret the words, the queen remembers Daniel who had helped Nebuchadnezzar with many mysteries (v10-16). Daniel recites the lesson Belshazzar should have learned from the life of Nebuchadnezzar: you have lifted up yourself and not God (v17-24). Daniel interprets the four words written on the wall by the divine hand (v25-29). Belshazzar's rule would meet its end at the hands of the Medes and the Persians that very night (v30-31).

Daniel 6:1-9 covers the story of Daniel being thrown in the den of lions. Daniel was one of the head governors over the new Medo-Persian kingdom. Acting out of jealousy the other rulers tried to find fault in Daniel, but could find none. The only way they could trap Daniel is in his relationship with God, so a decree was made that no one could petition any man or god except for the king. Daniel never wavered in his faithfulness to God as he continued to pray three times a day (v10). He was caught by the other rulers and found to be guilty of violating the king's decree and was thrown in the den of lions (v11-17). Darius could not eat or sleep, and prayed for Daniel's God to deliver him from the lions (v18-24). In returning to the den Darius found Daniel safe because the Lord had sent an angel to shut the mouths of the lions. Daniel's accusers and their families were thrown into the den of lions. In verses 25-28 Darius gave glory to God and proclaimed that God was alive as He acts in history, His rule is eternal, and He performs miracles to deliver His people.

Saturday • Hebrews 1-4

The book of Hebrews is a unique book, for only it pictures Jesus as our Great High Priest. Jesus is presented in this book as being greater than the prophets, the angels, Moses, Joshua, the high priest, the Levitical priests, and Abraham. He offers a better covenant, and He offered a greater sacrifice. This letter was written around 65-70 AD. It was written in the style of a sermon, to Jews who were wavering in their commitment to Christ around 65-70 AD because of the growing persecution of Christians. One thing this book does is show that Jesus reigns supreme, and that all Scripture points to Him.

Hebrews 1:1-4 shows that God spoke to man throughout the ages in many ways; such as a burning bush, a still small voice, in visions and dreams, and now through Jesus. The author of Hebrews points out 7 things about Jesus. He is the heir of all things, He made the worlds (creation), He is the express image (exact representation) of God, He upholds (sustains) all things, He has purged our sins, and He has sat down completing His work of salvation.

In verses 5-14 Jesus is presented as being greater than the angels through seven Old Testament Scriptures. What is foreign to believers today is the Jewish belief of angels. Angels play a prominent role in Scripture. They were created to worship God, and some of them rebelled against God. Many believe the Bible even speaks of guardian angels (Matt. 18:10). Scripture records that the heavens rejoice (including angels) at someone's salvation (Luke 15:10). Angels came to predict Jesus' birth, they ministered to Him, they announced His resurrection, His ascension, and they will come with Him at His second coming. Paul warns in Colossians 2:18 not to worship them. The Jews believed that angels controlled the movement of the stars even to the point of controlling time. Some believed that there were angels who controlled the rain, snow, and frost. According to Acts 7:51-53 and Galatians 3:19 the Jews believed that the angels mediated the Old Testament from God to man. If the writer of Hebrews was going to persuade those he was writing to that Jesus initiated a better covenant, he would have to prove that Jesus is greater than the angels.

Verse 5 is a quote from Psalm 2:7, which was sung at the crowning of a king, and from 2 Samuel 7:14. Both of these quotes show that Jesus is God's Son. Verse 6 is a quote from Psalm 97:7 and shows that Jesus is worshiped. Verse 7 is a quote from Psalm 104:4 which shows that Jesus is greater than the angels because He never changes. Verses 8-9 are a quote from Psalm 45:6-7 and are proofs of His deity. Verses 10-12 are from Psalm 102:25-27 and show that Jesus is eternal and creator. Verse 13 is from Psalm 110:1 shows that Jesus is the ruler of the universe. Sitting on the throne is a symbol of complete and final victory.

In Hebrews 2:1-4 the writer breaks from proving that Jesus is greater than the angels to focus on his audience. Because the writer of Hebrews has begun to prove that Jesus is greater than the angels, that means the words He spoke are greater (words of the New Covenant). In verses 1-4 the author of Hebrews warns them to pay attention to the words of the New Covenant. If they are not careful they will neglect the gospel and drift past it. Verses 2-3 compare the judgment that happened under the Old Covenant and was mediated by angels to the judgment that will come if they neglect the words of Christ and the New Covenant. Verse 4 offers proof that the New Covenant is greater than the Old Covenant.

Hebrews 2:5-9 teaches that Jesus is greater than the angels, and shows that Jesus was made lower than the angels (becoming a man) so He could provide salvation for man. Jesus' greatness is seen in the salvation He provided, because He became like those He came to save (v10-18). This passage says that Jesus is our Savior (v10), our Sanctifier (v11-13), our Satan defeater (v14-15), our Succourer (comes to the aid of, v16), and the Satisfier of our sins (v17-18).

In Hebrews 3:1-6, the author shows that Jesus is greater than Moses who is regarded by the Jews to be the greatest person of all. The author of Hebrews wants the readers to consider the life of Jesus and how He is greater than Moses. The word "consider" means to fix your thoughts on or to reflect on something. Verse 1 calls Jesus an Apostle (one who is sent) and our High Priest, emphasizing the sacrificial aspect of His mission. Also because Jesus is the Great High Priest He is holding an office that Moses never held-being a priest. The writer speaks of both Jesus and Moses being faithful (v2, Num. 12:7-8). Jesus is greater than Moses because He built the house and was a Son over the house (v2-6). Even Jesus taught the principle that being a son is greater than being a slave (John 8:35).

In verses 7-19 the author contrasts the Israelites disobedience in the wilderness to his present listeners, challenging them to walk closer to God. The writer builds on the theme of rest, which he sees now as being fulfilled in Christ. Verses 7-11 are from Psalm 95 and describe the wanderings in the wilderness after being delivered from Egyptian bondage. He is urging the readers that if they hear His voice they should not ignore it. He is also urging them to not be like the unfaithful Israelites, but to be faithful. If they would believe in Jesus they could enter that rest. Not all will enter into that rest, although they have the opportunity to do so (v12-19). The people were probably being tempted to go back to Judaism because it was an accepted religion that enjoyed rights and privileges, whereas Christianity did not.

Hebrews 4:1-10 explains that the rest is still available, and it was not done away with because the ancient Israelites failed to enter into it. Someone will enter the rest-those who believe the message spoken by Jesus and the prophets. Both have heard the same message but with the Israelites they never exercised faith in it. The only way to enter the rest is to place faith in Jesus. Today can be the day that by faith they enter rest (2 Cor. 6:2). Joshua could not lead them to rest but Jesus can, and they must enter it or be disobedient. Verse 9 has a different word for rest in the Greek. The word for rest in verse 9 means Sabbath rest. Sabbath rest was a time used to celebrate centered on praising God.

In verses 11-13 the author of Hebrews explains that God's Word can and will penetrate their heart because they can hide nothing from God. In verse 12 the Word of God is described. God's Word is described with five words. It is living (effective, life-giving), powerful (able to make happen), sharper (never fails to cut), piercing (cuts all way through), and discerning (exposes). God's Word is able to expose people's desires and attitudes.

Verse 13 describes the God of the Word. Everything is known to God and no one can hide from Him. The word "naked" means uncovered or to expose. The word "open" means to lay bare. This word was often used when slaughtering an animal for sacrifice exposing its throat. One day all will face judgment before God and give an account for their life. They can come to Jesus boldly and confidently. He knows our weaknesses because He is our High Priest, and has been in our place, suffering temptation but never sinning (v14-16).

Cover to Cover Challenge

Week 45

Sunday • Psalm 120-127

Welcome to week 45 of the *Cover to Cover Challenge*! Continue to pray for our understanding of the Word of God, that the presence of the Holy Spirit will be made known, and for the Lord to be honored and glorified through the *Cover to Cover Challenge*. Psalm 121:1-2 says "I will lift my eyes up to the hills, from where comes my help? My help comes from the Lord, who made heaven and earth".

Psalm 120-134 are the "Songs of the Ascents". Many believe this name comes from the people "ascending" to Jerusalem to celebrate the feasts. Psalm 120 is a psalm of lament. The psalmist is praying to God for deliverance from his enemies who are liars and deceivers (v1-4). He is a man dwelling among the ungodly striving for peace but his enemies only want war (v5-7).

In Psalm 121 the psalmist looks to the heavens for help from his Creator. It is God who keeps watch over His people (v3-4). God is pictured in this psalm as being the protector of His people (v5-6) and the preserver of His people (v7-8).

In Psalm 122:1-2 the psalmist finds joy each time he visits Jerusalem. When the people gather together in Jerusalem they give thanks to the Lord (v3-5). He urges all to pray for the peace of Jerusalem (v6-9). He specifically prays for all who love Jerusalem to prosper, and for those who live there to experience peace and prosperity.

Psalm 123 is a psalm of lament. In this psalm the people are looking to God, depending on Him for mercy (v1-2). They long to experience His mercy in the face of those who are proud and arrogant (v3-4).

Psalm 124 is a psalm of thanksgiving to God for delivering them from their enemies. The psalmist knows if the Lord had not delivered them they would have perished (v1-5). They have experienced the protecting and preserving hand of God (Ps. 121). They bless God because He has helped them during a great time of need (v6-8).

Psalm 125 is a song of confidence in the Lord. Those who trust in God have confidence in the Lord, knowing He will not allow them to be moved (v1-2). God had always promised to be the protector of His people if they would be obedient to Him (v3). The psalmist asks God to repay people according to their deeds, whether they are good or evil (v4-5). He asks this so there will be peace in Israel.

Psalm 126 concerns the return from exile. The people were filled with laughter and joy because the Lord had brought them back to their land (v1-3). This was also a witness to the nations that God was good in delivering His people. Upon their return, the land was not as it once was. The restoration of the land would be hard work, but once completed there would be joy in the land (v4-6).

Psalm 127 is a wisdom psalm. The building of the house in verses 1-2 may refer to raising a family (Gen. 16:2,

Ruth 4:11). If this is the case the Lord should be the center of the home because He will watch over and protect it. God will bless the family with an inheritance, security, and protection (v3-5).

Monday • Deuteronomy 10-12

In Deuteronomy 10:1-5, Moses continues with the rest of the story from chapter 9 and what takes place after their idolatry with the golden calf. What is shown here is that God is a forgiving God who gives the people another opportunity to believe in Him. Verses 6-9 tell of their travels, the death of Aaron, and the Levites being set apart as priests. In verses 12-22 Moses speaks about the importance of having a heart that is right with God in order to serve Him. This would require the people to love the Lord and be obedient to His commandments (v12-13). After speaking about God's choice of Israel (v14-15), Moses once again returns to the issue of the heart. Circumcision was a sign of the covenant made with Abraham, but the intent was always to be internal and not just external. No one will be loyal to the Lord unless it comes from the heart. In verses 17-22 Moses recalls God's faithfulness to the people and that they must worship and serve Him.

In Deuteronomy 11:1-7 Moses will continue to encourage the people to love God if they wanted to remain in the land He is giving them. All obedience starts with love (John 14:23, 15:10). They are also to recall what God has done for them in rescuing and providing for them. They are even to remember the disciplining hand of the Lord. In verses 8-25 their possession and blessing in the land is directly related to their obedience. Canaan would be more blessed than if they had stayed in Egypt. Moses warns against worshiping other gods in the land (v16). To prevent this, they were to always have God's Word before them dwelling in their hearts and minds (v18). With obedience there will be blessing and with disobedience there will be a curse (v26-32).

Deuteronomy 12:1-4 serves as a warning not to worship the gods of the people in the land of Canaan. They were to destroy everything that had to do with pagan worship to keep themselves from being tempted to worship other gods. Verses 5-28 cover where and how they are to worship God according to the way God had instructed. What is clear in verses 7, 12, 18 is that worship is a time that families gather to worship the Lord with joy. They were not going through the motions, but worshiping God for all of His blessings on them. Verses 29-32 serve as another warning not to worship the gods of the Canaanites. Verse 31 shows that child sacrifice was already being practiced by them. This is why Moses reiterates to them that they are to worship God the way God had instructed (v32).

Tuesday • 2 Kings 21-25

In 2 Kings 21 Hezekiah's son Manasseh rules over Judah for 55 years- the longest reign of any king. Verses 1-6 tell that he rebuilt all of the pagan religious sites that were torn down by his father. It is during Manasseh's reign that Judah became more wicked than the Amorites, whom God had driven from the land (v7-9). Because of this, Judah was destined to be judged by God and destroyed (v10-18). 2 Chronicles 33 records the repentance of Manasseh toward the end of his reign. Upon his death his son Amon, who followed Manasseh's ways, reigns for two years before he is assassinated by his own servants (v19-26).

2 Kings 22 Amon's son Josiah reigns in Judah. Josiah led one of the greatest revivals in Judah's history. Josiah followed in the footsteps of David, walking in the ways of the Lord (v1-2). His reform included repairing the temple (v3-7), returning to the word of God (v8-10), and repentance expressed by the king (v11-12). Josiah also

realized that they had been disobedient to God by not obeying the Lord (v13). Because Josiah humbled himself and grieved over Judah's sin, he would be spared from seeing God's judgment on Judah (v14-20).

In 2 Kings 23 Josiah brought sweeping reforms to the land of Judah and beyond. In verses 1-3 he leads the people to renew their covenant with God, and removes the pagan influences from temple (v4-7), and surrounding areas (v8-18). Josiah's reforms even went to places in the former northern kingdom of Israel (v19-20). The Passover was celebrated again according to the law (v21-25), and people from Israel celebrated with them (2 Chron. 35). Despite all of the reform, the judgment of God would still come (v26-27). Josiah would die in battle and his son Jehoahaz would become king (v28-30). Within 23 years the siege on Judah by the Babylonians would begin. Jehoahaz only reigned three months before being taken captive to Egypt and Jehoiakim, Josiah's son, would become king (v31-34). Jehoiakim's reign would last 11 years. His reign is noted in Jeremiah to be filled with opposition to God (Jer. 26:20-23, 36:21-23).

In 2 Kings 24:1-7 we see that during the reign of Jehoiakim Judah became a vassal state of Babylon. Because of their sin Judah would suffer at the hands of the Babylonians. After the death of Jehoiakim, his son Jehoiachin would reign for only 3 months (v8-16). Jehoiachin would be taken prisoner to Babylon, along with his family and officials. Josiah's son Zedekiah would then be king over Judah and would reign 11 years. Like those before him, he would do evil in the sight of the Lord and also rebel against Babylon (v17-20).

2 Kings 25:1-3 records the final siege by the Babylonians in which they surrounded the city, which caused a famine. For his rebellion, Zedekiah is caught trying to escape and is forced to watch his own sons be killed before having his eyes put out (v4-7). Nebuzaradan, the commander of Nebuchadnezzar's army, completes the destruction of Jerusalem and tears down the walls (v8-12). They also carry away the rest of the temple furnishings (v13-17). The officials who are not deported are executed, leaving no one behind to lead (v18-21). Nebuchadnezzar appoints Gedaliah governor over Judah, but he is soon killed by Ishmael (v22-26). Jehoichin is released from prison by Nebuchadnezzar's son, who gave him a seat at the king's table (v27-30).

Wednesday • Acts 13-14

In Acts 13:1-3, Antioch of Syria became the sending center of the church's mission. Here, Saul and Barnabas are called by the Holy Spirit to carry the gospel on their first missionary journey. Paul always went to the synagogues first to preach to the Jews (v4-12). John is John Mark (12:25), who is the writer of the gospel of Mark. In Cyprus they meet Sergius Paulus, who has asked to hear their message. Elymas the sorcerer is there to keep Sergius from hearing the gospel. Sergius is the highest ranking government official to be converted in the New Testament. Elymas' other name, Bar-Jesus, means "son of the Savior". Paul tells him he is a son of the devil. Different interpretations for the blindness have been offered. Some believe Paul asked for him to be made blind in the hope that the blindness would lead to repentance as it did for Paul. Others believe the blindness was symbolic of his own spiritual blindness. Beginning in verses 13-15, they went to Antioch of Pisidia and Paul preached in the synagogue there. It was customary to have visiting rabbis speak.

In verses 16-41 Paul's sermon has much in common with both Peter's sermon and the speech made by Stephen. In verses 16-25 Paul gives a sketch of Old Testament history that emphasizes God's promises to Israel. Stephen did this to show Israel's rebellion against God. Much like Peter, Paul gives Scriptural proof of how Jesus is the fulfillment of these promises (v26-37). In verses 38-41 Paul gives them an invitation to accept these promises that are fulfilled in Christ, and he also warns his audience against rejecting God's Word. Paul and Barnabas were invited back on the next Sabbath to speak with the Gentiles, who showed special interest in what they had spoken (v42-44). In verses 45-52 the Jews oppose the preaching of Paul and Barnabas. Paul explained to them that they were always supposed to be a light to the Gentiles (Isa. 49:6). With these words they turn to the Gentiles and many of them believe. The action of shaking the dust off your feet is a sign of disassociation.

In Acts 14:1-7 Paul and Barnabas go to Iconium to preach the gospel. When they arrive they once again meet opposition from the Jews. Paul's method was to go to the Jewish synagogues first. Not only would the Jews hear the gospel, but Gentiles who had converted to Judaism would have also heard it. From here they travel to Lystra, where Paul heals a man who had never walked (v8-18). This healing is similar in nature to the healing of the lame man (3:2-10) and the healing of Aeneas (9:32-35). In verses 15-17 Paul preaches his first message aimed at the Gentiles. He appeals to them through general revelation, by showing them that God is the Creator (v15). They also should know from God's common graces (v17) that God exists. Romans 1:18-25 testifies that through creation, and through His providence toward all people, it can be seen that God exists and can be known.

In verses 19-20, Paul is stoned by the Jews who followed them from Antioch and Iconium. This incident is probably what Paul is referring to in 2 Corinthians 11:25. Paul and Barnabas revisit all the places they went on their first missionary journey (v21-28). While they were there Paul and Barnabas did three things. First, they strengthened the disciples. This may be referring to further instruction and teaching. Second, they exhorted the new disciples to continue in the faith. Persecutions and sufferings would come because they believed in Jesus. Third, they appointed leadership within the churches. Those appointed would care for the church. It is believed Paul may have written Galatians when they returned to Antioch of Syria in order to report what God had done on the first missionary journey.

Thursday • Proverbs 29-30

Proverbs 29:1 can be seen as a warning not to harden our hearts when the Lord corrects us. Verse 2 teaches that a righteous ruler will bring rejoicing to the people. This can be seen from the lessons from the kings of the northern and southern kingdoms. Verse 3 is teaching that a son who follows wisdom brings joy to his father. Verse 4 teaches that a king who rules righteously will establish his kingdom, but the one who accepts bribes will have his kingdom overthrown. Verse 5 teaches that over exalting someone will cause them to eventually fall to pride. Verse 6 is teaching there are consequences to your actions. A righteous person will help the poor, but the wicked will not help them (v7). Rulers hardened by sin will cause others to suffer, but a wise ruler will not suffer wrath (v8). The wise person who continually argues with a fool will see no end to the arguing (v9). Verse 10 can be seen in the life of Cain and in loving one's enemies. The fool will speak his mind, but the wise will only speak at the right time (v11). In verse 12 the rulers are again warned against listening to and taking bad advice. Verses 13-14 are teaching that the poor and rich are equal in God's eyes. Disciplining our children will give them wisdom (v15, 17). Verse 16 is teaching that those who are righteous will see those who practice sin fall. Verse 18 does not refer to a man's vision for something, but to revelation from God. Verse 19 is teaching that it takes more than words of correction to correct stubborn people. Verse 20 is teaching that there is more hope for a fool than for a conceited person. Verse 21 is teaching about the impact that people in leadership positions can have on others. Verse 22 teaches that an angry man's temper will continually get worse. Verse 23 teaches that pride brings dishonor and humility brings honor. Verse 24 teaches that those who are brought together by sin will not tell the truth. Verse 25 teaches us to fear God above man. Verse 26 teaches that blessings come from the Lord and not man. Verse 27 shows the attitude of the wicked toward the righteous and the righteous toward the wicked. Both contend with one another. This ends the proverbs of Solomon.

Agur is the author of Proverbs 30. Some believe that Agur has been on a pursuit of human wisdom and finds that wisdom can only come from God, and that this divine wisdom is better than human wisdom (v1-3). The questions of verse 4 all should be answered with no one but God. Only in a relationship with God, through His Son Jesus, can true wisdom be found (Col 2:2-3). He urges the readers to place their trust in God and His Word because it is pure and true (v5-6). In verses 7-9 he asks God to remove deception and lies from him and to be content in his daily life. Verse 10 is a single proverb warning against oppression. Verses 11-14 discuss four types of fools. Verses 15-16 speak of things that will never be satisfied. Verse 17 is teaching us to honor our parents. Verses 18-20 teach four things that are wonderful and mysterious, and are to be contrasted with the adulterous woman. Verses 21-23 give four things that can cause unbearable situations. Verses 24-28 teach four things that are wise and to be learned from. Verses 29-31 are teaching fearlessness and confidence, while verses 32-33 warn against arrogance and exalting yourself.

Friday • Daniel 7-12

In chapter 7 Daniel recalls the vision he had during the reign of Belshazzar. The four beasts in the vision represented four coming world kingdoms. This also goes with chapter 2 and Nebuchadnezzar's dream of the statue, which represents four kingdoms. Verses 1-8 show the vision, and verses 15-27 are the interpretation. The first beast is a winged lion which corresponds to the golden head in chapter 2, and represents Babylon (v4). The second beast, which is a bear, represents Medo-Persia and corresponds to the silver chest and arms in chapter 2 (v5). The three ribs represent the three battles that Medo-Persia fought to gain control. The third beast is a four-winged leopard and corresponds to the bronze belly and thighs of chapter 2. This represents Greece (v6). Upon his death, Alexander's kingdom was separated into four divisions. The fourth beast is the most terrifying of all, and corresponds to the legs and toes of chapter 2- representing the Roman Empire (v7). The "little horn" is the ruler of the fourth kingdom (v8). The fifth and greatest kingdom is represented by the Ancient of Days (God the Father) and the Son of Man, which is Jesus (v9-14). They defeat the "little horn" and confine him to judgment in the burning flame. Verses 13-14 show Jesus before the Father receiving the Kingdom. Most of the interpretation in verses 15-28 concerns the fourth kingdom which disturbed Daniel the most, focusing on the nature of the kingdom (v19-22) and its ruler (v23-25).

Daniel records another vision in chapter 8. Daniel gives the vision in verses 1-14 and Gabriel interprets it for him in verses 15-25. The ram with two horns, with one higher than the other, is the Medo-Persian Empire (v20). The male goat with the large horn is Greece, and represents Alexander the Great. History records that within three years Greece became the dominant world power, conquering Medo-Persia. The four horns represent the division of Alexander's kingdom after his death. The "little horn" in 8:9 is not the one from chapter 7. Here it represents Antiochus Epiphanes IV, who oppressed the Jews. The Jews called him Epimanes ("Mad Man"). He desecrated the temple by putting up a statue of Zeus and offering swine on the altar. The Jews called this the "abomination of desolation" (Dan. 11:31, Matt. 24:15). Antiochus would be a type of "antichrist" that will come in the future. Hanukkah is the celebration of the defeat of Antiochus' army by Judas Maccabaeus.

In chapter 9 Daniel intercedes for his people (v3-19) and receives the answer to his prayers (v20-27). Daniel studied Scripture, and built the following prayer from it. From Jeremiah 25:11-13 and 29:10, Daniel knew that the time would be coming soon for God to fulfill his word and judge Babylon. Although it is not mentioned, Isaiah 44:28 predicted that Cyrus would be the one who would allow the Jews to go back to their homeland. Daniel also prepared himself to pray by fasting, putting on sackcloth, and sitting in ashes (v3). Here, for the first time in Daniel, he calls God YAHWEH which is the covenant name for God (v2, 4, 7, 8, 10, 13, 14). He asks God to forgive him and the people of their sin for their rejection of Him (v7-11). He also appeals to God's justice (v11-14) and for God to fulfill His Word for His name's sake (v15-19). Gabriel appears to give Daniel the answer to his prayer (v20-23). The prophecy of the 70 weeks is the unfolding of human history, and is divided into 3 periods of 7 weeks (49 years), 62 weeks (434 years), and 1 week (7 years). When the 70 weeks are complete, the six statements in verse 24 will be completely fulfilled. Verse 25 is the first set of 7 weeks, or 49 years, when the decree was given to rebuild Jerusalem and its walls (Neh. 2:1-8). Verse 26 is the 62 weeks, or 483 years, ending with Jesus' crucifixion. Verse 26 also predicts the destruction of the temple in 70 AD ("destroy the city and the sanctuary"). Verse 27 covers the final week of 7, years known to many as the tribulation period.

In Daniel 10:1-3 Daniel receives another vision from the Lord which caused him to mourn for three weeks. In verses 4-9 Daniel gives either the clearest description of an angel in all of Scripture, or what some believe to be a theophany (appearance of God). In verses 12-14 we see what happened in the spiritual realm when Daniel began to pray. The angel was sent with an answer to his prayer, but he was opposed by the "prince of Persia" (demonic power) for three weeks corresponding to the time Daniel began to pray. The vision that Daniel received is recorded in chapter 11, and pertains to the near future and the end of days concerning God's plan for Israel's future (v14). In verses 15-21 the angel strengthens Daniel, and assures him that the Lord is with him. Space will not permit to explain chapter 11 in detail because it covers a lot of history, but each part of it would come true just as God said it would. Verses 1-4 see the Persian Empire taken over by Alexander the Great. His kingdom is split into four groups (v5-20) with two dominating- the Ptolemies (king of the North) and the Seleucids (king of the South). These battles pave the way for Antiochus Epiphanes IV, who is the "little horn" of chapter 8 and a type of antichrist which will come in the future (v21-35). Antiochus may have had some of the characteristics in verses 36-39, but mainly these verses point to a future Antichrist. Verses 40-45 point to a time, future from our day, and describe the defeat of the Antichrist.

Daniel 12:1-3 refers to the end of days (Matt. 24:21). There will be a resurrection of believers and unbelievers, and all will be judged. Some believe verse 4 is teaching that as these days approach, people, especially believers, will understand that they are living in the last days. Much of these predictions will occur in what is called the Great Tribulation, or the last 3 ½ years of the tribulation period (v5-7). In verses 8-13 Daniel is told to seal the book, that many will be saved, and that he will receive an inheritance at his resurrection.

Saturday • Hebrews 5-8

In Hebrews 5, the author goes deeper in explaining the role of Jesus as High Priest. Verses 1-4 show the qualifications of the Aaronic priesthood, and in verses 5-11 he explains that Jesus not only met these qualifications but exceeded them. While both were appointed by God (v4-5), Jesus had a greater priesthood because He sacrificed Himself for sin (v8-9). Verses 6 and 10 introduce the theme of the Melchizedekian priesthood (Gen. 14:18-20). Verse 7 is a reference to the prayers of Jesus and will probably call to mind the scene in the Garden of Gethsemane where Jesus cried out to God before His crucifixion. Along with verses 8-9 this shows that believers have a compassionate High Priest in Jesus who is able to identify with His people in their times of suffering. The word "author" in verse 9 has two other meanings that apply to the passage. One other meaning of the word is source. Jesus is the source of salvation. The other meaning of the word is cause. So it could also be read that Jesus is the cause of salvation.

The writer of Hebrews is also concerned with his reader's spiritual maturity (v12-14). In verse 11 he mentions that they were "dull of hearing". In the Greek this phrase is in the perfect tense which shows that they were previously better at hearing than they were now. It could be because of persecution or simply a refusal to continue to learn of Christ. He tells them in verse 12 that they should already be teaching others what they know, but instead they need to be retaught the basics of the Christian faith. They were still "babes" who needed milk, but should be mature (full age) and desiring the "meat" of the word of God (v13-14). The word "unskilled" in verse 13 means someone who lacks experience and has not practiced what they have learned. In verse 14 he explains how to be mature in the Word. First, he says you have to apply what you have learned ("reason of use"). Second, he says you have to apply that knowledge into experience ("senses exercised"). Third, putting these two together will help someone live a mature life because they will be able to develop discernment knowing good from evil.

Hebrews 6:1-3 links with 5:12-14. He wants them to continue toward maturity. Verses 4-8 form what is possibly the most debated portion of Hebrews, along with 10:26-39. Some teach that these are hypothetical cases that could never happen. If this is the case, the warning is no warning at all because it could never happen. In these verses the writer is saying if they have experienced Christ to the point they understand what He has done for them, and turn away remaining in a state of unrepentance, they become as if they crucified Christ themselves. As 10:26-39 will explain, there is no other sacrifice for them because only Jesus provides salvation (John 14:6, Acts 4:12). Those who accept Christ will be blessed (v7), and those who reject will be cursed (v8).

In verses 9-12 the author of Hebrews goes on to encourage them to move toward maturity in Christ, which some apparently have (v9-12). He wants them to be eager (diligence) to continue their labor of love and ministering to the saints as these are evidences of salvation. Through the life of Abraham the readers are also encouraged to know that what God has promised to them He will do (v13-20). Verses 13-14 describe the covenant God made with Abraham, which was confirmed in Genesis 15 and reiterated throughout Genesis to his descendants. It is in Christ, and through the faith and patience described in verse 12, that Abraham and all other believers will inherit the promises of God (v15). God will never change what He has spoken, and in His words we have hope (v18). The two immutable (unchanging) things in verse 18 are God's promise and God's oath (Titus 1:2). Verses 19-20 show that the only hope anyone has is in the finished work of Christ. It is in Christ that there is stability, security, and fulfillment of the promises. Verse 20 also serves to open the discussion of Christ as High Priest.

In Hebrews 7:1-14 the writer develops the theme of the Melchizedek priesthood, showing the uniqueness of Jesus' priesthood (and kingship) and that it is superior to the Levitical priesthood. It is clear that the author of Hebrews sees significance in Melchizedek's name and the city he is king of. Melchizedek's name means "king of righteousness" and the city name means "king of peace." Jesus is also our righteousness (1 Cor. 1:30) and our peace (Eph. 4:12). This is the only place in Scripture that the word for "made like" is used (v3). It refers to something that is copied or modeled. This points out that Jesus is not like Melchizedek, but Melchizedek is like the Son of God. The author of Hebrews points out the greatness of Melchizedek in the fact that Abraham, the great patriarch, gave him a tenth of his plunder. In verse 5 he begins to show the greatness of the priesthood of Melchizedek over that of the Levites. He does this to show that with the tithe the recipient is always superior to the giver (v6-10). Now that the author has shown that the Melchizedek order of priests is superior to the Levitical order, he will now show that there is a need for a priest from the order of Melchizedek (v11-19). The Levitical (descendants of Aaron) priesthood nor the law could bring perfection (v11-12). He will now begin to show that it is Jesus who will be a priest from the order of Melchizedek. Priests did not come from the line of Judah, but from the line of Levi (v13).

Jesus' priesthood is superior because of His life (v15-19), the divine oath which guaranteed a better covenant (v19-22), the eternal nature of His priesthood (v23-24), and His sacrifice (v25-28). In verses 23-28 the author of Hebrews contrasts the Levitical priesthood with Jesus' priesthood. The Levitical priesthood had many priests, but Jesus is the only one in the Melchizedek line (v23-24). The Levitical priesthood was temporary, but Jesus' is eternal (v23-24). The Levitical priests had to offer sacrifices for themselves, but Jesus did not because He is holy and innocent (v26-27). The Levitical priesthood had to offer sacrifices daily, but Jesus' sacrifice was once and for all (v27). The Levitical priesthood offered animals while Jesus offered Himself (v27).

In Hebrews 8:1-6 the writer points out that Jesus, in becoming our High Priest, obtained a better ministry than the earthly priests; which also brought about a better covenant. His High Priestly duties are done in heaven at the actual tabernacle built by God (v2). The earthly priests performed their duties on copies made of the heavenly tabernacle (v3-5). Jesus, being a High Priest of Melchizedek, and through His sacrifice obtained a superior ministry to that of the Levitical order (v6). In doing this He also became the Mediator of a better covenant (New over Old). The New Covenant also has better promises.

A new covenant was needed because the first failed. But how was that to happen? This is made possible by Jesus' sacrifice, which brought in the New Covenant spoken of by Jeremiah in chapter 31:31-34 (v8-12). This is why the Old Covenant is obsolete, meaning it is ineffective or not able to meet their needs (v13). The word "obsolete" is in the perfect tense which shows that it has already become obsolete, which is evident in the present time.

Cover to Cover CHALLENGE

Week 46

Sunday • Psalm 128-133

Welcome to week 46 of the *Cover to Cover Challenge*! Continue to pray for our understanding of the Word of God, that the presence of the Holy Spirit will be made known, and for the Lord to be honored and glorified through the *Cover to Cover Challenge*. Psalm 130:3-4 says "If You, Lord, should mark iniquities, O Lord, who could stand? But there is forgiveness with You, that You may be feared".

Psalm 120-134 are the "Songs of the Ascents". Many believe this name comes from the people "ascending" to Jerusalem to celebrate the feasts. Psalm 128 is a wisdom psalm. Most believe it is primarily addressed to the man of the home in that he will be blessed if he fears the Lord (v1). His work will be prosperous, he will be happy, and his wife and children will be blessed (v2-4). A nation with men and families like this will also be blessed (v5-6).

Psalm 129 is a psalm of confidence in the deliverance the Lord will bring Israel against their enemies. Verses 1-4 give a brief description of Israel's long and difficult history, showing that it is the Lord who has delivered them. In verses 5-8 there is a curse pronounced upon the enemies of Israel and those who are against God.

Psalm 130 is a lament. In verses 1-2 the psalmist is asking God to hear his prayer for forgiveness. Verses 3-4 show that God forgives sin and hears the cries of those who seek His forgiveness. Because of this, the psalmist places his hope in the Lord (v5-6). God is the one who gives mercy and redeems people from their sin (v7-8).

Psalm 131 is a psalm of confidence in the Lord. In verse 1, David describes the condition of his heart. In describing his heart in this way David is showing that he is following the ways of the Lord, and that he is fully submitted to Him. Because of this David's soul is still (free from conflict) and quieted (v2). David prays that all people in Israel would place their hope in the Lord (v3).

Psalm 132 serves as a reminder of how special God's dwelling with His people was and a request for God's favor on the king. Verses 1-9 of the psalm deal with David's commitment to God, and verses 10-18 address God's promise to David. David did have a desire to build a house for the Lord but Solomon was the one who would build it (v1-5). David moved the ark from Kiriath Jearim to Jerusalem where it would become known as God's dwelling place and His footstool (v7-9). Verses 11-12 highlight the Davidic Covenant where God promised David that one of his descendants would sit on the throne forever (2 Sam. 7). God confirms David's choice of Jerusalem (v13-14) and all of the people are blessed (v15-16). In verses 17-18 God promises to grow David's kingdom and it will become powerful. These verses also remind the people of the coming promised Messiah.

Psalm 133 is a wisdom psalm. The blessings of being together in unity are praised (v1). In comparing unity to oil and dew, the psalmist is showing that dwelling in unity is refreshing and brings abundant blessing to all those who experience it (v2-3).

Monday • Deuteronomy 13-15

Deuteronomy 12 instructed the Israelites on proper worship and staying away from the false gods of the Canaanites. Deuteronomy 13 will warn against the following three different groups of people who are tempting them to worship other gods. The punishment for these individuals is death. Every generation will receive pressure to stray from the truth and it will likely come from one of these three areas. Verses 1-5 warn against following one of their own prophets who is tempting them to follow other gods. Verses 6-11 state that they are not to follow after anyone in their own family who is tempting them to follow other gods. In verses 12-18 there may be people from the general population of people who will tempt them to serve other gods. Once investigated and found to be true, they are to be sure they take care of it immediately.

Deuteronomy 14:1-21 mirrors the clean and unclean laws in Leviticus 11-15. The main purpose of these laws is listed in verses 2 and 21. The Israelites are to be holy unto the Lord. This would show the Israelites that in every walk of life they are to be holy because God is holy. In verses 22-29 is the law of the tithe. Moses speaks of three purposes for the tithe. First, it allows the whole family to worship (v13-16). Second, it provided for the welfare of others (v27-29). Third, it pointed out to them that God was the one who was blessing them (v29).

Deuteronomy 15:1-11 concerns the canceling of debt. They are to be cancelled every 7 years. One reason for this is because the land was also to lie fallow every seven years, and there would be no way to have income coming in. This was to be done so there would be no poverty in Israel (v4-8). Verses 12-18 deal with the freeing of servants who had sold themselves to repay debt. These laws make sure it was temporary (v12) and that they would be provided for when they left (v13-14). There is also provision made if they wanted to stay a servant to their master (v16). Verses 19-23 deal with the law of the firstborn, with the setting aside of the first born of the animals.

Tuesday • Ezra 1-5

Ezra follows on the same thoughts brought out in 1 and 2 Chronicles. It is basically a continuation of the story as 2 Chronicles 36:22-23 and Ezra 1:1-3 are nearly identical. The book of Ezra also switches from 3rd person to 1st person in chapter 7 which also suggests Ezra wrote the book. Ezra functions to show how God fulfills His promise to the Israelites in their return to the land.

Ezra 1:1-4 records the decree of Cyrus for the Jews to return and rebuild Jerusalem. It also shows that it was the Lord who stirred his heart to do so continuing the theme of the sovereignty of God from 1 and 2 Chronicles. The Lord also stirred the hearts of many of the exiles to return to their homeland (v5-11). Notice also the temple articles are sent along with them.

Ezra 2 provides a list for those who returned under the leadership of Zerubbabel (v1-2). Verses 2-20 list the men of Israel who returned, verses 21-35 involve people from villages and towns most are from the Benjamite territory, Verses 36-39 list four groups of priests, verses 40-42 lists the Levites and other temple personnel, verses 43-58 are the temple servants, and verses 59-63 are a small list of people who do not know their genealogy. These were excluded from serving in the temple. Verses 64-67 give totals for the total people and animals which returned to Jerusalem. Verses 68-70 tell of the offering given to support rebuilding the temple and tell that the people had settled in the cities.

In Ezra 3:1-6 they restore the altar for offering and begin once again to offer sacrifices and celebrate the Feast of Tabernacles. This established a pattern of worship. In verses 7-11 they start to plan, gather materials, and organize the rebuilding of the temple by laying the foundation. Some realize it will not have the splendor of the former temple and weep (v12-13).

In Ezra 4 persecution begins by those who oppose the rebuilding of the temple. In verses 1-5 men of the land come to offer help in rebuilding the temple, but they refuse their help. This causes the people there to stop working on the temple because they are filled with fear (v4-5). The letter sent by the men to king Artaxerxes gives, in detail, the many accusations that were brought against the rebuilding of the temple (v6-16). Because of this letter king Artaxerxes halts the rebuilding of the temple (v17-22) and it would not begin again until Darius becomes king, spanning about 18 years (v23-24).

Ezra 5 records the renewed efforts to rebuild the temple at the preaching of Haggai and Zechariah (v1-5). Because of their renewed efforts opposition to rebuilding the temple begins again and a letter is sent to king Darius (v6-17). In this letter we can see the response of the Jews to the question asked by Tattenai about who gave them authority to rebuild the temple, and why it was destroyed to begin with (v12-13).

Wednesday • Acts 15-16

Acts 15 is one of the most important chapters in the history of the church. The decision made here would affect the church positively or negatively, even to our own day. Verses 1-5 show the trouble was over circumcision and its part in salvation. The Judaizers believed that circumcision was a part of salvation, and that it must be done in order to be saved. The leaders of the church convene to make a decision on this in verses 6-19 and hear testimonies from Peter, Barnabas, and Paul of how God is moving among the Gentiles. Two things were at stake in this decision. One was the state of the church. If the wrong decision was made it would lead to the splitting of the church (Jewish/Gentile). Second, and most important, was the issue of salvation and how to be saved. James (Jesus' half-brother) quotes Amos 9:11-12 to show that God was rebuilding and restoring the kingdom through the preaching of Jesus. What they instructed the Gentiles to avoid in verse 20 are all parts of pagan rituals.

In verses 22-35 they send out letters containing the decision to all churches. The important decision made here protected salvation by grace alone through faith alone, preserved the purity and unity of the church, and protected Christianity from blending with other pagan religions. In verse 24 the word "troubled" means to plunder or tear down. It was a military word that described the plundering of a city. The Judaizers who believed circumcision and obeying the law was a requirement for salvation, were in fact tearing the church apart by what they believed. Verse 28 also serves to show that the decision reached was done not just in human wisdom, but by the Holy Spirit. Verses 30-35 record the Gentiles' reaction to the letter sent by the leadership in Jerusalem. The Gentiles were to be accepted into the church without circumcision and obeying the law. In verses 36-41 Paul and Barnabas part ways over John Mark and his earlier decision to leave them on their first missionary journey. Barnabas and John Mark are not mentioned again in Acts, while Paul and Silas begin the second missionary journey.

In Acts 16:1-5 Timothy joins Paul and Silas on their journey, where they are also delivering the decision of the Jerusalem council made in chapter 15. The Holy Spirit forbids them to go to certain places, but it is here that Paul receives a vision from the Lord to go to Macedonia (v6-10). At Philippi, Lydia is saved through Paul's preaching (v11-15). There was not much of a Jewish presence in Philippi because they are gathering by the rivers, which shows there was no synagogue there. As they are going with Lydia, they meet a girl possessed with a spirit of divination (v16-24). Divination in the Greek is *pythonas,* which is a mystical serpent or dragon. The python served as a symbol for the god Apollo, who was believed to predict the future. Because the girl seemed to have this gift she would have made her owners a lot of money. After casting the demon out, they are arrested and placed in jail.

In verses 25-34 the Philippian jailor is converted after experiencing the hand of God move to release Paul and Silas. This is similar to Acts 5:19-26 and 12:5-19 where the Lord intervenes and frees the apostles and Peter. When you see an earthquake in Scripture, God is moving and working (Ex. 19:18, Matt. 27:51-54, 28:2). This miracle did not take place so that Paul and Silas could be delivered from jail. The miracle took place so the jailor could be delivered from his sin. After being saved the Philippian jailor washed their stripes, he was baptized, he provided food for them, and he rejoiced. All these signs point toward his conversion. This shows the power of the gospel to change lives. The reason Paul insisted the leaders come and get them out in verses 35-40 was because that would ensure that any other Christian would receive the same treatment if they were arrested.

Thursday • Proverbs 31

Proverbs 31 was written by king Lemuel ("Belongs to God"), and is the words his mother taught him (v1). She offers him an early warning not to give himself to women or to habits that destroy kings (v2-3). He expands on the warning of strong drink in verses 4-7 because it will give him bad judgment and he will not keep the law. The king must keep his senses aware so he can speak up on behalf of those less fortunate (v8-9). Verses 10-31 praise the virtue of an excellent wife. Verse 10 functions to show how rare and precious the woman described in these verses is. Verses 11-12 show the trust her husband has in her to provide for their family, which she delights in (v13). She provides for her family and rises up early to show her compassionate and sacrificial heart (v14-15). She makes sound judgments and brings profit to her family (v16). She is also strong and works hard for her family (v17-20). She provides the best for her family and is committed to their well-being (v21-22). She also stands with her husband, bringing strength to their family (v23). She is confident and teaches wisdom and kindness to others (v24-26). She is attentive to her family, and hard working in all that she does (v27). Her husband and children publicly praise her for the woman she is (v28-29). Her husband believes she is the most excellent wife of all wives. The key to her life is not her beauty, but that she fears the Lord (v30). Only a fool would not want a wife like her.

Friday • Haggai-Zechariah 1-7

Haggai prophesied after the return of the exiles to Jerusalem. He is mentioned in Ezra 5:1 and 6:14, along with the prophet Zechariah. Based on Haggai 2:3, he may have been old enough to have seen Solomon's temple before it was destroyed. Haggai's prophecy is four oracles to encourage them to continue building the temple because 18 years had passed since they began the work.

Haggai 1:1-3 dates the prophecy of Haggai, and he addresses Zerubbabel (civil leader, descendant of Jehoiachin) and Joshua (religious leader, descendant of Aaron). The people were claiming it was not time for the Lord's house to be rebuilt, which was only because they were being opposed and feared them. Haggai rebukes them in verse 4 because they had put their own well-being before building the temple (v4-6). In verses 7-11 they are encouraged to continue building the temple so that the Lord can take pleasure in it and be honored by it. Verse 6 and verses 9-11 show their punishment for not obeying the Lord's command to rebuild the temple. Verses 12-15 show that three weeks had passed since Haggai began to speak and the people obeyed. The Lord also encourages them, letting them know that He is with them in all of their work.

Haggai 2:1-5 begins the second oracle, which also encourages the people to be strong and work because the Lord is with them. Apparently the main problem they now had was depression because the new temple was nothing like Solomon's. God also encourages them by reminding them His Spirit is with them and telling them that they have nothing to fear. In verses 6-9 God makes two promises to the people. First, the glory of the present temple would surpass that of the former. Second, God promised them that they would have peace which is something that they had not had in many years. The third oracle is in verses 10-19, and comes two months after the second. Verses 10-14 primarily concern their defilement by not rebuilding the temple. This caused others to put their personal needs ahead of God's in building the temple. When attitude is wrong, the gifts given to God are unacceptable. But, since they have been rebuilding the temple, God has met their needs (v15-19). Here God promises to meet their needs from this day forward. Obedience brings blessing, disobedience brings a curse. The fourth oracle concerns Zerubbabel and is a promise that one day God will overthrow all unrepentant Gentile kingdoms. Zerubbabel, as the signet ring, is represented in the genealogy of Jesus the Messiah (Matt. 1:11-12).

Zechariah ("The Lord Remembers") is a contemporary of Haggai. Like Jeremiah and Ezekiel he was a priest. Like Haggai, he encouraged the people to rebuild the temple. Haggai was used to begin the endeavor, and Zechariah can be seen as the motivator that kept it going. Zechariah's prophecies also concern the spiritual state of the people. One of his main themes in encouraging them to continue the rebuilding effort is because the Messiah will one day be in it. This book is said to be the most messianic, apocalyptic, and end-time focused book in the Old Testament and is known for its many visions.

Zechariah 1:1-6 is a call to repentance given by Zechariah to the Jews who are rebuilding the temple. If they would return to God, then He would bless them. Verses 7-17 begin the first of eight visions that Zechariah receives from the Lord. The date is 3 months after the call to repent and 5 months after they had resumed rebuilding the temple. This first vision teaches that although the nations who troubled Israel are at ease, God is going to restore His people because He is sovereign over the earth. The Angel of the Lord (preincarnate Christ) appears, interceding for the people of Israel to receive God's mercy which He promises to do. The second vision in verses 18-21 shows that the four horns who were against Israel will be judged by the four craftsmen. Many see the four horns as corresponding to Daniel's 4 world empires in Daniel 2 and 7, but it is not certain. The four immediate to this context are Assyria, Egypt, Babylon, and Medo-Persia.

Zechariah 2:1-5 is the vision of the measuring line, and shows the current rebuilding of Jerusalem and the restoring of the temple. Its ultimate purpose also shows the kingdom of God in the future. God's kingdom will grow to the point that it will overflow its walls. Even though it overflows its walls, the people will be protected by God. Verses 6-9 encourage the Jews still in Babylon to return to Jerusalem before God judges the nation. Verses 10-13 show the coming of the Lord to dwell among His people, bringing joy to them. God will bless His people with His presence, but also bring judgment upon those who defy Him.

Zechariah 3:1-5 is the vision of the high priest Joshua (Jeshua in Ezra) being cleansed of his filthy garments. Joshua represents Israel in this vision, being restored by the Lord as a kingdom of priests to God. His filthy garments are replaced by robes of righteousness given by the Lord. Satan also takes his role as accuser of the brethren in these verses. Also, Jesus is present as the Angel of the Lord. It is also a picture of salvation for each individual because it is by God's grace we are saved. Verses 6-10 are a prophecy of the coming of the Messiah, the Servant of the Lord. When their sin is forgiven God will provide peace and security for His people.

In Zechariah 4:1-7 the vision of the lampstand and two olive trees are for the encouragement of Zerubbabel and Joshua to continue their work because they have a divine source helping them complete the work. Zerubbabel and Joshua are the two olive branches and are to continue the work of building the temple by the Spirit of the Lord (v8-14).

Zechariah 5:1-4 is the 6th vision of the flying scroll. The scroll is open for all to read and contains a message of judgment for those who remain in their sin. There would be no way of escape for those who are going to be judged. Verses 6-11 are a vision of the woman in a basket which represents the wickedness that is in the land (Rev. 17:3-5). The basket is being carried to Shinar (Babylon), probably to be set up in a house to be worshiped. Babylon is pictured in the Bible as the originator of all false religions and worship.

Zechariah 6:1-8 is the last vision of Zechariah. It is thought the four chariots represent judgments of the Lord going throughout all of the earth (Rev. 6:1-8). The judgment of the north (Babylon) is coming for what they have done to God's own people. The crowning of Joshua pulls together themes that have been previously addressed (v9-14). The Branch (Messiah) will one day hold both the offices of Joshua (priest) and Zerubbabel (government leader, king). This is a picture of a future restored Israel, where the Messiah rules as King and Priest. He will help build the temple (future temple) and will sit on the throne ruling and reigning. Even the Gentiles will participate in building the temple and all who belong to Him will obey Him.

Zechariah 7 begins two years after the visions of Zechariah. In verses 1-3 the people are inquiring about fasting, especially the fast commemorating the day they were carried into captivity. In the Lord's response to them it appears that even in exile their fasting for this day had become just another ritual observance and was not real repentance out of obedience. In verses 8-14 they are reminded of their ancestors' disobedience and the consequences they had suffered. They are given four spiritual tests. First, did they administer true justice? Second, did they show mercy and compassion? Third, were they oppressing the disadvantaged? Fourth, did they continually think evil? Their ancestors refused and if they refused they would suffer the same fate.

Saturday • Hebrews 9-10

In Hebrews 9 the author presents the new covenant as greater than the old covenant. He will do this by contrasting the tabernacle and its earthly observances to Christ's sacrifice, which brought in a better covenant (v1-5). Verses 6-10 are concentrated on the Day of Atonement (Lev. 16). These verses serve to emphasize that the high priest could only go in once a year to offer sacrifices for himself and the people for their sins committed in ignorance. It also proves to show that he was the only one who had direct access to God. In verse 7 this sacrifice is done with blood. Leviticus 17:11 says "For the life of the flesh is in the blood, and I have given it to you upon the altar to make atonement for your souls, for it is the blood that makes atonement for the soul". The sacrifice on the Day of Atonement was only partial because it did not account for willful sin. According to verse 9 it was also an imperfect cleansing. It never freed anyone from a guilty conscience. Because of Christ's sacrifice, we all now can have direct access to the Father through Jesus (v11-14). These verses also disclose the reason the author used the tabernacle for comparison. Jesus and Paul both speak of our tent or tabernacle that we possess (our bodies). Jesus is said by John (1:14) to have tabernacled with us and sacrificed His own life for our sins, which bought our salvation. His sacrifice was once and for all, and needs not be repeated. According to verse 12 Jesus is a superior High Priest because He offered His own sinless blood, His sacrifice is offered only once, and His sacrifice obtained eternal redemption for all.

Verses 15-22 show the necessity of the shedding of blood in redemption and how Christ's sacrifice accomplished it to bring in the new covenant. The New Covenant did not become effective until Jesus' death (v16-17, Matt. 26:28). Without the shedding of Christ's blood there would be no New Covenant. The word "remission" in verse 22 means to send away. When people are forgiven, their sins are forgiven or sent away (Psalm 103:12). The author builds on this argument in verses 23-28 with the idea of Christ's sacrifice. His one-time sacrifice perfectly and eternally cleanses those who believe in Him for salvation. Christ is also pictured as returning again, not to sacrifice Himself again for sin, but to accomplish our glorification with Him (v27-28).

In Hebrews 10:1-4 the author contrasts the ancient system, which was only a shadow of things to come, with the once and for all sacrifice of Christ. The old system could never deal with sin the way Christ's sacrifice did. Jesus came to be the perfect sacrifice, atoning for the sins of man according to the will of God (v5-10). Christ's sacrifice was offered once, while the animal sacrifices were offered daily and continually. Even they never fully dealt with sin (v11-18). There is a contrast in verses 11-14 between the priests and Jesus. Priests continually stood to perform their duties because there was a need for sacrifices to be made for sin. On the other hand Jesus only offered one sacrifice (Himself) and then sat down at the right hand of God. Verses 15-17 show that Jesus' sacrifice brought about the New Covenant that was prophesied by Jeremiah. Jesus' sacrifice fully and finally dealt with sin, there is no longer any sacrifice needed or any sacrifice that can atone for sin (v18).

In verses 19-25 the author begins to apply what he has taught. If they truly believe in Jesus then they must live according to what He has revealed. What Jesus has done for them should lead them to "draw near" to God, "holdfast" to what they believe, "stir up" one another to love and good works, "not forsaking" one another but to "exhort" (encourage) one another. This is to be done because the Day of His return is quickly approaching. For those who have yet to believe, the author offers a warning here (v26-31). There is no other sacrifice for sin (10:18). Only through Jesus can they be saved (John 14:6, Acts 4:12). If they reject Christ they are trampling Him under their feet and counting His blood that He shed for them as something common or simple. It would be useless for them to continue following Judaism, because it cannot save them. The whole system has become obsolete because Christ has brought a better way. Verses 32-39 are a note of encouragement for them to believe in Jesus and continue in it even in the face of persecution. The word for "spectacle" in verse 33 is where our word theatre comes from. It would seem that the persecution they had endured or were enduring was public. They not only suffered themselves, but suffered because they belonged to Christ.

Cover to Cover Challenge

Week 47

Sunday • Psalm 134-136

Welcome to week 47 of the *Cover to Cover Challenge*! Continue to pray for understanding as we study the Word of God, and pray for the Lord to be honored and glorified. Psalm 136:1 says "Oh, give thanks to the Lord, for He is good! For His mercy endures forever".

Psalm 134 is the last of the Songs of Ascent. In verses 1-2 the priests lead the people in worship of the Lord. It would have been a time of praise with songs, musical instruments, and times of prayer. Verse 3 is the priest blessing all the people.

Psalm 135 is a hymn of praise to the Lord for His creative acts and sovereignty over history. This psalm may build off Psalm 134. It also begins with a call to worship, although it is more extensive here in this psalm (v1-4). Speaking from personal experience, the psalmist praises God for His acts in creation which show that He has all authority and power (v5-7). The Lord's power and strength are also seen in His acts in salvation history (v8-12). He alone called and saved His people from Egyptian bondage. Because God is Creator and the Author of salvation in delivering His people from bondage, His name will be remembered (v13-14). Verses 15-18 come from Psalm 115:4-8. These verses form a contrast with God who is powerful and sovereign, and the idols which are worthless. Verses 19-21 call upon everyone to praise the Lord.

Psalm 136 is also a hymn of praise that many believe was associated with Passover. Every verse praises God "For His mercy (loyal love) endures forever". Each act that God did for His people was out of His great love for them (and us). Verses 1-3 open the psalm with thanks because of God's acts in history and salvation. Verses 4-9 praise God for His acts of creation which show His glory. Verses 10-15 refer to the deliverance from Egypt showing God's strength. Verses 16-20 refer to the wilderness wanderings and show God's care for them. Verses 21-22 refer to the conquest of the land of Canaan and God delivering their enemies into their hands. From Egypt, to the wilderness, and to the conquest of the land, God rescued and provided for His people (v23-25). For all of this God is to be thanked (v26).

Monday • Deuteronomy 16-19

Deuteronomy 16:1-17 gives a summary of the three great feasts for the Israelites. Passover celebrates the angel of death passing over the homes of the Israelites (v1-8). Every male was required to celebrate at the central tabernacle and every family celebrated in their home. Verses 9-12 describe the Feast of Weeks (Pentecost). It is celebrated 7 weeks after the offering of new grain (freewill offering from first produce). Verses 13-17 describe the Feast of Tabernacles (Booths), which is celebrated at the fall harvest. The Israelites would camp in booths, reminding them of their camping in the wilderness following the exodus. All males were required to be at these three festivals. Verses 18-20 concern the appointment of judges and officers who administer justice and enforce God's laws. If the people obey they will be blessed by God. In verses 21-22 the people are told not to set up any pagan worship centers. In chapter 12 they were already instructed to tear down the ones in Canaan when they enter the land.

Deuteronomy 17 opens with instruction to not offer blemished sacrifices to God (v1). What follows are instructions for worship that pleases God (v2-7). One cannot follow other gods and serve the one true God. The person who is found guilty will be put to death. For cases that are hard to judge the people are to bring it before the priests, Levites, and the judges to discern (v8-13). The discipline recorded in chapter 17 is to ensure the obedience and faithfulness of the people. If deeds go unpunished, sin would become a normal way of life.

Deuteronomy 17:14-18:22 discusses the three main offices of the Old Testament: king (17:14-20), priests (18:1-8), and prophets (v15-22). In the discussion of a king God is not recommending a king, but allowing them to choose a king (1 Sam. 8:19-20). The instructions will allow for a godly king and reign. In 18:1-8 the priests are to come from the tribe of Levi and offer sacrifices on behalf of the people. They are also to be supported and provided for by the people. Verses 9-14 contain instructions for them to avoid the pagan practices of those in Canaan because these practices are not only forbidden by the Lord, but they are the reason He is driving them out. Verses 15-22 concern the office of the prophet. God promises to raise up a prophet like Moses from among them to deliver God's Word. All of these offices are to perform their calling in the name of the Lord. Jesus is the fulfillment of these verses. He also is the only One to hold all three offices. Today Jesus is the only Prophet, Priest, and King.

Tuesday • Ezra 6-10

Ezra 6:1-12 is the answer to the letter written by Tattenai to king Darius inquiring about the renewed efforts to rebuild the temple. In verses 1-5 a search was done of the archives in Media-Persia, and Cyrus' decree is found instructing the Jews to rebuild the temple. Darius instructs Tattenai and the people to support the Jews in rebuilding the temple and to not hinder it in any way (v6-12). With their help, the encouragement of Haggai and Zechariah, and the hard work of the people the temple was completed four years after they began (v13-15). The temple was dedicated in verses 16-18, and the Passover and the Feast of Unleavened Bread was celebrated (v19-22).

In Ezra 7:1-10 Ezra will lead another group of exiles back to Jerusalem some 60 years (some say 80) after the dedication of the temple. Ezra is a priest, a descendant of Aaron, and is skilled in the Law of Moses. Verses 12-26 are the letter from Artaxerxes to Ezra, supplying him with all he needs (and much more) to return to Jerusalem. These verses were also written in Aramaic so that all could read and understand that it was ordered by the king. Ezra recognizes that all of this is happening because of the Lord (v27-28).

Ezra 8:1-14 contains the list of the families who returned with Ezra. There were no Levites in the group so Ezra enquires about finding some Levites willing to join (v15-20). Ezra prays for protection over their journey to Jerusalem (v21-23). Ezra did not ask for armed protection for their journey, but Nehemiah will have armed escorts when he returns (Neh. 2:9). The priests are given their possessions to carry to the temple in Jerusalem in verses 24-30. What was given to them would be worth millions of dollars today. Four months later they arrive in Jerusalem (v31-36). Sacrifices were made in thanks to God, and a sin offering was also offered.

In Ezra 9:1-3 Ezra learns about the leaders marrying pagan women. The people listed are the original people who lived in Canaan before the Jews entered it. This great sin caused others to gather with Ezra at the evening sacrifice, which was a time of confession (v4-5). Ezra is grieved over the moral failure of the people. Verses 6-15 are his prayer before God, expressing his desire for them to be forgiven. God had been so gracious to them, and now they have sinned against God.

In Ezra 10:1-4 the people come weeping to Ezra, realizing they have sinned against God. They want to make a covenant with God and make things right between them and the Lord. Ezra gets the leaders of the priests, the Levites, and the people to swear an oath that they would do God's will in the matter (v5-15). After going in with the leaders, an assembly of the people is called in Jerusalem. After Ezra addresses their sin they confess that they have sinned against the Lord. A committee is formed to investigate and interview the men who had taken pagan wives (v16-17). Verses 18-43 contains the lists of those who had married pagan wives and who had agreed to put them away.

Wednesday • Acts 17-18

In Acts 17:1-9 Paul preaches the gospel in Thessalonica. It was located on the Egnatian Way, which was the main highway going east to west. The word "reasoned" in verse 2 shows that Paul used the Old Testament to support the message of the resurrection of Jesus. Many believed but Paul was forced out and went to Berea. The people of Berea were open minded to what Paul had to say and even searched the Scriptures to determine if what he was preaching was true (v10-15). In verse 11 the word "fair-minded" means open and tolerant. They listened with an open mind to what was being preached. Then, they searched the Scriptures for themselves to see if what they heard lined up with what Paul was preaching. It would be wise for every believer to put this method into practice.

Paul preaches the gospel in Athens after he sees that they are worshiping idols (v16-21). The Epicureans were materialistic, did not believe in any gods, and they tried to live their life free from pain and any kind of passion. They also had no belief in life after death. The Stoics believed in gods to the point that they believed god was in everything including themselves. Stoics did believe the soul lived on after death. They labeled Paul a "babbler" (v18). This word refers to someone who took parts of many ideas and made them their own. Both groups had trouble believing in Paul's Jesus and the resurrection because of their current beliefs. Paul will preach to them at the Areopagus (Mars Hill) about their "Unknown God", to show them that He is near and very knowable (v22-31). His message will show them that God is the Creator of the world (v24-25), teach them about God's providential care (v26-27), show that idolatry is foolish (v28-29), and teach about repentance and the judgment of God (v30-31). The reaction of the crowd shows that some only mocked him, others wanted to hear him again, and some believed (v32-34).

In Acts 18:1-17 Paul journeys to Corinth, which was known for its paganism and for its temple to Aphrodite (Diana). Here, he meets Priscilla and Aquila who are fellow tentmakers (v2). Paul preached in the synagogue there, but was opposed by many of the Jews (v6). Crispus, the leader of the synagogue, does believe and so do many Corinthians (v8). Jesus speaks to Paul in Corinth and encourages him by telling him of his divine protection (v9-10). Gallio was proconsul in Achaia in 50-51 AD which helps date the book of Acts and Paul's other writings (v12).

In verses 18-23 Paul goes to Ephesus on his way back to Antioch. The vow Paul took was a probably a temporary vow where his hair was offered as a sacrifice out of gratitude to God. Acts 18:23 marks the beginning of Paul's 3rd missionary journey. In verses 24-28 Apollos is introduced. He is well educated, strong in the Scriptures, and is enthused about the Lord. Apollos only knew about John's baptism, and was instructed by Priscilla and Aquila about Jesus and the gospel message.

Thursday • Ecclesiastes 1-2

Ecclesiastes ("Preacher") is believed to have been written by Solomon (1:1,12). Ecclesiastes 12:9 speaks of the author of the book as having wisdom, and many proverbs. It was more than likely written toward the end of his life, and it could be called his autobiography. The purpose of the book is to warn people not to follow after worldly things, but to pursue God in life (12:9-14). The word "vanity" (useless, meaningless) is used many times in the book to show that the pursuit of worldly things will leave you with nothing.

In Ecclesiastes 1:1-3 Solomon shows that the pursuit of worldly pleasures and meaning is vanity (useless, meaningless). Solomon shows, in verses 4-11, that meaning in life cannot be found in nature even though God is the Creator of it. Even with the wisdom Solomon had, life made no sense at times and was frustrating (v12-18). Solomon even made the point that his wisdom caused him much grief and sorrow in the pursuit of trying to understand worldly things.

In Ecclesiastes 2:1-11, Solomon seeks the answers to a meaningful life in many pleasures-laughter, drinking, large estates, lavish gardens, herds of cattle, his position as king, beautiful music, and his many wives. All of these pursuits did not result in lasting pleasure. They too were meaningless. In verses 12-23 he does see being a wise person as being better than the fool. Both will meet the same end-death. What use is it for a man to build up his kingdom only to have to leave it to a fool? Verses 24-26 do not promote a life seeking pleasure. Solomon is saying that whether anyone understands the meaning of life or not, they should look to God daily for their needs.

Friday • Zechariah 8-14

Zechariah 8:1-17 contrasts Israel's past disobedience with their future restoration. These verses are also called the deliverance or a salvation oracle promising their restoration. This oracle shows that God is standing behind each word (v2), the message of the salvation the people will experience (v3-8), God directly addressing the people (v9-17), and the proclamation not to be afraid (v13, 15). God is going to regather His people, be their God, and dwell among them. In verses 18-23 the Jews are also told that their mourning and times of fasting will cease and turn to joy. There will be a day when even the Gentiles will come to them and want to worship God (future Messianic kingdom).

Zechariah 9-14 primarily deals with the future, even from our day. In some of these prophecies there is an immediate fulfillment for them and a future fulfillment. Its focus is on the judgment and blessings for when the Messiah becomes King. Zechariah 9:1-8 shows the destruction of the nations mentioned in the text. This was accomplished by Alexander the Great who swiftly took over the regions mentioned, but when he came to Jerusalem he would not take it (v8). Verses 9-10 refer, in their context, to the future Messianic kingdom when Jesus comes again. He is described as righteous, saving, humble, and peaceful. It was also fulfilled in Jesus' Triumphal Entry into Jerusalem. The people will rejoice because He has come and for His kingdom, which is a kingdom of peace. Verses 11-13 show Him as being the conquering King who delivers the people from their enemies. This deliverance will result in the people experiencing God's protection and His blessings (v14-17).

In Zechariah 10:1-4 Zechariah explains that prayer to God brings blessing, but following idols will bring judgment and pain. They had followed false prophets (shepherds) in the past. God will judge the false shepherds and He will care for the people Himself. In the face of their enemies God will regather His people and reunite the nation (v5-7). He will regather them from far away nations and give them strength (v8-12).

Zechariah 11 describes the rejection of the Messiah. In verses 1-3 the whole region will be affected because of their rejection. It would also include the destruction of Jerusalem in 70 AD. In verses 4-14, Zechariah is instructed to act out the role of the good shepherd for the flock. The two staffs "Beauty" (Favor) and "Bonds" (Unity) represent Christ's ministry in leading and protecting His people in hopes of uniting them under Him. Upon His rejection, both staffs are broken. Verses 12-13 depict the severing of the relationship with the worker demanding his wages of 30 pieces of silver. This is quoted in the New Testament for the betrayal of Jesus for 30 pieces of silver. After the rejection of the Messiah, a worthless shepherd takes His place (v15-17). This worthless shepherd could be fulfilled with the rise of the Antichrist.

Zechariah 12:1-3 shows the future siege on Jerusalem and the Messiah delivering them at His return (Rev.16:16-21). In that day, Israel will be like an immovable rock because it is the Lord who will defend her. Verses 4-6 show their enemies experiencing the curses of the covenant for those who come against Israel. God is shown as being with them, going before them, and giving them strength (v7-9). At that time God will pour out His Spirit on the people and they will mourn over the rejected Messiah and repent (v10-14).

Zechariah 13:1-3 shows the cleansing of sin that can now be attained by the death of the Messiah. There will also be a cleansing in the land of false prophets, idols, and unclean spirits (v4-6). Verses 7-9 go back to the people's rejection of the Shepherd, and also show the death of the Shepherd (Matt. 26:31).

Zechariah 14 is about the return of the Lord and the setting up of His kingdom. Verses 1-2 could be speaking about Armageddon (Rev. 16:16-21). Verses 3-8 show the coming of Christ fulfilling not only these words, but also Acts 1:9-12 when He ascended from Mt. Olive. It will also be a day of signs and wonders in the skies, which is a common theme in all end time prophecies. He will establish His kingdom of peace in Jerusalem (v9-11), and He will punish all of those who have fought against His people (v12-15). People from all nations will come and worship the King (v16-21). His Kingdom will reign forever and ever (Rev. 19:16).

Saturday • Hebrews 11-13

In Hebrews 11:1-3 the writer discusses the topic of faith. Each of the people he names in this chapter placed their faith in God, not knowing what the future held. Their faith in God motivated them to continue moving forward no matter how difficult life became. Without faith it is impossible to please God. This chapter is also called the "Hall of Faith" chapter because the people listed are praised because of their devout faith in God. For the sake of space, I will not discuss each person. Faith was seen in people's lives before the flood (v4-7), and in the lives of Abraham (still in high regard among Jews) and Sarah (v8-12).

In verses 13-16 the author again praises these people of faith for being an example for us to embrace the promises of God by faith. The author returns to the patriarchs for examples of faith (v17-22) and turns to Moses (most revered among Jews), and gives 5 faith lessons from his life in verses 23-29. Verses 30-31 cover the exodus generation and verses 32-38 cover various people from different times in the Old Testament. All of these had a promise of the coming Savior, and the people the author of Hebrews is writing to have seen the fulfilment of that promise (v39-40).

Hebrews 12:1-3 also serves to encourage the readers of the letter to keep pressing on despite their hardships and persecutions, just like those he spoke of in chapter 11. They are to keep running their race, not looking at their hardships, but looking upon Jesus. He is encouraging them not to give in to sin (v1), not to lose focus (v2), and not to give up (v3). Verses 4-11 show that suffering is not because God does not love us, but because He does. The discipline of the Lord proves that one is a son (Prov. 3:11-12). When God disciplines believers it is so they will be fruitful in their lives. Building on this he encourages the people to live godly lives, and this will require their greatest effort (v12-13). They are to pursue (strive for) peace with all people (v14). This does not mean forsaking the truth for peace. Every believer must stand up for the truth, even if it causes difficulties in life. They are also to pursue (strive for) holiness. This command was first given in the Old Testament (Lev. 11:44-45) and stands today. In verse 15 they should be looking out for others who may fall short of God's grace. They are also to be careful and not let a root of bitterness spring up in themselves or others. The root of bitterness is pictured as sprouting and affecting others. They are also not to be immoral or profane (godless). The author of Hebrews gives the example of Esau selling his birthright. Most believe he uses this example to show someone who fell short of God's grace. If some of them are not careful they too may come to the point where they cannot repent (Rom. 1:28).

Verses 18-24 are a comparison between the fear at Mount Sinai when they received the law (Ex. 19:12-22, 20:18-21), and with the glory of Mount Zion. He does this to show that people who believe in Jesus can approach God. It is those who belong to the church and have all the rights of the firstborn (v23). In this verse God is also seen as the judge of all men, especially believers. In verse 24 Jesus is pictured as the Mediator of the New Covenant. It is by His blood that atonement has been made. Hebrews 11:4 mentions Abel's sacrifice being more excellent than Cain's because he offered it in faith. Here in the last part of verse 24, Jesus' blood is shown to be better than Abel's. In verses 25-29 the readers are also warned not to reject the voice of Him who speaks from heaven (Jesus) like those who in the past rejected His prophets (those who spoke on earth).

In Hebrews 13:1-6 the author encourages his readers to live a life of love, especially as it concerns the needs of others. Behavior of leadership is instrumental for those who are following them (v7). Leaders should be worth following. Verse 8 goes with verse 7. Earthly leaders will come and go, but there is One who is here forever and who never changes. Verse 9 is a warning to avoid false doctrines. Verses 10-16 are meant to show the readers that Jesus was sacrificed outside the camp, and believers must join Him outside of the camp- not participating in the world's practices. Leaders will also give an account for their leadership over God's people, and the people are encouraged not to make things hard for them so that they can lead (v17). The book of Hebrews ends with a prayer (v18-19) and a doxology praising the Lord for His sacrifice, His salvation, and His sanctifying work in the believer (v20-25).

Cover to Cover CHALLENGE

Week 48

Sunday • Psalm 137-139

Welcome to week 48 of the *Cover to Cover Challenge*! Continue to pray for our understanding of the Word of God, that the presence of the Holy Spirit will be made known, and for the Lord to be honored and glorified through the *Cover to Cover Challenge*. Psalm 139:23-24 says "Search me, O God, and know my heart; try me, and know my anxieties; and see if there is any wicked way in me, and lead me in the way of everlasting".

Psalm 137 is a lament that represents all of Israel while in captivity in Babylon. In verses 1-4 the people can be seen remembering and weeping over their lives they had in Jerusalem. The "Songs of Zion" in verse 3 were songs that celebrated God's protection over His people. In verses 5-6 the people vow never to forget God's promises to them while waiting on the Lord to deliver them. Verses 7-9 are a curse upon the Edomites and the Babylonians for their treatment of Israel.

Psalm 138 is a psalm of thanksgiving because the Lord is faithful to His people. David (representing Israel) praises the Lord for His love (lovingkindness), truth (faithfulness), and answered prayer (v1-3). In verses 4-6 all the kings (representing the nations) will praise the Lord because of His word (promises). Verses 7-8 are an expression of confidence in the Lord that He will deliver and save David from his enemies.

Psalm 139 is also a psalm of David where he speaks of how intimately God knows humanity. In verses 1-6 David speaks of the complete knowledge that God has of man. God knows man's moving, his thoughts, and He also protects him. Not only does God know man completely, but God's presence is everywhere (v7-12). God is also the Creator of all of humanity (v13-18). God knew each person before they were born and has given each person a distinct purpose in life. God's thoughts toward us are too many to be counted and too magnificent to comprehend. Verses 19-22 form a contrast with the rest of the psalm by speaking of the wicked who are the enemies of God. In verses 23-24 David asks God to search him for any wickedness that he may have because he knows the fate of the wicked.

Monday • Deuteronomy 20-22

Deuteronomy 20:1-4 is a reminder to the people that it is God who fights for them and wins the battles. Even this is based upon their obedience to God's commands. Verses 5-8 give exemptions for those who are not to fight in battles. Verses 10-15 are not for the inhabitants of Canaan, but for those in the land surrounding it. They could offer them peace; but if it was rejected they would attack, sparing only the women and children. Those inhabiting Canaan were not given an offer of peace, but were completely destroyed except for the trees that bore fruit (v17-20).

Deuteronomy 21:1-9 deals with unsolvable murders, which defile the land. The elders and judges of the nearest town were to kill a heifer by breaking its neck and washing their hands over it while asking forgiveness. Notice there was no bloodshed in this sacrifice. Wives taken from foreign lands were to go through the procedures in verses 10-14 before they married because it symbolized a complete break from their former life. Verses 15-17 concern the status of the firstborn. The man cannot show favoritism to the son of the woman he loves if the firstborn son is from the unloved wife. Verses 18-21 deal with rebellious children who do not obey their parents. If they cannot obey their parents, they will not function within the society and must be removed. Verses 22-23 show the seriousness of sin. Notice the person is already put to death before they are hanged on a tree. Paul quotes this in Galatians 3:13 in reference to Jesus bearing our sin on the cross.

Deuteronomy 22:1-4 shows the loving and caring nature all were to have toward their neighbor by watching over their possessions. Verse 5 is probably related to pagan rituals and also kept from gender confusion. Verses 6-7 are regarding conserving supplies for the future and verse 8 is building a fence around the roof of your home, which protects people from danger. Verses 9-12 also teach separation between different kinds. This is done because it is a reminder to Israel to remain separated from their pagan neighbors. The rest of the chapter concerns laws governing sexuality. Verses 14-21 are the law of virginity, verses 22-24 adultery, and verses 25-27 rape. A man was also not to take his father's wife as a wife for himself (v30).

Tuesday • Esther 1-5

The book of Esther takes place entirely in Susa (Shushan) during the reign of Xerxes (Ahasuerus). Many names have been suggested for who wrote the book, but no one knows for certain. It records the miraculous deliverance of the Jewish people by Esther. Even though God's name is not mentioned, God can be seen working out the deliverance of His people. The book of Esther does teach that God rewards faithfulness in His people.

Esther 1 provides the setting for the book and the beginning of the events that would cause Esther to rise to the throne. Ahasuerus (Xerxes) was the grandson of Cyrus the Great (v1-2). During the third year of his reign he provided a feast to show his wealth and glory that lasted for one week (v3-9). Queen Vashti also had a feast for all of the women. The king requested her presence, but she refuses to come (v10-12). Her rebellion toward the king led to a royal decree that a man should be ruler over his own house (v13-22). She could never again be in the presence of the king and her position would be given to another.

In Esther 2:1-4 the search begins for a new queen. All the women gathered were to be virgins, be beautiful, and be given special treatment for 12 months. In verses 5-11 we are introduced to Mordecai, who is Esther's cousin and is raising her as his own child. Mordecai also told her not to reveal to anyone that she was a Jew. After receiving her 12 months of beauty treatment (v12-14), Esther is brought before the king and she impressed everyone including the king (v15-18). Esther is made queen in the 7th year of the king's reign. In verses 19-23 Mordecai overhears a plot being made on the king's life and reveals it to Xerxes who has the men killed.

Esther 3:1-6 introduces Haman who will devise a plan to annihilate the Jews because Mordecai refuses to bow down to him. Jewish tradition teaches that Haman was a descendant of the Amalekites (enemies of Israel), who Saul failed to destroy in 1 Samuel 15. In verses 7-15 Haman goes to the king with his plan to destroy not just Mordecai, but all Jews from Persia. The Hebrew word for lot is pur, which is where the word Purim is derived from. Purim is celebrated today for when Esther (God's providence) delivered the Jews from Haman's wicked plan. The decree, which was sealed with the king's ring was for all people to kill every Jew one year from the date it was issued.

Esther 4:1-3 records Mordecai's mourning over the decree made by the king to annihilate the Jews. Esther learns of Mordecai's mourning, and sends Hathach to Mordecai where she learns of the decree by the king (v4-8). Mordecai urges Esther to intervene and plead for mercy on behalf of the Jews which would reveal her identity. Esther replies that no one could appear before the king unless they were called because they would be given the death penalty (v9-11). In verses 12-17 Mordecai again pleads with Esther to go before the king because she has been placed in her position for a time like this. She agrees to go, but asks all the Jews to fast for her for three days.

In Esther 5:1-8 after the 3 days of fasting, Esther appears before the king who tells her that he will grant any request she has. She invites the king and Haman to a banquet that she had prepared. Once again the king asks her about her request which she promises to reveal at another banquet the next day. In verses 9-14 Haman meets Mordecai who still refuses to bow down to him. He goes home and boasts about his riches, his sons, and the honor he was shown by the king and queen. Even all of this did not make him happy as long as Mordecai lived. His wife suggests he have gallows built to hang Mordecai on, and he has them built.

Wednesday • Acts 19-20

In Acts 19:1-10 Paul travels back to Ephesus, while Apollos is left at Corinth. The people there had only heard of John's baptism. Paul instructs them about Jesus, and they receive the Holy Spirit. Paul stays there for 2 years, preaching and teaching. The unusual miracles recorded in verses 11-20 had three purposes. First, they demonstrated God's ultimate power and authority. Second, they demonstrated that Paul was an apostle and a spokesman of God. Third, they demonstrated compassion and mercy on those in need. Paul's preaching led to many people being converted and leaving paganism. In verses 13-16 Jewish exorcists (who do not know Christ) use Jesus' name to exorcise a demon the way Paul did. This story shows that the power of God is only available to those who know Jesus personally. This chapter also gives insight on what the conditions were at Ephesus when you read the book of Ephesians. It is especially helpful for passages such as Ephesians 6:10-20, and in understanding spiritual warfare.

Paul's preaching of the gospel brought harm to the makers of the idols of Diana, who cause an uproar in the city (v21-41). The temple of Diana in Ephesus was one of the seven wonders of the world. The actual temple was 165 feet x 345 feet, with an altar area of over 20 feet. The altar area had a massive statue of Diana. Every spring there was a festival dedicated to her that brought in people from all over Asia. Diana was the worshipped throughout all of Asia. She was called lord, savior, and queen of the cosmos. Diana was believed to have power over nature, the underworld including demons, and the dead. Demetrius, the silversmith, brings three charges against Christianity. First, Christianity was a threat to them making a living. Second, Paul had told the people that the idols were not gods at all. Third, Paul's preaching had dethroned their god. Verse 32 gives an example of the mobs, and shows that most of them did not even know what they were there for. If not for the city clerk intervening in verse 35, the mob could have turned violent. The city clerk took Paul's side and reminded Demetrius that his actions were illegal (v38-41).

Acts 20:1-6 shows Paul's continuing missionary journey and those who went along with him. Those that went with him represented the church, showing its unity. Verses 7-12 record the raising of Eutychus ("Lucky One") after he fell asleep listening to Paul. Many see similarities in this miracle with those of Elijah (1 Kgs. 17:21) and Elisha (2 Kgs. 4:34). Verses 18-28 record Paul's speech to the elders at Ephesus. It is the only speech recorded in

Acts that is directed at believers, as he is giving it to prepare them for his absence. In verses 18-20 we see three characteristics of Paul and his ministry. Paul was humble (v18), he preached the gospel (v20), and he preached it to everyone (v21). In verses 22-23 Paul tells them he is being led by the Spirit to go to Jerusalem. Paul knew that he was under God's protection, similar to what he had experienced earlier in Corinth (Acts 18:9-10). Paul was also willing to die for the gospel if that is what the Lord wanted (v24).

In verses 25-27 Paul tells the elders at Ephesus he will see them no more. Similar to the watchman of Ezekiel 33, Paul declares that he has preached to all the whole counsel of God and he is no longer responsible for their lives. Paul had preached the message of the gospel to them and called for repentance. In verses 28-31 Paul warns the Ephesian elders of dangers to the church that are already present and those that will come in the future. Paul warns the elders to first watch out for themselves and then for the church. Leadership must not fall into being deceived, or else they cannot properly watch over the church. Satan will cause havoc in a church where there is not sound doctrine. Paul also shows that leadership is appointed by the Holy Spirit. Churches must follow the leadership of the Holy Spirit to appoint those who hold leadership positions. Verses 29-30 show that threats to the church will come from the outside and from within the church. The term "wolves" was often a designation for false prophets and teachers. In verses 32-35 Paul closes out his speech to the Ephesian elders with instruction for them to minister to the church in the same manner he practiced. With Paul's speech coming to an end, they pray together and escort Paul to the ship which will carry him to Jerusalem (v36-38).

Thursday • Ecclesiastes 3-4

Ecclesiastes 3:1-8 is teaching that humanity is to live one day at a time. On each day there is a right time for these things to be done. Today, believers are to listen to the leadership of the Holy Spirit to discern the right time. These things, done at the right time, produce fulfillment in the lives of man (v9-11) and cause rejoicing while they enjoy the fruit of their labor (v12-15). Again, the subject of death is addressed in verses 16-22. Man and animals are given life by their Creator but they both will die. Some people live as though they have all the time in the world, but here in these passages every person is confronted with the reality that death is coming and so is judgment.

Ecclesiastes 4:1-3 addresses those who are oppressed and powerless. For those who are suffering, Solomon praises those who are dead because they no longer have to suffer and better than this is to have never been born. In verses 4-6 he adds that both toil and success comes from envying one's neighbor. Three different types of workers are shown in the two proverbs that follow. One is a lazy person who does no work, the second only works as needed but knows how to rest, and third is the person who only works and knows no rest. The only one who is worse off is the one who works but has no one to share it with (v7-12). Having a friend is better than being alone, because with friends there is companionship and strength.

Friday • Malachi

Malachi ("My Messenger") is the last of the Old Testament prophets, and also the last book of the Old Testament. It was probably written during the time Nehemiah briefly returned to Persia (Neh.5:14; 13:6). It addresses many of the problems Nehemiah faced upon his return to Jerusalem: marrying foreign wives, withholding tithes, and social injustice. Malachi addresses these issues and will be the last time there is revelation from God for over 400 hundred years.

Malachi 1:1-5 opens with God's sovereign choice of Israel over all others with the example of Jacob and Esau. Verses 6-9 address the priests who were not honoring the Lord and bringing sacrifices that were worthless. The danger here is that the priests would lead the people into doing the same thing, taking them farther away from God. If the priests were going to do this, God says they should just shut the doors of the temple (v10-14). If the people reject God by doing this He will choose others who will praise His name (Gentiles, nations).

Malachi 2:1-9 continues the rebuke against the priests. The description of what the priests should have been did not describe the priests of Malachi's day. They were speaking lies instead of truth and leading people to sin instead of away from sin. The priests would suffer shame and be humiliated for what they have done and led the people to do. Verses 10-16 deal with intermarriage with foreign wives and the divorces that it caused. They should have married within their own people (v10-12; 2 Cor. 6:14-16). Verse 14 suggests that they may have divorced their aging wives for younger ones. God intends for marriage to be monogamous, and for it to last.

Malachi 3:1 describes the coming of John the Baptist to prepare the way for the long awaited Messiah. While verse 1 speaks of Jesus' first coming, verses 2-3 are about His second coming to judge, and verse 5 recognizes those He will judge. Verses 6-9 address the people to stop robbing God of tithes and offerings which harmed the priesthood and the nation as a whole. The remedy for their sin was they must start doing what is right in order to be blessed (v10-12). Part of the reason people did not tithe was because they had no faith in God, complaining that He is unfair in judgment (v13-15). For the faithful, God will protect them and they will be His people (v16-18).

Malachi 4:1-3 concerns the coming Day of the Lord where the wicked will be destroyed and those who are righteous will be healed. Malachi instructs them to do two things in verses 4-6. First, they are to listen and obey the Law of Moses. Second, when it is time for the Messiah's arrival He will send Elijah (John the Baptist) who will preach a message of repentance.

Saturday • Jude

Jude is the half-brother of Jesus and wrote this epistle around 68-70 AD. It is very similar to 2 Peter in its content; however Peter writes in future tense and Jude writes of false teachers who are already present. Other purposes of the book are to warn of judgment against those who rebel against God and to engage Christians to be active in sharing their faith. Believers today must heed the warnings of Jude, Paul (Acts 20:28-30) and Jesus (Matt. 7:15-20) about false teachers.

After the opening of the letter (v1-2), Jude reveals the purpose of his writing (v3-4). Jude wants believers to defend the truth of the gospel against those who are preaching a false gospel. In verses 5-10 he reminds his readers of false teachers from the past and the destructive doctrines they taught. Verse 5 is the sin of unbelief, verse 6 is the sin of rebellion, and verse 7 is the sin of immorality. False teachers live in their own world where they make up false doctrines and claim authority they do not have.

In verses 11-13 the false teachers will lead people to rebel against the Lord and His truth (Cain Gen. 4:5-8; Balaam Num. 22:5-7, 25:1-9; Korah Num. 16:13). Their teaching will have no substance, it will be dead words, it will produce shameful deeds, and they will vanish just as quickly as they appear. Verses 14-16 address the return of Christ as He comes to judge them of their ungodly deeds. Verses 17-19 are for believers to remember what they have been taught about the false teachers by the apostles. Verses 20-21 are an encouragement for them to remain firm in their faith and to continue to study the Word of God, to be praying, and to remain in the love of God. Verses 22-23 are a call for believers to rescue those who do not know Christ or who may be tempted to follow false teachers. Verse 24 is a reference to Jesus and his restraining influence in a believer's life. Jude closes with reverence of God in the form of a doxology, similar to the ones that are found in Revelation (v25).

Cover to Cover CHALLENGE

Week 49

Sunday • Psalm 140-142

Welcome to week 49 of the *Cover to Cover Challenge*! I pray that the Holy Spirit is teaching you great and mighty things from the Word of God. There is nothing greater that any of us can do than to be in the Word of God, and allow the Lord to speak to us through it. Continue to pray for the Lord to use this for His glory, and to work in the lives of all those participating. Psalm 141:1 says "Lord, I cry out to you; make haste to me! Give ear to my voice when I cry out to you".

Psalm 140 is a psalm of David and is a lament. In this psalm David cries out for the Lord to deliver him from evil men who are committing violence, saying evil things, and devising wicked plans (v1-5). In the midst of this David has full confidence that the Lord will deliver him and protect him (v6-8). David then prays for God to pay back the wicked for what they have done with His divine judgment (v9-11). In verses 12-13 David's cry for help turns into a song of victory as God delivers from the enemy.

Psalm 141 is also a lament spoken by David. In verses 1-2 David again cries out to God in prayer while lifting up his hands, symbolizing his dependence on the Lord. Verses 3-5 are actually a prayer filled with wisdom. David asks God not to let him sin with his lips, not to let his heart turn to sin, and to let him accept the rebuke of the righteous when he has sinned. As in Psalm 140, David prays for deliverance, but also for the Lord to repay the wicked for their evil deeds (v8-10).

Psalm 142 is another lament written by David. In verses 1-2 David again cries out to God during a trial in his life. Notice that he uses three different words to say this: cry out, pour out, and declare. At this point David is overwhelmed because his enemies are setting traps for him and there is no one to fight for him (v3-4). In this situation David knows that he can go to the Lord for help because he needs relief from his situation (v5-6). David needs the Lord to deliver him, and he will praise the Lord for delivering him.

Monday • Deuteronomy 23-25

Deuteronomy 23:1-8 concerns those to be excluded from corporate worship. These laws do not forbid someone from believing in God, they only exclude them from assembling with all of Israel to worship. No castrated man is allowed in the assembly to worship (v1), nor someone born from an illegitimate birth (v2). Verses 3-6 bar the Ammonites and Moabites from worshiping with Israel because of how they treated them in the past. They would also be excluded based upon verse 2 (Gen. 19:29-38). Verses 9-14 deal with uncleanness within an army camp, and also demonstrate that God is holy and must be respected. Verses 15-16 are probably foreign slaves who are seeking refuge. Prostitution is forbidden, especially if it is associated with paganism (v17-18). Loaning money to a fellow Israelite was not to be done with interest because this would only worsen their condition (v19-20). Verses 21-23 are about keeping vows and teach people to speak with honesty and integrity. Verses 24-25 are a provision for travelers, but they are not to take advantage of the generosity of their neighbors.

Deuteronomy 24:1-5 deals with laws concerning marriage. Verses 1-4 provide the woman protection and keep her from being rejected by society. They also give her freedom to remarry. It is also to prevent divorce for minor offenses and shows that God does not like divorce (Mal. 2:16; Matt. 19:3-9). Verse 5 prevents newly married men from going to war. If he is killed, he will have no offspring to carry on his name. Verse 6 prevents taking a millstone for collateral because this is how people got their daily provisions. Verse 7 says that the punishment for kidnapping is death. Verses 8-9 warn of following the priest's orders if leprosy breaks out, and also provide another warning through the life of Miriam who had disobeyed and was struck with leprosy. Verses 10-15 concern the borrower and lender relationship, emphasizing generosity and kindness. Verse 16 prevents unjust punishment for a crime not committed by the person. Verses 17-22 protect the less fortunate in society. Here, God reminds them of their previous situation in Egypt because they were once in the same situation.

Deuteronomy 25:1-3 teaches that justice was not to be taken in their own hands, but for judges to decide punishment for crimes. It also assured that the punishment should fit the crime. Verse 4 shows that mercy was to be shown to the animals that worked and helped provide in making a living. Verses 5-10 describe the laws concerning the levirate marriage, which you see in the story of Ruth. From many of the laws you can see that God cares deeply for offspring and families (v11-12). Verses 13-16 teach us to be honest in dealing with others, especially in business transactions. Verses 17-19 are a command to destroy the Amalekites for how they have treated Israel. This command would be disobeyed by Saul, and Jewish tradition teaches that Haman was a descendant of Amalek.

Tuesday • Esther 6-10

In Esther 6 the hand of God is definitely present as things begin to unravel for Haman and his evil plan. With the king unable to sleep, it is found out through the reading of the records that nothing was done for Mordecai when he discovered the plot to kill the king (v1-5). Haman was coming to bring his plot to hang Mordecai to the king (v6-11). The king is seeking to honor Mordecai for his good deed but Haman, in his pride, believed the king was going to honor him. Instead, Haman honored Mordecai and it humiliated him. When he returns home he tells the story of what happened to his wife and counselors (v12-14). They agree that Haman's plans will not stand against Mordecai and he will be ruined. Haman then is brought to the banquet prepared by Esther.

In Esther 7 the king and Haman go to the banquet prepared by Esther, and the king again asks Esther to share her request (v1-2). In verses 3-4 Esther pleads for her life and the life of her people, which also reveals she is a Jew. She reveals that Haman is the one who is behind the plot to annihilate all of the Jews (v5-6). The king leaves the palace and Haman remains behind, begging for his life on the couch Esther is sitting on (v7-8). When the king returns he accuses Haman of trying to rape Esther. Harbonah, a servant of the king, tells the king of Haman's plot to hang Mordecai who once saved the king's life (v9-10). The king orders Haman to be hanged and it is carried out immediately.

In Esther 8:1-2 the king gave Esther Haman's entire estate. She in turn gave it to Mordecai who had also received the king's signet ring. Mordecai now had Haman's wealth, title, and power. In verses 3-6, Esther begs the king to reverse the decree made by Haman to annihilate all of the Jews. The king orders them to write another decree offsetting the decree of Haman (v7-10). The new decree gave the Jews the right to protect themselves from anyone who attacked them and to get their property (v11-12). The new decree was carried throughout Persia and there was a celebration among the people and the Jews (v13-17). Some of the people in Persia actually became Jews as a result.

Esther 9:1-10 records that the time for both decrees to be performed had come. The Jews were also helped by the noblemen in the king's court because they feared Mordecai. The Jews showed no mercy, and even hunted those down who would destroy them. The Jews also did not take the plunder even though the decree said they could. This showed that they were not doing it to prosper themselves, but to protect themselves. In verses 11-17 the king grants Esther another request. She asks for one more day for the Jews to go against their enemies and for Haman's sons to be hanged for all to see. Throughout Persia over 75,000 Persians were killed. In verses 20-28 Mordecai writes a letter to all Jews in each province to celebrate this new holiday called Purim. The purpose of the letter was to establish Purim as a national holiday for Jews for all generations to come (v29-32). Esther closes showing the power of the king (v1), the recording of these events in Medo-Persia (v2), and the rise of Mordecai to his prominent position (v3).

Wednesday • Acts 21-22

Acts 21:1-14 records more of Paul's missionary journey. In Tyre, Paul is warned not to go to Jerusalem by the people there. It was revealed to them that Paul was going to suffer if he went. In Acts 23:11, God tells Paul directly to go to Jerusalem. Philip the evangelist was one of the seven original deacons, and a prominent figure in spreading the gospel to the Samaritans (Acts 8). His daughter's prophesying is not anything new in Scripture. There are many women who prophesied (Miriam Ex. 15:20; Deborah Judges 4:4; Huldah 2 Kgs. 22:14; Noadiah Neh. 6:14; Isaiah's wife Isa. 8:3; Anna Luke 2:36-38). Agabus also appears again (Acts 11:27-29), predicting Paul's arrest in Jerusalem. This story is similar to that of Jesus, who was also bound by the Jews and delivered to the Gentiles.

In verses 15-25, Paul arrives in Jerusalem and meets with James (Lord's brother) and the leaders of the church there. This would also bring to conclusion his third missionary journey. Paul is warned of opposition from the Jews and of how they have twisted his teachings (v20-22). It is recommended that Paul be purified along with four other men so the Jews can see that Paul's teachings are not unlawful (v23-25). When the gospel was not the issue, Paul was willing to become all things to all people so that they could be saved (1 Cor. 9:20). In verses 26-36 Paul carries the four men to the temple. He is recognized by the Jews who came from Asia to stir up a mob and they grab Paul and plan to kill him. Two of these charges were the same as those that were brought against Stephen (Acts 6:13). They also argue that Paul brought a Gentile into the temple, but they had no proof.

In Acts 21:37-Acts 22:21, Paul addresses the mob that has come against him. When on trial, Paul will speak in Hebrew and describes himself as a Jew and a Pharisee to identify with his listeners (v21:40-22:-3). Paul always used each opportunity to present the gospel. He also aligns himself with Gamaliel, who was the most honored rabbi of his day. He will give his testimony of his conversion to Christianity (v6-11), his visit from Ananias (v12-16) and his calling to go to the Gentiles (v17-21). Paul's testimony is given in Acts 9:1-30, Acts 22:6-21, and Acts 26:4-23.

In verses 22-23 the Jews want him to be killed (again similar to the treatment of Jesus). The commander orders him to be scourged, but Paul tells them he is a citizen of Rome. This protected him from being scourged and gave him a trial (v24-29). Verse 30 states that the next day he was released from his chains and would appear before the Sanhedrin.

Thursday • Ecclesiastes 5-6

In Ecclesiastes 5:1-7 Solomon warns that God's holiness is not meaningless. When you go to worship be cautious of your sacrifice, your prayers, and your vows. The person who never makes a vow is better off than the one who makes one and does not keep it. It is better to speak little and listen much in worship of God, who they are to fear. In verses 8-20 Solomon views wealth and the pursuit of it as vanity (meaningless, useless). It corrupts human authority (v8-9), you never have enough (v10), others get more (v11), and leads to unrest in life (v12). In verses 13-17 Solomon shows that wealth can lead to evil and unhappiness. You can keep it all for yourself (v13) or lose it all (v14). At death, wealth is also useless (v15-17). Very few find pleasure in wealth unless it is given to them by God (v18-20).

Ecclesiastes 6 continues the thought on wealth. Just as God has given some wealth to enjoy, He gives to some and they do not live to enjoy it (v1-2). A stillborn baby is better off than a rich man who does not get to enjoy their wealth (v3-6). The desire or getting of wealth does not satisfy in the end (v7-9). It is better for man to depend on God, because man understands very little about life.

Friday • Revelation 1-6

Revelation ("Unveiling") is the last book of the New Testament. It was written sometime between 90-98 AD by the apostle John on the island of Patmos where he was exiled for preaching the gospel (1:9). Much like Daniel it is written to assure God's people that He is still in control of the past, in control of the present, and also the future. Revelation contains a blessing for those who heed its words (1:3), and a warning for those who do not (22:18-19). Aside from the book of Hebrews, Revelation offers a unique picture of Jesus with 33 different names or descriptions of Him throughout the book.

Revelation 1:1-3 is the introduction to the book and also places a blessing on those who keep the words of the book, warning that the end is at hand. This is the first of seven blessings in the book of Revelation (14:13, 16:15, 19:9, 20:6, 22:7,14). Verse 1 shows how the book came to John. God gave it to Jesus, Jesus sends it by an angel, and an angel then gives it to John. John then writes Revelation to the seven churches in Asia, and gives one of the most complete descriptions of Jesus recorded in Scripture (v4-8, 12-18). In these verses Jesus is described as the faithful witness (John 18:37), the firstborn from the dead (1 Cor. 15:20), and the ruler over the kings of the earth (Ps. 89:27). The word used for love in verse 5 describes Jesus' continuing love for those who have been saved. Verse 7 is the purpose statement for the book of Revelation (Zech. 12:10), and is the first of seven references to Jesus' second coming (2:25, 3:3, 3:11, 22:7, 22:12, 22:20). Clouds in Scripture point to the presence of God (Ex. 19:16, Dan. 7:13-14, Matt. 24:30, 26:64, Acts 1:9, 1 Thess. 4:16-17).

John is on the isle of Patmos because of his witness of the gospel, and is asked to write what he is told in a book to the seven churches (v9-11,19-20). Verses 9-20 also show the relationship of Jesus to His church. In these verses Jesus is pictured as walking among the churches (v13). The description of Jesus is similar to the one found in Daniel 7:9 and 10:6. When John is in the presence of the Lord he falls on his face to worship (v17). All those in Scripture in the presence of God fall on their face to worship and/or to confess sin (Isa. 6:5, Dan. 10:8-9, Ez.

1:28, Luke 5:8, Acts 26:14). Jesus possessing the keys of Hades and Death shows that He has total control of them (John 11:25-26, Heb. 2:14-15).

Revelation 2 begins the letters to the seven churches. Each will address a specific church, a reference to Jesus, an examination of the church, words of praise or rebuke, a note of encouragement, a promise to those who overcome, and a command to listen to the Spirit. Many believe these churches represent ones in existence today, but no church is exempt from the warnings or the encouragements offered to these seven churches. Verses 1-7 are addressed to the church at Ephesus. Ephesus was probably the most prominent church in the area. Through Scripture we also see how the Ephesian church changes over time (Acts 18-19, Ephesians, 1-2 Timothy, Revelation). Ephesus was also known for its worship of Diana and was also a well-known sanctuary for criminals. It is also known as the loveless church, or as some call it, the backsliding church. While they have kept false teachers out of their church, they have left their first love (v4, Jesus-Matt. 22:36-38). The Ephesian church was now made of second and third generation Christians who continued to work, but had forgotten the One they were serving. Jesus wants them to remember from where they had fallen, repent, or He would remove their church.

Verses 8-11 are addressed to Smyrna, or the suffering church. Smyrna was once known as the most beautiful city in Asia. They receive no rebuke, but are encouraged to endure the persecution. The Christians in Smyrna would have been persecuted by the Jews and the residents of Smyrna for not worshiping the emperor. They are encouraged because even though they are physically poor, spiritually they are rich (v9). They are also encouraged to keep being faithful to the Lord (v10).

Verses 12-17 are addressed to Pergamos, which is also known as the compromising church or the worldly church. The city was also a center for pagan religions and they also worshiped Roma, which was the worship of Rome. The city also contained one of the largest libraries of its day and was known for its manufacturing of parchment. This church was on dangerous ground because it was mixing the worship of other religions with that of worship of Jesus (v14-15). It is believed that Antipas died standing up for his belief in Christ. Tradition says he was roasted alive inside a brass bull. The doctrine of Balaam can be viewed as immorality or being greedy for money (Num. 22-25). The doctrine of Nicolaitans may have been an early form of Gnosticism, where knowledge is salvation. It is also possible that it is a mixture of religions to look and seem Christian, but it is not.

Verses 18-29 are addressed to Thyatira, which is known as the corrupt church because they tolerate false teaching. This city was famous for its trade guilds which were much like unions today. Each trade guild had its own deity that was worshiped and had their own ceremonies. These ceremonies had three distinct elements. First, they poured out a cup of wine in worship of their god. Second, they ate a meal together which consisted of heavy drinking that was offered to their god. Third, they engaged in immorality. To hold a job or run a business they must belong to the trade guild. Christians faced the dilemma in this city of not just attending or not attending, but whether or not they had a job or a business. This scenario had led to corruption in the church. Their church was full of good works but it was being corrupted by false teaching, perhaps from the trade guilds' influence.

Revelation 3:1-6 is addressed to Sardis, or the dead or dying church. Sardis was a center for trade and also had a large military presence. It was known for its manufacturing of wool garments. The inhabitants of the city were known for being infatuated with death and immortality. This church had a reputation for being alive, but was dead because they depended on their past works. Jesus warns them to wake up from their present state and to strengthen themselves (v2). The people of Sardis also had a reputation of not being alert. Sardis was located 1500 feet above all roads and was situated like a fortress. Believing they could not be captured, no one watched. Twice in history they were captured, all because the people failed to watch.

Verses 7-13 are addressed to the church at Philadelphia, which is also known as the faithful church because they had suffered persecution and not denied the Lord's name. Philadelphia and Smyrna are the only churches not to receive any rebuke. Because of their faithfulness, the Lord had set before them an open door to minister (v8). Paul often prayed for doors to be open so he could minister (1 Cor. 6:9, 2 Cor. 2:12, Col. 4:3). Verse 10 is held to by many to prove that Christians will not suffer through the Tribulation period. The phrase "dwell on the earth" in Revelation is always a reference to unbelievers (Rev. 6:10, 8:13, 11:10, 13:8,12,14, 14:6, 17:2,8).

Verses 14-22 are addressed to Laodicea, otherwise known as the lukewarm or materialistic church. It is the church that wants to wear the crown, but not bear its cross. It is the church that believes they have it all, but actually has nothing. Today Sardis and Laodicea have no Christian presence, as they are the most severely rebuked of the churches. Ephesus would later be literally removed from its place (2:5). Smyrna and Philadelphia, the only two not rebuked, still have a Christian presence today.

In Revelation 4 we enter the throne room of heaven and see the worship of the Creator of the universe. The key word in this chapter is throne (14x), and the focus is on the One sitting on it. No human words can or could describe what John is seeing taking place. God's holiness and power are on full display in this chapter. This chapter serves to show that only God is to be worshiped, and all things should praise God because He has created all things (11).

Revelation 5 is also in the throne room of heaven. The focus of this chapter is worshiping the Lamb. He alone is worthy to be praised because He has provided redemption for man (v8-14). Throughout the Bible, redemption has been pictured through sacrifice. One ram died for one young man, one lamb died for the family, one lamb died for the nation, and one Lamb would die for the whole world. Many believe the scroll is the title deed of the earth, and only the Lamb can open it. These scriptures clearly point out that Jesus is the One who can open the scroll. The new song in verses 9-10 can only be sung by those who have been redeemed. Verse 12 shows the seven fold praise of the Lamb. He is praised for His power, riches, wisdom, strength, honor, and blessing. With the number seven being involved this can also be described as the perfect praise of the Lamb. It is also similar to the praise David offered to God in 1 Chronicles 29:11-12.

Revelation 6 begins the opening of the seven seals. The judgments of these seals are poured out upon the earth, and depict catastrophic events as God pours out His wrath upon the world. Verses 1-2 may depict the Antichrist riding on a white horse, who will come with a false peace. Verses 3-4 show a red horse that brings war and destruction. Verses 5-6 show the black horse that may refer to severe famine that will come because of economic crisis. A day's wages that could feed a family will barely buy enough to feed one person. Verses 7-8 depict the pale horse which brings death and the grave with it. With this seal, a fourth of the earth will die. Verses 9-11 show the souls of those who have been killed for proclaiming the Word of God. The Lord will avenge their blood when all who will give their life for the Word of God is complete. Verses 12-17 show the cosmic disturbances that will accompany end time events. These are foretold by Isaiah, Ezekiel, Joel, Amos, and by Christ Himself (Matt. 24). While the people represented in the verses are living apart from God, they do know that God is the one pouring out His wrath (v16).

Saturday • 1 John 1-3

1 John was written by the apostle John sometime in the early 90's AD. John wrote with four purposes in mind. First, he wrote to provide joy for believers (1:4). Second, he wrote to prevent sin and to remind them where to go when they did sin (2:1). Third, he wrote to refute false teaching (2:26). Fourth, he wrote to reassure believers of their salvation (5:13). John will leave no room- you either know Christ or you do not.

In 1 John 1:1-4 John opens the letter with an eyewitness testimony of Jesus. John and the others had heard, seen, looked upon (gaze), and handled Jesus. John wanted them to know that all believers have fellowship with one another because they have had a personal encounter with Jesus. This should provide joy for believers because they know that they have fellowship with the Father, Son, and all believers. Verses 5-10 build on the concept of light (God) and darkness (do not know God) to illustrate whether or not people actually have a relationship with Jesus. Light was a theme in John's gospel (John 1:4, 3:19, 8:12; Ps. 27:1, Ps. 119:1-5, 130). This can be seen from what they claim and compared to how they live their life (v6-7). Some in John's day taught that it was possible to reach a state of perfection where one did not sin anymore. John refutes this by saying that all are sinners, and if they claim otherwise they are making God a liar (v8-10).

1 John 2:1-2 goes with the previous chapter. It gives us another reason why John wrote-so you will not practice sin. The word "Advocate" is the same word used for the Holy Spirit in John's gospel. Jesus is our defense attorney, who intercedes on our behalf. The word "propitiation" means that Jesus died to satisfy God's wrath for our sin. Verses 3-11 also provide assurance of salvation. Believers can know they are saved because of how they live their lives in obedience to Jesus' word. If we truly love God there will be evidence of this in our daily lives, which will be seen through our love for other people. Verses 12-14 may describe three stages of spiritual growth within the church family. All are on different levels and are encouraged to keep growing in the Lord.

Verses 15-17 are a warning to avoid falling in love with the world. There are three primary avenues of temptation: lust of the flesh, lust of the eyes, and the pride of life. Lot looked toward Sodom, pitched his tent toward Sodom, then he moved to Sodom. In verses 18-27, John gives three ways to recognize the spirit of antichrist. First, they will depart from true fellowship (v19). Second, they will deny that Jesus came in the flesh (v22). Third, they will try to deceive believers (v26). John encourages believers to let the Word of God abide (remain) in them and to follow the Holy Spirit (v27, anointing). In verses 28-3:3 John encourages believers to love one another and keep themselves pure as they await the return of Jesus.

1 John 3:4-9 give two reasons that Jesus came. Jesus came to take away our sin (v5) and to destroy the works of the devil (v8). In verse 4 John describes sin as lawlessness. This is active disobedience against God's moral standards. Paul calls the future Antichrist the man of lawlessness in 2 Thessalonians 2. He will be someone who will deliberately disobey the moral standards of God. If believers are not careful, the lawlessness of our society can have an effect on the body of Christ. It can lead to indifference, where sin or evil does not bother us, and that which can lead to being unconcerned for the lost. Verse 6 shows that those who abide (remain) in Jesus will not practice sin. Whoever practices sin has not known Him (no relationship). Verse 7 shows that those who are righteous can only be righteous because they know Christ. In verse 8 it is shown that those who practice sin belong to the devil, and that he is the originator of sin (Isa. 14:9-17, Ez. 28:12-14). Jesus came to destroy (rob of power) the works of the devil. Verse 9 also proves that a practicing sinner cannot be a practicing Christian, and a practicing Christian cannot be a practicing sinner. Verses 10-15 teach that it is the nature of Christians to be loving. Those who do not love their brother do not belong to God either. In verse 12 John uses the example of Cain murdering Abel as an example of hate. In this act Cain resembles the devil (John 8:44). The world will hate those who imitate Christ (v13, John 15:18-19). Verse 14 is evidence for salvation. If you love your brothers you have been saved, while those who do not love have not been saved. The phrase "passed from death to life" means a permanent move from one place to another. Those who have been born again have moved permanently from darkness to light.

Those who love God should love others (v16-23). This is demonstrated by the love Christ had for when He laid down His own life (v16). This type of love should also be demonstrated by believers. This type of love meets needs (v17-18, James 2:15-16), brings assurance (v19-20), and enhances the prayer life of the saints (v21-23).

Cover to Cover CHALLENGE

Week 50

Sunday • Psalm 143-144

Welcome to week 50 of the *Cover to Cover Challenge*! Let us continue to pray that our eyes will be opened to the truth of God's Word, that the Holy Spirit will move in our lives, and for the Lord Jesus to get the glory and honor from it. Psalm 143:1 says "Hear my prayer, O Lord, give ear to my supplication! In Your faithfulness answer me, and in Your righteousness".

Psalm 143 is a psalm of lament written by David. He prays to God, depending on the Lord's faithfulness and righteousness (v1-2). David's enemies are pursuing him and he is discouraged (v3-4). In the midst of his trials he will remember, meditate, and consider God's past acts. He will continue to put his trust in the Lord while he prays for deliverance and guidance (v7-10). In closing David prays to be revived by the Lord, for help dealing with his enemies, and to remain God's servant.

Psalm 144 is a psalm of praise asking the Lord for help and for His continual blessings. From David's prayer in verses 1-2 it can be seen how dependent David was upon the Lord and what the Lord meant to him. David knows that he needs God to live and to rule over the people (v3-4). In verses 5-8 David prays for God to appear and destroy his enemies so that the people can be delivered. The new song David sings expresses confidence and trust in the Lord that He will deliver them (v9-10). David repeats his cry for deliverance (v7-8,11) and asks the Lord to continue to bless the nations (v12-15). This blessing is for their families to be blessed, their fields, and their livestock.

Monday • Deuteronomy 26-28

Deuteronomy 26:1-11 is to celebrate what God has given them by bringing Him the firstfruits of the land. Each person is to do this. It gives them an opportunity to worship before the Lord. The words they are to say are a summary of what God has done for them in bringing them into the land. Verses 12-15 are the tithe that is to be brought in the 3rd year they are in the land. This tithe is to be given to the Levites, strangers, orphans, and widows. Verses 16-19 tell Israel to be obedient to God. They are to obey God's commands and God will provide and meet all of their needs. In response to their obedience God promises to be their God and exalt the nation of Israel over all others.

In Deuteronomy 27:1-10 the people are commanded to obey the laws of God, to write the law on stones coated with plaster, and to set them up on Mount Ebal. They will also build an altar and make offerings to express their dependence and thankfulness to God. Once again they are called to obey God's laws because their livelihood depends on it. Verses 11-26 are the announcement of the curses. Six tribes are brought to Mount Gerizim to bless the people and six are brought to Mount Ebal to pronounce the curses. Curses are the divinely ordained consequences to those who violate the law. Eight of the twelve curses listed violate the Ten Commandments. Idolatry (v15), relationship with parents (v16), honesty (v17), abuse (v18), oppression (v19), immorality (v20-23), murder (v24-25), and breaking of any of God's laws (v26).

Deuteronomy 28 contains the blessing for obeying God's laws (v1-14) and the curses for disobeying (v15-68). God is showing them that without obedience there is no blessing, and every part of their life will be cursed. God gave them the land as He promised, but their success depends on their obedience (v1-2). They will be blessed in every part of the land (v3) and the offspring of both animals and humans (v4), they will have plenty of food (v5), they will never experience famine, they will have joy over their work (v6), they will enjoy military success (v7), their farming and families will prosper (v8,11), they will be a blessing to other nations (v9-10), and they will never have to borrow and will always lead (v12-13). Being disobedient to God's law brings a curse. The curses are designed to turn them from disobedience to obedience. Verses 16-19 are the exact opposite of the blessings in verses 3-6. They will suffer destruction (v20), disease (v21-22), drought (v23-24), defeat (v25-26), diseases of Egypt (v27-29), oppression and robbery (v30-35), exile (v36-37), crop failure and economic disaster (v38-48), be sieged by their enemies (v49-57), and disease that brings death and exile (v58-68).

Tuesday • Nehemiah 1-6

Nehemiah ("Jehovah Comforts") leads the third return to Jerusalem to rebuild its walls. Ezra 1-6 covered the first return under Zerubbabel and Joshua that included rebuilding the temple. Ezra 7-10 recounts the second return led by Ezra. The story of Esther took place in Persia during this time as Haman tried to execute all of the Jews. Artaxerxes is the king during the time of Nehemiah, and Nehemiah served as his cupbearer. Esther would have been Artaxerxes stepmother and may have influenced him to be favorable to the Jews.

In Nehemiah 1:1-4 Nehemiah hears of the condition of the walls of Jerusalem which have yet to be rebuilt, making them defenseless against their enemies. Ezra 4:7-23 does record an earlier attempt to rebuild the wall prior to Nehemiah. This news prompted Nehemiah to pray (v5-11). He confesses his own sin and the sins of the people and recalls God's promises to His people. Nehemiah especially prays that the Lord will show him mercy in sight of the king.

In Nehemiah 2:1-8 four months have passed since Nehemiah heard about the news of the wall. The king inquires as to why Nehemiah is sad, and after a prayer Nehemiah speaks from his heart. Nehemiah is known for his many prayers (1:5-11; 2:4; 4:4,9; 5:19; 6:9,14; 13:14). Nehemiah makes his request and it is granted along with letters for safe passage and for wood to rebuild. Nehemiah is given an armed escort, and meets Sanballat and Tobiah for the first time (v9-10). In verses 11-16 Nehemiah views the walls of the city at night because no one knows why he is there. It has been 140 years since the destruction of Jerusalem and its walls. Nehemiah explains to the leaders why he is there and God's favor was with him (v17-18). Once again Sanballat and Tobiah oppose the building of the wall (v19-20).

Nehemiah 3 lists 41 parties as participating in rebuilding the 42 sections of the walls. Verses 1-7 describe the work in the north, verses 8-13 the west, verse 14 the south, and verses 15-32 the eastern section. Men and women rebuilt the wall and the gates, which provides an example of what can be done when God's people work together.

In Nehemiah 4:1-3 Sanballat and Tobiah are angry over the progress of the wall and try their best to discourage them. Verse 3 is saying that if a fox jumped on the wall it would collapse. Nehemiah again goes to the Lord in prayer, asking for His help (v4-5). Their enemies turn from mocking to planning an attack on those who are rebuilding the wall (v6-15). During this time the people prayed to God (v8-9) and were worn out from all of the hard work (v10). Nehemiah constantly encouraged the people not to be afraid of their enemies. To counter their attacks Nehemiah instructed the workers to have weapons and be prepared to fight (v16-23). When their enemies would attack a trumpet would be blown, calling out for help.

Nehemiah 5:1-5 outlines the economic problems that existed as they tried to rebuild the walls. People were short on food, they mortgaged their property, they were forced to borrow money with interest, and they were forced to sell their children into slavery. Nehemiah became very angry over what was happening among the people and demanded that these things be made right (v6-13). Selling Hebrews as slaves to Gentiles was forbidden (Ex. 21:8). Nehemiah set the example of how the people were to live and treat one another (v14-19).

Nehemiah 6:1-9 lists many of the ways Tobiah and those who opposed the rebuilding of the wall attempted to catch Nehemiah in a trap. Nehemiah refused to be distracted or discouraged by the enemies' attacks. They even made up lies that Nehemiah was going to make himself king once the wall was completed. All of this was done to demoralize Nehemiah and the Jews. Tobiah even hired Shemaiah the priest and a false prophet to lie to Nehemiah that his life was being threatened (v10-14). Verses 15-19 record that the wall was completed in 52 days despite the opposition from their enemies. Even their enemies knew this could only be accomplished with God's help.

Wednesday • Acts 23-24

After being seized by the mob and rescued by the Roman commander in Acts 22, Paul prepares to speak before the Sanhedrin in Acts 23:1-10. When Paul calls the high priest a "whitewashed wall" he is calling him a hypocrite for having Paul slapped before he can present his defense (v3). Paul knows that the crowds who gathered are divided into Pharisees and Sadducees, so he takes advantage of the situation by bringing up that he is a Pharisee (v6-10). This causes an argument among the crowd and the Pharisees want to let him go. In verse 11 Jesus promises Paul that he will go to Rome to testify of Him. It also is a promise that God will protect Paul in Jerusalem.

Verses 12-22 reveal the plot to take Paul's life. Forty men have taken an oath to kill Paul. The word used here for oath is *anathematizeo*. It is not an oath, but a curse. For Jews it would begin with "May I be cursed" or "May I be eternally damned". This plot was also done in cooperation with the Sanhedrin (v14-15). Paul's nephew overhears the plot and it is averted (v16-22). Paul is taken to Caesarea to await trial where he will be heard by Felix with his accusers present (v23-35).

Acts chapters 24-26 center around three key political figures who will hear the gospel from Paul, fulfilling Acts 9:15-16. Paul will appear before Felix (ch.24), Festus (ch.25), and King Agrippa (ch.25-26). Each of these men will hear his testimony and hear the gospel. In Acts 24:1-9 Paul is brought before Felix so his case can be heard. Felix was governor from 52-59 AD. The Jews bring Tertullus, who brings three charges against Paul. First, Paul was a trouble maker and was causing riots. Second, Paul was the leader of an unrecognized sect. Third, he was caught defiling the temple. This third charge was designed to let Felix allow the Jews to kill Paul. Paul answers each charge in verses 10-21. Paul says he has not been in Jerusalem long enough to stir up a riot and that he only came to worship (1). He also ties Christianity (the Way comes from Isaiah 40) to the God of the Jewish people (2). He states that the reason he came to the temple was to bring money to the people and to offer sacrifices (3). By addressing the charges against him, Paul showed that he had broken no Jewish or Roman laws. The three issues he was being accused of only hid their real issue with Paul-his belief in the resurrection of the dead centered on Jesus Christ (v21).

Felix will delay his decision, but hears Paul speak numerous times about his faith in Christ (v22-27). The only reason there was a delay was because Felix did not want the Jews to riot against his rule. Paul preached to him about righteousness, self-control, and the judgment to come which would have been areas of conviction for Felix (v25). The only reason he kept sending for Paul was that he had hoped Paul would buy his freedom with a bribe (v26). After two years Porcius Festus will become governor (v27). Felix was more than likely at the point of conviction, but let his greed and desire to stay in power refuse the gospel message.

Thursday • Ecclesiastes 7-8

Ecclesiastes 7 answers the question from 6:12 with a series of proverbs relating to death (v1-2, 4,8) and wisdom/folly (v4-7, 9-12). It would be wise to consider what God has done and to make the most of our days on earth, whether they are good days or bad days (v13-14). Verses 15-22 show the limits of humanity whether in pursuing righteousness, wisdom, or folly. This section teaches that balance should be a part of our life. No person can be perfect, no matter how hard they pursue it, and no one can evade sin (v20-22). In verses 23-24 Solomon reminds the reader of his pursuit of meaning in life, which leads to his discussion in verses 25-8:1. On his journey to find meaning, Solomon learns three things about humanity. First, a manipulative woman is more bitter than death (v26). Second, an upright man is hard to find (v27-28) and the third lesson is that humanity has strayed from God (v29). Solomon's quest for wisdom has shown him that no person can attain it (v8:1).

Ecclesiastes 8:2-4 gives advice to obey the king because he can do as he wishes with his power. Obeying the king will also help avoid trouble (vv5-6), but there is no guarantee it will do so (v7-9). Solomon turns his attention on the wicked in the next verses. From his point of view, Solomon does not believe the wicked are being punished for their behavior (v10). This lack of punishment encourages others to act wickedly as well (v11). Because of this, he hopes that God will act in justice and repay them for their wickedness (v12-15). After observing these things he again concludes that God's work in the world cannot be fully known by man (v16-17).

Friday • Revelation 7-11

Revelation 7 answers the question asked in 6:17. Who is able to stand before God when He pours out His wrath? Verses 1-8 show that 12,000 will be sealed from each tribe of Israel totaling 144,000. Dan is replaced with Levi. This may be because they led Israel into idolatry (1 Kgs. 12:28-30). Ephraim is replaced with Joseph, and they too become consumed with idolatry. These 144,000 are the sealed servants of God, showing that He owns them and is protecting them during this terrible time. It also shows that God still has a plan for Israel. Some believe verses 9-17 are a scene from heaven just prior to the second coming of Christ. These are those who have lost their lives during the great tribulation and have been born again.

Revelation 8:1-6 opens with the opening of the 7th seal, which contains the 7 trumpets which are about to sound. The first four trumpets affect 1/3 of the earth, sea, water/springs, and sky (v7-12). The word "wormwood" has an interesting background that goes back to the Old Testament. It is mentioned in the Old Testament seven times and always refers to bitter judgment (Deut. 29:18, Prov. 5:4, Jer. 9:15, 23:15, Lam. 3:15, 19, Amos 5:7). The angel flying in verse 13 pronounces woes on those who remain on the earth because of the trumpets that are sounding next. Just as holy, holy, holy emphasizes God's holiness the repetition of the word "woe" emphasizes the judgments that are still to come. Even Jesus pronounced woes upon cities for not believing in Him (Matt. 11:21).

In Revelation 9:1-12 the 5th trumpet sounds and the bottomless pit is opened. Some believe these "locusts" are demons coming out of the bottomless pit (2 Pet. 2:4). They will torment all who do not have the seal of God on them for 5 months. The word for torture is *basanismos* and is one of the strongest words for torture and pain. The pain will be so great that men will seek death and will not be able to. This demonic army has a king over them. The name *Abaddon* in Hebrew describes the place of eternal punishment (Job 26:6; Ps. 88:11). In verses 13-19 the 6th trumpet sounds, and the army that is released by the angels also kills 1/3 of mankind. People are divided over whether this is a human or another demonic army. The fire, smoke, and brimstone will be the cause of death of millions. Verses 19-20 show the depravity of man. How they can experience these terrible judgments and still not repent of their sins?

Revelation 10:1-7 describes a mighty angel who holds a little book in his hand. Most believe this book is the whole Word of God, and by his actions he shows that God is the Creator and declares that time is quickly passing and God's plan is about to come to completion. In verses 8-11 John is given the little book and told to eat it. Ezekiel was told to do the same thing in Ezekiel 3:1-3,10. It represents taking God's Word into your own life and living it out. Verse 11 would be fulfilled when John wrote Revelation, and tradition says he was released from Patmos and preached once again.

In Revelation 11:1-2 John is told to measure the temple, but not the courtyard because it has been given over to the Gentiles for 3 ½ years. Measuring in the Bible shows ownership of something. There has been much speculation over the two witnesses in verses 3-14. Moses, Elijah, Enoch, Joshua, and Zerubbabel have all been considered, but no one truly knows. What is known is that these two witnesses will have a powerful Spirit-filled ministry during this time period. They will be killed by the beast (v7-10), and after 3 ½ days be resurrected by the Lord (v11-14). The 7th trumpet is blown in verses 15-19. Many believe this is a scene from the end of the tribulation, right before Christ returns.

Saturday • 1 John 4-5

1 John 4:1-6 provides a test to see whether or not a teaching or doctrine comes from the Lord. It will help us to discern between truth and error, and to see what the source of the teaching is. Some call this the Christological test because if a person does not believe that Jesus has come in the flesh, then their teaching did not come from God. The danger of false prophets and false doctrine is still prevalent today. These tests are here to get to the source of the teaching. Moses did the same thing in Deuteronomy 13:1-5 and 18:22 to know whether or not a prophet was speaking a message from God. The main false teaching John dealt with was called Docetism. This is the belief that Jesus was not human. Scripture makes it clear that Jesus is 100% human and also 100% God. John encourages believers to overcome in light of the false teachers and the doctrine they are spreading (v4-6). This is why it is necessary for believers to be in and to know the Word of God. There are warnings throughout Scripture on not being deceived.

Verses 7-8 return to the theme of love. The very definition of love is found in God, because God is love. Verses 9-19 are the display of love. God showed His love by sending His Son to die for our sins (John 3:16). Verses 20-5:5 are the demand of love. If someone loves God, then by their new nature, they will love others and be obedient to God's word. Faith also allows us to overcome the world.

Verses 20-5:5 are the demand of love. If someone loves God, then by their new nature, they will love others and be obedient to God's word. Faith also allows us to overcome the world. Rev. 12:11 says "And they overcame him (Satan) by the blood of the Lamb, and by the word of their testimony, and they did not love their lives to the death". Verses 6-13 give assurance to the believer that what they have believed is true. God will never leave Himself without a witness. The water and blood most likely are a reference to Jesus' baptism and crucifixion because God gives witnesses at both events that Jesus is His Son. Believers also have the inner witness of the Holy Spirit to provide assurance of salvation.

Verses 14-15 address the issue of prayer and praying according to God's will. The sin that leads to death is rejecting the gospel and the drawing of the Holy Spirit (v16-17). Verse 18 teaches that believers will not practice sin. In keeping yourself pure not only will you stay away from sin, but God will also protect you. Verse 19 is a warning that the world is opposed to God and is under the control of the devil. Verse 20 reminds us that to know God, one must have a relationship with Jesus. Verse 21 is a warning not to put anything in God's place and allow it to become an idol.

Cover to Cover Challenge

Week 51

Sunday • Psalm 145-147

Welcome to week 51 of the *Cover to Cover Challenge*! Continue to pray for understanding and that the Holy Spirit will teach each person participating in the *Cover to Cover Challenge*. Psalm 145:8 says "The Lord is gracious and full of compassion, slow to anger and great in mercy".

Psalm 145 is a psalm of David that praises the greatness of God in His mighty works. David opens this psalm by glorifying God, proclaiming that he will praise Him forever (v1-3). In verses 4-7 David praises the greatness of God as he will meditate (read, reflect, respond) and celebrate (utter the memory) God's greatness. In verses 8-13 David praises the grace of God because He has provided salvation, made him part of the kingdom, and for God's great power. David also praises the generosity of God because He helps the helpless, meets their needs, answers their prayers, saves them, and protects them (v14-21).

Psalms 146-150 are the last Hallel (praise) section. All of these are psalms of praise, describing God and His works. Verses 1-2 show that life's purpose for man is to praise God. In verses 3-4 the psalmist does not depend upon man to be saved because man cannot save. Verses 5-6 show that man is to place his hope in the Lord, who is the Creator of the heavens and the earth. The Creator also sustains those who are less fortunate, helps those who are hurting, and cares for the outcast of society (v7-9). The Lord will reign forever over His people (v10).

Psalm 147 is a hymn of praise. In verses 1-6 God is praised because He restores His people, is good to His creation, and works out justice on their behalf by judging the wicked and sustaining those in need. The psalmist thanks the Lord because He watches over and cares for all things He has created, especially those who place their hope in His love (v7-11). In verses 12-14 the psalmist praises God because He restores His people by strengthening them and giving them peace. God's power is shown through His work in nature (v15-18) and in His word (v19-20). The psalmist acknowledges that they are a blessed people to have received His word.

Monday • Deuteronomy 29-31

Deuteronomy 29 is a renewal of the covenant. In verses 1-8 Moses reviews Israel's disobedience and God's faithfulness to the people. One thing is clear: the people have yet to grasp fully what God has done for them and is doing through them. In verses 9-15 obedience to the covenant is stressed. They need to commit themselves today to obey God because not only will they be blessed, but future generations are dependent on it. Verses 16-29 are a stern warning to watch out for idolatry because when they enter the land these temptations will come once again. One person who falls into idolatry can bring down the whole nation and its judgment will be like Sodom and Gomorrah, plus they will lose their land.

Deuteronomy 29 leans towards the people becoming disobedient and being carried away from their land. Deuteronomy 30:1-10 deals with them being restored to the land. The problem is not their lack of understanding, but their heart (v11-14). Verses 15-20 reiterates obeying God's law. No one can be, or has been, saved through the law- but being obedient to it does bring blessings. The person who disobeys can be led back into idolatry, but those who obey will be passing this down to future generations.

In Deuteronomy 31:1-8 Moses tells the people to be obedient and not to fear because it is God who goes before them. Joshua would become the new leader of Israel as they prepare to enter the Promised Land. Moses also commands the reading of the law by the priests every seven years during the Feast of Tabernacles to remind them of what God requires of them. Moses and Joshua appear before God in the tabernacle for Joshua to be commissioned (v14-23). God reveals to Moses that the people will rebel once they enter the land and they will experience God's judgment. Moses will write a song as a witness against them that includes warnings of judgment and the path of repentance. God commands them to place the Book of the Law beside the ark (v24-29).

Tuesday • Nehemiah 7-10

In Nehemiah 7:1-3 the wall has been completed and guards are placed at each gate to guard the city. The gates were usually opened at dawn, but Nehemiah gives orders for them not to be opened until during the day. God wants Nehemiah to register the people by families (v4-5). During this time he finds a list of those who came during the first return under Zerubbabel (v6-73). This list is nearly identical with Ezra 2:1-70.

Nehemiah 8:1-12 records the great revival that started with the reading of the law. These people were hungry to hear the word of God (v1), were receptive to it (v3), were reverent toward it (v5), they agreed with it (v6), they worshiped the Lord through it (v6), they were given understanding by it (v8), they were convicted by it (v9), and they rejoiced in it (v10-12). On the next day people gathered to hear more from the word of the law (v13-18). From their reading, they celebrated the Feast of Booths which is a celebration of the completion of the harvest. It was a time of joy that matched the celebrations during the time of Joshua, after they first entered the land.

Nehemiah 9:1-5 begins 2 days after the celebration of the Feast of Booths and is a time of confession, reading of God's word, and worship. This prayer of confession goes through the history of Israel, and shows the goodness of God and the disobedience of the people. This prayer contains: praise to the Creator (v6), the choosing of Abraham and the covenant (v7-8), the deliverance from Egypt (v9-11), the wilderness wanderings and His leading them (v12-21), the defeat of their enemies and receiving the land (v22-25), His mercy and grace through the time of the judges (v26-28), His call for them to return to Him through the prophets (v29-31), and their current situation (v32-37). In verse 38 the people write out a covenant to be signed by the people to live according to God's word. The list of those who signed is in Nehemiah 10:1-27. It contains leaders, priests, Levites, and laymen- totaling 84 names. Verses 28-39 lay out the specifics of the covenant and include business dealings, the support for the temple upkeep, and offerings especially those concerning the firstfruits and supporting the Levites.

Wednesday • Acts 25-26

As Acts 25 begins, Paul has been in prison for two years. Festus is now the new governor of Judea and hears Paul's case (v1-12). The Jews again plot to kill him by asking Festus to send him to Jerusalem, but he declines. Upon arriving in Jerusalem the Jews make many accusations against Paul, but none can be proven. Festus wants Paul to be placed on trial in Jerusalem but Paul refuses. Knowing Festus may eventually hand him over to the Jews Paul appeals to Caesar, which will carry him to Rome (23:11).

In verses 13-27 Festus discusses Paul's case with King Herod Agrippa II and his sister Bernice. Verses 16-20 and 25 show that Paul was not breaking any law, but was there only because of his belief in Jesus Christ and His resurrection. Each of the descendants of Herod in the Bible have a confrontation with God, and each failed to realize the important decision that was before them. In God's providence this is also God's way of getting Paul to Rome. Paul's long journey through prison and in his trials placed him before kings and others in leadership positions that he otherwise would have never had contact with (Acts 9:15-16). Perhaps many of our trials are for others to get a chance to hear the gospel.

In Acts 26 Paul will stand before King Agrippa II and present his case. King Agrippa is the one who had Peter put in prison (Acts 12). This is the third time Paul will give his testimony and also is a fulfillment of Acts 9:15 that Paul would stand before kings. Paul begins his testimony in verses 1-11 by telling of his background (v4-8), and how he at one time had persecuted those who followed Jesus and believed in the resurrection (v9-11). Paul continues his testimony in verses 12-18 and speaks of meeting Jesus on the Damascus Road (Acts 9). In this passage he speaks of his conversion and focuses on his divine commission. Paul would be sent to "to open the eyes of unbelievers and to turn them from darkness to light so they could receive forgiveness of sins" (v18).

In verses 19-23 Paul speaks of his life after his belief in Jesus. Now Paul preaches repentance, encouraging people to turn to God and do works that show the fruit of their changed life (v20). After he speaks these things, King Agrippa believes that Paul has actually gone crazy (v24-25). Verses 26-32 show that while Paul was defending himself and the charges against him, he was also presenting the gospel to all of those in attendance. King Agrippa had a choice to make, and like his ancestors before him he makes the wrong choice. This passage also reveals that Paul would have been likely set free had he not appealed to Caesar (v32). This is the fifth time since Paul was in prison that his innocence was declared (23:9, 23:29, 25:18, 25:25, 26:32).

Thursday • Ecclesiastes 9-10

Ecclesiastes 9 returns once again to the subject of death. Just because one is righteous and wise does not mean you can control everything in life (v1-3). The good and the wicked both will experience death, but not until the end when God judges will their fate be seen (v5-6). Solomon offers the advice in verses 7-12 to seek pleasure in the things of life while they live because one will never know when tough times are coming. Verses 13-16 tell the story of a poor, wise man who saves a city only to be forgotten. This story is told to show that many things in life are meaningless to some. Beginning in 9:17-10:3, Solomon offers five proverbs to show why wisdom is greater than folly. Verses 4-7 are a story that shows how one foolish decision by someone in leadership can mess up things. Verses 8-11 are proverbs that show that life is unfair, even for wise people. But on the other hand, wisdom is better than being a fool (v12-15). Verses 16-17 return to the theme of leadership. Leadership, whether good or bad, is contagious. Verses 18-20 deal with laziness, money, and in dealing with leadership.

Friday • Revelation 12-17

Revelation 12-13 is a key part of the book. In these two chapters, 7 characters are revealed. The woman in verse 1 is the nation of Israel (Gen. 37:9) and the child in verse 2 is Jesus (Gen. 3:15, Micah 5:2-3). Verse 3 is Satan, and shows his power over the earth. With his tail he draws a third of the stars of heaven. Most believe this is a reference to the fall of Satan and the fallen angels. Satan has always desired to rid the world of the Jewish people because this would not allow the Messiah to be born. Pharaoh tried to eliminate the Jews, Saul tried to kill David, two times during the divided kingdom the messianic line was down to one child (2 Chron. 21:17, 22:10-12), Haman tried to destroy the Jews, even the people of Nazareth tried to throw Jesus off a cliff. The people of Israel will flee into the wilderness during this time, and most believe they will be supernaturally protected by God (v6, 12-17). Verses 7-12 describe the war in heaven between Michael and Satan. Michael is pictured in Scripture as being the protector of Israel (Dan. 10:13, 21; 12:1). This battle will be fought in the future as Satan is cast out of heaven, will no longer have access to God, and will accuse believers before Him. Satan will then begin wreaking havoc on earth, and believers will be able to overcome him (v11).

Revelation 13:1-10 describes a beast that rises out of the sea. This may refer to the Antichrist rising to become the political leader of the world. He will be worshiped by those who are not born again. He will also blaspheme God, be given power to conquer the saints, and be given power to control the world. The beast from the earth in verses 11-18 is referred to as the false prophet. The false prophet will lead people to worship and glorify the Antichrist. He will also perform "miracles" to deceive people. The mark of the beast will essentially be someone's allegiance to follow the Antichrist. Revelation 14:9-11 reveals that anyone who receives this mark will be sentenced to hell.

Revelation 14:1-5 describes the life and ministry of the 144,000 sealed in chapter 7. Verses 6-7 describe an angel that will preach the gospel to those on the earth. The second angel in verse 8 pronounces judgment upon the Antichrist's kingdom, and the third angel pronounces judgment upon those who have received the mark of the beast (v9-11). The believers who persevere during this time are those who have faith in Jesus and walk in His word (v12). Verse 13 is the second beatitude in Revelation, and focuses on those who will die during the tribulation. Verses 14-20 depict judgment upon the earth. Those who are not born again will experience the wrath of God.

Revelation 15 shows a scene from heaven just prior to the pouring out of the 7 bowls of judgment on the earth. Once the seven bowls are poured out the wrath of God will be complete (v1). In verse 2 the fire mentioned, along with the sea of glass, are probably a reference to judgment. Fire is often associated in Scripture with judgment (Num. 11:1, Deut. 9:3, Isa. 66:15). The song of Moses is found in Exodus 15:1-18 and is a song of victory and deliverance of the righteous, and also of judgment toward the enemies of God. Exodus 15:2 and Psalm 118:14 were believed to have been sung when the Israelites returned from captivity (Isa. 12). The song of the Lamb is also one of deliverance and victory. Only those who have been redeemed can sing these songs.

Revelation 16 begins the final outpouring of God's wrath. The first bowl is painful, and includes incurable boils on those who received the mark of the beast. The second and third bowls focus on water. With the fourth bowl, men are scorched with heat and still will not repent. The fifth bowl is poured out on the seat of the Antichrist's kingdom. The sixth bowl prepares and gathers all the nations together to fight in the war of Armageddon. The seventh bowl causes a great earthquake which signifies that the end of all things is very near. The third beatitude in Revelation is in verse 15, and warns believers to stay alert and watch for His coming.

Revelation 17 may refer to the religious portion of the Antichrist's kingdom (v1-6). The name of Babylon is found throughout Scripture and symbolizes resistance against God, especially in the area of religion. All false religions have their root in Babylon. All of those who are not born again will be deceived by this false religion, in whatever shape or form it takes, in the last days. In essence, what will unite the Antichrist's kingdom is a false religion that will help him acquire rulership over the kingdoms of the world (v7-18).

Saturday • 2 John

1-3 John were written by the apostle John sometime in the early 90's AD. 2 John is addressed to the "elect lady", who some believe refers to the church at large (v1-3). John is happy because there are people walking in the truth (v4). Walking in the truth should lead to loving one another because this is His command (v5-6). The main portion of this short letter is to warn of deceivers or false teachers (v7-11). It was a common custom in John's day to receive traveling preachers and have them preach. His warning here is aimed at those who do not confess that Jesus came in the flesh. They are instructed not to even bring them in their church or home. John had hoped to come to them and speak more about this in the future (v12-13).

Cover to Cover CHALLENGE

Week 52

Sunday • Psalm 148-150

Welcome to the final week of the *Cover to Cover Challenge*! Continue to pray that the Lord be honored and glorified through our study, and for understanding of His Word. This is also the final week of the *Cover to Cover Challenge*. I pray that you have been blessed by reading through God's Word and I encourage you to keep reading it. It has been a challenge, and for some it could be the first time you have completely read through it. Congratulations!

Psalm 148 continues with the last of the Hallel praise psalms. Verses 1-6 call for all of the heavens to praise the Lord because He is their Creator. Verses 7-12 are a call for all of the earth to praise the Lord. The psalmist list includes nature and humanity. When speaking of humanity, he lists the king first. If the king praised the Lord, then all the people of his kingdom will too. Verses 13-14 call upon all of God's creation to praise Him and exalt His name.

Psalm 149 is a hymn of victory. Verses 1-5 praise the Lord for winning the victory for His people. They are to sing new songs, dance, and play their instruments all to the praise of God. The victory is spoken of in verses 6-9. God will deliver His people from all of their enemies. God will judge the nations that have come against Israel for how they treated them. Psalm 150 is the closing doxology to the book of Psalms. God is to be praised in the heavens for His works and His greatness (v1-2). Those who play instruments are to praise Him with them (v3-5). All things that have breathe are called together to praise the Lord, partly because He is the one who has given them life (v6).

Monday • Deuteronomy 32-34

Deuteronomy 32 records the song of Moses. It consists of seven themes which begin with God's goodness and end with His grace toward His people. Verses 1-4 focus on the goodness and faithfulness of God, verses 5-9 are about the foolishness of the people as they rebel against God. Verses 10-14 return to the theme of God's goodness to His people as He cares for them. Verses 15-18 speak of their prosperity and their fall into idolatry. Jeshurun ("Upright One") is used as another name for Israel. In verses 19-27 we see that God is going to judge the people for their idolatry because it is also leading the coming generations into idolatry as well. They will continue down the path of going farther away from God, even after warnings from God. God will use other nations to judge them (v28-33). This judgment will be a sign of God's compassion for His people (v34-43). He will also hold the nations accountable for what they have done to His people. It is through this judgment that the people of Israel are to understand that He alone is God. Moses instructs the people to consider the words of the song because it will keep them from rebelling (v44-47). Moses is instructed to go up Mount Nebo to view the land of Canaan before he dies (v48-52).

In Deuteronomy 33 Moses will bless the people as a father does his family before their death. Moses was not just a father figure to the Israelites but was a man of God, set aside to be a servant of God (v1). Moses begins his blessing with praise of God (v2-5). His language shows that the giving of the law was a time of worship where the people were under God's rule and He became their King. Reuben's blessing is one of survival. Genesis 49:4 and Judges 5:15-16 already show that they will not excel. Judah's blessing is for military success through God. The Levites blessing is for the supernatural ability to use their skills in the Lord's work. Benjamin's blessing is for them to enjoy security and peace by the Lord's hand. The blessing on the tribe of Joseph is for material prosperity and military success. The blessing on Zebulun and Issachar is for their lives to be blessed, especially as they trade upon the sea. Gad is blessed because they help their fellow Israelites conquer in the land of Canaan. The blessing on Dan is one of potential strength. The blessing on Naphtali is for material blessings from God. The blessing on Asher is also for material prosperity. Verses 26-29 praise the power, protection, and prosperity God will bring the people.

In Deuteronomy 34:1-4 God allows Moses to see the Promised Land that He had promised to Abraham, Isaac, and Jacob. God is showing Moses that He is faithful to His promises. Moses dies communing with God on Mount Nebo (v5-9). Moses is honored by being buried by God in a place no one knows. Jude 9 mentions Michael and Satan fighting over the body of Moses. The period of mourning was usually 7 days, but the Israelites mourn over Moses for 30 days. Joshua assumes leadership over the Israelites and is empowered with the spirit of wisdom in order to lead. Moses' life displayed the power of God working through him to lead the children of Israel (v10-12).

Tuesday • Nehemiah 11-13

Nehemiah 11 records the selection and volunteering of the people who would live in Jerusalem (v1-2). Verses 3-6 record those from the tribe of Judah and verses 7-9 record those from the tribe of Benjamin. Priests (v10-14), Levites (v15-18), gatekeepers, and temple servants would all be needed in Jerusalem (v19-24). Verses 25-30 record the people from Judah who settled in cities outside of Jerusalem and verses 31-35 record those from Benjamin. Some of the Levites from Judah were transferred to Benjamin to even them out (v36).

Nehemiah 12:1-9 records the priests and Levites who returned under Zerubbabel. Verses 10-21 are the lists of priests and Levites since Joiakim the high priest. Verses 22-26 reveal the records kept in Persia of the priests and Levites while they were there. In verses 27-43 the wall is dedicated just as the temple was in Ezra 6. They purified everything before they proceeded with the ceremony (v30). There were two groups who sang. The first was led by Ezra and Hoshaiah, the second was led by Nehemiah. Both choirs had seven priests which blew trumpets while the Levites played instruments. They also made sacrifices and rejoiced over what God had done. In verses 44-47 the people of Judah made offerings to support the priests and Levites.

Nehemiah 13:5-6 records that Nehemiah had left and returned to Persia to the king. During his absence the people had returned to their old ways. Upon his return Nehemiah will set straight the sins they have committed. Verses 1-3 address the problem of mixed marriages as Jews had married pagans. Nehemiah also threw Tobiah out of the room provided for him by the high priest (v4-5, 8-9). The people had also neglected the offerings that provided for the priests and Levites (v10-14). Many of them had to go back to work to support themselves. The people had also begun to abuse the Sabbath by buying, selling, and trading (v15-22). Verses 23-29 return to the subject of mixed marriages. Nehemiah addressed each problem and provided a solution to each one. Nehemiah was a man that can be remembered as an example for his prayer life, vision, compassion, and his victory over opposition.

Wednesday • Acts 27-28

In Acts 27 Paul's journey to Rome to appear before Caesar begins. In verses 1-8 Paul is treated kindly by the centurion who was there to watch over him. They change to a larger ship in Myra and sail toward Fair Havens. Paul warns them in verses 9-12 not to keep sailing because it was nearing winter and the winds would be terrible during that time of year. The Euroclydon mentioned in verse 14 is where we get our word typhoon. These winds were known to tear ships apart. Not being able to see the sun or stars the sailors would have been unable to navigate the waters (v20).

In verses 21-26 Paul rebukes them for not listening to his advice. They are blessed to be in the presence of Paul because God intends for him to be brought to Rome. After running aground on Malta the soldiers wanted to kill all of the prisoners. The centurion watching over Paul kept them from doing so, preserving Paul's life (v39-44). If you were looking at a map, landing on Malta would be equal to finding a needle in a haystack.

Acts 28:1-10 records Paul's stay on the tiny island of Malta. The natives were very kind to Paul and the people. While gathering wood Paul is bitten by a viper and the natives believed Paul must have been a murderer. After they see he has not been harmed, they believe him to be a god. Paul also heals the father of Publius and many others on the island who were sick. After 3 months they continue their journey to Rome (v11-16). Paul gets to share the gospel with Jews in Rome upon his arrival and shows them from the Scriptures that Jesus is the Messiah (v17-25). The "hope of Israel" mentioned in verse 20 is the coming of the Messiah. Some believed Paul's message and others did not. Paul quotes Isaiah 6:9-10. This is a passage that warns of divine judgment for rejecting the message from God (26-29). Because of their rejection, the gospel will be spread among the Gentiles. Paul would remain in prison for two years in Rome (v30-31). From here he would write Ephesians, Colossians, Philippians, and Philemon. Acts also ends with the gospel going to the "uttermost parts of the earth" (Acts 1:8).

Thursday • Ecclesiastes 11-12

In Ecclesiastes 11:1-6 Solomon teaches that the future is uncertain and cannot be controlled by man because only God knows the future. The thought of verses 7-10 is to enjoy your youth, but these verses also warn that even for them one day death is coming. In contrast to the youth, verses 12:1-7 contemplate old age and the breaking down of the physical body. In concluding this section of the book, everything that Solomon had witnessed and pursued in the world he believed was meaningless (v8). Verses 9-14 are a fitting conclusion to the book. After all of his earthly pursuits the only thing that Solomon found pleasing and satisfying was to fear God and keep His commandments. In the end, everyone will give an account for what they do through life. Even though people may see things as meaningless we do not understand God's purposes in every situation. Only God can give meaning to life.

Friday • Revelation 18-22

Revelation 18 deals with the political side of his kingdom. It is God pouring out His wrath, which destroys Babylon and all those who depend on her wealth and have become drunk with her sins (v1-8). Just as the nations that persecuted Israel in the Old Testament received the curses of the covenant, Babylon will be repaid double for the sins she has committed. The people on earth (lost) will mourn over the destruction of Babylon (v9-19), while all of heaven rejoices (v20). In verses 21-24 the angel throws a millstone in the sea, symbolizing the final overthrow of Satan's kingdom on earth.

Revelation 19:1-10 continues the praise in heaven over the destruction of Babylon. The fourth beatitude of Revelation is in verse 9. This pronounces a blessing on all believers who will be at the marriage supper of the Lamb because they have been redeemed. Verse 10 reveals that the purpose of all prophecy is to testify and bring glory to Jesus. Verses 11-16 describe the second coming of Jesus. Riding on a white horse symbolizes victory in battle. Verses 16-21 describe the great feast prepared for the birds to feast on the dead of those who died in battle against the Lord. The beast and the false prophet are placed in the lake of fire where they will stay for an eternity.

Revelation 20:1-10 records the binding of Satan, the thousand year reign of Christ, and the final rebellion against God led by Satan. It is after these things that those who died apart from Christ will be judged at the Great White Throne Judgment (v11-15). This throne represents the holiness, justice, and purity of God. From John 12:48 we can probably conclude one of the books that will be at the judgment is God's Word. Whether you are saved or lost, both groups are judged based on their works. The difference between the Great White Throne and the Bema judgment is Jesus. Those at the Bema judgment have accepted Christ as Savior and those at the Great White Throne have not.

Revelation 21-22 describe the new heavens and new earth. Verses 1-8 describe the great change (v1), the great city (v2), the great fellowship (v3), the great comfort (v4), the great promise (v5), the great ending and the great invitation (v6), the great assurance (v7), and the great warning (v8). Verses 9-27 describe the holy Jerusalem coming down from heaven in all of its beauty. According to the measurements, the city will be 1400 miles high, wide, and deep. Just an example would be a building that is 396,000 stories high! There will no longer be a need for a temple because God will be there dwelling with His people (v22-22:1-5). Only those who have been born again and have their name written in the Lamb's Book of Life will see the glorious city of God. The sixth beatitude is in verse 7 and is for those who obey the words of this book. It also serves as a warning because Jesus says that He is coming quickly. The seventh of the beatitudes is in verse 14. It blesses those who have been born again by allowing them in to the city of God and to enjoy heaven. Verse 17 is an invitation to accept Christ from the Holy Spirit and from the bride which is the church. Verses 18-19 are a warning not to add or take away from the words of the book. Once more Jesus testifies that He is coming quickly (v20-21).

Saturday • 3 John

3 John was written by the apostle John sometime in the early 90's AD. 3 John is written to Gaius, whom John rejoices over because he lives in the truth (v1-4). Just as in 2 John, he rejoices when he hears that people are walking (living) according to the truth. In verses 5-8 John commends Gaius for his generosity (more than likely) toward those who are travelling preachers. John is commending him because those who travel preaching the truth of the gospel should be supported by fellow Christians. In verses 9-10 Diotrephes was a false teacher who was filled with pride, and who rejects those who preach the truth. He uses words to destroy those who preach

the truth and does not allow them to preach the truth, excommunicating them. In verse 11 John urges Gaius not to imitate Diotrephes' example, and gives him a way to identify those who are good and those who are evil. In verse 12 John does recommend Demetrius to Gaius because he has a good testimony from others and from John himself. John will not write anymore to Gaius because he wants to come visit him soon (v13-14).

Bibliography

Akin, Daniel L. *NAC: 1-3 John.* Nashville: Broadman & Holman, 2001.

Alden, Robert. *Job NAC.* Nashville: Broadman & Holman Publishers, 1993.

Barker, Kenneth L. *Expositor's Bible Commentary OT/NT.* Grand Rapids: Zondervan, 1994.

Barker, Kenneth L. NAC: *Micah, Nahum, Habakkuk, Zephaniah.* Nashville: Broadman & Holman Publishers, 1999.

Bergen, Robert D. *NAC: 1-2 Samuel.* Nashville: Broadman & Holman Publishers, 1996.

Bible Study Press. *The NET Bible First Edition Notes.* Biblical Studies Press, 2006.

Block, Daniel I. *NAC: Judges & Ruth.* Nashville: Broadman & Holman Publishers, 1999.

Bock, Darrell L. *Baker Exegetical Commentary: Luke.* Grand Rapids: Baker Academic, 1994.

Brooks, James A. *NAC: Mark.* Nashville: Broadman& Holman Publishers, 1991.

Bruce F.F. *TNTC: Romans.* Downers Grove: IVP Academic, 1985.

Carson, D.A. & Moo, Douglas. *An Introduction to the New Testament.* Grand Rapids: Zondervan, 2005.

Carson D.A. *PNTC: The Gospel According to John.* Grand Rapids: InterVaristy Press, 1991.

Cohen, Dr. Gary. *Revelation Visualized.* Chattanooga, TN. AMG Publishers, 1993.

Cole, R. Alan. *TNTC: Mark.* Downers Grove: InterVarsity Press, 1989.

Comfort, Philip W. *Life Application New Testament Commentary.* Carol Stream: Tyndale House Publishers, 2001.

Edwards, James R. *PNTC: Mark.* Grand Rapids: Eerdmans, 2002.

Fee, Gordon D. *IVP: Philippians.* Downers Grove: InterVarsity Press, 1999.

Garland, David E. *Baker Exegetical Commentary: 1 Corinthians.* Grand Rapids: Baker Academic, 2003.

Garland, David E. *Baker Exegetical Commentary: 2 Corinthians.* Grand Rapids: Baker Academic, 2003.

Garret, Duane A. NAC: *Hosea, Joel* . Nashville: Broadman & Holman Publishers, 1997.

George, Timothy. *NAC: Galatians.* Nashville: B&H Publishers, 1994.

Green, Gene L. *The Letter to the Thessalonians.* Grand Rapidss: Eerdmans Pub., 2002.

Grudem, Wayne A. *TNTC: 1 Peter.* Downers Grove: InterVarsity Press, 1988.

Guthrie, Donald. *TNTC: Hebrews: An Introduction and Commentary.* Downers Grove: InterVarsity Press, 1983.

Guthrie, Donald. *TNTC: The Pastoral Epistles.* Downers Grove: InterVarsity Press, 1990.

Gutierrez, Ben. *Living Out the Mind of Christ.* innovatechurch, Thomas Road Baptist Church, 2008.

Hansen, Walter G. *IVP: Galatians.* Downers Grove: InterVaristy Press, 1994.

Harrison, R.K. *TOTC: Jeremiah and Lamentations.* Downers Grove: InterVarsity Press, 1973.

Hindson, Ed. *The Book of Revelation: Unlocking the Future.* Chattanooga, TN. AMG Publishers, 2002.

Howard, David Jr. *Joshua NAC.* Nashville: Broadman & Holman Publishers, 1998.

Keener, Craig S. *Matthew IVP Commentary.* Downers Grove: InterVarsity Press, 1997.

Kidner, Derek. *TOTC: Ezra and Nehemiah.* Downers Grove: InterVarsity Press, 1979.

Kistemaker, S. J., & Hendriksen, W. NTC : *Exposition of the Book of Revelation*. Grand Rapids: Baker Book House, 2001.

Klein, George L. *NAC: Zechariah*. Nashville: B&H Publishing, 2008.

Kruse, Colin G. *2 Corinthians*. Downers Grove: InterVarsity Press, 1987.

Longman III, Tremper III. *Layman's Old Testament Bible Commentary*. Uhrichsville: Barbour Publishing, 2010.

MacArthur, John Jr. *The MacArthur Study Bible*. Nashville: Word Publishers, 1997.

MacArthur, J. F., Jr. *Revelation 1–11*. MacArthur New Testament Commentary. Chicago: Moody Press, 1999.

MacArthur, J. F., Jr. *Revelation 12–22*. MacArthur New Testament Commentary. Chicago: Moody Press, 1999.

MacArthur, John Jr. *1 Timothy*. . Chicago: Moody Press, 1995.

Mare, W. Harold. *NT Background Commentary: Words, Phrases, and Situations*. Rosshire: Mentor, 2004.

Marshall, I. Howard. *TNTC: Acts*. Downers Grove: InterVarsity Press, 1980.

Mathews, K.A. *Genesis 1-11:26 NAC*. Nashville: Broadman & Holman Publishers, 1996.

Melick, Richard R. *NAC: Philippians, Colossians, Philemon*. Nashville: B&H Publishers, 1991.

Moo, Douglas. *PNTC: The Letter of James*. Grand Rapids: Eerdmans, 2000.

Morris, Leon. *TNTC: 1 Corinthians*. Downers Grove: InterVarsity Press, 1985.

Morris, Leon. *TNTC: 1&2 Thessalonians: An Introduction and Commentary*. Downers Grove: InterVarsity Press, 1984.

Motyer, J.A. *TBST: The Message of Philippians*. Downers Grove: InterVarsity Press, 1984.

Osborne, G. R. *BECNT: Revelation*. Baker Grand Rapids, MI: Baker Academic, 2002.

Osborne, Grant. *Life Application New Testament Commentary*. Carol Stream: Tyndale House Publisher, 2001.

Phillips, John. *Exploring Revelation*. Grand Rapids, MI. Kregel Publications, 2001.

Polhill, John. *NAC: Acts*. Nashville: B&H Publishers, 1992.

Schreiner, Thomas R. *BECNT: Romans*. Grand Rapids: Baker Books, 1998.

Schreiner, Thomas R. *NAC: 1-2 Peter, Jude*. Nashville: B&H Publishers, 2003.

Selman, Martin J. *TOTC:1 Chronicles*. Downers Grove: InterVarsity Press, 1994.

Selman, Martin J. *TOTC:2 Chronicles*. Downers Grove: InterVarsity Press, 1994.

Silva, Moises. *BECNT: Philippians*. Grand Rapids: Baker Academic, 2005.

Smith, Billy K. & Page, Franklin. *Amos, Obadiah, Jonah NAC*. Nashville: Broadman & Holman Publishers, 1995.

Smith, Gary V. *NAC: Isaiah 1-39*. Nashville: B&H Publishing Group, 2007.

Stott, John R.W. *God's New Society: The Message of Ephesians*. Downers Grove: InterVarsity, 1979.

Wall, Robert W. *IVP: Colossians & Philemon*. Downers Grove: InterVarsity Press, 1995.

Walvoord, J. F., Zuck, R. B., & Dallas Theological Seminary. *Vol. 2: The Bible Knowledge Commentary: An Exposition of the Scriptures*. Wheaton, IL: Victor Books, 1985.

Wenham, Gordon J. *TOTC: Numbers*. Downers Grove: InterVarsity Press, 1981.

Wiersbe, Warren W. *Be Worshipful*. Colorado Springs: Cook Communications Ministries, 2004.

Willmington, H.L. *The Outline Bible*. Wheaton, IL: Tyndale House Publishers, 1999.

Wiseman, Donald J. *TOTC: Ezekiel*. Downers Grove: InterVaristy Press, 1969.

Wiseman, Donald J. *TOTC: Leviticus*. Downers Grove: InterVarsity Press, 1980.

Wiseman, Donald J. *TOTC: 1 & 2 Kings*. Downers Grove: InterVarsity Press, 1993.

Meet the Author

JASON BELL is the Senior Pastor of Nazareth Baptist Church in Rainsville, Alabama. Now serving in his second decade of ministry, Jason has previously served as Youth Minister, Children's Minister, Education Minister, and Associate Pastor at various churches. He is a graduate of Liberty University, and has earned a Bachelor's Degree in Religion and Master's Degree in Biblical Studies and Masters of Divinity in Theology. In addition to pastoral ministry at Nazareth Baptist Church, Jason serves as an Adjunct Professor at New Orleans Baptist Theological Seminary. He also serves as Vice-President on the Board of Directors for The Summit, which is a faith based 12 month residential intensive discipleship program for women struggling with life controlling problems (www.summitoffortpayne.com).

Married 21 years, Jason and wife Amber Bell have two children-Jacey, 19, and Noah, 16. Their home is in Rainsville, Alabama.

www.ingramcontent.com/pod-product-compliance
Lightning Source LLC
Chambersburg PA
CBHW080442090526
44586CB00047B/2172